MANAGERIAL ECONOMICS
EIGHTH EDITION

MANAGERIAL ECONOMICS
THEORY, APPLICATIONS, AND CASES

EIGHTH EDITION

W. Bruce Allen
The Wharton School
University of Pennsylvania

Neil A. Doherty
The Wharton School
University of Pennsylvania

Keith Weigelt
The Wharton School
University of Pennsylvania

Edwin Mansfield
late of University of Pennsylvania

W. W. NORTON & COMPANY
NEW YORK · LONDON

W. W. Norton & Company has been independent since its founding in 1923, when Wiliam Warder Norton and Mary D. Herter Norton first published lectures delivered at the People's Institute, the adult education division of New York City's Cooper Union. The firm soon expanded its program beyond the Institute, publishing books by celebrated academics from America and abroad. By midcentury, the two major pillars of Norton's publishing program—trade books and college texts—were firmly established. In the 1950s, the Norton family transferred control of the company to its employees, and today—with a staff of four hundred and a comparable number of trade, college, and professional titles published each year—W. W. Norton & Company stands as the largest and oldest publishing house owned wholly by its employees.

Editor: Jack Repcheck
Editorial assistant: Hannah Bachman
Project editor: Kate Feighery
Senior production manager, College: Benjamin Reynolds
Art direction: Rubina Yeh
Media editor: Cassie del Pilar
Associate media editor: Nicole Sawa
Assistant media editor: Carson Russell
Marketing manager, Economics : John Kresse
Composition: Jouve International—Brattleboro, VT
Manufacturing: Transcontinental

Library of Congress Cataloging-in-Publication Data
    Managerial economics: theory, applications, and cases/ W. Bruce Allen . . . [et al.]. – 8th ed.
        p. cm.
    Includes bibliographical references and index.
    ISBN 978-0-393-91277-7 (hardcover)
    1. Managerial economics.   I. Allen, W. Bruce.
    HD30.22.M354 2013
    338.5024'658–dc23
                                2012018763

W. W. Norton & Company, Inc., 500 Fifth Avenue, New York, N.Y. 10110
W. W. Norton & Company, Ltd., Castle House, 75/76 Wells Street, London W1T 3QT
wwnorton.com

1 2 3 4 5 6 7 8 9 0

To Edwin Mansfield, a pioneer of managerial economics

PART 1
THE NEED FOR A GUIDE

CHAPTER 1

INTRODUCTION

The main task of managers is to make good decisions. For better or worse, managers face a complex world, and they need a guide to help them choose well. This is that guide. Those who gain its understanding will increase the value of their decisions at personal and organizational levels.

This guide provides knowledge in the following sense. The ancient Chinese discuss knowledge as a temporal flow. Knowledge is not storage of memorized facts but an ability to understand the actions of others. With this knowledge, you better anticipate their behavior. Our guide will help you navigate through the managerial world of behavior.

We construct our guide within the framework of managerial economics. Managerial economics uses formal models to analyze managerial actions and their effect on firm performance. We use these models to shed light on business concepts such as cost, demand, profit, competition, pricing, compensation, market entry strategy, and auction strategy. All these concepts are under the control of managers, and they determine firm performance.

Contrary to the beliefs of many, managerial economics differs significantly from microeconomics: The focus of analysis is different. At best, the focus in microeconomics is at the firm level; many times the analysis is at the market level. In managerial economics, the focus is on managerial behavior. Managerial economics prescribes behavior, whereas the micro world describes the environment. This focus on managerial behavior provides powerful tools and frameworks to guide managers to better decisions. These tools allow managers to better identify the consequences of alternative courses of action.

Managerial economics plays two important roles in preparing students for managerial life. Concepts we will discuss in subsequent chapters are found in other functional business courses like accounting, finance, strategy, operations, and marketing. Our guide is what the great strategist Sun Tzu called the "general's seat," and it is characterized by what are known as *economies of scope*. That is, the better you understand the concepts we discuss, the easier will be your understanding of them when they arise in other business classes. And because managerial economics recognizes the complexity of the managerial world, it is arguably the most integrative of the functional business classes. This helps students learn the integrative mind-set that is essential for good management, and it also gets them to think past the short-term mentality and consider the long-term consequences.

THE THEORY OF THE FIRM

Managers work within a larger organization and ultimately determine its performance. To understand the behavioral world of managers, we must account for the behavior of firms. Of course, firms really don't behave on their own; you might think of them as marionettes with managers controlling the strings. Some management teams are good at pulling these strings, while others can't seem to get it right. But although management styles differ greatly in the millions of firms across the globe, there is surprisingly little variance in the goals of managers. Overwhelmingly, managers choose actions they believe will increase the value of their organization. So in our theory of the firm, the goals of managers focus on increasing this value. We understand there are many ways to create value in an organization; for example, to a microcredit organization with a double bottom line, value from its lending practices might consist of a profit measure and the gains to a local community's economy. But our models must account for behavior across a great number of firms, so we take the view that managers in profit-oriented organizations try to increase the net present value of expected future cash flows. We can formally present this managerial effort in the following

$$\text{Present value of expected future profits} = \frac{\pi_1}{1+i} + \frac{\pi_2}{(1+i)^2} + \cdots + \frac{\pi_n}{(1+i)^n}$$

$$\text{Present value of expected future profits} = \sum_{t=1}^{n} \frac{\pi_t}{(1+i)^t} \tag{1.1}$$

STRATEGY SESSION: Bono Sees Red, and Corporate Profits See Black

In 2007, rock star Bono started Red, a campaign that combines consumerism with altruism. When a consumer buys a Dell Red computer, a Motorola Red Motorazr, or Red items from the GAP, or uses an American Express Red card, a contribution is made into the global fund. Companies pay a licensing fee to label their products "Red" and then pay a portion of the sales from those products into the fund. According to the Red website (www.joinred.com/red/), $170 million has been generated by the Red campaign and been put to its intended use fighting AIDS, malaria, and tuberculosis in the African countries of Ghana, Rwanda, and Swaziland.

This concept has been branded *cause marketing* and was around long before Red—but without the publicity generated by a personality like Bono. For years McDonald's has sponsored Ronald McDonald Houses, where parents of sick children can find respite (and support groups) near the hospitals where their children are patients. Why do firms participate in cause marketing? Clearly, the companies can market themselves as being socially conscious. But equally clear is the cost of paying for the Red license and operating Ronald McDonald Houses. Where's the tangible benefit? According to a 2006 poll by Cone Inc. (a Boston marketing agency), 89% of Americans aged 13 to 25 (a large consumer group and one swayed by Bono) would switch to a brand associated with a "good cause" if the products and prices were comparable. There's the tangible benefit: Cause marketing also leads to a revenue stream (and presumably a profit stream). So incurring Red leads to seeing black as profits increase because of such actions. Cause marketing is in harmony with profit maximization.

Another phenomenon we are witnessing is the rise of "philantrepreneurs" such as Bill Gates, Warren Buffett, Richard Branson, and Ted Turner—individuals whose businesses make a lot of profit and wealth for themselves and then give a lot of that money to good causes. As of December 2010, in the United States, 57 billionaires have pledged to give a minimum of 50% of their wealth to good causes under something known as the "Giving Pledge." In addition to the billionaires named above, Paul G. Allen, Michael R. Bloomberg, Larry Ellison, Jon Huntsman, Carl Icahn, George Lucas, and Mark Zuckerberg are among those taking the pledge.

Source: "Bottom Line for (Red)," *The New York Times*, February 6, 2008; The Giving Pledge, www.givingpledge.org.

where π_t is the expected profit in year t, i is the interest rate, and t goes from 1 (next year) to n (the last year in the planning horizon). Because profit equals total revenue (TR) minus total cost (TC), this equation is also expressed as

$$\text{Present value of expected future profits} = \sum_{t=1}^{n} \frac{TR_t - TC_t}{(1 + i)^t} \qquad (1.2)$$

where TR_t is the firm's total revenue in year t, and TC_t is its total cost in year t.

Equation (1.2) shows why managers influence firm performance. Managerial decisions clearly determine both the revenues and costs for an organization. Consider, for example, the Toyota Motor Company. Its marketing managers and sales representatives work hard to increase its total revenues, while its production managers and manufacturing engineers strive to reduce its total costs. At the same time, its financial managers play a major role in obtaining capital and hence influence equation (1.2); its research and development personnel invent new products and processes to increase total revenues and reduce total costs. Managers of all these diverse groups make decisions to affect Toyota Motor's value, defined here as the present value of expected future profits.

Although managers want to increase their firm's value, they do not have total control over the level of value. If managerial life were that simple, you would not have to go to school to learn business techniques. What complicates managerial life are the operating constraints managers face. One constraint is that most resources are scarce. Within the firm, managerial decision making often involves allocating scarce inputs to support the production, distribution, and sales of goods and services that are sold at a price that exceeds their costs.

Other constraints that limit managerial actions are legal or contractual. For example, managers may be bound to pay wages exceeding a certain level because minimum wage laws stipulate that they must do so. Also, they must pay taxes in accord with federal, state, and local laws. Further, managers must comply with contracts with customers and suppliers—or take the legal consequences. A wide variety of laws (ranging from environmental laws to antitrust laws to tax laws) limit what managers can do, and contracts and other legal agreements further constrain their actions.

WHAT IS PROFIT?

As we have seen, firm value is largely a function of **profit**. Unlike in accounting, in managerial economics we measure profit after taking account of the capital and labor provided by the owners. For example, suppose a manager quits her position at a large firm to create a small start-up business. She receives no salary even though she puts in long hours trying to establish her business. If she worked these hours for her previous firm, she would have earned $65,000. And if she had invested the capital she used to begin her business in some alternative investment, she could have earned $24,000. Let's say in 2012 her start-up firm earned an accounting profit of $100,000. Her firm's profit in the managerial economics world is $100,000 − $65,000 − $24,000 = $11,000 rather than the $100,000 shown in accounting statements.

The differences between the profit concepts used by the accountant and the economist reflect a difference in focus. The accountant is concerned with controlling the firm's day-to-day operations, detecting fraud or embezzlement, satisfying tax and other laws, and producing records for various interested groups. The economist is concerned with decision making and rational choice among

Profit When economists speak of profit, they mean profit over and above what the owner's labor and capital employed in the business could earn elsewhere.

strategies. Although most of a firm's financial statements conform to the accountant's and not the managerial economist's concept of profit, the latter is more relevant for managerial decisions. (And this, of course, is recognized by sophisticated accountants.) For example, suppose the woman is trying to decide whether to continue operating her business. If she is interested in making as much money as possible, she should calculate her firm's profit based on our economist model. If the firm's economic profit is greater than zero, she should continue to operate the firm; otherwise she should close it and pursue other opportunities.

REASONS FOR THE EXISTENCE OF PROFIT

A firm's economic profit is generated by the actions of managers. Profit is one indicator of their decision-making skills. Three fertile profit-generating areas used by managers are innovation, risk, and market power. As we write this chapter, people are waiting for the chance to buy the iPhone 4S, the new model of Apple's iconic smartphones. And airlines are committing billions of dollars for the opportunity to purchase the 787 Dreamliner from Boeing. In both these markets, products already exist; but consumers apparently are more interested in new products. Both the iPhone and the 787 are considered pioneering products. They push the frontier relative to existing products in terms of functionality, technology, and style. As we write today, these managerial efforts both generate high profit—reportedly up to 40%. Future value depends on how each managerial team executes its strategy.

A hallmark of managerial decision making is the need to make risky choices. For managers this risk takes many forms. They are asked to make decisions whose future outcomes are unknown (How successful will this product be in the market?), when they don't know the reactions of rivals (If I raise my price, will my rivals raise theirs?), and when they do not know the likelihood of a future event (How likely is it a Democrat is elected our next president?). Profit is the reward to those who bear risk well.

As we will see later, managers also earn profit by exploiting market inefficiencies. Good managers understand how to create these to give their firm a sustainable competitive advantage. Common tactics in this area include building market entry barriers, sophisticated pricing strategies, diversification efforts, and output decisions. Such tactics, if done well, can generate a long stream of profit.

MANAGERIAL INTERESTS AND THE PRINCIPAL–AGENT PROBLEM

Although managerial economists generally assume that managers want to maximize profit (and hence firm value, as defined in equation (1.1)), they recognize additional goals. Some goals may enhance the firm's long-term value, like building market share or establishing a brand name. Other managerial goals have less to do with firm value and more to do with increasing managerial compensation.

As we will see, our model recognizes preferences of firm owners and managers sometimes diverge. And when managers make choices between maximizing a firm's value and increasing the payoffs to a single manager or management team, some choose the selfish path. This too is a trait of managerial behavior. The tendency to focus on self-interest is growing in importance because the separation between the ownership and management of firms is continuing to increase on a global scale. The owners of the firm—the stockholders—usually have little detailed knowledge of the firm's operations. Even a firm's board of directors has limited information relative to the management team. Managers are generally given a great deal of freedom as long as they perform adequately. Consequently, firm behavior is often driven by the interests of the nonowner management group. At the least, this behavior results in higher pay and more perquisites for managers; at worst, it creates an Enron spectacle.

Managerial economists call this **the principal–agent problem.** Managers are agents who work for the firm's owners, who are shareholders or principals. The principal–agent problem centers on whether managers may pursue their own objectives at a cost to the owners. We ask students in our class, "If we send you to Atlantic City with our money, would your behavior change?" Because the firm's owners find it difficult to adequately distinguish actions that maximize profit and those that do not, managers have incentives to enrich themselves.

To deal with this problem, owners often use contracts to converge their preferences and those of their agents. For example, owners may give managers a financial stake in future success. Many corporations use stock option plans, whereby managers can purchase shares of common stock at less than market price. These plans give managers incentives to increase firm profit and comply with owners' interest. There is some evidence these plans do change behavior. According to one study, if managers own between 5 and 20% of a firm, they are likely to perform better (that is, earn more profit) than if they own less than 5%. In some firms managers are forced to purchase stock, and boards of directors are compensated in stock. This and other moral hazard issues are discussed extensively in Chapter 15.

> **The principal–agent problem**
> When managers pursue their own objectives, even though this decreases the profit of the owners.

DEMAND AND SUPPLY: A FIRST LOOK

To understand behavior in any society, we must have a working knowledge of its institutions. The managerial world revolves around markets. Any manager, whether in Tokyo, New York, London, or Toronto, must understand basic market principles in order to anticipate behavior. A significant portion of this book is devoted to helping you understand the behavior of people in markets. We first give an overview of markets and then examine both the demand and supply sides in greater detail.

STRATEGY SESSION: Baseball Discovers the Law of Supply and Demand

It started several years ago with the Colorado Rockies looking for a way to obtain more revenue but at the same time not wishing to heap additional expense on their loyal season-ticket holders (who buy tickets for every game or an aggregation of games as a bundle). As of the 2003 season, the Rockies were joined by 11 other teams—slightly less than half of the 30 major league baseball teams. Doing what? Practicing what they call *variable pricing*. In lay terms, they are charging more for the exact same seat for games with desirable teams as opponents, such as teams that are traditional rivals, teams with superstars, and the like. And the trend continues. Almost every team now practices some sort of variable pricing.

Although this practice is nothing new for many goods and services (Miami Beach hotel rooms cost more in February than in July, ticket prices for Lady Gaga in the same seat in the same arena are more expensive than ticket prices for Carrie Underwood, etc.), it was new for baseball.

Historically, the price for seat X in the stadium was price Y for each of the team's 81 home games. Now seat X can be priced higher on opening day, on fireworks night, or when the New York Yankees or a traditional rival comes to town. The basic premise is the law of supply and demand. The number of seats in the ballpark remains fixed, but the attractiveness of the seat to a potential buyer is not constant.

Let's see what some of the teams are doing. Several teams, e.g., the Chicago Cubs, the New York Mets, the Tampa Bay Rays, and the Kansas City Royals, divide the games up into categories of perceived attractiveness. The Cubs have five categories (with the number of games in each category in parenthesis): Marquee (13), Platinum (13), Gold (31), Silver (13), and Bronze (11). The per-game price for the highest class seat (an Infield Club Box) for a Marquee game is $112, while the same seat for a bronze game is $58 (a 93% difference). The per-game price for the lowest class seat (Reserved Outfield Upper Deck) is $27 for a Marquee game and $8 for a Bronze game (a 237.5% difference). The Mets have four categories: Marquee (four-against the Yankees), Premium (22), Classic (25), and Value (30). Their highest class seats are Delta Club Platinum and Gold, and their price remained the same ($440 and $325) through all four categories. But their third highest class seat (Delta Club Silver) was priced at $280 for a Marquee game and $160 for a Value game (a 75% difference). Cheaper ticket classes followed the same 75% difference that exists in the Marquee to Value games. The Rays also have four categories: Diamond, Platinum, Gold, and Silver. Their highest class seat (Avantair Home Plate Club) sells for $300 for Diamond games and $210 for Silver Games (a 43% difference). Their cheapest class (Upper Reserved Party Deck) sells for $19 for Diamond games and $9 for Silver Games (an 111% difference). The Royals have two categories: Premium and Regular. The highest class seat (BATS Crown Club) sells for $250 for Premium games and $240 for Regular games (a 4.2% difference) and their lowest class seat (Hy-Vee View) sells for $15 for Premium games and $10 for Regular Games (a 50% difference). The Royals also charge an additional $1 or $2 fee for tickets purchased on the day of the game.

The St. Louis Cardinals price are based on day of the week and the opponent faced. For instance, for July 2011 Monday, Tuesday, and Wednesday games against the Reds and the Astros, the highest class seats (Diamond Box) was $110 for both, but Thursday games against the Diamondbacks and the Astros were $101 and $110 respectively. But Diamondback tickets for the Friday and Sunday games were $120, and the Saturday game against the Diamondbacks was $143. When the rival Cubs arrive two weeks later, the Friday and Saturday games are $158 and the Sunday game $130. Their cheaper seat classes follow a similar pattern.

The Atlanta Braves price based on the day of the week, regardless of the opposition faced. Monday through Thursday games are called Regular. Friday, Saturday, and July 4 are called Premium. Saturday is called Saturday and is their highest price category. Four of their 12 classes of seats have a fourth category (Value Days). Their highest seat class (Hank Aaron Seats) sells for $90 on Saturdays but $78 on Regular days (a 15.4% difference) and the lowest seat class (Upper Pavilion) sells for $8 regardless of the day. When the Value tickets are available, there's a 35–50% difference between them and the Regular tickets.

So some teams differentiate prices based on the opposition, some based on the day of the week, and others based on both.

We've reported on Major League Baseball ticket prices in boxes like this in previous editions of this book and on how teams use *pre-season* information on perceived demand for games to determine prices. But this is subject to a lot of uncertainty. While a rival will still be a rival, a pre-season predicted strong draw may not pan out (because the team does not live up to expectations, because superstars get injured or have off seasons, the weather may turn bad, etc.). When teams post their prices, they have to live with them.

However, we also stated that "true variable pricing will see price changing very close to game time." That, of course, has always taken place in the illegal selling of tickets by sleazy characters hanging out in the vicinity of stadiums and with legitimate resellers of tickets like StubHub. But now the San Francisco Giants have taken the concept to a whole new level.

It started in 2010 when the Giants noticed a surge in ticket sales for the Memorial Day game with the Colorado Rockies. Normally, a Memorial Day game is a tough sell, as families opt for parades and picnics rather than baseball games. But that Memorial Day, tickets were selling like hotcakes. Why? Because the Giant's pitching ace, Tim Lincecum, was facing the Rockies' pitching ace, Ubaldo Jimenez. So the Giants decided to raise ticket price for the game. For example, the Giants raised some ticket prices from $17 to up to $25. Even with such increases, the Giants sold 10,000 tickets on the weekend leading up to the Monday game, and the stadium was sold out for the game.

What the Giants noticed was that factors *during* the season, such as, weather, winning streaks, pitching matchups, and so on, that are only known as game time approaches can appreciably change the demand to see the game. Because the demand to see the game changes, the teams are now asking: Why shouldn't the game prices change? So the Giants are now changing their ticket prices *daily* depending on market conditions. The pricing is now almost truly dynamic (truly dynamic would be minute-to-minute changes as practiced by the scalpers).

The Giants didn't do this without experimenting. In 2009, they used the 2,000 least desirable seats in the stadium and raised or lowered prices based on their estimates of demand to see a game. They estimate that they sold 25,000 extra tickets yielding a gross revenue increase of $500,000. In 2010, pricing all tickets dynamically has led to an estimated revenue increase of 6%.

"We debated the merits of dynamic pricing for years, but there were numerous hurdles," says Giants CIO Bill Schlough, such as protecting season-ticket holders and choosing the right variables for the pricing model. And here's where it's wonderful to be an economist. Schlough goes on to say "Dynamic pricing enables us to capture a larger share of consumer surplus . . ." (See the definition of *consumer surplus* on p. 90).

Won't some fans complain about higher ticket prices? Sure. When the Giants always charged X for seat Y, fans who were willing to pay X or more bought tickets, and fans willing to pay less than X did not. (continued)

STRATEGY SESSION: Baseball Discovers the Law of Supply and Demand (*continued*)

Now, when the Giants charge $X + Z_1$ for the ticket, a number of fans still buy tickets (because they value seeing the game at $X + Z_1$ or greater). So some fans don't go to games anymore (those who value seeing the game at slightly less than $X + Z_1$ and X), and those that do attend pay more to the Giants. Neither of those types is likely to be overjoyed, but when the Giants charge $X - Z_2$ for a ticket, the people willing to pay X (or more) will purchase tickets, as will fans who have never purchased tickets before. This can lead to an expansion of the fan base. The Giants, being rational, wouldn't price this way unless it increased profits.

Like airline yield management models, sports teams beyond baseball, such as basketball and hockey, are using computers to analyze past ticket sales and data from the above mentioned legal secondary markets to try to price games based on what the markets will bear.

The models have many independent variables, and the game ticket price is the variable to be predicted. The models generate weights associated with each variable, such as day of the week, team perfor-

mance, pitching matchups, and so on, to yield a suggested ticket price for the seat for the game. Then a human being takes the recommended price and decides whether to adjust it and by how much.

The Giants make pricing decisions on future games *every morning*. So, as with airline fares, a price for a game two weeks from now could change daily up to game day. Fans seem to be accepting the process because they have become accustomed to it in the secondary market for tickets.

In the NBA (basketball), more than half the teams used a model to set season-ticket prices last year. A third of teams will use per-game pricing this year. In Cleveland (which had superstar Lebron James at the time), the Cavaliers priced 20,000 tickets on a daily basis and reported an average price increase of $9.25 per ticket.

Source: Various teams' websites; "Star Pitchers in a Duel? Tickets Will Cost More," *The New York Times*, June 28, 2010, at www.nytimes.com/2010/06/28/technology/28tickets.html; "San Francisco Giants, Dynamic Pricing Software Hits a Home Run," CIO, June 29, 2011, at www.cio.com/article/685312.

Market A group of firms and individuals that interact with each other to buy or sell a good.

One issue faced by managers long ago involved the facilitation of economic exchange. Whereas two individuals can negotiate face-to-face, coordination costs mount quickly as more people join. So managers had to devise a plan to reduce coordination costs and encourage more trade. They chose to create a social institution called a **market**.

A market exists when there is economic exchange; that is, multiple parties enter binding contracts. Countless markets exist in the world. The business world operates within these markets, and we need to examine (and understand) behavior in them. Surprisingly, given the number and diversity of markets, they all follow general principles. It is these principles we now focus on because knowing them is essential to understanding market behavior. We examine the behavior of individuals who enter contracts and on the aggregate effect that they create.

THE DEMAND SIDE OF A MARKET

Every market consists of demanders and suppliers. A manager needs to know how potential customers value a product or service, and must estimate the quantity of goods demanded at various prices. One goal of managers is to maximize firm value. The ability to focus on profit requires a thorough knowledge of demand, especially the behavior of revenue as price changes. Total revenue is equal to the number of units sold (Q) multiplied by the price (P) at which they were sold ($TR = P \times Q$).

The association of price and quantity demanded often depends on many variables, some controlled by the manager and some not. Possible influences include income and tastes, prices of substitutes and complementary products, advertising dollars, product quality (as well as the quality of substitutes and complements), and governmental fiat. The behavior of quantity demanded relative to price is called a firm's **demand function** (holding other possible influences constant).

A demand curve shows managers how many units they sell at a given price. Consider Figure 1.1, which shows the demand curve for copper in the world market

Demand function Quantity demanded relative to price, holding other possible influences constant.

FIGURE 1.1

The Market Demand Curve for Copper, World Market

The market demand curve for copper shows the amount of copper that buyers would like to purchase at various prices.

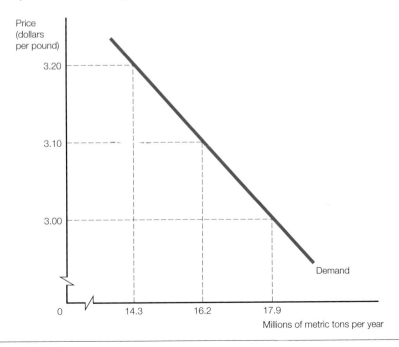

STRATEGY SESSION: Supply and Demand in Action

On any day, view the commodity pages in the financial section of the print media or online, and you'll see the law of supply and demand at work.

For instance, in *The Economic Times* of India on May 11, 2011, the headline read "Pineapple Prices Fall on Over Supply." Reading on in the story revealed that pineapple prices had "crashed" (about a 40% decline) following a "glut" of pineapples arriving in the market. The number of loads arriving in Mumbai (Bombay) had jumped threefold. In addition, other summer fruit, such as mangos and watermelon, were starting to come to market, suppressing the demand for pineapple. A rightward shifting supply curve and a leftward shifting demand curve will lead to a decline in price—just as the text analysis tells us. Last year, pineapple prices rose 20%. This contributed to the 2011 supply shift as pineapple producers planted more in 2011.

On May 13, 2011, four headlines and several smaller stories appeared in *The Economic Times* of India: "Crude Oil Climbs Above $100 on EU GDP Growth" (a rightward demand shift); "Speculation on Demand Pushed up Copper" (a rightward demand shift); "Brazil's Production Fall Lifts Sugar" (a leftward supply shift); "Buying Koreans Fuel US Meat Rally" (a rightward demand shift); and "Corn Rises in US on Rains" (a leftward supply shift).

U.S. beef prices have risen 13% in a year because of the added demand of Korean, Mexican, and Japanese consumers. While watching India and Thailand's sugar production, the world forgot about Brazil, where sugar production in one major region fell 69%. Brazil is the world's largest sugar producer. The headlines and the stories below them show that there are local markets (pineapples) and global markets (sugar, beef, copper, oil), and that one must be aware of supply-and-demand shifts both locally and internationally if one wants to predict prices.

But it's not just traditional consumption good commodities that exemplify the supply-demand model anymore. In an electronic world, more goods are now in active real-time supply-demand markets. For instance, the Boston Red Sox are normally a very strong baseball team. They should be: Their payroll is second to only the New York Yankees. But they started off the 2011 baseball season miserably, losing their first six games, all away from Boston. Their home games are usually sold out, but a secondary market exists in which people who have bought game tickets for speculative purposes or cannot attend a game for which they hold a ticket can offer these tickets for sale.

The first home game of the season, the season opener, is always a game where the demand for tickets is high. In addition, the first home game in 2011 was against the Red Sox's hated rival, the Yankees. However, ticket prices for the game were down about $100 according to Ace Ticket, the largest Red Sox ticket broker. FanSnap.com had 5,000 tickets for the game listed for sale at an average price of $253 on April 7, 2011, down about 23% from the April 1 average.

Two things likely happened here. First, demand shifted to the left as fickle fans are less enthusiastic about going to a game when the team is going bad (and the weather in Boston in early April is always iffy), and second, the supply is likely to shift rightward as ticket-holding fans are less enthusiastic about watching an underperforming team in the cold.

Sources: *The Economic Times*, May 11, 2011 and May 13, 2011; and "Boston Red Sox Prices Slump 40% as 0-6 Start is Worst Since 1945," *Bloomberg News*, April 8, 2011, at www.bloomberg .com/news/2011-04-07/boston-red-sox-start-season-0-6- for-first-time-since-45-in-cleveland-loss.html.

in 2012. The figure shows that 16.2 million metric tons of copper are demanded annually if the price is $3.10 per pound; 14.3 million metric tons if the price is $3.20 per pound; and 17.9 million metric tons if the price is $3.00 per pound. An important reason why copper has experienced recent growth in quantity demanded is its increasing use in emerging markets like China and India.

The demand curve in Figure 1.1 shows the global quantity of copper demanded at all prices. Any demand curve pertains to a particular period of time, and the shape and position of the demand curve can depend on the period length. The demand curve for copper slopes downward to the right. In mathematical terms, we say it has a *negative slope*; that is, the quantity of copper demanded increases as the price falls. This is true for most commodities: They almost always slope downward to the right. This makes sense; managers should expect price increases to result in lower sales.

Any demand curve is based on the assumption that other influences like tastes and incomes are held constant. Changes in any of these factors are likely to shift the position of a commodity's demand curve. So if consumers' tastes shift toward goods that use considerable copper or if consumers' incomes increase (and they thus buy more goods using copper), the demand curve for copper will shift to the right. In other words, holding the price of copper constant, more copper is demanded at any price. We will discuss this more fully in Chapter 2.

THE SUPPLY SIDE OF A MARKET

The supply side of a market is represented by a market supply curve that shows how many units of a commodity sellers will offer at any price. Figure 1.2 shows the supply curve for copper in the world market in 2012. According to the figure, 16.2 million metric tons of copper are supplied if the price of copper is $3.10 per pound, 17.4 million tons if the price is $3.20 per pound, and 14.9 million tons if the price is $3.00 per pound.

Note the supply curve slopes upward to the right. In mathematical terms, we say it has a *positive slope*; in other words, the quantity of copper supplied increases as the price rises. This seems plausible: Higher prices provide an incentive to suppliers to produce more copper to sell. Any supply curve is based on the assumption that production technology is held constant. If lower-cost production technology is developed, then managers will be willing to sell more units at any price. That is, technological change often causes a supply curve to shift to the right.

The supply curve for a product is affected by the cost of production inputs (labor, capital, and land). When costs of inputs decrease, managers realize lower production costs and are willing to supply a given amount at a lower price. So decreases in the cost of inputs cause supply curves to shift to the right. If input costs increase, managers are willing to supply a given amount only at a higher price (because their costs are higher). Hence the supply curve shifts to the left.

FIGURE 1.2

The Market Supply Curve for Copper, World Market

The market supply curve for copper shows the amount of copper that sellers would offer at various prices.

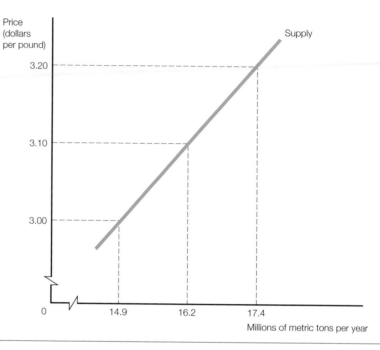

EQUILIBRIUM PRICE

Economists represent markets as the interaction of demand and supply curves. To illustrate, consider the world copper market shown in Figure 1.3. We construct the figure by overlaying the demand curve (Figure 1.1) with the supply curve (Figure 1.2). Now we can determine market behavior at various prices. For example, if the price of copper is $3.20 per pound, the demand curve indicates that 14.3 million metric tons of copper are demanded, while the supply curve indicates that 17.4 million metric tons are supplied. Therefore, if the market price is $3.20 per pound, there is a mismatch between the quantity supplied and the quantity demanded. Specifically, as shown in Figure 1.3, there is excess supply of 3.1 million metric tons. Some producers will not be able to sell all their inventories at this price; they may be tempted to cut their prices to reduce these inventories. Hence a market price of $3.20 per pound creates an unbalance in the market—there is too much supply. Because of this excess supply, producers will drop their prices, so $3.20 is not a sustainable market price.

If the price is $3.00 per pound, the demand curve indicates that 17.9 million metric tons are demanded, while the supply curve indicates that 14.9 million

FIGURE 1.3

Equilibrium Price of Copper, World Market

The equilibrium price is $3.10 per pound, since quantity demanded equals the quantity supplied at this price.

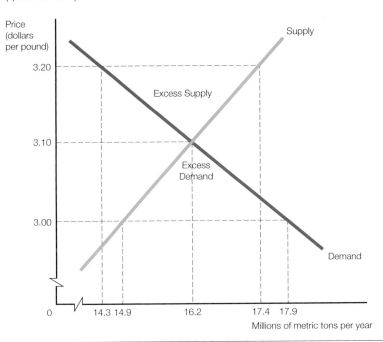

metric tons are supplied. So a market price of $3.00 also creates an unbalance in the market: There is not enough supply to satisfy demand. In fact, at this price consumers want to purchase an additional 3 million metric tons, but they can find no suppliers. When suppliers realize there is a shortage of copper they will increase their prices. Hence $3.00 is not a sustainable market price.

So what is a sustainable market price? A price is sustainable when the quantity demanded at a price is equal to the quantity supplied at that price. The market is in balance because individuals who want to purchase the good can, and everyone who wants to sell the good can. We say the market is at **equilibrium**. In Figure 1.3, the price at which the quantity supplied equals the quantity demanded is $3.10 per pound. This is also the point where the two curves intersect.

Equilibrium When the market is in balance because everyone who wants to purchase the good can and every seller who wants to sell the good can.

ACTUAL PRICE

Of course, price managers are interested in the actual price—the price that really prevails—not the equilibrium price. In general economists assume the actual price approximates the equilibrium price, which seems reasonable enough because the

---

STRATEGY SESSION: Using the Law of Supply and Demand to Invest in Stocks

Tax incentives designed to encourage homeowners and businesses in Italy and Germany are expiring, leading to a leftward shift in the demand curve for solar panels. At the same time, China's JA Solar Holdings Co. and Suntech (the two largest solar cell makers by capacity in the world) are greatly expanding their production capacity (as were other solar panel makers). This has led the supply curve to shift to the right. As discussed in this chapter, a leftward demand shift alone will cause prices to fall, and a rightward shift in supply alone will cause prices to fall. Put the two together, and prices really fall.

Investors watch for these market shifts. These price decreases do not bode well for firms making solar panels. Those with high production costs would be most hurt, but those with low production costs would still see a drop in profit margin. Savvy investors know that stock prices are generally positively correlated with profits, so investors sold solar panel companies' stocks short, with the intention of buying back shares on the cheap when solar panel firms' profits fell and hence stock prices fell.

First Solar Inc. of Tempe, Arizona, the world's largest producer of thin film solar panels, had 23% of their outstanding shares sell short. Q-Cells SE, a German company, had 54% of its shares sold short. Nine other large producers have large amounts of shares sold short (although none as much as First Solar and Q-Cells SE). The solar industries' stocks have a history of volatility, so much so that Shawn Kravetz of Esplanade Capital (a Boston hedge fund) and his colleagues have dubbed the industry: the "solarcoaster."

How does one make money by knowing about supply and demand? Watch for predicted price shifts and then buy or sell the product itself in the market, or buy or sell the stock in the market and cash out in the futures market. Sound easy? It actually takes nerve to be a speculator.

Source: "(BN) Shorts Sell 'Solarcoaster' as China Glut Sinks Panel Prices," *Bloomberg News*, June 19, 2011, at www .bloomberg.com/news/2011-06-19/short-sellers-hammer-solarcoaster-as-glut-of-chinese-panels-sinks-prices.html.

---

basic forces at work tend to push the actual price toward the equilibrium price. Therefore, if conditions remain fairly stable for a time, the actual price should move toward the equilibrium price.

To see this, consider the global market for copper, as described in Figure 1.3. What if the actual price of copper is $3.20 per pound? As we have seen, this price will cause downward pressure on the price of copper. Suppose the price, responding to this pressure, falls to $3.15 per pound. Comparing the quantity demanded with that supplied at $3.15 per pound, we see there is still downward pressure on price because supply exceeds demand. The price, responding to this pressure, may fall to $3.12 per pound; but comparing the quantity demanded with that supplied at this price, we find there is still downward pressure on price.

As long as the market price is greater than the equilibrium price, there is downward pressure on price. Similarly, as long as the actual price is less than the equilibrium price, there is upward pressure on price. Hence there is always a tendency for the actual price to move toward the equilibrium price. The speed of this adjustment can vary. Sometimes it takes a long time for the actual price to approach the equilibrium price, and sometimes it happens quickly.

This price adjustment process is what Adam Smith called the market's **invisible hand**. No governmental agency is needed to induce producers to drop or increase their prices. They act more or less in unison and cause the market price to change.

Invisible hand When no governmental agency is needed to induce producers to drop or increase their prices.

WHAT IF THE DEMAND CURVE SHIFTS?

Any supply and demand diagram like Figure 1.3 is essentially a snapshot of the situation at a particular time. The results in Figure 1.3 are limited to a particular period because demand and supply curves are not static; they shift in reaction to changes in the environment. What happens to the equilibrium price of a good when its demand curve changes? This is important to know because managers need to anticipate and forecast price changes.

To illustrate the effects of a rightward shift of a demand curve, consider the copper industry in 2010. Housing starts were increasing (copper tubing is often used for water lines) in the emerging markets of China and India. As indicated in the right panel of Figure 1.4, managers should have expected that such a rightward shift of the demand curve would cause an increase in the price of copper from P

FIGURE 1.4

Effects of Leftward and Rightward Shifts of the Demand Curve on the Equilibrium Price of Copper

A leftward shift of the demand curve results in a decrease in the equilibrium price; a rightward shift results in an increase in the equilibrium price.

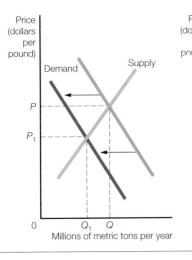

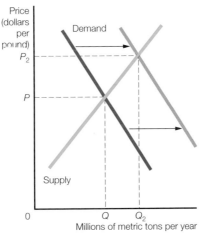

STRATEGY SESSION: Life During a Market Movement

When the market moves, planets can tremble. In early spring 2008, shifting demand and supply curves were impacting every country. The global food supply was in disequilibrium, and it appeared that the world was in a panic. During one week in early spring 2008, major governments worldwide used their sovereign powers to restrict trade in basic foods. Saudi Arabia cut import taxes on basic foodstuffs, India removed tariffs on edible oils while banning rice exports, and Vietnam cut its rice exports by 22%. Political unrest was beginning to erupt in countries as diverse as Egypt and Mexico over the rising cost of food. What is perhaps a mere inconvenience of paying $4.25 for a gallon of milk in the United States is one of life or death to those who live on the fringes. For the 300 million Chinese who live in poverty, food accounts for 50% of household expenses.

Look at what caused this commotion. The figure on the next page shows the behavior of food prices prior to mid-2008.

You can clearly see the acceleration of prices across major food groups. This is a shift in the demand curve. The *Financial Times* reported that the Philippine government paid $700 per ton of rice—almost double the price the government paid in December 2007. The price of corn increased by 73% between April 2007 and April 2008 (from $3.46 a bushel to $6 a bushel). Wheat increased by 123% in this same period (from $5.63 to $12.57 a bushel). In China, the price of pork increased by 63%. In early 2012, a bushel of corn cost $6.42 while a bushel of wheat was priced at $6.48.

This rightward shift in the demand curve for food was attributed to several factors. One theory was that Thomas Malthus's mathematical doomsday machine was finally reaching fruition. The world population continues to expand, while agricultural acreage continues to shrink. Many governments in developing countries have focused efforts on economic development rather than agriculture. A UN report shows the annual growth in agricultural productivity slowed to 1% by 2002. A growing middle class in large developing countries like China and India consumes more food. As people increase their income, they generally eat more food. In China, consumption of meat has

to P_2. In fact, the global price of copper in 2010 was roughly $2.65 per pound. By 2012 this price had increased to $3.82.

In mid-2009, we see a leftward shift in the demand curve for copper, as shown in the left panel of Figure 1.4. Because of slow economic growth in the United States and other countries, there was less demand for copper. This meant that the demand curve for copper shifted left, so there was less quantity demanded at any given price. Figure 1.4 shows a decrease in price from P to P_1.

WHAT IF THE SUPPLY CURVE SHIFTS?

What happens to the equilibrium price of a product when its supply curve changes? For example, suppose that because of technological advances in cop-

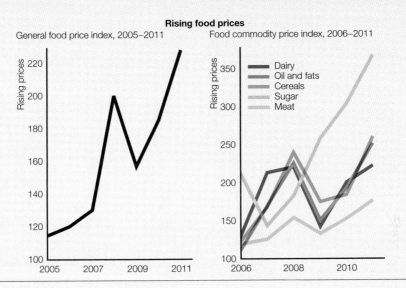

Rising food prices

General food price index, 2005–2011

Food commodity price index, 2006–2011

doubled as personal income has increased. Finally, the increased use of food stock, like corn, for the production of ethanol fuel has taken such products out of the food market. Also, more individuals are leaving rural areas (farms) in developing countries and moving to urban areas. These trends are apt to move the supply curve to the left and the demand curve to the right and put further upward price pressure on food.

Sources: "Countries Rush to Restrict Trade in Basic Foods," *Financial Times*, April 2, 2008, p. 1; "Food Prices Give Asian Nations a Wake-Up Call," *Financial Times*, April 3, 2008, p. 4.

per production, large producers like Codelco of Chile can supply more copper at a given price than they used to. This will cause the supply curve to shift to the right, as shown in the right panel of Figure 1.5. How will this shift affect the equilibrium price? Clearly it will fall from P (where the original supply curve intersects the demand curve) to P_4 (where the new supply curve intersects the demand curve).

On the other hand, suppose there is a significant increase in the wage rates of copper workers. This increase will cause the supply curve to shift to the left, as shown in the left panel of Figure 1.5. This shift will cause the equilibrium price to increase from P (where the original supply curve intersects the demand curve) to P_3 (where the new supply curve intersects the demand curve).

FIGURE 1.5

Effects of Leftward and Rightward Shifts of the Supply Curve on the Equilibrium Price of Copper

A leftward shift of the supply curve results in an increase in the equilibrium price; a rightward shift results in a decrease in the equilibrium price.

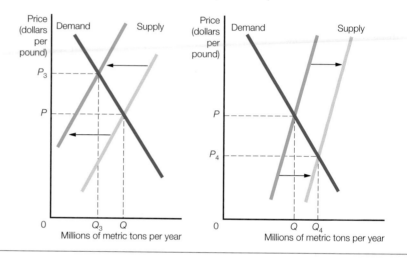

SUMMARY

1. The main task of managers is to make decisions. We offer a guide for the managerial world; it is based on the behavioral economics of the managerial model. In contrast to microeconomics, which is largely descriptive, managerial economics is prescriptive. Courses in managerial economics provide fundamental analytical tools as well as play a major integrating role. Our decision framework describes behavior found at a wide range of organizations, from non-business organizations like government agencies to single-owner entrepreneurial efforts.

2. To apply economics to managerial behavior, we need a theory of the firm. The theory accepted by most managerial economists is that the owners want to maximize its value, defined as the present value of its expected future net cash flows (which for now are equated with profit). However, this maximization occurs subject to constraints because the firm has limited inputs, particularly in the very short run, and must comply with a variety of laws and contracts.

3. Managerial economists define profit somewhat differently from the way accountants do. When economists speak of profit, they mean profit over and

above what the owners' labor and capital employed in the business could earn elsewhere. To a considerable extent, the differences between the concepts of profit used by the accountant and the economist reflect the difference in their functions.

4. Three important reasons for the existence of profit are innovation, risk, and market power. Profit and loss are the mainspring of a free enterprise economy. They are signals showing where resources are needed and where they are too abundant. They are important incentives for innovation and risk taking. They are society's reward for efficiency.

5. Although managerial economists generally assume that owners want to maximize profit (and hence their value), a principal–agent problem arises if managers pursue their own interests, even though this decreases the profit of the owners. To address this problem, owners often give managers a financial stake in the future success of a firm.

6. Every market has a demand side and a supply side. The market demand curve shows the amount of a product buyers will purchase at various prices. The market supply curve shows the amount of a product producers are willing to sell at various prices. The equilibrium price is the price where the quantity demanded equals the quantity supplied. This price is also called the market-clearing price.

7. Both demand curves and supply curves can shift over time. This results in changes in a product's price. Rightward shifts in the demand curve (and leftward shifts in the supply curve) tend to increase price. Leftward shifts in the demand curve (and rightward shifts in the supply curve) tend to decrease price.

PROBLEMS

wwnorton.com/studyspace

1. A book is to be written by Britney Spears. Batman Books agrees to pay Britney $6 million for the rights to this not-yet-written memoir. According to one leading publisher, Batman Books could earn a profit of roughly $1.2 million if it sold 625,000 copies in hardcover. On the other hand, if it sold 375,000 copies, managers would lose about $1.3 million. Publishing executives stated that it was hard to sell more than 500,000 copies of a nonfiction hardcover book, and very exceptional to sell 1 million copies. Were Batman managers taking a substantial risk in publishing this book?

2. Some say that any self-respecting top manager joining a company does so with a front-end signing bonus. In many cases this bonus is in the seven figures. At the same time, the entering manager may be given a bonus guarantee. No matter what happens to firm profit, he or she gets at least a percentage of that bonus. Do long-term bonus guarantees help to solve the principal–agent problem, or do they exacerbate it? Why?

3. If the interest rate is 10%, what is the present value of the Monroe Corporation's profit in the next 10 years?

Number of Years in the Future	Profit (Millions of Dollars)
1	8
2	10
3	12
4	14
5	15
6	16
7	17
8	15
9	13
10	10

4. Managers at Du Pont de Nemours and Company expect a profit of $2.9 billion in 2012. Does this mean that Du Pont's expected economic profit will equal $2.9 billion? Why or why not?

5. William Howe must decide whether to start a business renting beach umbrellas at an ocean resort during June, July, and August of next summer. He believes he can rent each umbrella to vacationers at $5 a day, and he intends to lease 50 umbrellas for the three-month period for $3,000. To operate this business, he does not have to hire anyone (but himself), and he has no expenses other than the leasing costs and a fee of $3,000 per month to rent the business location. Howe is a college student, and if he did not operate this business, he could earn $4,000 for the three-month period doing construction work.

   a. If there are 80 days during the summer when beach umbrellas are demanded and Howe rents all 50 of his umbrellas on each of these days, what will be his accounting profit for the summer?

   b. What will be his economic profit for the summer?

6. On March 3, 2008, a revival of *Gypsy*, the Stephen Sondheim musical, opened at the St. James Theater in New York. Ticket prices ranged from $117 to $42 per seat. The show's weekly gross revenues, operating costs, and profit were estimated as follows, depending on whether the average ticket price was $75 or $65

	Average Price of $75	Average Price of $65
Gross revenues	$765,000	$680,000
Operating costs	600,000	600,000
Profit	165,000	80,000

a. With a cast of 71 people, a 30-piece orchestra, and more than 500 costumes, *Gypsy* cost more than $10 million to stage. This investment was in addition to the operating costs (such as salaries and theater rent). How many weeks would it take before the investors got their money back, according to these estimates, if the average price was $65? If it was $75?

b. George Wachtel, director of research for the League of American Theaters and Producers, has said that about one in three shows opening on Broadway in recent years has at least broken even. Were the investors in *Gypsy* taking a substantial risk?

c. According to one Broadway producer, "Broadway isn't where you make the money any more. It's where you establish the project so you can make the money. When you mount a show now, you really have to think about where it's going to play later." If so, should the profit figures here be interpreted with caution?

d. If the investors in this revival of *Gypsy* make a profit, will this profit be, at least in part, a reward for bearing risk?

7. If the demand curve for wheat in the United States is

$$P = 12.4 - Q_D$$

where P is the farm price of wheat (in dollars per bushel) and Q_D is the quantity of wheat demanded (in billions of bushels), and the supply curve for wheat in the United States is

$$P = -2.6 + 2Q_S$$

where Q_S is the quantity of wheat supplied (in billions of bushels), what is the equilibrium price of wheat? What is the equilibrium quantity of wheat sold? Must the actual price equal the equilibrium price? Why or why not?

8. The lumber industry was hit hard by the downturn in housing starts in 2010 and 2011. Prices plunged from $290 per thousand board feet to less than $200 per thousand board feet. Many observers believed this price decrease was caused by the slowing of new home construction because of the glut of unsold homes on the market. Was this price decrease caused by a shift in the supply or demand curve?

9. From November 2010 to March 2011 the price of gold increased from $1,200 per ounce to over $1,800 per ounce. Newspaper articles during this period said there was little increased demand from the jewelry industry but significantly more demand from investors who were purchasing gold because of the falling dollar.

a. Was this price increase due to a shift in the demand curve for gold, a shift in the supply curve for gold, or both?

b. Did this price increase affect the supply curve for gold jewelry? If so, how?

EXCEL EXERCISE: DEMAND, SUPPLY, AND MARKET EQUILIBRIUM

Suppose you were given the following information about market demand:

Price (P)	Quantity Demanded (Q_D)
14	0
13	1
12	2
11	3
10	4
9	5
8	6
7	7
6	8
5	9
4	10
3	11
2	12
1	13
0	14

and the following information about market supply:

Price (P)	Quantity Supplied (Q_S)
2	0
3	1
4	2
5	3
6	4
7	5
8	6
9	7
10	8
11	9
12	10
13	11
14	12

You could predict market equilibrium in several ways.

Suppose you noticed that every number in the demand table corresponded to numbers generated by the formula

$$Q_D = 14 - P$$

Your statistics course will teach you how to fit an equation to data, but you may have encountered an SAT, GMAT, or GRE question that gave you a column of numbers and then asked you to continue the column for another one or two entries. If you answered that problem correctly, you implicitly solved for the above equation.

Suppose you noted that every number in the supply table corresponded to numbers generated by the formula

$$Q_S = -2 + P$$

You know from the text that in equilibrium, $Q_D = Q_S$, and so setting the two equal and solving for P gives

$$Q_D = 14 - P = -2 + P = Q_S$$

or

$$2P = 16$$

or

$$P = 8$$

Substituting $P = 8$ into the demand equation gives

$$Q_D = 14 - 8 = 6$$

Substituting $P = 8$ into the supply relationship gives

$$Q_S = -2 + 8 = 6$$

Thus market equilibrium is $P = 8$ and $Q = 6$.

But suppose that you couldn't estimate the demand and supply equations. Can you use a spreadsheet to calculate the equilibrium? Yes. Here's how.

Open your spreadsheet and put 14 in cell A1, then 13 in cell A2, and 12 in cell A3, and so on. Thus, you will have entered each price sequentially from 14 to 0.

Then put 0 in cell B1, 1 in cell B2, 2 in cell B3, and so on. Thus, you will have entered all the quantities demanded at their corresponding price.

Then put 12 in cell C1, 11 in cell C2, 10 in cell C3, down to 0 in cell C13. Thus, you will have entered all quantities supplied at their corresponding price.

Then in cell D1 enter the formula $= B1 - C1$ (Note: You must have the $=$ sign, and don't skip spaces) and in cell D2 enter the formula $= B2 - C2$, and so on. You don't actually have to enter the formulas multiple times. Just click on the cell D1 in the lower righthand corner, drag with your mouse down to cell D13, and the correct formulas will be transferred to cells D2 to D13.

The numbers that will appear in cells D1 to D13 will be the quantity demanded (Q_D) at the respective price minus the quantity supplied (Q_S) at the respective price (called the *excess demand*). As there is no excess demand at equilibrium, that is $Q_D = Q_S$, you look for the D column cell with a 0. If you've entered everything correctly, it'll be cell D7. Reading leftward across the seventh row, you'll see that $P = 8$ and $Q_D = Q_S = 6$.

The nice thing about the spreadsheet is that you can clearly see the amount of excess demand at each price above the market equilibrium, for example -10 at $P = 12$, and so you can imagine the pressure on the suppliers to lower the price to get rid of that 10 of inventory.

When the excess demand is negative (above the market equilibrium price), we usually multiply it through by -1 to make it positive and call it *excess supply*. Doing so enables us to see by how much Q_S exceeds Q_D when the market price is too high. When there is positive excess demand, the positive number shows the motivation of unsatisfied demanders with higher reservation prices to up their bids for the product (and the motivation for sellers to raise their prices).

Throughout the book, we will present other applications of using the spreadsheet to solve the economic problems facing managers.

What about case 2? Here the industry is entitled by law to a class 6 bridge. But another way of saying this is that the industry is entitled to profits of 250. The industry doesn't care where these profits come from as long as it gets 250.

Let's solve this one.

Enter 100 in cell A8, 150 in cell A9, and so on, until you've entered 250 in cell A13.

Enter 0 in cell B8, 25 in cell B9, and so on, until you've entered 120 in cell B13.

Columns A and B duplicate the initial data table.

Enter =A13−A8 in cell C8, =A13−A9 in cell C9, =A13−A10 in cell C10, =A13−A11 in cell C11, =A13−A12 in cell C12, and =A13−A13 in cell C13. Column C represents the amount of money the town owes the industry if the town decides to improve the bridge to a class that is not class 6. For instance, if the town decides to keep the bridge at class 1, the industry will earn 100 from sales of its product. But since the industry is entitled to the profits associated with a class 6 bridge (250), the town will have to pay the industry the difference, that is, 250−100 = A13−A9.

What are the town's total expenses for each bridge class? Enter =B8+C8 in cell D8 and click and drag until cell D13. Column D is the town's total cost for each bridge class, that is, the cost of upgrading the bridge plus the cost of compensating the industry for lost profit. Searching column D for the lowest number or entering =Min(D8:D13) in cell D14, yields 105 in cell D11. Note that this entails a class 4 bridge just as in case 1. Note also that the town incurs a 55 cost in upgrading the bridge and a 50 payment because the industry's profit is 200 with a class 4 bridge and the industry is guaranteed 250 with the class 6 bridge.

But if the industry wanted to, it could insist that the town upgrade the bridge to class 6. That would cost the town 120 − 55 = 65 more than to upgrade to the class 4 bridge. Going to a class 6 bridge would cost the town 65 more in bridge expense. But going to a class 6 bridge (from a class 4) would save the town 50 in terms of compensating the industry for its lost profits. Thus, if the industry wished, it could accept (at minimum) a 50 payment for its lost profits from having a class 4 bridge. Or it could hold out for slightly less than 65 (the extra cost the town would incur if the industry insisted on a class 6 bridge). Where between the 50 and 65 payment the actual payment would be depends on the bargaining skills of the parties. But since the leverage lies with the industry, we'd expect the payment to be closer to 65.

Notice that no matter who held the leverage, the optimal solution would be a class 4 bridge. Of course, the distribution of wealth differed significantly depending on who had the leverage (the property rights to having a class 1 or a class 6 bridge). This indifference solution is attributable to Coase.

CHAPTER 18

OPTIMIZATION TECHNIQUES

To begin this chapter, we describe marginal analysis—a powerful tool that illuminates many central aspects of decision making. Economists think at the margins. Virtually all the rules we study about optimal behavior of firms and managers are driven by this concept.

Next, we examine the basic elements of differential calculus, including the rules of differentiation and the use of a derivative to maximize a function such as profit or minimize one such as cost. Differentiation tells us what changes will occur in one variable (the dependent variable) when a small (marginal) change is made in another variable (the independent variable). Therefore, marginal analysis can be implemented by the use of differentiation.

Finally, we examine constrained optimization, including Lagrangian multipliers. When managers want to maximize profit, such maximization or minimization is often subject to constraints (such as producing a certain output to adhere to a contract or utilizing a certain amount of labor in a union agreement).

FUNCTIONAL RELATIONSHIPS

Frequently a relationship between economic variables is represented by a table or graph. Although tables and graphs are helpful, another way of expressing economic relationships is with equations. For example, how can the relationship between the number of units sold and the price be expressed in an equation? One way is to use the following functional notation

$$Q = f(P) \tag{18.1}$$

where Q is the number of units sold and P is price. This equation is read as "The number of units sold is a function of price," which means the number of units sold *depends* on price. In other words, the number of units sold is the *dependent* variable, and price is the *independent* variable.

Equation (18.1) is useful, but it does not tell us *how* the number of units sold depends on price. A more specific representation of this relationship is

$$Q = 200 - 5P \tag{18.2}$$

This equation says that if the price equals $10, the number of units sold should be $200 - 5(10) = 150$.

MARGINAL ANALYSIS

The **marginal value** of a dependent variable is defined as the change in this dependent variable associated with a one-unit change in a particular independent variable. As an illustration, consider Table 18.1, which shows in columns 1 and 2 the total profit of the Roland Corporation if we vary the number of units produced. In this case, total profit is the dependent variable and output is the independent variable. Therefore, the marginal value of profit, called the **marginal profit**, is the change in total profit associated with a one-unit change in output.

Column 3 of Table 18.1 shows the value of marginal profit. If output increases from zero to one unit, column 2 shows the total profit increases by $100 (from $0 to $100). Therefore, the marginal profit in column 3 equals $100 if the output is one unit. If the output increases from one to two units, the total profit increases by $150 (from $100 to $250). Therefore, the marginal profit in column 3 equals $150 if the output is increased from one to two units.

The central point about a marginal relationship of this sort is that the dependent variable—in this case, total profit—is maximized when its marginal value shifts from positive to negative. To see this, consider Table 18.1. So long as marginal profit is positive, the Roland Corporation can raise its total profit by increasing output. For example, if output increases from five to six units, the marginal profit is positive ($150); therefore, the firm's total profit goes up (by $150). But when marginal profit shifts from positive to negative, total profit *falls* with any further increase in output. In Table 18.1, this point is reached when the firm produces seven units of output. If output increases beyond seven units, marginal profit shifts from positive to negative—and total profit goes down (by $50). So we can see that the

Marginal value The change in the dependent variable associated with a one-unit change in a particular independent variable.

Marginal profit The change in total profit associated with a one-unit change in output.

TABLE 18.1

Relationship between Output and Profit: Roland Corporation

(1) Number of Units of Output per Day	(2) Total Profit	(3) Marginal Profit	(4) Average Profit
0	0	—	—
1	100	100	100
2	250	150	125
3	600	350	200
4	1,000	400	250
5	1,350	350	270
6	1,500	150	250
7	1,550	50	221.4
8	1,500	−50	187.5
9	1,400	−100	155.5
10	1,200	−200	120

---

dependent variable—in this case, total profit—is maximized when its marginal value shifts from positive to negative.

Because managers are interested in determining how to maximize profit (or other performance measures), this is a useful result. It emphasizes the importance of looking at marginal values—and the hazards that may arise if average values are used instead. In Table 18.1, **average profit**—that is, total profit divided by output—is shown in column 4. It may seem reasonable to choose the output level that gives the highest average profit; countless managers have done so. But this is not the correct decision if managers want to maximize profit. Instead, as stressed in the previous paragraph, managers should choose the output level at which marginal profit shifts from positive to negative.

To prove this, we need only find the output level in Table 18.1 at which average profit is highest. Based on a comparison of the figures in column 4, this output level is five units; and according to column 2, the total profit at this output level equals $1,350. But we found that the output level at which marginal profit shifts from positive to negative is seven units; and according to column 2, the total profit at this point equals $1,550. In other words, the total profit is $200 higher if the output level is seven rather than five units. Thus if managers of this firm were to choose the output level at which average profit is highest, they would sacrifice $200 per day in profits.

It is important to understand the relationship between average and marginal values. Because the marginal value represents the change in the total, the average

Average profit The total profit divided by output.

value must increase if the marginal value is greater than the average value. Similarly, the average value must decrease if the marginal value is less than the average value. Table 18.1 illustrates these propositions. For the first to fifth units of output, the marginal profit is greater than the average profit. Because the extra profit from each additional unit is greater than the average, the average is pulled up as more units are produced. For the sixth to tenth units of output, the marginal profit is less than the average profit. Because the extra profit from each additional unit is less than the average, the average value is pulled down as more units are produced.

RELATIONSHIPS AMONG TOTAL, MARGINAL, AND AVERAGE VALUES

To further explore the relationships among total, marginal, and average values, consider Figure 18.1, which shows the relationships among total, average, and marginal profit, on the one hand, and output, on the other hand, for the Roland Corporation. The relationship between output and profit is exactly the same as in Table 18.1; but rather than using particular numbers to designate output or profit, we use symbols such as Q_0 and Q_1 for output levels and π_0 for a profit level. This makes the results valid in general, not just for a particular set of numerical values.

Note that Figure 18.1 contains two panels. The upper panel (panel A) shows the relationship between total profit and output levels, whereas the lower panel (panel B) shows the relationship between average profit and marginal profit, on the one hand, and output levels, on the other. The horizontal scale of panel A is the same as that of panel B, so a given output level, like Q_0, is the same distance from the origin (along the horizontal axis) in panel A as in panel B.

In practice we seldom are presented with data concerning both (1) the relationship between total profit and output and (2) the relationship between average profit and output because it is relatively simple to derive the latter relationship from the former. How can this be done? Take any output level, say Q_0. *At this output level, the average profit equals the slope of the straight line from the origin to point E, the point on the total profit curve corresponding to output level Q_0.* To see that this is the case, note that the average profit at this output level equals π_0/Q_0, where π_0 is the level of total profit if the output level is Q_0. Because the slope of any straight line equals the vertical distance between two points on the line divided by the horizontal distance between them, the slope of the line from the origin to point E equals π_0/Q_0.[1] Thus the slope of line $0E$ equals the average profit at this output level. (In other words, K_0 in panel B of Figure 18.1 is equal to the slope of line $0E$.) To determine the relationship between average profit and output from the relationship between total profit and output, we repeat this procedure for each level of output, not just Q_0. The resulting average profit curve is shown in panel B.

Turning to the relationship between marginal profit and output (in panel B), it is relatively simple to derive this relationship also from the relationship between

1. The vertical distance between the origin and the point E equals π_0, and the horizontal distance between these two points equals Q_0. Therefore, the vertical distance divided by the horizontal distance equals π_0/Q_0.

FIGURE 18.1

Total Profit, Average Profit, and Marginal Profit: Roland Corporation

The average and marginal profit curves in panel B can be derived geometrically from the total profit curve in panel A.

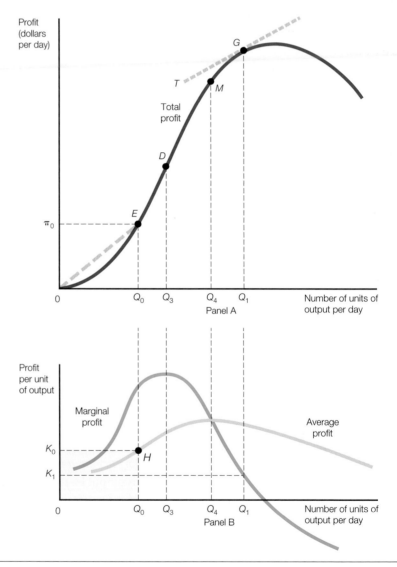

total profit and output (in panel A). Take any output level, say Q_1. *At this output level, the marginal profit equals the slope of the tangent to the total profit curve (in panel A) at the point where the output level is Q_1.* In other words, the marginal profit equals the slope of line T in Figure 18.1, which is tangent to the total profit curve at point G. As a first step toward seeing why this is true, consider Figure 18.2, which provides a magnified picture of the total profit curve in the neighborhood of point G.

Recall that marginal profit is defined as the extra profit resulting from a very small increase (specifically, a one-unit increase) in output. If the output level increases from Q_1 to Q_2, the total profit increases from π_1 to π_2, as shown in Figure 18.2. Therefore, the extra profit per unit of output is $(\pi_2 - \pi_1)/(Q_2 - Q_1)$, which is the slope of the GK line. But this increase in output is rather large. Suppose we decrease Q_2 so it is closer to Q_1. In particular, let the new value of Q_2 be Q_2'. If output increases from Q_1 to Q_2', the extra profit per unit of output equals $(\pi_2' - \pi_1)/(Q_2' - Q_1)$, which is the slope of the GL line. If we further decrease Q_2 until the distance between Q_1 and Q_2 is extremely small, the slope of the tangent (line T) at point G becomes a good estimate of $(\pi_2 - \pi_1)/(Q_2 - Q_1)$. In the limit, for changes in output in a very small neighborhood around Q_1, the slope of the tangent is marginal profit. (This slope equals K_1 in panel B of Figure 18.1.) To determine the relationship between marginal profit and output from the relationship between total profit and output, we repeat this procedure for each level

---

FIGURE 18.2

Marginal Profit Equals the Slope of the Tangent to the Total Profit Curve

As the distance between Q_1 and Q_2 becomes extremely small, the slope of line T becomes a good estimate of $(\pi_2 - \pi_1)/(Q_2 - Q_1)$.

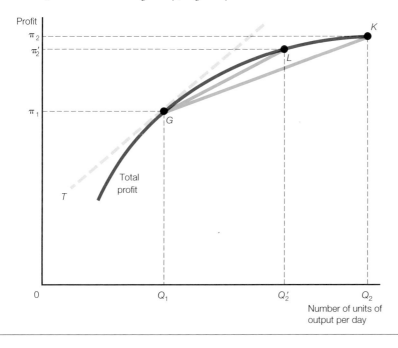

of output, not just Q_1. The resulting marginal profit curve is shown in panel B of Figure 18.1.

Sometimes we are given an average profit curve like that in panel B of Figure 18.1 but not the total profit curve. To derive the latter curve from the former, note that total profit equals average profit times output. Hence, if output equals Q_0, total profit equals K_0 times Q_0. In other words, π_0 in panel A equals the area of rectangle $0K_0HQ_0$ in panel B. To derive the relationship between total profit and output from the relationship between average profit and output, we repeat this procedure for each level of output. That is, we find the area of the appropriate rectangle of this sort corresponding to each output level, not just Q_0. The resulting total profit curve is shown in panel A.

Finally, two further points should be made concerning the total, average, and marginal profit curves in Figure 18.1. First, you should be able to tell by a glance at panel A that the marginal profit increases as the output level rises from zero to Q_3 and that it decreases as output rises further. Why is this so obvious from panel A? Because the slope of the total profit curve increases as we move from the origin to point D. In other words, lines drawn tangent to the total profit curve become steeper as we move from the origin to point D. Because marginal profit equals the slope of this tangent, it must increase as the output level rises from zero to Q_3. To the right of point D, the slope of the total profit curve decreases as the output level increases. That is, lines drawn tangent to the total profit curve become less steep as we move to the right of point D. Consequently, because marginal profit equals the slope of this tangent, it too must decrease when the output level rises beyond Q_3.

Second, panel B of Figure 18.1 confirms the following proposition: *The average profit curve must be rising if it is below the marginal profit curve, and it must be falling if it is above the marginal profit curve.* At output levels below Q_4, the average profit curve is below the marginal profit curve; therefore, the average profit curve is rising because the higher marginal profits are pulling up the average profits. At output levels above Q_4, the average profit curve is above the marginal profit curve; therefore, the average profit curve is falling because the lower marginal profits are pulling down the average profits. At Q_4, the straight line drawn from the origin to point M is just tangent to the total cost curve. Therefore, the average profit and marginal profit are equal at output level Q_4.

THE CONCEPT OF A DERIVATIVE

In the case of the Roland Corporation, we used Table 18.1 (which shows the relationship between the firm's output and profit) to find the profit-maximizing output level. Frequently a table of this sort is too cumbersome or inaccurate to be useful for this purpose. Instead we use an equation to represent the relationship between the variable we are trying to maximize (in this case, profit) and the variable or variables under the control of the decision maker (in this case, output).

Given an equation of this sort, we can employ the powerful concepts and techniques of differential calculus to find optimal decision solutions.

In previous sections, we defined the *marginal value* as the change in a dependent variable resulting from a one-unit change in an independent variable. If Y is the dependent variable and X is the independent variable

$$Y = f(X) \tag{18.3}$$

according to the notation in equation (18.1). Using Δ (called *delta*) to denote change, we can express a change in the independent variable as ΔX, and we can express a change in the dependent variable as ΔY. Thus the marginal value of Y is estimated by

$$\frac{\text{Change in } Y}{\text{Change in } X} = \frac{\Delta Y}{\Delta X} \tag{18.4}$$

For example, if a two-unit increase in X results in a one-unit increase in Y, $\Delta X = 2$ and $\Delta Y = 1$, then the marginal value of Y is about one-half. That is, the dependent variable Y increases by about one-half if the independent variable X increases by one.[2]

Unless the relationship between Y and X can be represented as a straight line (as in Figure 18.3), the value of $\Delta Y/\Delta X$ is not constant. For example, consider the relationship between Y and X in Figure 18.4. If a movement occurs from point G to point H, a relatively small change in X (from X_1 to X_2) is associated with a big change in Y (from Y_1 to Y_2). Therefore, between points G and H, the value of $\Delta Y/\Delta X$, which equals $(Y_2 - Y_1)/(X_2 - X_1)$, is relatively large. On the other hand, if a movement occurs from point K to point L, a relatively large change in X (from X_3 to X_4) is associated with a small change in Y (from Y_3 to Y_4). Consequently, between points K and L, the value of $\Delta Y/\Delta X$, which equals $(Y_4 - Y_3)/(X_4 - X_3)$, is relatively small.

The value of $\Delta Y/\Delta X$ is related to the steepness or flatness of the curve in Figure 18.4. Between points G and H the curve is relatively *steep*; this means a *small* change in X results in a *large* change in Y. Consequently $\Delta Y/\Delta X$ is relatively large. Between points K and L the curve is relatively *flat*; this means a *large* change in X results in a *small* change in Y. Consequently $\Delta Y/\Delta X$ is relatively small.

The derivative of Y with respect to X is defined as the limit of $\Delta Y/\Delta X$ as ΔX approaches zero. Because the derivative of Y with respect to X is denoted by dY/dX, this definition can be restated as

$$\frac{dY}{dX} = \lim_{\Delta X \to 0} \frac{\Delta Y}{\Delta X} \tag{18.5}$$

which is read "The derivative of Y with respect to X equals the limit of the ratio $\Delta Y/\Delta X$ as ΔX approaches zero." To understand what is meant by a limit, consider the function $(X - 2)$. What is the limit of this function as X approaches 2? Clearly,

2. Why do we say that Y increases by about ½ rather than by exactly ½? Because Y may not be linearly related to X.

FIGURE 18.3

Linear Relationships between Y and X

The relationship between Y and X can be represented as a straight line.

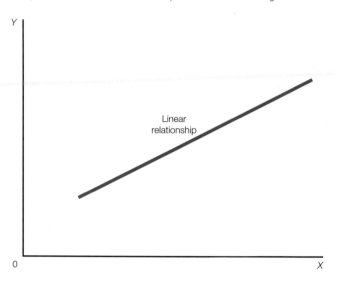

FIGURE 18.4

How the Value of $\Delta Y/\Delta X$ Varies Depending on the Steepness or Flatness of the Relationship between Y and X

Between points G and H, the curve is steep, so $\Delta Y/\Delta X$ is large. Between points K and L, the curve is flat, so $\Delta Y/\Delta X$ is small.

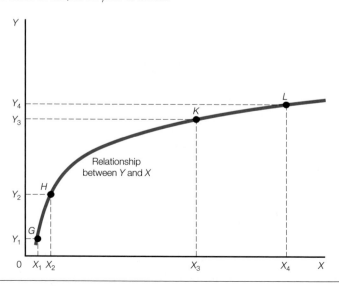

as X gets closer and closer to 2, $(X - 2)$ gets closer and closer to zero. What is the limit of this function as X approaches zero? Clearly, as X gets closer and closer to zero, $(X - 2)$ gets closer and closer to -2.

Graphically, the derivative of Y with respect to X equals the *slope* of the curve showing Y (on the vertical axis) as a function of X (on the horizontal axis). To see this, suppose we want to find the value of the derivative of Y with respect to X when X equals X_5 in Figure 18.5. A rough measure is the value of $\Delta Y/\Delta X$ when a movement is made from point A to point C; this measure equals

$$(Y_7 - Y_5)/(X_7 - X_5)$$

which is the slope of the AC line. A better measure is the value of $\Delta Y/\Delta X$ when a movement is made from point A to point B; this measure equals

$$(Y_6 - Y_5)/(X_6 - X_5)$$

which is the slope of the AB line. Why is the latter measure better than the former? Because the distance between points A and B is less than the distance between points A and C, and what we want is the value of $\Delta Y/\Delta X$ when ΔX is as small as possible. *Clearly, in the limit, as ΔX approaches zero, the ratio $\Delta Y/\Delta X$ is equal to the slope of the line M, which is drawn tangent to the curve at point A.*

FIGURE 18.5

Derivative as the Slope of the Curve

When X equals X_5, the derivative of Y with respect to X equals the slope of line M, the tangent to the curve at point A.

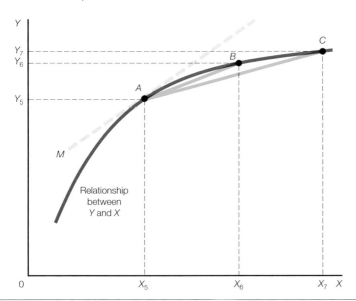

HOW TO FIND A DERIVATIVE

Managers want to know how to optimize performance. If Y is some measure of organizational performance and X is a variable under a particular manager's control, he or she would like to know the value of X that maximizes Y. To find out this value, managers want to approximate the derivative of Y with respect to X. In this section, we learn how to find this derivative.

Derivatives of Constants

If the dependent variable Y is a constant, its derivative with respect to X is always zero. That is, if $Y = a$ (where a is a constant)

$$\frac{dY}{dX} = 0 \qquad\qquad (18.6)$$

EXAMPLE Suppose $Y = 6$, as shown in Figure 18.6. Because the value of Y does not change as X varies, dY/dX is equal to zero. To see how this is shown geometrically, recall from the previous section that dY/dX equals the slope of the curve showing Y as a function of X. As is evident from Figure 18.6, this slope equals zero (since it is a horizontal line), which means dY/dX is equal to zero.

FIGURE 18.6

Case in Which $Y = 6$

In this case, dY/dX equals zero because the slope of this horizontal line equals zero.

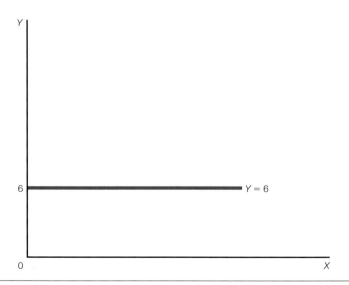

Derivatives of Power Functions

A power function can be expressed as

$$Y = aX^b$$

where a and b are constants. If the relationship between X and Y is of this kind, the derivative of Y with respect to X equals b times a multiplied by X raised to the $(b - 1)$ power

$$\frac{dY}{dX} = baX^{b-1} \tag{18.7}$$

EXAMPLE Suppose $Y = 3X$, which is graphed in panel A of Figure 18.7. Applying equation (18.7), we find that

$$\frac{dY}{dX} = 1 \times 3 \times X^0 = 3$$

because $a = 3$ and $b = 1$. Therefore, the value of dY/dX graphed in panel B of Figure 18.7 is 3, regardless of the value of X. This makes sense: The slope of the line in panel A is 3, regardless of the value of X. Recall once again from the previous section that dY/dX equals the slope of the curve showing Y as a function of X. In this case (as in Figure 18.6), the "curve" is a straight line.

EXAMPLE Suppose $Y = 2X^2$, which is graphed in panel A of Figure 18.8. Applying equation (18.7), we find that

$$\frac{dY}{dX} = 2 \times 2 \times X^1 = 4X$$

because $a = 2$ and $b = 2$. Therefore, the value of dY/dX, which is graphed in panel B of Figure 18.8, is proportional to X. As we would expect, dY/dX is negative when the slope of the curve in panel A is negative and positive when this slope is positive. Why? Because, as we have stressed repeatedly, dY/dX equals this slope.

We make a plea here for the actual ease of using calculus. All the calculus necessary to teach the concepts of managerial economics in this book can be summed up in one easy-to-remember formula.

If $y = kx^n$, where y is the dependent variable, that is, its value depends on the value of x, the independent variable. The value of X determines y's value. n and k are parameters (i.e., numbers). If you want to find the impact a change in the independent variable x has on the dependent variable y, you differentiate y with respect to x, that is, dy/dx. Now here's the easy-to-remember formula

$$dy/dx = nkx^{n-1}$$

FIGURE 18.7

Case in Which $Y = 3X$

In this case, dY/dX equals 3 because the slope of the line in panel A equals 3.

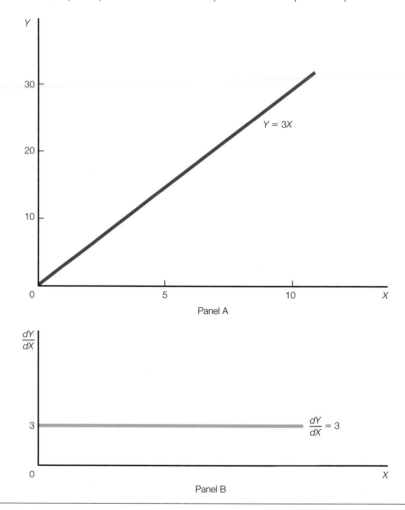

Panel A

Panel B

So if $y = 4x^3$, that is, $n = 3$ and $k = 4$, then $dy/dx = 12x^2$ with $nk = 3 \times 4 = 12$ and $n - 1 = 2$. Memorize the formula above, and you understand all the calculus to answer every numerical example in this book.

Derivatives of Sums and Differences

Suppose U and W are two variables, each of which depends on X. That is

$$U = g(X) \text{ and } W = h(X)$$

FIGURE 18.8

Case in Which $Y = 2X^2$

In this case, $dY/dX = 4X$ because the slope of the curve in panel A equals $4X$.

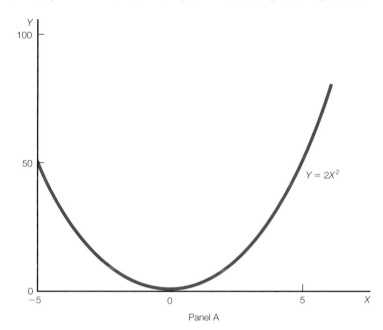

Panel A

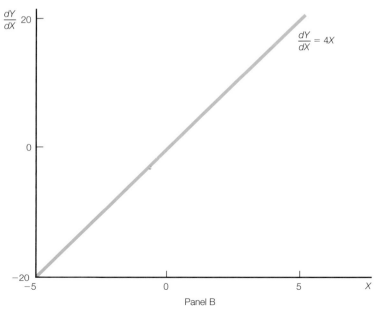

Panel B

The functional relationship between U and X is denoted by g, and that between W and X is denoted by h. Suppose further that

$$Y = U + W$$

In other words, Y is the sum of U and W. If so, the derivative of Y with respect to X equals the sum of the derivatives of the individual terms

$$\frac{dY}{dX} = \frac{dU}{dX} + \frac{dW}{dX} \tag{18.8}$$

On the other hand, if

$$Y = U - W$$

the derivative of Y with respect to X equals the difference between the derivatives of the individual terms

$$\frac{dY}{dX} = \frac{dU}{dX} - \frac{dW}{dX} \tag{18.9}$$

EXAMPLE Consider the case in which $U = g(X) = 3X^3$ and $W = h(X) = 4X^2$. If $Y = U + W = 3X^3 + 4X^2$

$$\frac{dY}{dX} = 9X^2 + 8X \tag{18.10}$$

To see why, recall from equation (18.8) that

$$\frac{dY}{dX} = \frac{dU}{dX} + \frac{dW}{dX} \tag{18.11}$$

Applying equation (18.7), we have

$$\frac{dU}{dX} = 9X^2 \text{ and } \frac{dW}{dX} = 8X$$

Substituting these values of the derivatives into equation (18.11), we obtain equation (18.10).

EXAMPLE Suppose $Y = U - W$, where $U = 8X^2$ and $W = 9X$. Then

$$\frac{dY}{dX} = 16X - 9$$

because, according to equation (18.9)

$$\frac{dY}{dX} = \frac{dU}{dX} - \frac{dW}{dX}$$

and, applying equation (18.7), we have

$$\frac{dU}{dX} = 16X \text{ and } \frac{dW}{dX} = 9$$

Derivatives of Products

The derivative of the product of two terms is equal to the sum of the first term multiplied by the derivative of the second plus the second term multiplied by the derivative of the first. Consequently, if $Y = UW$, we have

$$\frac{dY}{dX} = U\frac{dW}{dX} + W\frac{dU}{dX} \tag{18.12}$$

EXAMPLE If $Y = 6X(3 - X^2)$, we can let $U = 6X$ and $W = 3 - X^2$; then

$$\begin{aligned}
\frac{dY}{dX} &= 6X\frac{dW}{dX} + (3 - X^2)\frac{dU}{dX} \\
&= 6X(-2X) + (3 - X^2)(6) \\
&= -12X^2 + 18 - 6X^2 \\
&= 18 - 18X^2
\end{aligned}$$

The first term, $6X$, is multiplied by the derivative of the second term, $-2X$, and the result is added to the second term, $3 - X^2$, multiplied by the derivative of the first, 6. As indicated, the result is $18 - 18X^2$.

Derivatives of Quotients

If $Y = U/W$, the derivative of Y with respect to X equals

$$\frac{dY}{dX} = \frac{W(dU/dX) - U(dW/dX)}{W^2} \tag{18.13}$$

In other words, the derivative of the quotient of two terms equals the denominator times the derivative of the numerator minus the numerator times the derivative of the denominator—all divided by the square of the denominator.

EXAMPLE Consider the problem of finding the derivative of the expression

$$Y = \frac{5X^3}{3 - 4X}$$

If we let $U = 5X^3$ and $W = 3 - 4X$

$$\frac{dU}{dX} = 15X^2 \text{ and } \frac{dW}{dX} = -4$$

Consequently, applying equation (18.13), we have

$$\frac{dY}{dX} = \frac{(3 - 4X)(15X^2) - 5X^3(-4)}{(3 - 4X)^2}$$
$$= \frac{45X^2 - 60X^3 + 20X^3}{(3 - 4X)^2}$$
$$= \frac{45X^2 - 40X^3}{(3 - 4X)^2}$$

Derivatives of a Function of a Function (the Chain Rule)

Sometimes a variable depends on another variable, which in turn depends on a third variable. For example, suppose $Y = f(W)$ and $W = g(X)$. Under these circumstances, the derivative of Y with respect to X equals

$$\frac{dY}{dX} = \left(\frac{dY}{dW}\right)\left(\frac{dW}{dX}\right) \tag{18.14}$$

In other words, to find this derivative, we find the derivative of Y with respect to W and multiply it by the derivative of W with respect to X.

EXAMPLE Suppose $Y = 4W + W^3$ and $W = 3X^2$. To find dY/dX, we begin by finding dY/dW and dW/dX

$$\frac{dY}{dW} = 4 + 3W^2$$
$$= 4 + 3(3X^2)^2$$
$$= 4 + 27X^4$$
$$\frac{dW}{dX} = 6X$$

Then, to find dY/dX, we multiply dY/dW and dW/dX

$$\frac{dY}{dX} = (4 + 27X^4)(6X)$$
$$= 24X + 162X^5$$

USING DERIVATIVES TO SOLVE MAXIMIZATION AND MINIMIZATION PROBLEMS

Having determined how to find the derivative of Y with respect to X, we now see how to determine the value of X that maximizes or minimizes Y. *The central point is that a maximum or minimum point can occur only if the slope of the curve showing Y on the vertical axis and X on the horizontal axis equals zero.* To see this, suppose Y equals the profit of the Monroe Company and X is its output level. If the relationship between Y and X is as shown by the curve in panel A of Figure 18.9, the

FIGURE 18.9

Value of the Derivative When Y Is a Maximum

When Y is a maximum (at $X = 10$), dY/dX equals zero.

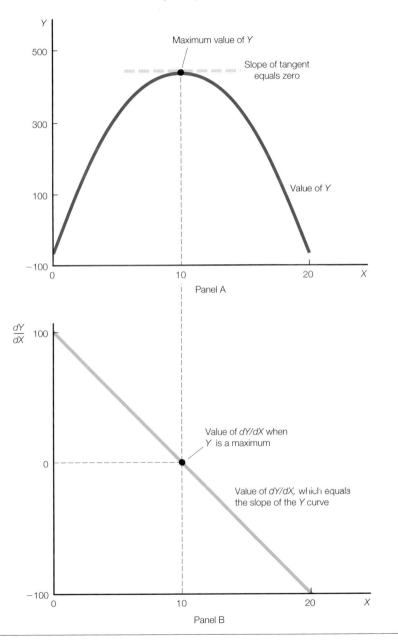

Panel A

Panel B

maximum value of Y occurs when $X = 10$, and at this value of X the slope of the curve equals zero.

Because the derivative of Y with respect to X equals the slope of this curve, it follows that Y is a maximum or minimum only if this derivative equals zero. To see that Y really is maximized when this derivative equals zero, note the relationship between Y and X in Figure 18.9 is

$$Y = -50 + 100X - 5X^2 \tag{18.15}$$

which means that

$$\frac{dY}{dX} = 100 - 10X \tag{18.16}$$

Therefore, if this derivative equals zero

$$100 - 10X = 0$$
$$X = 10$$

This is the value of X where Y is maximized. The key point here is that *to find the value of X that maximizes or minimizes Y, we must find the value of X where this derivative equals zero.* Panel B of Figure 18.9 shows graphically that this derivative equals zero when Y is maximized.

While we know the derivative equals 0 at $X = 10$, we must distinguish between a point on the curve where Y is maximized and a point where Y is minimized. For example, in Figure 18.10, this derivative is zero both when $X = 5$ and when $X = 15$. When $X = 15$, Y is a maximum; when $X = 5$, Y is a minimum. To distinguish between a maximum and a minimum, we must find the *second derivative of Y with respect to X, which is denoted d^2Y/dX^2 and is the derivative of dY/dX.* For example, in Figure 18.9, the second derivative of Y with respect to X is the derivative of the function in equation (18.16); therefore, it equals -10.

The second derivative measures the slope of the curve showing the relationship between dY/dX (the first derivative) and X. Just as the first derivative (that is, dY/dX) measures the slope of the Y curve in panel A of Figure 18.10, the second derivative (that is, d^2Y/dX^2) measures the slope of the dY/dX curve in panel B of Figure 18.10. In other words, just as the first derivative measures the slope of the total profit curve, the second derivative measures the slope of the marginal profit curve. The second derivative is important because it is always *negative* at a point of *maximization* and always *positive* at a point of *minimization.* Therefore, *to distinguish between maximization and minimization points, all we have to do is determine whether the second derivative at each point is positive or negative.*

To understand why the second derivative is always negative at a maximization point and always positive at a minimization point, consider Figure 18.10. When the second derivative is negative, this means the slope of the dY/dX curve in panel B is negative. Because dY/dX equals the slope of the Y curve in panel A,

FIGURE 18.10

Using the Second Derivative to Distinguish Maxima from Minima

At maxima (such as $X = 15$), d^2Y/dX^2 is negative; at minima (such as $X = 5$), d^2Y/dX^2 is positive.

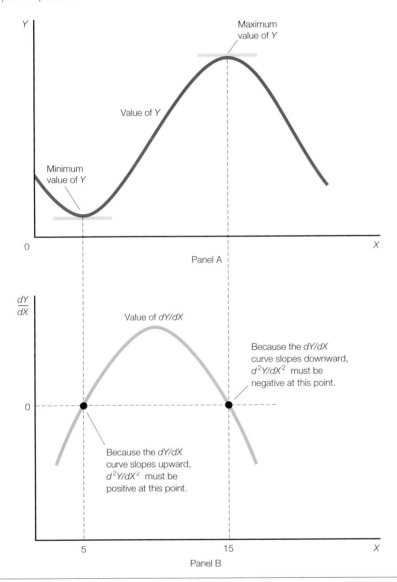

this in turn means the slope of the Y curve decreases as X increases. At a maximum point, such as when $X = 15$, this must be the case. On the other hand, when the second derivative is positive, this means the slope of the dY/dX curve in panel B is positive, which is another way of saying that the slope of the Y curve in panel A increases as X increases. At a minimum point, such as when $X = 5$, this must be the case.

EXAMPLE To illustrate how we can use derivatives to solve maximization and minimization problems, suppose the relationship between profit and output at the Kantor Corporation is

$$Y = -1 + 9X - 6X^2 + X^3$$

where Y equals annual profit (in millions of dollars) and X equals annual output (in millions of units). This equation is valid only for values of X that equal 3 or less; capacity limitations prevent the firm from producing more than 3 million units per year. To find the values of output that maximize or minimize profit, we find the derivative of Y with respect to X and set it equal to zero

$$\frac{dY}{dX} = 9 - 12X + 3X^2 = 0 \tag{18.17}$$

Solving this equation for X, we find that two values of X—1 and 3—result in this derivative being zero.[3]

To determine whether each of these two output levels maximizes or minimizes profit, we find the value of the second derivative at these two values of X. Taking the derivative of dY/dX, which is shown in equation (18.17) to equal $9 - 12X + 3X^2$, we find that

$$\frac{d^2Y}{dX^2} = -12 + 6X$$

If $X = 1$

$$\frac{d^2Y}{dX^2} = -12 + 6(1) = -6$$

Because the second derivative is negative, profit is a maximum (at 3) when output equals 1 million units. If $X = 3$

$$\frac{d^2Y}{dX^2} = -12 + 6(3) = 6$$

Because the second derivative is positive, profit is a minimum (at -1) when output equals 3 million units.

MARGINAL COST EQUALS MARGINAL REVENUE AND THE CALCULUS OF OPTIMIZATION

Once you know how elementary calculus is used to solve optimization problems, it is easy to see that the fundamental rule for profit maximization—set marginal

3. If an equation is of the general quadratic form, $Y = aX^2 + bX + c$, the values of X at which Y is 0 are

$$X = \frac{-b \pm (b^2 - 4ac)^{0.5}}{2a}$$

In the equation in the text, $a = 3$, $b = -12$, and $c = 9$. Hence

$$x = \frac{12 \pm (144 - 108)^{0.5}}{6}$$

$$= 2 \pm 1$$

Therefore, $dY/dX = 0$ when X equals 1 or 3.

FIGURE 18.11

Marginal Revenue Equals Marginal Cost Rule for Profit

At the profit-maximizing output of Q_1, marginal revenue (equal to the slope of line R) equals marginal cost (the slope of line S).

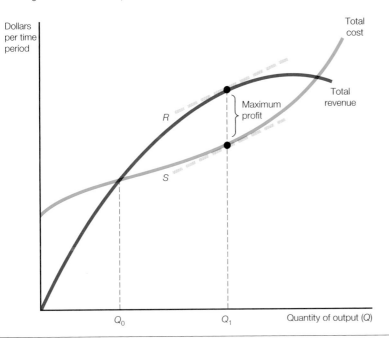

cost equal to marginal revenue—is based on the calculus of optimization. Figure 18.11 shows a firm's total cost and total revenue functions. Because total profit equals total revenue minus total cost, it equals the vertical distance between the total revenue and total cost curves at any level of output. This distance is maximized at output Q_1, where the slopes of the total revenue and total cost curves are equal. Because the slope of the total revenue curve is marginal revenue and the slope of the total cost curve is marginal cost, profit is maximized when marginal cost equals marginal revenue.

Inspection of Figure 18.11 shows that Q_1 must be the profit-maximizing output. Output levels below Q_0 result in losses (because total cost exceeds total revenue) and obviously do not maximize profit. As output increases beyond Q_0, total revenue rises more rapidly than total cost, so profit must be going up. So long as the slope of the total revenue curve (which equals marginal revenue) exceeds the slope of the total cost curve (which equals marginal cost), profit will continue to rise as output increases. But when these slopes become equal (that is, when marginal revenue equals marginal cost), profit no longer will rise but will be at a maximum. These slopes become equal at an output level of Q_1, and so this must be the profit-maximizing output level. After output Q_1, profit decreases because marginal cost exceeds marginal revenue.

Using calculus, we can readily understand why managers maximize profit by setting marginal cost equal to marginal revenue. The first thing to note is that

$$\pi = TR - TC$$

where π equals total profit, TR equals total revenue, and TC equals total cost. Taking the derivative of π with respect to Q (output), we find that

$$\frac{d\pi}{dQ} = \frac{dTR}{dQ} - \frac{dTC}{dQ}$$

For π to be a maximum, this derivative must be zero, so it must be true that

$$\frac{dTR}{dQ} = \frac{dTR}{dQ} \tag{18.18}$$

And because marginal revenue is defined as dTR/dQ and marginal cost is defined as dTC/dQ, marginal revenue must equal marginal cost.[4]

PARTIAL DIFFERENTIATION AND THE MAXIMIZATION OF MULTIVARIABLE FUNCTIONS

Up to this point, we have examined situations in which a variable depends on only one other variable. Although such situations exist, in many cases a variable depends on a number (often a large number) of other variables, not just one. For example, the Merrimack Company produces two goods, and its profit depends on the amount that it produces of each good. That is

$$\pi = f(Q_1, Q_2) \tag{18.19}$$

where π is the firm's profit, Q_1 is its output level of the first good, and Q_2 is its output level of the second good.

To find the value of each of the independent variables (Q_1 and Q_2 in this case) that maximizes the dependent variable (π in this case), we need to know the marginal effect of each independent variable on the dependent variable, *holding constant the effect of all other independent variables.* For example, in this case we need to know the marginal effect of Q_1 on π when Q_2 is held constant, and we need to know the marginal effect of Q_2 on π when Q_1 is held constant. To get this information, we obtain the partial derivative of π with respect to Q_1 and the partial derivative of π with respect to Q_2.

To obtain the partial derivative of π with respect to Q_1, denoted $\partial\pi/\partial Q_1$, we apply the rules for finding a derivative (on pages 738–44) to equation (18.19),

4. Two points should be noted. (1) For profit to be maximized, $d^2\pi/dQ^2$ must be negative. (2) The analysis in this section (as well as in earlier sections) results in the determination of a *local* maximum. Sometimes a local maximum is not a global maximum. For example, under some circumstances, the profit-maximizing (or loss-minimizing) output is zero.

but we treat Q_2 as a constant. Similarly, to obtain the partial derivative of π with respect to Q_2, denoted $\partial\pi/\partial Q_2$, we apply these rules to equation (18.19), but we treat Q_1 as a constant.

EXAMPLE Suppose the relationship between the Merrimack Company's profit (in thousands of dollars) and its output level of each good is

$$\pi = -20 + 113.75Q_1 + 80Q_2 - 10Q_1^2 - 10Q_2^2 - 5Q_1Q_2 \qquad (18.20)$$

To find the partial derivative of π with respect to Q_1, we treat Q_2 as a constant and find that

$$\frac{\partial\pi}{\partial Q_1} = 113.75 - 20Q_1 - 5Q_2$$

To find the partial derivative of π with respect to Q_2, we treat Q_1 as a constant and find that

$$\frac{\partial\pi}{\partial Q_2} = 80 - 20Q_2 - 5Q_1$$

Once we have obtained the partial derivatives, it is relatively simple to determine the values of the independent variables that maximize the dependent variable. All we have to do is *set all the partial derivatives equal to zero*. In the case of the Merrimack Company

$$\frac{\partial\pi}{\partial Q_1} = 113.75 - 20Q_1 - 5Q_2 = 0 \qquad (18.21)$$

$$\frac{\partial\pi}{\partial Q_2} = 80 - 20Q_2 - 5Q_1 = 0 \qquad (18.22)$$

Equations (18.21) and (18.22) are two equations in two unknowns. Solving them simultaneously, we find that profit is maximized when $Q_1 = 5.0$ and $Q_2 = 2.75$. In other words, to maximize profit, the firm should produce 5.0 units of the first good and 2.75 units of the second good per period of time. If it does this, its profit will equal $374,375 thousand per period of time.[5]

To see why all the partial derivatives should be set equal to zero, consider Figure 18.12, which shows the relationship in equation (18.20) among π, Q_1, and Q_2 in the range where π is close to its maximum value. As you can see, this relationship is represented by a three-dimensional surface. The maximum value of π is at point M, where this surface is level. A plane tangent to this surface at point M is parallel to the Q_1Q_2 plane; in other words, its slope with respect to either Q_1 or Q_2 must be zero. Because the partial derivatives in equations (18.21) and (18.22) equal these slopes, they too must equal zero at the maximum point M.[6]

5. Inserting 5.0 for Q_1 and 2.75 for Q_2 in equation (18.20), we find that $\pi = -20 + 113.75(5) + 80(2.75) - 10(5)^2 - 10(2.75)^2 - 5(5)(2.75) = 374.375$

6. The second-order conditions for distinguishing maxima from minima can be found in any calculus book. For present purposes, a discussion of these conditions is not essential.

FIGURE 18.12

Relationship among π, Q_1, and Q_2

At M, the point where π is a maximum, the surface representing this relationship is flat; its slope with regard to either Q_1 or Q_2 is zero.

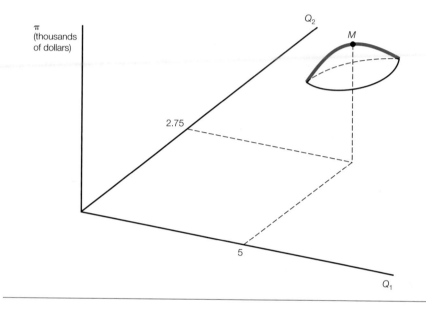

CONSTRAINED OPTIMIZATION

Managers of firms and other organizations generally face constraints that limit their options. A production manager may want to minimize his or her firm's costs but may not be permitted to produce less than is required to meet the firm's contracts with its customers. The managers of a firm may want to maximize profits; but in the short run, they may be unable to change its product or augment its plant and equipment.

Constrained optimization problems of this sort can be solved in a number of ways. In relatively simple cases in which there is only one constraint, we can use this constraint to express a decision variable—that is, one of the variables the decision maker can choose—as a function of the other decision variables. Then we can apply the techniques for unconstrained optimization described in the previous sections. In effect, we convert the problem to one of unconstrained maximization or minimization.

To illustrate, suppose the Kloster Company produces two products, and its total cost equals

$$TC = 4Q_1^2 + 5Q_2^2 - Q_1Q_2 \qquad (18.23)$$

where Q_1 equals its output per hour of the first product and Q_2 equals its output per hour of the second product. Because of commitments to customers, the number produced of both products combined cannot be less than 30 per hour. Kloster's president wants to know what output levels of the two products minimize the firm's costs, given that the output of the first product plus the output of the second product equals 30 per hour.

This constrained optimization problem can be expressed as follows

Minimize $\qquad\qquad TC = 4Q_1^2 + 5Q_2^2 - Q_1Q_2$

subject to $\qquad\qquad Q_1 + Q_2 = 30$

Of course the constraint is that $(Q_1 + Q_2)$ must equal 30. Solving this constraint for Q_1, we have

$$Q_1 = 30 - Q_2$$

Substituting $(30 - Q_2)$ for Q_1 in equation (18.23), it follows that

$$
\begin{aligned}
TC &= 4(30 - Q_2)^2 + 5Q_2^2 - (30 - Q_2)Q_2 \\
&= 4(900 - 60Q_2 + Q_2^2) + 5Q_2^2 - 30Q_2 + Q_2^2 \qquad (18.24) \\
TC &= 3{,}600 - 270Q_2 + 10Q_2^2
\end{aligned}
$$

The methods of unconstrained optimization just described can be used to find the value of Q_2 that minimizes TC. As indicated in earlier sections, we must obtain the derivative of TC with respect to Q_2 and set it equal to zero

$$
\begin{aligned}
\frac{dTC}{dQ_2} &= -270 + 20Q_2 = 0 \\
20Q_2 &= 270 \\
Q_2 &= 13.5
\end{aligned}
$$

To be sure this is a minimum, not a maximum, we obtain the second derivative, which is

$$\frac{d^2TC}{dQ_2^2} = 20$$

Because this is positive, we have found a minimum.

To find the value of Q_1 that minimizes total cost, recall that the constraint requires that

$$Q_1 + Q_2 = 30$$

which means that

$$Q_1 = 30 - Q_2$$

We know that the optimal value of Q_2 is 13.5, so the optimal value of Q_1 must be

$$Q_1 = 30 - 13.5 = 16.5$$

Summing up, if the Kloster Company wants to minimize total cost subject to the constraint that the sum of the output levels of its two products remains 30, it should produce 16.5 units of the first product and 13.5 units of the second product per hour.[7] In other words, it should produce 33 units of the first product and 27 units of the second product every two hours.

LAGRANGIAN MULTIPLIERS

If the technique described in the previous section is not feasible because the constraints are too numerous or complex, the method of Lagrangian multipliers can be used. This method of solving constrained optimization problems involves the construction of an equation—the so-called Lagrangian function—that combines the function to be minimized or maximized and the constraints. This equation is constructed so that two things are true:

1. When this equation is maximized (or minimized), the original function we want to maximize (or minimize) is in fact maximized (or minimized).
2. All the constraints are satisfied.

To illustrate how we create a Lagrangian function, reconsider the problem faced by the Kloster Company. As indicated in the previous section, this firm wants to minimize $TC = 4Q_1^2 + 5Q_2^2 - Q_1Q_2$, subject to the constraint that $Q_1 + Q_2 = 30$. The first step in constructing the Lagrangian function for this firm's problem is to restate the constraint so that an expression is formed that is equal to zero

$$30 - Q_1 - Q_2 = 0 \qquad (18.25)$$

If we multiply this form of the constraint by an unknown factor, designated λ (*lambda*), and add the result to the function we want to minimize (in equation (18.23)), we get the Lagrangian function, which is

$$L_{TC} = 4Q_1^2 + 5Q_2^2 - Q_1Q_2 + \lambda(30 - Q_1 - Q_2) \qquad (18.26)$$

For reasons specified in the next paragraph, we can be sure that if we find the unconstrained maximum (or minimum) of the Lagrangian function, the solution will be exactly the same as the solution of the original constrained maximization (or minimization) problem. In other words, to solve the constrained optimization problem, all we have to do is optimize the Lagrangian function. For example, in the case of the Kloster Company, we must find the values of Q_1, Q_2, and λ that minimize L_{TC} in equation (18.26). To do this, we must find the partial derivative of L_{TC} with respect to each of the three variables Q_1, Q_2, and λ

7. Substituting 16.5 for Q_1 and 13.5 for Q_2 in equation (18.23), we see that the firm's total cost will equal

$TC = 4(16.5)^2 + 5(13.5)^2 - (16.5)(13.5)$
$\quad = 4(272.25) + 5(182.25) - 222.75$
$\quad = 1089 + 911.25 - 222.75$
$\quad = 1,777.5$ or $1,777.50

$$\frac{\partial L_{TC}}{\partial Q_1} = 8Q_1 - Q_2 - \lambda$$

$$\frac{\partial L_{TC}}{\partial Q_2} = -Q_1 + 10Q_2 - \lambda$$

$$\frac{\partial L_{TC}}{\partial \lambda} = -Q_1 - Q_2 + 30$$

As indicated earlier, we must set all three of these partial derivatives equal to zero to minimize L_{TC}

$$8Q_1 - Q_2 - \lambda = 0 \qquad\qquad (18.27)$$
$$-Q_1 + 10Q_2 - \lambda = 0 \qquad\qquad (18.28)$$
$$-Q_1 - Q_2 + 30 = 0 \qquad\qquad (18.29)$$

It is important to note that the partial derivative of the Lagrangian function with regard to λ (that is, $\partial L_{TC}/\partial \lambda$), when it is set equal to zero (in equation (18.29)), is the constraint in our original optimization problem (recall equation (18.25)). This, of course, is always true because of the way the Lagrangian function is constructed. So if this derivative is zero, we can be sure this original constraint is satisfied. And if this constraint is satisfied, the last term on the right of the Lagrangian function is zero; so the Lagrangian function boils down to the original function that we wanted to maximize (or minimize). Consequently, by maximizing (or minimizing) the Lagrangian function, we solve the original constrained optimization problem.

Returning to the Kloster Company, equations (18.27), (18.28), and (18.29) are three simultaneous equations with three unknowns—Q_1, Q_2, and λ. If we solve this system of equations for Q_1 and Q_2, we get the optimal values of Q_1 and Q_2. Subtracting equation (18.28) from equation (18.27), we find that

$$9Q_1 - 11Q_2 = 0 \qquad\qquad (18.30)$$

Multiplying equation (18.29) by 9 and adding the result to equation (18.30), we can solve for Q_2

$$-9Q_1 - 9Q_2 + 270 = 0$$
$$\underline{9Q_1 - 11Q_2 = 0}$$
$$-20Q_2 + 270 = 0$$
$$Q_2 = 270/20 = 13.5$$

Therefore, the optimal value of Q_2 is 13.5. Substituting 13.5 for Q_2 in equation (18.29), we find the optimal value of Q_1 is 16.5.

The answer we get is precisely the same as in the previous section: The optimal value of Q_1 is 16.5, and the optimal value of Q_2 is 13.5. In other words, the managers at Kloster Company should produce 16.5 units of the first product and 13.5 units of the second product per hour. But the method of Lagrangian multipliers described in this section is more powerful than that described in the previous section for at least two reasons: (1) It can handle more than a single constraint, and (2) the value of λ provides interesting and useful information to the decision maker.

Specifically λ, called the *Lagrangian multiplier,* measures the change in the variable to be maximized or minimized (*TC* in this case) if the constraint is relaxed by one unit. For example, if managers at the Kloster Company want to minimize total cost subject to the constraint that the total output of both products is 31 rather than 30, the value of λ indicates by how much the minimum value of *TC* will increase. What is the value of λ? According to equation (18.27)

$$8Q_1 - Q_2 - \lambda = 0$$

Because $Q_1 = 16.5$ and $Q_2 = 13.5$

$$\lambda = 8(16.5) - 13.5 = 118.5$$

Consequently, if the constraint is relaxed so that total output is 31 rather than 30, the total cost will go up by $118.50.

For many managerial decisions, information of this sort is of great value. Suppose a customer offers the Kloster Company $115 for one of its products, but to make this product, Kloster would have to stretch its total output to 31 per hour. On the basis of the findings of the previous paragraph, Kloster managers would be foolish to accept this offer because this extra product will raise costs by $118.50, $3.50 more than the amount the customer offers to pay for it.

COMPARING INCREMENTAL COSTS WITH INCREMENTAL REVENUES

Before concluding this chapter, we must point out that many business decisions require comparing incremental costs with incremental revenues. Typically a manager must choose among courses of action, and the relevant decision factors are the differences in costs and revenues. For example, if the managers of a machinery company are considering whether to add a new product line, they should compare the incremental cost of adding the new product line (the extra cost resulting from its addition) with the incremental revenue (the extra revenue resulting from its addition). If the incremental revenue exceeds the incremental cost, the new product line will add to the firm's profits.

Incremental cost The extra cost from an output increase that may be substantial.

Incremental revenue The extra revenue from an output increase that may be substantial.

Note that *incremental* cost is not the same as *marginal* cost. Whereas marginal cost is the extra cost from a very small (one-unit) increase in output, **incremental cost** is the extra cost from an output increase that may be substantial. Similarly, **incremental revenue**, unlike marginal revenue, is the extra revenue from an output increase that may be substantial. For example, suppose you want to see whether a firm's profits will increase if it doubles its output. If the incremental cost of such an output increase is $5 million and the incremental revenue is $6 million, the firm will increase its profits by $1 million if it doubles its output. Marginal cost and marginal revenue cannot tell you this because they refer to only a very small increase in output, not to a doubling of it.

Although it may seem easy to compare incremental costs with incremental revenues, in fact there are many pitfalls. One of the most common errors is the failure to recognize the irrelevance of sunk costs. Costs incurred in the past are often irrelevant in making today's decisions. Suppose you are going to make a trip and you want to determine whether it will be cheaper to drive your car or to travel by plane. What costs should be included if you drive your car? Because the only incremental costs incurred are the gas and oil (and a certain amount of wear and tear on tires, engine, and so on), these are the only costs to be included. Costs incurred in the past, such as the original price of the car, and costs that are the same regardless of whether you make the trip by car or plane, such as your auto insurance, should not be included. On the other hand, if you are thinking about buying a car to make this and many other trips, these costs should be included.

To illustrate the proper reasoning, consider an airline that has deliberately run extra flights that return only a little more than their out-of-pocket costs. Assume this airline faces the decision of whether to run an extra flight between city *A* and city *B*. The fully allocated costs—the out-of-pocket costs plus a certain percentage of overhead, depreciation, insurance, and other such costs—are $5,500 for the flight. The out-of-pocket costs—the actual sum this airline has to disburse to run the flight—are $3,000, and the expected revenue from the flight is $4,100. In such a case, this airline will run the flight, which is the correct decision because the flight will add $1,100 to profit. The incremental revenue from the flight is $4,100, and the incremental cost is $3,000. Overhead, depreciation, and insurance are the same whether the flight is run or not. Therefore, fully allocated costs are misleading here; the relevant costs are out-of-pocket, not fully allocated, ones.

Errors of other kinds can also mar managerial estimates of incremental costs. For example, a firm may refuse to produce and sell some items because it is already working near capacity, and the incremental cost of producing them is judged to be high. In fact, however, the incremental cost may not be so high because managers may be able to produce these items during the slack season (when there is plenty of excess capacity), and the potential customers may be willing to accept delivery then.

Also, incremental revenue is frequently misjudged. Consider managers who are pondering the introduction of a new product. The firm's managers may estimate the incremental revenue from the new product without taking proper account of the effects of the new product's sales on the sales of existing products. They may think the new product will not cut into the sales of existing products; however, it may in fact do so, with the result that their estimate of incremental revenue is too high.

SUMMARY

1. Functional relationships can be represented by tables, graphs, or equations. The marginal value of a dependent variable is defined as the change in this variable associated with a 1-unit change in a particular independent variable. The dependent variable achieves a maximum when its marginal value shifts from positive to negative.

2. The derivative of Y with respect to X, denoted dY/dX, is the limit of the ratio $\Delta Y/\Delta X$ as ΔX approaches zero. Geometrically, it is the slope of the curve showing Y (on the vertical axis) as a function of X (on the horizontal axis). We have provided rules that enable us to find the value of this derivative.

3. To find the value of X that maximizes or minimizes Y, we determine the value of X where dY/dX equals zero. To tell whether this is a maximum or a minimum, we find the second derivative of Y with respect to X, denoted d^2Y/dX^2, which is the derivative of dY/dX. If this second derivative is negative, we have found a maximum; if it is positive, we have found a minimum.

4. A dependent variable often depends on a number of independent variables, not just one. To find the value of each of the independent variables that maximizes the dependent variable, we determine the partial derivative of Y with respect to each of the independent variables, denoted $\partial Y/\partial X$, and set it equal to zero. To obtain the partial derivative of Y with respect to X, we apply the ordinary rules for finding a derivative; however, all independent variables other than X are treated as constants.

5. Managers of firms and other organizations generally face constraints that limit the options available to them. In relatively simple cases in which there is only one constraint, we can use this constraint to express one of the decision variables as a function of the other decision variables, and we can apply the techniques for unconstrained optimization.

6. In more complex cases, constrained optimization problems can be solved by the method of Lagrangian multipliers. The Lagrangian function combines the function to be maximized or minimized and the constraints. To solve the constrained optimization problem, we optimize the Lagrangian function.

7. Many business decisions can and should be made by comparing incremental costs with incremental revenues. Typically, a manager must choose between two (or more) courses of action, and what is relevant is the difference between the costs of the two courses of action, as well as the difference between their revenues.

 wwnorton.com/studyspace

PROBLEMS

1. One very important question facing hospitals is this: How big must a hospital be (in terms of patient-days of care) to minimize the cost per patient-day?

According to one well-known study, the total cost (in dollars) of operating a hospital (of a particular type) can be approximated by

$$C = 4,700,000 + 0.00013X^2$$

where X is the number of patient-days.

a. Derive a formula for the relationship between cost per patient-day and the number of patient-days.

b. On the basis of the results of this study, how big must a hospital be (in terms of patient-days) to minimize the cost per patient-day?

c. Show that your result minimizes, rather than maximizes, the cost per patient-day.

2. The Trumbull Company has developed a new product. Trumbull's chairperson estimates that the new product will increase the firm's revenues by $5 million per year, and that it will result in extra out-of-pocket costs of $4 million per year, the fully allocated costs (including a percentage of overhead, depreciation, and insurance) being $5.5 million.

a. Trumbull's chairperson feels that it would not be profitable to introduce this new product. Is the chairperson right? Why or why not?

b. Trumbull's vice president for research argues that since the development of this product has already cost about $10 million, the firm has little choice but to introduce it. Is the vice president right? Why or why not?

3. For the Martin Corporation, the relationship between profit and output is the following:

Output (number of units per day)	Profit (thousands of dollars per day)
0	−10
1	−8
2	−5
3	0
4	2
5	7
6	12
7	21
8	22
9	23
10	20

a. What is the marginal profit when output is between 5 and 6 units per day? When output is between 9 and 10 units per day?

b. At what output is average profit a maximum?

    c. Should the Martin Corporation produce the output where average profit is a maximum? Why or why not?

4. Determine the first derivative of each of the following functions:
   a. $Y = 3 + 10X + 5X^2$
   b. $Y = 2X(4 + X^3)$
   c. $Y = 3X/(4 + X^3)$
   d. $Y = 4X/(X - 3)$

5. The total cost function at the Duemer Company is $TC = 100 + 4Q + 8Q^2$ where TC is total costs, and Q is the output.
   a. What is marginal cost when output is 10?
   b. What is marginal cost when output is 12?
   c. What is marginal cost when output is 20?

6. The Bartholomew Company's profit is related in the following way to its output: $\pi = -40 + 20Q - 3Q^2$, where π is total profit and Q is output.
   a. If the firm's output equals 8, what is its marginal profit?
   b. Derive an equation relating the firm's marginal profit to its output.
   c. What output maximizes the firm's profit?

7. Determine the second derivative of the following functions:
   a. $Y = 4 + 9X + 3X^2$
   b. $Y = 4X(3 + X^2)$
   c. $Y = 4X(2 + X^3)$
   d. $Y = (4/X) + 3$

8. The Mineola Corporation hires a consultant to estimate the relationship between its profit and its output. The consultant reports that the relationship is

$$\pi = -10 - 6Q + 5.5Q^2 - 2Q^3 + 0.25Q^4$$

    a. The consultant says that the firm should set Q equal to 1 to maximize profit. Is it true that $d\pi/dQ = 0$ when $Q = 1$? Is π at a maximum when $Q = 1$?

    b. Mineola's executive vice president says that the firm's profit is a maximum when $Q = 2$. Is this true?

    c. If you were the chief executive officer of the Mineola Corporation, would you accept the consultant's estimate of the relationship between profit and output as correct?

9. Find the partial derivative of Y with respect to X in each of the following cases:
   a. $Y = 10 + 3Z + 2X$
   b. $Y = 18Z^2 + 4X^3$
   c. $Y = Z^{0.2}X^{0.8}$
   d. $Y = 3Z/(4 + X)$

10. The Stock Corporation makes two products, paper and cardboard. The relationship between π, the firm's annual profit (in thousands of dollars), and its output of each good is

$$\pi = -50 + 40Q_1 + 30Q_2 - 5Q_1^2 - 4Q_2^2 - 3Q_1Q_2$$

where Q_1 is the firm's annual output of paper (in tons), and Q_2 is the firm's annual output of cardboard (in tons).

a. Find the output of each good that the Stock Corporation should produce if it wants to maximize profit.

b. If the community in which the firm is located imposes a tax of $5,000 per year on the firm, will this alter the answer to Part a? If so, how will the answer change?

11. The Miller Company uses skilled and unskilled labor to do a particular construction project. The cost of doing the project depends on the number of hours of skilled labor and the number of hours of unskilled labor that are used, the relationship being

$$C = 4 - 3X_1 - 4X_2 + 2X_1^2 + 3X_2^2 + X_1X_2$$

where C is cost (in thousands of dollars), X_1 is the number of hours (in thousands) of skilled labor, and X_2 is the number of hours (in thousands) of unskilled labor.

a. Find the number of hours of skilled labor and the number of hours of unskilled labor that will minimize the cost of doing the project.

b. If the Miller Company has to purchase a license costing $2,000 to do this project (and if the cost of this license is not included in C), will this alter the answer to Part a? If so, how will the answer change?

12. Ilona Stafford manages a small firm that produces wool rugs and cotton rugs. Her total cost per day (in dollars) equals

$$C = 7X_1^2 + 9X_2^2 - 1.5X_1X_2$$

where X_1 equals the number of cotton rugs produced per day, and X_2 equals the number of wool rugs produced per day. Because of commitments to retail stores that sell her rugs to consumers, she must produce ten rugs per day, but any mix of wool and cotton rugs is acceptable.

a. If she wants to minimize her costs (without violating her commitment to the retail stores), how many cotton rugs and wool rugs should she produce per day? (Do *not* use the method of Lagrangian multipliers.)

b. Does it seem reasonable that she would want to minimize cost in a situation of this sort? Why or why not?

c. Can she produce fractional numbers of rugs per day?

13. a. Use the method of Lagrangian multipliers to solve Problem 12.

b. Do you get the same answer as you do without using this method?

c. What does λ equal? What does this mean?

PART 2
THE NATURE OF MARKETS

CHAPTER 2

Elasticity Elasticity measures the
percentage change in one factor
given a small (marginal) percentage change in another factor.

DEMAND THEORY

An important determinant of profit is the nature of the demand for a firm's goods
or services. It is imperative that managers understand this multidimensional concept if they are to positively influence firm performance. Good managers learn to
understand the nature of demand for products and effectively manage it. Effective
management requires more knowledge than understanding the directional impact
on sales for a given price change. Many other factors besides price affect consumer
demand. Some of these factors are controlled by managers, such as advertising,
product quality, and distribution. Other factors, like the number of substitute
goods, the prices of rival products, and the advertising of rivals, are part of the
competitive dynamics of the product space. Finally, a few factors, like the state of
the economy or the level of disposable consumer income, are macroeconomic and
are not influenced by individual managers. Though these factors are outside their
control, managers still need to predict how their changes affect demand.

This chapter explains how managers can more precisely predict changes in
various environmental factors and quantify their impact on product demand.
The nature of product demand is that it is a process—and as such is dynamic.
Because many factors influence product demand, managers need to understand
how changes in these factors affect demand. Knowing the sensitivity of demand
to changes in environmental factors lets a manager effectively respond to these
changes. The sensitivity of one factor to another is called **elasticity**. Elasticity measures the percentage change in one factor given a small (marginal) percentage

change in another factor. The concept of elasticity is widespread in the business world. For example, elasticity is the basis for both a firm's operating and financial leverage. It is also used by managers to determine a product's most efficient mix of inputs.

THE MARKET DEMAND CURVE

One way to show how sales of a product are affected by its price is with a **market demand schedule**, which is a table showing the total quantity of the good purchased at each price. For example, suppose the market demand schedule for tablet computers in 2012 is as shown in Table 2.1. According to this table, 0.5 million tablet computers are demanded per year if the price is $200 per computer; 300,000 are demanded if the price is $300; and so on. Another way of presenting the data in Table 2.1 is with a **market demand curve**, which is a plot of the market demand schedule on a graph. The vertical axis of the graph measures the price per unit of the good, and the horizontal axis measures the quantity of the good demanded per unit of time. Figure 2.1 shows the market demand curve for tablet computers in 2012, based on the figures in Table 2.1.

In the previous chapter we introduced the concept of a market demand curve. Now we examine one in more detail. Note three things about Figure 2.1. First, the market demand curve shows the total quantity of tablet computers demanded at each price, not the quantity demanded from a particular firm. We discuss the demand for a particular firm's product later. Second, the market demand curve for tablets slopes downward to the right. That is, the quantity of tablets demanded increases as the price falls. As we pointed out in the last chapter, this is true for most products or services. Third, the market demand curve in Figure 2.1 pertains to a specified period: 2012. As you recall from the last chapter, any demand curve pertains to some particular time, and its shape and position depend on the length

Market demand schedule Table showing the total quantity of the good purchased at each price.

Market demand curve The plot of the market demand schedule on a graph.

TABLE 2.1

Market Demand Schedule for Tablets, 2012

Price per Tablet (Dollars)	Quantity Demanded (Thousands)
300	300
275	350
250	400
225	450
200	500

FIGURE 2.1

Demand Curve for Tablets

This demand curve is a graphical representation of the figures in Table 2.1.

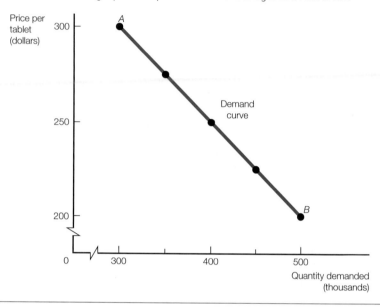

and other characteristics of this period. If we were to estimate the market demand curve for tablets for the first week in 2012, it would probably differ from the one in Figure 2.1. This difference arises partly because consumers adapt their purchases more fully to changes in the price of tablets in a year relative to a week.

In addition to the length of time, what factors determine the position and shape of a market demand curve? One important factor is the tastes of consumers. If consumers show an increasing preference for a product, the demand curve shifts to the right; that is, at each price consumers want to buy more than they did previously. Alternatively, for each quantity consumers are willing to pay a higher price. On the other hand, if consumers show a decreasing preference for a product, the demand curve shifts to the left because at each price consumers buy less than previously. Alternatively, for each quantity consumers are willing to pay only a lower price. For example, as shown in Figure 2.2, if people find that tablets are helpful and begin to use them more and give them in larger numbers to their children and others, the demand curve may shift to the right. The greater the shift in preferences, the farther the demand curve shifts.

Another factor that influences the position and shape of a product's market demand curve is the level of consumer incomes. For some products the demand curve shifts to the right if per capita income increases, whereas for other products

STRATEGY SESSION: The Customer Is Always Right—Wrong!

Some customers are viewed as angels. They purchase the big-ticket, big-markup items, want them right when they come out, and want each one of them. And some customers are viewed as devils. They wait for loss leader sales (items sold at a loss designed to entice consumers to the store, where the store hopes they will buy many other items—the devils only buy the loss leaders); buy items, return them, and then rebuy them as previously owned items at a discount; buy the most discounted items and then resell them (eliminating their customers from the store's pool); scour the Internet, circulars, and newspapers for the store's competitors' low prices and then make the store honor the competitors' prices because of the "we will not be undersold" pledge of the store; send in for rebates; and so on.

Big box electronics store Best Buy has had enough of the devils' tactics. Best Buy estimates that 20% of its store visits are by devils. And they'd like the devils to get out of their stores. They want to fire some of their customers! On the other hand, they have identified the true angels—the 20% of their customers that generate the bulk of their profits.

How do you get rid of the devils? You can't identify them and then not let them in your store. That would violate antidiscrimination laws. But you can eliminate the programs that draw them to your stores (and make sure they are not the same programs that draw the angels). For instance, stop direct mailing to the customers identified (by their past purchases) as devils; charge customers a restocking fee of 15% of the purchase price for returned items; prohibit reselling returned items on the Internet or at another store rather than at the original store; and break all ties with Internet sites (FatWallet.com, SlickDeals.net, TechBargains.com) that tipped the devils off to Best Buy bargains and buying strategies that Best Buy regarded as having a negative impact on profits. The financial services sector has solved this problem by catering to their angels (free checking for maintaining a certain balance) and penalizing the devils (transaction fees for ATM use, fees to deal with a teller, check fees, and so forth).

Source: "Analyzing Customers, Best Buy Decides Not All Are Welcome," *The Wall Street Journal*, November 8, 2004, p. A-1.

it shifts to the left if per capita income rises. In the case of tablets, we expect that an increase in per capita income will shift the demand curve to the right, as shown in Figure 2.3. Still another factor that influences the position and shape of a product's market demand curve is the level of other prices. For example, we expect the quantity of tablets demanded to increase if the price of applications falls drastically.

Finally, the position and shape of a product's market demand curve are affected by the size of the population in the relevant market. If the number of consumers increases, we expect that, if all other factors are held equal, the quantity of tablets demanded will increase. Of course, the population generally changes slowly, so this factor often has little effect in the short run.

FIGURE 2.2

Effect of an Increased Preference on the Market Demand Curve for Tablets

The demand curve for tablets shifts to the right.

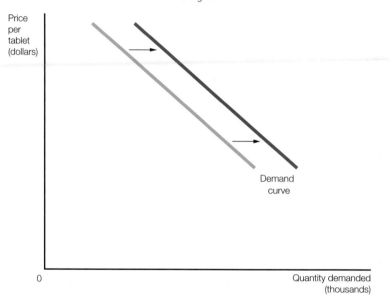

FIGURE 2.3

Effect of an Increase in Per Capita Income on the Market Demand Curve for Tablets

The demand curve shifts to the right.

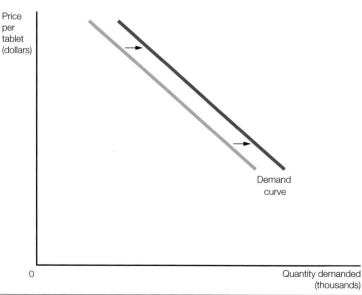

INDUSTRY AND FIRM DEMAND FUNCTIONS

Building on the results of the previous section, we define the **market demand function** for a product as the relationship between the quantity demanded and the various factors that influence this quantity. Put generally, this market demand function is written as

$$\text{Quantity demanded of good } X = Q = f \text{ (price of } X, \text{ incomes of consumers, tastes of consumers, prices of other goods, population, advertising expenditures, and so forth)}$$

Market demand function The relationship between the quantity demanded and the various factors that influence this quantity.

To be useful for analytical and forecasting purposes, this equation must be more specific. For example, if good X is tablet computers, the market demand function might be

$$Q = b_1 P + b_2 I + b_3 S + b_4 A \tag{2.1}$$

where in a particular year, Q equals the number of tablets demanded, P is the average price of tablets, I is per capita disposable income, S is the average price of applications for tablets and A is the amount spent on advertising by tablet producers. Equation (2.1) assumes that the relationship is linear. (Also, we assume the population in the relevant market is essentially constant.)

Going a step further, it is generally necessary for managers to obtain numerical estimates of the values of the b's in equation (2.1). Employing various statistical techniques, managers estimate these **parameters** of the demand function to increase their knowledge of the demand for their product. To illustrate the results we might obtain, we find that

Parameters Constant or variable terms used in the function that help managers determine the specific form of the function but not its general nature.

$$Q = -2{,}000P + 70I - 375S + 0.0001A \tag{2.2}$$

According to equation (2.2), a \$1 increase in the price of a tablet computer decreases the quantity demanded by 2,000 units per year; a \$1 increase in per capita disposable income results in a 70 unit increase in quantity demanded per year; a \$1 increase in the average price of applications reduces the quantity demanded by 375 units per year; and a \$1 increase in advertising raises the quantity demanded by 0.0001 units per year.

It is important to understand the relationship between the market demand function and the demand curve. The market demand curve shows the relationship between Q and P when all other relevant variables are held constant. For example, suppose we want to know the relationship between quantity demanded and price if per capita disposable income is \$13,000, the average price of applications is \$40, and advertising expenditure is \$50 million. Because $I = 13,000$, $S = 40$, and $A = 50,000,000$, equation (2.2) becomes

$$Q = -2,000P + 70(13,000) - 375(40) + 0.0001(50,000,000) \tag{2.3}$$

Or $\quad Q = 900,000 - 2,000P$ (2.4)

Solving this equation for P, we obtain

$$P = 450 - 0.0005Q$$

which is graphed Figure 2.1. This is the demand curve for tablets, given that I, S, and A are held constant at the stipulated levels.

Given the market demand function, managers can better understand how changes in variables can shift the demand curve. For example, how much of a shift will occur in the demand curve if the average price of applications falls from \$40 to \$20? Inserting 20 (rather than 40) for S in equation (2.3), we find that

$$Q = 907,500 - 2,000P \tag{2.5}$$

Solving this equation for P, we obtain

$$P = 453.75 - 0.0005Q \tag{2.6}$$

STRATEGY SESSION: Servicing Demand in Emerging Markets

Direct selling exists in the United States, as is illustrated by companies such as Herbalife, Avon, and Tupperware, and in other developed markets. Both Herbalife and Avon have recently outperformed analyst estimates of earnings. In general, however, these businesses are the Rodney Dangerfields of business—that is, they get no respect from their business colleagues.

But in less-developed parts of the world where small-scale shopping is performed, such as in very small stores, on sidewalks, and on street corners with no agglomeration commerce or one-stop shopping possibilities, the opportunities of direct marketing seem to be ready to proliferate. The CEO of Tupperware, Rick Goings, reports that women around the world are signing up "in droves" to be sales representatives, that is, holders of Tupperware parties. It's hard to advertise broadly in less-developed places. In environments where limited experience with new products is common due to low income and chance for exposure levels, customers seem to value the added personal touch and the testimonials.

Although the megamall and new products may seem remote possibilities in the less-developed world, word of mouth and the ability to see and handle the product in a personal setting may be the future of sales in such areas.

Source: Michelle Fox, "The Best Way to Sell Goods in Emerging Markets?" at www.cnbc.com, at www.cnbc.com/id/42876221.

FIGURE 2.4

Demand Curve for Tablets

If the price of applications falls from $40 to $20, the demand curve shifts to the right by 7,500 units.

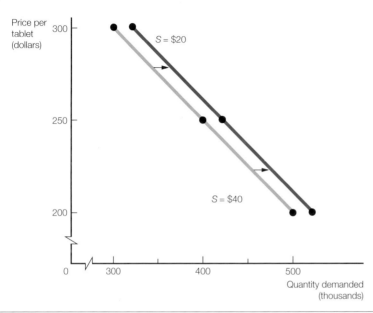

which is graphed (together with the demand curve based on $S = 40$) in Figure 2.4. Clearly the demand curve has shifted to the right: The quantity demanded is 7,500 more than when $S = 40$ (if P is held constant).

Managers are often more interested in the demand curves of their own brands rather than the market demand curve. We can derive these demand functions in a similar manner to predict the sales of an individual producer of tablet computers. In such an equation, the quantity demanded of the firm's product is still inversely related to its own price but is directly related to prices charged by its competitors. So if Dell increases its tablet prices, sales of Apple iPad 2 tablets will increase (all other factors being equal). It is important to distinguish between industry and firm demand functions because they are quite different. Although both are important for managers to understand, they are generally used for different purposes. Looking at the demand functions for individual firms is important in understanding the competitive dynamics of the market. Market demand curves tell managers more about substitute goods outside their product market and the general effects of macroeconomic factors like changes in disposable income on industry sales.

THE OWN-PRICE ELASTICITY OF DEMAND

The elasticity of a function is defined as the percentage change in the dependent variable in response to a 1% change in the independent variable. In $y = ax$, y is the dependent variable because by specifying x, we can determine y. A market demand curve is a function in which quantity demanded is dependent on a product's price. Market demand curves vary with regard to the sensitivity of quantity demanded to price. For some goods, a small price change results in a big change in quantity demanded; for other goods, a big price change results in a small change in quantity demanded. To indicate how sensitive quantity demanded is to price changes, economists use a measure called the **own-price elasticity of demand**. The word *own* is used to convey the idea that managers generally measure the price elasticity of demand for a product or service produced by their firm. More commonly, own-price elasticity of demand is simply referred to as the price elasticity of demand. The price elasticity of demand is defined as the percentage change in quantity demanded resulting from a 1% change in price. More precisely, it equals

Own-price elasticity of demand More simply referred to as price elasticity of demand, this is the concept managers use to measure their own percentage change in quantity demanded resulting from a 1% change in their own price.

$$\eta = \left(\frac{P}{Q}\right)\frac{\Delta Q}{\Delta P} \qquad (2.7)$$

$\Delta Q/\Delta P$ (horizontal change/vertical change) is the inverse of a line's slope. Because linear demand curves are downward-sloping, $\Delta Q/\Delta P$ is negative; hence the price elasticity of demand is expressed as a negative number. Suppose a 1% reduction in the price of Apple tablet computers results in a 1.3% increase in U.S. sales. If so, the price elasticity of demand for Apple tablets is -1.3. The price elasticity of demand generally changes as price varies along the demand curve. For instance, the price elasticity of demand may be higher in absolute value when the price of tablets is relatively high than when it is low. Similarly, the price elasticity of demand varies from market to market. India probably has a different price elasticity of demand for tablets than that of the United States.

We can classify the price elasticity of demand as falling into one of three possible "buckets." When a 1% change in price leads to a more than 1% change in quantity demanded, we say demand is **elastic**. When a 1% change in price leads to a less than 1% change in quantity demanded, we say demand is **inelastic**. And when a 1% change in price leads to a 1% change in quantity demanded, we say demand is **unitary elastic**. Because the price elasticity of demand is always negative for linear demand, we express this information as follows: When demand is elastic, $\eta < -1$; when demand is inelastic, $\eta > -1$; and when demand is unitary elastic, $\eta = -1$.

Elastic Elastic is used to describe demand when a 1% change in price leads to a more than 1% change in quantity demanded.

Inelastic Inelastic is used to describe demand when a 1% change in price leads to a less than 1% change in quantity demanded.

Unitary elastic Unitary elastic is used to describe demand when a 1% change in price leads to a 1% change in quantity demanded.

The price elasticity of demand for a product must lie between zero and negative infinity. If the price elasticity is zero, the demand curve is a vertical line; that is, the quantity demanded is unaffected by price. If the price elasticity is negative

FIGURE 2.5

Demand Curves with Zero and Infinite Price Elasticities of Demand

The demand curve is a vertical line if the price elasticity is zero and a horizontal line if it is negative infinity.

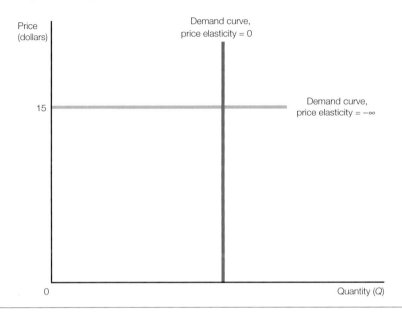

infinity, the demand curve is a horizontal line; that is, an unlimited amount can be sold at a particular price ($15 in Figure 2.5), but nothing is sold if the price is raised even slightly. Figure 2.5 shows these two limiting cases.

We know that $\Delta Q/\Delta P$ is constant along a linear function. However, the price elasticity of demand even for linear demand is not constant because the ratio of price to quantity (P/Q) varies as we move along the demand curve. This is illustrated in Figure 2.6. Point c represents a point on the demand curve. Price is very high, and quantity demanded is very low. Hence P/Q is a large positive number, so elasticity must be low ($\eta < -1$, and demand is elastic). At point z the opposite is true. Price is very low, and quantity demanded is very high; hence P/Q is less than 1. So elasticity is high ($\eta > -1$, and demand is inelastic). Hence for linear demand curves, when P is high, the price elasticity of demand is large (in absolute value terms). As we move down the demand curve, P is decreasing and Q is increasing. This causes the price elasticity to monotonically increase. As we approach the horizontal axis, by definition, P is low and Q is high, so the demand is inelastic. Because the price elasticity is high (above -1) when P is low, and low (below -1) when P is high, at some point on any linear demand curve, the price elasticity must be equal to -1 (unitary elasticity).

FIGURE 2.6

Values of the Price Elasticity of Demand at Various Points along a Linear Demand Curve

The price elasticity increases in absolute value as price rises, approaching negative infinity as quantity approaches zero.

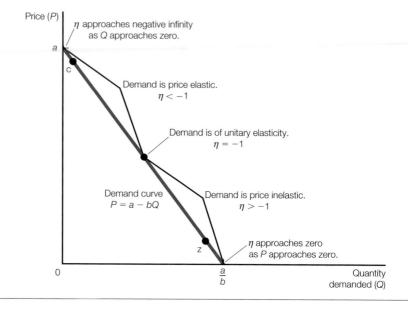

An alternative way of seeing how the price elasticity changes as we move along the demand curve is the following. If

$$P = a - bQ$$

where a is the intercept of the demand curve on the price axis and b is the slope (in absolute terms) of the demand curve, it follows that

$$Q = \frac{a}{b} - \frac{1}{b}P$$

Therefore, the price elasticity of demand is

$$\left(\frac{\Delta Q}{\Delta P}\right)\left(\frac{P}{Q}\right) = \left(\frac{-1}{b}\right)\frac{a - bQ}{Q}$$

Clearly, if the demand curve is linear, the price elasticity approaches zero as $P (= a - bQ)$ gets very small and approaches negative infinity as Q gets very small.

So for most demand curves, the elasticity of demand varies with price. That is, the magnitude of the sales response to price changes does not remain constant. This makes it more difficult for managers to estimate the effects of price changes on sales levels.

POINT AND ARC ELASTICITIES

If we have a market demand schedule showing the quantity of a product demanded at various prices, how can we estimate the price elasticity of market demand? Let ΔP be a change in the price of the good and ΔQ the resulting change in its quantity demanded. If ΔP is very small, we can compute the point elasticity of demand

$$\eta = \frac{\Delta Q}{Q} \div \frac{\Delta P}{P} \qquad (2.8)$$

For instance, consider Table 2.2, where data are given for very small increments in the price of a commodity. If we want to estimate the price elasticity of demand when the price is between $0.9995 and $1, we obtain

$$\eta = \frac{20{,}002 - 20{,}000}{20{,}000} \div \frac{99.95 - 100}{100} = -0.2$$

Note that we used $1 as P and 20,000 as Q. We could have used $0.9995 as P and 20,002 as Q, but it would have made no real difference to the answer.

But if we have data concerning only large changes in price (that is, ΔP and ΔQ are large), the answer may vary considerably depending on which values of P and Q are used in equation (2.8). Consider the example in Table 2.3. Suppose we want to estimate the price elasticity of demand in the price range between $4 and $5. Then, depending on which values of P and Q are used, the answer is

$$\eta = \frac{40 - 3}{3} \div \frac{4 - 5}{5} = -61.67$$

TABLE 2.2

Quantity Demanded at Various Prices (Small Increments in Price)

Price (Cents per Unit of Commodity)	Quantity Demanded per Unit of Time (Units of Commodity)
99.95	20,002
100.00	20,000
100.05	19,998

TABLE 2.3

Quantity Demanded at Various Prices (Large Increments in Price)

Price (Dollars per Unit of Commodity)	Quantity Demanded per Unit of Time (Units of Commodity)
3	50
4	40
5	3

---

or

$$\eta = \frac{3 - 40}{40} \div \frac{5 - 4}{4} = -3.70$$

The difference between these two results is very large. To avoid this difficulty, it is advisable to compute the arc elasticity of demand, which uses the average values of P and Q

$$\eta = \frac{\Delta Q}{(Q_1 + Q_2)/2} \div \frac{\Delta P}{(P_1 + P_2)/2}$$

$$\eta = \frac{\Delta Q(P_1 + P_2)}{\Delta P(Q_1 + Q_2)} \tag{2.9}$$

where P_1 and Q_1 are the first values of price and quantity demanded, and P_2 and Q_2 are the second set. Therefore, in Table 2.3,

$$\eta = \frac{40 - 3}{(40 + 3)/2} \div \frac{4 - 5}{(4 + 5)/2} = -7.74$$

USING THE DEMAND FUNCTION TO CALCULATE THE PRICE ELASTICITY OF DEMAND

Managers often estimate a demand function for their products. In equation (2.2) we provided the following hypothetical demand function for tablet computers

$$Q = -2,000P + 70I - 375S + 0.0001A$$

Given such a demand function, how can we calculate the price elasticity of demand?

The first step is to specify the point on the demand curve at which price elasticity is to be measured. Assuming per capita disposable income (I) is $13,000, the average price of applications is $40, and advertising expenditure is $50,000,000, we know from equation (2.4) that the relationship between quantity demanded and price is

$$Q = 900,000 - 2,000P \qquad (2.10)$$

Suppose we want to measure the price elasticity of demand when price equals $300. At this point on the demand curve (point A in Figure 2.1),

$$Q = 900,000 - 2,000(300) = 300,000$$

We can express $\Delta Q/\Delta P$ as the inverse of the slope. Hence in our example,

$$\Delta Q/\Delta P = -2,000 = -1/0.0005$$

According to equation (2.7), to obtain the price elasticity of demand, we must multiply $\Delta Q/\Delta P$ by P/Q. Performing this multiplication, we get

$$-2,000(300/300,000) = -2$$

which means the price elasticity of demand equals -2.

   As a further illustration, let us calculate the price elasticity of demand when price equals $200 rather than $300. At this point on the demand curve (point B in Figure 2.1),

$$Q = 900,000 - 2,000(200) = 500,000$$

Because $\Delta Q/\Delta P = -2,000$,

$$\eta = (\Delta Q/\Delta P)(P/Q) = -2,000(200/500,000) = -0.8$$

Therefore, the price elasticity of demand equals -0.8.

THE EFFECT OF PRICE ELASTICITY ON THE FIRM'S REVENUE

As we have seen, estimating the price elasticity of demand helps managers predict how a given price change will affect sales. We can also use price elasticities to determine how a price change will affect a firm's total revenue. Total revenue is equal to the price per unit multiplied by the number of units sold ($TR = P \times Q$). So as managers change the price of a product, sales generally vary. Good managers need to consider whether a price change will increase the firm's total revenue if their decisions are to improve firm performance. And whether a price change increases total revenue depends on the price elasticity of demand.

   Suppose at the current price, demand for a product is price elastic; that is, the price elasticity of demand is less than -1. In this situation, if the price is reduced, the percentage increase in quantity demanded is greater than the percentage reduction in price (this follows from the definition of elastic demand). That is, although all units are now being sold at a lower price, the increase in units sold because of the lower price more than makes up for the slightly lower unit price. Hence total revenue increases. Similarly, if demand is elastic at the current price and a manager increases the price, total revenue will decrease. Although we are selling each unit at a higher price, the decrease in sales (because of the higher price) more than offsets the slightly higher price per unit.

If the demand for the product at a given price is price inelastic, the price elasticity of demand is greater than -1. Following from our definition of inelastic demand, the percentage change in quantity is less than the percentage change in price. Hence if we increase price, total revenue will increase because the slightly higher price per unit sold will more than offset the decrease in units sold. If demand is inelastic and we decrease price, total revenue will decrease because the increase in units sold cannot offset the lower price per unit sold.

We can easily show this relationship formally. Let $TR = P \times Q$; then,

$$\frac{\Delta TR}{\Delta P} = Q\frac{\Delta P}{\Delta P} + P\frac{\Delta Q}{\Delta P}$$

$$Q\frac{\Delta P}{\Delta P} + Q\frac{P}{Q}\frac{\Delta Q}{\Delta P} = Q(1 + \eta)$$

$$\frac{\Delta TR/\Delta P}{Q} = 1 + \eta$$

QUANT OPTION

Although most students could hardly agree less, those who use calculus do find some measure of satisfaction in it. So here we derive the elasticity relationship using calculus

$$\frac{dTR}{dP} = Q\frac{dP}{dP} + P\frac{dQ}{dP}$$

$$Q\frac{dP}{dP} + Q\frac{P}{Q}\frac{dQ}{dP} = Q(1 + \eta)$$

$$\frac{dTR/dP}{Q} = 1 + \eta$$

If $\eta < -1$ (that is, elastic), $\frac{dTR/dP}{Q} < 0$ or $\frac{dTR}{dP} < 0$, so an increase in price will reduce TR. And if $\eta > -1$ (that is, inelastic), $\frac{dTR/dP}{Q} > 0$ or $\frac{dTR}{dP} > 0$, so an increase in price will increase TR.

PROBLEM SOLVED: Price Elasticity of Demand: Philip Morris

In 1993 Philip Morris cut cigarette prices by 18%. Its major competitor (RJ Reynolds) matched the price cut. Not surprisingly, the quantity sold of Philip Morris cigarettes increased (by 12.5%). In a June 13, 1994, article referring to the perils of a price cut, *Fortune* reported that Philip Morris profits fell by 25% as the result of a bad pricing strategy. Is there any evidence to determine whether this decision by Philip Morris managers decreased firm performance?

Although all the information is not available, we are not surprised by this result. We estimate the price elasticity of demand for Philip Morris brands (including the iconic Marlboro Man) as revealed by the market:

$$\eta_P = \frac{\%\Delta Q}{\%\Delta P} = \frac{12.5\%}{-18\%} = -0.694$$

Demand is inelastic, so any drop in price should surely decrease firm revenue. Total revenue decreased and total costs increased (because more cigarettes were produced), so profit was destined to fall.

Then if $\eta < -1$ (that is, elastic), $\dfrac{\Delta TR/\Delta P}{Q} < 0$ or $\dfrac{\Delta TR}{\Delta P} < 0$, so an increase in price will reduce TR. And if $\eta > -1$ (that is, inelastic), $\dfrac{\Delta TR/\Delta P}{Q} > 0$ or $\dfrac{\Delta TR}{\Delta P} > 0$, so an increase in price will increase TR.

FUNDING PUBLIC TRANSIT

Consider an example in which we can predict market behavior based on estimates of elasticity measures. The fare (price) elasticity for public transportation in the United States is about -0.3 (that is, fairly inelastic). All transit systems in the United States lose money. Keeping the deficit under control is a constant battle because the typical subsidizers (federal, state, and local governments) are often reluctant to fund public transit (because of their own deficit problems). Can we identify which transit systems have the most difficult time getting public funding?

We can use our knowledge of price elasticity of demand. Managers of transit systems depend on two sources of revenue: ticket sales and public funding. They know that increasing fares will result in higher revenues. Most likely costs will also drop because less capital and labor are used. However, increasing fares reduces ridership and makes public transit less affordable to many. So managers of transit systems that do not receive enough public funding must increase their fares to balance their budgets (and they know their revenues will increase because of their inelastic demand).

DETERMINANTS OF THE OWN-PRICE ELASTICITY OF DEMAND

Table 2.4 shows the price elasticity of demand for selected products in the United States. Managers need to understand the factors that determine a product's price elasticity of demand:

1. The price elasticity of demand for a product depends heavily on the number and similarity of available substitute products. A product with many close

---

TABLE 2.4

Own Price Elasticities of Demand, Selected Goods, and Services from Global Locations

Good/Service	Elasticity	Good/Service	Elasticity
Agricultural products		Cigarettes (U.S.)[7]	−1.107
Apples (U.S.)[1]	−1.159	Bread (U.K.)[3]	−0.26
Potatoes (U.K.)[3]	−0.13	Energy	
Oranges (U.S.)[2]	−0.62	Gasoline—short run (Canada)[8]	−0.01 to −0.2
Lettuce (U.S.)[2]	−2.58	Gasoline—long run (Canada)[8]	−0.4 to −0.8
Products from animals/fish		Transportation	
1 percent milk (U.S.)[5]	−0.54 to −0.74	Domestic cars (U.S.)[9]	−0.78
Cheese (U.K.)[3]	−1.36	European cars (U.S.)[9]	−1.09
Cheese (U.S.)[6]	−0.595	Other manufactured goods	
Meat (China)[4]	−0.06 to −0.18	Clothing and footwear (U.K./Ireland)[10]	−0.94
Beef/veal (U.K.)[3]	−1.45	Other goods (U.K./Ireland)[10]	−0.85
Manufactured agricultural products		Services	
Beer and malt beverages (U.S.)[6]	−2.83	Child care (North America)[11]	−0.570
Wine (U.K./Ireland)[7]	−1.12	Government health care (Kenyal)[12]	−0.100
Wine and brandy (U.S.)[6]	−0.198		

---

[1]C. Elmore, Chapter 10, "Use of 2.4-D in Orchard, Vineyard, and Soft Fruit Production in the United States," *Phenoxy Herbicides*, December 20, 1998.

[2]D. Suits, "Agriculture," in Walter Adams and James Brock, eds., *The Structure of American Industry*, (10th ed.; Englewood Cliffs, NJ: Prentice-Hall, 2000).

[3]AEF116: 1.6: Major market response concepts and measures 1: The demand side and its elasticities.

[4]Millennium Institute, China Agricultural Project.

[5]*A Regional Economic Analysis of Dairy Compacts: Implications for Missouri Dairy Producers*, Section IV—"Economic Analysis of Dairy Compact, circa 1999."

[6]Emilo Pagoulatos and Robert Sorensen, "What Determines the Elasticity of Industry Demand," *International Journal of Industrial Organization*, Vol. 4, 1986.

[7]C. O'Donoghue, "Carbon Dioxide, Energy Taxes, and Household Income," Department of Statistics and Social Policy, London School of Economics, October 13, 1998.

[8]"Potential for Fuel Taxes to Reduce Greenhouse Gas Emissions in Transportation," Hagler Bailly Canada for Department of Public Works and Government Services, Hull, Quebec, June 11, 1990.

[9]P. McCarthy, "Market Price and Income Elasticities of New Vehicle Demands," *Review of Economics and Statistics*, Vol. 78(3), August 1996, 543–547.

[10]E. Brynjolfsson, "Some Estimates of the Contribution of Information Technology to Consumer Welfare," MIT Sloan School, Working Paper 3647-094, January 1994.

[11]D. Chaplin et al., "The Price Elasticity of Child Care Demand: A Sensitivity Analysis."

[12]Section 4: "The Basics of Markets and Health Care Markets": Box 4.4: "Demand for Health Care in Kenya."

substitutes generally has elastic demand. If managers increase the product's price, consumers can easily switch to one of the several available substitutes. Conversely, if managers reduce the price of their product, they will see a significant increase in sales as consumers switch to their product. The extent to which a product has close substitutes largely depends on how well managers differentiate their product from similar ones.

2. The price elasticity of demand is also affected by a product's price relative to a consumer's total budget. Some claim that the demand for products like thimbles, rubber bands, and salt is quite inelastic, because the typical consumer spends only a very small fraction of her income on such goods. This is also why retail stores place items such as candy, soda, and magazines at the checkout counter. Because they are relatively inexpensive, consumers often buy them without thinking about the price. In contrast, products that command a larger percentage of the consumer's total budget tend to be more price elastic. Research has shown that when consumers consider purchasing items such as kitchen appliances or automobiles, they take the time to get several price quotes and gather information about brand attributes.

3. The price elasticity of demand for a product is also affected by the length of the period to which the demand curve pertains. For nondurable goods, demand is likely to be more elastic over a long period relative to a short period. This is because the longer the time period, the easier it is for consumers to substitute one good for another. If, for instance, the price of oil should decline relative to other fuels, the consumption of oil on the day after the price decline will probably increase very little. But over several years, people have an opportunity to react to the price decline in choosing types of home heating fuel; thus the price decline will have a greater effect on oil consumption than in the shorter period of one day. For durable goods, the opposite is true. Let's assume a consumer has just purchased a car. If the price of the car falls soon after the purchase, it is unlikely the consumer will run out and purchase another car; hence demand is inelastic.

THE STRATEGIC USE OF THE PRICE ELASTICITY OF DEMAND

Good managers not only display an avid interest in the price elasticity of demand for their products; they also take strategic actions to use the price elasticity to their benefit. Consider Table 2.5, which provides estimates of the price elasticity of demand for first-class, regular economy, and excursion air tickets between the United States and Europe. The price elasticity of demand for first-class air tickets is much lower in absolute value than for regular economy or excursion tickets, owing in part to the fact that the people who fly first class—often business travelers and relatively wealthy people—are unlikely to change their travel plans if moderate increases or decreases occur in the price of an air ticket. Airline executives study

STRATEGY SESSION: Elasticity in Use

Many of us are accustomed to see prices that end in 0s, 5s, or 9s. But prices that end in any integer are becoming more common. That's because firms are turning away from cost-plus pricing ("the pricing method still in use by the majority of manufacturers," IndustryWeek.com Leadership in Manufacturing) and turning toward strategic or value-based pricing. Profit margin improvements of as much as 21% are reported by Ralph Zuponcic, a managing partner of PricePoint Partners, one of many firms (such as SAP Khimetrics—an early entrant into this field) that now ply this market. Zuponcic notes that price changes are not usually huge (he states that typically a 1% price improvement can yield an 11% gain in profit margin for a firm with an 8% EBIT). Larry Robinson, director of Training and Development at PricePoint states that "adjusting prices for customer segments with varying sensitivity to value and price are the first steps to maximizing profits." This sensitivity is what we refer to in the text as price elasticity, and its precise role is shown in the text and later in this note.

Value-based pricing is one reason Wal-Mart has slashed prices (many to non-zero, five, or nine integers) and raised prices too. Longs Drug Stores (acquired by CVS) has also used such a model as has D'Agostino's (a New York–based grocery store chain). Not only do product prices go up or down from their current levels (as specified by the model), but they also differ for the same product from location to location. Why? Because that above-mentioned price sensitivity differs in different market segments. PricePoint refers to an industrial rubber parts manufacturer where the prices before the application of value pricing ranged from $8 to $12 for the same product. After the application of value pricing, some prices increased, some decreased, and the manufacturer's profit margin on the item rose 21%.

In the retail sector, rather than marking up costs, benchmarking competitors' prices, or guessing, price optimization models use data-mining techniques. Scanned transactions from cash registers, responses to sales promotions, and the like are used to estimate an individual demand curve for each product in each store. Much of this modeling is based on airline yield management systems (see Chapter 9). The goal driving the modeling is to find the crossover point between driving sales and giving away margin unnecessarily. That is consultant-speak. Let's put it into economist-speak.

Airline yield management models attempt to equate marginal expected revenues for each fare class. For instance, suppose two fare classes, 1 and 2, exist. As shown on page 52, marginal revenue (MR) is equal to $MR = P[1 + (1/\eta)]$, so equating marginal revenues for classes 1 and 2 yields

these data carefully and price these classes of tickets differently. For example, because the price elasticity of demand for first-class air tickets is relatively low in absolute value, they price these tickets relatively high. In early 2012 a consumer could purchase an economy airline ticket for a round-trip between Philadephia and Paris for under $900. A first-class ticket would cost the consumer more than $4,500.

Managers can also change the price elasticity of demand for their product. The most common way managers impact the price elasticity of their product is with differentiation strategies. Managers who successfully increase the differentiation

$$MR_1 = P_1[1 + (1/\eta_1)] = P_2[1 + (1/\eta_2)] = MR_2$$

Think about why a business with two different demand curves for the same product (such as business and leisure travelers for an airline seat, spring and summer demand for a bathing suit, location 1 and location 2 demand for Pampers) would want to equate the marginal revenues of these demand curves. If the marginal revenue from fare type 2 exceeds the marginal revenue from fare type 1, it would pay the airline to switch seats out of fare type 1 and into fare type 2. Because the costs of flying a person with fare type 1 is likely to be the same as the cost of flying a person with fare type 2, the airline can increase revenues while leaving costs the same by such a switch. Such a move must increase the airline's bottom line. (If the equated marginal revenues equal the marginal cost of moving a passenger, profits are not only improved, they are maximized.)

How would an elasticity model do this in retailing? Consider the optimal discounting of a product over time. The subscript 1 stands for the first time period, and the subscript 2 stands for the second time period. If the marginal revenue is higher in time period 2 than in period 1, you would want to shift some merchandise from period 1 to period 2 (or if 1 and 2 refer to stores, shift some product from store 1 to store 2).

Suppose that $\eta_1 = -2$ and $\eta_2 = -3$. Then

$$
\begin{aligned}
MR_1 &= P_1[1 + (1/-2)] = P_1[1 - (1/2)] = P_1/2 \\
&= P_2[1 + (1/-3)] = P_2[1 - (1/3)] \\
&= 2P_2/3 = MR_2
\end{aligned}
$$

Or $P_2 = 0.75P_1$; that is, the optimal discount on the product would be to sell the good in time period 2 for 25% off the price from time period 1. Lowering price increases the quantity demanded (because demand curves have an inverse relationship between price and quantity), hence the term *driving sales*. But lowering the price too much or too little will not give the seller the optimal profit margins; that is, the profit margin that yields maximum profit. This can be done only where $MR_1 = MR_2 = (MC)$.

An article in the *Economist* ("The Price is Wrong") notes that supermarket chains "can quickly and easily track customers 'elasticity'—how their buying habits change in response to a price rise or discount." Supermarkets such as D'Agostino's in New York and Dominicks in Chicago have used elasticity-based models to help them make pricing decisions.

Source: "Are You Getting Your Pricing Right or Leaving Money on the Table?" March 14, 2011, at www.industryweek.com/PrintArticle.aspx?ArticleID=24090.

of their product decrease (in absolute value) its price elasticity of demand. Simply put, differentiation strategies convince consumers the product is unique; hence it has fewer substitutes. Because consumers perceive fewer substitutes, they act as if they are more price inelastic. This gives managers more freedom to increase price because sales will fall less.

It is important for managers to understand that differentiation is not effective if consumers do not perceive it. Conversely, differentiation does not require tangible differences in products. For example, bleach is a commodity product; its chemical formula is well known. However, Clorox Bleach is able to command

TABLE 2.5

Elasticities of Demand for Air Tickets between the United States and Europe

Type of Ticket	Price Elasticity	Income Elasticity
First class	−0.45	1.50
Regular economy	−1.30	1.38
Excursion	−1.83	2.37

Source: J. Cigliano, "Price and Income Elasticities for Airline Travel: The North Atlantic Market," *Business Economics*, September 1980.

a retail price that is 300% higher than other brands of bleach. Most remarkably, this brand has been able to command such a high premium over several decades.

TOTAL REVENUE, MARGINAL REVENUE, AND PRICE ELASTICITY

We want to look more closely at the effect of the price elasticity of demand on a firm's total revenue. To a good's producer, the total amount of money paid by consumers equals the firm's revenue. Therefore, to the Toyota Motor Company, the total amount consumers spend on its cars is its total revenue. Suppose the demand curve for a firm's product is linear; that is,

$$P = a - bQ \qquad (2.11)$$

where a is the intercept on the price axis and b is the slope (in absolute terms), as shown in panel A of Figure 2.7. Thus the firm's total revenue equals

$$TR = PQ = (a - bQ)Q = aQ - bQ^2 \qquad (2.12)$$

Marginal revenue The incremental revenue earned from selling the nth unit of output.

An important concept to managers is that of **marginal revenue**, which is the incremental revenue earned from selling the nth unit of output. As we will see, managers must understand marginal revenue to maximize the firm's profit. Because this concept is central to firm performance, we need to understand how the price elasticity of demand affects it. In the present case,

$$MR = \frac{\Delta TR}{\Delta Q}$$

$$= \frac{\Delta(aQ - bQ^2)}{\Delta Q}$$

$$= a - 2bQ \qquad (2.13)$$

STRATEGY SESSION: Elasticity in Specialty Drugs

Specialty drugs are designed to treat illnesses that have major impacts on patients' lives, are difficult to treat, and don't affect a large number of people; these are very expensive to produce.

One such disease is multiple sclerosis (MS). It affects slightly over two million people worldwide, and a year's worth of drug treatment can approach $50,000.

A new oral medication, Novartis AG's Gilenya, has recently received FDA approval. Its yearly price tag is $48,000. MS sufferers are looking forward to the drug because its substitutes require injections, are much harder to self-administer, and can have nasty side effects. The side effects of Gilenya are not completely known, but its ease of use is creating optimism.

The makers of injectibles are sensing that the demand for their product will decline. A recent survey of neurologists by a Citigroup analyst showed that all other MS drugs will suffer from declines in sales in the next year. Some expect Gilenya will be the market leader by 2017.

So what are the producers of injectibles doing? They are raising their prices. They rose 39% last year (2010 to 2011). Analysts say that charging more for the old treatment is a way to "keep revenues steady as sales erode." Teva and Biogen Idec are two companies seeking to generate more revenue before

Gilenya wins significant market share, according to the source article.

Under what conditions can the injectibles achieve their goals? For revenues to be constant as prices rise and quantity falls, the elasticity must be unity, that is $\eta = -1$, and for revenues to increase when prices increase and quantity falls, the demand must be inelastic. Given the nature of the disease, it's not too difficult to believe that demand could be inelastic. Once one has found an injectible that "works," it's likely that the user would stick with it.

And maybe hope is on the way. There are three other oral MS drugs in the testing stages that may be a couple of years away. Hopefully, competition among the producers can bring the price down. However, if the drugs differ with respect to their effectiveness and side effects, the product differentiation could still lead to significant pricing power for each version. In addition, even with a homogenous product, competition driving the price down to cost could still lead to a hefty price for the drug given the high costs of production.

Source: Eva von Schaper and Naomi Kresge, "Novartis's $48,000 Pill Spurs US Price Increase for MS Drugs," *Bloomberg News*, March 22, 2011, at www.bloomberg.com/news/2011-03-21/novartis-s-48-000-pill-spurs-u-s-price-increases-for-ms-drugs.html.

---

which is also shown in panel A of Figure 2.7. Comparing the marginal revenue curve with the demand curve, we see that while both have the same intercept on the vertical axis (this intercept being a) the slope of the marginal revenue curve is twice that of the demand curve.

According to the definition in equation (2.7), the price elasticity of demand, η, equals $(\Delta Q/\Delta P)(P/Q)$. Because $\Delta Q/\Delta P = -1/b$ and $P = a - bQ$, it follows, in this case, that

$$\eta = \left(\frac{-1}{b}\right)\frac{a - bQ}{Q} \qquad (2.14)$$

FIGURE 2.7

Relationship between Price Elasticity, Marginal Revenue, and Total Revenue

If demand is price elastic, marginal revenue is positive and increases in quantity result in higher total revenue. If demand is price inelastic, marginal revenue is negative and increases in quantity result in lower total revenue.

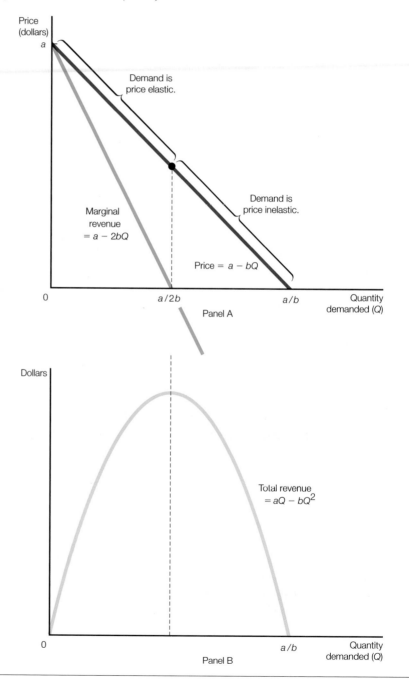

QUANT OPTION

We can see this relationship more clearly using calculus:

$$MR = \frac{dTR}{dQ}$$

$$= \frac{d(aQ - bQ^2)}{dQ}$$

$$= a - 2bQ$$

Therefore, whether η is greater than, equal to, or less than -1 depends on whether Q is greater than, equal to, or less than $a/2b$. As shown in Figure 2.7, demand is price elastic if $Q < a/2b$; it is of unitary elasticity if $Q = a/2b$; and it is price inelastic if $Q > a/2b$.

Panel B in Figure 2.7 plots the firm's total revenue against the quantity demanded of its product. Remember that marginal revenue is the incremental revenue earned from selling the next unit of output. As long as marginal revenue is positive, an increase in sales raises total revenue. However, at outputs where the incremental revenue is negative, total revenue will decrease. Some may ask, how can incremental revenue be negative? If a firm sells one more unit, it must receive a positive revenue from the person it sells to (unless it pays the person to take the good). But think about the effect on total revenue of that last unit sold.

STRATEGY SESSION: Beer—Elastic or Inelastic?

If you drink beer, you'd better hope your pants have some elasticity. But how about demand elasticity? InBev (brewers of Budweiser, Stella Artois, and Beck's) recently announced that due to high unemployment of young males in the United States, quantity demanded of their products fell by 0.4%, while prices rose. The direction of the change is no surprise given our knowledge of demand curves. But they also reported that total revenue rose by a whopping 5.6%. What does this tell us? That the quantity demanded stayed very high and in percentage terms dropped less than the percentage increase in price. Or in economic terms: The demand for their product is inelastic. But how inelastic? From the text, we have that $\Delta TR/\Delta Q = P(1 + [1/\eta])$. Multiplying both sides by Q/TR (or $Q/TR = Q/PQ = 1/P$) gives $(\Delta TR/TR)/(\Delta Q/Q) = \%\Delta TR/\%\Delta Q = 5.6/0.4 = -14 = (1 + [1/\eta])$ or $1/\eta = -15$ or $\eta = 1/-15 = -0.067$. This is very inelastic.

Source: "InBev Price Hike Outweighs Lower Volumes," at www.cnbc.com/id/42891391/.

If managers need to reduce the price to sell that last unit, they reduce the price of all the units sold. Hence selling one more unit can cause total revenue to be lower because the manager has reduced the price on all the units sold. Also, producing one more unit increases total costs. So if total revenue decreases and total cost increases, the manager is moving further from a profit-maximizing strategy. The important thing to remember is that managers do not want to produce at an output level where marginal revenue is negative.

Another thing to note about Figure 2.7 is that, at quantities where demand is price elastic, marginal revenue is positive; at quantities where it is of unitary elasticity, marginal revenue is zero; and at quantities where it is price inelastic, marginal revenue is negative. This is no accident. In general, whether or not the demand curve is linear, this is the case. To see why, recall that by definition,

$$MR = \frac{\Delta TR}{\Delta Q}$$

Because total revenue equals price times quantity, it follows that

$$MR = \frac{\Delta(PQ)}{\Delta Q}$$

We can transform this into

$$MR = P\frac{\Delta Q}{\Delta Q} + Q\frac{\Delta P}{\Delta Q}$$

Because $\Delta Q/\Delta Q = 1$,

$$MR = P + Q\frac{\Delta P}{\Delta Q}$$

$$= P\left[1 + \left(\frac{Q}{P}\right)\left(\frac{\Delta P}{\Delta Q}\right)\right]$$

And because the definition of the price elasticity of demand implies that $(Q/P)(\Delta P/\Delta Q) = 1/\eta$,

$$MR = P\left(1 + \frac{1}{\eta}\right) \tag{2.15}$$

Equation (2.15) shows that if $\eta < -1$, marginal revenue is positive; if $\eta > -1$, marginal revenue is negative; and if $\eta = -1$, marginal revenue is zero. In later chapters we use equation (2.15) repeatedly. Managers will find lots of uses for it. One way they use it is to estimate the value of marginal revenue. For example, what is the marginal revenue if the product price is $10 and the price elasticity of demand is -2? On the basis of equation (2.15), it equals $10(1 - 1/2) = \$5$.

QUANT OPTION

Equation (2.15) is so famous that we think it deserves a formal derivation

$$MR = \frac{dTR}{dQ}$$

$$MR = \frac{d(PQ)}{dQ}$$

$$MR = P\frac{dQ}{dQ} + Q\frac{dP}{dQ}$$

$$MR = P + Q\frac{dP}{dQ}$$

$$= P\left[1 + \left(\frac{Q}{P}\right)\left(\frac{dP}{dQ}\right)\right]$$

$$MR = P\left(1 + \frac{1}{\eta}\right)$$

THE INCOME ELASTICITY OF DEMAND

Price is not the only factor managers need to consider in predicting how many units they will sell. An important factor over which managers have little control is the level of consumer income. A consumer with relatively more money to spend is more likely to purchase various goods. For example, more cognac is sold on a per capita basis in cities populated by consumers with higher income levels, like New York City, than in cities like Fargo, North Dakota, where consumers have lower income levels. Managers need to understand the sensitivity of demand to changes in consumer incomes.

The **income elasticity of demand** for a particular good is defined as the percentage change in quantity demanded resulting from a 1% change in consumers' income. More precisely, it equals

$$\eta_I = \left(\frac{\Delta Q}{\Delta I}\right)\left(\frac{I}{Q}\right) \tag{2.16}$$

Income elasticity of demand The percentage change in quantity demanded resulting from a 1% change in consumers' income.

where Q is quantity demanded and I is consumers' income. For most products, the income elasticity of demand is positive. That is, when consumer incomes increase, they buy more of the product. Such goods are called *normal goods*. However, some products, called *inferior goods*, have negative income elasticities. For these goods, quantity demanded moves opposite to consumer incomes. When incomes increase, quantity demanded decreases; when incomes decrease, quantity demanded increases. Two examples of inferior goods in the United States are hamburgers and public transportation. When consumers' income increases, they generally consume fewer hamburgers. It is not that they eat less beef, but they eat steaks instead of burgers.

Managers must understand the impact of the income elasticity of demand on sales. Variance in sales is common in products with high income elasticities as sales react to the various stages of the business cycle. When the economy is expanding, products with high income elasticities will enjoy a significant increase in sales. However, when the economy enters a recession, these same products will see a significant decrease in sales. Though managers selling products with high income elasticities can do little to influence the business cycle, they can plan ahead to lessen the negative impact of economic fluctuations. For example, they can try to shift their cost structure toward fewer fixed costs and greater variable costs. One way of accomplishing this is by leasing capital goods instead of buying them. And in times of economic expansion, they must prepare for the probable significant increase in sales.

In forecasting the long-term growth of the quantity demanded for many major products, the income elasticity of demand is of key importance. According

STRATEGY SESSION: Estimating the Demand for Amtrak Rail Passenger Business

Amtrak (the national passenger railroad in the United States) has used an aggregate demand model to forecast system-wide passenger revenues. The first part of its model was a multivariate linear regression that forecast its system-wide passenger miles—the dependent variable (a passenger mile is one passenger moved one mile). Explanatory variables were disposable personal income; Amtrak's average fare; the ratio of Amtrak's fare to the airlines' average fare; retail gasoline prices; dummy variables to reflect such events as weather, holidays, strikes, and derailments; and dummy variables to reflect seasonal variation.

The most important determinant of rail passenger miles was disposable personal income (a proxy variable for the strength of the U.S. economy). From the regression, a 1% increase in disposable personal income was expected to yield a 1.8% increase in system-wide passenger miles.

1. Explain the rationale for each explanatory variable appearing in the model and what sign (positive or negative) you expect for its regression coefficient.

2. How did Amtrak use this forecast of system-wide passenger miles to obtain its estimate of system-wide passenger revenues?

3. What is Amtrak's estimate of income elasticity of demand for passenger service (based on the income level of the economy as a whole)? If U.S. disposable personal income per capita increases from $27,000 to $28,000, what's your prediction for the increase in train passenger miles in the new situation (all other independent variables remaining constant)? Will this prediction be 100% accurate? Why or why not?

4. Even though disposable personal income rose from 2000 through 2008 (on a real income basis by 13.26%), Amtrak's market share of U.S. passenger miles traveled has remained virtually constant (0.1105% in 2000 and 0.1120% in 2008). Can you explain this?

to studies done by the U.S. Department of Agriculture, the income elasticity of demand for milk is about 0.5, which means a 1% increase in disposable income is associated with about a 0.5% increase in the quantity demanded of milk. But in a study done in Britain, the income elasticity of bread was about −0.17, which means that a 1% increase in disposable income is associated with about a −0.17% decrease in the quantity demanded of bread. Table 2.5 shows that the income elasticity of demand for first-class air tickets between the United States and Europe is 1.5, which means that a 1% increase in disposable income is associated with a 1.5% increase in the quantity demanded of such tickets. Table 2.6 shows the income elasticity of demand for other commodities across the world. In measuring income elasticities, income can be defined as the aggregate income of consumers (as in Table 2.6) or as per capita income (as in the next section), depending on the circumstances.

CROSS-PRICE ELASTICITIES OF DEMAND

In addition to price and income, another factor influencing the quantity demanded of a product is the prices of rivals. Holding constant the product's own price (as well as the level of income) and allowing the price of another product to vary may result in important effects on the quantity demanded of the product in question.

TABLE 2.6

Income Elasticity of Demand, Selected Commodities, Global

Good	Elasticity	Good	Elasticity
Agricultural products		Cream (U.S.)[3]	+1.72
Grain (China)[1]	−0.12 to +0.15	Eggs (U.K.)[2]	−0.21
Potatoes (U.K.)[2]	−0.32	Eggs (U.S.)[3]	+0.57
Potatoes (U.S.)[3]	+0.15	Processed food products	
Oranges (U.S.)[3]	+0.83	Bread (U.K.)[2]	−0.17
Apples (U.S.)[3]	+1.32	Other cereal products (U.K.)[2]	+0.18
Lettuce (U.S.)[3]	+0.88	Automobiles	
Animal products		Domestic cars (U.S.)[4]	+1.62
Meat (China)[1]	+0.1 to +1.2	European cars (U.S.)[4]	+1.93
Milk (U.K.)[2]	+0.05	Asian cars (U.S.)[4]	+1.65
Milk (U.S.)[3]	+0.50		

[1]Millennium Institute, China Agricultural Project.
[2]AEF116: 1.6 "Major Market Response Concepts and Measures. 1: The Demand Side and Its Elasticities."
[3]D. Suits, "Agriculture," in *The Structure of American Industry*, ed. Adams and Brock.
[4]P. McCarthy, "Market Price and Income Elasticities of New Vehicle Demands."

By observing these effects, we can classify pairs of products as substitutes or complements, and we can measure how close consumers perceive the relationship (either substitute or complementary). Consider products X and Y. If Y's price goes up, what is the effect on Q_X, the quantity of X demanded? The **cross-price elasticity of demand** is defined as the percentage change in the quantity demanded of good X resulting from a 1% change in the price of good Y

Cross-price elasticity of demand
The percentage change in the quantity demanded of one good resulting from a 1% change in the price of another good.

$$\eta_{XY} = \left(\frac{\Delta Q_X}{\Delta P_Y}\right)\left(\frac{P_Y}{Q_X}\right) \tag{2.17}$$

Goods X and Y are classified as substitutes if the cross-price elasticity of demand is positive. For instance, an increase in the price of wheat, when the price of corn remains constant, tends to increase the quantity of corn demanded; therefore, η_{XY} is positive, and wheat and corn are classified as substitutes. On the other hand, if the cross-price elasticity of demand is negative, goods X and Y are classified as complements. For example, an increase in the price of software tends to decrease the purchase of laptop computers when the price of laptops remains constant; therefore, η_{XY} is negative, and software and laptops are classified as complements. If the cross-price elasticity of two products is around zero, then the products have independent demand levels. For example, if the price of butter increases, the demand for airline tickets remains constant.

PROBLEM SOLVED: Income Elasticity of Demand

In a previous section we learned how to calculate the price elasticity of demand based on a product's demand function. Here we see how to calculate the income elasticity of demand. Suppose the demand function for a product is

$$Q_X = 1,000 - 0.2P_X + 0.5P_Y + 0.04I$$

where Q_X is the quantity demanded of good X, P_X is the price of good X, P_Y is the price of good Y, and I is per capita disposable income. The income elasticity of demand is

$$\eta_I = \left(\frac{\Delta Q}{\Delta I}\right)\left(\frac{I}{Q}\right)$$

$$= 0.04\frac{I}{Q}$$

If $I = 10,000$ and $Q = 1,600$

$$\eta_I = 0.04\left(\frac{10,000}{1,600}\right) = 0.25$$

The income elasticity of demand equals 0.25, which means that a 1% increase in per capita disposable income is associated with a 0.25% increase in the quantity demanded of product X.

To illustrate the calculation of cross-price elasticities, suppose once again the demand function for our product is

$$Q_X = 1,000 - 0.2P_X + 0.5P_Y + 0.04I$$

where Q_X is the quantity demanded of product X, P_X is the price of X, P_Y is the price of product Y, and I is per capita disposable income. The cross-price elasticity of demand between products X and Y is

$$\eta_{XY} = \left(\frac{\Delta Q_X}{\Delta P_Y}\right)\left(\frac{P_Y}{Q_X}\right)$$
$$= 0.5\frac{P_Y}{Q_X}$$

Although the value of the cross-price elasticity depends on the values of P_Y and Q_X, the goods are always substitutes because η_{XY} is positive, regardless of the values of P_Y and Q_X. If $P_Y = 500$ and $Q_X = 2,000$,

$$\eta_{XY} = 0.5\left(\frac{500}{2,000}\right) = 0.125$$

The cross-price elasticity of demand is of fundamental importance to managers because they continually must anticipate what will happen to their own sales if rivals change their prices. To do so, they need information concerning the cross-price elasticities of demand. Table 2.7 shows the cross-price elasticities of demand for selected pairs of commodities.

The measure is also frequently used by antitrust authorities to evaluate proposed mergers. A high cross-price elasticity measure between products X and Y can cause concern that a merger between the producers of X and Y might result in consumers experiencing higher prices and fewer brand choices. A highly negative cross-price elasticity measure $(-\eta_{xy})$ signifies that the products are strong complements. Here the authorities may be concerned a merger between the products might lead to excessive control of the supply chain. That is, the merged firm may refuse to sell the intermediate product to other producers.

THE ADVERTISING ELASTICITY OF DEMAND

Although the price elasticity, income elasticity, and cross-price elasticities of demand are the most frequently used elasticity measures, they are not the only ones. For example, managers sometimes find it useful to calculate the **advertising elasticity of demand**. Suppose the demand function for a particular firm's product is

$$Q = 500 - 0.5P + 0.01I + 0.82A$$

where Q is the quantity demanded of the product, P is its price, I is per capita disposable income, and A is the firm's advertising expenditure. The advertising

Advertising elasticity of demand
The percentage change in the quantity demanded of the product resulting from a 1% change in the advertising expenditure.

TABLE 2.7

Cross-Price Elasticity of Demand, Selected Pairs of Commodities, Global

Change of Price of Good	Change of Quantity of Good	Cross-Price Elasticity
European/Asian cars	U.S. domestic cars	+0.28[1]
European/U.S. domestic cars	Asian cars	+0.61[1]
U.S. domestic/Asian cars	European cars	+0.76[1]
Australian public transit	Australian auto ownership	+0.1 to +0.3[2]
Irish coal	Irish natural gas	+0.4[3]
Irish coal	Irish oil	+0.7[3]
Kenyan government-provided health care	Mission- or private sector–provided health care in Kenya	+0.023[4]
U.S. durum wheat	U.S. hard red spring wheat	+0.04[5]
U.S. hard red winter wheat	U.S. white wheat	+1.80[5]
U.K. beef/veal	U.K. pork	0.00[6]
U.K. mutton/lamb	U.K. beef/veal	+0.25[6]

[1]P. McCarthy, "Market Price and Income Elasticities of New Vehicle Demand."

[2]J. Luk and S. Hepburn, "A Review of Australian Travel Demand Elasticities," Working Document No. TE 93/004, 1993, Australian Road Research Board.

[3]Competition Authority Decision of 30 January 1998, relating to a proceeding under Section 4 of the Competition Act 1991: Notification No. CA/15/97—Statoil Ireland Ltd./Clare Oil Company Ltd.—Share Purchase Agreement and Service Employment Agreement. Decision No. 490.

[4]"Section 4: The Basics of Markets and Health Care Markets: Box 4.4: Demand for Health Care in Kenya."

[5]Wheat Yearbook, March 30, 1998, Economic Research Services, U.S. Department of Agriculture, Washington, DC 20036-5831.

[6]AEF116: 1.6: "Major Market Response Concepts and Measures. 1: The Demand Side and Its Elasticities."

elasticity is defined as the percentage change in the quantity demanded of the product resulting from a 1% change in advertising expenditure. More precisely, it equals

$$\eta_A = \left(\frac{\Delta Q}{\Delta A}\right)\left(\frac{A}{Q}\right) \tag{2.18}$$

In this case, because $\Delta Q / \Delta A = 0.82$,

$$\eta_A = 0.82 \frac{A}{Q}$$

If A/Q, the amount of advertising per unit of the product demanded, is $2,

$$\eta_A = 0.82(2) = 1.64$$

This useful elasticity tells managers that a 1% increase in advertising expenditure results in a 1.64% increase in the quantity demanded. In later chapters we will see how information of this sort is used to help guide managerial decisions.

THE CONSTANT-ELASTICITY AND UNITARY ELASTIC DEMAND FUNCTION

In this chapter, we generally assume the demand function is linear. That is, the quantity demanded of a product is assumed to be a linear function of its price, the prices of other goods, consumer income, and other variables. Another mathematical form frequently used is the **constant-elasticity demand function**. If the quantity demanded (Q) depends only on the product's price (P) and consumer income (I), this mathematical form is

$$Q = aP^{-b_1/b_2} \tag{2.19}$$

Constant-elasticity demand function Mathematical form that always yields the same elasticity, regardless of the product's price and the consumers' income.

Therefore, if $a = 200$, $b_1 = 0.3$, and $b_2 = 2$,

$$Q = 200P^{-0.3/2}$$

An important property of this type of demand is that the price elasticity of demand equals $-b_1$, regardless of the value of P or I. (This accounts for it being called the constant-elasticity demand function.)

The constant-elasticity demand function is often used by managers and economists for several reasons. First, in contrast to the linear demand function, this mathematical form explicitly recognizes the effect of price on quantity demanded depends on income level and that the effect of income on quantity demanded depends on price. The multiplicative relationship in equation (2.19) is often more realistic than the additive relationship in equation (2.1). Second, like the linear demand function, the constant-elasticity demand function is relatively easy to estimate.

If the demand is of unitary elasticity (the price elasticity of demand equals -1), an increase or decrease in price has no effect on the amount spent on the good. As an illustration, consider the case shown in Figure 2.8. The demand curve shown is a rectangular hyperbola, which means that

$$Q = \frac{m}{P} \tag{2.20}$$

QUANT OPTION

Here is the formal derivation of the constant elasticity.

$$\eta = (P/Q)(\partial Q/\partial P) = (P/aP^{-b_1/b_2})(-ab_1P^{b_1-1/b_2}) = P(-b_1P^{-1}) = -b_1$$

FIGURE 2.8

Demand Curve with Unitary Elasticity at All Points

The demand curve is a rectangular hyperbola if the price elasticity of demand is always −1.

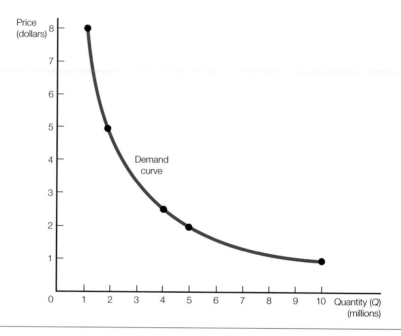

where Q is product demand, P is the price, and m is a constant. This type of demand is of unitary elasticity at all points. Hence changes in price have no effect on the total amount spent on the product. It is evident from equation (2.20) that, regardless of the price, the total expenditure for the product will be m ($10 million in Figure 2.8).

SUMMARY

1. The market demand curve for a product shows how much of the product is demanded at each price. The market demand curve shifts in response to changes in tastes, incomes, the prices of other products, advertising, and the size of the population.

2. The market demand function for a product is an equation showing how the quantity demanded depends on the product's price, the incomes of consumers, the prices of other products, advertising expenditure, and additional factors. Holding all factors other than the product's price constant, we can draw the market demand curve for the product from the market demand function. Market demand functions are formulated for individual firms as well as for entire industries.

3. The own-price elasticity of demand is the percentage change in quantity demanded resulting from a 1% change in price; more precisely, it equals $(\Delta Q/\Delta P)(P/Q)$. Whether a price increase (or decrease) results in an increase in the total amount spent by consumers on a product depends on the own-price elasticity of demand.

4. Marginal revenue is the change in total revenue resulting from a one-unit increase in quantity. Marginal revenue equals $P(1 + 1/\eta)$, where P is price and η is the own-price elasticity of demand.

5. The own-price elasticity of demand for a product tends to be elastic if the product has many close substitutes. Also, it often tends to be more elastic in the long run than in the short run. It is sometimes asserted a product's demand is relatively price inelastic if the product accounts for a very small percentage of the typical consumer's budget, but this need not be the case.

6. The income elasticity of demand is the percentage change in quantity demanded resulting from a 1% change in consumer income; that is, it equals $(\Delta Q/\Delta I)$ (I/Q), where I is the income of consumers. The income elasticity of demand may be positive or negative. Like the price elasticity of demand, it is of major importance in forecasting the long-term growth in the quantity demanded for products.

7. The cross-price elasticity of demand is the percentage change in the quantity demanded of product X resulting from a 1% change in the price of product Y; in other words, it equals $(\Delta Q_X/\Delta P_Y)(P_Y/Q_X)$. If X and Y are substitutes, it is positive; if they are complements, it is negative. This elasticity is important for managers because they must understand and forecast the effects of changes in other firms' prices on their own firm's sales.

8. If a demand curve is linear, the own-price elasticity of demand varies from point to point on the demand curve. As price approaches zero, the own-price elasticity of demand also approaches zero. As quantity demanded approaches zero, the own-price elasticity approaches negative infinity. In contrast, for a constant-elasticity demand function, the own-price elasticity of demand is the same regardless of the product's price. Both linear demand functions and constant-elasticity demand functions are used frequently by managers and managerial economists.

PROBLEMS

wwnorton.com/studyspace

1. The Dolan Corporation, a maker of small engines, determines that in 2012 the demand curve for its product is

$$P = 2,000 - 50Q$$

where P is the price (in dollars) of an engine and Q is the number of engines sold per month.

a. To sell 20 engines per month, what price would Dolan have to charge?

b. If managers set a price of $500, how many engines will Dolan sell per month?

c. What is the price elasticity of demand if price equals $500?

d. At what price, if any, will the demand for Dolan's engines be of unitary elasticity?

2. The Johnson Robot Company's marketing managers estimate that the demand curve for the company's robots in 2012 is

$$P = 3{,}000 - 40Q$$

where P is the price of a robot and Q is the number sold per month.

a. Derive the marginal revenue curve for the firm.

b. At what prices is the demand for the firm's product price elastic?

c. If the firm wants to maximize its dollar sales volume, what price should it charge?

3. After a careful statistical analysis, the Chidester Company concludes the demand function for its product is

$$Q = 500 - 3P + 2P_r + 0.1I$$

where Q is the quantity demanded of its product, P is the price of its product, P_r is the price of its rival's product, and I is per capita disposable income (in dollars). At present, $P = \$10$, $P_r = \$20$ and $I = \$6{,}000$.

a. What is the price elasticity of demand for the firm's product?

b. What is the income elasticity of demand for the firm's product?

c. What is the cross-price elasticity of demand between its product and its rival's product?

d. What is the implicit assumption regarding the population in the market?

4. The Haas Corporation's executive vice president circulates a memo to the firm's top management in which he argues for a reduction in the price of the firm's product. He says such a price cut will increase the firm's sales and profits.

a. The firm's marketing manager responds with a memo pointing out that the price elasticity of demand for the firm's product is about -0.5. Why is this fact relevant?

b. The firm's president concurs with the opinion of the executive vice president. Is she correct?

5. Managers of the Hanover Manufacturing Company believe the demand curve for its product is

$$P = 5 - Q$$

where P is the price of its product (in dollars) and Q is the number of millions of units of its product sold per day. It is currently charging $1 per unit for its product.

a. Evaluate the wisdom of the firm's pricing policy.
b. A marketing specialist says that the price elasticity of demand for the firm's product is -1.0. Is this correct?

6. On the basis of historical data, Richard Tennant has concluded, "The consumption of cigarettes is . . . [relatively] insensitive to changes in price. . . . In contrast, the demand for individual brands is highly elastic in its response to price. . . . In 1918, for example, Lucky Strike was sold for a short time at a higher retail price than Camel or Chesterfield and rapidly lost half its business."

a. Explain why the demand for a particular brand is more elastic than the demand for all cigarettes. If Lucky Strike raised its price by 1% in 1918, was the price elasticity of demand for its product greater than -2?
b. Do you think that the demand curve for cigarettes is the same now as it was in 1918? If not, describe in detail the factors that have shifted the demand curve and whether each has shifted it to the left or right.

7. According to S. Sackrin of the U.S. Department of Agriculture, the price elasticity of demand for cigarettes is between -0.3 and -0.4, and the income elasticity of demand is about 0.5.

a. Suppose the federal government, influenced by findings that link cigarettes and cancer, were to impose a tax on cigarettes that increased their price by 15%. What effect would this have on cigarette consumption?
b. Suppose a brokerage house advised you to buy cigarette stocks because if incomes were to rise by 50% in the next decade, cigarette sales would be likely to spurt enormously. What would be your reaction to this advice?

8. A survey of major U.S. firms estimates on average, the advertising elasticity of demand is only about 0.003. Doesn't this indicate that managers spend too much on advertising?

9. The McCauley Company hires a marketing consultant to estimate the demand function for its product. The consultant concludes that this demand function is

$$Q = 100P^{-3.1}I^{2.3}A^{0.1}$$

where Q is the quantity demanded per capita per month, P is the product's price (in dollars), I is per capita disposable income (in dollars), and A is the firm's advertising expenditures (in thousands of dollars).

a. What is the price elasticity of demand?
b. Will price increases result in increases or decreases in the amount spent on McCauley's product?
c. What is the income elasticity of demand?
d. What is the advertising elasticity of demand?
e. If the population in the market increases by 10%, what is the effect on the quantity demanded if P, I, and A are held constant?

10. The Schmidt Corporation estimates that its demand function is

$$Q = 400 - 3P + 4I + 0.6A$$

where Q is the quantity demanded per month, P is the product's price (in dollars), I is per capita disposable income (in thousands of dollars), and A is the firm's advertising expenditures (in thousands of dollars per month). Population is assumed to be constant.

a. During the next decade, per capita disposable income is expected to increase by $5,000. What effect will this have on the firm's sales?

b. If Schmidt wants to raise its price enough to offset the effect of the increase in per capita disposable income, by how much must it raise its price?

c. If Schmidt raises its price by this amount, will it increase or decrease the price elasticity of demand? Explain. Make sure your answers reflect the fact that elasticity is a negative number.

CHAPTER 3

CONSUMER BEHAVIOR AND RATIONAL CHOICE

We discussed market demand in Chapter 2. But as we will soon see, market demand for a product is the aggregate of individual demand for that product. So managers need to understand how individuals choose products. As you read this chapter, think about how you make decisions; certainly we all purchase much in our lives. More important, you need to understand how the variables controlled and directed by managers (prices, advertising, etc.) influence consumer choice.

Our model for consumer behavior is part of a larger whole. All of us make decisions every day. Most are decided with little effort: Either the choice is obvious or the impact is limited, so deep thought is not warranted. Occasionally we encounter decisions that require more thought and have high impact; in these situations we are likely to think harder about possible choices and their consequences. But whether we make a snap judgment or a systematic analysis, we are governed by an internal classification scheme that tells us we prefer one choice over another. Without preference ordering, we are reduced to random choices.

This chapter shows how economists model consumer purchase decisions. In later chapters we examine how individuals make decisions under risk (Chapter 14) and when they possess asymmetric information (Chapters 15 and 16).

Although some students may fret about the usefulness of economic principles in the business world, they cannot deny the usefulness of our decision models. It should be obvious that managers constantly face limited budgets to allocate across different uses. You as a consumer face this decision daily. For a problem of this sort, the economist's model of consumer behavior provides some guidelines. And good managers understand that they can take actions to influence consumer choice. This is the idea underlying the use of marketing, pricing, and distributional strategies.

In subsequent chapters we explain how this decision framework is applied to help improve managerial decision making. For now, you may want to try Problem 11 at the end of this chapter. See if you can figure out how this model sheds light on a state's choice between mass transit and highways. (The answer is provided at the end of the book.)

In examining how consumers choose, we initially assume a consumer is rational and wishes to maximize his or her well-being. That is, to the best of their knowledge, consumers do not make choices that cause them harm. A consumer's well-being is a function of the goods she or he chooses to purchase. However, this well-being is not unconstrained. If it were, we would see many more people driving expensive cars like a Porsche or a Bentley. Purchases are constrained by the income level of the consumer. A rational consumer maximizes his or her well-being given the prices of goods, personal tastes and preferences for goods, and income. We formally model this behavior by developing the concepts of utility functions, indifference curves, and budget lines. Using them, we derive the consumer's demand curve for products and show how demand shifts when income changes.

INDIFFERENCE CURVES

Indifference curve Contains points representing market bundles among which the consumer is indifferent.

To clarify important ideas, we initially assume consumers can purchase only food products and clothing products. All the implications we discuss apply to the more complex setting of the world. Consumer choice is modeled as a series of indifference curves. An **indifference curve** contains points representing market bundles among which the consumer is indifferent. To illustrate, consider Jennifer Popovich, a consumer in South Pasadena, California. Certain market bundles—that is, combinations of food and clothing—are equally desirable to her. For example, she may have a hard time choosing between a market bundle containing 50 pounds of food and 5 pieces of clothing and one containing 100 pounds of food and 2 pieces of clothing. These two bundles are represented by two points, K and L, in Figure 3.1. In addition, other market bundles, each of which is represented by a point in Figure 3.1, are just as desirable to Ms. Popovich. If we connect all these points, we derive a curve that represents equally desirable bundles to Ms. Popovich. Figure 3.1 maps these bundles as points on curve I_1 in Figure 3.1. Curve I_1 is an indifference curve.

We need to understand three things when modeling consumer indifference curves:

1. *A consumer has many indifference curves.* If Ms. Popovich is indifferent among all the market bundles represented by points on I_2 in Figure 3.1, I_2 is

FIGURE 3.1

Two of Ms. Popovich's Indifference Curves

The curves I_1 and I_2 are two of Ms. Popovich's indifference curves. Each shows market bundles that are equally desirable to Ms. Popovich.

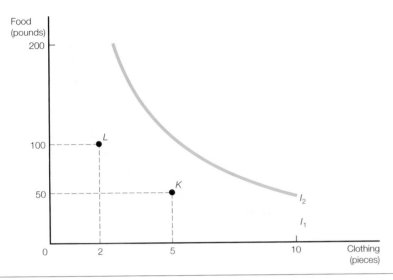

another of her indifference curves. Moreover, one thing is certain. She prefers any I_2 bundle to any one on I_1, because I_2 has bundles with as much clothing as and more food than (or as much food as and more clothing than) bundles on I_1. Implicitly we assume that consumers are sometimes insatiable. (Of course consumers sometimes become so satiated with a product that they prefer less of it to more, but we assume for simplicity that this is not the case here.) Consequently, market bundles on higher indifference curves like I_2 are preferred to bundles on lower indifference curves like I_1.

2. *Every indifference curve must slope downward and to the right, so long as the consumer prefers more of each commodity to less.* If one market bundle on an indifference curve has more of one product than a second bundle, it must have less of the other product than the second bundle. This is true so long as more of each product is preferred.

3. *Indifference curves cannot intersect.* If they did, this would contradict the assumption that more of a product is preferred. For example, suppose that I_1 and I_2 in Figure 3.2 are two intersecting indifference curves. If this is the case, the market bundle at point D is equivalent to the one represented by point C because both are on indifference curve I_1. Moreover, the market bundle represented by point E is equivalent in the eyes of the consumer to the one represented by point C because

FIGURE 3.2

Intersecting Indifference Curves: A Contradiction

Indifference curves cannot intersect. If they did, the consumer would be indifferent between D and C because both are on indifference curve I_1, and between E and C because both are on indifference curve I_2. But this implies that he or she must be indifferent between D and E, which is impossible because E contains the same amount of food and two more pieces of clothing than D, and we are assuming that more of a commodity is preferred to less.

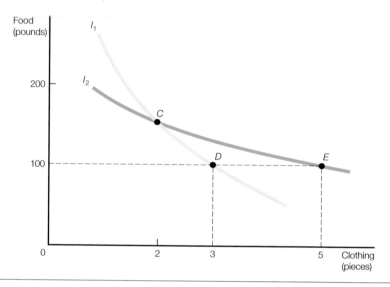

both are on indifference curve I_2. And this means the market bundle represented by point E is equivalent to the one represented by point D. But this is impossible because the bundle at E contains the same amount of food and two more pieces of clothing than bundle D. If we assume that more of a product is preferred, the bundle at E must be preferred to the bundle at D.

THE MARGINAL RATE OF SUBSTITUTION

Some consumers place a high value on obtaining an extra unit of a product; others place a low value on obtaining it. If managers are to understand consumer choice, it is useful to measure the relative importance a consumer places on acquiring an additional unit of a particular product. We measure this using what is called the marginal rate of substitution.

The **marginal rate of substitution** of product X for product Y is defined as the number of units of product Y that must be given up if the consumer, after receiving an extra unit of product X, is to maintain a constant level of satisfaction. Obviously the more units of product Y the consumer is willing to give up to get an

Marginal rate of substitution The number of units of product Y that must be given up if the consumer, after receiving an extra unit of product X, is to maintain a constant level of satisfaction.

FIGURE 3.3

Indifference Curves of Consumers with High and Low Marginal Rates of Substitution of Performance for Stylishness

The left panel shows the indifference curves of consumers who are willing to trade a lot of stylishness for a little extra performance. The right panel shows the indifference curves of consumers who are willing to trade a lot of performance for a little extra stylishness.

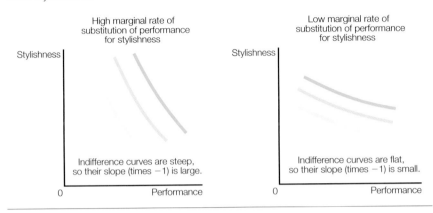

extra unit of X, the more important product X is (relative to Y) to the consumer. To estimate the marginal rate of substitution, we multiply the slope of the consumer's indifference curve by −1. This gives us the number of units of product Y the consumer is willing to give up for an extra unit of product X.

To illustrate, consider consumer preferences for attributes of automobiles. Two key attributes are stylishness and performance (for example, speed, gasoline mileage, and handling). Some consumers are willing to trade a lot of stylishness for a little extra performance. This behavior is shown in the left panel of Figure 3.3. The indifference curves here are steep. The marginal rate of substitution of performance for stylishness is relatively high because the slope of the indifference curves (times −1) is relatively large. Other consumers are willing to trade a lot of performance for a little extra stylishness. For these consumers the indifference curves in Figure 3.3 are relatively flat, as in the right panel of Figure 3.3. The marginal rate of substitution of performance for stylishness is relatively low because the slope of the indifference curves (times −1) is relatively small.

THE CONCEPT OF UTILITY

The consumer's indifference curves represent his or her tastes and preferences. Given all the indifference curves of a particular consumer, we attach a number, called a utility, to each of the available market bundles. **Utility** indicates the level of enjoyment or preference attached by a consumer to a particular market bundle.

Utility Indicates the level of enjoyment or preference attached by a consumer to a particular market bundle.

More specifically, it summarizes the preference ranking of market bundles; the higher the utility assigned to a bundle, the higher the level of satisfaction the consumer realizes from it. Because all market bundles on a given indifference curve yield the same amount of satisfaction, they all have the same utility. Market bundles on higher indifference curves have higher utilities than those on lower indifference curves.

When we assign utilities to market bundles, it tells us which bundles the consumer prefers. If the utility attached to one bundle is higher than that attached to another, the consumer prefers the first over the second. If the utility attached to the first bundle is lower than the second, he or she prefers the second over the first. If the utility attached to the first market bundle equals the second, he or she is indifferent between the two market bundles.

How do we rationally assign these utilities? Assume our consumer prefers market bundle R to bundle S, and bundle S to bundle T. The utility assigned to bundle R must be higher than that assigned to bundle S, while the utility assigned to bundle S must be higher than that assigned to bundle T. Any set of numbers conforming to these requirements is an adequate measure of utility. Therefore, the utility of market bundles R, S, and T may be 30, 20, and 10 or 6, 5, and 4, respectively. All that counts is that the utility of market bundle R is higher than that of bundle S, which in turn should be higher than that of bundle T. Put differently, both sets of utilities provide a correct ordering or ranking of market bundles in terms of levels of consumer satisfaction.

Indifference curves are also known as iso-utility curves. We can measure the slope described above as

$$-\Delta f/\Delta c = -(\Delta U/\Delta c)/(\Delta U/\Delta f) = -MU_c/MU_f$$

where MU_f is the marginal utility of food, that is, the increase in Ms. Popovich's utility if she obtains one more unit of food (holding the amount of clothing she possesses constant), and where MU_c is the marginal utility of clothing, that is, the increase in Ms. Popovich's utility if she obtains one more unit of clothing (holding the amount of food she possesses constant). Thus, Ms. Popovich's marginal rate of substitution is equal to the ratio of her marginal utility of clothing to her marginal utility of food. These marginal utilities are precisely what we were talking about earlier in this section when we referenced the value a consumer placed on obtaining an extra unit of a product.

THE BUDGET LINE

Consumers wish to maximize their utility, which means they want to consume bundles from the highest possible indifference curve. But whether a particular indifference curve is attainable depends on a consumer's income and product prices. To make things concrete, we return to our consumer, Jennifer Popovich. Suppose her total income is $600 per week, and she spends it on only food and clothing.

How much of each product Ms. Popovich can buy depends on the prices of food and clothing. Suppose a pound of food costs $3 and a piece of clothing costs $60. Then, if she spent all her income on food, she could buy 200 pounds of food per week. On the other hand, if she spent all her income on clothing, she could buy 10 pieces of clothing per week. Or she could, if she wished, buy some food and some clothing. There are many combinations of food and clothing she could buy, and each such combination can be represented by a point on the line in Figure 3.4. This line is called her budget line. A consumer's **budget line** shows the market bundles that he or she can purchase, given the consumer's income and prevailing market prices.

To obtain the equation for Jennifer Popovich's budget line, note that

$$YP_f + XP_c = I \qquad (3.1)$$

Budget line Shows the market bundles that the consumer can purchase, given the consumer's income and prevailing market prices.

FIGURE 3.4

Ms. Popovich's Budget Line

The consumer's budget line shows the market bundles that can be purchased, given the consumer's income and prevailing commodity prices. This budget line assumes that Ms. Popovich's income is $600 per week, that the price of a pound of food is $3, and that the price of a piece of clothing is $60.

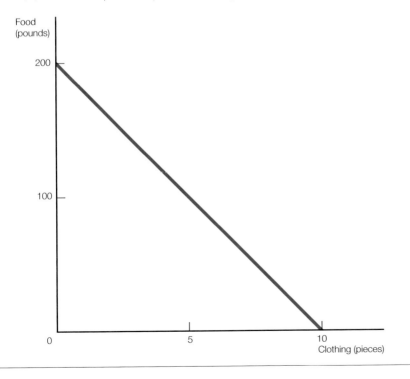

where Y is the amount of food she buys, X is the amount of clothing she buys, P_f is the price of food, P_c is the price of clothing, and I is her income. The left side of equation (3.1) equals the total amount she spends on food and clothing; what equation (3.1) says is that this amount must equal her income. For simplicity, we assume she saves nothing. (This assumption can be relaxed.) Solving equation (3.1) for Y, we obtain

$$Y = \frac{I}{P_f} - \frac{P_c}{P_f} X \qquad (3.2)$$

which is the equation for her budget line.

A shift occurs in a consumer's budget line if changes occur in the consumer's income or product prices. In particular, an increase in income raises the budget line, whereas a decrease in income causes the budget line to fall (parallel to the original line because a change in I does not affect the slope). This is illustrated in Figure 3.5, which shows Ms. Popovich's budget lines at incomes of $300, $600, and $900 per week. Her budget line moves upward as her income rises.

Also, the prices of products affect the budget line. A decrease in a product's price causes the budget line to intersect this product's axis at a point farther from

---

FIGURE 3.5

Ms. Popovich's Budget Lines at Incomes of $300, $600, and $900 per Week

The higher the consumer's income, the higher is the budget line. Holding commodity prices constant, the budget line's slope remains constant.

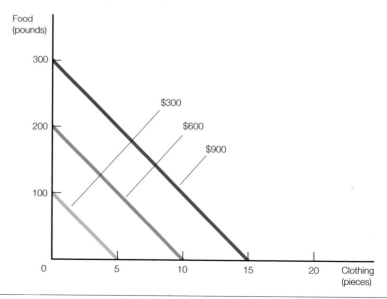

FIGURE 3.6

Ms. Popovich's Budget Line at Food Prices of $3 and $6 per Pound

Holding constant Ms. Popovich's income at $600 per week and the price of a piece of clothing at $60, the budget line intersects the vertical axis farther from the origin when the price of food is $3 than when it is $6.

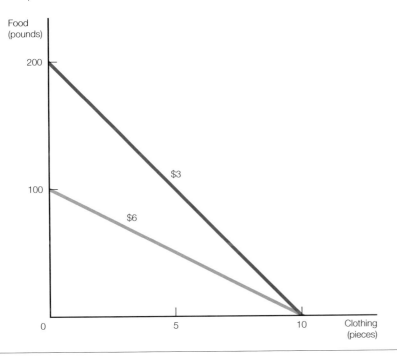

the origin. Figure 3.6 shows Ms. Popovich's budget line when the price of a pound of food is $3 and when it is $6. You can see the budget line meets the vertical, or food, axis farther from the origin when the price of food is $3 per pound. This is because the change in the price of food alters the slope of the budget line, which equals $-P_c/P_f$ (as shown in equation (3.2)).

THE EQUILIBRIUM MARKET BUNDLE

Given a consumer's indifference curves and budget line, we can determine the consumer's **equilibrium market bundle**—the market bundle that, among all the items the consumer can purchase, yields the maximum utility. The first step is to combine the indifference curves with the budget line on the same graph. Figure 3.7 brings together Ms. Popovich's indifference curves (from Figure 3.1) and her budget line (from Figure 3.4). On the basis of the information assembled in Figure 3.7, it is a simple matter to determine her equilibrium market bundle. Her indifference

Equilibrium market bundle The market bundle that, among all the items the consumer can purchase, yields the maximum utility.

FIGURE 3.7

Equilibrium Market Bundle

Ms. Popovich's equilibrium market bundle is at point *H*, containing 100 pounds of food and 5 pieces of clothing. This is the point on her budget line that is on the highest indifference curve she can attain, I_2.

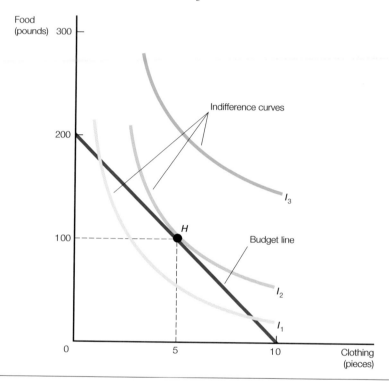

curves show what she wants: Specifically, she wants to attain the highest possible indifference curve. Therefore, she would rather be on indifference curve I_2 than on indifference curve I_1 and on indifference curve I_3 than on indifference curve I_2. But she cannot choose any market bundle she likes. The budget line shows which market bundles her income and product prices permit her to buy. Consequently she must choose a bundle on her budget line.

Clearly the consumer's choice boils down to choosing the market bundle on the budget line that is on the highest indifference curve. This is the equilibrium market bundle. For example, Ms. Popovich's equilibrium market bundle is at point *H* in Figure 3.7; it consists of 100 pounds of food and 5 pieces of clothing per week. This is her equilibrium market bundle because any other bundle on the budget line is on a lower indifference curve than point *H*. But will Ms. Popovich choose this bundle? It may take some time for her to realize this is the best market bundle under the circumstances, but eventually we should expect her to purchase this bundle.

STRATEGY SESSION: The Effect of a Time Constraint on Consumer Behavior

For consumers, time can be as important as money. For example, suppose Mildred Evans, an avid sports fan who goes regularly to baseball and football games, decides that she can devote no more than 24 hours per month to attending such games and that she can spend no more than $120 per month on baseball and football tickets. She lives much closer to the local baseball stadium than to the nearest football stadium, so it takes her 4 hours to see a baseball game but 6 hours to see a football game. The price of each baseball ticket is $10, and the price of each football ticket is $40.

Let B be the number of baseball games and F be the number of football games she attends per month. If she spends a total of $120 per month on tickets,

$$40F + 10B = 120 \qquad (3.3)$$

Why? Because $40F$ is the amount spent on football tickets, and $10B$ is the amount spent on baseball tickets, so $40F + 10B$ is the total amount spent per month on baseball and football tickets, which must equal $120. From equation (3.3), it follows that

$$F = 3 - B/4 \qquad (3.4)$$

This is the equation for the budget line, plotted in the following graph.

But this ignores the time constraint. If she spends a total of 24 hours per month at baseball and football games,

$$6F + 4B = 24 \qquad (3.5)$$

Why? Because $6F$ equals the number of hours spent at football games and $4B$ equals the number of hours spent at baseball games, so $6F + 4B$ equals the total number of hours spent at baseball and football games, which must equal 24. From equation (3.5), it follows that

$$F = 4 - 2B/3 \qquad (3.6)$$

This is the equation for the time constraint, plotted in the graph.

To keep within both the time and expenditure constraints, Mildred must pick a market bundle on line segment AE or line segment EC in the graph. Note that the time constraint cuts down on the number of feasible market bundles. Given that she wants to devote only 24 hours per month to attending baseball and football games, she must be content with market bundles along line segment EC rather than line segment ED, which would be available if there were no time constraint.

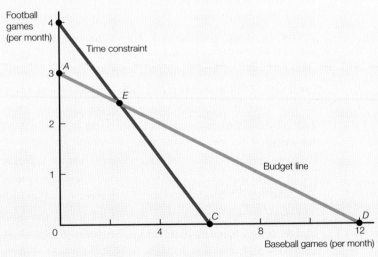

MAXIMIZING UTILITY: A CLOSER LOOK

Let us look more closely at the equilibrium market bundle at point H, the one Ms. Popovich chooses. Clearly this bundle is at the point where the budget line is tangent to an indifference curve. Because the slope of the indifference curve equals -1 times the marginal rate of substitution of clothing for food (see page 69) and the slope of the budget line is $-P_c/P_f$ (see page 73), it follows that Ms. Popovich, if she maximizes utility, chooses in equilibrium to allocate her income between food and clothing so that

$$MRS = P_c/P_f \qquad (3.7)$$

where MRS is the marginal rate of substitution of clothing for food.

To understand what this means, recall that the marginal rate of substitution is the rate at which the consumer is willing to substitute clothing for food, holding her total level of satisfaction constant. Hence if the marginal rate of substitution is 4, the consumer is willing to give up 4 pounds of food to obtain 1 more piece of clothing. On the other hand, the price ratio, P_c/P_f, is the rate at which the consumer is able to substitute clothing for food. So if P_c/P_f is 4, the consumer *must* give up 4 pounds of food to obtain one more piece of clothing.

What equation (3.7) is saying is this: The rate at which the consumer is willing to substitute clothing for food (holding satisfaction constant) must equal the rate at which he or she is able to substitute clothing for food. Otherwise, it is always possible to find another market bundle that increases the consumer's satisfaction.

To illustrate, suppose Ms. Popovich chooses a market bundle for which the marginal rate of substitution of clothing for food is 4. Suppose the price ratio, P_c/P_f, is 3. If this is the case, Ms. Popovich can obtain an extra piece of clothing if she buys 3 fewer pounds of food because the price ratio is 3. But an extra piece of clothing is worth 4 pounds of food to Ms. Popovich because the marginal rate of substitution is 4. Therefore, she can increase her satisfaction by substituting clothing for food—and this will continue to be the case so long as the marginal rate of substitution exceeds the price ratio. Conversely, if the marginal rate of substitution is less than the price ratio, Ms. Popovich can increase her satisfaction by substituting food for clothing. Only when the marginal rate of substitution equals the price ratio does her market bundle maximize her utility.

CORNER SOLUTIONS

Although in our example Ms. Popovich chooses the market bundle where the budget line is tangent to an indifference curve (the market basket at point H in Figure 3.7), this is not always true. A consumer may consume none of some

STRATEGY SESSION: A Manager's Trade-Off Between Output and Profit

In the corporate world, managers are often asked to choose between multiple goals. We can use indifference curves to estimate this behavior. Let's say a manager is driven by two goals: (1) She wants to make a large profit, and (2) she also wants to be noticed. And small firms don't tend to get noticed while big firms do.

For simplicity, assume she is a monopolist, so the market demand curve is her firm demand curve. The demand curve is

$$P = a - bQ$$

Hence $P = a$ when $Q = 0$ and $Q = a/b$ when P is 0. Total revenues are 0 when $P = 0$ and 0 when $Q = 0$. She can maximize revenues at a price where $\eta = -1$. If it costs a constant k to make a unit of product, total costs are $TC = kQ$. The figure below visualizes total revenue, total cost, and profit (the difference between the two).

The manager's utility curves have the usual shape: Utility increases if output is held constant and profit increases, and utility increases if profit is held constant and output increases. Of course she is

happiest if both output and profit increase. The profit curve now is her constraint curve. She will maximize utility with profit of Π_2 and output of Q_2 generating utility of U_2. Note that she does not maximize profit (which gives utility of only U_1) or quantity (because that gives her utility of only U_0—we're constraining her output size objectives to profitable output).

Now let's say our manager works for a large, publicly held corporation. You are a shareholder of that company, and you'd prefer to maximize profit. There is ample evidence to support your preference because higher profit is strongly associated with higher stock prices. We have just shown that the manager does not want to maximize profit. What can the shareholder do to revise the behavior of our manager so she also wants to maximize profit?

Such issues are faced by shareholders of most publicly held corporations. We will discuss these behaviors in Chapter 15 when we discuss the principal–agent issue. But as we can see from the figure, if we tie the manager's compensation to firm profit, our manager will care more about maximizing profit.

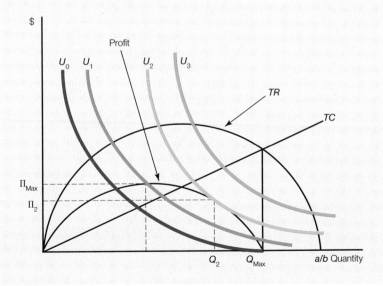

products because the cost does not justify the level of satisfaction they receive. For example, though many people have the income to afford a small amount of Beluga caviar, they do not purchase it because the cost is greater than the pleasure they receive from eating fish eggs.

Figure 3.8 shows this situation graphically. For simplicity, we assume the consumer can choose only between Beluga caviar and pizza. Given the position of these indifference curves, the consumer maximizes utility with bundle *W*, which contains all pizza and no Beluga caviar. This market bundle maximizes utility because it is on a higher indifference curve than any other bundle on the budget line. It is a **corner solution** in which the budget line touches the highest achievable indifference curve along an axis (in this case the vertical axis).

Corner solution When the budget line touches the highest achievable indifference curve along an axis.

We previously showed that if the consumer purchases some of both goods to maximize utility, the marginal rate of substitution is equal to the price ratio. But if the consumer maximizes utility with a corner solution, this is not the case.

FIGURE 3.8

Corner Solution

The market bundle that maximizes your utility is *W*, which lies on the vertical axis.

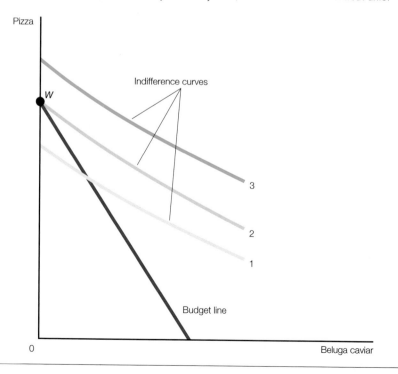

HOW MANAGERS CAN STRATEGICALLY INFLUENCE CONSUMER CHOICES

We just saw how Ms. Popovich's purchase decisions are influenced by her preferences, her income, and product prices. Although managers can do little to change
consumer incomes, they can influence preferences and the effect of a budget
constraint. For example, advertising is a direct action to influence preferences;
lowering prices may induce a consumer to purchase products. So managers can
influence budget constraints with their pricing policies. We have just portrayed
the budget constraint as linear to present the basic theory of consumer choice; but
in the real world managers price in ways that are consciously designed to make the
budget constraint nonlinear and to influence consumer choice.

A recent coupon offer by a leading grocery chain (Albertson's) offered its
customers $18 off their grocery bill if they spent at least $180 in one store visit.
Let's view the impact of such an offer on Ms. Popovich. Suppose her income is
$200. She can consume groceries at $1 per unit or clothing at $1 per unit. Thus,
before the coupon, her budget constraint and purchase decision (she purchases
C_0, units of clothing, G_0, units of groceries, and attains utility level U_0,) appears
in Figure 3.9.

By offering a coupon, Albertson's managers in effect shift Ms. Popovich's
budget constraint outward parallel to her old one. When her grocery bill reaches
$180 (so she consumes $20 of clothing), she receives $18 back (or pays $162 to
the grocery store) and now has the potential of spending $38 on clothing (if she
spends all her savings on clothing). Alternatively, she could spend $218 on grocer-
ies (if she took her $18 in savings and spent it on more groceries). Her new budget
constraint and purchase choices appear in Figure 3.10.

The coupon budget constraint looks like her no-coupon budget constraint
until she spends at least $180 on groceries. Then her budget constraint shifts
upward to the right by an additional $18. In effect, through their pricing deci-
sions, Albertson's managers have shifted Ms. Popovich's budget constraint. If
Ms. Popovich's indifference curves resemble the dashed line in Figure 3.10, the coupon does not affect her purchase behavior (her utility stays at U_0, and her purchases
are C_0, and G_0,). Nothing was gained by Albertson's managers, but the cost was trivial
(the printing of some coupons). However, had Ms. Popovich's initial indifference
curve been the solid U_0, the coupon would enable her to increase her utility to U_1.
The coupon was a good deal for Ms. Popovich. Was it a good strategy by Albertson's managers? Only if $G_1 - G_0 > 18$; that is, only if Ms. Popovich spent over
$18 more on groceries than she did without the coupon. Presumably the managers
felt that most consumers would spend more than $18 extra on groceries as a result
of the coupon. So we see that managers have a range of strategies they can use
to change the purchasing decisions of consumers in addition to advertising and
changing prices.

FIGURE 3.9

Ms. Popovich's Utility-Maximizing Purchase of Clothing and Groceries before Receiving the Coupon

With a budget of $200 and the price of a unit of clothing and a unit of groceries each $1, Ms. Popovich rationally chooses to consume $C_{0'}$ units of clothing and $G_{0'}$ units of groceries, attaining a utility of $U_{0'}$.

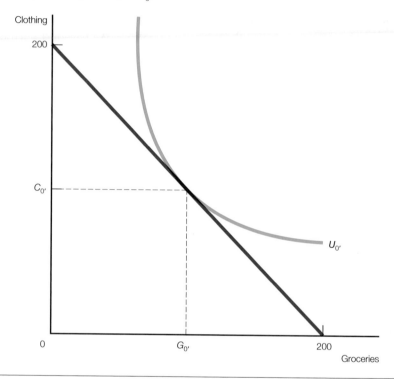

Another strategy for influencing the budget constraint of consumers is quantity discounts. Ms. Popovich pays a visit to Dunking Donuts. A single donut costs $.50, a half dozen costs $2, and a dozen costs $3. Suppose Ms. Popovich has $4 to spend on donuts and all other goods. The price of a unit of all other goods is $1. Thus if Ms. Popovich buys one donut, she will have $3.50 to spend on all other goods. If she buys two donuts, she will have $3 to spend on all other goods. If Ms. Popovich buys four donuts separately, she will spend $2 on donuts and $2 on all other goods—but she could buy a half dozen for $2. If more is indeed better (that is, if the marginal utility of donuts is positive), she should buy the half dozen rather than four or five donuts. If Ms. Popovich wants seven donuts, she should buy the half dozen for $2 and one donut separately for $0.50; this will leave her with $1.50 for all other goods. Should she wish to buy eight donuts, she should buy the dozen for $3. She could spend $2 for a half dozen and $0.50 each for donuts

FIGURE 3.10

Ms. Popovich's Utility-Maximizing Purchase of Clothing and Groceries after Receiving the Coupon

Part of Ms. Popovich's budget line shifts outward, parallel to her budget line without the coupon. Depending on the shape of her indifference curves, the coupon may or may not influence her purchases of clothing and groceries. If her indifference curves are similar to the dashed line here, her behavior is uninfluenced; but if her indifference curves are like the solid line, the coupon increases her utility (and perhaps firm revenue).

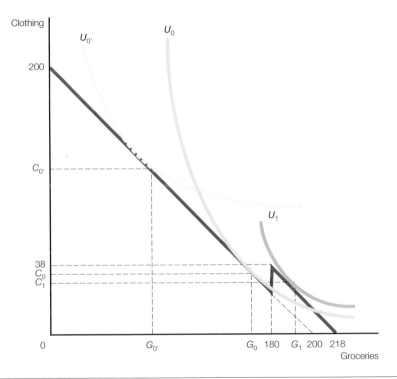

seven and eight, or she could get a dozen for the same $3. Thus she should never buy 8, 9, 10, or 11 donuts. Her budget constraint will appear as the step function in Figure 3.11.

In effect, what is the influence of the pricing strategy? Selling a half dozen donuts for $2 reduces the price per donut to $0.33, and selling a dozen donuts for $3 reduces the price per donut to $0.25. Why should the managers offer this price decrease? Perhaps because of the diminishing marginal utility of donuts. Consumers are willing to pay a lot for the first donut. But donuts are filling (and fattening). As the marginal utility of donuts decreases, the Dunking managers must lower the price to entice buyers.

FIGURE 3.11

Ms. Popovich's Utility-Maximizing Choices for Donuts and All Other Goods

The quantity discount for donuts creates a step function budget constraint and means that Ms. Popovich will never purchase 4, 5, 8, 9, 10, or 11 donuts. The quantity discount doesn't change her behavior if her indifference curves resemble the dashed line but raises her utility if her indifference curves resemble the solid line.

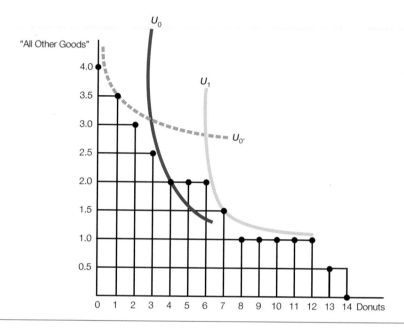

If the price of donuts was always $0.50/donut, Ms. Popovich's budget constraint intercept on the donuts axis would occur at 8 donuts. With the quantity discount, her budget constraint intercept is at 14 donuts. If Ms. Popovich's indifference curve is the dashed one, the quantity discount strategy will not change her behavior; but if it is the solid one, she is induced to move from buying 4 donuts to 7 while increasing her utility from U_0 to U_1. Both managers and consumers can benefit from this strategy.

You face this situation anytime you are offered a quantity discount. Remember this the next time you encounter one and see whether the pricing strategy changes your behavior.

We can also use shifts in the budget constraint to explain why most individuals prefer cash to a specific gift (unless they requested the gift). At every holiday season, consumers decide what gifts to buy for friends and family. Suppose Ms. Popovich is already maximizing her utility subject to her budget constraint (I_0) with A_0 units of all other goods and G_0 units of the gift good and receiving U_0 units of satisfaction. Let the unit price of all other goods, P_A, be 1. Suppose

Ms. Popovich's well-meaning mother-in-law gives her another unit of the gift item for the holidays. Assuming the marginal utility of the gift item is positive, Ms. Popovich's utility has increased. Gift giving has been a success as far as her mother-in-law is concerned. But how about for Ms. Popovich? Consider the situation depicted in Figure 3.12.

After receiving the gift unit from her mother-in-law, if Ms. Popovich's high-level utility resembles the dashed line, she will have A_0 units of all other goods and $G_0 + 1$ units of the gift good and will maximize her utility at level $U_{1'}$. By spending P_G on a gift unit, the mother-in law got it right on. The mother-in-law is happy that Ms. Popovich appreciates the gift, and Ms. Popovich is happy because her utility is increased. You will be lucky if all your gift giving turns out this way. Unfortunately, in many cases the most likely scenario is depicted by the solid higher-level indifference curves (U_1 and U_2). We can state two things. If the

---

FIGURE 3.12

Ms. Popovich's Utility and Consumption of All Other Goods and Gift Goods under Various Scenarios of Gift Receiving

A gift will, at best, give Ms. Popovich the exact consumption of the gift good and all other goods had Ms. Popovich made the choice herself. But most likely a smaller cash gift from the gift giver will yield Ms. Popovich the same utility as the gift; or a gift of cash to Ms. Popovich equal to what the gift giver spent will yield a higher level of utility than did the gift.

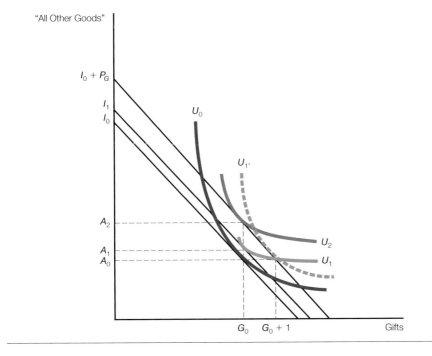

mother-in-law's objective is to get Ms. Popovich to a level of satisfaction U_1, she could do so with a smaller expenditure ($I_1 < I_0 + P_G$), giving Ms. Popovich no gift units and instead $A_1 - A_0$ units of all other goods. Ms. Popovich will get the same level of utility as with the gift if she had A_1 units of all other goods and G_0 gift units. In general, from a utility standpoint, gift giving is more expensive than it has to be. A second point is that if the mother-in-law gives Ms. Popovich the cash she spent on her gift (P_G), Ms. Popovich's budget line will shift outward to $I_0 + P_G$ and Ms. Popovich will maximize her utility by consuming A_2 units of all other goods and G_0 units of the gift good. That is, a cash gift equal to the unit cost of the gift good will increase Ms. Popovich's utility to U_2, which is higher than the U_1 level attained with the gift. Thus the mother-in-law could spend less and give Ms. Popovich the same level of satisfaction by buying Ms. Popovich more units of all other goods (that is, by giving cash) rather than the gift she bought her.

Our colleague Joel Waldfogel has received much "Grinch" publicity since his article about this deadweight loss of Christmas was published in 1993.[1] In fact, every year around Christmas he gets calls from newspapers looking for seasonal stories about Christmas. If you look at the proliferation of gift cards in recent years, you might conclude that his concept is getting through. However, gift cards tie the recipient to a particular store: A gift card to an apparel store may not be good if you really want electronics. General gift cards, like those from American Express, are less constraining but aren't universally accepted; cash is accepted in all brick-and-mortar stores. We should point out, though, that our analysis does not account for sentimental value. You may hate the gift that your grandmother gives you but be happy knowing that she loves you enough to select and purchase it.

DERIVING THE INDIVIDUAL DEMAND CURVE

A consumer's demand curve shows how much product a person will purchase at various prices (when other prices, preferences, and income are held constant). It reveals the inner desires of purchase behavior. Let us return to Ms. Popovich.

Ms. Popovich can choose between two products: food and clothing. Her weekly income is $600, and the price of clothing is $60 per piece. Ms. Popovich's budget is budget line 1 in Figure 3.13 when the price of food is $3 per pound. As we saw in Figure 3.7, she will buy 100 pounds of food per week.

How will she purchase when the price of food increases to $6 per pound? If her income and the price of clothing remain constant, her budget is budget line 2 in Figure 3.14. She attains her greatest utility by reaching her highest indifference curve, I_1. She chooses the bundle at point K, which contains 50 pounds of food per week. If the price of food is $6 per pound, she will make a weekly purchase of 50 pounds of food per week.

We have derived two points on Ms. Popovich's demand curve for food, those corresponding to food prices of $3 and $6 per pound. Figure 3.14 shows these

1. J. Waldfogel, "The Deadweight Loss of Christmas," *American Economic Review* Vol. 83(5) (December 1993), pp. 1328–1336.

FIGURE 3.13

Effect of a Change in Price on Ms. Popovich's Equilibrium Market Bundle

If the price of a pound of food is $3, Ms. Popovich's budget line is such that her equilibrium market bundle is at point H, where she buys 100 pounds of food per week. If the price of a pound of food is $6, Ms. Popovich's budget line is such that her equilibrium market bundle is at point K, where she buys 50 pounds of food per week.

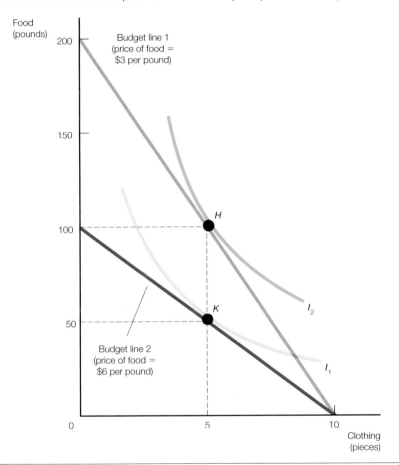

two points, U and V. To obtain more points on her demand curve, all we do is assume a particular price of food, construct the budget line corresponding to this price (holding her income and the price of clothing constant), and find the market bundle that is on her highest indifference curve. Plotting the level of food in this bundle relative to the assumed price of food, we obtain a new point on her demand curve for food. Connecting all these points, we estimate her complete demand curve for food, in Figure 3.14. (In our scenario, the level of clothing consumed remains constant. This does not have to be the case.)

PROBLEM SOLVED: Do I Stay or Do I Go? Use of Indifference Curves

Ms. Popovich is a self-employed business owner who is also raising a family. Her business is growing, and she finds it could literally demand 18–20 hours per day. Of course she feels the same about her children. What is she to do? We call the time spent engaged in business *work* and time spent not working *leisure*.[a] Unlike money budget constraints, which vary with an individual's income, the time constraint is a great equalizer: There are 24 hours each day whether you are rich or poor. Thus Ms. Popovich is directed by a time budget constraint of $H_W + H_L = 24$, where H_W is the hours worked and H_L is the hours spent in leisure pursuits. We express hours worked as $H_W = 24 - H_L$.

In every hour working, Ms. Popovich receives a wage of W. We use that knowledge to estimate a time budget constraint with income. Her utility (level of satisfaction) is a function of income (I) and leisure (L): $U = U(I, L)$. As in a purchase decision, she must choose between the two. For a given level of income, she'd be happier with more leisure, and for a given time in leisure, she'd be happier with more income. Her indifference curves are downward-sloping and convex to the origin (the "normal" shape).

We estimate Ms. Popovich's income as the hourly wage (W) times the hours worked

$$W \times (24 - H_L) = 24W - W \times H_L$$

We presuppose that time is money and show why with a budget constraint. If she chooses all work and no play, $H_W = 24$ and $H_L = 0$, her income is $24W$. If she chooses all play and no work, $H_W = 0$ and $H_L = 24$, her income is 0. Her utility-maximizing behavior is shown in the figure.

The slope of the time constraint is $-W = -24W/24$; that is, the market will pay her W to work an hour (or alternatively, she forgoes W for every hour of leisure). The slope of her indifference curve is

$$\frac{-\Delta I}{\Delta L} = \left(\frac{-\Delta I}{\Delta L}\right)\left(\frac{\Delta U}{\Delta U}\right)$$

$$= -\left(\frac{\Delta U}{\Delta L}\right)\bigg/\left(\frac{\Delta U}{\Delta I}\right) = -\frac{MU_L}{MU_I}$$

Or more elegantly,

$$-\frac{MU_L}{MU_I} = -\left(\frac{dU}{dL}\right)\bigg/\left(\frac{dU}{dI}\right)$$

We estimate that Ms. Popovich will act as if setting $MU_L/MU_I = W$, that is, the slope of the indifference curve, is equal to the slope of the constraint. That is, she works up to the point where her trade-off of leisure for income equals the wage rate. By changing the wage rate (for instance, from W to a greater rate W'), we can estimate how Ms. Popovich changes her demand for leisure (in this case choosing less of it, $H_{L'} < H_L$, and preferring more income). We can change the wage rate and virtually trace out Ms. Popovich's supply curve for labor. But, if we pay Ms. Popovich too much, she may actually choose to work less. She has attained enough income to make her comfortable and now wants to spend more time with her family. So if the wage rate rises to W'', Ms. Popovich will decrease her working time to $24 - H_L$ hours.

[a] Arguably, it might be the other way around.

Ms. Popovich's Dilemma of Balancing Work and Leisure

Ms. Popovich gets utility from work (income) and leisure (family and friends). If the wage rate is W, she will work $24 - H_L$ hours. If the wage rate increases to W', she will increase her work hours to $24 - H_{L'}$.

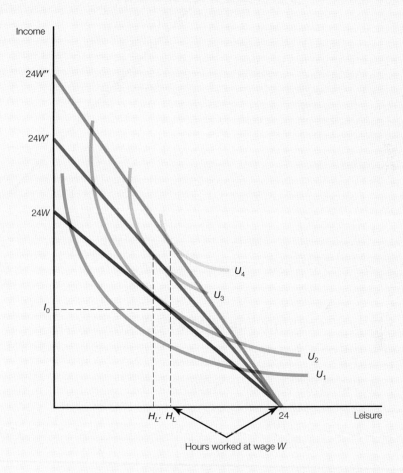

FIGURE 3.14

Ms. Popovich's Individual Demand Curve for Food

Ms. Popovich's individual demand curve for food shows the amount of food she would buy at various prices.

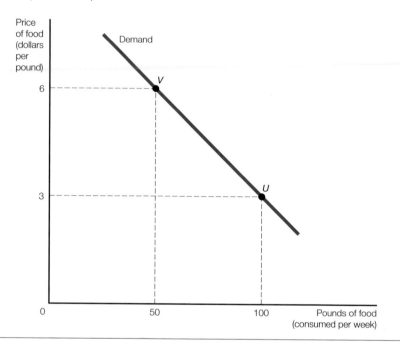

DERIVING THE MARKET DEMAND CURVE

We have just shown how to estimate a consumer's demand curve for a product, given the consumer's tastes and income as well as the prices of other products. What if we estimate the individual demand curve for each consumer in the market? How can they help us understand the market?

The answer is easy. Think of the market demand curve as representing the sum of tastes and preferences of individual consumers. It summarizes the demand curves of all individuals in the market. To derive the market demand curve, we estimate the horizontal sum of all the individual demand curves. At each pricing point we estimate the market total by summing the purchases of all individuals at that price.

Table 3.1 shows the demand schedules for food of four families: the Moores, Sarafians, Chases, and Grubers. For simplicity, suppose these four families constitute the entire market for food; then the market demand curve for food is shown in the last column of Table 3.1. Figure 3.15 shows the families' demand curves for food as well as the resulting market demand curve. To illustrate how the market demand curve is derived, suppose the price of food is $3 per pound; the market quantity demanded is 103 hundreds of pounds per month. This is the sum of the

TABLE 3.1

Individual Demand Curves and Market Demand Curve for Food

Price of Food (Dollars per Pound)	Individual Demand Curves (Hundreds of Pounds per Month)				Market Demand
	Moore	Sarafian	Chase	Gruber	
3.00	51.0	45.0	5.0	2.0	103
3.20	43.0	44.0	4.2	1.8	93
3.40	36.0	43.0	3.4	1.6	84
3.60	30.0	42.0	2.6	1.4	76
3.80	26.0	41.4	2.4	1.2	71
4.00	21.0	41.0	2.0	1.0	65

quantities demanded by the four families. (As shown in Table 3.1, this sum equals 51.0 + 45.0 + 5.0 + 2.0, or 103 hundreds of pounds.)

Figure 3.15 clearly illustrates that within a single product market, demand is not composed of homogeneous buyers. A market is generally composed of buyers with different tastes and preferences. We will see later that managers can strategically exploit this heterogeneity by identifying submarkets and charging each submarket a different price.

FIGURE 3.15

Individual Demand Curves and Market Demand Curve for Food
The market demand curve is the horizontal sum of all the individual demand curves.

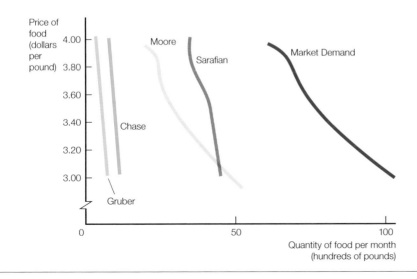

We also see why managers like to expand their markets. As more consumers enter the market, the demand curve is pushed out to the right due to horizontal summation. As this occurs (and the supply curve remains constant), the market price increases.

Finally, while demand for a firm's product or service is necessarily a fraction of total market demand, the demand curve facing managers of a firm is generally not a parallel, scaled-down version of market demand. The choices of managers can significantly influence demand for their products. Managers who are better able to influence consumers realize higher performance relative to rivals.

CONSUMER SURPLUS

One key insight managers need to understand is that many consumers value a product at a premium. They are willing to pay a higher price than that of the market, as illustrated in Figure 3.16. This is a simple but powerful (and potentially profitable) fact that managers need to exploit. An individual's demand curve estimates the unit price (P_X) she is willing to pay to purchase a given number of product units (say X). Because the demand curve (usually) is downward-sloping, the curve indicates that the consumer values products $X - 1, X - 2$, and so forth at a higher amount than the value of the Xth good purchased (say at values P_{X-1}, P_{X-2}). The price at which the consumer values each number of units demanded is called the **consumer's reservation price** for that particular unit of good. It is also known as the willingness to pay (WTP). The reservation price is the highest price the consumer is willing to pay for that unit of product or service. If we try to charge any price above the WTP, the consumer will not purchase from us.

The difference between what an individual is willing to pay and what that individual has to pay (the market price) for a product is called **consumer surplus**. It is the actual price paid subtracted from the reservation price.

When a market is at equilibrium, the marginal individuals to purchase are those whose reservation price just equals the market price. They receive no consumer surplus from the purchase; they value it for the amount of money they paid for it. But all other purchasers have reservation prices exceeding the market price. They all gained a surplus because they paid less for the product than they were willing to pay (they got what many term a "good deal"). If we aggregate all the individuals' consumer surpluses, we estimate the consumer surplus of the market at that given price. Visually, a product's consumer surplus is the area below the demand curve but above the market price (area A in Figure 3.16).

We will say more about consumer surplus later, when we introduce the analogous idea of producer surplus, and the summation of consumer and producer surplus, called the total surplus. Economists use these concepts to describe the efficiency of markets and the social benefits of market transactions. We draw a simpler observation. As long as the demand curve for a product is downward-sloping

Consumer's reservation price The price at which the consumer values each number of units demanded.

Consumer surplus The difference between what an individual is willing to pay (their reservation price) and what that individual has to pay (the market price) for a product.

STRATEGY SESSION: The Trade-Off between Risk and Return

As investors in developing countries like India and China begin to diversify their savings from simple saving accounts to bonds and stocks, they will show behavior regarding their risk–return profiles. A recent article in *The Times of India* discussed the need for investors to understand their "risk profile."[a] We can operationalize this risk profile using indifference curves.

Assume our investor Devi Bangerjee has $1 million, which she must allocate between stocks and government bonds. If she invests in government bonds, she will receive a return of 5%, and there is no risk. If she invests $1 million in common stock, she expects a return of 10% and endures considerable risk. If she invests half in bonds and half in common stocks, she expects a return of 7.5% and there is some risk. Line *RT* in the graph that follows shows her expected return with its corresponding risk for combinations of the two investments. People differ in their risk tolerance; this is part of human nature. We represent hers in the form of indifference curves.

But because we differ in risk tolerance does not mean we are totally idiosyncratic. For most of us,

indifference curves slope upward to the right. Risk is fundamentally different from purchase decisions, for which indifference curves slope downward to the right.

The risk indifference curves slope upward to the right because Devi prefers less risk to more when the expected return is held constant. If there is an increase in risk, she needs a higher expected return to maintain the same level of satisfaction. She must choose some point on line *RT*. The point on *RT* that is tangent with the highest indifference curve is point *S*. Here her expected return is 7.5%. Hence she should purchase $500,000 of government bonds and $500,000 of common stock. We will look at such investment decisions in greater detail in Chapter 14.

There are websites around the globe (www.amp .co.nz; www.tools.asiapacific.hsbc.com) with risk profile calculators. Using a short series of questions, these calculators approximate the indifference curve of the investor.

[a]D. Ghosh, "Know Your Appetite for Risk-Taking," *The Times of India*, April 15, 2008.

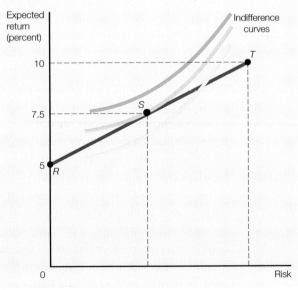

FIGURE 3.16

The Consumer Surplus for a Price of P_x

The consumer surplus for an individual is the area under the demand curve but above the price (P_x) paid (area A). The same definition holds for a market demand curve.

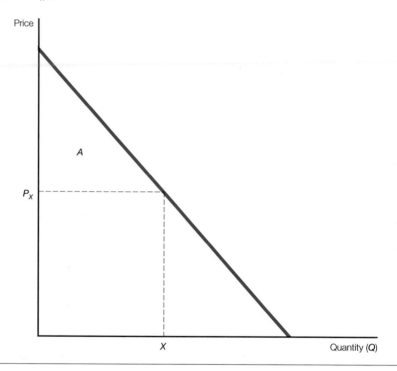

(and most are), a manager will generate more revenue if she charges each consumer his or her reservation price. Managers can also increase revenue by charging higher prices to consumers who value the product more highly. This is called price discrimination. Relative to a simple single-price strategy, this captures consumer surplus for the benefit of the firm. Even though various legal, practical, and economic constraints limit the extent to which managers can charge different prices for the same product, the practice is widespread. Examples include airline tickets, automobiles sold at dealerships where haggling is the norm, and goods and services offered at discounts through coupon systems and other special offers. We explore these strategies in greater detail later.

SUMMARY

1. An indifference curve contains points representing market bundles among which the consumer is indifferent. If the consumer prefers more to less of both commodities, an indifference curve must have a negative slope.

2. Market bundles on higher indifference curves provide more satisfaction than those on lower indifference curves. Utility is a number that indexes the level of satisfaction derived from a particular market bundle. Market bundles with higher utilities are preferred over those with lower utilities.

3. The marginal rate of substitution shows how many units of one good must be given up if the consumer, after getting an extra unit of another good, is to maintain a constant level of satisfaction. To obtain the marginal rate of substitution, multiply the slope of the indifference curve by -1.

4. The budget line contains all the market bundles the consumer can buy, given his or her money income and the level of each price. Increases in income push the budget line upward and parallel to the old budget line; changes in the price ratio alter the budget line's slope.

5. To attain the highest level of satisfaction compatible with the budget line, the consumer must choose the market bundle on the budget line that is on the highest indifference curve. This market bundle is at a point where the budget line is tangent to an indifference curve (unless there is a corner solution).

6. The consumer who maximizes utility will choose in equilibrium to allocate his or her income so that the marginal rate of substitution of one good for another good equals the ratio of the prices of the two goods (unless there is a corner solution).

7. The theory of consumer behavior is often used to represent the process of rational choice. Frequently a person or organization has a certain amount of money to spend and must decide how much to allocate to a number of different uses. This theory indicates how such decisions should be made.

8. A consumer's demand curve shows how much the consumer would purchase of a good at various prices of the good when other prices, preferences, and the consumer's income are held constant. The theory of consumer behavior can be used to derive the consumer's demand curve, and the market demand curve can be obtained by summing the individual demand curves horizontally.

9. Consumer surplus is the difference between what a consumer is willing to pay for a good and what the consumer pays for the good in the market. Clever managers want to figure out pricing policies to extract consumer surplus from consumers.

PROBLEMS

wwnorton.com/studyspace

1. The market for sports performance drinks experienced a big shift in 2012 as sales of low-calorie sports drinks grew by over 25%. Many attributed this shift to greater use by women who wanted a sports drink without many calories.

   a. If a woman desires two containers of low-calorie sports drink as much as one container of high-calorie sports drink, what do her indifference curves (between low- and high-calories sports drinks) look like?

b. Do they have the typical shape of indifference curves? Why or why not?

2. In recent years fresh bagel sales have been growing at about 30% per year. Once considered an ethnic food to be eaten with cream cheese and lox, bagels now "have become the new donut to bring to the office," according to Michael Goldstein of Goldstein's Bagel Bakery in Pasadena, California. But one problem with bagels is that they get stale fast. In the words of Ray Lahvic, editor emeritus of *Bakery Production and Marketing*, "the worst thing in the world is a day-old bagel." If a market researcher asserts that the slope of the typical consumer's indifference curves between fresh bagels and day-old bagels is -1, would you agree with this assertion? Why or why not?

3. On a piece of graph paper, plot the quantity of lamb consumed by Ms. Turner along the vertical axis and the quantity of rice she consumes along the horizontal axis. Draw the indifference curve that includes the following market bundles. Each of these market bundles gives equal satisfaction

Market Bundle	Lamb (Pounds)	Rice (Pounds)
1	2	8
2	3	7
3	4	6
4	5	5
5	6	4
6	7	3
7	8	2
8	9	1

4. In the previous question, what is the marginal rate of substitution of rice for lamb? How does the marginal rate of substitution vary as Ms. Turner consumes more lamb and less rice? Is this realistic?

5. Suppose Richard has an after-tax income of $500 per week and must spend it all on food or clothing. If food is $5 per pound and clothing is $10 per piece, draw his budget line on a piece of graph paper, where the amount of food is measured along the vertical axis and the amount of clothing is measured along the horizontal axis.

6. In the previous problem, what is the budget line if Richard's weekly income increases to $600? What is his budget line if his income is $500, but the price of food increases to $10 per pound? What is his budget line if his income is $500, but the price of clothing increases to $20 per piece? Draw each of these budget lines on the piece of graph paper used in the previous problem.

7. Maria has budgeted a total of $9 to spend on two goods: chips and salsa. She likes to consume a unit of chips in combination with a unit of salsa. Any unit of chips that she cannot consume in combination with a unit of salsa is useless. Similarly, any unit of salsa that she cannot consume in combination with a unit of chips is useless. If the price of a unit of chips is $0.50 and the price of a unit of salsa is $0.10, how many units of each good does she purchase?

8. In the following diagram, we show one of Jane's indifference curves and her budget line.
   a. If the price of good X is $100, what is her income?
   b. What is the equation for her budget line?
   c. What is the slope of her budget line?
   d. What is the price of good Y?
   e. What is Jane's marginal rate of substitution in equilibrium?

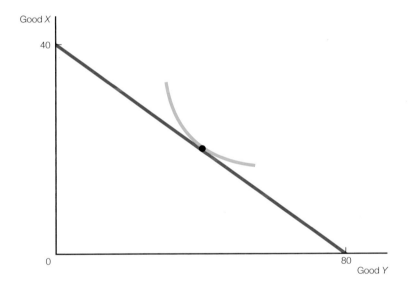

9. Sarah has $300 to allocate between opera tickets and movie tickets. The price of each opera ticket is $60, and the price of each movie ticket is $6. Her marginal rate of substitution of opera tickets for movie tickets equals 5, regardless of what market bundle she chooses. How many opera tickets does she purchase?

10. Suppose Milton has $50 to be divided between corn and beans and that the price of beans is $0.50 per pound. What will be the relationship between the price of corn and the amount of corn he will buy if $U = \log Q_c + 4 \log Q_b$, where U is his utility, Q_c is the quantity of corn he consumes (in pounds), and Q_b is the quantity of beans he consumes (in pounds)?

11. The state of New York receives $3 billion (from federal sources and a state petroleum tax) to be spent on highways and/or mass transit (subways, buses,

and urban rail lines), both of which could be used to meet the transportation needs of the state's population.

a. If each mile of mass transit costs $20 million, what is the maximum number of miles of mass transit that these funds would have enabled the state to construct?

b. If each mile of highway costs $10 million, what is the maximum number of miles of highways that these funds would have enabled the state to construct?

c. If the number of miles of mass transit constructed is put on the vertical axis of a graph and the number of miles of highways constucted is put on the horizontal axis, can a budget line (showing the maximum number of miles of mass transit that can be constructed, given each number of miles of highways constructed) be drawn for the state? If so, what is the slope of this budget line? (Assume that the $3 billion is the only source of funds for mass transit or highway construction.)

d. If the public and the state government agree that every extra mile of mass transit adds three times as much to the state's transportation capability as an extra mile of highways, how much of the $3 billion should be spent on mass transit if the objective is to maximize transportation capability?

PART 3

PRODUCTION AND COST

CHAPTER 5

PRODUCTION THEORY

Once managers determine the demand for the firm's product or service, their job is far from over. Now they must choose the optimal method to produce. Managers need to be as efficient as possible. Resources are costly, and using them wisely is the hallmark of good managers. Efficiency requires an understanding of the production process. Simply stated, a production process explains how scarce resources (inputs) are used to produce a good or service (output). The production function precisely specifies the relationship between inputs and outputs.

Production issues are not confined to the physical transformation of inputs into outputs. In business, production involves all activities associated with providing goods and services, such as employment practices, acquisition of capital resources, and product distribution. Today, at firms like investment banks and consulting practices, managers are concerned with efficiently producing intellectual resources.

Understanding the production process is fundamental to gaining insight into cost analysis. Control of costs, along with an understanding of demand, is required for managers to optimize profit. But costs evolve from the production process. Managers cannot understand their firm's cost structure unless they understand the production process.

STRATEGY SESSION: **The Yankees' Deal for Alex Rodriguez**

In February 2004 the New York Yankees assumed the richest contract in sports by trading players to the Texas Rangers for shortstop Alex Rodriguez. Rodriguez was working under a 10-year, $252 million contract that he signed with the Rangers in 2000. As soon as the deal was announced, commentators speculated about whether the contract was economically sensible. In fact, when we look at the underlying economics, the Yankees appear to have gotten the best player in baseball at a relatively bargain price.

First, the Yankees received $67 million in cash from the Rangers—the largest sum to trade hands in the history of baseball. This reduced the Yankees' liability to Rodriguez to roughly $112 million. The expected payouts to the players the Yankees got rid of in the trade were approximately $13.3 million. Rodriguez was to receive $15 million in 2004, but he agreed to defer $1 million. Hence the added cost of Rodriguez to the Yankees' payroll in 2004 was roughly $750,000.

For future years, the payouts to Rodriguez would be the following: $15 million for the next three seasons; $16 million in 2007–2008; $17 million in 2009; and $18 million in 2010. Rodriguez would defer $1 million for the first four years at no interest and receive the $4 million in 2011.

Because of their high payroll costs, the Yankees must pay a luxury tax (which is split among the other baseball teams). In 2004 the Yankees estimated their payroll would equal $190 million (this was higher than the 10 lowest-payroll teams). A payroll of $190 million would cost the Yankees $21 million in luxury taxes.

The total revenue for the Yankees was estimated to be $330 million in 2004. Approximately $110 million was generated from 3.5 million paying customers (ticket prices increased by an average of 10% for the 2004 season). The Yankees received $60 million from the YES Network, $10 million from WCBS radio, and over $30 million from national television, licensing, and sponsorship revenues. The team also received revenue from local sponsorships and game concessions.

The Yankees expected the addition of Alex Rodriguez to increase attendance even in the face of increasing ticket prices (after the trade was announced, the ticket office was swamped with ticket requests). These additional fans also presumably would spend more at the games on snacks, drinks, and merchandise.

After all the factors are considered, most experts believe the marginal benefit to the Yankees was greater than the additional costs for Rodriguez's contract.

Source: "Sports Business: Steinbrenner Has Got It, and He Loves to Flaunt It," *New York Times*, February 17, 2004.

THE PRODUCTION FUNCTION WITH ONE VARIABLE INPUT

The production function is a table, a graph, or an equation showing the maximum product output achieved from any specified set of inputs. The function summarizes the characteristics of existing technology at a given time; it shows the technological constraints managers face. Any manager should want to use the most efficient process known. So we assume managers presuppose technical efficiency. Unfortunately many managers view processes as static. Production is dynamic: Methods, designs, and factor costs change. Changes beget changes and may require different input mixes.

Say a process uses two inputs. If X_1 is the level of the first input and X_2 is the level of the second input, the production function is

$$Q = f(X_1, X_2)$$ (5.1)

where Q is the firm's output rate.

Cognitively, the simplest case has one input whose quantity is fixed and one input whose quantity is variable. Fixed inputs cannot be changed in the short run. To be sure, economists assume the time needed to change an asset is the beginning of what is called the long term. Fixed inputs often require capital (buildings, machinery, land). Variable inputs can be changed in the short run; labor is an example. In the long run, all inputs are variable.

John Thomas is an entrepreneur who currently owns five CNC machine tools. He works as a contractor in the airplane industry. He wants to know the effect

TABLE 5.1

Output of Metal Parts When Various Amounts of Labor Are Applied to Five Machine Tools, Thomas Machine Company

Amount of Labor (L)	Amount of Capital (Number of Machines)	Output of Parts (Q, hundreds per year)
0	5	0
1	5	49
2	5	132
3	5	243
4	5	376
5	5	525
6	5	684
6.67	5	792.59
7	5	847
8	5	1,008
9	5	1,161
10	5	1,300
11	5	1,419
12	5	1,512
13	5	1,573
14	5	1,596
15	5	1,575

on annual output if he were to hire various numbers of machinists. (Please note that the following output numbers are expressed in hundreds.) Thomas estimates that one machinist produces 49 parts per year. Thomas can produce more parts by hiring more workers, as we see in Table 5.1. This table represents a production function for Thomas Machine Company when five machine tools are used. More visually, the curve in Figure 5.1 presents exactly the same results. In fact, the

FIGURE 5.1

Relationship between Total Output and Amount of Labor Used on Five Machine Tools, Thomas Machine Company

Total output increases as labor increases at an increasing rate (up to 6.67 units of labor) and increases at a decreasing rate (until slightly more than 14 units of labor). Thereafter, output decreases as more units of labor are deployed. Managers will never willfully deploy labor in the latter circumstance. The production function shows the relationship between output (in this case number of parts produced) and input (in this case units of labor).

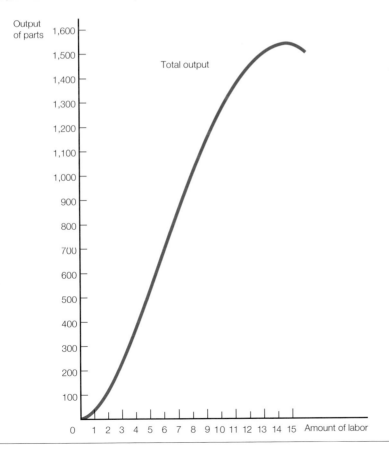

TABLE 5.2

Average and Marginal Products of Labor, Thomas Machine Company

Amount of Labor (Units)	Amount of Capital (Number of Machines)	Output of Parts (Q, Hundreds of Parts)	Average Product (Q/L)	Marginal Product $(\Delta Q/\Delta L)^a$	Marginal Product $(dQ/dL)^a$
0	5	0	—	—	—
1	5	49	49	49	67
2	5	132	66	83	98
3	5	243	81	111	123
4	5	376	94	133	142
5	5	525	105	149	155
6	5	684	114	159	162
6.67	5	792.59	118.89	162.89	163.33
7	5	847	121	_163_	163
8	5	1,008	126	161	158
9	5	1,161	129	153	147
10	5	1,300	_130_	139	_130_
11	5	1,419	129	119	107
12	5	1,512	126	93	78
13	5	1,573	121	61	43
14	5	1,596	114	23	2
15	5	1,575	105	−19	−45

^{a}The figures in the $\Delta Q/\Delta L$ column pertain to the interval between the indicated amount of labor and one unit less than the indicated amount of labor. The figures in the dQ/dL column are the continuous marginal product—that is, $dQ/dL = MP_L = 30 + 40L - 3L^2$.

numbers in Table 5.1 (and Table 5.2) are derived from the production function equal to $Q = 30L + 20L^2 - L^3$. L is equal to the number of machinists.

We can think of the production function as giving insights into the manager's technology use. Thomas is clearly interested in knowing how output changes as the number of machinists varies. One common measure used by many managers is *output per worker*. This measure is what economists call **average product (AP)**. Because we are varying machinists, this is output per worker or

Average product (AP) Common measuring device for estimating the units of output, on average per input unit.

$$AP = \frac{Q}{X_1}, \text{ holding } X_2 \text{ constant}$$

Average product tells Thomas how many units of output, on average, each machinist is responsible for. If he wants a better metric to estimate the efficiency of each worker, he should use what economists call the **marginal product (MP)**. The input's MP is equal to the incremental change in output created by a small change in input

$$MP = \frac{\Delta Q}{\Delta X_1}, \text{ holding } X_2 \text{ constant}$$

Marginal product (MP) Metric for estimating the efficiency of each input in which the input's MP is equal to the incremental change in output created by a small change in the input.

For machinists, the marginal product represents the impact on output of a unit change in machinists. If Thomas adds a machinist, the question is, "How many more units did we produce because I hired this last machinist?" If he must let one go, it is, "How many fewer units did we produce because I let this machinist go?" The marginal product is what Thomas wants to measure.

We calculate the average product and marginal product of labor, based on our estimated $Q = 30L + 20L^2 - L^3$. Both vary, of course, as we allocate the machinists to our five machines. If $Q(L)$ is total output with L units of labor per year, the average product is $Q(L)/L$. The marginal product of labor MP, when between L and $(L - 1)$ units of labor per year, is $Q(L) - Q(L - 1)$. From Table 5.2 we see that the average product of our first machinist is 49 parts and the marginal product is 83 parts per machinist between the first and second hires. Results for other machinist hires are shown in Table 5.2.

QUANT OPTION

More precisely, the marginal product of an input is the derivative of output with regard to the quantity of the input. That is, if Q is the output and x is the quantity of the input, the marginal product of the input equals dQ/dx if the quantities of all other inputs are fixed.

The average and marginal products of machinists are shown in Figure 5.2; the numbers are derived from Table 5.1. The curve is representative of most production processes. The average product of machinists (with five machines) reaches a maximum (at $L = 10$ and $Q/L = 130$), then falls. The marginal product of labor follows a similar pattern: It initially increases, reaches a maximum (at $L = 6.67$ and marginal product $= 163.33$), then falls. This, too, is typical of most production processes. Figure 5.2 shows that the marginal product equals the average product when the latter reaches a maximum; that is, $MP = AP = 130$ when $L = 10$.

We use two definitions of marginal product in Table 5.2. The first $(\Delta Q/\Delta L)$ assumes that Thomas employs labor in discrete units, as in a machinist or a machinist-hour. This may be due to employment laws or negotiated contracts with

---

FIGURE 5.2

Average and Marginal Product Curves for Labor

Marginal product exceeds average product when the latter is increasing and is less than average product when the latter is decreasing. (Output per unit of labor is measured in hundreds of parts.)

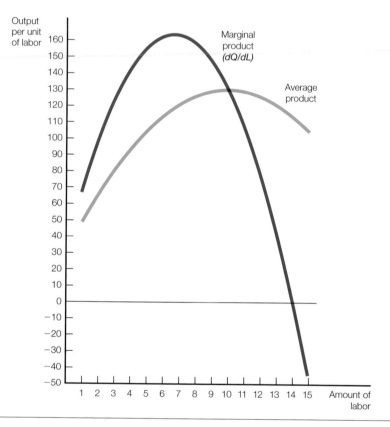

labor. The second (dQ/dL) assumes that Thomas can employ labor continuously, as in 1.25 workers or 1.33 workers. This could be achieved by using part-time workers or workers who work more or less time than in a standard day's work.

We need to understand why *MP* equals *AP* when *AP* is maximized. A simple intuitive frame may help. Assume your professor is grading papers. She is keeping a running average of test scores by calculating a new average after each paper she corrects. After grading three papers her average is 86. If the next (marginal) test score is higher than 86, the average must increase. If it is lower than 86, the average must decrease. This is a natural law of mathematics. So as long as *MP* is greater than *AP*, *AP* must be increasing. When *MP* is less than *AP*, *AP* must be decreasing. *MP* intersects with *AP* when *AP* is at a maximum.

Enough chat; let's get serious. If x is the input with Q as the output, then AP is Q/x and MP is dQ/dx

$$\frac{d(Q/x)}{dx} = \frac{x(dQ/dx) - Q(dx/dx)}{x^2}$$

$$= \frac{1}{x}\left(\frac{dQ}{dx} - \frac{Q}{x}\right)$$

When the average product is at a maximum, $d(Q/x)/dx$ equals zero. Therefore,

$$\frac{d(Q/x)}{dx} = \frac{1}{x}\left(\frac{dQ}{dx} - \frac{Q}{x}\right) = 0$$

And hence

$$MP = \frac{dQ}{dx} = \frac{Q}{x} = AP$$

THE LAW OF DIMINISHING MARGINAL RETURNS

The **law of diminishing returns** is a well-known constraint in managerial economics and a good one for managers to understand. It teaches managers to remain in balance. For most production processes, if managers add equal increments of an input while holding other input levels constant, the incremental gains (MP) to output get smaller, and if pushed to the extreme, are counterproductive. It is not hard to see why diminishing marginal returns are found in most production functions.

We see in Table 5.2 that if Thomas hires an eighth machinist, marginal product will decrease. Why? Because Thomas has only five machines. As more machinists are hired, they will have to ration machines, or new hires will be assigned to less important tasks.

Choosing the optimal input bundle is not an easy managerial task. Managers cannot hold all inputs but one constant; and they cannot expect that adding more units will always result in large increases in output. It is not as simple as that, as we will see later.

Law of diminishing returns A well-known occurrence where when managers add equal increments of an input while holding other input levels constant, the incremental gains to output eventually get smaller.

THE PRODUCTION FUNCTION WITH TWO VARIABLE INPUTS

Now we want to complicate John Thomas' world. With a longer time horizon, the formerly fixed input of five CNC machines becomes variable. Table 5.3 shows the extra input combinations to consider. Though Thomas will have to consider more choices, the process is similar to that of the one-variable input case.

TABLE 5.3

Production Function, Two Variable Inputs, Thomas Machine Company

Amount of Labor (Units)	Quantity of Machine Tools (Hundreds of Parts Produced per Year)			
	3	4	5	6
1	5	11	18	24
2	14	30	50	72
3	22	60	80	99
4	30	81	107	125
5	35	84	130	144

To illustrate, suppose Thomas is considering whether to purchase additional CNC machines. Engineers estimate the production function of additional machines and derive Table 5.3. The average product of either machine tools or machinists is computed by dividing the total output by the amount of either machine tools or machinists used. The marginal product of each input is obtained by holding the other input constant. For example, the marginal product of an additional machine tool when using four machinists and three machine tools is 5,100 parts per machine tool; the marginal product of an additional machinist when using three machinists and four CNC machines is 2,100 parts per unit. If X_1 is the amount of the first input and X_2 is the amount of the second input, the production function is

$$Q = f(X_1, X_2)$$

where Q is the firm's output rate. The marginal product of the first input is $\Delta Q / \Delta X_1$; the marginal product of the second input is $\Delta Q / \Delta X_2$.

QUANT OPTION

For the fastidious, we have

$$MP_1 = \frac{\partial Q}{\partial X_1} \quad MP_2 = \frac{\partial Q}{\partial X_2}$$

1. This surface is not meant to represent the numerical values in Table 5.3 but is a general representation of how a production surface of this sort is likely to appear.

Visually, we can represent the production function by a surface, as shown in Figure 5.3. The production surface is *OAQB*.[1] We measure output for any

STRATEGY SESSION: Substitution of Capital for Labor in Legal Proceedings

In lawsuits, the parties must submit documents to each other that are requested and ordered by the court. This enables each side to discover what the other side knows and to prepare an offense or defense against it. This process is called *discovery*. The traditional tactic used by the defense in large cases is to overload the plaintiff with documents, e-mails, and so on, including many materials the defense knows are irrelevant to the case. The plaintiff must then separate the wheat from the chaff—often a daunting task. Who performs the work? Often an army of paralegals and lawyers who are compensated handsomely (especially the lawyers) for many, many hours of work. In a classic example, one case (a U.S. Department of Justice antitrust case involving five television studios in 1978), 6 million documents were examined at a cost of $2.2 million.

Enter the world of artificial intelligence (AI) and the computer. What's called "e-discovery" software can quickly scan documents and e-mails for key words and phrases. In addition, the software can point to patterns of behavior over multiple documents and develop timelines of who knew what when. In January of 2011, Blackstone Discovery helped analyze 1.5 million documents for a price that was less than $100,000. In 2010, Clearwell (an e-discovery firm) analyzed 570,000 documents in two days and distilled them to 3,070 documents that were relevant to the case. The labor savings can be on the order of 99%; in other words, one lawyer can do what before had taken 100 to do. Mike Lynch, the founder of Autonomy (another e-discovery firm), predicts that one lawyer will soon be able to do the work of 500, and that new generations of software will enable one lawyer to do the work of 1,000.

Interestingly enough, good develops from bad. The rapid development of AI for the legal community came from the massive amount of documentation the U.S. Department of Justice accumulated in the Enron fraud case. More than 5 million pieces of documentation were involved. When researchers got their hands on the documentation, they learned how participants conversed about nefarious activities and how social networks are formed.

Here's how sophisticated the programs are becoming. The programs focus on "linguistics" and "sociology." Linguistics has moved from just searching for keywords to linking those words to related words: synonyms, antonyms, activities associated with a word, and so on. An example might be that a search for cat would also give you *feline*, *meow*, *cuddly*, and *mice*. Sociology traces who's talking with whom about what, can trace changes in communications in terms of tone and content, and can even analyze whether certain words, phrases, or documents indicate stress levels of the sender or receiver. Examples here are when communications turn from casual to stiff or communication length/frequency changes. Words like *let's continue this offline* usually indicate that something is going on.

AI has penetrated into the computer industry itself. Software has replaced logic designers and draftsmen in the computer chip industry, and it now performs many of the tasks of loan officers in banks and of tax accountants (think TurboTax). This puts middle management jobs at risk and the trend could continue to upper management jobs.

But one more question arises: The computer is fast, but is it good? A major chemical company lawyer tested e-discovery software on old cases of his company. He found that his company's lawyers were only 60% accurate relative to the computer. He points out that people get bored, get distracted, don't feel well, have bad days, and so on, but computers don't.

Source: John Markoff, "Armies of Expensive Lawyers, Replaced by Cheaper Software," *New York Times*, at www.nytimes.com/2011/03/05/science/05legal.

FIGURE 5.3

Production Function, Two Variable Inputs

The production surface, *OAQB*, shows the amount of total output that can be obtained from various combinations of machine tools and labor.

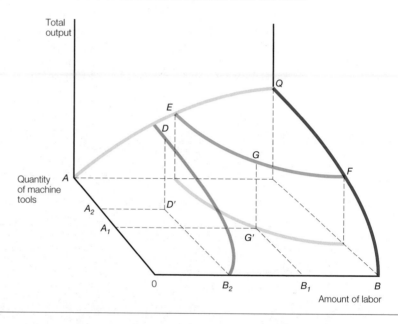

input bundle as height on the surface. Dropping a perpendicular down from a point on the surface to the "floor" defines the corresponding input bundle. For example, producing $G'G$ units of output requires OB_1 $(= A_1G')$ machinists and OA_1 $(= B_1G')$ machine tools. Conversely, we can take any amounts of machine tools and machinists, say OA_2 machine tools and OB_2 machinists, and find their output levels by measuring the height of the production surface at D', the point where machinists is OB_2 and machine tool input is OA_2. According to Figure 5.3, the output equals $D'D$. Input bundles that produce identical output have the same height.

ISOQUANTS

Isoquant Curve showing all possible (efficient) input bundles capable of producing a given output level.

An **isoquant** is a curve showing all possible (efficient) input bundles capable of producing a given output level. An isoquant is composed of all the points having the same height in the production surface of Figure 5.3. Suppose we want to find the isoquant corresponding to an output of $G'G$. All we need to do is cut the surface at the height of $G'G$ parallel to the base plane, the result being *EGF*, and drop perpendiculars from *EGF* to the base. Clearly this results in a curve that includes

STRATEGY SESSION: How Nucor Stays on the Production Function

Nucor is the largest steel firm in the United States, although it did not focus on steel production until the 1960s. Net sales for the first 39 weeks of 2011 were over $15 billion. More remarkably, the company has paid a cash dividend for 154 consecutive quarters. This performance has far outstripped that of more traditional (integrated) steel manufacturers like U.S.X. For example, when the average integrated steel company in the United States produced 400 tons of steel per employee, Nucor produced about 980 tons per employee. What actions have Nucor's managers implemented to achieve this superior performance?

One difference is that Nucor is a "minimill," not an integrated steel firm. Minimills have a different production function than do integrated mills. They use electric arc furnaces to make steel products from scrap metal. In 2007 Nucor was the nation's largest recycler, reprocessing one ton of steel every two seconds.

The primary reason for Nucor's outstanding performance is the company's focus on the efficient use of resources. Management has executed strategies that keep the company on an efficient production function. Being efficient is not caused by random luck. It is clearly governed by managerial decisions and requires an integrated set of policies. In Nucor's case, the firm employs roughly 12,000 people. How do Nucor managers keep employees focused on efficient production?

Nucor uses the following multipronged approach:

1. It maintains a simple, streamlined organizational structure that encourages decentralized decision making. Most divisions use only three layers of management. Each division is treated as a profit center and is expected to earn a 25% return on total assets.

2. The company acts as the general contractor in building new plants. It locates plants in rural areas where land is cheap (and unions are weak). Also, each plant is located near water and is served by at least two railroad lines to keep freight rates low.

Nucor recruits employees to help build the plant; this allows it to observe the work habits of individuals. Those with good work habits are recruited to work in the plant when it opens. It also brings workers from other plants (who have already built plants) to join the constuction team. Using these methods, Nucor can build a plant at a lower cost and in about 33% less time than competitors.

3. All employees are subject to performance-related compensation plans. For example, production employees are paid weekly bonuses based on the productivity of their work group. Using this team approach, Nucor can lower its monitoring costs because employees monitor each other. Bonuses are based on the capabilities of the equipment and average 80% to 150% of an employee's base pay. The more output a team produces, the higher are its bonuses.

4. Nucor treats all employees equally. Benefits are the same regardless of organizational position. There are no company cars, executive dining rooms, or corporate jets.

5. The firm's focus on output does not mean that quality suffers. Employees are committed to providing the highest-quality steel at a competitive price. To reinforce this commitment to quality, most of Nucor's divisions are ISO 9000 certified.[a]

6. Finally, Nucor regards itself as a technological leader. It was the first firm to produce thin-slab casting at a minimill and searches worldwide for new developments in steel production. This emphasis on innovation is reinforced by the firm's flat organizational structure. Decisions can be made and implemented quickly.

[a]ISO 9000 is a set of quality standards. To receive ISO 9000 certification, managers must fulfill various quality assurance requirements and be audited by an external registrar. If a firm's quality assurance system is approved by this registrar, the firm is awarded an ISO 9000 certification and is allowed to advertise this fact to all customers.

all efficient combinations of machine tools and machinists that can produce $G'G$ metal parts. Using the notation in equation (5.1), an isoquant shows all combinations of X_1 and X_2 such that $f(X_1, X_2)$ equals a certain output.

Several isoquants, each pertaining to a different output rate, are shown in Figure 5.4. The two axes measure the quantities of inputs. In contrast to the previous diagrams, we assume labor and capital—not machinists and machine tools (a particular form of labor and capital)—are the relevant inputs. The curves show the various input bundles that produce 100, 200, and 300 units of output. For example, consider the isoquant for 100 units of output. This isoquant shows it is possible to produce 100 units if L_0 units of labor and K_0 units of capital are used per time period. Alternatively, this output rate can be attained with L_1 units of labor and K_1 units of capital—or L_2 units of labor and K_2 units of capital.

Figure 5.4 illustrates several properties of isoquants. The farther the isoquant is from the origin, the greater the output it represents. Because we assume continuous production functions, we can draw an isoquant for any input bundle. Each isoquant represents an infinite number of possible input combinations. Isoquants are always downward-sloping and convex to the origin (we will see why in the next section).

FIGURE 5.4

Isoquants

These three isoquants show the various combinations of capital and labor that can produce 100, 200, and 300 units of output.

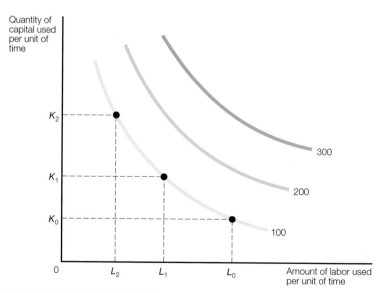

Firms now have manager job titles that weren't around a few years ago. One of those titles reads something like Chief Innovation Officer. A search of LinkedIn found at least 700 people who claimed this title in their firm and that an additional 25,000 had the word innovation somewhere in their job title. And who knows how many other managers innovate under a different job title. So what's new in innovation? The developments seem to fall into three areas: (1) Take a wide view and think out of the box; (2) Think entrepreneurially like those guys in the Silicon Valley; and (3) Listen to what customers are saying that they want and are missing and try to serve these needs. Thus, the innovators wish to explore new goods and services and how to produce them and existing goods and services more efficiently.

For instance, consider developments (1) and (2) from the previous paragraph. Weyerhauser (which produces paper and pulp) has discovered a new use for a chemical compound called *lignin*. It's a by-product of trees from pulp making and had been recycled as a fuel in the process of paper making. But some analysis showed that it could be used to produce the carbon fiber that automakers use to replace metal (to lower car weight and thus improve fuel efficiency). Lignin is worth 10 to 20 times more in the production of carbon fiber than it is as a fuel in a paper plant. The automobile industry is changing its production function by substituting carbon fiber for metal, and the pulp industry is changing its production function by substituting another fuel for lignin.

Citigroup's Chief Innovation Officer is applying development (3) and changing the bank's focus to customers and away from banking products, asking what do customers want rather than asking what Citibank wants to sell? Affluent customers were grouped into four affinity groups ranging from up-and-comers (30 year olds) to retiring baby boomers and two groups in between. Then customer service and marketing were retooled to what those customers wanted.

The new banks are digital, featuring touch-screen workstations and videoconferencing links to financial experts. The new banks are virtually paperless (traditional banks use as many as 100 forms). Thus, capital has replaced labor, and virtual banking has replaced paper banking. The production function for banking is changing.

Source: Steve Lohr, "Innovate, Yes, but Make It Practical," *New York Times*, at www.nytimes.com/2010/08/15/business/15unboxed.html.

THE MARGINAL RATE OF TECHNICAL SUBSTITUTION

Generally a particular output can be produced with a number of input bundles. As we move along a particular isoquant, the **marginal rate of technical substitution (MRTS)** shows the rate at which one input is substituted for another (with output remaining constant). If, as in equation (5.1), the output produced is a function of two inputs,

Marginal rate of technical substitution (MRTS) MRTS shows the rate at which one input is substituted for another (with output remaining constant).

$$Q = f(X_1, X_2)$$

MRTS is

$$MRTS = -\frac{\Delta X_2}{\Delta X_1} \qquad (5.2)$$

given that Q (output) is held constant.

Geometrically the marginal rate of technical substitution is -1 times the slope of the isoquant. This makes sense because $\Delta X_2 / \Delta X_1$ measures the slope, which is downward or negative (so X_2 is on the y axis and X_1 is on the x axis).

It is useful for managers to think of MRTS as the ratio of marginal products, MP_1 / MP_2, for inputs 1 and 2. Managers need to be efficient. The marginal product metric shows the incremental effect on output of the last unit of input. In spirit, managers want to increase the use of inputs with relatively high marginal products, though they must also consider the costs of inputs.

The rate of substitutability between inputs is varied. In some production processes, one type of labor is easily substituted for another; in others, specialized inputs are required. In extreme cases, no substitution among inputs is possible; to produce a unit of output, a fixed amount of each input is required, and inputs must be used in fixed proportions. Figure 5.5 shows the firm's isoquants in such a case; as you can see, they are right angles. Few production processes allow no substitution among inputs, but in some, substitutability is limited. If perfect substitutability of inputs is possible, isoquants are straight lines connecting the two axes.

QUANT OPTION

It's time for some fun!

$$dQ = \left(\frac{\partial Q}{\partial X_1}\right)dX_1 + \left(\frac{\partial Q}{\partial X_2}\right)dX_2 = 0$$

Therefore,

$$\frac{dX_2}{dX_1} = \frac{-(\partial Q/\partial X_1)}{\partial Q/\partial X_2} = -\frac{MP_1}{MP_2} \qquad (5.3)$$

Mathematically, isoquants may have positively sloped segments or bend back on themselves, as shown in Figure 5.6. Above OU and below OV, the isoquant slopes are positive, implying that increases in both capital and labor are required to maintain a specified output rate. If this is the case, the marginal product of one or the other input is negative. Above OU, the marginal product of capital is negative; therefore, output increases if less capital is used while the level of labor is held constant. Below OV, the marginal product of labor is negative; output increases if

FIGURE 5.5

Isoquants in the Case of Fixed Proportions

If inputs must be used in fixed proportions, the isoquants are right angles.

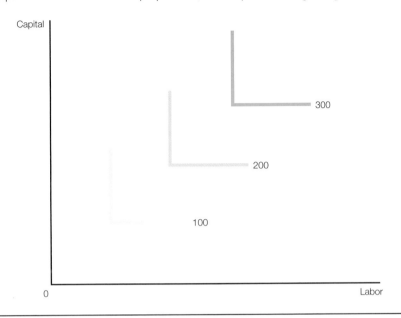

FIGURE 5.6

Economic Region of Production

No profit-maximizing firm operates at a point outside the ridge lines, *OU* and *OV*.

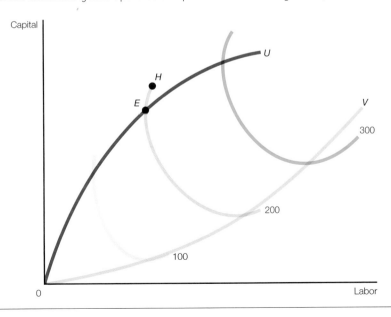

STRATEGY SESSION: Innovations in Payments for Goods and Services

Is the cash register a thing of the past? Already "cashiers" don't key in item prices—UPC codes are scanned. Cashiers may take money and make change, but many payments are made by credit and debit cards. Some stores such as Home Depot, are already offering self-checkout lines. What's next? How about a big arch near the exit that you walk your cart through that scans all your items purchased and puts the total on your credit card or reduces your bank balance by the amount of your purchases? It's like an E-Z Pass for groceries or purchases from other retailers.

But how about paying by just swiping your smartphone? Deutsche Telekom, France Télécom, Google, Visa, and other companies are scrambling to get into what are called *near-field communication (NFC)* payment systems that will enable consumers to shop at the corner store and pay with a swipe of the phone. The telecoms are hoping that their existing payments system and billing arrangements with customers will be a first-mover advantage against

technology giants like Google (who bills virtually no one). The NFC market is estimated to account for up to a third of the global market in mobile transactions by 2014 (a $1.3 trillion market). Not only cash registers but credit cards may be replaced.

The arrival of Google's Android and Samsung's Nexus S, as well as speculation that Apple (which knows how to bill) may enter the NFC market, make the future in this area very interesting.

Infrastructure investment will be significant. Gazillions of point of sales terminals must be put in place and then all phones will have to be NFC compatible. The most likely way all this will come about is through some partnership between the telecom experts and the financial services industry.

Source: Matthew Campbell and Jonathan Browning, "'Mega' Payments Race Pits Google, Visa Against Phone Operators," *Bloomberg News*, February 21, 2011, at www.bloomberg.com/news/2011-02-20/-mega-payments-race-pits-google-visa-against-phone-operators.html.

Ridge lines The lines that profit-maximizing firms operate within, because outside of them, marginal products of inputs are negative.

less labor is used while the amount of capital is held constant. The lines *OU* and *OV* are called **ridge lines.**

No profit-maximizing manager will operate at a point outside the ridge lines because she can produce the same output with less of both inputs. This choice is strictly less costly. Consider point *H* in Figure 5.6. This point is located on a positively sloped segment of the isoquant (and so outside the ridge lines). It will always require greater levels of both labor and capital than a point inside the ridge lines (for example, point *E*) on the same isoquant. Because both capital and labor have positive prices, it is cheaper to operate at point *E* than at point *H*. The moral is this: Managers cannot use input bundles outside the ridge lines if they want to maximize profit.

THE OPTIMAL COMBINATION OF INPUTS

The previous analysis did not include the costs of inputs. Managers must consider costs because the inputs are scarce. A manager who wants to maximize profit will try to minimize the cost of producing a given output or maximize the output derived from a given level of cost.[2] Suppose a manager takes input prices as given and uses two inputs, capital and labor, that vary in the relevant period. What combination of capital and labor should the manager choose to maximize the output derived from the given level of cost?

First we determine the various input combinations that can be obtained for a given cost. If capital and labor are the inputs and the price of labor is P_L per unit and the price of capital is P_K per unit, the input combinations that are obtained for a total outlay of M are such that

$$P_L L + P_K K = M \tag{5.4}$$

where L is the level of labor and K is the level of capital. Given M, P_L, and P_K, it follows that

$$K = \frac{M}{P_K} - \frac{P_L L}{P_K} \tag{5.5}$$

The various bundles of capital and labor that can be purchased, given P_L, P_K, and M, are represented by the straight line shown in Figure 5.7. (Capital is plotted on the vertical axis, and labor is plotted on the horizontal axis.) This line, which has an intercept on the vertical axis equal to M/P_K and a slope of $-P_L/P_K$, is called an

---

FIGURE 5.7

Isocost Curve

The isocost curve shows the combinations of inputs that can be obtained for a total outlay of M.

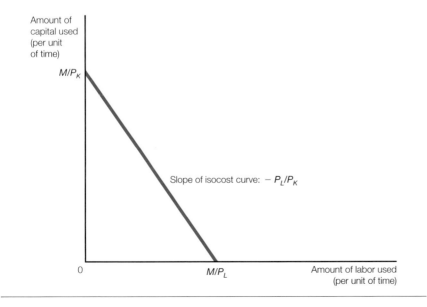

2. The conditions for minimizing the cost of producing a given output are the same as those for maximizing the output from a given cost. This is shown in the present section. Therefore, we can view the firm's problem in either way.

Isocost curve Curve showing all the input bundles that can be purchased at a specified cost.

isocost curve. It shows all the input bundles that can be purchased at a specified cost (M).

If we superimpose the relevant isocost curve on the isoquant map, we see the input bundle that maximizes output for a given cost. An efficient manager should choose the point on the isocost curve that is tangent to the highest-valued isoquant—for example, R in Figure 5.8. Because the slope of the isocost curve is the negative of P_L/P_K and the slope of the isoquant is the negative of MP_L/MP_K (as we pointed out in the previous section), it follows that the optimal combination of inputs is one where $MP_L/MP_K = P_L/P_K$. Put differently, the firm should choose an input combination where $MP_L/P_L = MP_K/P_K$.

So efficient managers need to choose an input bundle where the marginal products per dollar spent of labor and capital are identical. If they are not, the manager should increase the use of the input with the higher marginal product per dollar value.

If there are more than two inputs, the manager maximizes output by distributing costs among the various inputs so the marginal product of a dollar's worth of one input is equal to the marginal product of a dollar's worth of any other input used. In spirit, the manager chooses an input bundle such that

$$\frac{MP_a}{P_a} = \frac{MP_b}{P_b} = \cdots = \frac{MP_n}{P_n} \tag{5.6}$$

FIGURE 5.8

Maximization of Output for a Given Cost

To maximize the output for a given cost, the firm should choose the input combination at point R.

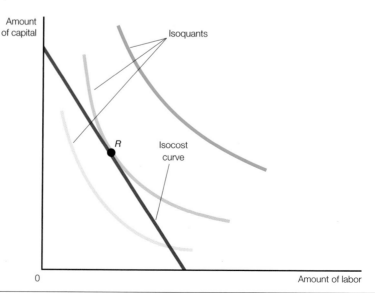

where MP_a, MP_b, ..., MP_n are the marginal products of inputs a, b, ..., n; and P_a, P_b, ..., P_n are the prices of inputs a, b, ..., n.

To determine the input bundle that minimizes production costs, we use a graph similar to Figure 5.8. Moving along the isoquant of the stipulated output level, we find the point that lies on the lowest isocost curve—for example, S in Figure 5.9. Input bundles on isocost curves like C_0 that lie below S are cheaper than S, but they cannot produce the desired output. Input bundles on isocost curves like C_2 that lie above S produce the desired output but at a higher cost than S. It is obvious that the optimal bundle S is a point where the isocost curve is tangent to the isoquant. Therefore, to minimize the cost of producing a given output or to maximize the output from a given cost outlay, the firm must equate

STRATEGY SESSION: The Substitution of Inputs in Baseball

The regular baseball season is a grueling 162-game odyssey that leads eight teams to the playoffs and, ultimately, two teams to the World Series. Surviving the 162 games and arriving at the playoffs entails luck and skill. Pitching is a large percentage of the game. Most teams operate with a four or five starting-pitcher rotation (meaning that each pitcher starts between 30 and 40 games and gets about four days rest between starts). Over the long haul of the season, a pitcher needs that time between starts to avoid wear and tear on his arm.

But when teams make it to the playoffs, things change. Because of strategic scheduling of games and because there is only a short time until the pitchers can rest during the off-season, teams are able to go with their best three (or four) pitchers instead of using their fourth or fifth starters. By using their best pitchers, post season ERAs (earned run averages) have been lower in the post season than in the regular season in 13 of the last 15 years. In 2001, the ERA in the post season was 1.3 runs less than in the regular season (almost a 30% decrease).

Which pitchers are the best pitchers for the playoffs? The power pitchers, such as Josh Beckett, John Smoltz, "CC" Sabathia, Curt Schilling, and Randy Johnson are best. While some finesse pitchers

have done well, including Cliff Lee and Cole Hamels, other regular season finesse pitchers, such as Greg Maddux and Tom Glavine, have been subpar in the post season. The power pitchers tend to dominate during the playoffs.

Why does management (i.e., the managers and coaches) substitute power for finesse? John Smoltz—a former power pitcher, playoff Most Valuable Player, and holder of a 15-4 playoff win-loss record and a 2.67 playoff ERA, and now a baseball color commentator—states, "If I had to orchestrate a team, the front end of my rotation would have power guys. Whether or not they were super successful during the regular season, they have a better chance of dominating in a short series." Tampa Bay Ray's pitching coach Jim Hickey says, "I think every team would prefer to go with power arms. If you get a dominant pitcher who strikes people out, there are no other variables." Power pitchers control their destiny with strikeouts whereas finesse pitchers let batters make contact with the ball and hence create the possibility of hits and errors.

Source: Jorge L. Ortiz, "Pitching Rules in Playoffs: ERAs Drop, Strikeouts Go Up," *USA Today*, October 5, 2010, at www.usatoday.com/sports/baseball/playoffs/2010-10-05.

FIGURE 5.9

Minimization of Cost for a Given Output

To minimize the cost of producing the amount of output corresponding to this isoquant, the manager should choose the input combination at point S.

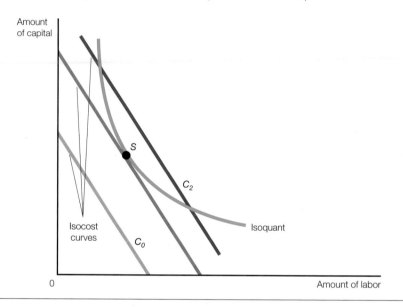

MP_L/MP_K and P_L/P_K; this means that $MP_L/P_L = MP_K/P_K$. And if more than two inputs are needed, the manager must satisfy equation (5.6).

CORNER SOLUTIONS

Just as in consumption theory in Chapter 3, it is possible to have corner solutions—that is, optimal input bundles with just one input deployed. Given the production technology and the prices of the inputs, there may be no tangency of an isoquant with an isocost curve. In the two-input case, this means that just one input is used to produce the product in the least expensive way (or to produce the most output with a given cost). Equation 5.6 will now be an inequality reading $MP_K/P_K > MP_L/P_L$ for cases where just capital is used and $MP_K/P_K < MP_L/P_L$ for cases where just labor is used. The former case is shown in Figure 5.10.

RETURNS TO SCALE

We have seen how managers can represent technology as a production function and use concepts like marginal and average product to operate more efficiently. We want to continue this theme and examine some long-term considerations

FIGURE 5.10

A Corner Solution Where Only One Input Is Used

With outlay of M, the most that can be produced is Q_3 using only capital (M/P_K units). If only labor were used, the firm could produce only Q_1 units with outlay M. The cheapest way to produce Q_3 units is with just M/P_K units of capital and with no labor. Q_3 units could be produced with an outlay of $M' > M$ by using both capital and labor, but that would be inefficient.

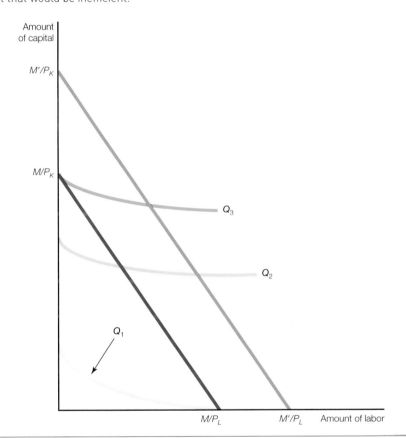

managers face. These focus on scale. Basically, what is the incremental change to output as managers increase their use of capital and labor?

Suppose we consider a long-term situation where all inputs are variable, and managers increase the level of inputs by the same proportion. What will happen to output? Clearly there are three possibilities. First, output may increase by a larger proportion than inputs; for example, doubling all inputs may more than double output. This is the case of **increasing returns to scale**. Or output may increase by a smaller proportion than inputs; for example, doubling all inputs

Increasing return to scale When output increases by a larger proportion than inputs.

Decreasing returns to scale
When output increases by a smaller proportion than inputs.

Constant returns to scale When output increases by exactly the same proportion as inputs.

may lead to less than a doubling of output. This is the case of **decreasing returns to scale**. Finally, output may increase by exactly the same proportion as inputs; for example, doubling all inputs may double output. This is the case of **constant returns to scale**.

At first glance, some managers may believe that production functions necessarily exhibit constant returns to scale. After all, if a manager can build two factories with the same plant size and types of workers, can't she achieve the same output with a single plant twice the size? But things are not this simple. If managers double the size of a plant, they may employ techniques that are economically infeasible at the smaller scale. Some inputs are not available in small units; for example, we

---

PROBLEM SOLVED: What Skills Do We Need?

Consider the Beiswanger Company, a small firm engaged in engineering analysis. Beiswanger's president has estimated that the firm's output per month (Q) is related in the following way to the number of engineers (E) and technicians used (T)

$$Q = 20E - E^2 + 12T - 0.5T^2 \qquad (5.7)$$

The monthly wage of an engineer is $4,000, and the monthly wage of a technician is $2,000. If the president allots $28,000 per month for the combined wages of engineers and technicians, what mix of engineers and technicians should he hire?

If the president is to maximize output (for his $28,000 budget), he must choose a bundle of engineers and technicians such that

$$\frac{MP_E}{P_E} = \frac{MP_T}{P_T} \qquad (5.8)$$

where MP_E is the marginal product of an engineer, MP_T is the marginal product of a technician, P_E is the wage of an engineer, and P_T is the wage of a technician. Viewing the change in equation (5.7) with respect to E and T, we find that

$$MP_E = \frac{\Delta Q}{\Delta E} = 20 - 2E \qquad (5.9a)$$

$$MP_T = \frac{\Delta Q}{\Delta T} = 12 - T \qquad (5.9b)$$

Inserting these expressions for MP_E and MP_T into equation (5.8) and noting that $P_E = 4,000$ and $P_T = 2,000$, it follows that

$$\frac{20 - 2E}{4,000} = \frac{12 - T}{2,000}$$
$$\frac{2,000(20 - 2E)}{4,000} = 12 - T$$
$$10 - E = 12 - T$$
$$T = E + 2$$

Because Beiswanger allocates $28,000 per month for the total wages of engineers and technicians, we have

$$4,000E + 2,000T = 28,000$$

Substituting ($E + 2$) for T gives us

$$4,000E + 2,000(E + 2) = 28,000$$

This means that $E = 4$ (and $T = 6$). So to maximize output from the $28,000 outlay on wages, the president should hire four engineers and six technicians.

PROBLEM SOLVED: The Efficient Minds of Managers

Managers need to search for input bundles to minimize costs for a given output. Intuitively they need to balance the productivity of an input with its cost. As we will show in Chapter 6, there are easier metrics for managers to use, like costs. But the ability to control costs is enhanced by understanding production functions. Consider the issues facing managers at the Miller Company, for which the relationship between output per hour (Q) and the number of workers (L) and machines (K) used per hour is

$$Q = 10(LK)^{0.5}$$

The wage of a worker is \$80 per hour, and the price of a machine is \$20 per hour. If the Miller Company produces 800 units of output per hour, how many workers and machines should managers use?

According to equation (5.8), the Miller Company should choose an input combination such that

$$\frac{MP_L}{P_L} = \frac{MP_K}{P_K}$$

where MP_L is the marginal product of a worker, MP_K is the marginal product of a machine, P_L is the wage

of a worker, and P_K is the price of using a machine. Because $Q = 10(LK)^{0.5}$,

$$MP_L = \frac{\Delta Q}{\Delta L} = 5\left(\frac{K}{L}\right)^{0.5}$$

$$MP_K = \frac{\Delta Q}{\Delta K} = 5\left(\frac{L}{K}\right)^{0.5}$$

So if $MP_L/P_L = MP_K/P_K$

$$\frac{5(K/L)^{0.5}}{80} = \frac{5(L/K)^{0.5}}{20}$$

Multiplying both sides of this equation by $(K/L)^{0.5}$, we get

$$\frac{5K}{80L} = \frac{5}{20}$$

which means that $K = 4L$. Because $Q = 800$,

$$10(LK)^{0.5} = 800$$
$$10[L(4L)]^{0.5} = 800$$
$$L = 40$$
$$K = 160$$

Therefore, to minimize cost, managers at the Miller Company should hire 40 workers and use 160 machines.

---

cannot install half a robot. Because of indivisibilities of this sort, larger plants may have increasing returns to scale. So when managers think about efficient choice, building one large factory relative to two smaller ones may be better.

Larger plants also let managers subdivide tasks and use inputs more narrowly. This specialization strategy increases production efficiency; so investment bankers specialize in designated areas, and airlines dedicate computers to handling reservations. Larger size may also generate probabilistic efficiencies; for example, because the aggregate behavior of a larger number of customers tends to be more stable, a firm's inventory may not have to increase in proportion to its sales.

Increasing returns to scale also arise because of certain geometrical relations. Because the volume of a box that is $2 \times 2 \times 2$ feet is eight times as great as the volume of a box that is $1 \times 1 \times 1$ foot, the former box can carry eight times as much as the latter box. But the area of the six sides of the $2 \times 2 \times 2$ box is 24 square feet and the area of the six sides of the $1 \times 1 \times 1$ box is six square feet, so the former box requires only four times as much wood as the latter.

It turns out that bigger is not always better; managers can experience decreasing returns to scale. The most common culprit is the challenge of coordinating a large organization. It can be difficult even in a small firm for managers to obtain the necessary information to make important decisions; in a large firm such problems tend to be greater. As we show in Chapter 15, managers often have difficulties in designing efficient incentive schemes in larger firms. Though the advantages of a large organization are obvious, scale can generate inefficiencies. For example, in certain kinds of research and development, large teams tend to be less effective than smaller ones.

Whether scale returns are constant, increasing, or decreasing is an empirical question that must be settled case by case. There is no simple, all-encompassing answer. In some industries the evidence suggests that returns increase over a certain range of output; but the answer is likely to depend on the output considered. There may be increasing returns to scale at small output levels and constant or decreasing returns to scale at higher levels. In addition, managers need to know how output changes when inputs are not all increased or decreased in the same proportion.

THE OUTPUT ELASTICITY

Output elasticity The percentage of change in output resulting from a 1% increase in all inputs.

To measure whether there are increasing, decreasing, or constant returns to scale, the output elasticity is computed. The **output elasticity** is defined as the percentage of change in output resulting from a 1% increase in all inputs. If the output elasticity exceeds 1, there are increasing returns to scale; if it equals 1, there are constant returns to scale; and if it is less than 1, there are decreasing returns to scale.

As an illustration, consider the Lone Star Company, a maker of aircraft parts, which has the following production function

$$Q = 0.8L^{0.3}K^{0.8}$$

Here Q is the number of parts produced per year (measured in millions of parts), L is the number of workers hired, and K is the amount of capital used. This is the commonly used Cobb-Douglas production function (named after Charles Cobb and Paul Douglas, who pioneered its application).

To calculate the output elasticity at the Lone Star Company, let's see what will happen to Q if we multiply both inputs (L and K) by 1.01. Clearly the new value of Q (that is, Q') equals

$$\begin{aligned}
Q' &= 0.8(1.01L)^{0.3}(1.01K)^{0.8} \\
&= 0.8(1.01)^{1.1}L^{0.3}K^{0.8} \\
&= (1.01)^{1.1}(0.8L^{0.3}K^{0.8}) \\
&= (1.01)^{1.1}Q \\
&= 1.011005484Q
\end{aligned}$$

Therefore, if a manager increases the use of both inputs by 1%, output increases by slightly more than 1.1%; this means the output elasticity is approximately 1.1. It is exactly 1.1 for an infinitesimal change in input use (of both inputs). Because a 1% change is larger than infinitesimal, the increase in output is slightly larger than 1.1.

ESTIMATIONS OF PRODUCTION FUNCTIONS

Managers need to estimate production functions. One of the first steps in estimating a production function is to choose its mathematical form. Managers commonly use the Cobb-Douglas form. With only two inputs, this form is

$$Q = aL^bK^c \tag{5.10}$$

where Q is the number of parts produced per year (measured in millions of parts), L is the number of workers hired, and K is the amount of capital used. One advantage of this form is that the marginal productivity of each input depends on the level of all inputs employed, which is often realistic. Consider the marginal product of labor, which equals

$$\frac{\Delta Q}{\Delta L} = baL^{b-1}K^c = b\left(\frac{Q}{L}\right) = b(AP_L)$$

QUANT OPTION

$\partial Q/\partial L = baL^{b-1}K^c = baL^{b-1}K^c(L/L) = baL^bK^c/L = b(Q/L) = b(AP_L)$

Obviously the marginal product of labor depends on the values of both L and K. Another advantage is that if logarithms are taken of both sides of equation (5.10),

$$\log Q = \log a + b \log L + c \log K \tag{5.11}$$

PROBLEM SOLVED: Finding the Optimal Mix

Consider the production of broiler chickens, which is a big industry in the United States (2010 production value: $20.8 billion). At one company, managers ran an experiment in which broilers were fed various amounts of corn and soybean oilmeal and the gain in weight of each broiler was measured. The managers then used regression to estimate the production function for broilers

$$G = 0.03 + 0.48C + 0.64S$$
$$- 0.02C^2 - 0.05S^2 - 0.02CS \quad (5.12)$$

Here G is the gain in weight (in pounds per broiler), C is pounds of corn per broiler, and S is pounds of soybean oilmeal per broiler. The multiple coefficient of determination (R^2) is very high—about 0.998.

Using equation (5.12), managers can estimate isoquants for poultry production. Suppose they want to estimate the isoquant pertaining to a weight gain of one pound. In other words, they want to find the various combinations of corn per broiler and soybean oilmeal per broiler that results in a weight gain per broiler of one pound. To find these combinations, set $G = 1$

$$1 = 0.03 + 0.48C + 0.64S$$
$$- 0.02C^2 - 0.05S^2 - 0.02CS \quad (5.13)$$

Then we set C equal to various values and determine each resulting value of S. For example, suppose $C = 1$. Then

$$1 = 0.03 + 0.48(1) + 0.64S$$
$$- 0.02(1^2) - 0.05S^2 - 0.02(1)S$$

or

$$1 = 0.03 + 0.48 - 0.02 + (0.64 - 0.02)S - 0.05S^2$$

Solving $0.05S^2 - 0.62S + 0.51 = 0$ by the quadratic formula yields

$$S = [0.62 \pm (0.62^2 - 4(0.05)(0.51))^{0.5}]/2(0.05)$$
$$= [0.62 \pm (0.3844 - 0.0102)^{0.5}]/0.1$$
$$= [0.62 \pm (0.2824)^{0.5}]/0.1$$
$$= (0.62 \pm 0.5314)/0.1$$

Therefore, $S = 1.1514/0.1 = 11.514$, or $S = 0.08858/0.1 = 0.886$. Consequently, if a broiler is to gain one pound of weight, it must be fed 0.886 pounds of soybean oilmeal, as well as one pound of corn.[a]

If we let $C = 1.1$, we can find the corresponding value of S by substituting 1.1 for C in equation (5.13) and solving for S. If we let $C = 1.2$, we can find the corresponding value of S by substituting 1.2 for C in equation (5.13) and solving for S. Proceeding in this way, we can find more and more points on the isoquant corresponding to a weight gain of one pound. The resulting isoquant is shown in the figure. Isoquants of this sort are of great importance to managers. Coupled with data regarding input prices, they can be used to determine which input bundles will minimize costs (recall Figure 5.9).

Managers use the isoquant in the figure shown on page 163 to determine how much corn and soybean oilmeal to feed a broiler if they want a one-pound weight gain. To see how, suppose the price of a pound of corn is three-quarters the price of a pound of soybean oilmeal. Then the slope of each isocost curve in the figure equals $-\frac{3}{4}$ because, as pointed out in Figure 5.7, the slope equals -1 times the price of the input on the horizontal axis (corn) divided by the price of the input on the vertical axis (soybean oilmeal). For the cost of the weight gain to be at a minimum, the isocost curve should be tangent to the isoquant; this means that the slope of the isoquant should also equal $-\frac{3}{4}$. As shown in the figure,

Isoquant for a One-Pound Weight Gain for a Broiler and Isocost Curve If Corn Price Is ¾ of Soybean Oilmeal Price

The optimal input combination is 1.35 pounds of corn and 0.61 pounds of soybean oilmeal.
Source: Organization for Economic Cooperation and Development, Interdisciplinary Research

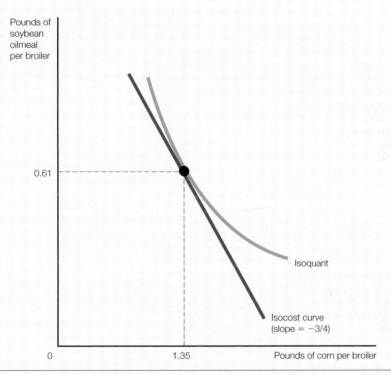

this occurs when 1.35 pounds of corn and 0.61 pounds of soybean oilmeal are used. Therefore, this is the optimal input combination if the price of a pound of corn is three-quarters the price of a pound of soybean oilmeal.

[a] There is another possible value of S, which corresponds to the use of the plus sign (rather than the minus sign) before $(b^2 - 4ac)^{0.5}$ in this formula; but this other value is not relevant here.

STRATEGY SESSION: Economies in Oil Tankers

Over 65% of crude oil output is transported by oil tankers. Oil is the largest commodity in transocean trade, accounting for 40% of all ocean shipments by weight. Oil tankers can be regarded as large cylinders. The surface area of a cylinder is not proportional to its volume; instead, as a cylinder's volume increases, its surface area goes up less than proportionately. Therefore, a tanker that can carry 300,000 deadweight tonnes (dwt) is only about twice as broad, long, and deep as one that can carry 30,000 tonnes.

Since the 1970s, the size of oil tankers has increased, as shown here:

Year	Average Oil Tanker Size (Thousands of dwt)
1973	64.0
1978	103.0
1985	146.0
2000	220.0
2008	273.0
2011	300.0

There is a strong cost incentive for larger tankers to be built. The cost of constructing an oil tanker is largely based on the cost of steel. A manager can increase the capacity of a tanker eight times by only using four times the amount of steel. A 280,000 dwt tanker costs roughly $85 million to build, whereas a 28,000 dwt tanker costs roughly $20 million to build.

Larger tankers can also operate with relatively smaller crews. An oil tanker of over 200,000 dwt today operates with a crew of 24—roughly half the crew size of a ship half that size in the 1980s. Onshore personnel costs are also relatively lower with larger tankers because these are based on the number of ships and not total tonnage. Finally, fuel costs of larger tankers are relatively lower. For example, a 60,000 dwt tanker generally requires 16,000 horsepower to travel at 15 knots. A 260,000 dwt tanker requires 42,500 horsepower to do the same. So 2.7 times the energy enables 4.3 times as much cargo to be shipped.

Sources: www.oceanatlas.com/unatlas/uses/transportation

Note that if managers use the Cobb-Douglas form, they can easily estimate the returns to scale. If the sum of the exponents (that is, $b + c$) exceeds 1, increasing returns to scale are indicated; if the sum of the exponents equals 1, constant returns to scale prevail; and if the sum of the exponents is less than 1, decreasing returns to scale are indicated. This is true because if the Cobb-Douglas production function prevails, the output elasticity equals the sum of the exponents. For example, in the previous section the output elasticity of the Lone Star Company was 1.1, which equaled the sum of the exponents (0.3 and 0.8).

There is no cut-and-dried way to determine which mathematical form is best because the answer depends on the particular situation. Frequently a good procedure is to try more than one mathematical form and see which fits the data best. The important thing is that the chosen form provide a faithful representation of the actual situation. To determine whether this is the case, it often is useful to see how well a particular estimated production function can forecast the quantity of output resulting from the combination of inputs actually used.

SUMMARY

1. The production function defines the relationship among various inputs and the maximum quantity of a good that can be produced. Managers study production functions to gain insights into the firm's cost structure.

2. An isoquant is a curve showing all possible (efficient) combinations of inputs capable of producing a particular quantity of output. The marginal rate of technical substitution shows the rate at which one input can be substituted for another input if output remains constant. No profit-maximizing manager will operate at a point where the isoquant is positively sloped.

3. To minimize the cost of producing a particular output, a manager should allocate expenditures among various inputs so that the ratio of the marginal product to the input price is the same for all inputs used. Graphically, this amounts to choosing the input combination where the relevant isoquant is tangent to an isocost curve.

4. If a manager increases all inputs by the same proportion and output increases by more (less) than this proportion, there are increasing (decreasing) returns to scale. Increasing returns to scale may occur because of indivisibility of inputs, various geometrical relations, or specialization. Decreasing returns to scale can also occur; the most frequently cited reason is the difficulty of managing a huge enterprise. Whether there are constant, increasing, or decreasing returns to scale is an empirical question that must be settled case by case.

5. Managers have estimated production functions in many firms and industries. Many studies show that a Cobb-Douglas function is the best fit for the data.

PROBLEMS

wwnorton.com/studyspace

1. In the Elwyn Company, the relationship between output (Q) and the number of hours of skilled labor (S) and unskilled labor (U) is

    $$Q = 300S + 200U - 0.2S^2 - 0.3U^2$$

    The hourly wage of skilled labor is $10, and the hourly wage of unskilled labor is $5. The firm can hire as much labor as it wants at these wage rates.

    a. Elwyn's chief engineer recommends that the firm hire 400 hours of skilled labor and 100 hours of unskilled labor. Evaluate this recommendation.

    b. If the Elwyn Company decides to spend a total of $5,000 on skilled and unskilled labor, how many hours of each type of labor should it hire?

    c. If the price of a unit of output is $10 (and does not vary with output level), how many hours of unskilled labor should the company hire?

2. A consulting firm specializing in agriculture determines that the following combinations of hay and grain consumption per lamb will result in a 25-pound gain for a lamb:

Pounds of Hay	Pounds of Grain
40	130.9
50	125.1
60	120.1
70	115.7
80	111.8
90	108.3
110	102.3
130	97.4
150	93.8

    a. The firm's president wants to estimate the marginal product of a pound of grain in producing lamb. Can he do so on the basis of these data?

    b. The firm's president is convinced that constant returns to scale prevail in lamb production. If this is true and hay and grain consumption per lamb are the only inputs, how much gain accrues if the hay consumption per lamb is 100 pounds and the grain consumption per lamb is 250.2 pounds?

    c. What is the marginal rate of technical substitution of hay for grain when between 40 and 50 pounds of hay (and between 130.9 and 125.1 pounds of grain) are consumed per lamb?

    d. A major advance in technology occurs that allows farmers to produce a 25-pound gain per lamb with less hay and grain than the preceding table indicates. If the marginal rate of technical substitution (at each rate of consumption of each input) is the same after the technological advance as before, can you draw the new isoquant corresponding to a 25-pound gain per lamb?

3. The Ascot Corporation, which produces stationery, hires a consultant to estimate its production function. The consultant concludes that

$$Q = 0.9P + 0.06L$$

where Q is the number of pounds of stationery produced by Ascot per year, L is the number of hours of labor per year, and P is the number of pounds of paper used per year.

    a. Does this production function seem to include all the relevant inputs? Explain.

b. Does this production function seem reasonable if it is applied to all possible values of *L*? Explain.

c. Does this production function exhibit diminishing marginal returns?

4. A Cobb-Douglas production function was estimated for six types of farms. There were five inputs in the production function: (1) land, (2) labor, (3) equipment, (4) livestock and feed, and (5) other resource services. The exponent of each input was as follows:

				Exponent	
Farm Type	Land	Labor	Equipment	Livestock and Feed	Other Resource Services
Crop farms	0.24	0.07	0.08	0.53	0.02
Hog farms	0.07	0.02	0.10	0.74	0.03
Dairy farms	0.10	0.01	0.06	0.63	0.02
General farms	0.17	0.12	0.16	0.46	0.03
Large farms	0.28	0.01	0.11	0.53	0.03
Small farms	0.21	0.05	0.08	0.43	0.03

a. Do there appear to be increasing returns to scale in any of these six types of farms?

b. In what type of farm does a 1% increase in labor have the largest percentage effect on output?

c. Based on these results, would you expect output to increase if many of the farms included in this sample were merged?

5. According to the chief engineer at the Zodiac Company, $Q = AL^\alpha K^\beta$, where Q is the output rate, L is the rate of labor input, and K is the rate of capital input. Statistical analysis indicates that $\alpha = 0.8$ and $\beta = 0.3$. The firm's owner claims the plant has increasing returns to scale.

a. Is the owner correct?

b. If β were 0.2 rather than 0.3, would she be correct?

c. Does output per unit of labor depend only on α and β? Why or why not?

6. According to data obtained by the U.S. Department of Agriculture, the relationship between a cow's total output of milk and the amount of grain it is fed is as follows:

Amount of Grain (Pounds)	Amount of Milk (Pounds)
1,200	5,917
1,800	7,250
2,400	8,379
3,000	9,371

(This relationship assumes that forage input is fixed at 6,500 pounds of hay.)

    a. Calculate the average product of grain when each amount is used.

    b. Estimate the marginal product of grain when between 1,200 and 1,800 pounds are fed, when between 1,800 and 2,400 pounds are fed, and when between 2,400 and 3,000 pounds are fed.

    c. Does this production function exhibit diminishing marginal returns?

7. An electronics plant's production function is $Q = 5LK$, where Q is its output rate, L is the amount of labor it uses per period, and K is the amount of capital it uses per period. The price of labor is \$1 per unit of labor, and the price of capital is \$2 per unit of capital. The firm's vice president for manufacturing hires you to determine which combination of inputs the plant should use to produce 20 units of output per period.

    a. What advice would you give him?

    b. Suppose the price of labor increases to \$2 per unit. What effect will this have on output per unit of labor?

    c. Is this plant subject to decreasing returns to scale? Why or why not?

8. Volvo A.B., the Swedish auto firm, operated a car assembly plant at Uddevalla in 1988. The idea was to have a small team of highly skilled workers build an entire car. According to the proponents, this would reduce the tedium associated with the conventional assembly line and cut absenteeism and turnover among workers. In 1991 there were reports that it took 50 hours of labor to assemble a car at Uddevalla, in contrast to 25 hours at Volvo's conventional assembly plant at Ghent, Belgium. If you were Volvo's chief executive officer, what questions would you ask Uddevalla's managers, and what steps would you take?

APPENDIX: LAGRANGIAN MULTIPLIERS AND OPTIMAL INPUT COMBINATIONS

In this chapter we stated that equation (5.6) must be satisfied if a firm is to maximize output for a given expenditure level or if it is to minimize the cost of producing a specified amount of output. In this appendix we show how the decision rule in equation (5.6) is derived using the method of Lagrangian multipliers. To keep things relatively simple, we assume the manager is using only two inputs.

Maximizing Output from a Specified Expenditure Level

Suppose a firm's production function is

$$Q = f(X_1, X_2)$$

where Q is output, X_1 is the amount used of the first input, and X_2 is the amount used of the second input. The firm's total expenditure on both inputs is specified to equal E^*. Therefore,

$$X_1 P_1 + X_2 P_2 = E^*$$

where P_1 is the price of the first input and P_2 is the price of the second input. The manager seeks to maximize output for this specified level of expenditure. So she wants to maximize Q, where

$$Q = f(X_1, X_2) \qquad (5.14)$$

subject to the constraint that

$$E^* - X_1 P_1 - X_2 P_2 = 0 \qquad (5.15)$$

We first construct the Lagrangian function, which is the right side of equation (5.14) plus λ times the left side of equation (5.15)

$$L_1 = f(X_1, X_2) + \lambda(E^* - X_1 P_1 - X_2 P_2)$$

where λ is the Lagrangian multiplier. Taking the partial derivatives of L_1 with respect to X_1, X_2, and λ and setting them all equal to zero, we obtain

$$\frac{\partial L_1}{\partial X_1} = \frac{\partial f(X_1, X_2)}{\partial X_1} - \lambda P_1 = 0 \qquad (5.16)$$

$$\frac{\partial L_1}{\partial X_2} = \frac{\partial f(X_1, X_2)}{\partial X_2} - \lambda P_2 = 0 \qquad (5.17)$$

$$\frac{\partial L_1}{\partial \lambda} = E^* - X_1 P_1 - X_2 P_2 = 0 \qquad (5.18)$$

These are the conditions for output maximization subject to the expenditure constraint.

MP_1 is the marginal product of input one and MP_2 is that for input two. By definition, we know the following is true

$$\frac{\partial f(X_1, X_2)}{\partial X_1} = \frac{\partial Q}{\partial X_1} = MP_1$$

$$\frac{\partial f(X_1, X_2)}{\partial X_2} = \frac{\partial Q}{\partial X_2} = MP_2$$

Equations (5.16) and (5.17) can be restated as

$$MP_1 - \lambda P_1 = 0$$
$$MP_2 - \lambda P_2 = 0$$

which implies that

$$MP_1 = \lambda P_1 \qquad (5.19)$$
$$MP_2 = \lambda P_2 \qquad (5.20)$$

Dividing each side of equation (5.19) by the corresponding side of equation (5.20), we find that

$$\frac{MP_1}{MP_2} = \frac{P_1}{P_2}$$

or

$$\frac{MP_1}{P_1} = \frac{MP_2}{P_2} \tag{5.21}$$

which is the decision rule in equation (5.6) when there are only two inputs. Thus we have shown why managers want to equate the marginal product per dollar spent across all inputs using the method of Lagrangian multipliers when the object is to maximize output subject to an expenditure constraint.

Minimizing the Cost of a Specified Amount of Output

Suppose a manager is committed to produce a specified quantity of output, Q^*, which means that

$$f(X_1, X_2) = Q^*$$

Her problem is to minimize costs, which equal

$$C = X_1 P_1 + X_2 P_2 \tag{5.22}$$

subject to the constraint that

$$Q^* - f(X_1, X_2) = 0 \tag{5.23}$$

We use Lagrangian multipliers to solve this problem. Again, we first construct the Lagrangian function, which is the right side of equation (5.22) plus λ times the left side of equation (5.23)

$$L_2 = X_1 P_1 + X_2 P_2 + \lambda[Q^* - f(X_1, X_2)]$$

where λ is the Lagrangian multiplier. Taking the partial derivatives of L_2 with respect to X_1, X_2, and λ and setting them all equal to zero, we obtain

$$\frac{\partial L_2}{\partial X_1} = P_1 - \lambda \frac{\partial f(X_1, X_2)}{\partial X_1} = 0 \tag{5.24}$$

$$\frac{\partial L_2}{\partial X_2} = P_2 - \lambda \frac{\partial f(X_1, X_2)}{\partial X_2} = 0 \tag{5.25}$$

$$\frac{\partial L_2}{\partial \lambda} = Q^* - f(X_1, X_2) = 0 \tag{5.26}$$

These are the conditions for cost minimization subject to the output constraint.

Substituting MP_1 for $\partial f(X_1, X_2)/\partial X_1$ and MP_2 for $\partial f(X_1, X_2)/\partial X_2$ in equations (5.24) and (5.25), we get

$$P_1 - \lambda MP_1 = 0$$
$$P_2 - \lambda MP_2 = 0$$

which implies that

$$P_1 = \lambda MP_1 \qquad\qquad\qquad (5.27)$$
$$P_2 = \lambda MP_2 \qquad\qquad\qquad (5.28)$$

Dividing each side of equation (5.27) by the corresponding side of equation (5.28), we find that

$$\frac{P_1}{P_2} = \frac{MP_1}{MP_2}$$

or

$$\frac{MP_1}{P_1} = \frac{MP_2}{P_2}$$

which is our decision rule in equation (5.6).

CHAPTER 6

THE ANALYSIS OF COSTS

Even a manager who fully understands the relationship between inputs and outputs still cannot make optimal (profit-maximizing) decisions without cost information. The key question managers must ponder is this: How are costs related to output? A full understanding of costs is necessary because virtually all business decisions require comparisons of costs and benefits. A manager wants to undertake an action if the additional (marginal) revenue attributable to that action exceeds its additional (marginal) cost. As we will see, to maximize profit, a manager wishes to produce at an output level where the marginal revenue equals the marginal cost. Obviously this calculation is not possible without a knowledge of the cost structure.

Cost (like many four-lettered words) invokes multiple interpretations. Managers find that what seems like a simple concept often provokes controversy over the nature of costs, how they are defined, and their scope and relevance in a decision (hence the basis for cost accounting in virtually every MBA program). A thorough understanding of cost is necessary for a variety of basic managerial decisions: pricing, output, transfer pricing, cost control, and planning for future production.

Managerial consideration of costs must include both short-run and long-run components. A focus on just one of these components, especially the short term, can have catastrophic consequences for an organization. As we detail in later chapters, most managerial decisions require long-term vision.

This chapter explains the basics of cost analysis and describes models to help managers create competitive advantages using cost analysis.

OPPORTUNITY COSTS

Managerial economists define the opportunity cost of producing a particular product as the revenue a manager could have received if she had used her resources to produce the next best alternative product or service. That is, opportunity costs are the revenues forgone if resources (inputs) are not optimally used. They are one reason why managers want to use resources as efficiently as possible; managers need to reduce opportunity costs.

We encounter opportunity costs throughout our lives. Those of you who were accepted at more than one college already have. Those of you who are married or in committed relationships also should understand the concept.

The opportunity cost of General Electric managers' decision to produce large gas turbines is the revenue they could have earned if the labor, equipment, and materials used in the production of turbines were used to produce another GE product—say debt financing. Or GE managers could even have invested outside their firm. Economists believe the true costs of inputs are their values when used in the most productive way. These costs, together with the firm's production costs (the accounting costs of producing a product), determine the economic cost of production. This is called the **opportunity cost doctrine**.

The opportunity cost of an input may not equal its **historical cost**, which is defined as the money managers actually paid for it. For example, if a manager invests $1 million in equipment that is quickly outmoded and inefficient relative to new equipment, its value is clearly not $1 million. Although conventional accounting rules place great emphasis on historical costs, managerial economists believe historical costs can be misleading.

Managers must be concerned with two types of costs, both of which are important. The first type is **explicit costs**, which are the ordinary items accountants include as the firm's expenses. These include the firm's payroll, payments for raw materials, and so on. The second type is **Implicit costs**, which include the forgone value of resources that managers did not put to their best use (i.e., opportunity costs). Unfortunately accountants and managers, in calculating the costs to a firm, often omit implicit costs.

Think of opportunity costs in the context of MBA students. The total cost (including room and board) of a year's schooling at the Wharton School is roughly $100,000. This is the cash outlay that most students pay. However, many MBA students held jobs before coming back to school. Assume the compensation of the average MBA student in the previous year was $70,000. If we asked an accountant the average yearly cost of attending Wharton, he would say about $100,000. If we pose that same question to economists, most would say $170,000.

Opportunity cost doctrine The inputs' values (when used in their most productive way) together with production costs (the accounting costs of producing a product) determine the economic cost of production.

Historical cost The money that managers actually paid for an input.

Explicit costs The ordinary items accountants include as the firm's expenses.

Implicit costs The forgone value of resources that managers did not put to their best use.

Consider John Harvey, the proprietor of a firm who invests his own labor and capital in the business. These inputs should be valued at the amount he would have received if he had used them in a different manner. If he could have received a salary of $65,000 working for someone else and he could have received dividends of $20,000 by investing his capital elsewhere, he should value his labor and capital at these rates. Excluding these implicit costs can be a serious mistake.

Economists also follow the doctrine of **sunk costs**. Sunk costs are resources that are spent and cannot be recovered. For example, if a company builds a plant for $12 million but then disposes of it for a price of $4 million, it incurs sunk costs of $8 million. Sunk costs equal the difference between what a resource costs and what it is sold for in the future.

Ignoring sunk costs is difficult for managers—and in fact perplexes most folks. For example, many people stay in unhealthy relationships because of the time they have invested. You may have given a partner the best five years of your life, but that is no reason to remain in a relationship you don't like. No matter what you do, you cannot recapture the five years, so ignore them in deciding your future.

Rational managers must ignore sunk costs and choose between possible strategies by evaluating only future costs and benefits. For example, if a manager has already spent $6 million on an advertising campaign, those costs are sunk (they cannot be recovered). So she cannot argue that she has already spent $6 million and needs only $1 million more to "turn the corner." The expected return of that $1 million in the campaign must be compared to the expected return of $1 million across alternative investments.

SHORT-RUN COST FUNCTIONS

Given a firm's cost of producing each level of output, we can define the firm's cost structure. A **cost function** shows various relationships between input costs and output. The firm's production function and the input prices determine the firm's cost structure.

Similar to what we saw with production functions, cost functions are either for the short or long run. The short run is a period so short that a manager cannot alter the quantity of some inputs. As the length of time increases, more inputs become variable. The time span between one where the quantity of no input is variable and one where the quantities of all inputs are variable is called the **short run**. However, a more restrictive definition is generally employed: We say the short run is the time interval so brief that a manager cannot alter the quantities of plant and equipment. These are the firm's **fixed inputs**, and they determine the firm's **scale of plant**. Inputs like labor, which a manager can vary in quantity in the short run, are the firm's **variable inputs**.

Sunk costs Sunk costs are resources that are spent and cannot be recovered.

Cost function Function showing various relationships between input costs and output rate.

Short run The time span between one where the quantity of no input is variable and one where the quantities of all inputs are variable.

Fixed inputs When the quantities of plant and equipment cannot be altered.

Scale of plant This scale is determined by fixed inputs.

Variable inputs Inputs that a manager can vary in quantity in the short run.

TABLE 6.1

Fixed, Variable, and Total Costs: Media Corporation

Units of Output Q	Total Fixed Cost (Dollars per Day) TFC	Total Variable Cost (Dollars per Day) TVC	Total Cost (Dollars per Day) TC
0	100	0	100
1	100	40	140
2	100	64	164
3	100	78	178
4	100	88	188
5	100	100	200
5.5	100	108.625	208.625
6	100	120	220
6.64	100	139.6	239.6
7	100	154	254
8	100	208	308
9	100	288	388
10	100	400	500

We consider three short-run cost concepts: fixed, variable, and total. **Total fixed cost** (*TFC*) is the total cost per period of time incurred for fixed inputs. Because the level of fixed inputs is constant (by definition), the firm's total fixed cost does not vary with output. Examples of fixed costs are depreciation of plant and equipment and property taxes. Table 6.1 shows that the fixed cost of the Media Corporation, a producer of sofas, is $100 per day. This is visually shown in Figure 6.1. If Q is equal to total output, the values in Table 6.1 (and in Table 6.2) come from the total cost relationship

$$TC = 100 + 50Q - 11Q^2 + Q^3$$

Total variable cost (*TVC*) is the total cost incurred by managers for variable inputs. These costs increase as output rises because greater output requires more inputs and higher variable costs. For example, the greater the output of a woolen mill, the larger the quantity of wool used and the higher the total cost of the wool. The Media Corporation's total variable cost schedule is shown in Table 6.1. Figure 6.1 shows the corresponding total variable cost function. Up to a particular output rate (four units of output), total variable costs rise at a decreasing rate; beyond that output level, they increase at an increasing rate. This characteristic of the total variable cost function follows from the law of diminishing marginal

Total fixed cost (*TFC*) The total cost per period of time incurred for fixed inputs.

Total variable cost (*TVC*) The total cost incurred by managers for variable inputs.

175

FIGURE 6.1

Fixed, Variable, and Total Costs: Media Corporation

Fixed costs do not vary with output, so the fixed cost curve is a horizontal line. Variable costs at first increase with output at a decreasing rate and then increase with output at an increasing rate. The total cost curve is the vertical summation of the fixed cost curve and the average variable cost curve. The total cost function and the total variable cost function have the same shape because they differ by only a constant amount, which is total fixed cost.

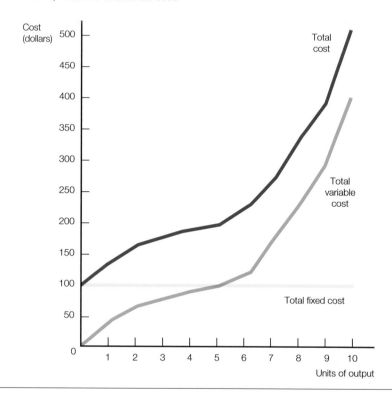

returns. At low levels of output, increasing the variable inputs may increase productivity, with the result that total variable costs rise with output but at a decreasing rate. (More will be said about this later.)

Finally, **total cost** (*TC*) is the sum of total fixed and total variable costs. To derive the total cost column in Table 6.1, add the total fixed cost and total variable cost at each output level. The total cost function for the Media Corporation is also shown in Figure 6.1. The total cost function and the total variable cost function have the same shape because they differ by only a constant amount, which is total fixed cost.

Managers want to allocate resources efficiently (remember, they are scarce). They want to choose the input bundle that produces a given output at the lowest

Total cost (*TC*) The sum of total fixed and total variable costs.

possible cost. Costs are a function of the production process and input prices, so managers need to understand the behavior of costs as output changes. One indicator of this behavior is found in average and marginal costs.

AVERAGE AND MARGINAL COSTS

Although the total cost of producing a product is important, from an operational viewpoint, knowledge of the average and marginal cost functions is key. These functions predict the behavior of costs as output changes. There are three average cost functions, corresponding to the three total cost functions. **Average fixed cost** (*AFC*) is total fixed cost divided by output. *AFC* necessarily declines with increases in output; mathematically, the function is a rectangular hyperbola. Table 6.2 and Figure 6.2 show the *AFC* function for the Media Corporation.

Average fixed cost (*AFC*) The total fixed cost divided by output.

     Average variable cost (*AVC*) is total variable cost divided by output. This indicator tells managers the variable cost, on average, of each unit of output. For the Media Corporation, the *AVC* function is shown in Table 6.2 and Figure 6.2. Initially,

Average variable cost (*AVC*) The total variable cost divided by output.

TABLE 6.2

Average and Marginal Costs: Media Corporation

Units of Output Q	Average Fixed Cost (Dollars) TFC/Q	Average Variable Cost (Dollars) TVC/Q	Average Total Cost (Dollars) TC/Q	Marginal Cost (Dollars) $\Delta TC/\Delta Q$[a]	Marginal Cost (Dollars) dTC/dQ[a]
0	—	—	—	—	—
1	100	40	140	40	31
2	50	32	82	24	18
3	33.33	26	59.33	14	11
4	25	22	47	10	10
5	20	20	40	12	15
5.5	18.18	19.75	37.93		19.75
6	16.67	20	36.67	20	26
6.64	15.06	21.04	36.11		36.11
7	14.29	22	36.29	34	43
8	12.5	26	38.5	54	66
9	11.11	32	43.11	80	95
10	10	40	50	112	130

[a] The figures in the $\Delta TC/\Delta Q$ column pertain to the interval between the indicated amount of quantity and one unit less than the indicated amount of quantity. The figures in the dTC/dQ column are the continuous marginal cost—that is $dTC/dQ = MC = 50 - 22Q + 3Q^2$.

FIGURE 6.2

Average and Marginal Cost Curves: Media Corporation

Average fixed cost continually decreases as output increases. Average variable cost and average total cost at first decrease, reach a minimum, then increase as output increases. The minimum of the average total cost occurs at a higher output than the minimum of the average variable cost. The average total cost curve is the vertical summation of the average fixed cost and the average variable cost curves. Marginal cost passes through the minimum of both average cost curves, and when marginal cost is below the average cost, average cost falls and vice versa. Average total cost achieves its minimum at a higher output rate (6.64) than average variable cost (5.5) because the increases in average variable cost are, up to a point, more than offset by decreases in average fixed cost.

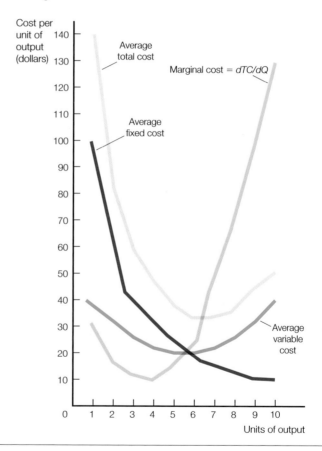

increasing output results in decreases in *AVC*. However, as output increases, at some point of increased production, *AVC* rises, thus increasing the average variable cost per unit.

Last chapter we said the behavior of cost is largely determined by the production function. Now we can show why. *AVC* is simply total variable cost divided by the number of units produced (TVC/Q). Let U be the number of input units used and W the cost per unit of input. It is then true that

$$AVC = \frac{TVC}{Q} = W\frac{U}{Q}$$

We defined average product in Chapter 5 as

$$AP = \frac{Q}{U}$$

Hence AP is the inverse of U/Q. Now we can express AVC as

$$AVC = W\frac{1}{AP} \qquad (6.1)$$

So one way for managers to think of AVC is as the inverse of average product times the cost per unit of input. Recall the behavior of the average product. It initially increases with output, reaches a maximum, and then begins to decrease. Because of their inverse relationship, AVC mirrors the behavior of AP. When AP increases, AVC decreases; when AP decreases, AVC increases. So we expect AVC to initially decrease, hit a minimum, and then increase.

Average total cost (ATC) is total cost divided by output. For the Media Corporation, the ATC function is shown in Table 6.2 and Figure 6.2. ATC is simply the sum of $AFC + AVC$. Its shape is similar to AVC but higher at all output levels due to the effect of fixed costs. At output levels where both AFC and AVC decrease, ATC must decrease too. However, ATC reaches its minimum at output levels relatively higher than AVC because increases in average variable cost are for a time more than offset by decreases in average fixed cost (which must decrease as output increases).

Average total cost (ATC) The total cost divided by output.

Marginal cost (MC) is the incremental cost of producing an additional unit of output. If $C(Q)$ is the total cost of producing Q units of output, the marginal cost between Q and $(Q - 1)$ units of output is $C(Q) - C(Q - 1)$. For the Media Corporation, the marginal cost function is shown in Table 6.2 and Figure 6.2. At low output levels, MC may decrease (as it does in Figure 6.2) with increases in output; but after reaching a minimum, it increases (like AVC) with additional output. We saw why this is true last chapter when we discussed diminishing marginal returns. If ΔTVC is the change in total variable costs resulting from a change in output of ΔQ and if ΔTFC is the change in total fixed costs resulting from a change in output of ΔQ then

Marginal cost (MC) The incremental cost of producing an additional unit of output.

$$MC = \frac{\Delta TVC + \Delta TFC}{\Delta Q}$$

But ΔTFC is zero because fixed costs can't vary; therefore

$$MC = \frac{\Delta TVC}{\Delta Q}$$

Hence the cost of the input is given by $\Delta TVC = W(\Delta U)$, where W is the cost per unit of input and ΔU is the change in the units of input needed to produce the increase of ΔQ in output. Consequently,

$$MC = W\frac{\Delta U}{\Delta Q}$$

Last chapter we defined MP as

$$MP = \frac{\Delta Q}{\Delta L}$$

Hence we can define MC as

$$MC = W\frac{1}{MP}$$

So like the inverse nature of AP and AVC, the behavior of MP is inverse to that of MC. Marginal cost is simply the cost per unit of input times the inverse of its marginal product. Let's think about why this is true. Say a unit of labor costs $10. If the MP of a unit of labor is 10, the MC of producing the last unit of output is $1 ($10/10). But if the MP of that unit of labor is 1, the MC is $10. As MP increases, MC decreases; and when MP decreases, MC increases. We saw that the behavior of marginal product is to increase, attain a maximum, and then decline with increases in output; marginal cost normally decreases, attains a minimum, and then increases.

QUANT OPTION

If the total cost function is continuous, marginal cost is defined as dTC/dQ, where TC is total cost. Suppose, for example, using the Media Corporation's total cost function,

$$TC = 100 + 50Q - 11Q^2 + Q^3$$

where TC is expressed in thousands of dollars and Q is expressed in units of output. This firm's marginal cost function is

$$MC = \frac{dTC}{dQ} = 50 - 22Q + 3Q^2$$

TABLE 6.3

Relationship of Average Product and Marginal Product to Average Variable Cost and Marginal Cost: Thomas Machine Company

L	Q	AP_L	$MP_L =$ dQ/dL	W	$AVC =$ W/AP_L	$MC =$ W/MP_L
0	0	—	—	390	—	—
1	49	49	67	390	7.96	5.82
2	132	66	98	390	5.91	3.98
3	243	81	123	390	4.81	3.17
4	376	94	142	390	4.15	2.75
5	525	105	155	390	3.71	2.52
6	684	114	162	390	3.42	2.41
6.67	792.6	118.9	163.33	390	3.28	2.388 ← MP_L max
7	847	121	163	390	3.22	2.393 so MC min
8	1008	126	158	390	3.10	2.47
9	1161	129	147	390	3.02	2.65
10	1300	130	130	390	3.00 ← AP_L max	3.00
11	1419	129	107	390	3.02 so AVC min	3.64
12	1512	126	78	390	3.10	5.00
13	1573	121	43	390	3.22	9.07
14	1596	114	2	390	3.42	195.00
15	1575	105	−45	390	3.71	—

The relationship between production and cost is shown in Table 6.3. Consider the previous definitions of the production function of the Thomas Machine Company ($Q = 30L + 20L^2 - L^3$) from the last chapter. If the wage rate is 390, Table 6.3 shows the relationship between average product and average variable cost and between marginal product and marginal cost. As you can see, when AP is maximized, AVC is minimized. Likewise, we see that MC equals AVC when average variable cost is minimized. This is to be expected because $MP = AP$ when AP is maximized. Average product is maximized when 10 units of labor are employed (at 130); average variable cost is minimized when 10 units of labor are employed (at 3); and marginal cost is also equal to 3 when 10 units of labor are employed.

Marginal cost always equals average variable cost when the latter is at a minimum (because $MP = AP$, when AP is maximized). If the cost function of Thomas is $TC = 100 + 50Q - 11Q^2 + Q^3$, then the firm's AVC is

$$AVC = \frac{TVC}{Q} = 50 - 11Q + Q^2$$

If we take the ΔAVC with respect to ΔQ and set it equal to zero, we find the value of Q where AVC is at a minimum

$$\frac{\Delta AVC}{\Delta Q} = -11 + 2Q = 0$$

$$Q = 5.5$$

When Q equals 5.5, both marginal cost and average variable cost equal \$19.75. (Substitute 5.5 for Q in the preceding equations for MC and AVC and see for yourself that this is true.) Therefore, as pointed out, $MC = AVC$ when AVC is at a minimum. Note also that marginal cost equals average total cost when the latter is at a minimum. The firm's average total cost is

$$ATC = (100/Q) + 50 - 11Q + Q^2$$

If we take ΔATC with respect to ΔQ and set it equal to zero, we find the value of Q where ATC is at a minimum

$$\frac{\Delta ATC}{\Delta Q} = \left(\frac{-100}{Q^2}\right) - 11 + 2Q = 0$$

Or

$$2Q^3 - 11Q^2 - 100 = 0$$

This is solved for $Q = 6.64$. Substituting 6.64 into the ATC and MC equations yields $MC = ATC = 36.11$.

QUANT OPTION

Here's some fun!

$$\frac{dAVC}{dQ} = \frac{d\left(\frac{VC}{Q}\right)}{dQ}$$

$$\frac{\left[Q\left(\frac{dVC}{dQ}\right) - VC\left(\frac{dQ}{dQ}\right)\right]}{Q^2}$$

$$\frac{\left[\left(\frac{dVC}{dQ}\right) - \left(\frac{VC}{Q}\right)\right]}{Q} = 0$$

which implies

$$\left(\frac{dVC}{dQ}\right) - \left(\frac{VC}{Q}\right) = MC - AVC = 0$$

Or
$$MC = AVC$$

PROBLEM SOLVED: The Effects of Output on the Cost of Producing Aircraft

The National Research Council conducted a study of the U.S. aircraft industry, which stresses the importance to airplane manufacturers of serving the entire world market. As evidence, the council presents the following graph.

Problems

1. As indicated in this graph, the cost per airplane of producing 525 aircraft of a particular type is about 10% higher than the cost per airplane of producing 700 aircraft of this type. Assuming this graph pertains to the short run, by what percentage does average fixed cost increase if 525 rather than 700 aircraft are produced?

2. If average fixed cost is 30% of average total cost if 700 aircraft are produced and 36% of average total cost if 525 aircraft are produced, is it true that aver-

age total cost is about 10% higher if 525 rather than 700 aircraft are produced?

Solutions

1. If the number of aircraft produced is 525 rather than 700, average fixed cost is $TFC/525$ rather than $TFC/700$, where TFC equals total fixed cost. Therefore, average fixed cost increases by 33%.

2. For 700 aircraft, average total cost equals $X/0.30 = 3.33X$, where X is average fixed cost when 700 aircraft are produced. For 525 aircraft, average total cost equals $1.33X/0.36 = 3.69X$ because average fixed cost equals $1.33X$ when 525 aircraft are produced. Therefore, average total cost increases by about 11% (from $3.33X$ to $3.69X$) if 525 rather than 700 aircraft are produced.

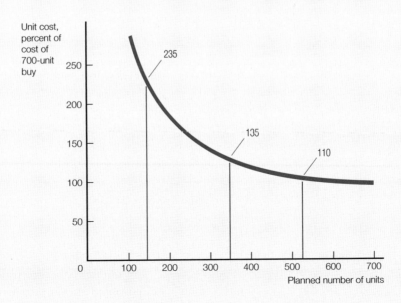

Note that we define marginal cost in two ways. The first ($\Delta TC/\Delta Q$) assumes we can produce only in discrete units, like a car or a cake. The second (dTC/dQ) assumes we can produce on a continuous basis, as in 3.14 tons of grain or 10.33 gallons of gasoline. Which definition managers use depends on the situation: Is the manager constrained to an integer output level or can she produce fractions of the product?

LONG-RUN COST FUNCTIONS

In the long run all inputs are variable, and managers can build any scale or type of plant. There are no fixed costs in the long run because no inputs are fixed; so there is nothing to stop a manager from being as efficient as possible. Thinking about the long run requires managers to focus more on the destination rather than the route. As we show in Chapters 11 and 12, managers need to actively anticipate the future and think toward it.

When Toyota managers consider building a new U.S. plant, they can build one of any size at any location; there are boundless choices. But once the investment is made, type and size of plant and equipment are to a considerable extent frozen.

Assume managers are looking to construct one of three alternative scales of plant; the short-run average cost functions for these scales of plant are represented by $G_1G_{1'}$, $G_2G_{2'}$, and $G_3G_{3'}$, in Figure 6.3. In the long run managers can choose any of the three plants. Which scale is most profitable? Obviously the answer depends on the manager's beliefs about long-run product demand because she needs to produce at the minimum average cost.

We can see this in Figure 6.3. If the manager anticipates product demand of around Q, she should build the smallest plant. At these sales, the average cost per unit sold is equal to C. If the manager builds the medium-sized or largest plant, the average cost per unit is higher at Q. If the manager believes that demand will be equal to S, she should build the largest plant (G_3).

Long-run average cost function *(LAC)* Function showing the mini-mum cost per unit of all output levels when any desired size plant is built.

The **long-run average cost function** (*LAC*) shows the minimum cost per unit of all output levels when any desired size plant is built. In Figure 6.3 the long-run average cost function is the solid portion of the short-run average cost functions, $G_1DEG_{3'}$. Any point on the long-run average cost function is also a point on a short-run average cost function. In fact, it is a point on the lowest-cost short-run cost function for the given output level. So when given the freedom (that is, in the long run), managers want to choose the plant scale that minimizes average cost. The broken-line segments of the short-run functions are not included because they are not the lowest average costs, as is obvious from the figure.

Toyota managers can choose from more than three plant scales: They can choose from an infinite number of possibilities. However, managers must understand that once they commit funds to building a plant, they immediately shift to a short-run cost function. Figure 6.4 depicts this decision. The minimum average

FIGURE 6.3

Short-Run Average Cost Functions for Various Scales of Plant

The long-run average cost function is the solid portion of the short-run average cost functions, G_1DEG_3'.

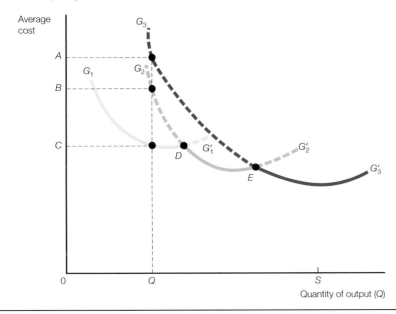

FIGURE 6.4

Long-Run Average Cost Function

The long-run average cost function, which shows the minimum long-run cost per unit of producing each output level, is the envelope of the short-run functions.

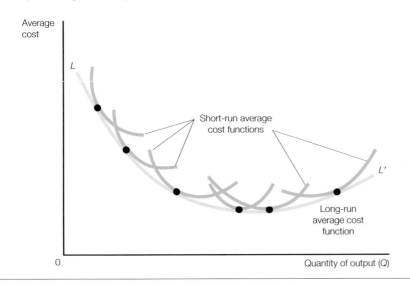

PROBLEM SOLVED: Managerial Use of Cost Functions

To illustrate the relationship between a firm's long-run and short-run cost functions, consider a Martin division that produces MP3 players. Managers have been told to cut costs, so they need to create an efficient input bundle. Engineers estimate the division's production function as

$$Q = 4(KL)^{0.5} \qquad (6.2)$$

where Q is output (in thousands of MP3 players per month), K is the capital used per month (in thousands of units), and L is the number of hours of labor employed per month (in thousands). Because laborers are paid \$8 per hour and capital costs equal \$2 per unit, Martin's total cost (in thousands of dollars per month) equals

$$TC = 8L + 2K = \frac{Q^2}{2K} + 2K \qquad (6.3)$$

Equation (6.2) implies that

$$L = \frac{Q^2}{16K}$$

In the short run, managers cannot vary their level of capital, so K is fixed. The division presently uses 10,000 units of capital ($K = 10$). Substituting 10 for K in equation (6.3), we find that the short-run cost function is

$$TC_S = \frac{Q^2}{20} + 20 \qquad (6.4)$$

where TC_S is short-run total cost. Therefore, the short-run average total cost function is

$$AC_S = \frac{TC_S}{Q} = \frac{Q}{20} + \frac{20}{Q}$$

and the short-run marginal cost function is

$$MC_S = \frac{\Delta TC_S}{\Delta Q} = \frac{Q}{10}$$

In the long run, managers can buy new machines or sell current ones, so no input is fixed. If Martin managers want to minimize total costs, they need to choose the optimal level of capital needed to produce Q MP3 players. Basing their estimates on equation (6.3), they find that

$$\frac{\Delta TC}{\Delta K} = -\frac{Q^2}{2K^2} + 2$$

Setting this equal to zero, we find that the cost-minimizing value of K is

$$K = \frac{Q}{2}$$

This decision rule tells the managers to estimate expected demand and then purchase capital equal to one-half of demand. Substituting $Q/2$ for K in equation (6.3), we see that the long-run cost function is

$$TC_L = 2Q \qquad (6.5)$$

where TC_L is long-run total cost. Because $TC_L/Q = 2$, the long-run average cost equals \$2 per MP3 player. The long-run marginal cost is also \$2 for MP3 players because $\Delta TC_L/\Delta Q = 2$.

Short-Run Average and Marginal Costs and Long-Run Average Cost, Martin Division

Because the long-run average cost function is horizontal, it is tangent to the short-run average cost function at the latter's minimum point.

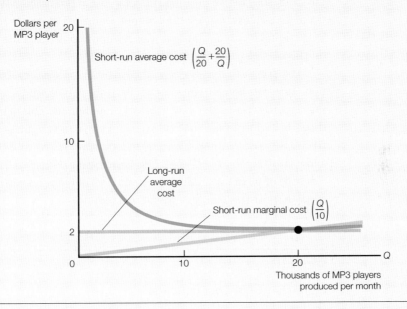

The figure shows the relationship between Martin's short run average and marginal costs and its long-run average costs. As managers expect, the short-run marginal cost function intersects the short-run average cost function at its minimum point, where $Q = 20$ and $AC_S = 2$, in this case. Because it is horizontal (owing to constant returns to scale), the long-run average cost function is tangent to the short-run average cost function at the latter's minimum point. Many long-run average cost functions are not horizontal. Instead they have what we call *scale economies*: As the plant size varies, so does the average unit cost. As discussed in the following section, there are economies of scale (over at least some range of output) in a wide variety of markets and processes. Smart managers use these scale economies to create competitive advantage.

cost of producing all outputs is given by the long-run *AC* function, *LL'*. Each point on *LL'* is also a point on a short-run *AC* function. At that output level, it is a point on the lowest-cost short-run *AC* function; it is the best an efficient manager can do. The two functions are tangent at that point. (Mathematically, the long-run average cost function is the envelope of the short-run functions.)

Managers who estimate the long-run average cost of producing any given output can readily derive the long-run total cost of production: It is simply the product of long-run average cost and output. Figure 6.5 shows the relationship between long-run total cost and output; this relationship is called the **long-run total cost function**.

Managers can readily derive the **long-run marginal cost function**. This function represents how varying output affects the cost of producing the last unit if the manager has chosen the most efficient input bundle. This marginal cost function shows behavior similar to average costs. Long-run marginal cost is less than *LAC* when *LAC* is decreasing; it is equal to long-run *LAC* when *LAC* is at a minimum; and it is greater than *LAC* when *LAC* is increasing. When managers build the optimal scale of plant for producing a given level of output, long-run marginal cost is equal to short-run marginal cost at that output.

Long-run total cost function The relationship between long-run total cost and output.

Long-run marginal cost function Function representing how varying output affects the cost of producing the last unit if the manager has chosen the most efficient input bundle.

FIGURE 6.5

Long-Run Total Cost Function

The long-run total cost of a given output level equals the long-run average cost (given in Figure 6.4) times output.

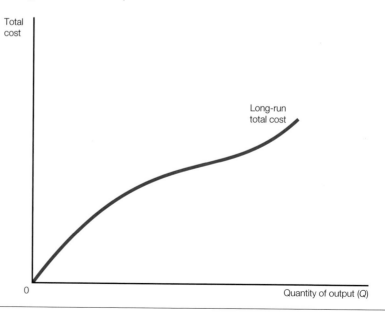

QUANT OPTION

Never believe everything you read; always ask for the proof.

Suppose the long-run average cost of producing an output rate of Q is $L(Q)$, and the short-run AC of producing it with the ith scale of plant is $A_i(Q)$. Let $M(Q)$ be the long-run MC and $R_i(Q)$ be the short-run MC with the ith scale of plant. If the manager maximizes profit, she is operating where short-run and long-run average costs are equal; in other words, $L(Q) = A_i(Q)$. This means that

$$\frac{dL(Q)}{dQ} = \frac{dA_i(Q)}{dQ} \text{ and } Q\frac{dL(Q)}{dQ} = Q\frac{dA_i(Q)}{dQ}$$

From these conditions, it is easy to prove that the long-run marginal cost, $M(Q)$, equals the short-run marginal cost, $R_i(Q)$

$$M(Q) = \frac{d[QL(Q)]}{dQ} = L(Q) + \frac{QdL(Q)}{dQ}$$

$$R_i(Q) = \frac{d[QA_i(Q)]}{dQ} = A_i(Q) + \frac{QdA_i(Q)}{dQ}$$

We know from the previous paragraph that $L(Q) = A_i(Q)$ and $QdL(Q)/dQ = QdA_i(Q)/dQ$; so it follows that $R_i(Q)$ must equal $M(Q)$.

QUANT OPTION

$$dTC_S/dQ = Q/10$$

$$dTC/dK = -(Q^2/2K^2) + 2 = 0$$

$$dTC_L/dQ = 2$$

MANAGERIAL USE OF SCALE ECONOMIES

Long-run average cost curves tell managers whether bigger is better: They show whether, and to what extent, larger plants have cost advantages over smaller ones. **Economies of scale** occur when the firm's average unit cost decreases as output increases. To illustrate, consider nursing homes, which make up an industry with

Economies of scale When the firm's average unit cost decreases as output increases.

FIGURE 6.6

Long-Run Average Cost Curve for Texas Nursing Homes

For nursing homes with fewer than 60,000 patient–days, there seem to be substantial economies of scale.

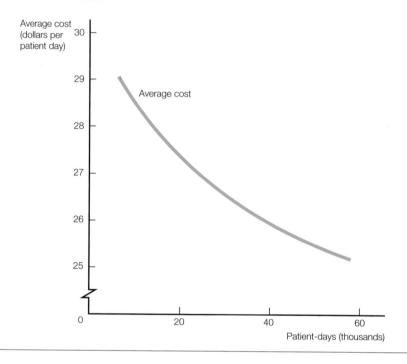

annual sales of over $190 billion in 2011. Figure 6.6 shows the long-run average cost curve for a nursing home.

As you can see, there are substantial economies of scale. If a nursing home provides 10,000 patient–days of service per year, the cost per patient–day is almost $29; if it provides about 50,000 patient–days of service per year, the cost per patient–day is under $26. Curves like Figure 6.6 are estimated by engineers and economists for a wide variety of plants and processes; they help managers choose optimal input bundles.

Scale economies are not confined to plants. In our global economy, managers often use more than one plant to produce their product. Nike is a good example. Managers at such companies have the opportunity to exploit possible scale economies at the firm level. For example, holding the size of each plant constant, average cost may decrease in response to increases in the number of plants operated by Nike. Managers could create cost savings for several reasons, including centralized purchasing, better management techniques, or an improved ability to build or lease plants.

Managers use many sources of scale economies to create competitive advantages. Managers at UPS use them in their distribution network to decrease costs. Exxon Mobil managers use them to decrease costs in their refining and chemical process. Managers at BskyB, the British pay television server, can pay more for some content because of scale economies in its large network. Finally, the size of cruise ships keeps growing because larger ships have a lower cost per passenger thanks to scale economies. Royal Caribbean continues this trend with the launching of the *Oasis of the Seas* ship in 2010; this 225,000-ton ship can carry 6,296 passengers. When asked why bigger is better, Harri Kulovaara of Royal Caribbean noted, "Having more real estate, we can provide more deck area. That means more entertainment options and better amenities."[1]

Managers must understand their cost relationships to recognize where to best exploit scale economies. As we have seen, scale economies are not confined to production; they are found in distribution, raising capital, advertising, and most business processes. All managers have the opportunity to exploit scale economies in some form, though some fail to recognize their opportunities.

However, bigger is not always better. As plants, distribution networks, or cruise ships get bigger, at some point managing them gets harder. Increasing size eventually causes **diseconomies of scale**: Average costs per unit of output increase, usually because of the complexity of managing and coordinating all the necessary activities.

Diseconomies of scale When the average costs per unit of output increase.

MANAGERIAL USE OF SCOPE ECONOMIES

Scale economies are not the only cost economies managers can exploit. A cost efficiency strategy available to managers of multiproduct firms is called **economies of scope**. These economies exist when the cost of producing two (or more) products jointly is less than the cost of producing each one alone. For example, suppose managers of the Martin Company can produce 1,000 milling machines and 500 lathes per year at a cost of $15 million, whereas if the firm produced only 1,000 milling machines, the cost would be $12 million, and if it produced only 500 lathes, the cost would be $6 million. In this case the cost of producing both the milling machines and the lathes is less than the total cost of producing each separately. Hence there are scope economies.

Economies of scope Exist when the cost of jointly producing two (or more) products is less than the cost of producing each one alone.

A simple way for managers to estimate the extent of their scope economies is to use the following measure

$$S = \frac{C(Q_1) + C(Q_2) - C(Q_1 + Q_2)}{C(Q_1 + Q_2)}$$

(6.6)

Here S is the degree of economies of scope, $C(Q_1)$ is the cost of producing Q_1 units of the first product alone, $C(Q_2)$ is the cost of producing Q_2 units of the second product alone, and $C(Q_1 + Q_2)$ is the cost of producing Q_1 units of the

1. J. Wise, "World's Largest Cruise Ship Pulls 360s with Joystick," *Popular Mechanics*, June 2007.

first product in combination with Q_2 units of the second product. If there are economies of scope, S is greater than zero because the cost of producing both products together—$C(Q_1 + Q_2)$—is less than the cost of producing each alone—$C(Q_1) + C(Q_2)$. Clearly S measures the percentage of saving that results from producing them jointly rather than individually. Managers of the Martin Company calculate the following

$$S = \frac{\$12 \text{ million} + \$6 \text{ million} - \$15 \text{ million}}{\$15 \text{ million}} = 0.20$$

which means scope economies have lowered their costs by an estimated 20%. Strategically, managers of Martin have created a 20% cost advantage relative to managers of single-product firms. Obviously, the larger is the value of S, the greater are the scope economies.

STRATEGY SESSION: Economies of Scope in Advertising Agencies

In recent years there has been considerable controversy over the extent to which there are economies of scope in the advertising industry. An advertising agency can use many media, including network television, general magazines, newspapers, radio, outdoor ads, the Internet, and cell phones.

Researchers have looked at the percentage of cost reduction from joint production at several hundred advertising agencies and found the following cost savings.

As you can see, the cost savings from joint production of these products range from essentially zero to about 86%, depending on which advertising agency is considered. On the average, the cost saving is about 26%. Clearly advertising has very substantial economies of scope; and smaller firms seem to enjoy greater scope economies than larger firms.

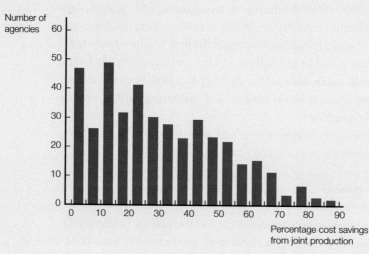

STRATEGY SESSION: Economies of Scope

First we had individual firms, then conglomerates, and now perhaps a trend of returning to individual firms focusing on core competencies.

The argument for conglomerates were those of economies of scope—that is, one could produce X and Y cheaper together, $C(X, Y)$, than producing X and Y separately, $C(X) + C(Y)$, on the supply side. Conglomerates also serve as a portfolio diversified "mutual fund" for investors on the demand side. The leader of conglomerates is ITT, which had over 300 separate businesses in the 1960s.

But some have argued that the emperor had no clothes, that conglomerates had overpaid (acquisitions are usually at a premium), and that managers often knew little of the intricacies of the businesses they had acquired. Economies of scope didn't materialize in many conglomerates and, in fact, evidence of diseconomies existed—does Daimler-Chrysler ring a bell? If investors wanted to diversify their portfolios, they could make their own portfolio by purchasing the stocks of separate companies or buying existing mutual funds.

Recently ITT, Fortune Brands, Marathon Oil, and Cargill, among others, have announced breakups of their companies. These would be what are called spin-

offs. In a spinoff, the base company (say ITT) issues shares specifically for the division they wish to spin-off and distributes them on a pro rata basis to their base shareholders. These shareholders can hold the shares or sell them. Spinoffs are used, for example, when the base company can't sell the subsidiary. Sometimes the base company loads the spinoff with weak portions of the base company's management and debt. Not a recipe for success of the spinoff.

Some conglomerates, such as General Electric, Berkshire Hathaway, and United Technologies, have been historically successful, constantly reinventing themselves by adding new subsidiaries and shedding old ones, but always with the goal of economies of scope and risk diversifying and not growth for growth's sake. Some recent acquisitions, such as Disney's acquisition of Marvel and eBay's acquisition of PayPal, would seem to make sense from a scope perspective and because of their demand complementarities.

Source: Steven M. Davidoff, "A Test to See If the Parts Are Worth More Than the Whole," *New York Times*, January 18, 2011, at http://dealbook.nytimes.com/2011/1/18.

Like scale economies, managers can exploit scope economies across a range of markets, processes, and behavior. Oil firms like Exxon Mobil and British Petroleum produce both petroleum and chemical products; drug firms like Merck and GlaxoSmithKline produce both vaccines and tranquilizers; and publisher W. W. Norton publishes both economics and literature textbooks. Both Coca-Cola and Pepsi use single trucks to deliver an assortment of flavors and sizes of drinks. Most airlines fly both passengers and cargo. Managers use scope economies to create cost advantages by producing multiple products rather than just one. Often these cost savings arise because the products share either processes (like distribution) or resources (such as components). However, just as with diseconomies of scale, there can be diseconomies of scope. Many conglomerates, such as General

Why do some firms organize as conglomerates whereas others produce in just one line of business? The latter argue for "core competency"—doing what they do best, whereas the former argue for economies of scope and diversification of risk. Those who have disassembled conglomerates argue that the whole is worth less than the sum of its parts (for example, Cendent, which was built and then dismantled by Henry Silverman). Those who favor con-

glomerates, such as General Electric and Siemens, argue the reverse and point to synergies of idea generation and the ability to use personnel across businesses.

On the risk-diversification side, critics argue that as capital markets have become more sophisticated, global, and liquid, fund managers maintain that they can diversify risk and increase returns by purchasing securities across multiple sectors.

Electric, continue to subtract (and add) from their lines of business when it is no longer profitable for them to produce a particular product.

TRANSACTIONS COSTS CAN TAKE MANY FORMS

Consider our consumer, Ms. Popovich. She may not know the price of the unit of food in Chapter 3 precisely. But she may know that it typically ranges from P_{Fmax} to P_{Fmin}. Suppose that she currently finds the item at P_{F2}, near the high of P_{Fmax}. She may wish to continue to search for the item knowing that it's likely that she will find it for a lower price. However, searching takes time (even online) and may involve transportation costs (traveling among potential suppliers). What should Ms. Popovich do? She should consider the expected benefits of more search (a lower price) versus the costs of the search (time and money).

The same analysis would apply for a manager faced with input costs that vary. Consider a corporate recruiter. Should she interview at schools X, Y, and B, or just at X? If her experience at school X has been that she most often finds the right person for the job there, she may not visit the other schools. But if her experience is that sometimes X yields the best person and sometimes Y does, she may want to schedule both schools. And what about up and coming school B? Of course, the more schools she visits, the larger the costs, such as the opportunity costs of work she would be doing for her firm if not recruiting—travel, and lodging costs, and so on. The authors are always amazed at the number of management personnel from investment banks and consulting firms that come to Philadelphia for a corporate show and tell. As with Ms. Popovich, the recruiter must consider the expected benefits of more search with the costs of the search.

Another transaction cost is negotiation. Consider our case of the Haddonfield Brewery and the Cherry Hill Chemical Company in Chapter 17. In this example, *in the absence of negotiation costs*, the cheapest (and societially optimal) way to solve the problem was for Haddonfield to pay Cherry Hill to filter its own effluent if Cherry Hill is not liable for the damages its effluent causes or for Cherry Hill to filter its own effluent if Cherry Hill is liable for its damages.

But suppose that Cherry Hill is not liable, and negotiation costs are $10,001, with Cherry Hill's cost N_C and Haddonfield's costs N_H, where $N_C + N_H = 10,001$ or $N_H = 10,001 - N_C$. Recall that Cherry Hill can filter its outgoing water for a cost of $40,000, whereas Haddonfield can filter its incoming water for a cost of $50,000.

Since Cherry Hill is not liable, it is entitled to make its full profit of $500,000. In order for Cherry Hill to filter its outgoing water, Haddonfield must pay Cherry Hill at least the costs ($40,000) of Cherry Hill's filtering (since Cherry Hill is not obligated to do so). Call this payment P. Clearly, Haddonfield won't pay Cherry Hill more than $50,000 (since Haddonfield could filter the incoming water themselves for $50,000). With Haddonfield currently filtering its incoming water for $50,000, Haddonfield's profits are $200,000. For Haddonfield to be willing to negotiate, they must make more than their current profit of $200,000.

Thus for Cherry Hill to be willing to negotiate with Haddonfield, the following condition must hold

$$\$500,000 - \$40,000 + P - N_C \geq \$500,000$$

Or
$$P - N_C \geq \$40,000$$

For Haddonfield to be willing to negotiate with Cherry Hill, the following condition must hold

$$\$250,000 - P - N_H \geq \$200,000$$

Or
$$\$250,000 - P - (\$10,000 - N_C) \geq \$200,000$$

Or
$$\$240,000 - P + N_C \geq \$200,000$$

Or
$$\$40,000 \geq P - N_C$$

Clearly $P - N_C$ can't be simultaneously greater and less than $40,000 and so negotiation costs greater than $10,000 will preclude the socially optimal outcome (and lead to the more expensive way of cleaning up the pollution problem—that is, Haddonfield paying $50,000 to filter the incoming water).

The important lesson is that inclusion of transaction costs can change some of our outcomes. If negotiation costs were less than $10,000, the most efficient solution (Cherry Hill filtering for $40,000) would occur.

When we considered sophisticated pricing in Chapters 9 and 10, it was necessary to "segment and seal" the markets. The segmenting entails more sophisticated demand analysis than a single price monopoly requires. Such analysis requires more time and money to carry out. First-degree price discrimination (Chapter 9) may require bargaining (haggling) between the buyer and the seller. This requires more salespeople as compared to a single posted price strategy. In addition, the sophisticated pricer must seal the market to prevent resale from a low-price buyer to a high-price buyer. This entails some sort of screening, such as Disney's technique of requiring visitors to show a driver's license at the time of entry to their parks. Such screening costs money, for it takes extra time to screen each buyer. In the example of Honest Sanjay in Chapter 9, as long as these extra costs of segmenting and sealing the market are less than $15.5, Sanjay will practice first-degree price discrimination. Since so many real world firms practice price discrimination, we conclude that the transaction costs of doing so are exceeded by the benefits of practicing sophisticated pricing. One of the advantages of auctions cited in Chapter 13 is the elimination of haggling transaction costs for items when the seller had a difficult time identifying the reservation price of the potential buyers.

Firms have used transaction costs to lock in customers. Consider the long-term cell phone contracts. With a two-year contract with company X, you're less likely to switch to company Y when you see Y's new phone and rates, which might appear attractive to a new buyer. That's because the penalty costs associated with breaking the contract with X exceed the benefits of the new phone/plan with Y. Most consumers, when confronted by a side-by-side comparison of Colgate and Crest toothpastes in the grocery store in which one brand was $0.50 more expensive, would switch brands in a heartbeat to the cheaper one. We should all remember our lessons about sunk costs when doing our benefit/transaction cost analysis.

Consider the transaction costs your instructor faces when switching textbooks. She is already very familiar with her current adoption. She has tailored her notes and examples to the book. A new text will have different notation and examples. In addition, publishers provide slide decks, teaching guides, test banks, links to current events relevant to the text. All of these services are available with a new text. But adopting a new text means learning how to use these new systems and revising ones notes. These are costs. Are the benefits of another text enough to offset these costs of switching? The same situation occurs when one contemplates switching from one word-processing system to another or from one spreadsheet program to another.

Game theory (Chapter 12) involves strategic thinking. How can I strike a deal that is most advantageous to me? Many large railroads sold off their sparsely used branch lines after railroad deregulation in 1980, preferring to become wholesalers concentrating on their mainline business. Branch lines were expensive for unionized large railroads to use because of their low-traffic density and their low speeds (due to poor track condition), which ate up available unionized labor hours. Non-unionized short lines took over many of these routes. Virtually no traffic both originates and terminates on the same short line. Where does the short line originated/terminated traffic go/come from? From the large railroads. And from which main lines? Generally they originate from the original owner of the branch line. Many of the short lines have only one connection. This lowers the short line's bargaining power to deal with the shares of the revenue (called *divisions*) from moving the traffic. Even when branch lines have connections with multiple main lines, contracts with the selling (or leasing) main line require that the short line tender traffic to the original owning railroad. This is a "holdup" effect, an increased cost to the short line of doing business. And it's a very clever strategy by the selling railroad, which now delivers and picks up an aggregate of cars (think wholesale) at the junction of the main line and the short line instead of engaging in the previous very costly retail business of picking up and delivering cars one or two at a time.

Transaction costs are also involved in information asymmetries (Chapters 14, 15, and 16). Individuals and firms unaware of these costs may make decisions differently if they know of these costs. Legislation such as truth in lending lets borrowers know the true cost of borrowing. Warnings that smoking cigarettes may be harmful to your health let you know that you may incur health care costs in addition to the cost of the cigarettes. Your insurance coverage may require you to undergo certain medical tests before you are allowed to pay your premium and be insured and may require certain subsequent expenditure or behavioral modifications if you are to continue to be insured. These are all costs a person needs to consider beyond the insurance premium.

Virtually all of the actions discussed in this book entail transactions costs that enable the transaction to occur (or prevent the transaction from occurring). These costs are above and beyond the obvious costs we have discussed. We have concentrated on the simple concept that there is a "cost" or a "price" to simplify the analysis, but the basic concept is always the same: You do something if the benefits exceed the costs, whereas you don't do something if the reverse is true.

For example, consider our discussion of the full costs of transportation later in this chapter on pages 218 and 219. If we consider the volume or freight moved as a function of the cost of moving freight, we will conclude that the two are inversely related. But what is that cost? It's not just the freight rate charged by the transportation mode. It's also the cost of the time in transit (opportunity cost of inventory in transit—after all, goods are dollar bills in disguise), transit time reliability (which affects safety stock—an amount of inventory held in case delivery is not on time), loss and damage cost, packaging cost, and so on. All freight demand modeling looks at all these costs in total, not just the freight rate charged by the carrier.

NETWORK ECONOMIES

Many industries involve networks. Can you imagine Alexander Graham Bell with his telephone asking Watson "Are you there," if Watson didn't have a telephone? Or if American Airlines only flew from its hub at Dallas-Fort Worth to Dallas-Fort Worth? Or if you went on Facebook and found you were the only one there? What if you could only tweet to yourself? The list goes on and on. These industries only have value because multiple people can participate. The larger the network, the more people can participate, and hence the greater their value. Because the secret of the value is in the size of the network, the first entrant in the market can secure a great advantage.

Suppose a world of six people, two of which are the above-mentioned misters Bell and Watson. If just those two have phones, then while they can call each other; the four others can't be called and none of the other four can call each other. But if Bell can get the other four people to join his phone network, then everyone can talk to everyone else. This means that $6 \times 5 = 30$ possible phone connections can be made. Going from two people with phones to six people with phones leads to a 15 times increase in the amount of potential phone calls. The cost increase to serve the additional customers can be less than 15 times (especially if the people are close together). Thus Mr. Bell can take advantage of economies of scale and scope. He has a fixed investment of running wires from each customer's home to a phone routing center (that directs the call from person A to person B), but after that investment is made, adding additional customers entails minor adjustments to the routing center and additional wire from the street to the new customer's house.

Suppose a seventh customer moves into the area and a potential new entrant is considering starting a phone service. The new entrant would have to duplicate Mr. Bell's investment and then convince potential customers that they had someone they could call. But if Mr. Bell has the first six customers tied up, the new consumer won't join the new company (there's no one to call) and would likely join Mr. Bell's network. Note that Mr. Bell's network has now become even more attractive to his existing customers because now there are 42 ($=7 \times 6$) possible connections to be made. Adding the seventh customer (a 16.67% increase) increased potential output by 40%. And these advantages for the incumbent keep rising. Adding one more customer when there are already 100 customers is a 1% increase in customers. But potential connections rise from 100×99 to 100×101, a 2.02% increase. If n is the current number of customers, an increase of one more customer (a $100/n$ percent increase) will increase the number of potential connections by $200/(n-1)$ percent. The advantage continues (and only approaches zero as n approaches infinity).

Let's define a network. To do so, and continue with the logic shown above, we'll consider a hypothetical example of Federal Express. Suppose that five communities exist that require overnight air service for one unit of product. Four of them (A through D) lie along a square with length 1 and the fifth (E) lies at the intersection of the two main diagonals. The scenario is shown in Figure 6.7.

The distances between each city pair are shown on the figure. The distances from A to D and from B to C are 1.414.

Suppose that aircraft are very expensive and that to travel one distance unit takes one time unit. Each plane can travel 1.6 distance units in the time that it takes to get a good from its origin to its destination absolutely-positively overnight. Also assume that each city wants to ship one unit of product to each other city. Planes can be purchased with any amount of capacity with larger planes being more expensive to run but with costs increasing less proportional to size because pilot/ co-pilots are necessary on any aircraft. Operating costs of an aircraft that can carry four units of product are one per distance unit while operating costs on aircraft that can carry one unit of product are 0.75 per distance unit.

One possibility (but not the only one) is to provide point-to-point service for each city pair. If this is done, there are 5 × 4 or 20 shipments required each night. This would require 20 planes and a total cost shown in Table 6.4. Each plane would operate with capacity of one. The operating cost of running this system is 14.484.

Suppose, alternatively, that point E is treated as a hub airport. All four units shipped from A (destined to B, C, D, and E) are placed on one plane with operating costs of one per distance unit. The same is true for all four shipments from B and from C and from F. Once at E, the E destined shipments are culled out. The A to B shipment is then combined with the C to B shipment and the D to B shipment,

---

FIGURE 6.7

The Network for a Hypothetical Federal Express

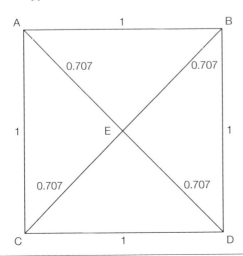

TABLE 6.4

Operating Cost if Each City Pair was Served in Point-to-Point Service

Route	Operating Cost
A to B	$0.75 = 1 \times 0.75$
B to A	0.75
A to C	0.75
C to A	0.75
A to D	$1.0605 = 0.75 \times 1.414$
D to A	1.0605
A to E	$0.53025 = 0.75 \times 0.707$
E to A	0.52025
B to C	1.0605
C to B	1.0605
B to D	0.75
D to B	0.75
B to E	0.53025
E to B	0.53025
C to D	0.75
D to C	0.75
C to E	0.53025
E to C	0.53025
D to E	0.53025
E to D	0.53025
Total	**14.484**

and the E to B shipment and all four units are shipped to B on the aircraft that came from B. The same is true for all shipments destined to A, C, and D. No plane has exceeded the 1.6 constraint, so long as this sorting at E takes less than $1.6 - 1.414$ in time. So four larger aircraft can now do the job of 20 smaller aircraft (or think that four pilots and co-pilots can now do the job of 20 pilots and co-pilots). Under this scenario, the total costs are shown in Table 6.5.

Using the hub network involves a 61% operating cost saving to provide the same output as the point-to-point service because you can do it with 20% of the aircraft and 20% of the pilots/co-pilots. When the aircraft cost, the operating cost of the aircraft, and the operating cost of the hub are combined, it turns out that it's the cheapest way to move the traffic subject to the absolutely, positively overnight constraint.

TABLE 6.5

Operating Costs if Each City is Served Via a Hub at E

Flight	Cost
A to E	$0.707 = 1 \times 0.707$
E to A	0.707
B to E	0.707
E to B	0.707
C to E	0.707
E to C	0.707
D to E	0.707
E to D	0.707
Total	**5.656**

MANAGERIAL USE OF BREAK-EVEN ANALYSIS

The concept of breaking even is a cost-based analysis that is both useful and simple. Break-even analysis looks at the relative positioning of costs and revenues; managers use it to estimate how possible pricing changes affect firm performance. Figure 6.8 shows the situation facing Martin divisional managers. They face fixed costs of $600,000 per month and average variable costs of $2 per unit. They sell their component for $3 per unit. Because average variable cost is constant, the cost of an extra unit (marginal cost) is also constant and equal to average variable cost. Given the $3 per-unit price, the revenue curve is a straight line through the origin. Martin managers create a break-even chart by plotting the firm's total revenue curve with its total cost function. The chart estimates monthly profit for all possible sales. For example, Figure 6.8 shows that if Martin managers have sales of 300,000 units per month, managers realize a loss of $300,000. The chart also estimates the **break-even point**, which is the output level that must be reached if managers are to avoid losses. This is the intersection of the cost and revenue functions; in Figure 6.8 the break-even point is 600,000 units. A useful way to represent the difference between a product's price and its average variable costs is as the money needed to "cover" the fixed costs. Once managers cover their fixed costs, the difference represents the profit per unit. For the Martin managers, each unit they sell can cover a dollar of fixed costs ($3 − $2). Because fixed costs are $600,000, they need to sell 600,000 units given this $1 difference. At the 600,000th unit, the firm's profit is $0; and after 600,000 units are sold, each unit increases profit by $1.

Break-even analysis offers useful estimates of the relationships among sales and costs, receipts, and profit. For example, managers use this analysis to predict how a projected decline in sales will impact profit. Or they use it to estimate how

Break-even point The output level that must be reached if managers are to avoid losses.

FIGURE 6.8

Break-Even Chart: Martin Company

The break-even point—the output level that must be reached if the firm is to avoid losses—is 600,000 units of output per month.

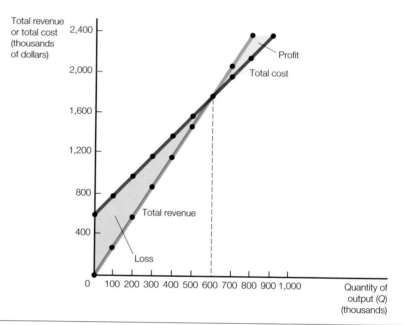

QUANT OPTION

Let P be the price of the component, Q the quantity sold, AVC the average variable cost, and TFC the fixed cost. The break-even unit is the output, Q_B, at which $TR = TC$. Because TR is PQ and total cost is $TFC + AVC(Q)$, it follows that

$$PQ_B = TFC + AVC \times (Q_B)$$
$$(P - AVC)Q_B = TFC$$
$$Q_B = \frac{TFC}{P - AVC} \qquad (6.7)$$

In the case of the Martin managers, $P = \$3$, $AVC = \$2$, and $TFC = \$600,000$. Consequently,

$$Q_B = \frac{\$600,000}{3 - 2} = 600,000$$

a price change might affect profit. Like most models, the analysis has limitations. High variance in prices or difficulties in estimating the cost structure can decrease the accuracy of results.

It is worth noting that although we worked with a linear cost function, this assumption is easily relaxed. Often a curvilinear cost function is used to estimate the cost structure. Many times, for fairly small changes in output, a linear approximation is good enough. This guideline is supported by many empirical studies suggesting that cost functions are often close to linear, as long as managers are not operating at or close to capacity.

PROFIT CONTRIBUTION ANALYSIS

Managers also use break-even analysis to understand the relationship between price and profit; this analysis is known as **profit contribution analysis**. As we have already discussed, profit contribution is the difference between total revenue and

Profit contribution analysis A break-even analysis to understand the relationship between price and profit.

STRATEGY SESSION: Mr. Martin Gets Chewed Out by the Boss

John Martin, an accountant at a small company that manufactures and sells three types of desks, constructed a break-even chart for the company as a whole. He used as a measure of output the total number of desks produced during each year. To estimate the average variable cost of a desk, he took the mean of the average variable costs of the three types of desks. To estimate the price of a desk, he took the mean of the prices of the three types of desks. Using these figures, he constructed a break-even chart (based on linear total cost and total revenue curves) indicating that the company was operating at an output level well above the break-even point and that profit would increase rapidly as output increased.

When Martin presented these findings, the company's president, Susan Rogers, said they were misleading because the analysis lumped together the three types of desks. For one type, the plant was operating at capacity, and marginal cost would increase substantially if output were increased. For another type of desk, it had become increasingly

obvious that the price was too high, and it was about to be reduced. For the third type of desk, only a few were produced, so it was incorrect to weight it as heavily as the other two types in the analysis. Rogers also pointed out that as the firm's output increased, the first and second types accounted for bigger and bigger shares of total output.

How should Martin respond to these comments? (Sometimes it is best just to admit you are wrong and thank the president for the information.) The fact that the product mix changes with increases in output is important, and Martin should have recognized this. It is also misleading to lump all three products together. And contrary to the assumption that the total cost curve is linear, the marginal cost of the first type of desk rises with increases in output. Finally, the price Martin used for the second type of desk is not the relevant one.

Note: This section is based on an actual case, although the numbers and situation have been disguised somewhat.

total variable cost; on a per-unit basis, it is equal to price minus average variable cost. In the case of the Martin Company, price is $3 and average variable cost is $2, so the per-unit profit contribution is $3 − $2, or $1.

Suppose managers at Martin want to estimate the sales level that will earn them a profit of $1 million per month. The required sales equal

$$Q = \frac{\text{Total fixed cost} + \text{Profit target}}{\text{Profit contribution (per unit)}}$$

$$= \frac{\$600,000 + \$1,000,000}{\$1}$$

$$= 1,600,000 \text{ units}$$

Or if managers sell only 500,000 units per month, the firm loses $100,000. The marketing team hope to land an order for 50,000 units of product. How much will this order reduce the firm's loss? To find out, multiply the order size (50,000 units) by the per-unit profit contribution ($1) to get the increase in profit (or reduction in loss, which is the case here); the result is $50,000.

SUMMARY

1. Managerial economists define a product's opportunity cost as the value of other products that could have been produced with the money used to produce the product. Hence a product's opportunity cost may differ from its historical cost, which is generally the basis for accounting statements.

2. In the short run it is important to distinguish between a firm's fixed and variable costs. Managers should be able to chart total, average, and marginal costs against output. The resulting cost functions, or cost curves (as they are often called), show how changes in output affect a firm's costs.

3. The long-run average cost function shows the minimum cost per unit of producing a given output level when any desired scale of plant can be built. The long-run average cost function is tangent to each of the short-run average cost functions at the output where the plant corresponding to the short-run average cost function is optimal. The long-run average cost curve is important to managers because it shows the extent to which larger plants have cost advantages over smaller ones.

4. Economies of scope occur when the cost of producing two (or more) products jointly is less than the cost of producing them separately. Such economies may arise because the production facilities used to make one product can also be used to make another product, or by-products resulting from the making of one product can be useful in making other products.

5. Break-even analysis compares total revenue and total cost, graphically or algebraically. A break-even chart combines the total cost function and the total

revenue curve, both of which are generally assumed to be linear, and shows the profit or loss resulting from each sales level. The break-even point is the sales level that must be achieved if the firm is to avoid losses. Managers often find it useful to carry out various types of profit contribution analysis. The profit contribution is the difference between total revenue and total variable cost; on a per-unit basis, it is equal to price minus average variable cost.

PROBLEMS

wwnorton.com/studyspace

1. An MIT study has estimated costs for producing steel with three different technologies: (1) coke, blast furnace, basic oxygen furnace, ingots, and finishing mills; (2) coke, blast furnace, basic oxygen furnace, continuous casting, and finishing mills; and (3) steel scrap, electric arc furnace, continuous casting, and finishing mills. Under reasonable assumptions concerning input prices, the estimated average costs per ton are as follows:

Cost Category	Coke, Blast Furnace, Basic Oxygen Furnace, Ingots, Finishing Mills	Coke, Blast Furnace, Basic Oxygen Furnace, Continuous Casting, Finishing Mills	Steel Scrap, Electric Arc Furnace, Continuous Casting, Finishing Mills
Process materials	$148.34	$136.19	$122.78
Energy	21.15	15.98	41.58
Direct labor	83.43	75.09	67.43
Capital	102.06	99.93	54.08
Other	46.74	41.67	24.47
Total	$401.72	$368.86	$310.34

a. The MIT report concludes that "unless significant changes occur in other technologies, the electric-furnace continuous-casting route will dominate domestic production." Why?

b. At the same time, the report notes that the price of scrap (which is used in this route) "could increase as electric furnace production expands because of the increased demand." Why is this relevant?

c. The report also concludes that regardless of which of these technologies is used, cost per ton is about 25 to 30% higher if wages are $26 per hour rather than $2 per hour. What does this imply about the competitiveness of U.S. steel producers relative to producers in other countries that pay wages far below U.S. levels?

d. If these cost figures are long-run average costs, under what circumstances would they also equal long-run marginal costs?

2. The Haverford Company is considering three types of plants to make a particular electronic device. Plant A is much more highly automated than plant B, which in turn is more highly automated than plant C. For each type of plant, average variable cost is constant so long as output is less than capacity, which is the maximum output of the plant. The cost structure for each type of plant is as follows:

Average Variable Costs	Plant A	Plant B	Plant C
Labor	$1.10	$2.40	$3.70
Materials	0.90	1.20	1.80
Other	0.50	2.40	2.00
Total	$2.50	$6.00	$7.50
Total fixed costs	$300,000	$ 75,000	$25,000
Annual capacity	200,000	100,000	50,000

a. Derive the average costs of producing 100,000, 200,000, 300,000, and 400,000 devices per year with plant A. (For output exceeding the capacity of a single plant, assume that more than one plant of this type is built.)

b. Derive the average costs of producing 100,000, 200,000, 300,000, and 400,000 devices per year with plant B.

c. Derive the average costs of producing 100,000, 200,000, 300,000, and 400,000 devices per year with plant C.

d. Using the results of parts (a) through (c), plot the points on the long-run average cost curve for the production of these electronic devices for outputs of 100,000, 200,000, 300,000 and 400,000 devices per year.

3. The Abner Corporation, a retail seller of television sets, wants to determine how many television sets it must sell to earn a profit of $10,000 per month. The price of each television set is $300, and the average variable cost is $100.

a. What is the required sales volume if the Abner Corporation's monthly fixed costs are $5,000 per month?

b. If the firm sells each television set at a price of $350 rather than $300, what is the required sales volume?

c. If the price is $350, and if average variable cost is $85 rather than $100, what is the required sales volume?

4. According to a statistical study, the following relationship exists between an electric power plant's fuel costs (C) and its eight-hour output as a percentage of capacity (Q)

$$C = 16.68 + 0.125Q + 0.00439Q^2$$

a. When Q increases from 50 to 51, what is the increase in the cost of fuel for this electric plant?

b. Of what use might the result in part (a) be to the plant's managers?

c. Derive the marginal (fuel) cost curve for this plant, and indicate how it might be used by the plant's managers.

5. The following table pertains to the Lincoln Company. Fill in the blanks:

Output	Total Cost	Total Fixed Cost	Total Variable Cost	Average Fixed Cost	Average Variable Cost
0	50	____	____	____	____
1	75	____	____	____	____
2	100	____	____	____	____
3	120	____	____	____	____
4	135	____	____	____	____
5	150	____	____	____	____
6	190	____	____	____	____
7	260	____	____	____	____

6. The Deering Manufacturing Company's short-run average cost function in 2012 was

$$AC = 3 + 4Q$$

where AC is the firm's average cost (in dollars per pound of the product), and Q is its output rate.

a. Obtain an equation for the firm's short-run total cost function.
b. Does the firm have any fixed costs? Explain.
c. If the price of the Deering Manufacturing Company's product (per pound) is $3, is the firm making profit or loss? Explain.
d. Derive an equation for the firm's marginal cost function.

7. The president of the Tacke Corporation believes that statistical research by his staff shows that the firm's long-run total cost curve can be represented as

$$TC = \alpha_0 Q^{\alpha 1} P_L^{\alpha 2} P_K^{\alpha 3}$$

where TC is the firm's total cost, Q is its output, P_L is the price of labor, and P_K is the price of capital.

a. Tacke's president says that α_1 measures the elasticity of cost with respect to output—that is, the percentage change in total cost resulting from a 1% change in output. Is he correct? Why or why not?
b. He also says that if $\alpha_1 < 1$, economies of scale are indicated, whereas if $\alpha_1 > 1$, diseconomies of scale are indicated. Is he correct? Why or why not?
c. According to Tacke's president, the value of α_3 can be estimated by regressing log (TC/P_K) on log Q and log (P_L/P_K). Is he correct? Why or why not?

8. Engineers sometimes rely on the "0.6 rule," which states that the increase in cost is given by the increase in capacity raised to the 0.6 power; that is,

$$C_2 = C_1(X_2/X_1)^{0.6}$$

where C_1 and C_2 are the costs of two pieces of equipment, and X_1 and X_2 are their respective capacities.

a. Does the 0.6 rule suggest economies of scale?

b. Some experts have stated that in the chemical and metal industries, the 0.6 rule can be applied to entire plants rather than individual pieces of equipment. If so, will the long-run average cost curve in these industries tend to be negatively sloped?

c. Can you think of a way to test whether this rule is correct?

9. The Dijon Company's total variable cost function is

$$TVC = 50Q - 10Q^2 + Q^3$$

where Q is the number of units of output produced.

a. What is the output level where marginal cost is a minimum?

b. What is the output level where average variable cost is a minimum?

c. What is the value of average variable cost and marginal cost at the output specified in the answer to part (b)?

10. The Berwyn Company is considering the addition of a new product to its product line. The firm has plenty of excess manufacturing capacity to produce the new product, and its total fixed costs would be unaffected if the new product were added to its line. Nonetheless, the firm's accountants decide that a reasonable share of the firm's present fixed costs should be allocated to the new product. Specifically, they decide that a $300,000 fixed charge will be absorbed by the new product. The variable cost per unit of making and selling the new product is $14, which is composed of the following:

Direct labor	$8.20
Direct materials	1.90
Other	3.90
Total	$14.00

a. Should the Berwyn Company add the new product to its line if it can sell about 10,000 units of this product at a price of $25?

b. Should it add the new product if it can sell about 10,000 units at a price of $20?

c. Should it add the new product if it can sell about 10,000 units at a price of $15?

d. What is the minimum price for the new product that will make it worth-while for Berwyn to add the new product to its line?

11. The Jolson Corporation produces 1,000 wood cabinets and 500 wood desks per year, the total cost being $30,000. If the firm produced 1,000 wood cabinets only, the cost would be $23,000. If the firm produced 500 wood desks only, the cost would be $11,000.

a. Calculate the degree of economies of scope.

b. Why do economies of scope exist?

12. The Smith Company made and sold 10,000 metal tables last year. When output was between 5,000 and 10,000 tables, its average variable cost was $24. In this output range, each table contributed 60% of its revenue to fixed costs and profit.

a. What was the price per table?

b. If the Smith Company increases its price by 10%, how many tables will it have to sell next year to obtain the same profit as last year?

c. If the Smith Company increases its price by 10%, and if its average variable cost increases by 8% as a result of wage increases, how many tables will it have to sell next year to obtain the same profit as last year?

EXCEL EXERCISE: PRODUCTION AND COST

Suppose that your industrial engineers presented you with the following technically efficient ways of combining labor (L) with the two units of capital (K) you possess.

Capital	Labor	Quantity
2	0.00	0
2	0.25	1
2	0.60	2
2	1.05	3
2	1.60	4
2	2.25	5
2	3.00	6
2	3.85	7
2	4.80	8

You also know that the cost of a unit of capital (r) is 2.5 and that the cost of a unit of labor (w) is 10. Is this enough information to derive the firm's total cost function (and other associated costs of the firm)? The answer is yes; let's see how the spreadsheet eases that calculation.

Open up your spreadsheet. Enter 2 in cell A1. Then click the lower right hand corner of cell A1 and drag down until you reach cell A9, then release. This should leave with a column of nine 2s.

Then enter 0 in cell B1, 0.25 in cell B2, 0.6 in cell B3, and so on, until you've entered 4.8 in cell B9.

Then enter 0 in cell C1, 1 in cell C2, and so on, until you've entered 8 in cell C9.

You have now replicated the table in the spreadsheet.

Then enter $=C2/B2$ in cell D2, $=C3/B3$ in cell D3, and so on. You can use the click-and-drag method to fill all the cells from D3 to D9. You have calculated the average product of labor—that is, $AP_L = Q/L$, the famous labor productivity measure.

Then enter $=(C2-C1)/(B2-B1)$ in cell E2 and $=(C3-C2)/(B3-B2)$ in cell E3, and so on. You can use the click-and-drag method to fill all the cells from E3 to E9. You have calculated the marginal product of labor—that is, $MP_L = \Delta Q/\Delta L$.

Then enter 10 in cell F1 and drag and click until you reach cell F9. That should give you a column of 10s, which is the wage rate the firm faces for each unit of labor it hires (and as can be seen from column 2, it can hire labor in fractional units—think part-time workers).

Then enter $=F2/E2$ in cell G2, $=F3/E3$ in cell G3, and so on via the click-and-drag method, until you reach cell G9. You now have the firm's marginal cost in column G. Recall from the text that $MC = w/MP_L$.

Then enter $=F2/D2$ in cell H2, $=F3/D3$ in cell H3, and so on via the click-and-drag method, until you reach cell H9. You now have the firm's average variable cost in column H. Recall from the text that $AVC = w/AP_L$.

Then enter 2.5 in cell I1 and drag and click till cell I9. You should have a column of 2.5s which is the cost of a unit of capital.

Then enter $=A1*I1$ in cell J1, and $=A2*I2$ in cell J2, and so on via the click-and-drag method. This should give you a column of 5s, the firm's fixed cost $(FC = rK)$.

Then enter $=B1*F1$ in cell K1 and $=B2*F2$ in cell K2, and so on via click-and-drag. This will give you the firm's variable cost $(VC = wL)$.

Then enter $=J1+K1$ in cell L1, and $=J2+K2$ in cell L2, and so on via click-and-drag. This will give you the firm's total cost $(TC = FC + VC)$.

You might even be able to discern a relationship between variable cost and quantity. Note that every number in column K (using the Qs in column C) can be calculated from the formula $VC = 2Q + 0.5Q^2$. Thus, the firm's total cost function is $TC = 5 + 2Q + 0.5Q^2$.

But you don't have to know that relationship because you were able to enumerate the firm's costs by using the production function given to you by your industrial engineers in the table above along with the unit prices of your inputs, r and w.

APPENDIX A: BREAK-EVEN ANALYSIS AND OPERATING LEVERAGE

Managers must continually compare alternative systems of production. Should one type of plant be replaced by another? How does your plant stack up against your competitor's? Break-even is used to help make such comparisons more effective. In this appendix we show managers how to analyze changes in total cost and profit, depending on how automated or mechanized a plant may be. This is an important topic because top-level managers often have to make such comparisons.

At the outset it is essential to recognize that some plants, because they are more mechanized than others, have relatively high fixed costs but relatively low average variable costs. Consider firms I, II, and III in Figure 6.9. Firm I's plant has fixed costs of $100,000 per month, which are much higher than those of the plants operated by firm II or III; however, its average variable cost of $2 is much lower than that of firm II or III. Essentially firm I has substituted capital for labor and materials. Managers have built a highly automated plant with high fixed costs but low average variable cost.

At the opposite extreme, managers of firm III have built a plant with low fixed costs but high average variable cost. Because they have not invested a great deal in plant and equipment, total fixed costs are only $25,000 per month, which is much less than that for firm I or II. However, because of the relatively low level of automation at its plant, firm III's average variable cost is $4—considerably higher than at the other two firms. Relative to firm I, firm III uses more labor and materials and less capital.

Firm II's plant occupies a middle position (between firms I and III) in this regard. Its total fixed cost of $60,000 is less than firm I's but more than firm III's, and its average variable cost of $3 is greater than firm I's but less than firm III's. It has not automated its plant to the extent that firm I has, but it has automated more than firm III.

In comparing these plants, an important issue to consider is the degree of operating leverage, which is defined as the percentage change in profit resulting from a 1% change in the number of units of product sold. Specifically,

$$\text{Degree of operating leverage} = \frac{\text{Percentage change in profit}}{\text{Percentage change in quantity sold}}$$

$$= \frac{\Delta\pi/\pi}{\Delta Q/Q}$$

$$= \frac{\Delta\pi}{\Delta Q}\left(\frac{Q}{\pi}\right) \quad \text{or} \quad \frac{d\pi}{dQ}\left(\frac{Q}{\pi}\right) \tag{6.8}$$

where π is the firm's profit, and Q is the quantity sold.

FIGURE 6.9

Break-Even Analysis and Operating Leverage

Firm I has relatively high fixed costs and low variable costs; firm III has relatively low fixed costs and high variable costs; and firm II is in the middle.

Firm I

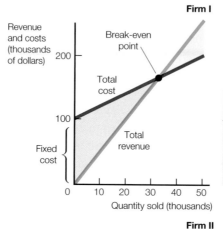

Total fixed cost = $100,000

Average variable cost = $2

Selling price = $5

Quantity sold	Total revenue	Total cost	Total profit
10,000	$ 50,000	$120,000	$−70,000
20,000	100,000	140,000	−40,000
30,000	150,000	160,000	−10,000
40,000	200,000	180,000	20,000
50,000	250,000	200,000	50,000

Firm II

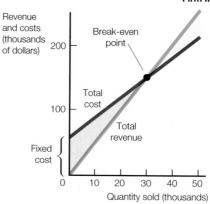

Total fixed cost = $60,000

Average variable cost = $3

Selling price = $5

Quantity sold	Total revenue	Total cost	Total profit
10,000	$ 50,000	$ 90,000	$−40,000
20,000	100,000	120,000	−20,000
30,000	150,000	150,000	0
40,000	200,000	180,000	20,000
50,000	250,000	210,000	40,000

Firm III

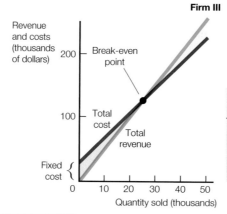

Total fixed cost = $25,000

Average variable cost = $4

Selling price = $5

Quantity sold	Total revenue	Total cost	Total profit
10,000	$ 50,000	$ 65,000	$−15,000
20,000	100,000	105,000	−5,000
30,000	150,000	145,000	5,000
40,000	200,000	185,000	15,000
50,000	250,000	225,000	25,000

The degree of operating leverage, because it measures how a given change in sales volume affects profit, is of great importance. If firm I is selling 40,000 units per month, and if we let $\Delta Q = 10,000$ units, the degree of operating leverage equals

$$\frac{\Delta \pi}{\Delta Q}\left(\frac{Q}{\pi}\right) = \frac{\$50,000 - \$20,000}{10,000}\left(\frac{40,000}{\$20,000}\right) = 6$$

because Figure 6.9 shows that if $\Delta Q = 10,000$ units, $\Delta \pi = \$50,000 - \$20,000$. (Why? Because if Q changes from 40,000 to 50,000 units, π changes from $20,000 to $50,000.) Thus a 1% increase in quantity sold gives a 6% increase in profit.

If both the total revenue curve and the total cost function are linear, as in Figure 6.9, a simple way to calculate the degree of operating leverage when output equals Q is to use the following formula

$$\text{Degree of operating leverage} = \frac{Q(P - AVC)}{Q(P - AVC) - TFC} \tag{6.9}$$

where P equals selling price, AVC equals average variable cost, and TFC equals total fixed cost. It can be shown that if both the total revenue curve and the total cost function are linear, equation (6.9) yields the same result as equation (6.8). Thus for firm I, if $Q = 40,000$, equation (6.9) says that the degree of operating leverage equals

$$\frac{Q(P - AVC)}{Q(P - AVC) - TFC} = \frac{\$40,000(\$5 - \$2)}{40,000(\$5 - \$2) - \$100,000}$$

$$= \frac{\$120,000}{\$120,000 - \$100,000} = 6$$

because P equals $5, AVC equals $2, and TFC equals $100,000. The result is the same as in the previous paragraph. (In both cases it is 6.)

It is interesting and important to compare the degree of operating leverage of the three firms; this comparison reveals a great deal about how the operation of each plant differs from that of the other. If $Q = 40,000$, the degree of operating leverage for firm II equals

$$\frac{Q(P - AVC)}{Q(P - AVC) - TFC} = \frac{\$40,000(\$5 - \$3)}{40,000(\$5 - \$3) - \$60,000} = 4$$

For firm III, it equals

$$\frac{Q(P - AVC)}{Q(P - AVC) - TFC} = \frac{\$40,000(\$5 - \$4)}{40,000(\$5 - \$4) - \$25,000} = 2.67$$

STRATEGY SESSION: Water, Water, Not Everywhere

In an economy that still has a number of command-and-control aspects, one way to handle a water shortage in China would be to ration supply by decreeing what amount one could use. But markets are growing in China, so another solution is to raise the price, and that's what just about every major city has done in the last decade; they need to conserve water because of the great demand relative to supply, but this requires high prices, and the constituency is accustomed to low water prices. Prices are scheduled to rise by 40 to 48% in Luoyang. Shanghai raised its prices by 25% in June 2009 and planned a 22% increase in November 2010. Zhengzhou raised its water fees by 25% in April 2009 and says that fees will have to change more rapidly in the future. In Nanjing, rates rose by 12% in April 2009. Several other major cities have also recently raised their rates. Even in cities that didn't recently raise rates, such as Beijing (which almost doubled its water rates five years ago), citizens think that water is already expensive and don't want to see increases.

Chinese officials now believe that low prices are a major part of China's water shortage problem. The low prices give little incentive for residences and business to use water prudently. At one time, it was estimated that 20% of supply was lost through leaky pipes.

To see how China's water prices compare with the rest of the world, Deutsche Bank estimated the price of a cubic meter of water, expressed in U.S. dollars, in major developed countries throughout the world. The table below shows the results.

Germany	$3.01
United Kingdom	$2.37
France	$2.00
Australia	$1.82
Italy	$1.58
Canada	$1.02
South Africa	$1.02
United States	$0.74
Brazil	$0.65
China	$0.31

Thus a 1% increase in sales volume results in a 6% increase in profit at firm I, a 4% increase in profit at firm II, and a 2.67% increase in profit at firm III. Clearly firm I's profit are much more sensitive to changes in sales volume than are firm III's profit; firm II is in the middle in this regard.

APPENDIX B: MEASUREMENT OF SHORT-RUN COST FUNCTIONS: THE CHOICE OF A MATHEMATICAL FORM

Smart managers understand the need to estimate cost functions for their informational value. In business these are often called cost curves. One step in estimating a cost curve is to choose the mathematical relationship between output and cost. As a first approximation, managers often assume that short-run total cost is

The cost of water in Germany is 10 times that in China. Of course these prices reflect differing supply-and-demand situations in each country and different pricing levels for all goods and services. Nevertheless, the consensus is that water is priced too low in China. Per-capita water availability is one quarter of the world average. A study by the World Bank estimates that water shortages cost China 1.3% of its yearly economic output. A lot of the water in China is polluted and that further cuts economic output by 1%.[a]

There's a lesson in supply and demand here. If prices rose, people would reduce waste, and the allocation of water across users would improve (the allocatable efficiency of the price system) on the demand side. Higher prices would also encourage investment in projects, such as desalination, that would increase supply. In fact, "if China moved more aggressively to price water in a manner that reflected supply and demand," says Peter Orszag, vice chairman of global banking at Citicorp and former head of the federal Office of Management and Budget (OMB), "it could teach the U.S. a lesson in using market economics to address environmental issues." Orszag notes that water prices in China are much too low to ensure that water is used efficiently enough to sustain the supply. Water has never been priced efficiently in the United States, claims a Citicorp analyst (note our low cost in the table above), it is heavily subsidized. Orszag states that "market forces can work wonders for the environment, but only if we have the political courage to create them."[b]

[a] Andrew Batson, "China Cities Raise Water Prices in Bid to Conserve," *The Wall Street Journal*, July 31, 2009, at http://online.wsj.article/SB124897577003694405.html.
[b] Peter Orszag, "Why We Care about the Price of Water in China: Peter Orszag," *Bloomberg News*, July 6, 2011, at www.bloomberg.com/2011-07-06/why-we-care-about-the-price-of-water-in-china-Peter-orszag.html.

a linear function of output, which means marginal cost tends to be constant in the relevant output range (see Figure 6.10). In fact, this simple linear approximation often fits the data for particular firms and plants quite well in the short run. However, managers need to note that although marginal costs may vary little over a wide range of output, it is inconceivable that they do not eventually rise with increases in output. Therefore, a linear function is likely to be appropriate only for a restricted range of output.

It is also possible to assume total cost is a quadratic or cubic function of output. If the quadratic form is chosen, marginal cost increases with output, as shown in Figure 6.11. If the cubic form is chosen (and c is large enough), marginal cost first decreases then increases with output, as shown in Figure 6.12. Whether these forms are better than the linear form depends on whether they fit the data better. In many cases, they fit the data slightly better than the linear form.

FIGURE 6.10

Average Cost and Marginal Cost: Linear Total Cost Function
Marginal cost is constant.

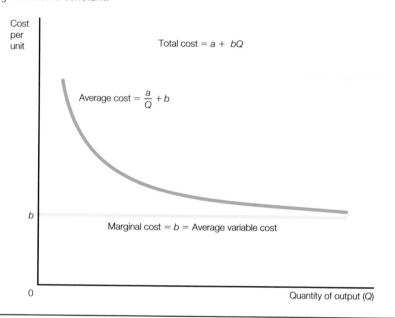

FIGURE 6.11

Average Cost and Marginal Cost: Quadratic Total Cost Function
Marginal cost increases as output rises.

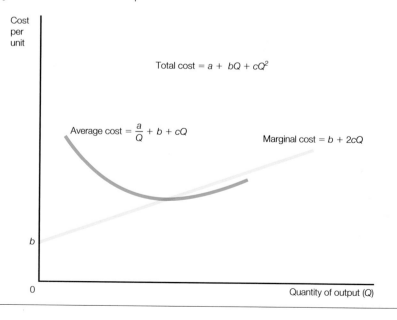

FIGURE 6.12

Average Cost and Marginal Cost: Cubic Total Cost Function

Marginal cost first falls then rises as output increases.

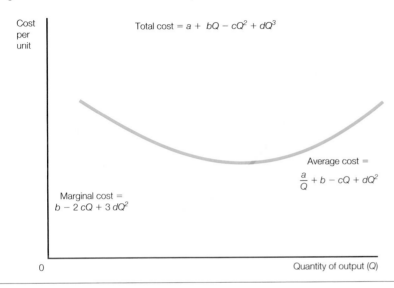

Cost per unit

Total cost $= a + bQ - cQ^2 + dQ^3$

Average cost $=$
$\dfrac{a}{Q} + b - cQ + dQ^2$

Marginal cost $=$
$b - 2cQ + 3dQ^2$

0

Quantity of output (Q)

Key Steps in the Estimation Process

When managers have chosen a mathematical form and decided on their data set, the following six items should be given careful thought:

1. *Definition of cost*: As we said at the beginning of this chapter, the relevant concept of cost for managers is opportunity cost, not cost based on accounting data. We must be careful to ensure that the accounting data—or engineering data, for that matter—on which an estimated cost function is based are reasonably indicative of opportunity costs. If not, adjust the data. For example, suppose historical data regarding a firm's depreciation costs are based on tax laws rather than on opportunity costs of the relevant equipment. Managers need to revise the cost data to better reflect both opportunity costs and tax conventions.

2. *Correction for price level changes*: When managers use time series data to estimate cost functions, it is important that changes over time in the input prices be recognized and measured. What managers need is a cost function based on next year's input prices if next year is the period to which the analysis pertains. Because historical data are based on input prices at various times in the past, we need a price index to allow us to adjust our historical cost data for changes in various input prices. Moreover, because various inputs may experience quite different rates of inflation, managers should construct a separate price index for

STRATEGY SESSION: The Value of Time and the Full Price of Transportation

Transportation economists have written for years about the full cost of using a transportation mode. It's not just the fare or the gas and parking costs but also the time spent on accessing and egressing the mode; the costs associated with unreliable transport time; safety costs; the ability to pursue other activities while being transported; and so on. Generally the most important cost component (at least for higher-income people) is travel time.

We can get a feel for this by observing what happens in markets where consumers have options. Take State Route 91 in California, for example. Toll lanes were built in the median of an existing freeway. The freeway is heavily congested and often takes two hours to drive in peak periods. In the toll lanes, however, the same trip takes a half hour. The top cost? $9.45 during the 4 pm to 5 pm hour on Thursdays going eastbound. So what's saving an hour and a half worth? At least $6.30/hour (that is, 9.45/1.5), or a rational driver wouldn't use such lanes. The lanes are continuously priced so that a "free flow" (a flow at the posted speed limit) is maintained. This is supply and demand at work. If too many cars want to use the toll lanes so that the posted speed can't be maintained, the toll is increased (and users can choose whether or not to enter the lanes if they wish). Likewise, if the toll lanes can tolerate more cars and still maintain the posted speed limit, the tolls are lowered.

If $9.45 seems steep, consider that such a policy encourages car pools. Cars with three or more occupants can use the toll lanes for 50% of the toll during evening rush hour and a minimum of $1.30 at all other times. Cars with multiple occupants can split the toll, mitigating some of its impact. California also is pricing Interstate 15 in San Diego. The states of Washington, Virginia, and Texas are now considering toll roads. The Bush administration proposed congestion pricing in the 2007 State of the Union message. Singapore has been using congestion pricing for over 36 years, and the system was adopted over eight years ago in London and more recently in Stockholm. Mayor Bloomberg of New York City has proposed an $8 prime time weekday toll for Manhattan south of 86th Street.

But offers to save time are not limited to highways. You've perhaps experienced a long delay in an airport security line. Would you like to bypass such lines? Even if the line isn't long, you have to report to the airport early because the line might be long. In such cases you spend long times in the secure area of the airport—time you probably would rather spend elsewhere.

A firm called Verified Identity Pass will allow (for a fee of $99.95 per year) British Airways travelers to avoid the typical security wait. Certain airports (Orlando, Indianapolis, Cincinnati, and San Jose) are interested in establishing lanes where passengers have been precleared and only have to verify their identity by a fingerprint or an iris scan. If you were a businessperson flying the New York–London route 10 times a year, you'd pay perhaps $10 to avoid a half-hour delay each time you flew. A weekly commuter on the same route would pay only $2 to save that half hour.

The time spent in security, the airlines' cutting service to small airports, and the fact that virtually all service between small airports is through a hub airport (with the resulting waiting time for connecting flights) is spawning another industry: an air taxi service. With the production of very light jets at the relatively low price of $1.8–$2.4 million, which can fly up to 1,200 miles nonstop and can land at over 5,000 U.S. general aviation airports (there are general aviation airports almost everywhere), several entrepreneurs are contemplating entering the air taxi service market.

Why do they believe this will be lucrative? Because of the full costs of travel via conventional carriers to and from as well as between small markets. Such a service will allow customers to fly directly from origin to destination, transforming many trips to home and back in a day rather than the current two–three day trips with their accompanying meals and hotel accommodations.

Such taxis will be easy to catch at the general aviation airports in the suburbs of big cities; but taxis may be unwilling to fly to locations where generating return fares will not be easy.

Several airlines once flew the lucrative New York–London route offering all business-class service. They priced this service in the $1,975 range compared with the business-class services offered by the legacy carriers, such as British Airways, Virgin Atlantic, and American Airlines, which charged around $5,925. While the legacy carriers go to London Heathrow, the new carriers went to Stansted (farther from central London). In addition, connections at Stansted are mostly with discount carriers (like Ryanair); so after transatlantic luxury, a beyond-London traveler would face minimal service.

But why wouldn't a London-destined business traveler want to save $3,950 on her fare? It's the full pricing again. British Air runs 10 round-trips per day, and Virgin offers five round-trips per day, whereas the all-business-class airlines usually offered one. Many businesspeople value the ability to go when they want to; this is called schedule delay and is measured by the difference between when the customer wants to go and when the carrier is scheduled to leave. And don't forget the legacy carriers' loyalty awards and frequent-flier miles. One can go anywhere in the world on British Air. Finally, because this service caters to business travelers, they aren't paying the bill (the company is); and a business expense is tax deductible, so the cost difference isn't as great as it initially appears. Alas, focusing on business-class-only customers does have a downside. During the economic crisis of 2008–2012, most business-class-only airlines went bankrupt as business travel plummeted.

Are there hidden full costs for nontransportation goods and services? Because most goods take time to consume and may require other expenditures (say, user assembly time and electricity and repair costs), all rational decision makers should consider the full costs of each product and service.

Sources: Timothy Egan, "Paying on the Highway to Get Out of First Gear," *New York Times*, April 28, 2005, at www.nytimes.com/2005/04/28/natural/28toll.html; Patrick McGeehan, "For a Price, a Faster Way through Local Airports," *New York Times*, December 5, 2006, at www.nytimes.com/2006/12/05/nyregion/05screen.html; Joe Sharkey, "Standing on a Runway Hailing an Air Taxi," *New York Times*, February 28, 2006, at www.nytimes.com/2006/02/28/business/28road.html; Joe Sharkey, "TransAtlantic Luxury for Less," *New York Times*, February 21, 2006, at www.nytimes.com/2006/02/21/business/21compete.html; and "Get Moving on Traffic Relief," *New York Times*, May 25, 2007, at www.nytimes.com/2007/05/25opinion/25fri2.html.

each major input. Using these price indexes, managers can convert the available historical cost data into cost data reflecting next year's input prices, not those of the past.

3. *Relating cost to output*: For an estimated cost function to be reasonably accurate, it is important that cost data distinguish properly between costs that vary with output and those that do not. For many types of equipment, as well as other assets, depreciation depends on both the passage of time and the extent of use, with the result that it is difficult or impossible to determine solely from accounting data how much the depreciation cost varies with output alone. Also, some costs do not vary with output so long as output does not exceed a critical level. Above this critical level, these costs may increase considerably. For example, up to some output level, managers need just one machine tool of a particular type; but beyond that output level they need to obtain an additional machine tool.

4. *Matching time periods*: Major errors sometimes occur because cost data do not pertain to the same time periods as output data. To see what mayhem this can cause, suppose we were to plot a firm's 2012 cost against its 2011 output. Would the resulting chart be a good estimate of the firm's cost function? Of course not. Instead managers need to relate a firm's costs in a particular period to its output in that same period. Managers need to modify this guideline in cases in which some costs of producing output in one period do not arise until subsequent periods. These delayed costs must be recognized, measured, and charged against the period in which the output occurred. For example, the costs of maintenance and repairs, when they are delayed, should be treated in this way.

5. *Controlling product, technology, and plant*: Managers need to estimate a firm's cost function on the basis of a fixed definition of the firm's product, as well as on a fixed level of technology and (for short-run cost functions) a fixed scale of plant. This means that managers should be careful to ensure that the firm's product mix does not significantly change over time. Also, the observations used in the analysis should not cover so long a period that they pertain to different levels of technology (or different scales of plant).

6. *Length of period and sample size*: Although managers should prefer a larger sample size, they cannot extend the data gathering phase too long. No simple rule can specify the best length of time. In deciding how long to wait, managers need to consider issues like the level of technology change, seasonal effects, and product changes.

Nature and Limitations of Available Data

Having chosen a mathematical form, managers must select the type of data to use in estimating a cost function. One possibility is to use time series data. Another possibility is to use cross-section data and relate the total costs of a variety of firms (during the same period) to their output levels. Figure 6.13 plots the 2012 output of eight firms in a given industry against their 2012 total costs. Here, too, regres-

FIGURE 6.13

Relationship between Total Cost and Output, Cross Section

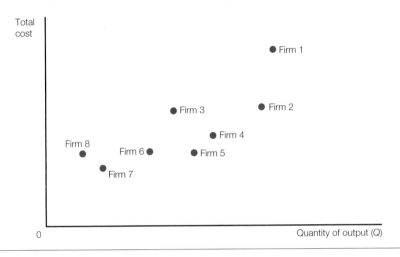

sion analysis can be used to estimate the relationship. A third possibility is to use engineering data to construct cost functions.

Regardless of which types of data are used, there are a number of important issues in estimating cost functions. Accounting data, which are generally the only cost data available, suffer from a number of possible deficiencies. Accountants may use arbitrary allocations of overhead and joint costs. The depreciation of an asset is determined largely by tax laws rather than economic criteria. Many inputs are valued at historical cost and do not include opportunity cost.

Engineering data also may contain possible issues. An inherent arbitrariness is involved in allocating costs jointly when producing more than one product in multiproduct firms.

PART 4
MARKET STRUCTURE AND SIMPLE PRICING STRATEGIES

CHAPTER 7

PERFECT COMPETITION

We are at a natural point to review our path. We first looked at behavior in simple markets and the laws of supply and demand that govern them. We next focused on the supply side of the market, looking at production and cost structures. Our goal was to provide tools and understanding to help managers improve their operating efficiency. Now we want to switch to the demand side and examine managerial behavior and pricing decisions. Only after managers understand both sides of the market can they consider maximizing profit.

Our decision model, like most rational models, assumes managers want to maximize firm value. In the strictest sense this means maximizing profit, though we believe value is more than a simple financial measure. Managers can bring value to their firms by thinking about long-term reputational effects. All decisions have short- and long-term consequences; the foresight to maximize firm value is the benchmark by which managerial ability is judged.

Managers live within a constrained world. They make decisions subject to the limits imposed by technology, reources, economics, politics, and avarice. A dominant constraint in pricing decisions is the market structure. Market structure is important because it largely determines the potential pricing power of managers. We say potential because many managers fail to price optimally. We discuss this further when we introduce sophisticated pricing in Chapters 9 and 10.

Managers should classify markets based on their degree of pricing power. At one end is a perfectly competitive market in which managers have no market power. The other end is anchored by monopoly markets, where managers face no competition and possess plenty of market power.

We begin by examining pricing behavior in perfectly competitive markets. From a strategic view, these markets are less interesting because individual managers have no effect on price. Instead they are ruled by the "invisible hand" described by Adam Smith. Managers are price takers: They accept the decisions of the aggregate market. However, perfectly competitive markets serve as good benchmarks to evaluate any value created by managers. They also lay the groundwork for our journey through more strategically interesting markets where managers must consider and anticipate the actions of others (consumers and rivals) in setting prices.

In many markets managers operate with no market power. For example, as a small participant in a large market where the market supply and demand curves determine the price, the manager maximizes the firm's profit given the market-determined price. Other examples occur when the government sets the price (either via price controls or by virtue of being in a regulated industry) or where the firm is a follower firm in a market where a price leader sets the market price. Managers with no market power have no control over price; they are at the whim of the market.

If you find yourself in such a market, here is what you should expect. You will still face the supply-side challenges of efficient production and cost control. This is true for all managers at all times. From the demand side, managers must choose the profit-maximizing output when the price is given. In all other markets, managers can vary both output and price.

In perfectly competitive markets, managers cannot overrule the price set by the interaction of the aggregate market demand and supply curves. An individual manager cannot influence the market price. It is often suggested that the farmer is in this position. While not controlling price, the farmer does decide on quantity—that is, how much of each crop to plant. This decision must be made months before the crop comes to market. To minimize risk, a farmer may sell a crop for future delivery, but most do not. After the crop is planted, the price may change as conditions influencing demand (tastes, income) and supply (weather, crop disease) change. The farmer makes a second quantity decision at harvest time: How much of the crop to harvest. Farmers may also stop growing a crop before it matures, replow, and plant another crop because of changes in market prices. What is common in all these cases is that the farmer makes quantity decisions only, and they are based on a price over which the farmer has no control.

MARKET STRUCTURE

This situation of a price-taking producer is one of four general categories of market structure we investigate. We preview all four categories in this section, then spend the rest of this chapter discussing the perfect competition (price taker) category. As we pointed out in Chapter 1, a market consists of a group of firms and individuals that buy or sell some good or service. Economists have generally found it useful to classify markets into four broad types: perfect competition, monopoly, monopolistic competition, and oligopoly. In **perfect competition** and **monopolistic competition** there are many sellers, each of which produces only a small part of the industry's output. **Monopoly** markets, on the other hand, consist of only a single seller. **Oligopoly** is an intermediate case where there are a few sellers; this is the most prevalent category in present-day business. Hence American Water (which serves 16.2 million customers in 32 states and Ontario), if it is the only supplier of water in a particular market, is a monopoly. And because there are only a few automobile manufacturers, the market for automobiles is an oligopoly.

Market structures vary substantially in the extent to which managers can control price. Managers in perfectly competitive markets have no control over price. For example, a farmer producing corn has no control over the price of corn. On the other hand, a monopolist is likely to have considerable control over price. In the absence of public regulation, American Water would have considerable control over the price of water in the locations it serves. A manager operating under monopolistic competition or oligopoly is likely to have less control over price than a monopolist and more control over price than a manager in a perfectly competitive market.

These market structures also vary in the extent to which the firms in an industry produce standardized (that is, identical) products. Firms in a perfectly competitive market all produce identical products. One farmer's wheat is essentially the same as another farmer's. In a monopolistically competitive industry like shirt manufacturing, firms produce somewhat different products. One firm's shirts differ in style and quality from another firm's shirts. In an oligopoly, firms sometimes, but not always, produce identical products; for example, in steel and aluminum they do, whereas in cars, they do not. And in a monopoly there can be no difference among firms' products because the industry contains only one firm.

How easily firms can enter an industry differs from one market structure to another. In perfect competition **barriers to entry** are low. For example, only a small investment is required to enter many parts of agriculture. Similarly, there are low barriers to entry in monopolistic competition. But oligopolies such as automobile manufacturing and oil refining tend to feature considerable barriers to entry: It is very expensive to build an automobile plant or an oil refinery. In a monopoly entry is blocked; if entry occurs, the monopoly no longer exists.

Market structures also differ in the extent to which managers compete on the basis of advertising, public relations, and different product characteristics, rather than price. In perfect competition there is no nonprice competition. (If every farmer produces identical corn and has to accept the market price, why devote funds to advertising?) In monopolistic competition considerable emphasis is placed on managers using nonprice competition. Much of this nonprice competition centers around the ability of managers to differentiate their products; this

Perfect competition When there are many firms that are small relative to the entire market and produce similar products.

Monopolistic competition When there are many firms and consumers, just as in perfect competition; however, each firm produces a product that is slightly different from the products produced by the other firms.

Monopoly Markets with a single seller.

Oligopoly Markets with a few sellers.

Barriers to entry Barriers that determine how easily firms can enter an industry, depending on the market structure.

TABLE 7.1

Characteristics of Perfect Competition, Monopolistic Competition, Oligopoly, and Monopoly

Market Structure	Examples	Number of Producers	Type of Product	Power of Firm over Price	Barriers to Entry	Nonprice Competition
Perfect competition	Some sectors of agriculture	Many	Standardized	None	Low	None
Monopolistic competition	Retail trade	Many	Differentiated	Some	Low	Advertising and product differentiation
Oligopoly	Computers, oil, steel	Few	Standardized or differentiated	Some	High	Advertising and product differentiation
Monopoly	Public utilities	One	Unique product	Considerable	Very high	Advertising

differentiation gives managers the power to overrule the market price. Managers of oligopolies that produce differentiated products also tend to rely heavily on nonprice competition, whereas managers of oligopolies that produce nondifferentiated products do not. For example, computer firms try to increase their sales by building better computers and by advertising, whereas steel companies do little advertising. Monopolists also engage in advertising and public relations, although these activities are directed not at capturing the sales of other firms in the industry (no other firms exist) but rather at increasing total market demand and insulating the firm from the negative connotations sometimes associated with monopoly.

Table 7.1 summarizes many key features of each market structure. Be sure to look over this table before proceeding further. This chapter discusses perfect competition. Chapter 8 covers monopoly and monopolistic competition. Chapters 9 and 10 extend the monopoly model to consider sophisticated monopoly pricing strategies. Chapter 11 considers oligopoly.

MARKET PRICE IN PERFECT COMPETITION

In a perfectly competitive industry, market price, as we saw in Chapter 1, is determined by the intersection of the market demand and supply curves. The market demand curve shows the total amount that individual buyers of the commodity will purchase at any price; the market supply curve shows the total amount that individual suppliers of the commodity will supply at any price. Figure 7.1 shows

FIGURE 7.1

Determination of Price in a Perfectly Competitive Market

Equilibrium price is $10, and equilibrium quantity is 24,000 units.

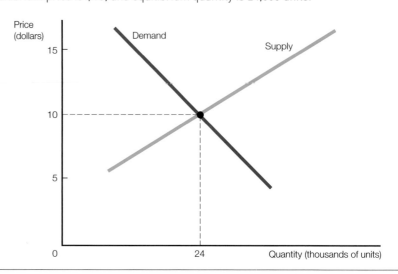

the market demand and supply curves for a good produced in a perfectly competitive market. As is ordinarily the case, the market supply curve slopes upward to the right; that is, price increases generally result in higher industry output because managers find it profitable to expand production. Also, in accord with Chapters 1 and 2, the market demand curve slopes downward to the right; that is, price increases generally result in less product being demanded.

To determine the equilibrium price, which is the price that will eventually prevail in this market, we must find the price at which market supply equals market demand.[1] The demand curve in Figure 7.1 is

$$P = 22 - 0.5Q_D \tag{7.1}$$

where P is the price (in dollars) of this good and Q_D is the quantity demanded (in thousands of units). The supply curve in Figure 7.1 is

$$P = 4 + 0.25Q_S \tag{7.2}$$

where Q_S is the quantity supplied (in thousands of units). Because the equilibrium price is at the level where Q_D (the quantity demanded) equals Q_S (the quantity supplied),

$$P_D = 22 - 0.5Q = 4 + 0.25Q = P_S$$
$$0.75Q = 18$$
$$Q = 24$$

1. Recall from Chapter 1 that an equilibrium price is a price that can be maintained. If conditions do not change, the actual price tends to equal the equilibrium price.

Substituting 24 for Q_D in equation (7.1), we find that $P = \$10$. (If we substitute 24 for Q_S in equation (7.2), we get the same result.) Therefore, as shown in Figure 7.1, price is expected to equal \$10, and output is expected to equal 24,000 units.

Although Figure 7.1 shows that both total quantity demanded and total quantity supplied depend on price, this does not mean an individual manager can affect price. According to the market demand curve in equation (7.1),

$$P = 22 - 0.5Q_D$$

If 1,000 firms are in this market, each produces, on the average, only 24 units of the product. Even if an individual firm doubles its output (from 24 to 48 units), the effect on price is minuscule. Specifically, an output increase of 24 units results in a price reduction of only 1.2 cents, or about 0.1%.[2] This means that managers in this market essentially face a horizontal demand curve. No matter how many units one manager sells, the market price remains the same. Whereas the demand curve for the output of the entire industry slopes downward to the right (as shown in Figure 7.1), the demand curve for the output of any single firm is regarded as horizontal (at a price of \$10 in this case).

SHIFTS IN SUPPLY AND DEMAND CURVES

Shifts in the market supply or demand curves result in price changes (recall Chapter 1). For example, if the supply curve in Figure 7.1 shifts to the left, the price is expected to rise. Shifts in market supply and demand curves have significant consequences for firm performance, and managers must try to anticipate them and respond as best they can.

For present purposes, managers must understand the factors affecting the supply and demand curves of the products they buy and sell. There is no need here to dwell at length on the factors causing shifts in demand curves; they have been discussed in Chapter 2. But it is worth recalling from Chapter 1 that two of the most important factors causing shifts in supply curves are technological advancements and changes in input prices. Improvements in technology tend to shift a product's supply curve to the right because they often permit managers to reduce their costs. On the other hand, increases in input prices tend to shift a product's supply curve to the left because they push up the firm's costs.

THE OUTPUT DECISION OF A PERFECTLY COMPETITIVE FIRM

How much output should managers at a perfectly competitive firm produce? As we discussed previously, managers in a perfectly competitive firm cannot affect the market price of their product, and they must sell any output (within their capabilities) at the market price. To illustrate the manager's situation, consider the example in Table 7.2. The market price is \$10 per unit, and the manager can

2. If output increases by 24 units, Q increases by 0.024 because Q is measured in thousands of units. If Q increases by 0.024, P falls by $0.5(0.024) = 0.012$, according to the demand curve in equation (7.1). P is measured in dollars, so this amounts to 1.2 cents.

TABLE 7.2

Cost and Revenues of a Perfectly Competitive Firm

Units of Output Period	Price (Dollars)	Total Revenue (Dollars)	Total Fixed Costs (Dollars)	Total Variable Costs (Dollars)	Total Cost (Dollars)	Total Profit (Dollars)
0	10	0	1	0	1	−1
1	10	10	1	3	4	6
2	10	20	1	8	9	11
3	10	30	1	15	16	14
4	10	40	1	24	25	15
5	10	50	1	35	36	14
6	10	60	1	48	49	11
7	10	70	1	63	64	6
8	10	80	1	80	81	−1
9	10	90	1	99	100	−10

produce as much as she chooses. Hence the firm's total revenue at various output rates is given in column 3 of Table 7.2. The firm's total fixed cost (1), total variable cost, $(2Q + Q^2)$, and total cost $(1 + 2Q + Q^2)$ are given in columns 4, 5, and 6 of Table 7.2. Finally, the last column shows the firm's total profit.

Figure 7.2 shows the relationship between total revenue and cost and output. The vertical distance between the total revenue and total cost curves is the profit at the corresponding output. Below one unit of output and above seven units of output, this distance is negative. Because the manager can sell either large or small volumes of output at the same price per unit, the total revenue curve is a straight line through the origin with a slope equal to the fixed price. (Specifically, $TR = P*Q$; because the price is constant, total revenue is proportional to quantity.) Because a manager in a perfectly competitive firm takes the price as given, the slope of the total revenue is always the market price.

The firm's profit (π) is expressed as total revenue (TR) minus total cost (TC)

$$\pi = TR - TC$$

It follows that

$$\frac{\Delta \pi}{\Delta Q} = \frac{\Delta TR}{\Delta Q} - \frac{\Delta TC}{\Delta Q}$$

FIGURE 7.2

Relationship between Total Cost and Total Revenue of a Perfectly Competitive Firm

The output rate that would maximize the firm's profit is four units per time period. The profit (total revenue minus total cost) equals $15.

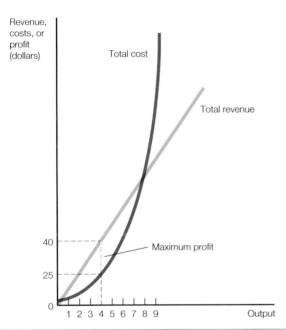

If

$$\frac{\Delta\pi}{\Delta Q} = 0$$

then

$$\frac{\Delta TR}{\Delta Q} - \frac{\Delta TC}{\Delta Q} = 0$$

so

$$\frac{\Delta TR}{\Delta Q} = \frac{\Delta TC}{\Delta Q}$$

Here $\Delta TR/\Delta Q$ is the firm's marginal revenue. It represents a change in total revenue when the output changes by a small amount (usually $\Delta Q = 1$). The firm's total revenue is price times quantity or PQ. Therefore, marginal revenue is

QUANT OPTION

$$\pi = TR - TC$$

$$\frac{d\pi}{dQ} = \frac{dTR}{dQ} - \frac{dTC}{dQ}$$

To maximize profit,

$$0 = \frac{dTR}{dQ} - \frac{dTC}{dQ}$$

so

$$\frac{dTR}{dQ} = \frac{dTC}{dQ}$$

or

$$MR = MC$$

$\Delta TR/\Delta Q = P$. So the firm's marginal revenue is the product's price. This is not surprising. If the firm sells five units, its total revenue is $5P$; if it sells six units, its total revenue is $6P$; if it sells seven units, its total revenue is $7P$; and so on. Every time another unit is sold, total revenue rises by P. In this case $P = \$10$, so the firm's marginal revenue (always equal to price for a price taker) is $10.

Consider the firm's total cost ($TC = 1 + 2Q + Q^2$). Therefore, $\Delta TC/\Delta Q = 2 + 2Q$, and $\Delta TC/\Delta Q$ is called the firm's marginal cost. It represents a change in the total cost (or variable cost) when output changes by a small amount (usually by $\Delta Q = 1$).

The condition $\Delta TR/\Delta Q = \Delta TC/\Delta Q$ is restated as $MR = MC$; that is, to maximize profit, the manager must set marginal revenue equal to marginal cost (if marginal cost is increasing). In the case of a price taker, the profit-maximizing condition reads $P = MC$ (because $P = MR$). This is why managers want to avoid these markets: The nature of competition is to grind the price down to marginal cost. The competitive pressure is relentless. There is no above-normal economic profit, nor should managers expect any (except in the short run). Clearly managers should never produce output where the marginal cost is greater than the marginal revenue. Hence

$$P = 10 = 2 + 2Q = MC \text{ or } Q = 4 \tag{7.3}$$

One other condition must exist for the $P = MC$ rule to yield a profit maximum. It must be the case that $\Delta(\Delta\pi/\Delta Q)/\Delta Q < 0$. Since $\Delta\pi/\Delta Q = P - MC$, this means that $\Delta P/\Delta Q - \Delta MC/\Delta Q < 0$. Since $\Delta P/\Delta Q = 0$, then $-\Delta MC/\Delta Q < 0$ or $\Delta MC/\Delta Q > 0$. That is, the marginal cost must be increasing.

QUANT OPTION

For a maximum to occur, the sign of the second derivative of the profit function must be negative.

$$\frac{d^2\pi}{dQ^2} = d\left(\frac{\dfrac{d\pi}{dQ}}{dQ}\right)$$

$$= d\left(\frac{\dfrac{dTR}{dQ}}{dQ}\right) - d\left(\frac{\dfrac{dTC}{dQ}}{dQ}\right)$$

$$= \frac{dMR}{dQ} - \frac{dMC}{dQ} < 0$$

Because $MR = P$ and doesn't change as Q changes,

$$\frac{dMR}{dQ} = 0$$

Thus dMC/dQ must be positive because it has a negative sign in front of it and the whole equation must be negative.

Table 7.2, Figures 7.2 and 7.3, and equation (7.3) show that managers maximize the firm's profit at four units per time period. At this output level, the profit figure in the last column of Table 7.2 is the highest; the vertical distance between the total revenue and cost curves in Figure 7.2 is the largest; and the profit curve in Figure 7.3 is the highest.

QUANT OPTION

Of course the marginal revenue of the firm is $dTR/dQ = P$ because Q is not a function of P. The marginal cost is

$$dTC/dQ = 2 + 2Q$$

FIGURE 7.3

Relationship of Profit and Output of a Perfectly Competitive Firm

The output rate that maximizes profit is four units per time period. To maximize profit, the slope of the profit function ($\Delta\pi/\Delta Q$) must be zero.

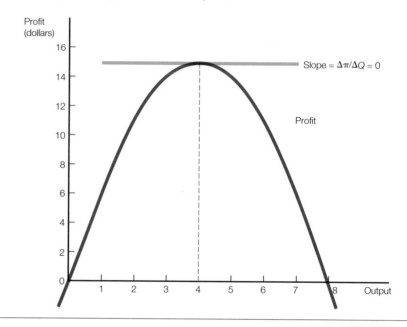

It is worthwhile to present the marginal revenue and marginal cost curves as well as the total revenue and total cost curves. Table 7.3 shows the firm's marginal revenue and marginal costs at each output rate.

Figure 7.4 shows the resulting marginal revenue and marginal cost at each output rate. Because the manager takes the price as given, it is constant for all output levels ($P = MR$). Hence the marginal revenue curve is also the firm's demand curve, which (for the reasons discussed already) is horizontal.

The central point to note is that managers maximize profit at the output where the price (or marginal revenue) equals the marginal cost. Both the numbers in Table 7.3 and the curves in Figure 7.4 indicate that the price equals the marginal cost at an output rate of four units, which we know from Table 7.2, Figures 7.2 and 7.3, and equation (7.3) to be the profit-maximizing output.

SETTING THE MARGINAL COST EQUAL TO THE PRICE

Earlier we showed that if managers want to maximize firm value, they should set price equal to marginal cost when marginal cost is increasing. As we can see in Table 7.3 and Figure 7.4, this is true.[3]

3. Recall from Chapter 6 that in the short run, $MC = W/MP$, where W is the fixed wage of labor and MP is the marginal product of labor. Therefore, if the marginal cost is increasing, the marginal product of labor must be decreasing. A price-taking situation, therefore, implies diminishing marginal productivity of labor in the short run.

TABLE 7.3

Marginal Revenue and Marginal Cost: Perfectly Competitive Firm

Output per Period	Marginal Revenue	Marginal Cost[a]
0	10	2
1	10	4
2	10	6
3	10	8
4	10	10
5	10	12
6	10	14
7	10	16
8	10	18

[a]This column was calculated from $MC = 2 + 2Q$. This assumes that output can be sold and produced in noninteger, continuous amounts. Many goods meet this criteria—for example, gasoline, deli meats, and bulk agricultural products. Although these goods are priced on a per-unit basis (by the gallon, per pound), seldom do we purchase integer units. Other goods are produced and consumed only in integer units, such as cars, televisions, and compact disks. In this case, the marginal cost for output level n is calculated as the total cost at output level n minus the total cost for output level $n - 1$. For instance, the total cost at $Q = 3$ is 16, at $Q = 4$ is 25, at $Q = 5$ is 36 (see Table 7.2). Therefore, the marginal cost at $Q = 4$ is 9 and at $Q = 5$ is 11 (as opposed to 10 and 12 shown in this table). Under these conditions, the manager wants to produce the fourth unit because the marginal revenue from doing so ($10) exceeds the marginal cost ($9). However, the manager would not produce the fifth unit because the marginal cost of doing so ($11) exceeds the marginal revenue ($10). Therefore, the manager produces four units in the integer output case and in the continuous output case.

Managers in perfectly competitive markets often accrue negative profits, even if they satisfy the preceding rules ($P = MC$ and MC increasing). If the price is P_2 in Figure 7.5, the short-run average total cost exceeds the price at all possible outputs. Because the short run is too short (by definition) to permit the manager to alter the scale of plant, all she can do is produce at a loss or discontinue production. The decision to close a plant should answer one question: Does the product's price cover the average variable costs? For any output where price exceeds average variable costs, managers should produce, even though the price does not cover average total costs. If there is no output rate at which price exceeds the average variable cost, the manager is better off shutting the plant. Hence if the average variable cost curve is as shown in Figure 7.5, the manager will produce if the price is P_2 but not if it is P_1.

It is essential to recognize that if managers shut a plant, they still incur fixed costs. Therefore, if the loss from producing is less than the firm's fixed costs (the loss of shutting down), it is more profitable (a smaller deficit) to produce than

FIGURE 7.4

Marginal Revenue and Marginal Cost of a Perfectly Competitive Firm

When output is at the profit maximizing level of four units, price (= marginal revenue) equals marginal cost.

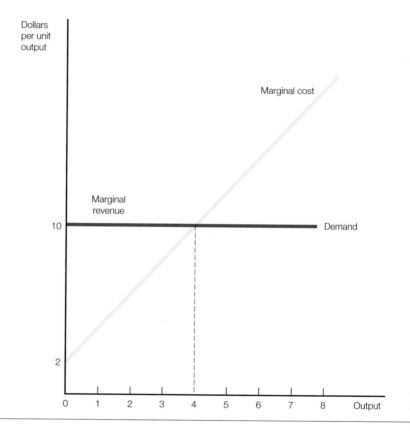

to discontinue production. Another way of expressing this is if the loss per unit of output is less than the average fixed cost—that is, if $ATC - P < AFC$, where ATC is average total cost, P is price, and AFC is average fixed cost. This is true if $ATC < AFC + P$ because P is merely added to both sides of the inequality. Subtracting AFC from both sides results in $ATC - AFC < P$. $ATC - AFC$ is the average variable cost; thus it is better to produce than to shut down production if the price exceeds the average variable cost.

Managers must manage the cash flow they control, which is total revenue (because managers control the Q of P^*Q). They must also manage variable cost because it is a function of Q. But the fixed cost is not part of controllable short-run

In the eastern part of the United States, (Delaware, Illinois, Indiana, Kentucky, Maryland, Michigan, New Jersey, North Carolina, Ohio, Pennsylvania, Tennessee, Virginia, West Virginia, and the District of Columbia), power can be transmitted among power companies on the PJM Interconnection (a regional transmission organization). There are 650 member companies and 1,325 generating stations on the network. It is the largest competitive wholesale electric market in the world. Companies that have excess power can sell it to the highest bidder, and companies that require more power can buy power from the grid. The grid operator has an independent monitor, Monitoring Analytics. The monitor reports that PJM's prices were set by marginal units operating at or near their marginal cost. Joseph Bowring, president of Monitoring Analytics, reports that "this is evidence of competitive behavior and competitive market outcomes." That's what the theory tells us.

Historically, the international iron ore market tended to operate on an annual price that was reset every year. Customers and suppliers signed contracts based on this rate, despite the fact that demand or supply conditions arising during the course of that year could cause more to be demanded at that price than supplied or more supplied than demanded. Prices were not free to go up in the former case or down in the latter case. But over time, a spot market developed reflecting the market conditions in supply and demand in real time.

Marius Kloppers, head of BHP Billiton, is a major advocate of the spot market. Kloppers notes that spot pricing "will mean that the cost of the highest marginal tonne (read highest seller's reservation price) in any particular system, be it iron ore, coking or thermal coal, or manganese, will be more efficiently transferred into the global price. And that means, over the longer haul, the lowest-cost operators (those with the lowest seller's reservation price) will secure both a greater share of overall demand and better prices." With respect to exports to China, Kloppers notes that true market prices encourage

Australian producers to expand more vigorously (as demand is growing) and that the new Australian tonnes to meet the expanded Chinese demand replace the most expensive Chinese domestic production. "And each time someone (a high marginal cost producer) is squeezed out, the highest marginal cost is lowered and thus the reference price falls too." Ah, the beauty of price equals marginal cost in action.

Kloppers appears again in a bid to acquire Potash Corp of Saskatchewan, Canada. If successful, his strategy will be to operate the mines at full capacity. Because they are low-cost mines, Kloppers believes that such a move would lower prices in the short run. However, he believes that such production will lead to higher prices over the long run "as rival marginal high-cost production is deferred."

The market share of the big three cement producers in central Africa (initially 93%) has fallen by 14% as new producers have entered the market with cheaper prices. The new entrants' factories have lower maintenance costs and higher energy efficiency. In addition, they have lower clinker (a mineral element that goes into cement production) costs. Finally, the new entrants are already in the building supplies industry and can add the cement into their existing distribution network. These lower costs are passed on to consumers, and the lower marginal cost has shifted the supply curve of cement downward yielding lower cement prices.

Sources: "PJM Wholesale Power Price Rises in 2010, but Markets Still Competitive, Monitor Says," *Platts Inside FERC*, August 16, 2010, at www.lexisnexis.com/Inacui2api/; Matt Stevens, "Shift to Rational Pricing Will End Annual Conflict," February 13, 2010, at www.theaustralian.com.au/business/opinion/shift-to-rational-pricing-will-end-annual-conflict/story-e6frg9if-1225829866038; Andy Stevens and Brenda Bouw, "Chinese Bid for Potash Corp Would Cut Revenues, BHP Warns," *The Globe and Mail*, September 21, 2010, at www.theglobeandmail.com/globe-investor/potash/Chinese-bid-for-potash-corp-would-cut-revenues-bhp-warns/article1716883; Moses Michira, "New Cement Firms Ride on Low Prices to Grow Sales," *Business Daily*, January 27, 2011, at www.businessdailyafrica.com/New-cement-firms-ride-on-low-prices-to-grow-sales/-/539552/1096296/-/oemr6i-index.html.

FIGURE 7.5

Short-Run Average and Marginal Cost Curves

If the price is P_0, the firm will produce an output of X; if price is P_2, it will produce an output of Y; and if price is less than P_3 (that is, when P_3 equals the minimum of average variable cost), the firm will produce nothing.

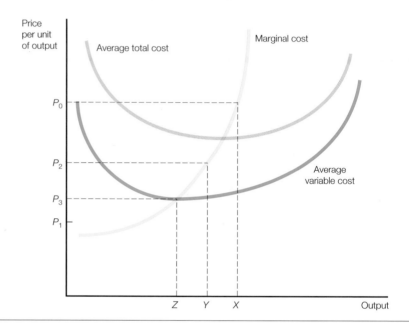

cash flow. Thus managers want TR to exceed VC by as much as possible—that is, maximizing the controllable cash flow. If VC exceeds TR, they shouldn't produce because controllable cash flow is negative. If TR exceeds VC, they should produce because controllable cash flow is positive. Dividing both sides in the preceding sentence by Q yields $TR/Q = P > VC/Q = AVC$. Thus in addition to $P = MC$, P must exceed AVC.

The manager will be indifferent at P_3, the price that is equal to the minimum point of average costs (output Z). The point (Z, P_3) is called the **shutdown point** because at that point, the price equals the minimum average variable cost. Price is also equal to marginal cost because it intersects with average variable cost at this point. The future is clear: At this price, the manager loses money equal to fixed cost if he produces, or he loses that money if he shuts down. At any price below P_3, the manager shuts the plant. Therefore, the marginal cost curve (above the minimum average variable cost) is the supply curve of the firm; that is, if the price is P_2, the firm produces Y, and if the price is P_0, the firm produces X. These points (Y, P_2) and (X, P_0) are also points on the firm's marginal cost curve.

Shutdown point When the price equals the minimum average variable cost.

STRATEGY SESSION: Forecasting the Price of Salmon

Managers at a large diversified food firm set out to forecast the price of fresh salmon three years ahead. Such a forecast is needed because these managers must decide whether they should enter the business of supplying salmon. The firm's analysts estimate the quantity of fresh salmon to be supplied three years ahead. Because of substantial plans to expand the production of farmed Atlantic and Pacific salmon in Canada, Chile, Japan, and Ireland, this projected supply is considerably greater than the actual current supply. In addition, the analysts estimate the quantity of fresh salmon that is demanded three years ahead. Their results show that if the price of salmon remains unchanged over the next three years, the quantity supplied will exceed the quantity demanded by about 15% at the end of the three-year period.

The firm's analysts also estimate the price elasticity of demand for fresh salmon to be about −1.5. This estimate, too, is based on the techniques described in previous chapters. Like the other estimates presented here, it is regarded as rough but useful.

Before they can determine whether to enter the salmon market, managers need to estimate the future price of salmon. (The firm's analysts believed that the quantity supplied three years hence will be approximately equal to their estimates, regardless of whatever changes occur in price during this three-year period.) Using the previous estimates, they envision that the quantity demanded will increase by 15% to reduce the gap between quantity supplied and quantity demanded. Because they estimate that the price elasticity of salmon is −1.5, a 10% decrease in price will increase the quantity demanded by about 15%.

Note: This section is based on an actual case, although the numbers and situation have been disguised somewhat.

PROBLEM SOLVED: The Kadda Company

As an illustration, consider the Kadda Company, a perfectly competitive firm with the following total cost function

$$TC = 800 + 6Q + 2Q^2$$

where TC is the total cost (in dollars) and Q is the firm's output per day. The firm's marginal cost is therefore

$$\Delta TC/\Delta Q = MC = 6 + 4Q$$

If the price of Kadda's product equals $30, the manager should set output so that

$$MC = \Delta TC/\Delta Q = 6 + 4Q = 30 = P \qquad (7.4)$$

In other words, the manager should set marginal cost equal to price ($30). Solving equation (7.4) for Q, we find the manager should set output equal to six units per day. To make sure the price is not less than average variable cost at that output, we note that because the firm's total variable cost equals $6Q + 2Q^2$, its average variable cost (AVC) equals

$$AVC = (6Q + 2Q^2)/Q = 6 + 2Q$$

Therefore, if $Q = 6$, average variable cost equals $6 + 2(6)$ or $18, which is less than the price of $30.

QUANT OPTION

Kadda's marginal cost is

$$dTC/dQ = MC = 6 + 4Q$$

To summarize, if the manager maximizes profit or minimizes loss, the output is set so the short-run marginal cost equals the price and the marginal cost is rising. But this proposition has an exception: If the market price is below the firm's average variable costs at every output level, the manager minimizes loss by discontinuing production.

ANOTHER WAY OF VIEWING THE PRICE EQUALS MARGINAL COST PROFIT-MAXIMIZING RULE

If a firm has one fixed input (say capital) and one variable input (say labor), how much of its variable input should it utilize? This is an important question for managers of firms large and small. To answer it, we must define the marginal revenue product of the variable input and the marginal expenditure of the variable input.

Marginal revenue product (MRP)
The amount an additional unit of the variable input adds to the firm's total revenue.

The **marginal revenue product (MRP)** is the amount an additional unit of the variable input adds to the firm's total revenue. The input adds to total revenue because it allows managers to produce more output. Letting MRP_L be the marginal revenue product of the labor input,

$$MRP_L = \Delta TR/\Delta L \tag{7.5}$$

where ΔTR is the change in total revenue resulting from a change of L, the amount of labor input used by the firm. It can easily be proven that MRP_L equals labor's marginal product times the firm's marginal revenue. To see this, note that marginal revenue (MR) equals $\Delta TR/\Delta Q$, where ΔQ is the change in the firm's output, and that

$$MRP_L = \Delta TR/\Delta L = (\Delta TR/\Delta Q)(\Delta Q/\Delta L)$$

Because $\Delta Q/\Delta L$ equals labor's marginal product (MP_L), it follows that

$$MRP_L = (MR)(MP_L) \tag{7.6}$$

which is what we set out to prove. Let's view the intuition. If managers use ΔL more labor, they produce ΔQ more units of the firm's product—that is, the marginal product of labor. If managers take these additional ΔQ units to market, they will generate ΔTR in revenue (marginal revenue). The marginal revenue per unit times the number of units gives the additional revenue obtained by managers as the result of using an additional unit of labor.

The marginal expenditure (ME) is the amount an additional unit of labor adds to the firm's total costs. That is, letting ME_L be the marginal expenditure on labor,

$$ME_L = \Delta TC/\Delta L \tag{7.7}$$

where ΔTC is the change in total cost resulting from a change in the amount of labor, ΔL. If managers can buy all the labor they want at the price of \$10 per unit, ME_L equals \$10. In some cases, however, managers must pay a higher price for labor to get more of it; in such cases, ME_L exceeds the price of labor (as we will show in the monopsony section of Chapter 8). Note that $\Delta TC/\Delta L$ can be written as $(\Delta TC/\Delta Q)(\Delta Q/\Delta L)$, where $\Delta TC/\Delta Q$ is the change in the firm's total cost (ΔTC) divided by the firm's change in output (ΔQ). $\Delta TC/\Delta Q$ is the firm's marginal cost (MC), or the change in the firm's total cost as its output is changed by a small amount.

QUANT OPTION

In more technical terms,

$$MRP_L = dTR/dL$$

and

$$ME_L = dTC/dL$$

To maximize profit, managers should use labor where its marginal revenue product equals its marginal expenditure. In other words, managers should set

$$MRP_L = ME_L \tag{7.8}$$

Again, let's view the intuition. To maximize profit, managers need to expand any activity as long as the marginal benefit exceeds the marginal cost. They should stop expanding it when the marginal benefit (in this case MRP_L) equals the marginal cost (in this case ME_L). To generalize this further, rewrite equation (7.8) as

$$\left(\frac{\Delta TR}{\Delta Q}\right)\left(\frac{\Delta Q}{\Delta L}\right) = \left(\frac{\Delta TC}{\Delta Q}\right)\left(\frac{\Delta Q}{\Delta L}\right)$$

or

$$\frac{\Delta TR}{\Delta Q} = \frac{\Delta TC}{\Delta Q}$$

or

$$MR = MC$$

We have again verified one of the most important rules of managerial economics: Managers should stop expanding output when marginal revenue equals marginal cost.

In the case of perfect competition, $MR = P$. So our rule becomes $P \times MP_L = ME_L = P_L$, where P_L is the price of a unit of labor. Consider the intuition once again. Hiring another unit of labor costs managers P_L. That laborer generates MP_L additional output, which, when managers take it to market, generates $P \times MP_L$ additional revenue for the firm. Managers should continue to hire more labor as long as $P \times MP_L > P_L$, and they won't hire labor if $P \times MP_L < P_L$. The stopping rule to maximize profit is $P \times MP_L = P_L$. Dividing both sides by MP_L gives $P = P_L/MP_L$. As was shown in Chapter 6, $P_L/MP_L = MC$. Thus to maximize profit in the perfectly competitive market, managers should expand production until $P = MC$.

PRODUCER SURPLUS IN THE SHORT RUN

In Chapter 3 we examined consumer surplus and saw that it equals the difference between the market price and the price consumers are willing to pay (their reservation price). Now we introduce a parallel idea, called producer surplus, from the supply side of the market. **Producer surplus** is the difference between the market price and the price the producer is willing to receive for a good or service (the producer's reservation price). As we showed in our analysis of a perfectly competitive market, a producer's reservation price is the marginal cost of producing a good or service (above the break-even point of the firm). Panel A of Figure 7.6 shows this surplus in the shaded area. The firm's profit before accounting for fixed cost (its variable cost profit $P^*BC'D' = P^*BE$) is just total revenue (P^*Q^*) minus variable cost ($D'C'Q^*O$). But the variable cost is also just the area under the marginal cost up to output Q^*; that is, EBQ^*O. This variable-cost profit is also the shaded area in Panel A of Figure 7.6; that is, P^*BE. Note the difference between profit (P^*BCD) and producer surplus. To arrive at a producer surplus, managers subtract only the variable cost from the total revenue, whereas to calculate their profit, they subtract both the fixed and variable costs from total revenue. Hence the variable-cost profit is larger than profit (by the level of fixed cost), and producer surplus and variable-cost profit are the same. Because the perfectly competitive firm's marginal cost represents its supply curve, we can view producer surplus as the difference between the supply curve and the price received for the good (area B in Panel B of Figure 7.6).

Figure 7.7 shows the market equilibrium. Just as market demand is the horizontal summation of individuals' demand curves for the product, market supply

Producer surplus The difference between the market price and the price the producer is willing to receive for a good or service (the producer's reservation price).

FIGURE 7.6

Producer Surplus and Variable-Cost Profit

Producer surplus for the firm is its variable-cost profit, or total revenue minus variable cost. Producer surplus for the market is the area above the supply curve but below the price received for the good because the supply curve is the horizontal summation of the competitive firms' marginal cost curves.

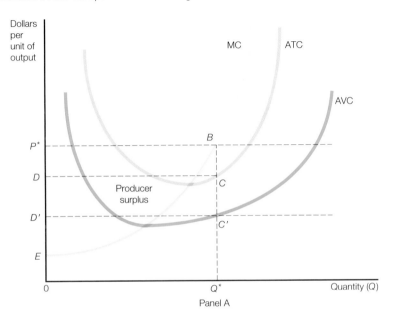

Panel A

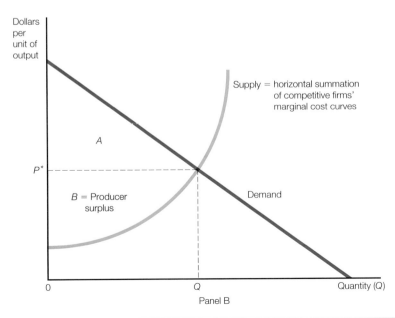

Panel B

FIGURE 7.7

Market Social Welfare (A + B) of a Perfectly Competitive Price Policy, P*

Social welfare at a given price (P*) is measured by the sum of the consumer surplus (A) and the producer surplus (B).

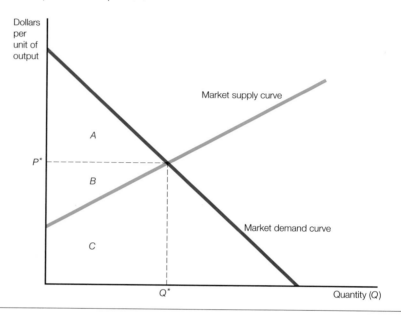

is the horizontal summation of individual firms' supply curves for the product. Using the results for consumer surplus, we can see from Figure 7.7 that the market equilibrium price of P* yields a consumer surplus of A and a producer surplus of B.

The sum of A and B, the total surplus, is the economist's measure of social welfare at the price P* and the quantity Q*. To understand this idea, think about the total benefit and cost that consumers and producers assign to the goods in the market. For consumers, this is the area beneath the demand curve, left of the equilibrium quantity—that is, the total amount consumers are willing to pay for the goods (areas A, B, and C in Figure 7.7). For producers, the total variable cost of supplying quantity Q* is the area beneath the supply curve and left of the equilibrium quantity (area C in Figure 7.7). In the market consumers pay and producers receive P*. Yet P* is less than the total benefit and greater than the variable cost of the goods. In this sense the market exchange generates value for participants, represented by consumer, producer, and total surplus. In this case the difference between what the demanders are willing to spend (A, B, and C) and what the suppliers are willing to receive (C) is the measure of social welfare—that is, A + B.

Clearly the magnitude of the total surplus and its distribution between consumers and producers depend on the shape of the demand and supply curves. For instance, keeping the equilibrium at P^*, Q^*, a more gently sloped supply curve reduces producer surplus, whereas a more gently sloped demand curve reduces consumer surplus. But the thing to remember is that market exchanges, generally speaking, provide opportunities for gains; and as we see later, savvy managers can devise ways to capture a greater share of those gains for their firms.

We use this measure of social welfare to show the rationale of antitrust policy and the gains from trade in Chapter 17.

LONG-RUN EQUILIBRIUM OF THE FIRM

In the long run, how much will managers of a competitive firm produce? The long-run equilibrium position of the firm is at the point where its long-run average total cost curve[4] equals the price. If the price exceeeds the average total cost, economic profit is earned and new firms enter the industry. This increases supply, thereby driving down price and hence profit. If the price is less than the

4. This is also called the *long-run average cost curve*. Because all costs are variable in the long run, there is no need for an adjective in front of average costs, as there is in the short run, to distinguish between average total, average variable, and average fixed costs. There are only average costs in the long run.

PROBLEM SOLVED: Output at the Bergey Company

For example, suppose the Bergey Company's long-run average cost curve is

$$AC = 200 - 4Q + 0.05Q^2 \qquad (7.9)$$

where AC is long-run average cost (in dollars) and Q is the firm's output per day. Because the Bergey Company operates in a perfectly competitive market, its output in the long run equals the value of Q that minimizes AC. Note from Figure 7.8 that the slope of the long-run average total cost curve when it is a minimum is $\Delta AC/\Delta Q = 0$; that is, GG' is tangent to AC at the output level V in Figure 7.8.

Forming $\Delta AC/\Delta Q$ from equation (7.9) and setting it $= 0$ gives $Q = 40$. Therefore, if managers at Bergey maximize profit, in the long run they will maintain an output of 40 units per day.

As indicated previously, the average cost equals the marginal cost at this output. To see this, note that because total cost equals Q times AC,

$$TC = Q(200 - 4Q + 0.05Q^2)$$
$$= 200Q - 4Q^2 + 0.05Q^3$$

where TC is total cost.

The firm's marginal cost is $MC = \Delta TC/\Delta Q$. Therefore, $MC = \Delta TC/\Delta Q = 200 - 8Q + 0.15Q^2$. Because $Q = 40$,

$$MC = 200 - 8(40) + 0.15(40)^2 = 120$$

Also, inserting 40 for Q in equation (7.9),

$$AC = 200 - 4(40) + 0.05(40)^2 = 120$$

Therefore, marginal cost equals average cost when $Q = 40$. (Both marginal cost and average cost equal $120. This means that the long-run equilibrium price is $120.)

average total costs for any firm, that firm will exit the industry. As firms exit, supply falls, causing price and profit to rise. Only when economic profit is zero (which means that long-run average cost equals price) is a firm in long-run equilibrium.

Recall from Chapter 1 that economic profit is not the same as accounting profit. Economic profit is profit above and beyond what the owners could obtain elsewhere from the resources they invest in the firm. Therefore, long-run equilibrium occurs when the owners receive no more (and no less) than they could obtain elsewhere from these resources.

More specifically, the price must equal the *lowest value* of the long-run average total cost. That is, in equilibrium managers produce at the minimum point on their long-run average cost curves. To see why, note that if managers maximize their profit, they must operate where price equals long-run marginal cost. Also, we just saw that they must operate where price equals long-run average cost. If both of these conditions are satisfied, it follows that long-run marginal cost must equal long-run average cost. And we know from Chapter 6 that long-run marginal cost is equal to long-run average cost only at the point at which long-run average cost is a minimum. Consequently this point is the equilibrium position of the firm.

To illustrate this equilibrium position, consider Figure 7.8. When all the adjustments are made, price equals G. Because price is constant, the demand curve

---

FIGURE 7.8

Long-Run Equilibrium of a Perfectly Competitive Firm

In long-run equilibrium, the firm produces an output of *V*, and price = marginal cost (both long-run and short-run) = average cost (both long-run and short-run).

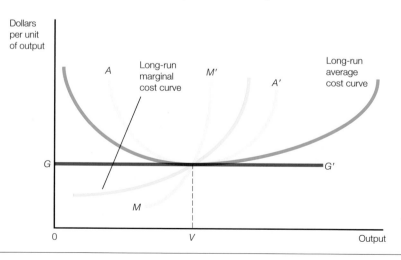

is horizontal, and therefore the marginal revenue curve is the same as the demand curve, both being GG'. The equilibrium output of the firm is V, and its optimally sized plant is described by the short-run average and marginal cost curves AA' and MM'. At this output and with this plant, we see that long-run marginal cost equals short-run marginal cost equals price. This ensures that the manager maximizes profit. Also, long-run average cost equals the short-run average cost equals price; this ensures that economic profit is zero. Because long-run marginal cost and long-run average cost must be equal, the equilibrium point is at the bottom of the long-run average cost curve.

THE LONG-RUN ADJUSTMENT PROCESS: A CONSTANT-COST INDUSTRY

Having looked at the behavior of managers at a perfectly competitive firm in the short and long runs, we turn to the long-run adjustment process of a perfectly competitive industry. We assume that this industry is a *constant-cost industry*, which means that expansion of the industry does not increase input prices. Figure 7.9 shows long-run equilibrium under conditions of constant cost. The top panel shows the short-run and long-run cost curves of a typical firm in the industry. The bottom panel shows the demand and supply curves in the market as a whole, D being the original demand curve and S the original short-run supply curve. We assume the industry is in long-run equilibrium, with the result that the price ($6 perunit) equals the minimum value of the long-run (and short-run) average cost.

Suppose now that the demand curve shifts to D_1. In the short run, with the number of firms fixed, the product price rises from $6 to $7 per unit; each firm expands its output from 5,000 to 6,000 units per day; and each firm makes economic profit because the new price, $7, exceeds the short-run average costs of the firm when the output is 6,000 units per day. The result is that firms enter the industry and the supply curve shifts to the right. In a constant-cost industry, entrance of new firms does not influence the costs of existing firms. The inputs used by this industry are used by other industries as well, and new firms in this industry do not bid up the price of inputs and hence raise the costs of existing firms. Neither does the entry of new firms reduce existing firms' costs.

Hence a constant-cost industry has a horizontal long-run supply curve. Because output can be increased by increasing the number of firms producing 5,000 units of output per day at an average cost of $6 per unit, the long-run supply curve is horizontal at $6 per unit. So long as the industry remains in a state of constant costs, its output can be increased indefinitely. If price exceeds $6 per unit, firms enter the industry; if price is less than $6 per unit, firms leave the industry.

FIGURE 7.9

Long-Run Equilibrium in a Constant-Cost Industry

A constant-cost industry has a horizontal long-run supply curve, as shown in panel B. If demand shifts upward from D to D_1, the consequent increase in price (to $7 per unit) results in the entry of firms, which shifts the supply curve to the right (to S_1), thus pushing the price back to its original level ($6 per unit).

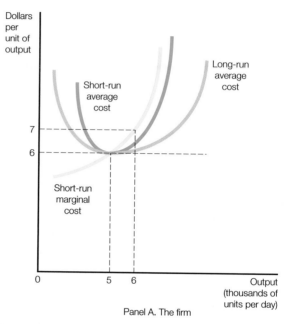

Panel A. The firm

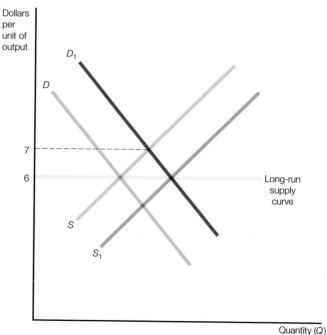

Panel B. The industry

Therefore long-run equilibrium can occur in this industry only when price is $6 per unit. And industry output can be raised or lowered, in accord with demand conditions, without changing this long-run equilibrium price.

THE LONG-RUN ADJUSTMENT PROCESS: AN INCREASING-COST INDUSTRY

Not all industries are constant-cost industries. Next we consider the case of an *increasing-cost industry*, which occurs when industry expansion increases input prices.[5] An increasing-cost industry is shown in Figure 7.10. The original conditions are the same as in Figure 7.9: In panel B, D is the original demand curve, S is the original supply curve, $6 per unit is the equilibrium price, and LL' and AA' in the top panel are the long-run and short-run average cost curves of each firm. As in Figure 7.9, the original position is one of long-run equilibrium because price equals the minimum value of long-run (and short-run) average cost.

Assume now that the demand curve shifts to D_1, with the result that the product price goes up and the firms earn economic profit, attracting new entrants. More and more inputs are needed by the industry, and in an increasing-cost industry, the prices of the inputs rise with the amount used by the industry. Therefore, the cost of inputs increases for established firms as well as entrants, and the average cost curves are pushed up to $L_1L'_1$ and $A_1A'_1$.

If each firm's marginal cost curve is shifted to the left by the increase in input prices, the industry supply curve tends to shift to the left. But this tendency is more than counterbalanced by the increase in the number of firms, which shifts the industry supply curve to the right. The latter effect *must* more than offset the former effect because otherwise there is no expansion in total industry output. (No new resources are attracted to the industry.) This process of adjustment must go on until a new point of long-run equilibrium is reached. In Figure 7.10 this point is where the price of the product is $7 per unit and each firm produces 6,000 units per day.[6]

An increasing-cost industry has a positively sloped long-run supply curve. That is, after long-run equilibrium is achieved, increases in output require increases in the price of the product. For example, points X and Y in Figure 7.10 are on the long-run supply curve for the industry. The difference between constant-cost and increasing-cost industries is this: In constant-cost industries, new firms enter in response to an increase in demand until the price returns to its original level; whereas in increasing-cost industries, new firms enter until the minimum point on the long-run average cost curve has increased to the point where it equals the new, higher price.[7]

Finally, some industries are neither constant-cost nor increasing-cost industries: They are decreasing-cost industries. Their long-run supply curves

5. In addition to constant-cost and increasing-cost industries, there are also decreasing-cost industries, which are the most unusual case, although quite young industries may fall into the category. External economies, which are cost reductions that occur when an industry expands, may be responsible for the existence of decreasing-cost industries. For example, the expansion of an industry may improve transportation and reduce the costs of each firm in the industry. A decreasing-cost industry has a negatively sloped long-run supply curve.

6. We cannot be sure that the firm's new output exceeds its old output as shown in Figure 7.10. It is possible for its new output to be less than or equal to its old output.

7. This is not the only way in which equilibrium can be achieved in increasing-cost industries. It is also possible that the increase in input prices (due to the expansion of industry output) raises average cost more than the increase in demand raises average revenue. Therefore, firms may experience losses, some may leave the industry, and the remaining firms may produce more.

FIGURE 7.10

Long-Run Equilibrium in an Increasing-Cost Industry

An increasing-cost industry has a positively sloped long-run supply curve, as shown in panel B. After long-run equilibrium is achieved, increases in output require increases in the price of the product.

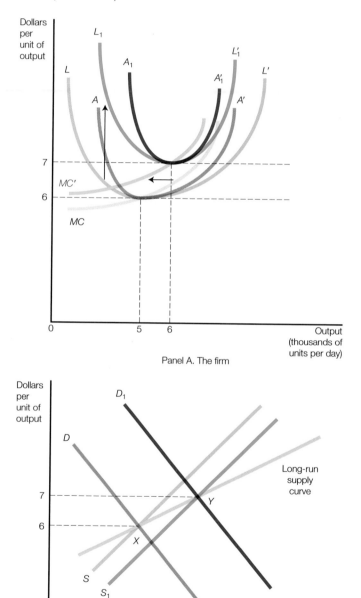

Panel A. The firm

Panel B. The industry

are negatively sloped. For further discussion of these industries, which are encountered less frequently than constant-cost or increasing-cost industries, see footnote 5.

HOW A PERFECTLY COMPETITIVE ECONOMY ALLOCATES RESOURCES

It is important for managers to understand how a competitive economy allocates resources. Without such an understanding, they cannot interpret or anticipate the fundamental changes that may occur. To illustrate this allocation process, we take a simple case: Consumers become more favorably disposed toward corn and less favorably disposed toward rice than in the past. What happens in the short run? The rising demand for corn increases its price and results in some increase in the output of corn. However, corn output cannot be increased substantially because the capacity of the industry cannot be expanded in the short run. Similarly, the falling demand for rice reduces its price and results in some reduction in the output of rice. But the output of rice cannot be curtailed greatly because firms continue to produce as long as they can cover their variable costs. Because of the increased price of corn and the decreased price of rice, corn producers earn economic profit and rice producers show economic loss. Producers reallocate resources to correct this imbalance.

When short-run equilibrium is achieved in both the corn and rice industries, the reallocation of resources is not yet complete because there has not been enough time for producers to build new capacity or liquidate old capacity. In particular, neither industry operates at minimum average cost. The corn producers may operate at greater than the output level where average cost is a minimum; and the rice producers may operate at less than the output level where average cost is a minimum.

What occurs in the long run? The shift in consumer demand from rice to corn results in greater adjustments in output and smaller adjustments in price than in the short run. In the long run, existing firms can leave rice production and new firms can enter corn production. As firms leave rice production, the supply curve shifts to the left, causing the price to rise above its short-run level. The transfer of resources out of rice production ceases when the price has increased and costs have decreased to the point where loss no longer occurs.

Whereas rice production loses resources, corn production gains them. The short-run profit in corn production stimulates the entry of new firms. The increased demand for inputs raises input prices and cost curves in corn production, and the price of corn is depressed by the movement to the right of the supply curve because of the entry of new firms. Entry stops when economic profit is no longer being earned. At that point, when long-run equilibrium is achieved, more firms and more resources are used in the corn industry than in the short run.

SUMMARY

1. Managers of perfectly competitive firms set output levels so that price equals marginal cost. If there is an output level where price exceeds average variable cost, it pays for managers to produce in the short run, even though price does not cover average total costs. But if there is no output level where price exceeds average variable cost, managers are better off to produce nothing at all. In the long run, managers produce at the minimum point on their long-run average total cost curve. The price tends to be at the level where the market demand curve intersects the market supply curve. The short-run supply curve of a perfectly competitive firm is its marginal cost curve above the point of the minimum average variable cost.

2. Producer surplus is equivalent to the firm's variable-cost profit—that is, total revenue less variable costs. The producer surplus is the difference between the price a seller receives for its product and the seller's reservation price (the minimum price at which she would sell her product). This is a measure of welfare from a producer's perspective. When combined with the consumer surplus introduced in Chapter 3, the sum of the producer and consumer surpluses gives a measure of social welfare. We can use this measure to compare the benefits of different pricing proposals and the benefits of trade (as shown in Chapter 17).

3. A constant-cost industry has a horizontal long-run supply curve; an increasing-cost industry has a positively sloped long-run supply curve. If a constant-cost industry expands, there is no increase (or decrease) in input prices; if an increasing-cost industry expands, there is an increase in input prices.

wwnorton.com/studyspace

PROBLEMS

1. The Hamilton Company is a member of a perfectly competitive industry. Like all members of the industry, its total cost function is

$$TC = 25{,}000 + 150Q + 3Q^2$$

where TC is the firm's monthly total cost (in dollars) and Q is the firm's monthly output.

   a. If the industry is in long-run equilibrium, what is the price of the Hamilton Company's product?

   b. What is the firm's monthly output?

2. In 2012, the box industry was perfectly competitive. The lowest point on the long-run average cost curve of each of the identical box producers was $4, and this minimum point occurred at an output of 1,000 boxes per month. The market demand curve for boxes was

$$Q_D = 140{,}000 - 10{,}000P$$

where P was the price of a box (in dollars per box) and Q_D was the quantity of boxes demanded per month. The market supply curve for boxes was

$$Q_S = 80{,}000 + 5{,}000P$$

where Q_S was the quantity of boxes supplied per month.

a. What was the equilibrium price of a box? Is this the long-run equilibrium price?

b. How many firms are in this industry when it is in long-run equilibrium?

3. The Burr Corporation's total cost function (where TC is the total cost in dollars and Q is quantity) is

$$TC = 200 + 4Q + 2Q^2$$

a. If the firm is perfectly competitive and the price of its product is $24, what is its optimal output rate?

b. At this output rate, what is its profit?

4. The supply and demand curves for pears are

$$Q_S = 10{,}000P$$
$$Q_D = 25{,}000 - 15{,}000P$$

where Q_S is the quantity (tons) supplied, Q_D is the quantity (tons) demanded, and P is the price per pear (in hundreds of dollars per ton).

a. Plot the supply and demand curves.

b. What is the equilibrium price?

c. What is the equilibrium quantity?

5. The White Company is a member of the lamp industry, which is perfectly competitive. The price of a lamp is $50. The firm's total cost function is

$$TC = 1{,}000 + 20Q + 5Q^2$$

where TC is total cost (in dollars) and Q is hourly output.

a. What output maximizes profit?

b. What is the firm's economic profit at this output?

c. What is the firm's average cost at this output?

d. If other firms in the lamp industry have the same cost function as this firm, is the industry in equilibrium? Why or why not?

6. The long-run supply curve for a particular type of kitchen knife is a horizontal line at a price of $3 per knife. The demand curve for such a kitchen knife is

$$Q_D = 50 - 2P$$

where Q_D is the quantity of knives demanded (in millions per year) and P is the price per knife (in dollars).

a. What is the equilibrium output of such knives?
b. If a tax of $1 is imposed on each knife, what is the equilibrium output of such knives? (Assume the tax is collected by the government from the suppliers of knives.)
c. After the tax is imposed, you buy such a knife for $3.75. Is this the long-run equilibrium price?

EXCEL EXERCISE: PERFECT COMPETITION

Suppose that you are a price taker and the market price is given to you as 8 (from our market demand and supply exercise in Chapter 1). Your total cost is given as the total cost function determined in the Excel exercise on production and cost (Chapter 6), i.e., $TC = 5 + 2Q + 0.5Q^2$. From the text, we know that the profit-maximizing rule for a price taker is $P = MC$. From the above total cost formula,

$$MC = dTC/dQ = 2 + Q$$

(which assumes that the product can only be produced in integers)

the firm thus sets $\qquad P = 8 = 2 + Q = MC$

or $\qquad Q = 6$

The firm's total revenue is $TR = P*Q = 8*6 = 48$. The firm's total cost is $TC = 5 + 2Q + 0.5Q^2 = 5 + 2*6 + 0.5*6*6 = 5 + 12 + 18 = 35$. The firm's profit is $= \pi = TR - TC = 48 - 35 = 13$.

But suppose that you didn't know the above rule but instead knew that the market price was 8 and that the total cost relationship for your firm was

Quantity	Fixed Cost	Variable Cost	Total Cost
0	5	0.0	5.0
1	5	2.5	7.5
2	5	6.0	11.0
3	5	10.5	15.5
4	5	16.0	21.0
5	5	22.5	27.5
6	5	30.0	35.0
7	5	38.5	43.5
8	5	48.0	53.0
9	5	58.5	63.5

(continued)

Quantity	Fixed Cost	Variable Cost	Total Cost
10	5	70.0	75.0
11	5	82.5	87.5
12	5	96.0	101.0

Could you still determine the firm's profit-maximizing output and profit? Of course. Here's how with a spreadsheet:

Enter 0 in cell A1, 1 in cell A2, and so on, until you enter 12 in cell A13, replicating the quantity column in the table above.

Enter 5 in cell B1 and click on the lower-right-hand corner and drag down to cell B13. That should yield you a column of 5s, the firm's fixed cost.

Enter 0 in cell C1, 2.5 in cell C2, and continue until you enter 96 in cell C13. This gives you the firm's variable cost from the table.

Enter =B1+C1 in cell D1. Then click on the lower-right-hand corner and drag down to cell D13. This gives you the firm's total cost from the table.

You have now replicated the above table in the spreadsheet.

Enter =D2−D1 in cell E2, =D3−D2 in cell E3, and so on via the click-and-drag method. This will yield the firm's discrete marginal cost, which assumes that the firm can only produce output in integers.

For reference purposes, we will put the firm's continuous marginal cost (which assumes that the firm can produce output along a continuous spectrum—think gasoline production and gasoline sales) in column F. From above, the continuous marginal cost is $MC = 2 + Q$.

Enter =2+A1 in cell F1, =2+A2 in cell F2, and so on via click-and-drag. Notice that the continuous and discrete marginal costs are different, which reflects the different incremental changes in output. The continuous marginal cost exceeds the discrete marginal cost.

Enter 8 in cell G1. Click and drag this to cell G13. This will give you a column of 8s, the market price of the good.

Enter =A1*G1 in cell H1, =A2*G2 in cell H2, and so on, via click and drag. This will yield the firm's total revenue ($TR = P*Q$).

Enter =H2−H1 in cell I2, =H3−H2 in cell I3, and so on, via click and drag. This yields the firm's marginal revenue, i.e., its change in total revenue from making an additional sale.

Enter =H1−D1 in cell J1, =H2−D2 in cell J2, and so on, via click and drag. This yields a column of the firm's profits, $\pi = TR - TC$.

Now just search column J for the highest number. You should find 13 in the seventh row with the associated output of 6. Note that the continuous marginal cost (8) equals the price (8) at the output of 6 (as we showed at the beginning). You can also find the highest number by adding =Max(J1:J13) in cell J14.

But we get the same results without the calculus. View the discrete output case. At output 6, the marginal revenue (price) is 8 and the discrete marginal cost is 7.5. Of course, the firm would want to produce the sixth unit, since cash flow in (8) exceeds cash flow out (7.5). But view the marginal revenue of the seventh unit (8) and the discrete marginal cost of producing the seventh unit (8.5). Clearly managers would not want to produce the seventh unit, because the cash flow in (8) is exceeded by the cash flow out (8.5).

Thus, both methods, the continuous (knowing calculus) and the discrete (with no calculus) yield the same solution.

CHAPTER 8

MONOPOLY AND MONOPOLISTIC COMPETITION

The question faced by most managers is how to set prices and output when they have market power. As we will see, when managers possess market power, they have the ability to overrule the invisible hand described by Adam Smith. In these markets the equilibrium price set by the intersection of the supply and demand curves is rarely seen. We will first investigate this important issue by looking at how managers act when they have monopoly power. Managers with monopoly power do not have to consider the actions of market rivals because there are none. For example, US Airways is the only carrier flying between Ithaca, New York, and Philadelphia, Pennsylvania. In the winter Kubel's Restaurant is the only restaurant open in Barnegat Light, New Jersey. Only one supermarket may be open all night long in your area. The Philadelphia Gas Works is the only supplier of natural gas in Philadelphia, Pennsylvania.

The market demand curve for air travel between Ithaca and Philadelphia *is* the demand curve for US Airways. The market demand for winter restaurant meals in Barnegat Light is the demand curve seen by managers at Kubel's. Likewise, the market demand for overnight supermarket shopping and natural gas in Philadelphia are the demand curves facing those firm managers. Monopolies have no intramarket competition, and firm demand is equal to market demand.

The demand faced by managers of monopolies is downward-sloping; that is, as price increases, quantity demanded decreases. Managers with market power face a pleasantly more complex decision relative to those in perfectly competitive markets. They must decide both price and quantity; they are no longer passive price takers. Relative to managers of perfectly competitive firms, they have more strategic power and are rewarded with higher economic profit. We now want to look at how managers maximize profit in such an environment.

Although being a monopolist comes with some degree of market power, it does not give managers carte blanche; they need to manage the demand characteristics of their product. If no one wants to fly between Ithaca and Philadelphia or shop at 3 A.M. or eat in a restaurant in the winter in Barnegat Light, the managers monopoly power is virtually worthless. And even if managers create demand for their products, they still must efficiently manage costs and resources. Finally, monopolists still must worry about potential competitors. It is only 183 miles between Ithaca and Philadelphia, so driving or taking a bus is an option for many consumers. And though Barnegat Light has only one winter restaurant, a restaurant exists in a town three miles away, and home-cooked meals are a substitute. Many grocery stores are open all day and in the early evening, so customers can easily shop at times other than 3 A.M. Consumers need not heat their homes or hot water with gas; many choose to use oil or electricity. Cross elasticities (see Chapter 2) can tell us what goods, locations, and times are substitutes for a "monopoly" product.

So even when there is no intramarket competition, managers must work hard if substitute products, locations, and times exist. Managers need to understand product, spatial, and temporal competition, or they can make serious mistakes. Also, the higher the profit, the more others will test your market defenses and try to enter your market. Finally, if managers do too good a job and generate what is viewed as excess profit, authorities may try to regulate their actions in some way.

In this chapter, we examine issues the monopolist manager must consider in choosing the optimal price and quantity combination. We show how market power changes the thought process of managers, though the decision rule remains to produce where marginal revenue equals marginal cost. This simple rule dictates managerial behavior in all market structures.

We also show the profit-maximizing rule for managers in monopolistic competitive markets. In these markets managers still have market power, but they must deal with intramarket rivals. Although managers still face a downward-sloping demand curve, a lack of entry barriers allows others into the market. The world is more complicated; managers must consider the actions of these rivals in choosing their optimal strategy. Industries such as shirt manufacturing approximate monopolistic competition.

PRICING AND OUTPUT DECISIONS IN MONOPOLY

The monopolist behaves differently than the perfect competitor of Chapter 7. An unregulated monopolist maximizes profit by choosing the price and output where the difference between total revenue and total cost is the largest. For example, consider a monopolist with a demand curve of

$$P = 10 - Q$$

where P is the price per unit of the product and Q is the number of units demanded at that price. The monopolist has a total cost curve of

$$TC = 1 + Q + 0.5Q^2$$

The monopolist's total revenue is $TR = PQ$, or

$$TR = (10 - Q)Q = 10Q - Q^2$$

The total revenue and total cost for the monopolist at various levels of output are shown in Table 8.1. The manager maximizes profit at the output where total revenue exceeds total cost by the greatest amount. Figures 8.1 and 8.2 show the situation graphically.

TABLE 8.1

Cost, Revenue, and Profit of a Monopolist

Output	Price (Dollars)	Total Revenue (Dollars)	Variable Cost (Dollars)	Total Cost (Dollars)	Total Profit (Dollars)	Variable-Cost Profit (Dollars)
0	10	0	0	1	−1	0
1	9	9	1.5	2.5	6.5	7.5
2	8	16	4	5	11	12
3	7	21	7.5	8.5	12.5	13.5
4	6	24	12	13	11	12
4.5	5.5	24.75	14.625	15.625	9.125	10.125
5	5	25	17.5	18.5	6.5	7.5
6	4	24	24	25	−1	0
7	3	21	31.5	32.5	−11.5	−10.5
8	2	16	40	41	−25	−24
9	1	9	49.5	50.5	−41.5	−40.5
10	0	0	60	61	−61	−60

FIGURE 8.1

Total Revenue, Total Cost, and Total Profit of a Monopolist

To maximize profit, the monopolist chooses an output rate of three units per period of time and a price of $7.

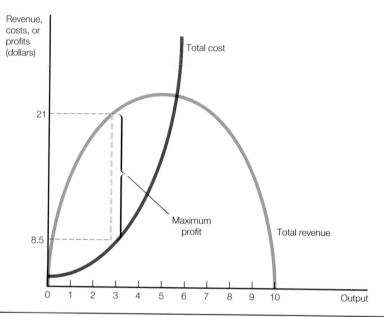

FIGURE 8.2

Profit and Output of a Monopolist

To maximize profit, the monopolist chooses an output rate of three units per time period and makes a profit of $12.5.

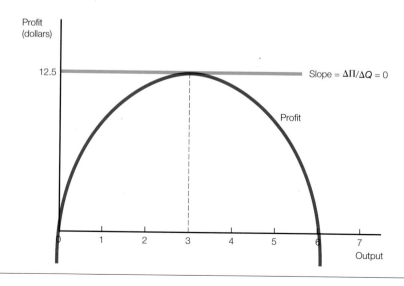

Under monopoly, as under perfect competition, managers maximize profit if they set output at the point where marginal cost equals marginal revenue. As can be seen in Figure 8.2, profit is maximized when $\Delta\pi/\Delta Q = 0$. Recall from Chapter 7 that $\pi = TR - TC$ (that is, profit equals total revenue minus total cost) and that

$$\frac{\Delta\pi}{\Delta Q} = \frac{\Delta TR}{\Delta Q} - \frac{\Delta TC}{\Delta Q} = 0$$

which implies that $MR - MC = 0$ or that $MR = MC$.

Let us investigate the situation in Table 8.1 and Figures 8.1 and 8.2 in greater detail. The marginal revenue $= MR = \Delta TR/\Delta Q = 10 - 2Q$.

With a linear demand curve, the marginal revenue curve has the same dollar intercept as the demand curve (10) but it falls at twice the speed; that is, the marginal revenue curve has twice the slope of the demand curve. This is always true for linear demand curves (which we almost always use for illustrative purposes—of course, in the real world, demand curves could take any form that shows an inverse relationship of price and quantity). Therefore, a demand curve of $P = 250 - 12.5Q$ has a corresponding marginal revenue curve of $MR = 250 - 25Q$.[1]

The total cost function is $TC = 1 + Q + 0.5Q^2$. Therefore, marginal cost $= MC = \Delta TC/\Delta Q = 1 + Q$.

Setting marginal revenue equal to marginal cost gives

$$MR = 10 - 2Q = 1 + Q = MC, \text{ or } Q = 3 \tag{8.1}$$

and hence $P = 10 - 3 = \$7$.

Unlike firms in a perfectly competitive market, the firms marginal revenue is no longer constant; nor is it equal to price. Recall from Chapter 2 that

$$MR = P\left[1 + \left(\frac{1}{\eta}\right)\right]$$

$$= P\left[1 - \left(\frac{1}{|\eta|}\right)\right]$$

$$= P - \left(\frac{P}{|\eta|}\right) \tag{8.2}$$

QUANT OPTION

The monopolist's marginal revenue is

$$dTR/dQ = MR = 10 - 2Q$$

The monopolist's marginal cost is

$$dTC/dQ = MC = 1 + Q$$

1. Total revenue would be $TR = (250 - 12.5Q)Q = 250Q - 12.5Q^2$ and so $MR = dTR/dQ = 250 - 25Q$.

where MR is marginal revenue, P is price, and η is the price elasticity of demand. Because $\eta < 0$, the marginal revenue equals price minus $P/|\eta|$. Hence marginal revenue is price minus something positive—so price must exceed marginal revenue. In addition, no rational manager produces where marginal revenue is negative. (This implies that selling another unit decreases total revenue; because producing another unit would increase total costs, the manager could not maximize profit.) If managers are to produce where marginal revenue equals marginal cost, a negative marginal revenue implies a negative marginal cost. Total costs increase (not decrease) when managers increase production. If marginal revenue is positive, then from equation (8.2), $\eta < -1$ (that is, $|\eta| > 1$), which implies an elastic demand.[2] Thus a monopolist can not produce in the inelastic range of her demand curve if she is maximizing profit.

Table 8.2 and Figure 8.3 present the marginal revenue and marginal cost numbers for these functions; they substantiate that profit is maximized when marginal revenue equals marginal cost.

Note at the optimal output of three units (price $=$ \$7), the demand is elastic (-2.33) and the marginal revenue is positive (\$4). It is also true that in a monopoly, price must exceed average variable cost if managers are to maximize profit (and from Table 8.1, we calculate at a production of three units, AVC is equal to \$2.5; that is, $AVC = VC/Q = \$7.5/3 = \$2.5$). If not, the monopolist is not covering variable cost and should shut the operation to reduce losses to only fixed cost.

2. From equation (8.2), if $|\eta| > 1$, then $1/|\eta| < 1$ and $[1 - (1/|\eta|)] > 0$. This makes $MR > 0$, because P must be positive.

STRATEGY SESSION: Why Monopoly Power Attracts Warren Buffett

Warren Buffett states that when he judges businesses, he does so based on their ability to raise prices way above the ability of the management team. Pricing power is his single most important criteria in evaluating a business. He says, "If you owned the only newspaper in town, up until the last five years or so, you had pricing power and you didn't have to go to the office." That's what a monopoly does: It gives the manager the ability to raise prices above marginal cost. He also says, "If you've got the power to raise prices without losing business to a competitor, you've got a very good business. And if you have to have a prayer session before raising the price by 10%, then you have a terrible business."

So monopoly is good. Buffett, of course, must also be sure that price covers average variable cost as we have shown in the text. Monopoly power without cost control is not a guaranteed ticket to success. Looking at the success of Berkshire Hathaway would suggest that Buffett is very good at covering all his costs.

Source: Andrew Frye and Dakin Campbell, "Buffett Says Pricing Power More Important Than Good Management," *Bloomberg News*, February 18, 2011, at www.bloomberg.com/news/2011-02-18/buffett-says-pricing-power-more-important-than-good-management.html.

TABLE 8.2

Marginal Cost and Marginal Revenue of a Monopolist

Price	Output	Marginal Cost[a]	Marginal Revenue[b]	Total Profit[c]	Elasticity
10	0	1	10	−1	−∞
9	1	2	8	6.5	−9
8	2	3	6	11	−4
7	3	4	4	12.5	−2.33
6	4	5	2	11	−1.5
5.5	4.5	5.5	1	9.125	−1.22
5	5	6	0	6.5	−1
4	6	7	−2	−1	−0.67
3	7	8	−4	−11.5	−0.43
2	8	9	−6	−25	−0.25
1	9	10	−8	−41.5	−0.11
0	10	11	−10	−61	0

[a]The marginal cost is calculated from the equation $MC = 1 + Q$. This assumes that the product is produced in continuous amounts, like gasoline. If the product can be produced only in discrete amounts, like cars, the marginal cost for output n is defined as the total cost of producing n units minus the total cost of producing $n - 1$ units. Using the total cost information from Table 8.1, the marginal cost of producing two units is $2.5 (that is, $5 − $2.5); the marginal cost of producing three units is $3.5 (that is, $8.5 − $5); and the marginal cost of producing four units is $4.5 (that is, $13 − $8.5). Why does this differ from the marginal cost of $5 shown for output 4 in the table? Because the costs differ if you can produce continuously as opposed to only in discrete integer units.

[b]The marginal revenue is calculated from the equation $MR = 10 − 2Q$. This assumes that the product can be sold in continous amounts, like gasoline. If the product can be sold only in discrete amounts, like cars, the marginal revenue for output n is defined as the total revenue from selling n units minus the total revenue of selling $n - 1$ units. Using the total revenue information from Table 8.1, the marginal revenue of selling two units is $7 (that is, $16 − $9); the marginal revenue of selling three units is $5 (that is, $21 − $16); and the marginal revenue of selling four units is $3 (that is, $24 − $21).

[c]Note that using the discrete marginal revenue and the marginal cost gives the same result as the continuous analysis; that is, the profit-maximizing output is three units. In the discrete case, the firm would clearly produce the second unit because the marginal revenue exceeds the marginal cost ($7 > $2.5) and hence would increase profit. Likewise, it would produce the third unit because the marginal revenue exceeds the marginal cost ($5 > $3.5) and hence would increase profit. However, the firm would not produce the fourth unit because the marginal revenue is exceeded by the marginal cost ($3 < $4.5) and hence would decrease profit.

FIGURE 8.3

Marginal Revenue and Marginal Cost of a Monopolist

At the monopolist's profit-maximizing output (three units), the marginal cost equals the marginal revenue (at $4).

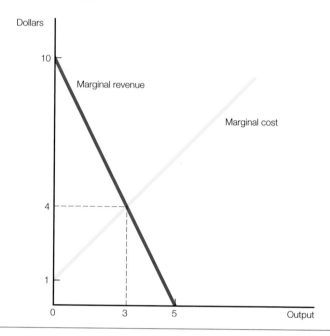

It is easy to graphically show the price and output decision facing managers. Figure 8.4 shows the demand curve, the marginal revenue curve, the marginal cost curve, the average total cost curve, and the average variable cost curve faced by managers. To maximize profit, managers need to produce the output Q_M where the marginal cost curve intersects that of marginal revenue. If the monopolist produces Q_M, she will set a price of P_M. Because she is the only member of her market, her firm's demand curve is the industry demand curve. This is in contrast to perfect competition, where the demand curve for a firm's output is horizontal. The demand curve for the monopolist's output slopes downward to the right, as shown in Figure 8.4.

In Figure 8.4 managers generate profit per unit of $P_M - ATC$. This, multiplied by the number of units, Q_M, is the shaded area of the figure and equals total profit. Note also that $P_M > AVC$ to fulfill the second managerial rule of profit maximization.

Relative to managers in perfectly competitive markets, monopolists choose a higher price and lower output. This lets them charge a price higher than marginal cost and hence generate economic profit. Managers in perfectly competitive

FIGURE 8.4

Output and Price Decisions of a Monopolist

In equilibrium, the monopolist produces Q_M units of output and sets a price of P_M. (Note that, in contrast to perfect competition, the demand curve slopes downward to the right.)

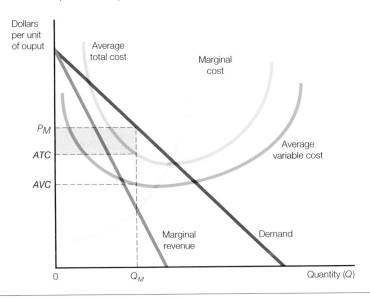

markets can only set price equal to marginal cost. In the preceding example, if managers were forced to behave as a perfect competitor, they would set price equal to marginal cost; that is, $P = 10 - Q = 1 + Q = MC$. This yields $2Q = 9$ or an output of 4.5 and a price of 5.5; that is, $P = 10 - 4.5$. Therefore, output is curtailed under monopoly (from 4.5 to 3), price is increased (from $5.5 to $7), and profit is increased (from $9.125 to $12.5)—see Table 8.1.

To see that the monopolist's price exceeds marginal cost, recall that

$$MR = P[1 - (1/|\eta|)]$$

and that the monopolist sets marginal revenue equal to marginal cost. Therefore,

$$MC = P\left[1 - \left(\frac{1}{|\eta|}\right)\right] \text{ or} \qquad (8.3)$$

$$P = \frac{MC}{\left[1 - \left(\frac{1}{|\eta|}\right)\right]}$$

Because $|\eta| > 1$, it follows that $[1 - (1/|\eta|)] < 1$, which means P must exceed MC.

What happens when a franchiser with monopoly power has a different objective than a franchisee has? Consider the case of McDonald's, where the franchiser makes its money by collecting a percentage of each store's gross sales or total revenues (formally called a *royalty*). Therefore the franchiser wants to maximize the total revenue from the sales of its hamburgers by having each store maximize its total revenues (and by adding more stores). We assume that franchisees wish to maximize their profit. To do so, the franchisee would set $MR = MC$ (in the elastic range of demand where $|\eta| > 1$). But maximizing total revenue requires that $MR = 0$ (and that $|\eta| = 1$). Because the objectives of the franchiser and the franchisee cannot be accomplished with the same pricing policy, they are in conflict. The situation is depicted in the figure.[a]

Note that this conflict exists in other situations such as book publishing. Authors generally receive a percentage of book sales as a royalty. Therefore, authors would like publishers to maximize total revenues. Publishers, on the other hand, want to maximize profit. Hence the author's objective would entail lower book prices than the publisher's; don't blame us for the high price of this book!

The royalty rates[b] (as a percentage of monthly sales) for some popular franchises are shown here:

McDonald's	4% of gross sales
DQ Grill and Chill Restaurants	4% of gross sales
DQ Treat Centers	6% of gross sales
Motel 6	4% of gross room revenues
Studio 6	5% of gross room revenues
UPS Store	5% of gross sales and gross commissions
Ben and Jerry's	3% of gross sales
Jiffy Lube	5% of gross sales

In addition, there is generally a marketing or sales promotion fee (for advertising) of 2–6% of sales for most franchises as well as a one-time franchise fee. Papa John's, however, has a royalty fee of 5% of *net* sales (and hence the incentives of the franchiser and franchisees are aligned).

[a]*Businessweek*, June 2, 1997.
[b]Company websites, May 2008.
A monopolist produces at $P_{Franchisee}$, $Q_{Franchisee}$ as dictated by the rule that marginal revenue equals marginal cost. A revenue maximizer produces where marginal revenue is zero $(P_{Franchiser}, Q_{Franchiser})$—that is, where $|\eta| = 1$.

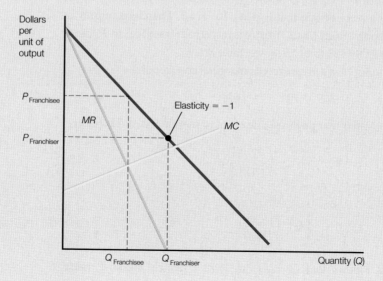

PROBLEM SOLVED: **The McComb Company**

To illustrate how managers choose price and output to maximize profit, consider the situation facing managers at the McComb Company, a monopolist producing and selling a product with the demand curve

$$P = 30 - 6Q \qquad (8.4)$$

where P is price (in thousands of dollars) and Q is the firm's output (in thousands of units). The firms total cost function is

$$TC = 14 + 3Q + 3Q^2 \qquad (8.5)$$

where TC is total cost (in millions of dollars).

From the demand curve in equation (8.4), we determine the firm's total revenue (in millions of dollars), which is

$$TR = PQ = (30 - 6Q)Q = 30Q - 6Q^2$$

Therefore, marginal revenue equals $\Delta TR/\Delta Q = 30 - 12Q$.

From the total cost function in equation (8.5), we determine that marginal cost is

$$\Delta TC/\Delta Q = 3 + 6Q$$

Setting marginal revenue equal to marginal cost gives us

$$MR = 30 - 12Q = 3 + 6Q = MC$$

This means that $Q = 1.5$. Inserting 1.5 for Q in the demand equation (8.4), we find that $P = 30 - 6(1.5)$, or $21. So to maximize profit, managers should set a price of $21,000 and produce and sell 1,500 units. Doing so will result in profit equal to $[30(1.5) - 6(1.5)^2] - [14 + 3(1.5) + 3(1.5)^2] = 6.25 million.

The extra profit earned by monopoly managers is generated by their ability to choose a price greater than marginal cost, whereas the perfect competitor merely charges the marginal cost. Of course managers in both markets must choose a price that is higher than average variable cost.

COST-PLUS PRICING

Unfortunately academic studies of pricing behavior consistently suggest that many managers do not price optimally. Instead they use the simple heuristic of **cost-plus pricing** (see Strategy Session: Markup Pricing on the iPad2, page 268).

Many managers act as if cost is the primary driver of price. Although this simple strategy guarantees that price is higher than the estimated average cost, it does not necessarily optimize profit. The behavior has many variations but follows a guiding principle: Price is set as a function of cost. Managers first allocate unit costs conditional on a given output level (such as 70% capacity). Then they add a profit margin. This margin is generally a percentage of costs and is added to the estimated average costs. The markup is meant to cover costs that are difficult to allocate to specific products and as a return on firm investment.

Cost-plus pricing Simplistic strategy that guarantees that price is higher than the estimated average cost.

STRATEGY SESSION: Markup Pricing on the iPad2

Just like iPods and iPhones, the new iPads have taken the market by storm and are flying off the shelves and at a rate that rippled the robust debut sales of the first iPad.

Responding to strong consumer demand and competition from Motorola Mobility, Samsung, Research in Motion, Hewlett-Packard, and 59 other companies, iPad has captured the imagination of the market (bringing in many first-time buyers).

How does such monopoly power standing translate into a price markup over cost? According to IHS iSuppli (a research firm), materials for the iPad2 cost about $326.60 for a version with 32 gigabytes of memory that works with the mobile phone standard

known as global system for mobile communications. This is a 2% increase over the costs of an earlier model.

The price of an iPad2 ranges from $499 to $829. Thus, the ratio of price to cost is somewhere between 1.53 and 2.54 creating a tidy variable profit (profit excluding fixed cost) for the "gadget of the year."

Source: Adam Satariano, "Apple May Have Sold 500,000 iPad2 Tablets on Debut Weekend, Analyst Says," *Bloomberg News*, March 14, 2011, at www.bloomberg.com/news/2011-03-14/apple-may-have-sold-500-000-ipad-2-tablets-analyst-estimates.html.

In basic algebra, the percentage markup of this strategy is expressed as

$$\text{Markup} = (\text{Price} - \text{Cost})/\text{Cost} \tag{8.6}$$

Profit margin The price of a product minus its cost.

where the numerator (Price − Cost) is the **profit margin**. If the cost of a paperback book is $4 and its price is $6,

$$\text{Markup} = (6 - 4)/4 = 0.50$$

or 50%. If we solve equation (8.6) for price, the result is

$$\text{Price} = \text{Cost}(1 + \text{Markup}) \tag{8.7}$$

which is the pricing formula described in the previous paragraph. In the case of the paperback book,

$$\text{Price} = 4(1 + 0.5) = \$6$$

because the markup is 50%.

Target return What managers hope to earn and what determines the markup.

Managers may also choose a **target return** they hope to earn, which determines the markup. For example, General Electric at times has established a target rate of return of 20%. Under a target rate of return pricing, price is set equal to

$$P = L + M + K + (F/Q) + (\pi A/Q) \tag{8.8}$$

where P is price, L is unit labor cost, M is unit material cost, K is unit marketing cost, F is total fixed or indirect costs, Q is the number of units managers plan to produce during the relevant planning period, A is total gross operating assets, and π is the desired profit rate on those assets. If managers estimate unit labor cost at $2, unit material cost at $1, unit marketing cost at $3, total fixed cost at $10,000, output at 1,000 units, with assets of $100,000 and a target rate of return of 15%, they should set price at

$$P = 2 + 1 + 3 + (10,000/1,000) + [0.15(100,000)/1,000] = \$31$$

One issue facing managers who produce more than one product is the charge for indirect cost, or overhead. Often managers use the heuristic of allocating this cost among the firm's products on the basis of their average variable costs. If a firm's total annual indirect costs (for all products) are estimated to be $3 million and the total annual variable costs (for all products) are estimated to be $2 million, indirect costs would be allocated to products at a rate of 150% of variable costs. For example, if the average variable cost of product Y is estimated to be $10, managers should add a charge of $1.50 \times \$10$, or $15, for indirect cost. Adding this charge to the average variable cost, the manager estimates the fully allocated cost of $10 + $15, or $25. Managers then set a price that is higher than this cost to generate profit. For example, if the markup is 40%, the price is $1.40 \times \$25$, or $35.

COST-PLUS PRICING AT THERMA-STENT

Cost-plus pricing is widely used in medical group purchasing organizations. Therma-Stent is a producer of graft stents. Managers set price by estimating the average production costs (including indirect ones). They then add a 40% markup to set the product's market price

$$\text{Factory cost/unit} = \$2,300 \text{ (at production of 20,000)}$$
$$40\% \text{ markup} = \$920$$
$$\text{U.S. list price} = \$3,220$$

Using the heuristic eases the complexity of setting price by ignoring market considerations. For instance, price is set without considering prices of rival products. This pricing scheme works better when products are differentiated. Therma-Stent produces graft stents that are unique in form and surface structure.

COST-PLUS PRICING AT INTERNET COMPANIES AND GOVERNMENT-REGULATED INDUSTRIES

Managers at many online companies seem to have adopted a cost-plus pricing scheme. Consider OnSale, an online store. Managers have structured a pricing policy called "At Cost" where they sell products based at the wholesale price plus a fixed transaction fee (the markup).[3]

3. Henry Norr, "Egghead Whips Up a $400 Million Deal with Onsale," *San Francisco Chronicle*, July 15, 1999.

STRATEGY SESSION: When Is the Price Too High?

Monopolists mark price up above marginal cost (which would be the price if the market were perfectly competitive), as we know from the text. They wouldn't (assuming rationality) charge a price higher than the one that would maximize their profit. But is that price/profit too high? From a social welfare perspective, we know that the answer is yes (because pricing at marginal cost maximizes social welfare). But we have many prices that exceed marginal costs in our markets, so when should we intervene and say that the markup is too high?

We have captive shipper provisions in the U.S. rail industry where the Surface Transportation Board can still regulate rates in what is basically a deregulated U.S. rail industry. Regulation can occur under a very specific set of conditions related to the overall revenue adequacy of the railroad, the ratio of the rate to the variable cost of the movement, and the cost of building a stand-alone railroad specifically to serve the captive shipper in question, among other things. Basically no rail carrier rates have been declared too high (although the shippers believe this to be the case, they can't win in a proceeding before the Surface Transportation Board).

But we aren't alone in this situation. Transnet Freight Rail in South Africa has recently raised its rates on a coal export railway line to Richards Bay by 26.3% over last year. The clients of the railroad have agreed to the increase. A lawyer has stated that since Transnet is the dominant rail carrier in South Africa, the rate is subject to the country's Competition Act, which states that the dominant group can't charge excessively to the detriment of consumers. A case can be won, the lawyer claims, if it is shown that the rates were raised without the carrier experiencing a corresponding increase in costs.

This would seem to be an answer in search of a problem. The customers of the railroad have not filed a complaint. Transnet argues that costs have indeed increased. A director for Venmyn, a firm that advises mining companies on legal compliance with the law and project valuation, notes that if that's what it costs to put up and maintain that infrastructure, that's what one has to pay.

As in the United States, these cases are not brought before the competition authorities because they are "notoriously" difficult to prove as no one can determine what excessive pricing is. Only one case has been brought in South Africa, and it didn't lead to any conclusion and the parties settled.

So whereas laws in the United States and South Africa exist to prevent prices (rates) from becoming too high in the railroad industry (indicating that legislators were convinced that situations could exist where prices were too high), in practice, the implementation of these laws in both countries has been sparse (indicating that the potential plaintiffs in these cases don't believe that it is possible to prove such a case even though they believe the prices are too high).

Source: Allan Seccombe, "Transnet Freight Rail Tariffs Run into Criticism," *Business Day* (South Africa), April 5, 2011, at www .businessday.co.za/Articles/Content.apsx?id-139223.

4. Cost Appliances and Electronics: Lowest Prices on the Web, at www .bybb.com.

Online sellers in other product lines have adopted the same pricing scheme. Managers at www.bybb.com sell major household appliances (GE and Hotpoint washers, dryers, refrigerators, and ovens) and electronics (Toshiba, Mitsubishi, and Sony TVs and MP3 players) on a cost-plus basis, where the purchaser is shown the wholesale price of the item.[4]

Many automobile dealers also use a cost-plus pricing scheme, though they tend to make it difficult for consumers to accurately determine cost. Auto dealer invoices contain some items such as area allowances, which are hard for the novice consumer to interpret, and manufacturer givebacks are not included in the invoice. Therefore consumers do not see the true price the dealer paid for the car. In addition, many customers trade in their old vehicles. In haggling with a customer, the dealers are concerned with how much money they can make in the package—the trade-in plus the sale of the new vehicle. This makes buying from the auto dealer harder than buying from the appliance seller (where trade-ins are nonexistent).

Government regulators also use cost-plus pricing in industries they regulate or control. For instance, the Coal Ministry in India recently allowed Rajmahal coal to be priced at cost plus Rs143 per tonne after meeting production costs.[5] The danger of such a pricing scheme in a government-controlled industry is that, when the profit is guaranteed, firm managers may lose the incentive to be cost efficient. This tends to create a larger government regulatory bureaucracy to monitor costs.

CAN COST-PLUS PRICING MAXIMIZE PROFIT?

The important question we need to consider is how good a heuristic cost-plus pricing is for managers to use. So far it seems unlikely that cost-plus pricing will often maximize profit. Indeed, this pricing technique seems simple-minded in that it does not explicitly account for important factors on both the demand and supply sides. It certainly does not explicitly consider the extent of demand or the product's price elasticity, including the pricing behavior of rivals. On the supply side it looks at average, not marginal, cost. Nevertheless, if applied well, cost-plus pricing may result in managers almost maximizing profit. The possibility that cost-plus pricing is sometimes a good heuristic revolves around what factors managers consider in determining the size of the percentage markup or the target rate of return. For example, why was the markup on the paperback book cited earlier 50%? Why not 25% or 150%?

In choosing a markup to maximize profit, managers must estimate the book's price elasticity of demand. To understand why this is true, recall from equation (8.3) that

$$MC = P\left[1 - \left(\frac{1}{|\eta|}\right)\right]$$

Dividing both sides of the equation by $1 - (1/|\eta|)$, we get

$$P = MC\left\{\frac{1}{\left[1 - \left(\frac{1}{|\eta|}\right)\right]}\right\}$$

5. B. Sanyal, "Cost-Plus Pricing Helps Rajmahal Expansion," August 26, 1996, at www.hindubusinessline.com/1996/08/26/BLFP.08.html.

So in setting price, if managers want to maximize profit, they need to understand how marginal cost and price elasticity of demand are associated. Formally, managers need to set price so it equals the products marginal cost multiplied by

$$\left\{ \frac{1}{\left[1 - \left(\frac{1}{|\eta|} \right) \right]} \right\}$$

Intuitively, equation (8.7) says that in cost-plus pricing, managers choose a price equal to cost multiplied by (1 + Markup). If managers use marginal (not average) cost, then a markup of

$$\text{Markup} = |\eta| / (|\eta| - 1) \tag{8.9}$$

will maximize profit.

Put differently, a manager can maximize profit using cost-plus pricing with a markup equal to the value specified in equation (8.9). As equation (8.9) clearly shows, the optimal markup depends on the product's price elasticity of demand. To help managers think about this, we have constructed Table 8.3, which shows the profit-maximizing markup corresponding to elasticity values. For example, if a product's price elasticity of demand equals -1.2, the optimal markup is 500%. If its price elasticity is -21, the optimal markup is only 5%. Table 8.3 should be studied carefully because it provides useful information to help managers choose an effective pricing policy.

Note the negative association between elasticity and markup. As the price elasticity of demand decreases (in absolute value), the optimal markup increases. Table 8.3 shows this clearly. To see that the inverse relationship in Table 8.3 between markup and price elasticity is reasonable, ask yourself the following question: If the quantity demanded of a product is not very sensitive to its price, should I set

---

TABLE 8.3

Relationship between Optimal Markup and Price Elasticity of Demand

Price Elasticity of Demand	Optimal Percentage Markup of Marginal Cost
−1.2	500
−1.4	250
−1.8	125
−2.5	66.67
−5.0	25
−11.0	10
−21.0	5
−51.0	2

PROBLEM SOLVED: The Humphrey Corporation

To illustrate how managers can use cost-plus pricing and maximize profit, consider the Humphrey Corporation, a seller of office furniture. One of Humphrey's major products is a metal desk for which the company pays $76 per desk, including transportation and related costs. Although managers at Humphrey face a variety of overhead and marketing costs, these costs are essentially fixed, so marginal cost is approximately $76. Given that many firms in Humphrey's geographic area sell reasonably comparable desks, Humphrey's managers estimate that the demand for desks is fairly price elastic—about −2.5. On the basis of Table 8.3, managers should choose a markup of 66.67% to maximize profit.

According to equation (8.7), the optimal price is

$$\text{Price} = \text{Cost}(1 + \text{Markup})$$
$$= 76(1 + 0.6667)$$
$$= \$126.67$$

So if managers want to maximize profit, they should choose the price of $127 per desk. In so doing, managers will approximate profit-maximizing behavior. Behavior is only approximated because values of factors like marginal cost and price elasticity of demand must be estimated. Recognizing that this is the case, Humphrey's managers should be prepared to slightly alter the price once they see the market reaction to it.

---

a relatively high or low price for this product? Obviously you should set a high price if you want to make as much money as possible. Since this is what Table 8.3 tells us, it accords with common sense.

THE MULTIPLE-PRODUCT FIRM: DEMAND INTERRELATIONSHIPS

Managers at monopolies that produce multiple products face a more complex decision. Managers need to recognize that a change in the price or quantity sold of one product may influence the demand for other products. For example, if the Akkina Company produces and sells two products, X and Y, its total revenue (that is, sales) is represented as

$$TR = TR_X + TR_Y \tag{8.10}$$

where TR_X is its total revenue from product X and TR_Y is the total revenue from product Y. The marginal revenue from product X is

$$MR_X = \frac{\Delta TR_X}{\Delta Q_X} + \frac{\Delta TR_Y}{\Delta Q_X} \tag{8.11a}$$

and the marginal revenue from product Y is

$$MR_Y = \frac{\Delta TR_Y}{\Delta Q_Y} + \frac{\Delta TR_X}{\Delta Q_Y} \tag{8.11b}$$

The last term in each of these equations represents the demand interrelationship between the two products. In equation (8.11a), the last term shows the effect of an increase in the quantity sold of product X on the total revenue from product Y. This effect can be positive or negative. If products X and Y are complements, this effect is positive because an increase in the quantity sold of one product increases the total revenue from the other product. On the other hand, if products X and Y are substitutes, this effect is negative: An increase in the quantity sold of one product reduces the total revenue of the other product.

Managers who do not understand or pay proper attention to demand interrelationships of this sort can make serious pricing mistakes. For example, if product X is a fairly close substitute for product Y and the division of the Akkina Company producing product X launches a campaign to increase its sales, the results may be good for the division but bad for the company as a whole. Why? Because the resulting increase in product X's sales may occur largely at the expense of product Y's sales.

PRICING OF JOINT PRODUCTS: FIXED PROPORTIONS

In addition to being interrelated on the demand side, some products also have interrelated production characteristics. For example, products sometimes are produced in a fixed ratio, as in the case of cattle, where beef and hide are obtained from each animal. In such a situation there is no reason to distinguish between the products from the point of view of production or costs; managers should think of them as a bundle. One hide and two sides of beef might be such a bundle in the case of cattle because they are produced from each animal. With such jointly produced products, there is no economically correct way to allocate the cost of producing each bundle to the individual products.

To determine the optimal price and output of each such bundled product, managers need to compare the marginal revenue generated by the bundle to its marginal cost of production. If the marginal revenue—that is, the sum of the

---

QUANT OPTION

The marginal revenue from product X is

$$MR_X = \frac{\partial TR_X}{\partial Q_X} - \frac{\partial TR_Y}{\partial Q_X}$$

and the marginal revenue from product Y is

$$MR_Y = \frac{\partial TR_Y}{\partial Q_Y} - \frac{\partial TR_X}{\partial Q_Y}$$

If you want a steak in New York City, a top-notch place to go is one of the four Palm restaurants in the city. They are owned by the Palm Management Corporation, which has 26 U.S. locations (and one in London), all with the same menu. The price of a 9-ounce filet mignon steak in each of these 26 U.S. restaurants in April 2011 was as follows:

New York (4 locations), Chicago, East Hampton, Las Vegas, Los Angeles (2 locations)	$43
Atlantic City, Boston, Charlotte, Denver, Houston, Miami, Nashville, Orlando, San Diego, San Juan, Tyson's Corner, Washington, DC	$42
Atlanta, Dallas, Philadelphia, San Antonio, Tampa	$41

Problems

1. Suppose that the corporate management at Palm notes that people in various cities, such as San Antonio, are more price conscious than people in other cities, such as New York, and that local managers must know what price to charge to be competitive in their local market. Assuming that the market for restaurant food is monopolistically competitive in each of these cities, is the demand for filet mignon at the Palm restaurant in San Antonio the same as at one of the Palm restaurants in New York? If not, how does it differ?

2. Suppose corporate management also states that their labor costs in New York are higher than they pay in other cities, such as San Antonio. Is the marginal cost curve for a filet mignon at a Palm restaurant in New York the same as at the Palm restaurant in San Antonio? If not, how does it differ?

3. Why is the price of a filet mignon dinner higher in New York than in San Antonio?

4. If the marginal cost is 20% higher in New York than in San Antonio, and the price elasticity of demand is −3 in New York and −4 in San Antonio,

what would you expect to be the percentage price differential between New York and San Antonio?

Solutions

1. No. On the basis of corporate management's statement, the demand curve is more price elastic in San Antonio than in New York. A 1% price increase is likely to reduce the quantity demanded by a larger percentage in San Antonio than in New York.

2. No. The marginal cost curve is lower in San Antonio than in New York.

3. As pointed out on page 265, the profit-maximizing price equals

$$P = MC/(1 - [1/|\eta|])$$

where MC equals marginal cost and $|\eta|$ equals the absolute value of the price elasticity of demand. (This is true under any market structure.) Because MC is higher and η is less elastic in New York than in San Antonio, the profit-maximizing price is higher in New York than in San Antonio.

4. If P_S is the price in San Antonio and P_N is the price in New York, MC_S is the marginal cost in San Antonio, MC_N is the marginal cost in New York, η_S is the price elasticity of demand in San Antonio, and η_N is the price elasticity of demand in New York, then

$$
\begin{aligned}
P_S/P_N &= \{MC_S/(1 - [1/|\eta_S|])\}/\{MC_N/(1 - [1/|\eta_N|])\} \\
&= \{MC_S/(1 - [1/|-4|])\}/\{MC_N/(1 - [1/|-3|])\} \\
&= \{MC_S/(1 - [1/4])\}/\{MC_N/(1 - [1/3])\} \\
&= \{MC_S/(3/4)\}/\{MC_N/(2/3)\} \\
&= \{(4/3)MC_S\}/\{(3/2)(1.2MC_S)\} \\
&= 1.33/1.8 = 0.74
\end{aligned}
$$

Therefore, we would expect the price in San Antonio to be about 26% below the price in New York.

Source: http://www.thepalm.com/files/files/AprilDinner, accessed on July 28, 2011.

marginal revenues obtained from each product in the package—is greater than its marginal cost, managers should expand output. Assuming there are two joint products (*A* and *B*), Figure 8.5 shows the demand and marginal revenue curves for each, as well as the marginal cost of the bundled product (*AB*) in the fixed proportion in which it is produced.[6] The **total marginal revenue curve** is the vertical summation of the two marginal revenue curves for the individual products (*A* and *B*) because each *AB* bundle of output yields revenues from both products. Consequently, the profit-maximizing output in Figure 8.5 is *Q*, where the total marginal revenue equals marginal cost. The optimal price for product *A* is P_A, and the optimal price for product *B* is P_B.

Note that the total marginal revenue curve coincides with the marginal revenue curve for product *A* at all outputs beyond Q_0 in Figure 8.5. This is true because managers should never sell product *B* at a level where its marginal revenue is negative. A negative marginal revenue means managers can increase revenue by selling fewer units. Therefore, if the total output exceeds Q_0, managers should sell only part of the product *B* produced; specifically, they want to sell the amount corre-

Total marginal revenue curve
The vertical summation of the two marginal revenue curves for individual products.

FIGURE 8.5

Optimal Pricing for Joint Products Produced in Fixed Proportions (Case 1)

The price of product *A* is set at P_A, the price of product *B* is set at P_B, and output is set at *Q*.

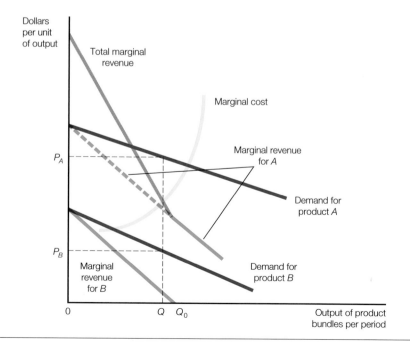

6. For simplicity, we assume that the demand curve for product *A* is not influenced by the price of product *B* and vice versa.

FIGURE 8.6

Optimal Pricing for Joint Products Produced in Fixed Proportions (Case 2)

The price of product A is set at P_A, the price of product B is set at P_B, and not all of product B is sold.

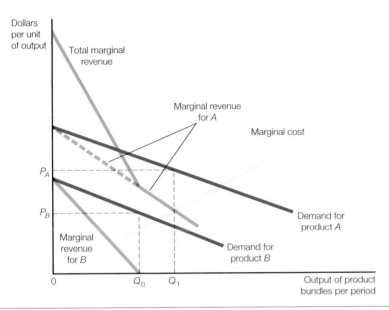

sponding to an output of Q_0 product bundles. Consequently, if output exceeds Q_0, the total marginal revenue equals the marginal revenue of product A alone.

What should managers do if the marginal cost curve intersects the total marginal revenue curve to the right of Q_0 in Figure 8.5? In particular, suppose managers face the situation shown in Figure 8.6, where the marginal cost curve is lower than in Figure 8.5 (but the other curves are the same). The profit-maximizing output is Q_1, where the marginal cost and total marginal revenue curves intersect. All of product A produced is sold, the price being P_A; but not all of product B is sold. Instead the amount sold is limited to the amount of output Q_0, so that the price of product B is P_B. The "surplus" amount of product B (that is, $Q_1 - Q_0$) must be kept off the market to avoid depressing its price.

OUTPUT OF JOINT PRODUCTS: VARIABLE PROPORTIONS

Having discussed the case in which two joint products are produced in fixed proportions, we turn to the case in which they are produced in variable proportions. This generally is a more realistic case, particularly if a manager is considering

PROBLEM SOLVED: Profit Maximizing at Humphrey

Humphrey managers now face the following situation. They manufacture two different conference table legs that are cut from the same piece of metal. They differ in their design but are jointly produced in equal quantities. That is, for every unit of the modern design produced, Humphrey also produces a unit of classical design. Managers face the total cost function

$$TC = 100 + Q + 2Q^2 \qquad (8.12)$$

where Q is the number of units (in tens) of output. (Each unit contains one classic leg and one modern leg.) The demand curves for the firm's two products are

$$P_A = 200 - Q_A \qquad (8.13)$$
$$P_B = 150 - 2Q_B \qquad (8.14)$$

where P_A and Q_A are the price and output (in tens) of the modern leg and P_B and Q_B are the price and output (in tens) of the classic leg.

Humphrey managers need to know how many units of each leg they should produce to maximize profit. The firm's total revenue is equal to the total revenues from its two products

$$TR = P_A Q_A + P_B Q_B \qquad (8.15)$$

Substituting the right sides of equations (8.13) and (8.14) for P_A and P_B, respectively, it follows that

$$TR = (200 - Q_A)Q_A + (150 - 2Q_B)Q_B$$
$$= 200Q_A - Q_A^2 + 150Q_B - 2Q_B^2$$

Assuming that Humphrey managers want to sell all they produce of both products, $Q_A = Q_B = Q$ because a unit of one product is produced whenever a unit of the other product is produced. Therefore,

$$TR = 200Q - Q^2 + 150Q - 2Q^2$$
$$= 350Q - 3Q^2 \qquad (8.16)$$

To obtain total profit, π, managers must subtract the total cost in equation (8.12) from the total revenue in equation (8.16)

$$\pi = (350Q - 3Q^2) - (100 + Q + 2Q^2)$$
$$= -100 + 349Q - 5Q^2$$

To maximize profit, we need to set $\Delta\pi/\Delta Q = 0$

$$\Delta\pi/\Delta Q = 349 - 10Q = 0$$

or

$$10Q = 349$$

Isocost curve Curve showing the amounts of goods produced at the same total cost.

Isorevenue lines Lines showing the combinations of outputs of products that yield the same total revenue.

a fairly long period. Even cattle's proportions of hides and beef can be altered because the animals can be bred to produce more or less beef relative to hide.

Suppose a firm produces and sells two products, A and B, and that each **isocost curve** (labeled TC in Figure 8.7) shows the amounts of these goods produced at the same total cost. The isocost curve labeled $TC = 13$ shows the various combinations of outputs—for example, 26 units of product A and 10 units of product B or 8 units of product A and 30 units of product B—that can be produced at a total cost of $13,000 per day.

Also included in Figure 8.7 are **isorevenue lines** (labeled TR), each of which shows the combinations of outputs of the two products that yield the same total revenue. For example, the isorevenue line labeled $TR = 52$ shows the various

or

$$Q = 34.9$$

In other words, to maximize profit, Humphrey managers should produce 34.9 (tens of) legs of each design. Equation (8.13) tells managers they need to choose a price of $165.10 to sell 34.9 (tens of) modern legs

$$P_A = 200 - 34.9 = \$165.10$$

And equation (8.14) tells managers they need to price classic legs at

$$P_B = 150 - 2(34.9) = \$80.20$$

to sell 34.9 (tens of) of them.

Managers are not quite through with the analysis yet. As indicated, we assume that Humphrey sells all it produces of both products. To see whether this is true, we must see whether, if $Q = 34.9$. the marginal revenues of both products are nonnegative. Only then will Humphrey managers sell all that is produced of both products (recall Figure 8.6). From equations (8.13) and (8.14), we find that TR_A, the total revenue from product A, equals

$$TR_A = P_A Q_A = (200 - Q_A)Q_A = 200Q_A - Q_A^2$$

and that TR_B, the total revenue from product B, equals

$$TR_B = P_B Q_B = (150 - 2Q_B)Q_B = 150Q_B - 2Q_B^2$$

Hence the marginal revenue of product A is

$$MR_A = \Delta TR_A / \Delta Q_A = 200 - 2Q_A = 130.2$$
$$\text{(when } Q_A = 34.9)$$

And the marginal revenue of product B is

$$MR_B = \Delta TR_B / \Delta Q_B = 150 - 4Q_B = 10.4$$
$$\text{(when } Q_B = 34.9)$$

Because both marginal revenues (MR_A and MR_B) are nonnegative when Q_A and $Q_B = 34.9$, the assumption underlying the analysis is valid.[a]

[a] If one product's marginal revenue had been negative when Q_A and Q_B equaled 34.9, the optimal solution would have involved producing more of this product than is sold, as indicated in Figure 8.6. The firm would sell only the amount of this product where the marginal revenue is zero. The marginal revenue for the other product would be used to determine its optimal amount level, as shown in Figure 8.6.

QUANT OPTION

$$d\pi/dQ = 349 - 10Q = 0 \text{ so that } 10Q = 349 \text{ or } Q = 34.9$$

The marginal revenue for product A is

$$MR_A = dTR_A/dQ_A = 200 - 2Q_A = 130.2 \text{ (when } Q_A = 34.9)$$

The marginal revenue for product B is

$$MR_B = dTR_B/dQ_B = 150 - 4Q_B = 10.4 \text{ (when } Q_B = 34.9)$$

FIGURE 8.7

Optimal Outputs for Joint Products Produced in Variable Proportions

The optimal point, which must be at a point where an isorevenue line is tangent to an isocost curve, is at point *M*, where profit per day is $7,000.

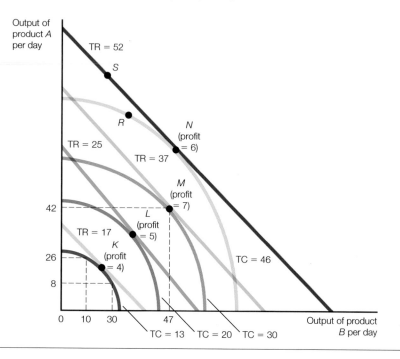

combinations of outputs, such as those corresponding to points *S* or *N*, that yield a total revenue of $52,000 per day. Other isorevenue lines show the output combinations that yield total revenues of $17,000, $25,000, and $37,000, respectively.

The problem facing the manager is to determine how much of products *A* and *B* to produce. The first step toward solving this problem is to observe that if an output combination is at a point where an isorevenue line is *not* tangent to an isocost curve, it *cannot* be the optimal output combination. To see this, note that if an output combination is at a point where an isorevenue line is not tangent to an isocost curve (say point *R*), it is possible to increase revenue (without changing cost) by moving to a point (on the same isocost curve) where an isorevenue line *is* tangent to the isocost curve (say point *N*). Therefore, any output combination that is not at a tangency point cannot be the profit-maximizing output combination because we indicated how profit can be increased if the firm is at such a nontangency point.

Given that this is the case, we find the optimal output combination by comparing the profit level at each tangency point and choosing the point where the profit level is the highest. For example, four tangency points are shown in Figure 8.7: points K, L, M, and N. As indicated in Figure 8.7, the profit levels corresponding to these four points are $4,000, $5,000, $7,000, and $6,000, respectively. So if we must choose among the output combinations on the isocost curves in Figure 8.7, the optimal output combination for this firm is point M, where the managers produce and sell 42 units of product A and 47 units of product B per day and make a profit of $7,000.

MONOPSONY

Whereas monopoly occurs when there is one seller, **monopsony** occurs when there is one buyer. As in monopoly, the monopsonist controls price. Consider the market for busboys for New York City restaurants. There are many restaurants and many aspiring busboys. If a restaurant wants to hire an additional busboy, it can pay the prevailing wage for busboys, and that wage won't change as a result of its hiring. However, consider The Company in a company town. When it wishes to hire another worker, because it employs such a large proportion of the labor force, it will influence the wage.

The demand for labor is labor's marginal revenue product—that is, the incremental revenue that an additional worker will generate for The Company and the additional benefit of hiring another worker. Formally, it is The Company's marginal revenue multiplied by the marginal product of labor. It is downward-sloping because marginal revenue falls as output increases and because labor's marginal product falls as more labor is employed (recall the law of diminishing marginal productivity from Chapter 5). Denote the labor supply curve as $P = c + eQ$, where P is the wage of labor and Q is the number of workers willing to work at that wage. Note that it is upward-sloping, reflecting the influence that the monopsonist has on the prevailing wage rate; that is, to hire another worker, The Company must increase the wage to entice a worker either into the workforce or away from another job (and by so doing will have to pay all its workers the new higher wage).

The Company's total expenditure on labor (total cost) is

$$C = PQ = (c + eQ)Q = cQ + eQ^2$$

Monopsony Markets that consist of a single buyer.

QUANT OPTION

The marginal cost of hiring another worker is

$$dC/dQ = c + 2eQ$$

FIGURE 8.8

Optimal Monopsony Pricing

The optimal number of workers hired under monopsony is less (Q_1) than the optimal number of workers hired under perfect competition (Q_2); and the optimal wage under monopsony (P_1) is less than the optimal wage under perfect competition (P_2).

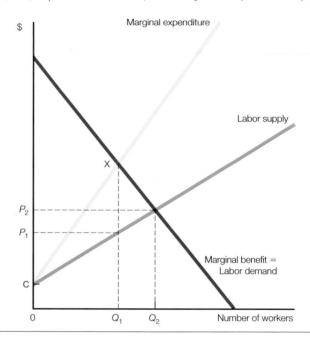

To maximize profit, managers will equate the marginal benefit of hiring another worker with the marginal expenditure (marginal cost) of hiring another worker

$$\Delta C / \Delta Q = c + 2eQ = MC$$

Figure 8.8 shows the optimal amount of labor and the wage paid by the monopsonist. The marginal benefit equals the marginal expenditure at point X with Q_1 workers. Dropping down to the labor supply curve yields a wage of P_1. Note that the monopsonist restricts the amount of labor hired (Q_1) and pays a lower wage (P_1) than it would if the labor market were perfectly competitive (Q_2 and P_2).

MONOPOLISTIC COMPETITION

We now turn our attention to monopolistic competition. From a managerial point of view, a central characteristic of monopolistic competition is product differentiation. Unlike perfect competition, in which all managers sell an identical product, firms in monopolistic competition sell similar but not identical products. Hence consumers can associate specific products with a given firm. For example, in retail markets both American Apparel and Gap sell similar tank tops for women. Managers at each firm make their tank tops slightly different (color, fabric, design). Managers could also offer different services or use different distribution channels to differentiate their products. Due to the differences among their products, managers have some control over product price, though price differentials are relatively small because the products of other firms are so similar.

In perfectly competitive markets, the firms included in an industry are easy to determine because they all produce an identical product. But when managers can differentiate their products, it is not as simple to accurately define an industry. Each firm produces a somewhat different product. Nevertheless, it is often useful to group together firms that produce similar products and call them a **product group**. We can define a product group called *neckties* or *toothbrushes* or *shirts*. The process by which we combine firms into product groups is somewhat arbitrary; there is no way to decide how close a pair of substitute products must be to belong to the same product group. Clearly the broader the definition of a product group, the greater the number of firms included.

Product group Group of firms that produce similar products.

In addition to product differentiation, other conditions must be met for an industry to qualify as one of monopolistic competition:

1. *There must be many firms in the product group.* The product must be produced by perhaps fifty to a hundred or more firms, with each firm's product a fairly close substitute for the products of the other firms in the product group.

2. *The number of firms in the product group must be large enough that each firm expects its actions to go unheeded by its rivals and unimpeded by possible retaliatory moves on their part.* Hence, when formulating their own price and output policies, they do not explicitly concern themselves with their rivals' responses. If there are many firms, this condition normally is met.

3. *Entry into the product group must be relatively easy, and there must be no collusion, such as price fixing or market sharing, among managers in the product group.* It generally is difficult, if not impossible, for a great many firms to collude.

Price and Output Decisions under Monopolistic Competition

If each firm produces a somewhat different product, it follows that the demand curve facing each manager slopes downward to the right. That is, if the firm raises its price slightly, it will lose some, but by no means all, of its customers to other firms. And if it lowers its price slightly, it will gain some, but not all, of its competitors' customers.

Figure 8.9 shows the short-run equilibrium of a monopolistically competitive firm. Managers, in the short run, set price at P_0 and output at Q_0 because this combination of price and output maximizes profit. We can be sure this combination of

FIGURE 8.9

Short-Run Equilibrium in Monopolistic Competition

The firm will set its price at P_0 and its output rate at Q_0 because marginal cost equals marginal revenue at this output. It will earn a profit of $P_0 - C_0$ per unit of output.

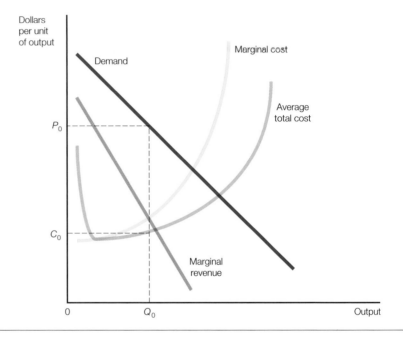

price and output maximizes profit because marginal cost equals marginal revenue at this output level. Economic profit is earned because price, P_0, exceeds average total cost, C_0. As in the case of monopoly and perfect competition, price must exceed average variable cost for profit to be maximized (clearly this occurs in Figure 8.9—average variable cost lies below average total cost).

One condition for long-run equilibrium in these markets is that each firm makes no economic profit or loss because entry or exit of firms will occur otherwise—and entry and exit are incompatible with long-run equilibrium. Another condition for long-run equilibrium is that each firm maximize its profit. At what price and output are both these conditions fulfilled? Figure 8.10 shows that the long-run equilibrium is at a price of P_1 and an output of Q_1. The zero economic profit condition is met at this combination of price and output because the firm's average cost at this output equals the price, P_1. And the profit maximization condition is met because the marginal revenue curve intersects the marginal cost curve at Q_1.[7]

7. The seminal work in the theory of monopolistic competition was E. Chamberlin, *The Theory of Monopolistic Competition* (Cambridge, MA: Harvard University Press, 1933).

FIGURE 8.10

Long-Run Equilibrium in Monopolistic Competition

The long-run equilibrium is at price P_1 and output Q_1. There is zero profit because long-run average cost equals price. Profit is maximized because marginal cost equals marginal revenue at this output.

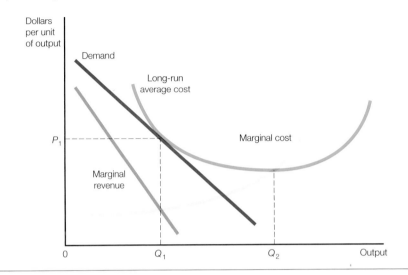

ADVERTISING EXPENDITURES: A SIMPLE RULE

Managers in monopolistic competition, as well as in other market structures, spend huge amounts on advertising. How much should a profit-maximizing manager spend on advertising? This section derives a simple rule to help managers answer this question.[8] The quantity a firm sells of its product is assumed to be a function of its price and the level of its advertising expenditures. We assume diminishing marginal returns to advertising expenditures, which means that beyond some point, successive advertising outlays yield smaller increases in sales. (Table 8.4 shows an illustrative case in which successive increments of $100,000 in advertising outlays result in smaller increases in quantity sold. For example, the quantity sold increases by 2 million units when advertising expenditures rise from $800,000 to $900,000, but by only 1.5 million units when they rise from $900,000 to $1 million.)

Let P be the price of a unit of the product and MC the marginal cost of production. If we assume that neither price nor marginal cost is altered by small changes in advertising expenditure, managers realize an increase in gross profit of $(P - MC)$ from each additional unit of product. Why is this the *gross* profit of selling an additional unit of output? Because it takes no account of whatever additional advertising expenditures are required to sell this extra unit of output. To

8. This rule, put forth by R. Dorfman and P. Steiner, applies to monopolistic or oligopolistic (see Chapter 11) firms as well as monopolistically competitive firms.

TABLE 8.4

Relationship between Advertising Expenditures and Quantity

Advertising Expenditures (Millions of Dollars)	Quantity Sold of Product (Millions of Units)
0.8	15.0
0.9	17.0
1.0	18.5
1.1	19.5
1.2	20.0

obtain the net profit, managers must deduct these additional advertising outlays from the gross profit.

To maximize net profit, a manager must set advertising expenditures at the level where an extra dollar of advertising results in extra gross profit equal to the extra dollar of advertising cost. Unless this is the case, a manager can increase the firm's total net profit by changing advertising outlays. If an extra dollar of advertising results in more than a dollar of increase in gross profit, the extra dollar should be spent on advertising (because this increases the total net profit). If the extra dollar (as well as the last dollar) of advertising results in less than a dollar's increase in gross profit, advertising outlays should be cut.[9] Therefore, if ΔQ is the number of extra units of output sold as a result of an extra dollar of advertising, the manager should set advertising expenditures so that

$$\Delta Q(P - MC) = 1 \qquad (8.17)$$

because the right side of this equation equals the extra dollar of advertising cost and the left side equals the extra gross profit resulting from this advertising dollar.

If we multiply both sides of equation (8.17) by $P/(P - MC)$, we obtain

$$P\Delta Q = P/(P - MC) \qquad (8.18)$$

Because the manager is maximizing profit, he is producing an output level at which marginal cost (MC) equals marginal revenue (MR). Therefore, we can substitute MR for MC in equation (8.18), the result being

$$P\Delta Q = P/(P - MR) \qquad (8.19)$$

Using equation (8.2), we can show that the right side of equation (8.19) equals $|\eta|$, the negative of the price elasticity of demand for the firm's product.[10] The left side of equation (8.19) is the marginal revenue from an extra dollar of advertising (it equals the price times the extra number of units sold as a result of

9. For simplicity, we assume that the gross profit resulting from an extra dollar spent on advertising is essentially equal to the gross profit resulting from the last dollar spent. This is an innocuous assumption.

10. Recall from equation (8.2) that $MR = P[1 - (1/|\eta|)]$. Therefore, $[1 - (1/|\eta|)] = MR/P$ and $1/|\eta| = 1 - (MR/P)$; this means that $|\eta| = 1/[1 - (MR/P)] = P/(P - MR)$ which is the right side of equation (8.19).

an extra dollar of advertising). To maximize profit, the manager should set advertising expenditure so that

$$\text{Marginal revenue from an extra dollar of advertising} = |\eta| \qquad (8.20)$$

This rule can be very helpful to managers.[11] Consider managers at the Humphrey Corporation, who estimate the price elasticity of demand for its product equals −1.6. To maximize profit, managers must set the marginal revenue from an extra dollar of advertising equal to 1.6, according to the rule in equation (8.20). Suppose managers believe an extra $100,000 of advertising will increase sales by $200,000. This association implies that the marginal revenue from an extra dollar of advertising is about $200,000/$100,000, or 2.0 rather than 1.6. Because the marginal revenue exceeds the absolute value of the price elasticity, managers can increase profit by advertising more.[12] To maximize profit, managers should increase advertising to the point where the marginal revenue from an extra dollar of advertising falls to 1.6—that is, the absolute value of the price elasticity of demand.

USING GRAPHS TO HELP DETERMINE ADVERTISING EXPENDITURE

A simple graphical technique can help managers identify optimal advertising expenditures. Take the case of the Hertzfeld Chemical Company. Curve A in Figure 8.11 shows the relationship between a product's price elasticity of demand and the amount managers spend on advertising. Managers should think of price elasticity as a proxy for the effectiveness of their differentiation strategies. Advertising is a strategic variable managers use to convey their differentiating message. The graph shows a curvilinear association between advertising and price elasticity. With little or no advertising, differentiation is slight between rival products; hence the price elasticity is high (in absolute value).

But because effective advertising can induce consumers to attach economic value to product attributes, increases in advertising spending reduce the product's price elasticity (in absolute value) considerably (by decreasing the product's perceived substitutability with other goods).[13] For any advertising level, the B curve shows the marginal revenue from an extra dollar of advertising. Because the A curve intersects the B curve when Hertzfeld's advertising expenditure is R dollars, this, on the basis of equation (8.20), is the estimated optimal advertising spending.

Clearly the optimal advertising level depends on the position and shape of the B and A curves. For example, suppose Hertzfeld's B curve shifts rightward to B', as shown in Figure 8.11. Such a shift might occur if managers increase advertising effectiveness. Because advertising is more effective, marginal revenue increases, so managers want to increase their ad spending. Hence we see the optimal level of advertising increases (to S dollars in Figure 8.11).

11. However, this rule is based on many simplifying assumptions and is not a complete solution to this complex problem.

12. Had Humphrey's managers believed that the marginal revenue from an extra dollar of advertising was *less* than the price elasticity of demand, a *reduction* in the firm's advertising expenditures would increase profit.

13. This is true for some products, but not for others. In some cases the absolute value of price elasticity of demand is directly, not inversely, related to the amount spent on advertising.

FIGURE 8.11

Optimal Advertising Expenditure

The firm's optimal advertising expenditure is R if the marginal revenue curve is B (or S if the marginal revenue curve is B').

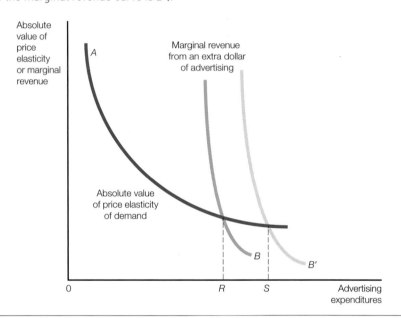

ADVERTISING, PRICE ELASTICITY, AND BRAND EQUITY: EVIDENCE ON MANAGERIAL BEHAVIOR

Promotions and advertising tend to be two sides of the same coin. Although they both seek to improve market performance, promotions appeal to the price-sensitive, whereas ads build brand loyalty. Promotions use a price-oriented message to test the limits of brand loyalty; advertising illuminates brand worth and does not mention price. Both strategies persuade consumers by influencing the price sensitivities of consumers. Promotions increase price elasticity and, in the long run, limit the price consumers are willing to pay for brand quality. Understanding these effects on consumer behavior certainly helps managers better understand the consequences of their actions.

So can we find real-world evidence of the effectiveness of these strategies? Yes. A large body of evidence shows that promotions increase the price elasticities of consumers.[14] These studies also show that the change in elasticities varies across consumers and time. In addition, brand loyalty does protect against promotions: Promotional strategies have less effect on the elasticities of brand loyalists relative to nonloyalists. And promotion is characterized as decaying in time. Short-term

14. K. Pauwells, D. Hanssens, and S. Siddarth, "The Long-Term Effects of Price Promotions on Category Incidence, Brand Choice, and Purchase Quantity," *Journal of Marketing Research*, vol. 39 (November 2002), pp. 421–436; C. Mela, S. Gupta, and D. Lehmann, "The Long-Term Impact of Promotion and Advertising on Consumer Brand Choice," *Journal of Marketing Research*, vol. 34 (May 1997), pp. 248–262.

change is greater, as if consumers operate with a high discount rate; or they may have short memories.

Mela, Gupta, and Lehmann report on a mature good market in which the ratio of advertising to promotions shifted from spending $250 million on advertising and offering promotions less than 10% of the time to spending less than $100 million on advertising and giving discounts more than 25% of the time. They found that the price elasticity of the average nonloyalist was twice that of the average brand loyalist. Loyalty is measured as frequency of repeat purchases. A drop in advertising messages affects all consumers, but the effect is much greater on the nonloyal crowd. In fact, a drop in advertising leads to a larger number of nonloyalists. Without reinforcement, a brand is eroded by price. Frequent promotions encourage nonloyalists to look for them, so their price sensitivities increase. The effect of promotions on the price sensitivity of nonloyalists is four times that of loyalists.

Pauwells, Hanssens, and Siddarth report on the soup and yogurt markets. They studied buying habits over a two-year period by analyzing purchases of over 690,000 ounces of yogurt and 535,000 ounces of soup. In both markets they find the effects of a promotion on price sensitivities was the greatest within the two-week period following its announcement. After this initial period, the effect grew weaker. The frequency of promotions also varied across firms, as did the amount of the discounts. These findings indicated that promotions are used more frequently by managers whose brand loyalty is weaker.

SUMMARY

1. Under monopoly, a manager maximizes profit by setting output at the point where marginal revenue equals marginal cost. It does not follow that managers in monopoly markets always earn significant profit. If the monopolist cannot cover its variable costs, it, like a perfectly competitive firm, will shut down, even in the short run.

2. An industry that is monopolized generally sets a higher price and a lower output than if it were perfectly competitive. The perfectly competitive firm operates at a point where price equals marginal cost, whereas the monopolist operates at a point at which marginal revenue equals marginal cost (and price exceeds marginal cost).

3. Empirical studies indicate that cost-plus pricing is used by many managers. In this approach, a manager estimates the cost per unit of output (based on some assumed output level) and adds a markup to include costs that cannot be allocated to any specific product and to provide a return on the firm's investment. On the surface, it is questionable whether this approach can maximize profit; but if marginal cost (not average cost) is really what is being marked up and the size of

the markup is determined (in the appropriate way) by the product's price elasticity of demand, cost-plus pricing can approximate profit maximization.

4. Firms generally sell more than one product. It is important for managers to recognize the demand interrelationships among the products they sell. Also, products are often interrelated in production. If two products are produced jointly in fixed proportions, the profit-maximizing output occurs where the total marginal revenue curve (the vertical summation of the marginal revenue curves for the individual products) intersects the marginal cost curve for the bundle of products, assuming the marginal revenue of each product is nonnegative.

5. If two products are produced jointly in variable proportions, we can construct isocost curves, each of which shows the combinations of outputs that can be produced at the same total cost. Also, isorevenue lines can be constructed, each of which shows the combination of outputs that yield the same total revenue. For an output combination to be optimal, it must be at a point where an isorevenue line is tangent to an isocost curve. To determine which output combination is optimal, we compare the profit levels at the tangency points. The tangency point where profit is the highest is the optimal output combination.

6. Monopsony occurs when there is only one buyer. Analogous to monopoly, the monopsonist restricts the amount purchased to less than what would occur if perfect competition existed and decreases the price paid relative to the price that would prevail under perfect competition.

7. In contrast to perfect competition, where all firms sell an identical product, firms under monopolistic competition sell somewhat different products. Producers differentiate their products from those of other producers. Therefore, the demand curve facing each firm slopes downward to the right—and is not horizontal, as it would be under perfect competition. Each firm sets marginal revenue equal to marginal cost if it maximizes profit.

8. Managers of monopolistically competitive firms spend large amounts on advertising. To maximize its profit, a manager should set an advertising level so the marginal revenue from an extra dollar of advertising equals the absolute value of the price elasticity of demand (under the conditions discussed).

9. Advertising of price changes may increase the price elasticity of demand for the product whose price has changed. This happens because the advertising makes consumers more aware of the price changes. Measures of brand loyalty are useful in guiding decisions concerning promotional activities to increase sales of particular brands.

PROBLEMS

1. Harry Smith owns a metal-producing firm that is an unregulated monopoly. After considerable experimentation and research, he finds that the firm's marginal cost curve can be approximated by a straight line, $MC = 60 + 2Q$

where MC is marginal cost (in dollars) and Q is output. The demand curve for the product is $P = 100 - Q$, where P is the product price (in dollars) and Q is output.

a. If Smith wants to maximize profit, what output should he choose?

b. What price should he charge?

2. The Wilson Company's marketing manager has determined that the price elasticity of demand for its product equals -2.2. According to studies she carried out, the relationship between the amount spent by the firm on advertising and its sales is as follows:

Advertising Expenditure	Sales
$100,000	$1.0 million
200,000	1.3 million
300,000	1.5 million
400,000	1.6 million

a. If the Wilson Company spends $200,000 on advertising, what is the marginal revenue from an extra dollar of advertising?

b. Is $200,000 the optimal amount for the firm to spend on advertising?

c. If $200,000 is not the optimal amount, would you recommend that the firm spend more or less on advertising?

3. The Coolidge Corporation is the only producer of a particular type of laser. The demand curve for its product is

$$Q = 8,300 - 2.1P$$

and its total cost function is

$$TC = 2,200 + 480Q + 20Q^2$$

where P is price (in dollars), TC is total cost (in dollars), and Q is monthly output.

a. Derive an expression for the firm's marginal revenue curve.

b. To maximize profit, how many lasers should the firm produce and sell per month?

c. If this number were produced and sold, what would be the firm's monthly profit?

4. The Madison Corporation, a monopolist, receives a report from a consulting firm concluding that the demand function for its product is

$$Q = 78 - 1.1P + 2.3Y + 0.9A$$

where Q is the number of units sold, P is the price of its product (in dollars), Y is per capita income (in thousands of dollars), and A is the firm's advertising expenditure (in thousands of dollars). The firm's average variable cost function is

$$AVC = 42 - 8Q + 1.5Q^2$$

where AVC is average variable cost (in dollars).

a. Can we determine the firm's marginal cost curve?

b. Can we determine the firm's marginal revenue curve?

c. If per capita income is $4,000 and advertising expenditure is $200,000, can we determine the price and output where marginal revenue equals marginal cost? If so, what are they?

5. The Wilcox Company has two plants with the marginal cost functions[15]

$$MC_1 = 20 + 2Q_1$$
$$MC_2 = 10 + 5Q_2$$

where MC_1 is marginal cost in the first plant, MC_2 is marginal cost in the second plant, Q_1 is output in the first plant, and Q_2 is output in the second plant.

a. If the Wilcox Company minimizes its costs and produces five units of output in the first plant, how many units of output does it produce in the second plant? Explain.

b. What is the marginal cost function for the firm as a whole?

c. Can we determine from these data the average cost function for each plant? Why or why not?

6. If the Rhine Company ignores the possibility that other firms may enter its market, it should set a price of $10,000 for its product, which is a power tool. But if it does so, other firms will begin to enter the market. During the next two years it will earn $4 million per year, but in the following two years it will earn $1 million per year. On the other hand, if it sets a price of $7,000, it will earn $2.5 million in each of the next four years because no entrants will appear.

a. If the interest rate is 10%, should the Rhine Company set a price of $7,000 or $10,000? Why? (Consider only the next four years.)

b. If the interest rate is 8%, should the Rhine Company set a price of $7,000 or $10,000? Why? (Consider only the next four years.)

c. The results in parts (a) and (b) pertain to only the next four years. How can the firm's managers extend the planning horizon?

7. During recessions and economic hard times, many people—particularly those who have difficulty getting bank loans—turn to pawnshops to raise cash. But even during boom years, pawnshops can be profitable. Because the collateral that customers put up (such as jewelry, guns, or electric guitars) is generally worth at least double what is lent, it generally can be sold at a profit. And because usury laws allow higher interest ceilings for pawnshops than for other lending institutions, pawnshops often charge spectacularly high rates of inter-

15. This question pertains to the chapter appendix.

est. For example, Florida's pawnshops charge interest rates of 20% or more *per month*. According to Steven Kent, an analyst at Goldman, Sachs, pawnshops make 20% gross profit on defaulted loans and 205% interest on loans repaid.

a. In 2012 there were about 15,000 pawnshops in the United States. This was much higher than in 2007, when the number was about 12,000. Why did the number increase?

b. In a particular small city, do the pawnshops constitute a perfectly competitive industry? If not, what is the market structure of the industry?

c. Are there considerable barriers to entry in the pawnshop industry? (*Note*: A pawnshop can be opened for less than $250,000, but a number of states have tightened licensing requirements for pawnshops.)

8. In 1996 dairy farmers, hurt by a decade of low milk prices, began reducing their herds. Subsequently Kenneth Hein, a Wisconsin farmer, said he was getting $16 per 100 pounds of milk, rather than $12, which he had gotten earlier.[16]

a. Why did the price increase?

b. Dairy cattle are often fed corn. When Hein got $16 per 100 pounds of milk, he paid $5 a bushel for corn; but when he got $12 per 100 pounds of milk, he paid $2.50 a bushel for corn. Does this mean that Hein made less money when the price of milk was $16 than when it was $12?

9. The demand for diamonds is given by

$$P_Z = 980 - 2Q_Z$$

where Q_Z is the number of diamonds demanded if the price is P_Z per diamond. The total cost (TC_Z) of the De Beers Company (a monopolist) is given by

$$TC_Z = 100 + 50Q_Z + 0.5Q_Z^2$$

where Q_Z is the number of diamonds produced and put on the market by the De Beers Company. Suppose the government could force De Beers to behave as if it were a perfect competitor—that is, via regulation, force the firm to price diamonds at marginal cost.

a. What is social welfare when De Beers acts as a single-price monopolist?

b. What is social welfare when De Beers acts as a perfect competitor?

c. How much does social welfare increase when De Beers moves from monopoly to competition?

10. The Hassman Company produces two joint products, X and Y. The isocost curve corresponding to a total cost of $500,000 is

$$Q_Y = 1,000 - 10Q_X - 5Q_X^2$$

where Q_Y is the quantity of product Y produced by the firm and Q_X is the quantity of product X produced. The price of product X is 50 times that of product Y.

16. *Philadelphia Inquirer*, September 14, 1996.

    a. If the optimal output combination lies on this isocost curve, what is the optimal output of product X?

    b. What is the optimal output of product Y?

    c. Can you be sure that the optimal output combination lies on this isocost curve? Why or why not?

11. The McDermott Company estimates its average total cost to be $10 per unit of output when it produces 10,000 units, which it regards as 80% of capacity. Its goal is to earn 20% on its total investment, which is $250,000.

    a. If the company uses cost-plus pricing, what price should it set?

    b. Can it be sure of selling 10,000 units if it sets this price?

    c. What are the arguments for and against a pricing policy of this sort?

12. The Morrison Company produces tennis rackets, the marginal cost of a racket being $20. Because there are many substitutes for the firm's rackets, the price elasticity of demand for its rackets equals about -2. In the relevant range of output, average variable cost is very close to marginal cost.

    a. The president of the Morrison Company feels that cost-plus pricing is appropriate for his firm. He marks up average variable cost by 100% to set price. Comment on this procedure.

    b. Because of heightened competition, the price elasticity of demand for the firm's rackets increases to -3. The president continues to use the same cost-plus pricing formula. Comment on its adequacy.

13. The Backus Corporation makes two products, X and Y. For every unit of good X that the firm produces, it produces two units of good Y. Backus's total cost function is

$$TC = 500 + 3Q + 9Q^2$$

where Q is the number of units of output (where each unit contains one unit of good X and two units of good Y) and TC is total cost (in dollars). The demand curves for the firm's two products are

$$P_X = 400 - Q_X$$
$$P_Y = 300 - 3Q_Y$$

where P_X and Q_X are the price and output of product X and P_Y and Q_Y are the price and output of product Y.

    a. How much of each product should the Backus Corporation produce and sell per period?

    b. What price should it charge for each product?

EXCEL EXERCISE: SIMPLE MONOPOLY

Suppose that the monopolist has the following estimate for her demand curve:

Price (P)	Quantity Demanded (Q)
14	0
13	1
12	2
11	3
10	4
9	5
8	6
7	7
6	8
5	9
4	10
3	11
2	12
1	13
0	14

and has the following estimate of her variable cost of producing each output:

Quantity Produced	Variable Cost
0	0
1	2.5
2	6.0
3	10.5
4	16.0
5	22.5
6	30.0
7	38.5
8	48.0
9	58.5
10	70.0
11	82.5
12	96.0
13	110.5
14	126.0

The firm has fixed costs of 5.

From the first spreadsheet exercise in Chapter 1, we know the demand equation is $Q = 14 - P$, which can also be expressed as $P = 14 - Q$ (by adding P to both sides of the equation and subtracting Q from both sides of the equation). As shown in the text, the firm's marginal revenue curve given this demand curve is $MR = 14 - 2Q$—that is, same intercept, double the slope.

Determining the relationship between quantity produced and variable cost is a bit tougher, but it can be shown that every number in the variable cost column comes from the formula $VC = 2Q + 0.5Q^2$. We know from the text that marginal cost $MC = dVC/dQ = 2 + Q$ and that to maximize profit, the firm sets $MR = MC$. Doing so yields

$$MR = 14 - 2Q = 2 + Q = MC$$

or $$3Q = 12$$

or $$Q = 4$$

Substituting $Q = 4$ into the demand curve gives $P = 14 - 4 = 10$.

The firm's total revenue (TR) is $TR = P^*Q = 10^*4 = 40$.

The firm's variable cost (VC) is $VC = 2Q + 0.5Q^2 = 2^*4 + 0.5^*4^*4 = 8 + 8 = 16$.

The firm's fixed cost (FC) = 5.

The firm's profit (π) = $\pi = TR - TC - FC = 40 - 16 - 5 = 19$.

But suppose you didn't have the above equations and did not know the calculus. Could you still calculate what the profit-maximizing output and price are and how much profit you will make?

The answer is yes, and with the spreadsheet, complete enumeration is quite simple.

Open up the spreadsheet and enter 14 in cell A1, then 13 in cell A2, and so on until you've sequentially ordered all the prices in the first table above.

Then enter 0 in cell B1, 1 in cell B2, and so on, until you've entered all quantities demanded from the table above opposite their respective prices.

Then enter =A1*B1 in cell C1. This is the firm's total revenue if it sells at price 14. You only have to enter the formula in cell C1. You then click on the lower right-hand corner of cell C1 with your mouse and drag down to cell C15. That will transform the correct total revenue formula to each cell. You can then see from column C how total revenue first rises, reaches a maximum, and then falls as price is decreased as described in the text.

Then enter =C2−C1 in cell D2. This shows the change in total revenue as you go from making no sales at $P = 14$ to making one sale at $P = 13$—that is your marginal revenue from making the first sale. As with the total revenue, you don't have to add the formula each time; just use the same click-and-drag method described for total revenue. This marginal revenue column enables you to see how marginal revenue decreases as sales increase and how it ultimately becomes negative (which, as we show on page 262, is a place no profit-maximizing manager wants to go). We call this the *discrete marginal revenue* because it assumes that one can only sell products in integers (think of buying automobiles or cans of beans).

In our formula version above ($MR = 14 - 2Q$), we assume that output can be purchased on a continuous basis (think of your purchases of gasoline or ham at the deli). For reference, enter $=14-2*B1$ in cell E1, and so on, to compare the continuous marginal revenue with the discrete marginal revenue. As above, you only have to enter the one formula in cell E1, and then click and drag.

You will notice that the discrete marginal revenue is different (and greater) than the continuous marginal revenue. This reflects the difference between integer changes in output and very small changes in output. Notice that where total revenue is maximized, the continuous marginal revenue is 0, as shown on page 266.

Enter 5 in cell F1, and so on. This is the firm's fixed cost (*FC*). Use the click-and-drag method to fill out the column.

Enter 0 in cell G1, 2.5 in cell G2, 6 in cell G3, and so on; in other words, enter the numbers from the variable cost (*VC*) table above.

Enter $=F1+G1$ in cell H1 and so on via click and drag after the first entry. Column H is the firm's total cost—that is, $TC = FC + VC$.

Enter $=H2-H1$ in cell I2, and so on. Fill the column via click and drag. This column measures the firm's discrete marginal cost, or how total cost changes as one increases output by an integer (think of the production of automobiles).

The formula used above ($MC = 2 + Q$) to solve for the profit-maximizing output was the continuous marginal cost, assuming that you could produce output in very small increments (think gasoline production). In column J, we present the continuous marginal cost to compare with the discrete marginal cost of column I. Enter $=2+B1$ in cell J1, and so on, via click and drag. Notice that the discrete and continuous marginal costs differ reflecting the increments of output assumed and that the continuous marginal cost exceeds the discrete marginal cost.

Column K is our objective. It is the profit column, total revenue minus total cost. Enter $=C1-H1$ in cell K1, and so on, via click and drag.

Now search column K for the highest number. If you entered everything correctly, you should find 19 in profit and, reading leftward, find in row 5 that the price is 10 and the quantity is 4. You may also enter $= Max(K1:K15)$ in cell K16 to find the highest profit.

Thus without any calculus, you were able to find the profit-maximizing price and quantity. Note that at $P = 10$, the continuous marginal revenue equaled the continuous marginal cost ($=6$). Note also that at $P = 10$, the discrete marginal revenue equaled 7, while the discrete marginal cost equaled 5.5. Because cash flow in (7) exceeds cash flow out (5.5), the producer who can only produce in integers wants to produce the fourth unit. Note that at $Q = 5$, the discrete marginal revenue is 5 and the discrete marginal cost is 6.5. Because cash flow in (5) is exceeded by cash flow out (6.5), the producer who can only produce in integers will not want to produce the fifth unit. Thus, regardless of whether we use the discrete or continuous numbers, we come to the same conclusion: Profit is maximized when four units are produced and sold at price 10.

We can also see from the table that monopolists mark price up over marginal cost (10 versus either 6 or 5.5).

Column L calculates the firm's price elasticity of demand. Recall the formula from the text is $\eta_D = (P/Q)(\Delta Q/\Delta P)$. From the first table $\Delta Q/\Delta P = -1$, and so $\eta_D = -P/Q$. Enter $=-A2/B2$ in cell L2 and fill the column via click and drag. Notice the profit-maximizing firm produces in the elastic range of the demand curve (as we showed on page 262), and the elastic range of the demand curve exists where the marginal revenue is positive (and the inelastic range of the demand curve is where the marginal revenue is negative). You can also observe how total revenue changes when prices change in the elastic and inelastic ranges of the demand curve (as shown on page 263).

APPENDIX: ALLOCATION OF OUTPUT AMONG PLANTS

Many firms own and operate more than one plant. In this appendix we show how managers should allocate output among various plants. This is an important decision, and our results have major direct practical value. We consider the case of the Johnson Company, a monopolist; but our results are valid for any manager who exercises market power.

The Johnson Company, a monopolist that makes a particular type of fixture, operates two plants with marginal cost curves shown in columns 2 and 3 of Table 8.5, output being shown in column 1. Clearly, if the managers decide to produce only one unit of output per hour, they should use plant I because the marginal cost between zero and one unit of output is lower in plant I than in plant II. Hence for the firm as a whole, the marginal cost between zero and one unit of output is $10 (the marginal cost between zero and one unit for plant I). Similarly, if the managers decide to produce two units of output per hour, both should be produced in plant I, and the marginal cost between the first and second units of output for the firm as a whole is $12 (the marginal cost between the first and second units in plant I). If managers decide to produce three units of output per hour, two should be produced in plant I and one in plant II, and the marginal cost between the second and third units of output for the firm as a whole is $14 (the marginal cost between zero and one unit of output for plant II). Alternatively, all three could be produced at plant I (the marginal cost between the second and third units of output in plant I is also $14).

Going on in this way, we can derive the marginal cost curve for the firm as a whole, shown in column 4 of Table 8.5. To maximize profit, the manager should find the output level at which the marginal revenue equals the marginal cost of the firm as a whole. This is the profit-maximizing output level. In this case it is three or four units per hour. Suppose managers choose to produce four units.[17] To

17. The firm is indifferent between producing three or four units. If it produces four, its total revenue is $92,000 (23 × 4) and its variable cost is $50,000 (10 + 12 + 14 + 14), yielding a variable-cost profit of $42,000. If it produces three, the total revenue is $78,000 (26 × 3) and the variable cost is $36,000 (10 + 12 + 14), yielding a variable-cost profit of $42,000. Because both plants already exist, their fixed costs must be paid and therefore are irrelevant in the short run. In the long run (if demand were predicted to remain constant), the firm could divest itself of plant II.

TABLE 8.5

Costs of the Johnson Company

Output per Hour	Marginal Cost[a] Plant I (Dollars)	Plant II (Dollars)	Marginal Cost for Firm[a] (Dollars)	Price (Dollars)	Marginal Revenue[a] (Dollars)
1	10	14	10	40	—
2	12	18	12	30	20
3	14	22	14	26	18
4	20	26	14	23	14
5	24	30	18	20.8	12

[a]These figures pertain to the interval between the indicated output and one unit less than the indicated output.

determine what price to charge, they must estimate what price corresponds to this output on the demand curve. In this case, the answer is $23.

At this point we have solved most of the Johnson Company's problems, but not quite all. Given that managers will produce four units of output per hour, how should they divide this production between the two plants? The answer is that they need to set the marginal cost in plant I equal to the marginal cost in plant II. Table 8.5 shows this means that plant I would produce three units per hour and plant II would produce one unit per hour. The common value of the marginal costs of the two plants is the marginal cost of the firm as a whole; this common value must be set equal to the marginal revenue if the firm maximizes profit.

Many managers use this technique to allocate output among plants. For example, electric power companies have developed computer programs to facilitate the job of allocating electricity demand (or "load") among plants in accord with this theoretical rule. These programs allow a central dispatcher, who is in constant communication with the plants, to compute quickly the optimal allocation among plants. The result has been millions of dollars of savings.

As a further illustration, consider the Chou Company, which has plants at Altoona, Pennsylvania, and at High Point, North Carolina. The total cost function for the Altoona plant is

$$TC_A = 5 + 9Q_A + Q_A{}^2$$

where TC_A is the daily total cost (in thousands of dollars) at this plant and Q_A is its output (in units per day). The total cost curve for the High Point plant is

$$TC_H = 4 + 10Q_H + Q_H{}^2$$

where TC_H is the daily total cost (in thousands of dollars) at this plant, and Q_H is its output (in units per day).

The Chou Company's demand curve is

$$P = 31 - Q$$

and its total revenue is

$$TR = PQ = (31 - Q)Q = 31Q - Q^2$$

Therefore the Chou Company's marginal revenue curve is

$$MR = \Delta TR/\Delta Q = 31 - 2Q$$

Note that $Q = Q_A + Q_H$, P is price, and MR is the marginal revenue (in thousands of dollars per unit).

To maximize profit, managers must choose a price and output such that

$$MC_A = MC_H = MR \qquad (8.21)$$

where MC_A is the marginal cost (in thousands of dollars) at the Altoona plant and MC_H is the marginal cost (in thousands of dollars) at the High Point plant.

The Altoona plant's marginal cost is

$$MC_A = \Delta TC_A/\Delta Q_A = 9 + 2Q_A$$

The High Point plant's marginal cost is

$$MC_H = \Delta TC_H/\Delta Q_H = 10 + Q_H$$

According to equation (8.21), MC_A must equal MC_H. Therefore,

$$9 + 2Q_A = 10 + Q_H$$

or

$$Q_H = -1 + 2Q_A$$

Also, because equation (8.21) states that MC_A must equal MR,

$$
\begin{aligned}
9 + 2Q_A &= 31 - 2(Q_A + Q_H) \\
&= 31 - 2(Q_A - 1 + 2Q_A) \\
&= 33 - 6Q_A
\end{aligned}
$$

or

$$8Q_A = 24$$

Consequently, $Q_A = 3$. And because $Q_H = -1 + 2Q_A$, it follows that $Q_H = 5$. Moreover, $P = 23$ because $P = 31 - (Q_A + Q_H)$. In a nutshell, managers should charge \$23,000 per unit and produce three units per day at the Altoona plant and five units per day at the High Point plant.

PART 5
SOPHISTICATED MARKET PRICING

CHAPTER 9

MANAGERIAL USE OF PRICE DISCRIMINATION

Price discrimination is common across many markets and products. A car dealership aims to sell each vehicle for the highest price it can get (as long as that price is higher than its reservation price). Airline managers segment their markets and sell the same seats at significantly different prices depending on when the tickets are purchased, whether the tickets are refundable, penalities for changing flight plans, and the like. College administrators use a price discrimination policy by awarding financial aid; there is a wide variety of aid packages within the student population.

In general, managers try to identify submarkets on the basis of an individual's price elasticity of demand. A car dealership is an example of first-degree price discrimination, where the dealer attempts to extract the reservation price of each buyer. In effect each buyer is a submarket. The airlines use one general pricing model to divide the market into at least two submarkets: a relatively price-insensitive business class and a relatively price-sensitive leisure class. Airlines are an example of third-degree price discrimination, where each airline tries to extract the average reservation price of those similar in price sensitivity. The airline pricing model is compromised somewhat by Internet firms such as Expedia, which search airline databases for the lowest fares. This gives the consumer more information about the range of fares available and enables the consumer to potentially get a lower fare than that available from dealing directly with the carrier.

MOTIVATION FOR PRICE DISCRIMINATION

Consider Figure 9.1, which shows the profit-maximizing price and quantity for a single-price monopolist. By charging price P_M, the monopolist sells Q_M units. But aside from the customer whose reservation price was P_M, all other purchasing customers in area AB of the demand curve value the good at a price higher than P_M, but they are asked to pay only P_M for it. Consumers can retain a significant amount of consumer surplus—money they are willing to pay the producer but are not asked to do so. The amount of that consumer surplus is V (the area shaded in dark blue).

Consumers in area BC of the demand curve are unwilling to spend P_M for the good but have reservation prices that exceed the marginal cost of producing the good and hence represent potential profitable sales. These sales are not made by

---

FIGURE 9.1

Single-Price Monopolist Profit-Maximizing Outcome

The single-price monopolist prices at P_M and produces and sells Q_M units. Consumers in region AB are willing to pay a higher price than P_M yet are not asked to do so. Consumers in region BC are unwilling to pay a price as high as P_M but will pay a price higher than it costs the producer to make the good. Both these situations are potentially profitable sales that are not made.

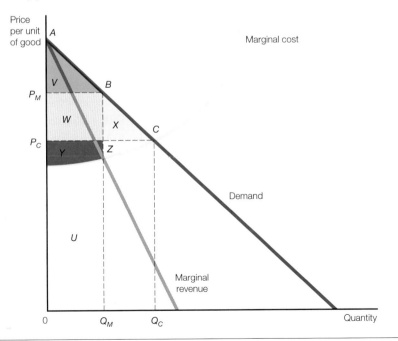

the single-price monopolist, who curtails output at Q_M, whereas profitable sales could continue up to Q_C. The amount of profit represented by those potential sales is $X + Z$.

Instead the single-price monopolist settles for a variable-cost profit of $W + Y$: the gray plus red areas where total revenue is $P_M Q_M = W + Y + U$ and variable cost is the area U, under the marginal cost curve (as shown in Chapter 6).

If the monopolist raises the price above P_M to capture some of the consumer surplus in area V, area $X + Z$ becomes greater. If the manager lowers the price below P_M to capture some of the potential profit in area $X + Z$, area V becomes bigger. We know that managers cannot increase profit by deviating from P_M because it is the profit-maximizing price for the single-price monopolist. If the manager is going to capture some (or all) of region V and some (or all) of region $X + Z$, she cannot do it with a single-price strategy. Managers can capture surplus from area V and profit from areas $X + Z$ only with a strategy that involves two or more prices. We now explore what those strategies should be. Their motivation is capturing the additional profit in area V and areas $X + Z$. If the benefit of capturing that profit exceeds the costs of doing so (remember that sophisticated pricing is more costly to implement than simple single pricing), then our manager should do so.

PRICE DISCRIMINATION

Price discrimination When the same product is sold at more than one price.

Price discrimination occurs when the same product is sold at more than one price. For example, an airline may sell tickets on a particular flight at a higher price to business travelers than to college students. An automobile dealer may sell the exact same equipped make and model at different prices on the same day to different buyers. Even if the products are not precisely the same, price discrimination is said to occur if similar products are sold at prices that are in different ratios to their marginal costs. If managers sell boxes of candy with a label (costing $0.02) saying "Premium Quality" in rich neighborhoods for $12 and sell the same boxes of candy without this label in poor neighborhoods for $5, this is price discrimination. Differences in price among similar products are not evidence of discrimination unless these differences do not reflect cost differences.

First-Degree Price Discrimination

Managers need to master three basic types of price discrimination: first, second, and third degree. The auto dealer is an example of the first degree, whereas the airline and candy firm are examples of the third degree. Selling electricity to certain customers is an example of the second degree. By examining price discrimination in a bit more detail, managers can better understand how to use all three types.

Consider again the diagram of a simple monopoly (single-price) profit maximizer shown in Figure 9.1. To reiterate, consumers in segment AB of the demand

STRATEGY SESSION: When Can You Haggle?

In general, Americans hate to haggle. They do so at car dealers (and detest the experience), in real estate transactions, in dealings with contractors for home repairs, in contract negotiations, and at flea markets; but most of their purchases involve posted prices, and most Americans accept that. However, haggling is the norm in many places around the world, and more haggling is drifting into the United States. Why is that?

According to a *Consumer Reports* National Research Center survey of over 2,000 shoppers, 61% bargained for products such as cell phones, furniture, medical bills, home electronics, household appliances, jewelry, antiques, and the like during the previous three years. In the home furnishings category, 94% reported paying less than the posted price. Of those who negotiated successfully, 61% reported savings of between $50 and $99; 26% reported savings of between $1 and $49; and 14% reported savings of $100 or more.

Our MBA students play a series of managerial economics games against each other and MBA students at INSEAD's campuses in Fontainebleau and Singapore. Because they are French, INSEAD Fontainebleau gave a bottle of fine French champagne to the team that scored the highest. We decided to do the same. We teach 12 sections and hence needed 12 bottles. One of our faculty members went to several New Jersey liquor stores and negotiated a price for the champagne that was significantly below the posted price.

Here are *Consumer Reports'* tips for hagglers:

1. Use the power of timing. For service contracts, negotiate for discounts and perks at the time of the initial contract or at its renewal.

2. Offer cash. Credit and debit card companies charge merchants 2–8% for card use.

3. Look for flaws—scratches and dents that don't impair the performance of the product and can be hidden or covered by the purchaser.

4. Buy multiple units and ask for a quantity discount.

This opportunity to haggle is good news for consumers who don't buy goods at their posted prices because they are above their reservation prices. But it's got to be a good deal for the sellers too. Otherwise why would sellers negotiate?

However, it's potentially not good news for people who don't mind posted prices. If buying a bar stool becomes more like buying a car, many people are going to hate shopping. Even if you accept the posted price of the stool (which you know is high relative to the seller's reservation price given your car-buying experience), you'll worry that you paid too much; and you'll worry that your neighbor will quiz you about what you paid and then humble you when she tells you what she paid. At least when you both pay the same posted price, you feel equal to her.

Source: "Haggle Even at Stores; Survey Shows It Works," *Philadelphia Inquirer*, May 18, 2008, p. M-2.

curve are willing to pay more than the single monopoly price of P_M. Consumers in segment BC of the demand curve are willing to pay more for the good than it costs the producer to produce it—that is, the firm's marginal cost.

The simple monopolist makes a variable-cost profit of $W + Y$, as shown in Figure 9.1, and leaves the consumer surplus of V with the consumers of segment AB. If managers could perfectly price discriminate (another term for first-degree

---

PROBLEM SOLVED: Honest Sanjay's Use of First-Degree Price Discrimination

We now view an example of first-degree price discrimination versus simple monopoly pricing. Honest Sanjay sells used cars. The market demand for Sanjay's used cars is $P = 12 - Q$, where P is the price in thousands and Q is the quantity of cars sold per month.

Sanjay has two strategies of selling cars. He can set a price and merely pay a general manager to write the paperwork. The total cost of selling each car under such an arrangement is $2 (thousand), so Sanjay's marginal cost is $2 (thousand). This is also Sanjay's average variable cost of selling a car. Sanjay faces fixed costs of $5 (thousand) per month.

To maximize profit under simple monopoly pricing, Sanjay should set marginal revenue equal to marginal cost. Sanjay's total revenue is $TR = PQ = (12 - Q)Q = 12Q - Q^2$. Sanjay's marginal revenue, $MR = \Delta TR / \Delta Q$, is

$$MR = 12 - 2Q$$

Setting Sanjay's marginal revenue equal to his marginal cost,

$$MR = 12 - 2Q = 2 = MC$$

gives $Q = 5$, which implies that the price of cars is $P = 12 - 5 = 7$ or $7,000.

Sanjay's total revenue per month is $35 (that is, $PQ = (\$7)(5) = \$35,000$), variable costs are $10 (that is, $(AVC)Q = (\$2)(5) = \$10,000$), and fixed costs are $5 (thousand), resulting in a monthly profit of $20 (thousand) from simple monopoly pricing.

Sanjay could also sell cars the more common way—customers haggling with salespeople. Sanjay can hire a slick salesforce. By chatting with customers, a salesperson can pretty well estimate a customer's reservation price of a car; for example, salespeople often come right out and ask a customer how much the customer is looking to spend or are more subtle by asking, "What do you do for a living? Do you want to drive the car home tonight?" Salespeople who are not good at estimating customers' reservation prices tend not to be employed for long in the automobile business. A general manager is still needed to write the paperwork, and the salespeople are paid strictly on commission: $1 (thousand) for each car they sell. Under this model of sales, Sanjay's marginal cost is $3 (thousand) per car. The haggle model is first-degree price discrimination in action. As mentioned, practicing price discrimination does carry costs not incurred by managers charging a single price.

Under this model, Sanjay sells cars up to the point where the reservation price equals marginal cost

$$P = 12 - Q = 3 = MC \text{ or } Q = 9$$

---

price discrimination), they would charge the consumers in segment AB their reservation prices, capturing all the consumer surplus and turning it into producer surplus (that is, variable-cost profit). Note that when managers can perfectly discriminate in segment AB, the firm's variable-cost profit increases to $V + W + Y$.

First-degree discrimination lets managers expand sales. Because managers are not constrained by a single price, they can serve consumers in segment BC. This increases variable-cost profit by $X + Z$ because the reservation price of the consumers in segment BC exceeds the additional cost of producing the units

First-Degree Price Discrimination

The first-degree price discriminator captures all consumer surplus *J* and turns it into producer surplus (variable-cost profit).

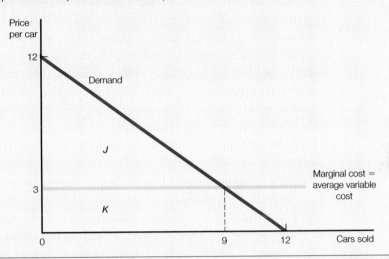

All consumer surplus (*J* in the figure shown) is captured. Sanjay's profit is total revenue (*J* + *K*) less total cost (variable cost, *K*, plus fixed cost). In this case total revenue is $67.5[a] (thousand), variable cost is $27 (($AVC$)($Q$) = ($3)(9) = $27,000), and fixed cost is $5 (thousand), resulting in a profit of $35.5 (thousand).

Sanjay prefers the haggle model over the simple monopoly posted-price model (because $35.5 > $20).

Presumably this explains why most auto dealers have not switched to the posted-price model and continue haggling to sell cars.

[a]The area of trapezoid *J* + *K* is one-half the height (9) times the sum of the trapezoid's two sides (12 + 3). Therefore 0.5(9)(15) = 67.5.

involved: $Q_C - Q_M$. By perfectly discriminating in both the AB and the BC segments, managers increase the firm's variable-cost profit (and hence its profit) by $V + X + Z$. This is precisely all the area we saw that the simple monopolist was not exploiting in Figure 9.1. The potential for this additional profit gets creative managers thinking about pricing strategies to capture it.

If managers can capture all of $V + X + Z$, we say they are practicing discrimination of the first degree. Managers always want to find ways to use first-degree price discrimination. In essence, the strategy allows them to charge each consumer his or her reservation price. By so doing, they guarantee that consumer surplus is zero. Clearly managers are willing to do this up to Q_C units in Figure 9.1. The additional revenue managers generate by selling an additional unit of product is the reservation price of the consumer. Managers sell to a consumer as long as the reservation price (which the manager can charge and the consumer is willing to pay) exceeds the marginal cost of production. In essence, in perfect discrimination the firm's demand curve becomes the firm's marginal revenue curve. Therefore, managers will not sell more than Q_C items because the marginal cost of producing them exceeds the revenue they will generate for the firm—that is, their reservation price.

Thus the profit-maximizing rule developed in Chapters 7 and 8 holds. The perfectly discriminating manager maximizes profit by producing until marginal revenue (represented by the demand curve) is equal to the output's marginal cost.

One interesting outcome of first-degree price discrimination is that it produces the same output as if the monopolist were in a perfectly competitive market—that is, Q_C. The difference between the two scenarios is in the distribution of consumer and producer surplus. In essence, using first-degree price discrimination, the manager gets to bake the cake and eat it too. In Figure 9.1, under perfectly competitive pricing (P_C), consumer surplus is $V + W + X$ and producer surplus is $Y + Z$. Because total welfare is the sum of consumer and producer surplus, social welfare is V through Z. Under first-degree discrimination, consumer surplus is zero (it has all been captured) and producer surplus is V through Z. Therefore, the welfare is the same under both pricing mechanisms, V through Z, but consumers benefit under perfect competition and producers get *all* the benefit of first-degree price discrimination. Because the output is the same in each pricing scheme, social welfare is identical.

For first-degree price discrimination, managers usually must have a relatively small number of buyers and must be able to estimate the maximum prices they are willing to accept. In addition, other conditions must hold that are elaborated on when we discuss third-degree price discrimination. For these reasons, the two-part tariff method of pricing (discussed later) is a simpler way to operationalize first-degree price discrimination in many situations.

The general retail market in the United States is not well suited to first-degree price discrimination. The market is predominantly posted price, so there is no haggling (with the exception of car buying, home buying, dealing with housing contractors, and yard sales). In other cultures haggling is more prevalent. For example, in the bazaars of Asia, buyers are expected to haggle with sellers. In the finest pearl establishments of Hyderabad, India (a pearl capital of the world), transactions are all done by haggling (unless an unsuspecting tourist from a no-haggle country is uninformed enough to pay the price listed for the pearls). Negotiation is much more prevalent in business-to-business transactions in the United States.

Second-Degree Price Discrimination

Second-degree price discrimination is most common in utility pricing. According to some authorities, second-degree price discrimination plays an important role in the schedule of rates charged by many public utilities—gas, water, electricity, and others.[1]

Consider a gas company, *each* of whose customers has the demand curve shown in Figure 9.2. The company charges a high price, P_0, if the consumer purchases fewer than X units of gas per month. For an amount beyond X units per month, the company charges a medium price, P_1. For purchases beyond Y, the company charges an even lower price, P_2. Consequently the company's total revenues from each consumer are equal to the shaded area in Figure 9.2 because

---

FIGURE 9.2

Second-Degree Price Discrimination

The company charges a different price (P_0, P_1, or P_2) depending on how much the consumer purchases, thus increasing its total revenue and profit.

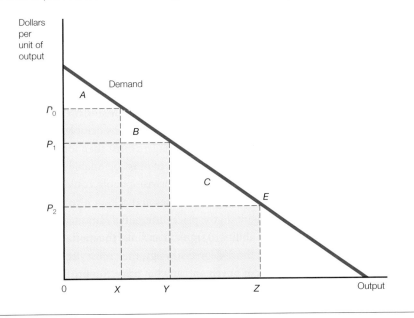

1. Of course, this assumes for simplicity that each consumer purchases Z units and that each price considered exceeds the firm's marginal cost. Also, other simplifying assumptions (which need not concern us here) are made in this and the next paragraph.

the consumer purchases X units at a price of P_0, $(Y - X)$ units at a price of P_1, and $(Z - Y)$ units at a price of P_2.

The manager, by charging different prices for various amounts of the commodity, increases revenues and profit. After all, if she charged only a single price and wanted to sell Z units, she would charge a price of P_2. Thus the firm's total revenue would equal the rectangle $0P_2EZ$, which is considerably less than the shaded area in Figure 9.2. By charging different prices, managers increase profit relative to a single-price strategy. Unlike first-degree price discrimination, managers leave a consumer surplus of $A + B + C$. Because second-degree (and third-degree) discrimination occurs at the group level and not at that of the individual, consumers retain some surplus.

Third-Degree Price Discrimination

We now consider the most common form of price discrimination: third-degree price discrimination. Three conditions must hold true for this pricing strategy to succeed. Demand must be heterogeneous, managers must be able to identify and segregate the different segments, and markets must be successfully sealed. As we previously discussed, individuals within a market have different preferences toward a product. The differences in their price elasticity of demand may be due to differences among classes in income levels, tastes, or the availability of substitutes. For example, the price elasticity of demand for the boxes of candy discussed earlier may be lower (in absolute value) for the rich than for the poor.

Think of it like this: Managers would prefer to identify the preferences of individuals (first-degree price discrimination). For various possible reasons, they can't (or don't want to because it is too expensive). So they choose the next best alternative, which is to identify individuals with similar traits and group them together. Managers then appeal to the group.

Students are a good example of third-degree discrimination. Students have relatively limited income, so they tend to have high price elasticities of demand—they are price sensitive. Thus many times they are sold a good or a service at a lower price. They get a discount, and all they must do is to show student identification.

Buyers of the product must fall into classes with considerable differences in price elasticity of demand for the product. Managers must then identify and segregate these classes at moderate cost. Also, buyers must be unable to transfer the product easily from one class to another; otherwise people could make money by buying the product from the low-price classes and selling it to the high-price classes, making it difficult to maintain the price differentials among classes. We call these latter two conditions the ability to *segment* and *seal* the market.[2]

If managers want to use a third-degree strategy, they must decide how much output to allocate to each class of buyer, and at what price. Suppose there are only two classes of buyers. Managers have already chosen total output, so they need to allocate output across the two markets. Managers will maximize profit by allocat-

2. Segmenting and sealing can have another meaning. In 2000, customers of Amazon.com discovered (via an Internet chat room) that they had been charged significantly different prices by Amazon for the same DVD. When they expressed their displeasure and made the price differences public, Amazon announced that it no longer would engage in such pricing. If the customers had not discovered the price differences, they would have been satisfied (as revealed by their purchase of the DVD), and Amazon could have continued selling the same product at different prices. See David Streitfeld, "On the Web, Price Tags Blur," *Washington Post*, September 27, 2000.

STRATEGY SESSION: That Darling Little Mouse Is Really a Price Discriminator

It's been a long, cold winter in Green Bay. Let's reward the kids with a spring break vacation at Disneyland and Disney California Adventure Park. They'll love Mickey, Minnie, Donald, and Snow White, and it'll be warm. Family A of four (two adults, two kids ages five and seven) packs up and heads for Anaheim.

It's another day in paradise. Should we go to the ocean, take a ride to the mountains, or go to Disneyland and Disney California Adventure Park? So many choices for the Los Angeles family, and so many times those same choices are available. Family B of four (two adults, two kids ages five and seven) hops in the family car and heads for Anaheim.

Both families buy the One-Day Park Hopper (which lets them visit both parks). The bill for the Griswolds from Green Bay is $312. The bill for the family from Los Angeles is $292. It costs Disney the same to serve the Los Angeles family as the Green Bay family. So why the $20 price difference? And how can Disney

tell the two families apart? It's the Wisconsin driver's license that family A is carrying and the driver's license showing a Southern California address that family B is carrying. That's how the market is sealed. How is it segmented?

The Griswolds came all the way from Green Bay to see Mickey, and Dad's not going to disappoint those children for a mere $20. On the other hand, family B could have gone to the ocean or the mountains or could see Mickey tomorrow. Simply put, the Griswolds had a much less elastic demand than family B, who had plenty of substitutes.

That mouse is a clever third-degree price discriminator!

Sources: http://disneyland.disney.go.com/disneyland/en_US/reserve/ticketListing?year=2007 for Southern California prices and http://disneyland.disney.go.com/disneyland/en_US/reserve/ticketListing?name=TicketListin for other prices.

ing the total output so that the marginal revenue in one class is equal to the marginal revenue in the other. For example, if the marginal revenue in the first class is $25 and that in the second class is $10, the allocation is not optimal. Managers can increase profit by allocating one less unit of output to the second class and one more unit to the first class. In fact, managers want to allocate so the marginal revenue of both classes is equal. When this is true, the ratio of the price in the first class to that in the second class equals

$$\frac{P_1}{P_2} = \left[\frac{1 - \left(\frac{1}{|\eta_2|} \right)}{1 - \left(\frac{1}{|\eta_1|} \right)} \right]$$

(9.1)

where η_1 is the price elasticity of demand in the first class and η_2 is that in the second class.[3] We can now see why it does not pay to discriminate if the two price elasticities are equal: $|\eta_1| = |\eta_2|$ implies that $P_1 = P_2$. Moreover, segments with a lower (absolute values) price elasticity are charged a higher price.

3. Recall from equation (2.15) that marginal revenue equals $P[1 + (1/\eta)]$, where P is price and η is the price elasticity of demand. Therefore, if marginal revenue is the same in the two classes, $P_1[1 - (1/|\eta_1|)] = P_2[1 - (1/|\eta_2|)]$. Hence $P_1/P_2 = [1 - (1/|\eta_2|)]/[1 - (1/|\eta_1|)]$.

Turning to the more realistic case in which managers choose total output, it is obvious they must look at costs as well as demand in the two classes. The manager will then optimize profit when the marginal cost of the entire output is equal to the common value of the marginal revenue in the two classes. The firm's profit (π) is

$$\pi = TR_1 + TR_2 - TC$$

where TR_1 is the total revenue from class 1, TR_2 is the total revenue from class 2, and TC is the total cost. The total cost is a function of the total amount of the good (Q) produced and sold, and it is allocated Q_1 to class 1 and Q_2 to class 2.

The monopolist has two output choices, so profit is maximized when $\Delta\pi/\Delta Q_1 = 0$ and $\Delta\pi/\Delta Q_2 = 0$. Note that $\Delta\pi/\Delta Q_1 = (\Delta TR_1/\Delta Q_1) - (\Delta TC/\Delta Q_1)$ and $(\Delta TR_2/\Delta Q_1) = 0$ because revenues in class 2 are independent of sales in class 1. Likewise, $\Delta\pi/\Delta Q_2 = (\Delta TR_2/\Delta Q_2) - (\Delta TC/\Delta Q_2)$ and $(\Delta TR_1/\Delta Q_2) = 0$ because revenues in class 1 are independent of sales in class 2. These two relationships are rewritten as

$$\Delta\pi/\Delta Q_1 = MR_1 - MC = 0$$
$$\Delta\pi/\Delta Q_2 = MR_2 - MC = 0$$

(9.2)

Note that both $\Delta TC/\Delta Q_1$ and $\Delta TC/\Delta Q_2$ equal MC (and not MC_1 and MC_2) because the plant manager knows only that producing another unit incurs additional costs. It is the marketing or sales department's job to decide whether the good is destined for class 1 or class 2 demanders.

QUANT OPTION

Profits are maximized when $\partial\pi/\partial Q_1 = 0$ and when $\partial\pi/\partial Q_2 = 0$. Partial derivatives are used when just one of the outputs is changing but not the other. Note that $\partial\pi/\partial Q_1 = (\partial TR_1/\partial Q_1) - (\partial TC/\partial Q_1)$ and $(\partial TR_2/\partial Q_1) = 0$ because revenues in class 2 are independent of sales in class 1. Likewise, $\partial\pi/\partial Q_2 = (\partial TR_2/\partial Q_2) - (\partial TC/\partial Q_2)$ and $(\partial TR_1/\partial Q_2) = 0$ because revenues in class 1 are independent of sales in class 2.

The equations (9.2) state that to maximize profit, managers must choose output so $MR_1 = MC$ and $MR_2 = MC$, implying that $MR_1 = MR_2 = MC$. Had there been n classes of demanders, the profit-maximizing rule would be $MR_1 = MR_2 = \ldots = MR_n = MC$. To see this in the two-class case, consider Figure 9.3, which shows D_1, the demand curve in class 1; D_2, the demand curve in class 2; R_1, the marginal revenue curve in class 1; R_2, the marginal revenue curve in class 2; and the firm's marginal cost curve. The curve representing the horizontal summation of the two marginal revenue curves is G. This curve shows, for each

FIGURE 9.3

Third-Degree Price Discrimination

To maximize profit, the firm produces a total output of Q units and sets a price of P_1 in the class 1 market and P_2 in the class 2 market.

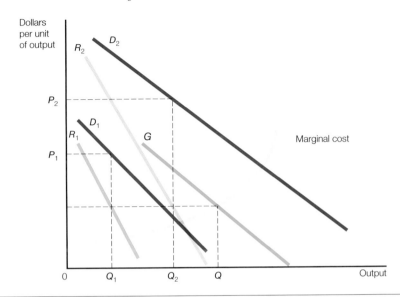

level of marginal revenue, the total output needed if marginal revenue in each class is to be maintained at this level. The optimal output is shown by the point where the G curve intersects the marginal cost curve because marginal cost must be equal to the common value of the marginal revenue in each class. If this were not true, profit could be increased by expanding output (if marginal cost were less than marginal revenue) or contracting output (if marginal cost were greater than the marginal revenue). Therefore, managers produce an output of Q units and sell Q_1 units in the class 1 market and Q_2 units in the class 2 market. The price is P_1 in the class 1 market and P_2 in the class 2 market. This results in a higher profit than if the firm quoted the same price in both markets.

Managerial Use of Third-Degree Price Discrimination

Perhaps the most frequently cited example of third-degree price discrimination is the case of airline tickets. The airlines often charge a lower fare for essentially the same ticket if it is purchased in advance as opposed to the day of the flight or based on the day of the week for which the ticket is valid. However, there is a penalty paid on these low-price tickets if the trip is canceled or changed. As an example of different prices for the same service, in 2011 the price of a round-trip coach ticket from New York to San Francisco ranged from about $580 to $674 for flights leaving and returning on similar dates.

315

STRATEGY SESSION: Mickey Mouse Pricing at Amusement Parks

Going to an amusement park used to mean paying the admission charge (and perhaps an additional fee inside the park to ride the hot new attraction); but that was it. The prices were transparent. But now you need a scorecard to know how to play and what prices are available. Attendance fell after 9/11. Despite that, most parks raised their base gate prices.

But in general, that gate price is the highest price to get into a park. There are web-based sales with 17–27% discounts for those who purchase on the web and print their tickets. Others offer further discounts for the observant buyer. For instance, the gate price at Knott's Berry Farm in California is $43, $35 online, and $28.95 on its all-you-can-eat barbecue days. King's Dominion north of Richmond, Virginia, has a $43.99 gate price, a $34.99 online price, and a $29.99 four-day advance purchase price. Five rival parks in California (Disney and Knott's included) teamed together to sell City Pass, which allowed admission to all five parks at a substantial discount. Multiday and annual passes are also generally available only online.

Some of the discounts are cost-based. Online tickets save a park money by not having more sales personnel at the gates and eliminate queues at entrances that annoy customers.

The parks are also exploring other types of tickets. For instance, some people do not want to use a park's attractions but would rather watch others use them—such as grandparents who wish to see their grandchildren enjoy the attractions but who would rather skip riding the "Rebel Yell" roller coaster. The full price may deter onlookers from coming to the park, but a reduced price can mean additional profit because they don't contribute much to costs, are likely to consume high markup concessions and souvenirs, and might preclude the whole family from attending if they didn't attend.

More diverse pricing structures can be based on both the cost and demand sides of the equation.

Source: Eleena De Lisser, "A New Twist in Theme Park Pricing," *The Wall Street Journal*, June 24, 2004, at online.wsj.com/article/SB108802974024445871.html.

One reason for these price differences is that the price elasticity of demand for business travel is much less elastic than that for vacation travel. Business travelers must meet with clients, suppliers, and associates at particular times, often as soon as possible. Regardless of the price of an airline ticket (so long as it remains within reasonable bounds), many of these trips are well worth making. On the other hand, vacation travelers often plan their trips well in advance, are relatively flexible with regard to the timing of their trips, and are sensitive to moderate differences in ticket price. From the discussion in the previous section, it seems likely that airline managers, to maximize profit, would like to set higher prices for business travelers than for vacation travelers. And this is the effect of the price differences just cited because business travelers are much less likely than vacation travelers to buy their tickets ahead of time and they desire the flexibility of being able to change their flight schedules.

STRATEGY SESSION: Yield Management and Airline Performance

A recent survey has shown that yield management is a major factor in airline profitability. The managers of American Airlines used yield models to generate over $1 billion in savings over a three-year period. Yield management models are a nice example of how mathematical models apparently capture the complexity of our social structure, using only a few variables. They also show how the intellectual effort of managers generates profit for the firm.

Yield management models are complex pricing mechanisms. They are dynamic in the sense that prices respond to customer behavior. At any time several classes of seats are priced at different levels. Prices at each level depend on a real-time demand forecasting model that analyzes market behavior and then optimizes pricing behavior. The firm prices as if it were practicing third-degree price discrimination.

The models can handle the complexity of reality only by looking at a simplified version of it—as if life is abridged. Yield management models focus on a few key variables and ignore everything else. Most focus on overbooking, discount allocation, and traffic management. Managers build models that look at the revenue potential of a complex menu of price and itinerary pairs.

For example, consider overbooking. Airlines must overbook because some customers never claim their reservations. If they did not overbook, then some aircraft that should fly full based on demand (customer behavior) would fly with unused capacity. So managers build models that balance the trade-offs between the increased revenue of more passengers and the costs of having passengers take the next flight (ideally).

Modeling the situation is not easy. Clearly reputational costs with customers are involved if overbooking becomes too common. There are also real economic costs. Passengers not permitted to board the plane because of overbooking must be compensated. Many are given vouchers for discounts on future flights, and some must be fed or given hotel rooms.

Managers build the models to maximize expected net revenue. The optimal overbooking rule is to overbook until the expected marginal revenue from one more passenger on a flight is equal to the marginal cost of an additional overbooking. The actual point chosen reflects concerns for customer satisfaction, so it is constrained a bit.

Other variables are modeled using similar decision rules. For example, in discount allocation models, the objective is to balance the expected marginal revenue of a specific fare request against the expected marginal net revenue of all other fares. To see how sophisticated the models are, consider the inclusion of "sell-up" probabilities. These probabilities are used in discounting models to predict which customers will buy a higher-priced ticket if they are not offered a low price.

The models require sophisticated hardware and software to operate efficiently. Computerized reservation systems like SABRE play an integral part in yield management. These systems interface with the market; their ability to capture and analyze data allows the models to constantly update pricing levels. They also control seat inventory.

Given the competitive nature of the airline market, airlines have not been able to keep all the surplus generated by yield management programs. The programs generate some benefits for airline customers, mainly in the form of lower ticket prices and more efficient use of equipment.

Sources: "Yield Management—A Growth Key Driver"; "Airline Ties Profitability Yield to Management," *The Travel Tightwad*, May 28, 2002.

At the same time, it is also worth noting that because the airlines can reduce their costs if demand is predictable (as a result of better scheduling of equipment and personnel), they may enjoy savings if travelers buy their tickets in advance. Also, if a ticket is not refundable, it clearly benefits the airline more than a ticket that is refundable, even though the penalty involved in changing it may be relatively small.

In recent years entrepreneurs have stepped in with a business model that mitigates some of the airlines' ability to practice third-degree price discrimination. Internet firms such as Expedia scour airline databases continuously looking for cheap fares. Consumers use Expedia and its competitors, such as CheapTicket or Travelocity, to view such fares. These additional information sources can lead to lower fares than if the customer dealt with the air carrier alone. This is not always the case, however. In addition, customers must take the time to search the sites. Because airlines change fares continuously, if the sites are not updated frequently, the customer may not get the cheapest fare. A recent search of two such sites visited within seconds of each other revealed a $500 difference between the cheapest fares from Philadelphia to Hyderabad, India. Because the airlines release the sale of these seats to the sites, they are still falling into a managerial pricing plan (that plan, however, would be different if the sites were not present). In addition, some sites, like Priceline, follow more of a first-degree strategy. Consumers are asked to name their target price (say X). If the cost of the seat to Priceline was price Y (less than X), then managers have created a surplus of $X - Y$.

USING COUPONS AND REBATES FOR PRICE DISCRIMINATION

One way managers can implement a price discrimination strategy is with coupons and rebates. Basically these devices reduce the price of products. But why don't managers simply reduce prices? Primarily because coupons are used to price discriminate. Not all consumers use coupons. Of 332 billion coupons distributed in the United States in 2010, only 3.3 billion were redeemed. Of consumers, 78.3% reported coupon use in 2010.[4] This demand segment is more price sensitive and on the more elastic part of the demand curve. Hence managers use coupons and rebates to price discriminate because other consumers (on the less elastic part of the demand curve) are willing to pay more—that is, to buy the good without a coupon.

By estimating the elasticity of demand, managers can figure out how coupons should be priced. Suppose managers at the Barnegat Light Fish Company sell their product, a special blend of crab cake, in a market where managers think two types of consumers exist: a more affluent group (R) with an estimated price elasticity for Barnegat Light crab cakes of -2 ($|\eta_R| = 2$) and a less affluent group (S) with an estimated price elasticity for Barnegat Light crab cakes of -5 ($|\eta_S| = 5$). Managers at the fish company choose a posted price (P) but then issue a coupon for $$X$

4. Santella and Associates, *Coupon Trends Report*, 2011, www.santella.com/Trends.htm.

off in the newspaper local to the consumer types. Every buyer pays the nominal price of P per unit for Barnegat Light crab cakes on the grocers' sales receipt; but at the bottom of the sales receipt, an $X credit appears for those who tender a coupon. Thus although all buyers pay the same price P, in reality buyers without coupons pay P while coupon tenderers pay $P - X$. What should the values of P and X be? As we saw, to maximize profit, the marginal revenue in each market should be equal and they, in turn, should equal Barnegat Light's marginal cost (MC). Therefore,

$$P[1 - (1/|\eta_R|)] = (P - X)[1 - (1/|\eta_S|)] = MC$$

Suppose Barnegat Light's marginal cost is a constant $2

$$MR_R = P[1 - (1/2)] = P/2 = 2 = MC \text{ or } P = \$4$$

and

$$MR_S = (4 - X)[1 - (1/5)] = (4 - X)(0.8) = 2 = MC$$

or

$$3.2 - 0.8X = 2 \text{ or } X = \$1.5$$

Managers should price crab cakes at $4 per unit and offer a $1.50 off coupon. The more affluent buyers pay $4/unit for the crab cakes, and the less affluent ones clip the coupon and pay $2.50/unit for the *same* crab cakes. Those who are more price elastic (the less affluent in this case) use coupons; the less price elastic people (the affluent in this case) do not. So by issuing coupons (or rebates) managers can price discriminate (and increase their profit).

PEAK LOAD PRICING

The demand for goods or services may shift with the time of day, week, or year. For example, the demand for highway and transit services is greatest during the morning and evening rush hours, lower during midday, and lower still overnight. Roads to resorts are likely to see greater demand on the weekend than during the week. And Miami Beach hotels have greater demand in February when it is cold in the northern United States than in the summer when it's warm almost everywhere in the United States.

Because these temporal differences in demand are coupled with a plant capacity that does not change over the demand cycle, managers facing these demand conditions should charge different prices in the peak (high ones = P_P) and in the trough (low ones = P_T). The rule to follow is that marginal revenue equals marginal cost. However, the marginal revenue curves differ because the service demand curves change between the peak and trough. The marginal cost is usually high in the peak because the supplier is operating at or

PROBLEM SOLVED: Third-Degree Price Discrimination

To illustrate how price discrimination is used, suppose a drug manufacturer sells a major drug in Europe and the United States. Because of legal restrictions, the drug cannot be bought in one country and sold in another. The demand curve for the drug in Europe is

$$P_E = 10 - Q_E \qquad (9.3)$$

where P_E is the price (in dollars per pound) in Europe and Q_E is the amount (in millions of pounds) sold there. The demand curve for the drug in the United States is

$$P_U = 20 - 1.5Q_U \qquad (9.4)$$

where P_U is the price (in dollars per pound) in the United States and Q_U is the amount (in millions of pounds) sold there. The total cost (in millions of dollars) of producing the drug for sale worldwide is

$$TC = 4 + 2(Q_E + Q_U) \qquad (9.5)$$

The firm's total profit (π) from both Europe and the United States is

$$
\begin{aligned}
\pi &= P_E Q_E + P_U Q_U - TC \\
&= (10 - Q_E)Q_E + (20 - 1.5Q_U)Q_U - [4 + 2(Q_E + Q_U)] \\
&= 10Q_E - Q_E^2 + 20Q_U - 1.5Q_U^2 - 4 - 2Q_E - 2Q_U \\
&= -4 + 8Q_E - Q_E^2 + 18Q_U - 1.5Q_U^2 \qquad (9.6)
\end{aligned}
$$

To maximize profit with respect to Q_E and Q_U, we must set $\Delta\pi/\Delta Q_E = 0$ and $\Delta\pi/\Delta Q_U = 0$. Hence $\Delta\pi/\Delta Q_E = 8 - 2Q_E = 0$ and $\Delta\pi/\Delta Q_U = 18 - 3Q_U = 0$.

Solving these equations for Q_E and Q_U, we find that managers should sell 4 million pounds of the drug in Europe and 6 million pounds in the United States.

To find the optimal prices in Europe and the United States, we substitute 4 for Q_E and 6 for Q_U in equations (9.3) and (9.4); the result is that managers set a European price of $6 per pound and a U.S. price of $11 per pound. Substituting these values of P_E and P_U, as well as the foregoing values of Q_E and Q_U, into equation (9.6), we find that the firm's profit equals

$$\pi = -4 + 8(4) - 4^2 + 18(6) - 1.5(6^2) = 66$$

or $66 million.

Note that if we use the graphical technique shown in the previous section, we will obtain identical results. Whether the graphical technique or the mathematical technique is used, the answer is the same.

How much additional profit do managers generate? If price discrimination were not possible (perhaps because the submarkets could not be segmented and sealed), P_E would equal P_U. Letting this common price be P, it follows from equation (9.3) that $Q_E = 10 - P$, and from equation (9.4) that $Q_U = (1/1.5)(20 - P) = (40/3) - (2/3)P$. Therefore, the firm's total amount sold in Europe and the United States combined is

$$
\begin{aligned}
Q = Q_E + Q_U &= (30/3) - (3/3)P + (40/3) - (2/3)P \\
&= (70/3) - (5/3)P
\end{aligned}
$$

which implies that[a]

$$P = 14 - 0.6Q \qquad (9.7)$$

QUANT OPTION

To be elegantly fashionable, setting $\partial\pi/\partial Q_E = 0$ and $\partial\pi/\partial Q_U = 0$ will maximize profit. Hence $\partial\pi/\partial Q_E = 8 - 2Q_E = 0$ and $\partial\pi/\partial Q_U = 18 - 3Q_U = 0$.

for $P \leq \$10$ or for $Q \geq 20/3$. (For $P \geq \$10$ or $Q \leq 20/3$, $P = 20 - 1.5Q$ because only the United States purchases the drug if the price exceeds $10.) Hence managers generate profit of only

$$\pi = PQ - TC$$
$$= (14 - 0.6Q)Q - (4 + 2Q)$$
$$= 14Q - 0.6Q^2 - 4 - 2Q$$
$$= -4 + 12Q - 0.6Q^2 \tag{9.8}$$

because $Q = Q_E + Q_U$.

To maximize profit, the manager selects Q so that $\Delta\pi/\Delta Q = 0$. Therefore,

$$\Delta\pi/\Delta Q = 12 - 1.2Q$$

Solving for Q, we find if managers do not engage in price discrimination, they choose output of 10 million pounds of the drug (which is the same as the output produced when they discriminated).[b] Substituting 10 for Q in equations (9.7) and (9.8), it follows that

$$P = 14 - 0.6(10) = \$8$$
$$\pi = -4 + 12(10) - 0.6(10^2) = \$56$$

Therefore, if managers do not engage in price discrimination, profit is $56 million rather than the $66 million they earn by using price discrimination.

Because 10 million pounds are produced under both pricing schemes, the cost of production is the same in both cases: $4 + 2(10) = \$24$. So the total revenues are $80 (= 64 + 16) when there is no discrimination and $90 (= 66 + 24) when there is discrimination. With no discrimination, the average revenue per unit

is just the price (80/10 = $8); but with discrimination, the average revenue per unit is $9 (90/10). The profit-enhancing property of third-degree discrimination is that it raises the average revenue above the price on the demand curve for a given quantity.

If segmenting and sealing the market are possible but costly, the preceding example tells us that managers should be willing to pay up to the difference in the profit of the two pricing schemes (but no more) to segment and seal—that is, up to $10 million.

Finally, note that at a price of $6, 4 million pounds of the drug are sold in Europe (from $Q_E = 10 - 6$) and that at a price of $11, 6 million pounds are sold in the United States (from $Q_U = (40/3) - (2/3)11$). Also, note that $\Delta Q_E/\Delta P_E = -1$ and $\Delta Q_U/\Delta P_U = -2/3$. Recall from Chapter 2 that elasticity is $|\eta| = (P/Q)(\Delta Q/\Delta P)$. So $|\eta_E| = (6/4)(|-1|) = |-1.5|$ and $|\eta_U| = (11/6)(|-2/3|) = |-1.22|$. Therefore, the price is raised (from $8 to $11) for the less elastic demander and lowered (from $8 to $6) for the more elastic demander—just as we would expect from equation (9.1).

[a] This means that $(5/3)P = (70/3) - (3/3)Q$ or $5P = 70 - 3Q$ or $P = 14 - 0.6Q$.
[b] If the demand curves are curvilinear, the output of the third-degree discriminator and the single-price monopolist are not necessarily the same, and it's possible that prices fall in all markets.

QUANT OPTION

Touché!
Setting $d\pi/dQ = 0$ will maximize profit. Thus, $d\pi/dQ = 12 - 1.2Q$.

near capacity, and it is usually low in the trough because much excess capacity exists. Note that this is not the same as third-degree price discrimination. Both the third-degree price discrimination and peak trough situations have separate marginal revenues for each demand class; but in third-degree price discrimination, the demand classes share the *same* supplier capacity at the *same* time. Therefore, marginal cost in third-degree price discrimination is a function of $Q_1 + Q_2$; that is, the two demands are interdependent in how they influence marginal cost. But in the intertemporal demand case, the demanders use the *same* capacity at *different* times. Therefore, there are separate levels of marginal cost for Q_1 and Q_2; that is, the demands are independent in their influence on marginal cost. The optimal solution for third-degree price discrimination is $MR_1(Q_1) = MR_2(Q_2) = MC(Q_1 + Q_2)$, whereas the optimal solution for peak–trough pricing is $MR_1(Q_1) = MC_1(Q_1)$ and $MR_2(Q_2) = MC_2(Q_2)$. The parentheses indicate "a function of." These conditions are shown in Figure 9.4.

The Strategy Session box discusses peaks and troughs in electricity demand. Consider the situation on roadways. The Texas Transportation Institute reports that American drivers in the largest 101 urban areas on average lost 40 hours in 2010 to road congestion.[5] This indicates severe auto congestion in some areas. The worst is in Washington, DC, where the typical driver could save 74 hours

---

FIGURE 9.4

Determination of Peak and Trough Prices

The optimal peak price (P_P) is determined by where the peak marginal revenue equals the firm's marginal cost; the optimal trough price (P_T) is determined by where the trough marginal revenue equals the firm's marginal cost.

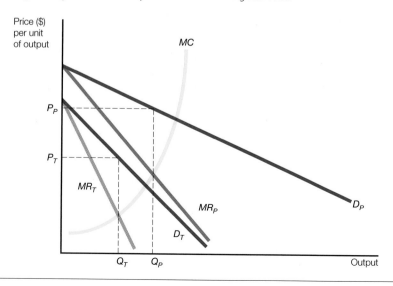

5. David Schrank and Tim Lomax, *The 2011 Urban Mobility Report* (College Station: Texas Transportation Institute, Texas A & M University, September 2011).

STRATEGY SESSION: The Future Is Now: The Futures Market for Super Bowl Tickets

Your team is going to the Super Bowl. You'd like to go. You could have bought tickets way in advance of the game, but you didn't know your team was going until they won their league championship game (and you're only interested in being there if your team is playing). So you go online and see if you can buy tickets on eBay, or you call a ticket broker, or you go to the Super Bowl city on game day and seek a ticket scalper outside the stadium. You could have bought the tickets before you knew who was in the game and then sold them on eBay if your team did not make the game.

But a new market has grown up for you. Commodities have had futures markets for years. Now there's a futures market for Super Bowl tickets. In such markets both buyers and sellers can lock in a price and reduce uncertainty. If you wait until your team makes it, you don't know what the ticket price will be.

Yoonew.com, TheTicketReserve.com, and Super bowlOption.com sold options on the 2006 Super Bowl. A client pays $X for the option of getting a ticket for the game. If his or her team makes the Super Bowl, he or she gets a ticket. If not, the option is worthless. The futures contracts are for a specific team, so the price will vary from team to team based on the likelihood of that team making the Super Bowl. Prices change as more information becomes available. For instance, if a team clinches their division crown, that guarantees them a slot in the playoffs (and increases their chances of being in the Super Bowl). This raises the price of their option. If the team wins the first round of their divisional playoffs, this puts them a step closer to the Super Bowl and hence increases the price of their option. If they win the second-round playoff game, they are in the Super Bowl. Even then the value of the option will change based on the collective demand of fans to see the game (because the supply is fixed—the stadium has a certain capacity). Data suggests that gambling odds from Sporting-betUSA explained 96% of the variability in one options market's prices.

Alan Krueger, an economist at Princeton, gives the following example of how the market works. Suppose there's a 10% chance a fan's team will reach the Super Bowl, and a futures contract costs $250, whereas a ticket when the Super Bowl participants are known is $2,500. Note that the expected value of a $2,500 ticket is $250 ($0.1 \times $2,500). Suppose a risk-loving fan would pay $2,500 for a ticket to see his team play and a risk-averse fan would pay $250 for a futures contract. But there's more. A risk-averse fan will be willing to pay more for a futures contract. As with an insurance policy, ticket futures sell at a premium over their expected value because they help risk-averse fans hedge against uncertainty.

What premium? The fan could guarantee a ticket to the Super Bowl by buying a futures contract on every team in a conference. This is a sure thing. If fans were risk-neutral, the sure-thing price would equal the price the tickets were expected to be at game time (say $2,500). The excess of the sure-thing price over $2,500 is a measure of the market valuation of insuring against risk. For the 2006 Super Bowl, the premium for a sure-thing ticket ranged from 35 to 60% during the season (which is not far from the risk premium in some lines of regular insurance). However, this premium fell substantially as the playoffs advanced. Krueger hypothesizes that this occurred because fans overestimated their teams' chances of getting in the Super Bowl earlier in the season.

Source: Alan B. Krueger, "Wait Till Next Year, but Lock In the Ticket Price Now," *New York Times*, February 2, 2006, at www .nytimes.com/2006/02/02/business/02scene.html.

per year if he or she could drive at free flow rates on the roadway—that is, at the posted speed limit. One reason why such levels of congestion exist is that roadways, in general, are not peak–trough priced in the United States. Singapore has used peak–trough pricing in its central city since the 1970s. In 2003 London instituted a £5 (now £8, and the pricing area has expanded geographically) price for driving in central London. Initial reports are that driving has decreased by 20%. (Are you surprised by the direction of this change? Having studied managerial economics, we hope you are not.) State Route 91 in Orange County, California, has priced recently constructed lanes (where the price varies in real time to keep the lanes operating at free flow level) and kept the existing lanes free (where rush hour traffic moves at 10–25 mph). Many transit systems run 10 times as much equipment during peak rush hours compared to off-peak periods. However, many transport systems charge a flat fee to use the system, independent of the time of use. In fact, many systems actually reward peak use by selling weekly or monthly passes at a discount compared to purchasing single rides for each commute. Therefore, some peak riders actually pay less per ride compared with off-peak riders—just the opposite of what we stated was optimal.[6] Some systems, such as the Metro system in Washington, DC, practice peak–trough pricing.

Another version of intertemporal pricing exists. Some consumers have to read the best-selling book on the *New York Times* list as soon as it reaches that position (or perhaps before it reaches that position if they are truly trendsetters). Others must see the latest Harry Potter or Daniel Day-Lewis movie the first weekend it opens (or soon thereafter). Such individuals can discuss the book or movie at the next cocktail party or around the water cooler and be judged "worthy" by their peers. These people have a high demand to be "with it" and hence pay a high price for hardcover books and first-run movies.

Others have an interest in such books or movies but not at the prices that the trendsetters will pay. After about a year, the paperback version of the best seller appears at 20–40% of the price of the hardcover book. And after about six months, the DVD of the movie is available for purchase for less than two admissions to the first-run movie theater (and you can see it again and again, pause while you do something else, and rewind to see a favorite scene).

So book and movie suppliers realize that there are leaders and followers in the markets for their services and have figured out how to cater to both with high prices for those who cannot wait and low prices for those who can.

TWO-PART TARIFFS

Often managers will implement a first-degree price discrimination strategy through a **two-part tariff**. Managers set prices so that consumers pay an *entry fee* and then a *use fee* for each unit of the product they consume. Two-part tariffs are

Two-part tariff When managers set prices so that consumers pay an entry fee and then a use fee for each unit of the product they consume.

6. Such a pricing policy may be related to the fact that transit's competition (the highway system) has a zero price during peaks and troughs.

STRATEGY SESSION: Why Do Your Laundry at 3 A.M.?

Gertrude Stein once wrote that "a rose is a rose is a rose." In most states a kilowatt-hour is a kilowatt-hour—but not in Florida, Pennsylvania, Washington, and Wisconsin. These states allow electric utilities to practice time-of-day pricing to residential customers who opt to be charged in this way. Otherwise, consumers can stick with the traditional plan, where they pay the same flat rate per kilowatt-hour all the time for power. In the new pricing schemes, prices of a kilowatt-hour can change every several hours. (A Pennsylvania utility, Allegheny Power, has experimented with rates that change every hour.) Not surprisingly, in these states it costs more to consume a kilowatt-hour in the peak periods, when demand is greatest, and less during the trough periods, when demand is the lowest. Many states have allowed time-of-day pricing for commercial and industrial customers for quite some time.

In Florida, Gulf Power of Pensacola charges $0.042 cents per kilowatt-hour at night, on weekends, and on holidays. Demand is less during those periods because the 9-to-5 workday crowd is not at work. Gulf charges $0.10 cents per kilowatt-hour on weekday afternoons when residential and commercial power demand peaks because of air conditioning use. A third rate is a "critical rate" of $0.309 cents when supplies of kilowatt-hours go

extremely short (less than 1% of the time). These rates compare to the alternative residential plan of a flat $0.063 cents per kilowatt-hour regardless of the time. A customer utilizing the plan estimates that he shaved $600 off his annual power bill by shifting a third of his power consumption to the off-peak periods. In Washington, Puget Sound Energy has estimated that running the same dishwasher in the off-peak time saves a user 25% off the peak rate. With about one-third of customers participating in the off-peak plan, Puget Energy Inc. (the biggest residential time-of-use provider) estimates that peak demand has been cut by 5%. This saves the energy company big money. If it cannot handle peak loads, it enters the power grid market to buy the required power at spot market rates (which are usually expensive) or brings its least efficient (most expensive) capacity on line. By restricting the quantity demanded in the peak via pricing, it need not resort to these expensive alternatives. In addition, by bolstering trough demand, it utilizes its capital plants better.

Source: R. Gavin, "Cut Your Electric Bill: Do Laundry at 3 A.M.," *The Wall Street Journal*, August 22, 2002.

common in the business world. Membership fees for golf clubs are the entry fee, and a greens fee for playing a round of golf is the use fee. Wireless phone users are asked to pay an initial fee and then are charged monthly fees in exchange for access to the network. Some are even charged a use fee for each message unit. Other examples include razors and blades, health clubs, and computer printers. An innovative (and lucrative) use of a two-part tariff is the personal seat license (PSL) for sports stadiums. While the stadium is being constructed, fans are asked to pay a PSL. This is a fixed fee (usually thousands of dollars) that gives the fan the right to purchase tickets to attend a game. It is also an important source of revenue for

STRATEGY SESSION: A Change from Markup Pricing to Sophisticated Pricing

Parker Hannifin produces over 800,000 individual parts. Many (about a third) are virtually one of a kind with limited or no competition. How should these items be priced? Until 2001 the answer was cost plus (the cost of making the part plus a 35% markup). Sophisticated computer models costed out an item and then added on 35% (approximately, with some discretion given to sales where competition and hence price comparisons were easier for clients).

This pricing mechanism created several results counter to the best profit interests of the firm. First, if Parker became more efficient and reduced its costs, it automatically reduced its price. This might make sense if competitors were lowering their prices or if lowering Parker's prices would yield more profitable business; but if there was limited competition, this was a missed profit opportunity. Second, if Parker improved its product at the same cost and thus added value to the customer, Parker maintained its price and got nothing for its value-enhanced product. It's estimated by Thomas Nagle of the Monitor Group that as many as 60% of U.S. manufacturers use cost-plus pricing.

When Donald Washkewicz became CEO of Parker in 2001, he decided to practice strategic pricing (defined as basing prices on determining what a customer was willing to pay as opposed to what it costs to make a product). Since Parker implemented strategic pricing, operating income increased by $200 million, net income increased by $543 million, return on invested capital increased to 21% (from 7%), and Parker's share prices rose by 88% (all in the 2002–2006 time frame).

Washkewicz views the change of corporate culture as being like pulling teeth. His vice president of corporate strategic pricing defines it as messing with the company's DNA. Washkewicz had to terminate some executives who couldn't get with the new program. Now each of the company's 115 divisions has at least one pricing guru to implement its strategic pricing. One guru describes the previous cost-plus pricing policy as one where no one asked, Why not a 45% markup?

Parker has divided its 800,000 products into five categories. A core product is highly competitive with many external reference prices. Prices in this category fell modestly (in some cases by 3%) but also increased (in some cases by 5%). Two classes (B and C) of partially differentiated (from the market) products exist. In B the differentiation adds value to the customer; prices here increased by 0–5%. In C the products were niche in nature with no close competitors; here prices increased by 0–9%. The differentiated product systems were tailored to improve customer profitability and productivity, and prices in this category increased by 0–25%. The last category was custom designed, and only Parker could do it. Here prices increased by over 25%.

Although some customers balked at the price increases, virtually all stuck with Parker, especially because Parker promoted the value-added properties of its products to customers. Adopting strategic pricing also has impacted how Parker thinks about new product development. One dimension now considered is the ability of each product to yield a pricing premium.

With the financial gains shown by Parker, one wonders what the other 60% of companies that practice cost-plus pricing are thinking.

Source: Timothy Aeppel, "Seeking Perfect Prices, CEO Tears Up the Rules," *The Wall Street Journal*, March 27, 2007, p. 1.

construction costs. In effect, managers use PSLs to generate revenue from an asset that hasn't yet been built.

One decision facing managers is to set the appropriate fixed upfront fee and variable usage fee to maximize profit. The upfront fee is designed to extract consumer surplus, so managers use it for first-degree price discrimination. One example is a country club (which actually practices a three-part tariff). Before you can play a round of golf, you must be approved for membership. With that comes a one-time initiation fee, then yearly dues. Both payments are made before you can play and are independent of the number of rounds you play. In this sense the initiation fee and the dues are like the fixed costs managers face. But should you wish to play a round of golf, having been selected as a member and being a member in good standing, you must also pay a greens fee (that is, a use fee for the service the club provides). The greens fee is analogous to the variable costs managers face. Eating clubs, tennis clubs, health clubs, and amusement parks all practice similar pricing policies. In some amusement parks, one fee (the entry fee) gets you inside the park, where the fee to go on the rides (the use fee) is zero for many rides; but some rides (the newest or the most popular) often require additional fees for rides taken.

Managers in other markets also use two-part tariffs. Walmart's Sam's Club is one example. After paying a membership fee, members are admitted to a Sam's Club store, where they pay individually for every item purchased. As another example, it is estimated that Costco earns over 50% of its profit from its entry fee. This bodes well for Costco customers because it means individual items are being priced close to marginal cost.

Managers at Internet service providers also use this pricing strategy. For a fixed monthly fee (the entry fee), customers get access to the Internet. Then they are charged for each time unit they are online (the use fee). In many cases the use fee is zero for the first X minutes; but after the X minutes, a per-minute fee is assessed.

We start with a simple example to demonstrate this pricing principle. Suppose all demanders for a service are perfect clones; *each* demander has the same demand curve. That is, they all have identical preferences. We assume the demand curve is linear of the form $P = a - bQ$, where P is the price per unit and Q is the number of units demanded at price P. In addition, we assume managers face a constant marginal cost of production.

The profit-maximizing optimal two-part tariff requires pricing the use fee at marginal cost and the entry fee equal to the resulting consumer surplus. So managers must choose their use fee before pricing the entry fee. Consider the situation in Figure 9.5. The use fee (P^*) equals MC. At P^*, the demander consumes Q^* units. The resulting consumer surplus A^* is the optimal entry fee.[7] The use fee covers the manager's variable cost of serving the consumer (because $MC = AVC$ and $(AVC)Q^* = VC$) when marginal costs are constant, and the variable-cost profit

7. Technically, $A^* - \varepsilon$ will break the indifference of the consumer to joining or not joining. Hereafter we'll call it A^*, recognizing that the nonambiguous entry fee is $A^* - \varepsilon$.

STRATEGY SESSION: Making Them Pay Twice: Personal Seat Licenses for Sports Teams

Charlotte, North Carolina, is a city on the move. It is the banking capital of the southeastern United States. One way that many upcoming cities "get on the map" is to obtain a professional sports franchise. Charlotte acquired a National Football League franchise for the Carolina Panthers. But it needed a stadium. How should it finance such a large capital expense?

Enter Max Muhlemann. Charlotte was excited about its new team, and fans were supportive. Muhlemann suggested that the Panthers sell personal seat licenses for the new stadium. The concept was that a fan would have to purchase a personal seat license to be able to purchase a ticket to see the Panthers play football. The personal seat license was an entry fee. The use fee was the price of a game ticket.

Demand for the licenses was strong; they sold for prices that reflected the desirability of the seats. The average price of a personal seat license was $2,400. The Panthers sold 62,500 personal seat licenses. That's $149 million received by the team *before* a game was ever played in the stadium. That's $149 million in consumer surplus that fans were willing to spend just for the *right* to purchase tickets to see the games. After obtaining the personal seat license, the holder would buy a game ticket at a price no different than other football teams charge. The big difference was that other teams were not collecting the consumer surplus as the Panthers were.

The use of personal seat licenses to finance new stadiums and stadium improvements is growing. The New York Jets and the New York Giants are building a $1.6 billion new stadium to be shared by both teams in New Jersey. Although this has not yet been announced, virtually all commentators and fans expect both teams to use personal seat licenses to help finance the stadium. If they sell them, it is expected that all 9,200 club seats (the category below luxury suites) would be sold as personal seat licenses, along with a number of other seats. Twelve NFL teams have used

seat licenses since the mid-1990s and have raised almost $900 million in the process. The Philadelphia Eagles sold 29,000 such licenses at prices ranging from $1,800 to $3,700 and raised $70 million toward the cost of their new field. Dallas has sold one for its yet-to-be-built stadium at $150,000. Other Dallas luxury seats are going for $16,000, $35,000, $50,000, and $100,000. The Cowboys' senior vice president for sales and marketing has said that "it was an internal feeling that that was what the market could bear"— which is what price discrimination is all about. Half of the Dallas licenses sold in a four-month period. It is estimated that the Cowboys could raise $300 million. The Chicago Bears sold 45% of their seats with the highest price being $10,000. The remaining 55% of the seats carried no licenses.

Although some fans complain about the licenses because of an active resale market, other fans (in cities where attendance and demand for tickets are high) view the licenses as an appreciating asset. Some Chicago fans (of the 55% who did not have to purchase licenses) approached the Bears *and requested that their seats be licensed.* The Bears did so. The licenses are resold in many ways. One is via Seasonticketrights .com. Its founder reports that the average gain on the resale of a Bears license is about $8,300 (which shows that the Bears underpriced their licenses). To demonstrate that fans have a higher reservation price than they are currently charged, one Giants fan who currently pays $80 per game ticket says, "I'm going to buy my tickets whether there are licenses or not. Do I want to pay? No." But he says he will.

Source: F. Klein, "Growing Plague: Buying the Right to Buy a Ticket," *The Wall Street Journal*, September 26, 1996; and Richard Sandomir, "Jets and Giants Fans May Pay for the Right to Pay for Tickets," *New York Times*, March 22, 2008, at www .nytimes.com/2008/03/22/sports/football/22seat.html?scp= 1&sq="jets+and+giants+fans+may+pay+for+the+right+to+pay+ for+tickets"&st=nyt.

"People laughed at the idea of charging someone to shop at your warehouse, but our membership fees are north of $1 billion per year," states Joel Benoliel, a senior vice president at Costco. There are more than 24 million members in the United States and Canada. Current yearly membership fees are $50 per person, per family, or per business and $100 for an executive membership (which entitles the customer to other services). Note that 24 million members at $50 per member is $1.2 billion, and because some are executive members, that $1.2 billion is a conservative estimate.

Steve Hoch, a professor of marketing at the Wharton School, states that most of Costco's profit is from the annual membership fee (the entry fee). But profit also occurs from the markup of items' costs. There is a scale advantage here too: The larger the Costco membership, the larger the item quantities Costco buys. That greater buying power gives Costco a lower cost of obtaining items and the ability to offer items at lower prices.

Source: Julie Bick, "24 Rolls of Toilet Paper, a Tub of Salsa, and a Plasma TV," *New York Times*, January 28, 2007, at www.nytimes.com/2007/01/28/business/yourmoney/28costco.html?scp=1&sq="24+rolls+of+toilet+paper"&st=nyt.

of the firm for serving this consumer is $A^* + P^*Q^* - (AVC)Q^* = A^*$ (because $AVC = P^*$). Multiplying A^* by the number of clones and subtracting the firm's fixed cost gives managers their profit.

Intuitively, a two-part tariff lets managers act as first-degree price discriminators. Managers capture the entire consumer surplus through the entry fee and convert it into producer surplus (variable-cost profit). Note that managers produce until price equals marginal cost.

A two-part tariff is simpler for managers to implement than first-degree price discrimination because they need not charge individuals different prices for each unit of the good consumed. This pricing strategy also gives managers two other advantages. First, the entry fee is collected at the beginning of the demand period. First-degree price discrimination collects as the consumer consumes the product or service. Money now is worth more than the same amount of money later. Second, though most managers understand there are some units that are highly valued (the first round of golf after a long Minnesota winter) and some units whose value to consumers is low (a round of golf in a downpour), they are not certain of individuals' reservation prices. With the two-part tariff, all a manager must know is that over the demand period, consumers will show variance in their reservation prices. By using a two-part tariff strategy, managers need not worry about this variance. They have already collected their surplus with the entry fee.

Managers also use two-part tariffs to get customers to reveal their preferences. Because it is costly to induce customers to reveal their demand functions, many

---

FIGURE 9.5

Optimal Two-Part Tariff When All Demanders Are the Same

The optimal two-part tariff when all demanders are clones is a use fee equal to marginal cost $(P^* = MC)$ and an entry fee equal to the consumer surplus resulting from such a use fee (A^*).

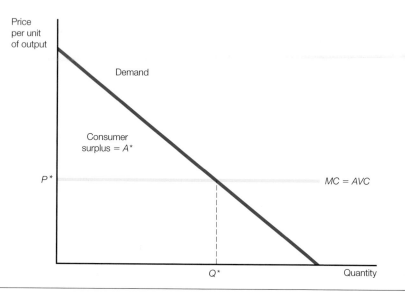

---

managers offer a pricing menu to customers. Consider the wireless phone industry. Managers offer customers different plans that vary in monthly charges and use fees. Customers choose the plans they believe are optimal for them; hence they reveal their preferences.

A Two-Part Tariff with a Rising Marginal Cost

What if managers face marginal costs that are upward-sloping rather than constant? The optimal rule for managers remains the same: Charge a use fee equal to marginal cost and an entry fee equal to the resulting consumer surplus. The only difference, relative to constant marginal cost, is that managers realize additional profit from the use fee (see area X^*) as well as their entry fee, as shown in Figure 9.6.

Charging a use fee of P^* results in selling Q^* to the consumer. This yields revenues of $P^*Q^* = X^* + Y^*$ from the use fee. The variable cost of selling Q^* units to the customer is the area under the marginal cost curve (Y^*). Therefore, the revenue from the use fee more than covers the variable-costs of serving the customer, and managers earn a variable-cost profit from serving the customer of X^* from the use fee. The entry fee is the consumer surplus that results from charging the use fee of P^* (that is, A^*). Hence the variable-cost profit of serving this customer is $A^* + X^*$.

STRATEGY SESSION: Verizon Local Calling Plans

Telephone service is a classic example of a two-part tariff. A subscriber pays the phone company a monthly fee for the privilege of receiving a dial tone. This fee must be paid regardless of whether there are zero, tens, or hundreds of incoming or outgoing calls per month. It is an entry fee for having the service available (although one could avoid this fee by using pay phones, albeit at a higher use fee for outgoing calls).

Managers of phone companies are becoming more adept at using sophisticated pricing strategies. Consider Verizon's local calling plans in New Jersey. Because Verizon managers do not know, with certainty, the demand curve of individual consumers, they let the consumers reveal their preference function by offering a menu of pricing plans. Although most of the plans are primarily two-part tariff pricing, managers combine this pricing strategy with bundling and price discrimination.

In 2008 Verizon offered the following local calling plans in New Jersey:

- *Low-use message rate service*—$5.20/month: This plan has a monthly allowance of 20 message units per month with every unit over 20 costing $0.10/unit. A message unit is a local call of five minutes.
- *Moderate message rate service*—$7.40/month: This plan has a monthly allowance of 75 message units per month with every unit over 75 costing $0.065/unit.

- *Flat-rate service*—$8.95/month: This plan gives the consumer unlimited message units of local outgoing calls during the month.
- *Verizon local package*—$25.99/month: This plan gives the consumer unlimited message units of local outgoing calls during the month and a choice of up to three calling features.
- *Verizon local service package extra*—$29.99/month: This plan gives the consumer unlimited message units of local outgoing calls during the month and a choice of four or more calling features.
- *Verizon regional package unlimited*—$38.00/month: This plan gives the consumer unlimited message units of local outgoing calls, unlimited message units of regional outgoing calls, and a choice of up to three calling features.
- *Verizon regional package*—$42.95/month: This plan gives the consumer unlimited message units of local outgoing calls, unlimited message units of regional outgoing calls, and five calling features including home voice mail.

Special features include unlimited directory assistance and calling features. Features include caller ID, three-way calling, and call waiting.

Source: www.verizon.com, accessed on March 24, 2008.

A Two-Part Tariff with Different Demand Curves

In most markets consumers do not all have identical demand functions. What is the optimal two-part tariff when there are multiple types of demanders in the market? Consider the case with relatively strong and weak demanders. The strong demander is willing to purchase more units than the weak at any given price. Managers should consider at least two two-part tariff pricing options. If

PROBLEM SOLVED: Two-Part Tariff Pricing

Let's demonstrate the use of a two-part tariff pricing strategy. Managers at C-Pal Industries face 100 identical individuals, each with a demand curve of $P = 10 - Q$. C-Pal has a constant marginal cost of $4 per unit produced and a fixed cost of $500. C-Pal's situation is depicted in the figure.

Managers at C-Pal charge a use fee of $4 (= MC) for each good a consumer purchases. Consumers purchase six goods apiece; the demand can be rewritten as $Q = 10 - P = 10 - 4 = 6$. C-Pal's total revenue from the use fee from one customer is $P^*Q^* = ($4)(6) = 24, and C-Pal's variable cost for serving one customer is $(AVC)Q^* = ($4)(6) = 24. The consumer surplus when six goods are demanded at a price of $4 for a customer is $0.5(10 - 4)6 = 18, and managers charge this as an entry fee. The total revenue from one customer is $24 + $18 = 42, and the variable cost of serving that customer is $24, yielding C-Pal a variable-cost profit of serving a customer of $42 - $24 = 18; this is the consumer surplus captured from the consumer and converted into producer surplus. Because there are 100 clones, managers earn a total

variable-cost profit of 100($18) = $1,800. C-Pal's profit is the variable-cost profit minus the fixed costs: $1,300 = $1,800 - $500.

One point of confusion in using a two-part tariff is what happens when a demander conceives of a two-part tariff as a one-part tariff. Consider one of C-Pal's customers. He is paying (on average) $7 for each item he consumes—that is, $4 from the use fee and $3 (= $18/6) from the entry fee. But if C-Pal had merely put a flat charge on each item sold of $7, the customer would purchase only three units $(Q = 10 - P = 10 - 7 = 3)$. The individual demand curve derived in Chapter 3 shows the amount the consumer pays for *each* unit. Indeed, if C-Pal's customers face a price of $7, they will purchase only three units. But that is not the deal they have been offered. The *only* way they can buy the good is to pay an entry fee of $18 for the privilege of purchasing each unit at a price of $4. They choose to purchase six because their benefits equal their costs of doing so. That is why the two-part tariff is so clever. It extracts all the consumer surplus (which a single price does not).

A Two-Part Tariff Example: C-Pal Industries

C-Pal's optimal two-part tariff entails charging a use fee of $4 (= MC) for each item consumed and an entry fee of $18.

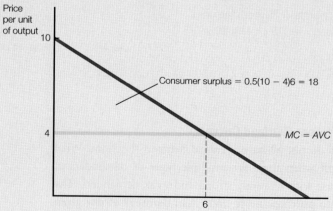

FIGURE 9.6

Optimal Two-Part Tariff When Marginal Cost Is Rising

The optimal two-part tariff is to charge a use fee P^* equal to marginal cost and an entry fee equal to the resulting consumer surplus (A^*). The firm's variable-cost profit is now $A^* + X^*$ because the firm's use revenues now exceed its variable cost (Y^*).

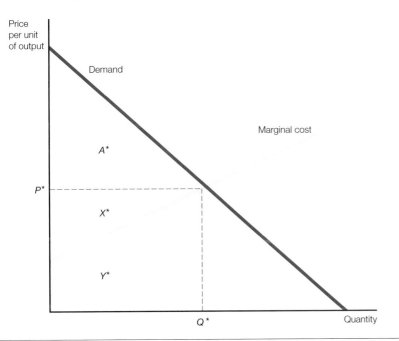

the strong demander is willing to buy significantly more units at any price, then it is more profitable to charge a use fee equal to marginal cost and an entry fee equal to the resulting consumer surplus of the strong demander. This strategy excludes the weak demander from the market. The weak demander's consumer surplus is smaller than that of the strong demander and so the weak demander is not willing to pay the entry fee. From her point of view, the marginal cost (entry fee) is greater than the marginal benefit (consumer surplus). It is not unusual for managers to use pricing policies that exclude demanders from markets. In single-price scenario, no consumer whose reservation price is below the market price participates in that market.

The other pricing policy is used when the strong demand is not that much stronger than the weak demand. In these markets, managers should set the use fee at or above marginal cost and set the entry fee equal to the resulting consumer surplus of the weak demander. In doing so, managers cannot use first-degree price

---

STRATEGY SESSION: Academic Institutions Practice What They Preach

While the professional teams have opted for the two-part tariff pricing structure called "personal seat licenses" (in which a fan purchases a seat license—the entry fee—for the right to purchase game tickets—the use fee), some universities, such as the University of California at Berkeley and the University of Kansas, have opted for a variant. With personal seat licenses, the price of game tickets can vary from year to year. The university version (called Equity Seats Rights, or ESR) has an entry fee and a use fee, but the ESR fee guarantees the ERS holder that the use fee (ticket price) won't go up for a certain period of time (10 years in the case of KU and 30 years in the case of UC Berkeley). KU's rights could cost as much as $105,000, while UC Berkeley's rights could cost as much as $225,000. The rights can be paid in a lump sum or in installments that are likened to a mortgage—that is, like a $105,000 mortgage with yearly installments of principal and interest due.

What's the advantage to the buyer over a PSA? The first advantage is the guaranteed use fee. The second is that 70% of the purchase price can be deducted from federal taxes because it's treated as a contribution to a nonprofit institution. KU projects that about 20% of the expected revenues from its ESR will be spent on academic programs, with the remaining 80% going to athletic programs. UC Berkeley had sold 1,800 of 3,000 available seats by March 2010 and had raised $150 million. KU has been less successful.

Will the pro teams go in the same direction? They haven't so far. The Chicago Cubs baseball team nixed the concept. The Sacramento Kings basketball team was considering the concept as was the Tottenham (English Premier League) soccer team.

Sources: David Sweet, "Cal's Unique Seat-pricing Concept," *sportsbizonMSNBC.com*, November 19, 2008, at www.msnbc.com/id/27788392/ns/business_sports_biz/t/new_seating_concept_could_net_cal_million/#.Ts8P13HWNsQ; and Associated Press, "Colleges 'Mortgage' Top Seats," March 30, 2010, at http://cjonline.com/sports/2010-03-30/colleges_mortgage_top_seats#.Ts8QGXHWNSQ.

---

discrimination against the strong demander and this demander will realize some consumer surplus. The situation is depicted in Figure 9.7

If managers want to exclude the weak demander, they should set the use fee equal to marginal cost ($= AVC$) and the entry fee equal to the relevant consumer surplus of the strong demander. The revenue from the use fee equals the variable cost incurred serving the strong demander. The variable-cost profit is the entry fee (areas A^* through F). If managers want to include the weak demander, they must choose the use fee P^*, which maximizes the area $2A^* + 2C + D + E$ or $2A^* + 2C + 2D$, whichever is larger. $2A^* + 2C + D + E$ occurs if $P^* > MC$ and $2A^* + 2C + 2D$ occurs if $P^* = MC$. Once P^* is chosen, it determines the consumer surplus (either A^* or $A^* + C + D$).

STRATEGY SESSION: Scientific Pricing—Even for Great Art?

A number of firms have been practicing scientific pricing for some time. Airlines have milked their databases to learn the booking trends on routes each hour until takeoff and how those booking rates respond to price changes at various times. They also factor in forward-looking information such as conventions and major sporting events. Long's Drug Stores and D'Agostino Supermarkets have developed prices for specific products at specific stores (and prices for item *X* may differ from store to store even if the stores are close). But pricing salsa based on ethnic characteristics has got to be different than pricing Picassos, doesn't it?

Apparently not, according to David Galenson, an economist (and art lover and collector) from the University of Chicago. Galenson has developed a model to explain the value of great art, and it works fairly well. After collecting price data on works of great artists, Galenson found the following pattern. Young great artists (Gauguin, Picasso, Van Gogh) seemed to have epiphanies (something came to them and they put it down on canvas quickly). At the other end of the spectrum were the old great artists (like Cezanne), whose great paintings were modifications and evolutions of previous work. Galenson claims the same poles exist for novelists, too.

While economists understand how to model human behavior (or so we think) and use data to test the model, behaviorists feel that human behavior is too complex to be captured in a regression equation. This type of debate also rages in sports. Many professional sports teams have computerized every play of every game and look for patterns in coaches' play calling in certain situations to predict the behavior of a coach in a current situation. In addition, they document players' performances in every play. As an example, they know whether baseball player *X* tends to hit better against left-handed or right-handed pitchers (and which pitchers) and how he performs in pressure situations. Old-time scouts say you need a feel for the game that a computer can't give you. Some doctors also abhor "evidence-based medicine," in which data point to the diagnosis and remedy; they prefer a doctor's clinical judgment.

In the meantime, don't overpay for your next work of great art. That Picasso, painted by the old man, isn't worth much relative to the young Picasso's work; and that painting Cezanne did as a young man isn't worth as much as the work of the mature Cezanne.

Source: David Leonhardt, "The Art of Pricing Great Art," *New York Times*, November 15, 2006, at www.nytimes.com/2006/11/15/business/15leonhardt.html.

Because both demanders are willing to pay A^* in the case of $P^* > MC$, managers realize $2A^*$ in revenues. The revenues from the use fee more than cover the variable cost of serving the consumers. At the use fee of $P^*(>MC)$, the weak demander wants Q_W units of the good and the strong demander wants Q_S units of the good. Area C represents the variable-cost profit managers realize from the use fee revenues from the weak demander, and area $C + D + E$ represents the

PROBLEM SOLVED: A Two-Part Tariff with Different Demands

The Will and Dylan Company has a strong demander (with a demand curve of $P_S = 8 - Q_S$) and a weak demander (with a demand curve of $P_W = 6 - Q_W$). Managers face a constant marginal cost of production of $2. They want to consider several two-part tariff pricing options in order to increase firm value. They first consider charging a use fee of $2 (the firm's marginal cost) and an entry fee equal to the resulting consumer surplus of the strong demander. We can rewrite the strong demand curve as $Q_S = 8 - P_S$. If the use fee is $2, the strong demander will purchase six units. The resulting consumer surplus is $0.5(8 - 2)6 = \$18$. The managers choose this as the entry fee. Under this strategy, managers earn a variable-cost profit of $18. Managers next consider charging a use fee of $2 and an entry fee equal to the consumer surplus of the weak demander. Because we can rewrite the weak demand as $Q_W = 6 - P_W$, if the use fee is $2, the weak demander will purchase four units. The resulting consumer surplus for the weak demander equals $0.5(6 - 2)4 = \$8$. If this is charged as the entry fee, both demand types will pay it, and the firm's variable-cost profit will be $16.

Finally, managers consider charging a use fee greater than marginal cost and an entry fee equal to the resulting consumer surplus of the weak demander. How should managers choose the optimal use fee ($P*$)? If managers charge a use fee of $P*$, the strong demander will purchase $Q_S = 8 - P*$ units and the weak demander will purchase $Q_W = 6 - P*$ units. Because $P* > MC = AVC$, managers will realize a variable-cost profit (of $P* - 2$) from every unit they sell (and they sell $8 - P* + 6 - P* = 14 - 2P*$ units). The variable-cost profit from the use fee is $(P* - 2)(14 - 2P*) = -2P*^2 + 18P* - 28$. With $6 - P*$ units sold to weak demanders, their resulting consumer surplus is $0.5(6 - P*)(6 - P*) = 18 - 6P* + 0.5P*^2$. This is the entry fee; and because both demanders will pay it, the variable-cost profit from the entry fee is $36 - 12P* + P*^2$. The total variable cost profit then is

$$VC\pi = -2P*^2 + 18P* - 28 + 36 - 12P* + P*^2$$
$$= -P*^2 + 6P* + 8 \qquad (9.9)$$

The variable-cost profit is maximized when $\Delta VC\pi / \Delta P* = 0$. Therefore,

variable-cost profit realized from the use fee revenues from the strong demander. Therefore, the total variable-cost profit is $2A* + 2C + D + E$ from serving both demander types if $P* > MC$.

If the use fee $P*$ is set equal to marginal cost, the resulting consumer surplus of the weak demander is $A* + C + D$. Both demanders will pay it. There is no profit from the use fee because it equals marginal cost (= average variable cost). The profit managers earn is thus $2A* + 2C + 2D$. We must then compare $2A* + 2C + 2D$ with $2A* + 2C + D + E$ to see which is largest. That determines (if we serve both demanders) whether the use fee is greater than or equal to marginal cost. Once we determine the best profit from serving both demanders, we must compare it with the profit from serving just the strong

$$\Delta VC\pi / \Delta P^* = 0 = -2P^* + 6$$

or

$$P^* = \$3$$

Substituting $P^* = \$3$ in equation (9.9) gives

$$VC\pi = -(3^2) + 6(3) + 8 = \$17$$

Managers compare the resulting variable-cost profit from each strategy, and choose to serve the strong demander only. This gives them the highest variable-cost profit of $18.[a][b]

The managers consider one last pricing option. Suppose they combine the concept of price discrimination and the two-part tariff. They calculated the consumer surplus of the weak demander when the use fee is a marginal cost (= $2) of $8, and that of the strong demander when the use fee is marginal cost which is $18. Therefore, they propose to set the use fee equal to marginal cost, charge the weak demander an entry fee of $8, and charge the strong demander an entry fee of $18. This yields a variable-cost profit of $26. Price discrimination takes place not on the use fees but on the entry fees.

Think about this last pricing policy in the real world. Clubs have full members, associate members, junior members, and the like. Each has a different initiation and dues structure. Usually there is some restriction on use (perhaps not all members can play golf on Wednesday afternoons, when the doctors play). But can you see the motivation behind these different classes of membership?

[a] If the strong demand had been $P_S = 7 - Q_S$, serving only the strong demander would yield a variable-cost profit of $12.5, whereas serving both demand types with a use fee equal to marginal cost would yield a variable-cost profit of $16. If a use fee greater than marginal cost is chosen (optimal fee $2.5) and the resulting consumer surplus of the weak demander is the entry fee ($6.125), the variable-cost profit is $16.25, which is the best of the three options considered.

[b] We showed the case of $P^* = MC = 2$ explicitly. We did not need to do this. If $P^* = MC = 2$ was the profit-maximizing use fee, it would be the solution to the maximization of the variable-cost profit equation (9.9).

QUANT OPTION

Setting $dVC\pi / dP^* = 0$ will maximize profit. Thus, $dVC\pi / dP^* = -2P^* + 6 = 0$.

---

demander. When we solve this problem with the calculus (see Problem Solved), the two calculations for the weak demander collapse to one and the calculus shows whether $P^* > MC$ or $P^* = MC$ maximizes profit if the manager serves both demanders.

FIGURE 9.7

Optimal Two-Part Tariff with Two Demand Types

The use fee should be set equal to marginal cost and the entry fee equal to the resulting consumer surplus of the strong demander (areas A^* through F) if areas A^* through F exceed the maximum of $2A^* + 2C + D + E$ and $2A^* + 2C + 2D$. The use fee should be set equal to $P^*[>MC]$ and the entry fee equal to the resulting consumer surplus of the weak demander (A^*) if $2A^* + 2C + D + E$ exceeds areas A^* through F or equal to $P^* = MC$ and the entry fee equal to the resulting consumer surplus of the weak demander $(A^* + C + D)$ if the above condition holds and $2A^* + 2C + 2D$ exceeds $2A^* + 2C + D + E$.

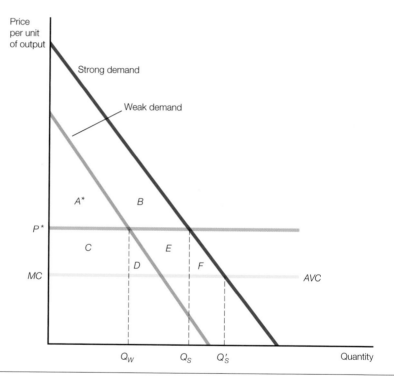

Consider the best possible scenario for managers: perfectly price discriminate on the basis of entry fees. Managers will charge all demanders a usage fee equal to marginal cost. Weak demanders are willing to pay an entry fee equal to $A^* + C + D$. Stronger demanders will pay an entry fee of $A^* + C + D + B + E + F$. Managers then realize profits of $2A^* + 2C + 2D + B + E + F$. All consumer surplus is converted to producer surplus. We see managers using this strategy. For example, health clubs may have silver, gold, platinum, and diamond membership fees.

Two-part tariff pricing schemes can get complicated fairly quickly. If demand curves intersect, the analysis becomes more complex than our discussion here. We treat this more difficult case in the chapter appendix. Fortunately, complex cases can be modeled so that a number of demanders with varying demand characteristics are considered. Managers need to understand the potential increase in profit due to two-part tariff pricing. Several available models examine more complex demand in markets.

SUMMARY

1. Managers practice price discrimination either when they sell physically identical products at different prices or when similar products are sold at prices with different ratios to marginal cost. The strategy works best in markets with various classes of buyers who are differentiated in price elasticities of demand; where segments can be identified and segregated with relatively low costs (lower than the added expected revenue); and where markets can be sealed so goods cannot be transferred easily from one class to another. Once managers choose a discriminating strategy, they maximize profit by allocating outputs across markets so the marginal revenues are equal to each other and to the total marginal cost. This is called third-degree price discrimination. Managers use second-degree price discrimination when they can price increments of output at different rates, usually charging higher rates for initial increments of output, then lower rates as consumption increases. First-degree price discrimination entails pricing goods at the reservation price of each consumer. This practice captures all the consumer surplus and converts it to producer surplus or variable-cost profit. It is the strategy of first choice because of this. However, it is difficult to estimate each consumer's reservation price, and this scheme is more costly to implement than the other degrees of price discrimination.

2. Two-part tariffs are a strategy to enable managers to use first-degree price discrimination. This pricing strategy has managers charge the consumer an "entry" fee for the right to pay a "use" fee to actually purchase the product. In the simplest case, where all demanders are the same, the optimal use fee is the marginal cost of the product and the entry fee is the consumer surplus available when that use fee is charged. If consumers have different demand curves, managers may exclude weaker demanders from the market and follow the preceding rule with the stronger demanders. Or managers could include all demanders by pricing the use fee at or above its marginal cost and choosing an entry fee equal to the resulting consumer surplus of the weak demander. Managers who practice price discrimination on the entry fee, while charging all consumers the marginal cost as a use fee, realize the maximum profit.

3. Consumer preferences tend to show temporal variation (by day, week, or season). To account for these variations in temporal behavioral, managers many times charge high prices during the peaks and lower prices during the troughs (as opposed to a single price across the whole temporal cycle). The rule for managers to optimize price is to set the relevant marginal revenue equal to marginal cost.

PROBLEMS

wwnorton.com/studyspace

1. Managers at the Ridgeway Corporation produce a medical device that they sell in Japan, Europe, and the United States. Transportation costs are a negligible proportion of the product's total costs. The price elasticity of demand for the product is −4.0 in Japan, −2.0 in the United States, and −1.33 in Europe. Because of legal limitations, this medical device, once sold to a customer in one country, cannot be resold to a buyer in another country.

   a. The firm's vice president for marketing circulates a memo recommending that the price of the device be $1,000 in Japan, $2,000 in the United States, and $3,000 in Europe. Comment on his recommendations.

   b. His recommendations are accepted. Sales managers send reports to corporate headquarters saying that the quantity of the devices being sold in the United States is lower than expected. Comment on their reports.

   c. After considerable argument, the U.S. sales manager agrees to lower the price in the United States to $1,500. Is this a wise decision? Why or why not?

   d. Can you be sure that managers are maximizing profit? Why or why not?

2. Ann McCutcheon is hired as a consultant to a firm producing ball bearings. This firm sells in two distinct markets, each of which is completely sealed off from the other. The demand curve for the firm's output in the first market is $P_1 = 160 − 8Q_1$, where P_1 is the price of the product and Q_1 is the amount sold in the first market. The demand curve for the firm's output in the second market is $P_2 = 80 − 2Q_2$, where P_2 is the price of the product and Q_2 is the amount sold in the second market. The firm's marginal cost curve is $5 + Q$, where Q is the firm's entire output (destined for either market). Managers ask Ann McCutcheon to suggest a pricing policy.

   a. How many units of output should she tell managers to sell in the second market?

   b. How many units of output should she tell managers to sell in the first market?

   c. What price should managers charge in each market?

3. The Lone Star Transportation Company hauls coal and manufactured goods. The demand curve for its services by the coal producers is

$$P_C = 495 - 5Q_C$$

where P_C is the price (in dollars) per ton-mile of coal hauled and Q_C is the number of ton-miles of coal hauled (in thousands). The demand curve for its services by the producers of manufactured goods is

$$P_M = 750 - 10Q_M$$

where P_M is the price (in dollars) per ton-mile of manufactured goods hauled, and Q_M is the number of ton-miles of manufactured goods hauled (in thousands). The firm's total cost function is

$$TC = 410 + 8(Q_C + Q_M)$$

where TC is total cost (in thousands of dollars).
   a. What price should managers charge to haul coal?
   b. What price should managers charge to haul manufactured goods?
   c. If a regulatory agency were to require managers to charge the same price to haul both coal and manufactured goods, would this reduce the firm's profit? If so, by how much?

4. Electric companies typically have 5–10 different rate schedules for their main customer groups. The average price charged to large industrial users may differ substantially from that charged to residences. Moreover, many consumers pay a price for electricity based on the time of day they use it. For example, the prices charged by Consolidated Edison, a large New York electric utility, and Pacific Gas and Electric, a major California electric utility, are as follows:

Price	
Company and Time of Day of Electricity Use (Cents per Kilowatt-Hour)	
Consolidated Edison	
8 A.M.–10 P.M. (peak hours)	27
10 P.M.–8 A.M.(off-peak hours)	4[a]
Pacific Gas and Electric	
Summer	
Noon–6 P.M. (peak hours)	28.3
6 P.M.–noon (off-peak hours)	9.2
Winter	
Noon–6 P.M. (peak hours)	11.3
6 P.M.–noon (off-peak hours)	8.0

[a]Approximate figure.

Electric utilities use their cheapest generators continuously and start up their more costly ones as demand goes up. Consequently, at 3 A.M., a utility might meet its requirements from a hydroelectric dam that produces electricity for $0.02 per kilowatt-hour. However, on a hot day in August, when air conditioners are running full blast, demand would be so great that the utility would be forced to use its most costly generators—perhaps an oil-fired plant where electricity costs $0.07 per kilowatt-hour.

   a. Does price discrimination occur in the market for electricity?

   b. Why have some state regulatory commissions, including the Public Service Commission of New York, ordered that time-of-day rates be phased in for residential consumers?

   c. In many areas, both residential and industrial consumers tend to pay a lower price per kilowatt-hour if they use more rather than less electricity. Is this price discrimination? If so, what kind of price discrimination is it?

   d. Explain why price discrimination is used by managers of electric companies.[8]

5. In the town of Oz, there are two types of tennis players: wizards and imps. Wizards and imps do not socialize, so it would be impossible to start a tennis club that both types would join. Imps have access to credit but a weak demand for tennis as follows.

$$P_I = 30 - Q_I$$

where Q_I refers to the number of games they would play if the price of a game were P_I.

Because of their access to credit, they would be willing to pay an upfront fee to join the club.

Wizards live from paycheck to paycheck and would be willing to pay for each tennis game as they go along. Their demand is

$$P_W = 40 - Q_W$$

where Q_W refers to the number of games they would play if the price of a game were P_W.

There are an equal number of wizards and imps (for simplicity, assume one of each). The marginal cost of one game of tennis is a constant 2.

You can design your tennis facility to attract either wizards or imps (but not both). Which clientele would you like to attract and what would be your profit per "person"?

6. The managers of Roosevelt's (a local yet upscale bar) are considering charging an admission fee on Thursday nights. They contemplate how to charge. Should they

   Option 1. Use just a beverage charge per beverage ordered *or*

   Option 2. Use an admission charge (a fee to enter the establishment) *and* a beverage charge per beverage ordered?

8. For further discussion, see W. Shepherd and C. Wilcox, *Public Policies toward Business* (Homewood, IL: Irwin, 1979); and *New York Times*, June 9, 1990.

There are two types of people who frequent Roosevelt's: Over 21 Students (S) and Over 21 Student Wannabees (W). Each Student has a demand for beverages of

$$P = 8 - Q_S$$

where Q_S is the quantity of beverages demanded if the price of a beverage is P. Each Wannabee has a demand for beverages of

$$P = 8 - 2Q_W$$

where Q_W is the quantity of beverages demanded if the price of a beverage is P.

The marginal cost of serving a beverage is a constant \$2.

For simplicity, assume there is one demander of each type. Roosevelt's must (by law) charge all customers the same admission charge and the same per beverage charge. Beverages do not have to be sold in integer amounts and prices do not have to be in integer amounts.

a. Under option 1, what is the profit maximizing price per beverage?
b. Under option 2, what is the profit maximizing two-part tariff?
c. What is Roosevelt's profit under Roosevelt's best choice?

7. The demand for a strong demander for a round of golf is

$$P_S = 6 - Q_S$$

where Q_S is the number of rounds demanded by a strong demander when the price of a round of golf is P_S.

The demand for a weak demander for a round of golf is

$$P_W = 4 - Q_W$$

where Q_W is the number of rounds demanded by a weak demander when the price of a round of golf is P_W.

The cost of providing an additional round of golf to either type of golfer is a constant 2.

There is one golfer of each type.

The club has decided that the best pricing policy is a two-part tariff. However, it's your job to tell the club the optimal entry fee and the optimal use fee to maximize the club's profit. The club cannot price discriminate on either the use or the entry fee. The club's fixed cost is 1.

What are the club's optimal use fee and the optimal entry fee?

8. The university museum has two types of visitors. One type is university employees; and the other type is people nonaffiliated with the university. All university employees have identical annual demands for museum visits, given by

$$P_P = 30 - Q_P \qquad (\textit{for each university employee})$$

where Q_P is the number of visits demanded if the price is P_P per visit. Non-affiliated people all have identical annual demands for museum visits, but differ from university employees

$$P_N = 100 - Q_N \quad (\textit{for each nonaffiliated person})$$

where Q_N is the number of visits demanded if the price is P_N per visit. The museum can identify university employees by their university ID card, while a nonaffiliated person does not possess a university ID.

The university's profit-maximizing museum is contemplating two different pricing policies:

Policy 1
- For university employees: An annual membership fee and an additional price-per-visit. (Only university employees are eligible for this membership plan.)
- For nonaffiliated visitors: A single price-per-visit, with no membership fee. (This price per visit is not necessarily the same as the university employee price per visit.)

Policy 2
- This policy would offer a *different* price-per-visit for each type of visitor, but no membership fees at all.

The museum has a constant marginal cost of $6 per visit, regardless of the visitor's type. For simplicity, assume that there is one university employee and one nonaffiliated person in the target population.

How much more profit does the best policy yield than the other policy?

EXCEL EXERCISE: PERFECT PRICE DISCRIMINATION

Suppose our monopolist takes their demand curve ($P = 14 - Q$) and charges each demander they wish to serve the buyer's reservation price. Recall that the firm's total cost is $TC = 5 + 2Q + 0.5Q^2$, and the firm's marginal cost is $MC = 2 + Q$. We assume here that the good can be produced and sold on a continuous basis, that is, in non-integer amounts.

The perfectly discriminating firm's demand curve becomes the firm's marginal revenue curve (as shown in the text). Therefore, the firm will produce where marginal revenue (MR) equals MC, that is,

$$MR = 14 - Q = 2 + Q = MC$$

or $\qquad 2Q = 12$

or $\qquad Q = 6$

and the last item sold is to the demander with the reservation price of 8.

The firm receives total revenue equal to the trapezoid running from $P = 14$ at $Q = 0$ to $P = 8$ at $Q = 6$ or

$$TR = 0.5*(14 + 8)*6 = 0.5*22*6 = 66$$

The firm's total cost is

$$TC = 5 + 2Q + 0.5Q^2 = 5 + 2*6 + 0.5*6*6 = 5 + 12 + 18 = 35$$

Thus, the perfectly discriminating firm's profit is

$$\pi = TR - TC = 66 - 35 = 31$$

(substantially better than the 19 shown in the excel exercise on simple monopoly pricing in Chapter 8).

Can we do perfect price discrimination with spreadsheets? Yes we can.

We will assume now that our product can only be produced and consumed in integers.

Call up your spreadsheet. Enter 14 in cell A1, 13 in cell A2, and continue until you enter 0 in cell A15. Then enter 0 in cell B1, 1 in cell B2, and so on, until you enter 14 in cell B15. With columns A and B, you have entered the firm's demand curve.

Then enter 0 in cell C1, =A2 in cell C2, =C2+A3 in cell C3. Then click on the lower right-hand corner of cell C3 with your mouse and drag down until cell C15. This will give you a column of the firm's total revenue at each quantity if you perfectly price discriminate, that is, charge each demander their reservation price.

Then enter =C2−C1 in cell D2, =C3−C2 in cell D3, and so on. You may do this by clicking on the lower right-hand corner of cell D2 and dragging down with your mouse until you reach cell D15. This gives you the firm's marginal revenue curve. Note that the result is exactly the same as column A, that is, the perfectly discriminating monopolist's demand curve and its marginal revenue curve coincide.

Then enter =5 in cell E1, and so on, via click and drag until cell E15. This is a column of the firm's fixed cost.

Then enter =2*B1+0.5*B1^2 in cell F1, and so on via click and drag, until cell F15. This is a column of the firm's variable cost.

Then enter =E1+F1 in cell G1, and so on via click and drag, until cell G15. This is a column of the firm's total cost.

Then enter =G2−G1 in cell H2, and so on via click and drag, until cell H15. This is a column of the firm's discrete marginal costs, the additional cost incurred when producing another unit of product.

From above, we know that the firm's continuous marginal cost is $MC = 2 + Q$. For comparison, we'll enter the continuous marginal cost curve in column I. Enter =2+B1 in cell I1 and so on via click and drag until cell I15. Note that the two marginal costs differ because of the size of the increments considered (i.e., integer versus continuous), and that the continuous marginal cost exceeds the discrete marginal cost.

Column J is our objective, that is, the firm's profit. Enter =C1−G1 in cell J1, and so on via click and drag, until cell J15. Then search column J for the largest number. You may enter =Max(J1:J15) in cell J16 to have the spreadsheet do this for you. The largest profit will be 28 in cell J7, and as you read leftward in the seventh row, you will notice that this occurs when you produce and sell six units (the same as the above with the continuous demand and cost quantities).

For the continuous case, marginal revenue = 8 and marginal cost = 8 at six units of output. In the discrete case, marginal revenue = 8 and marginal cost = 7.5 at six units of output so the firm wants to produce and sell the sixth unit since the cash flow in (8) exceeds the cash flow out (7.5). The discrete firm does not want to go beyond six units because the marginal cost of the seventh unit = 8.5 exceeds the marginal revenue of the seventh unit = 7. Since cash flow in (7) is exceeded by cash flow out (8.5), the firm will not produce the seventh unit.

Why does the profit differ between the continuous model (31) and the discrete model (28)? This is because of the difference in the changes in output. The continuous demand model is $P = 14 - Q$, whereas the discrete demand function is a step function. Let's look at the continuous demand function from output zero to output one. The total revenue over this demand range is the trapezoid with area of

$$TR = 0.5*(14 + 13)*1 = 13.5$$

whereas the total revenue for the discrete demand curve in this demand range is 13 (the additional revenue from going from selling zero units to selling one unit). That's a difference of 0.5. There's an additional 0.5 between outputs one and two, and yet another between outputs two and three. This continues up to output six. There are six of these 0.5 values. Hence, $6*0.5 = 3$ which accounts for the 31–28 difference in profits.

EXCEL EXERCISE: THIRD-DEGREE PRICE DISCRIMINATION

Suppose that you know the demand for your product is made up of the demand from strong demanders and the demand from weak demanders. The strong demanders have a demand curve of

$$P_S = 14 - Q_S \text{ or } Q_S = 14 - P_S$$

and the weak demanders have a demand curve of

$$P_W = 10 - Q_W \text{ or } Q_W = 10 - P_W$$

The total demand for your product can be expressed as

$$Q = Q_S + Q_W = 14 - P + 10 - P = 24 - 2P$$

or $\qquad 2P = 24 - Q$

or $\qquad P = 12 - 0.5Q \text{ for } P \leq 10 \text{ and } Q \geq 4$

The firm's marginal revenue (as shown in the text) has the same intercept as and double the slope of the demand curve, that is,

$$MR = 12 - Q$$

The firm's total cost function is

$$TC = 5 + 2Q$$

The firm's marginal cost is

$$MC = \Delta TC / \Delta Q = 2$$

The firm's average variable cost is

$$AVC = VC/Q = 2Q/2 = 2$$

To maximize profit, the simple monopoly firm will set $MR = MC$ (as shown in the text), that is,

$$MR = 12 - Q = 2 = MC$$

or $\qquad Q = 10$

Substituting $Q = 10$ into the demand curve gives

$$P = 12 - 0.5 * 10 = 12 - 5 = 7$$

Total Revenue $= TR = P * Q = 7 * 10 = 70$
Total Cost $= TC = 5 + 2Q = 5 + 2 * 10 = 5 + 20 = 25$
Profit $- \pi = TR - TC = 70 - 25 = 45$
If the firm followed third-degree price discrimination, they would set $MR_S = MC$ and $MR_W = MC$ (as shown in the text). In other words,

$$MR_S = 14 - 2Q_S = 2 = MC$$

or $\qquad 2Q_S = 12$

or $\qquad Q_S = 6$

Substituting $Q_S = 6$ into the strong demand curve gives

$$P_S = 14 - Q_S = 14 - 6 = 8$$

and $\qquad MR_W = 10 - 2Q_W = 2 = MC$

or $$2Q_W = 8$$

or $$Q_W = 4$$

Substituting $Q_W = 4$ into the weak demand curve gives

$$P_W = 10 - Q_W = 10 - 4 = 6$$

Note that $Q = Q_S + Q_W = 6 + 4 = 10$
Total Revenue Strong Market $= TR_S = P_S * Q_S = 8 * 6 = 48$
Total Revenue Weak Market $= TR_W = P_W * Q_W = 6 * 4 = 24$
Total Revenue Total $= TR = TR_S + TR_W = 48 + 24 = 72$
Total Cost $= TC = 5 + 2Q = 5 + 2 * 10 = 5 + 20 = 25$
Profit $= \pi = TR - TC = 72 - 25 = 47$

Thus following third-degree price discrimination increases profit by $47 - 45 = 2$.

Let's suppose we didn't know the calculus derived rules for profit maximization but were given the following estimates of market demand by our demand consultants:

Price	Strong Quantity Demanded	Weak Quantity Demanded
14	0	0
13	1	0
12	2	0
11	3	0
10	4	0
9	5	1
8	6	2
7	7	3
6	8	4
5	9	5
4	10	6
3	11	7
2	12	8
1	13	9
0	14	10

Can we find the simple monopoly price with this information? Yes.

Open your spreadsheet. Enter 14 in cell A1, 13 in cell A2, and so on, until you enter 0 in cell A15. Column A is the price (P) column.

Enter 0 in cell B1, 1 in cell B2, and so on, until you enter 14 in cell B15. Column B is the strong demander's quantity demanded (Q_S).

Enter 0 in cell C1, 0 in cell C2, 0 in cell C3, 0 in cell C4, 0 in cell C5, 1 in cell C6, 2 in cell C7, and so on, until you enter 10 in cell C15. Column C is the weak demander's quantity demanded (Q_W).

Enter =B1+C1 in cell D1 and so on. You can do this easily by clicking on the lower right-hand corner of cell D1 and dragging your mouse down until you reach cell D15. Columns A and D give the simple monopolist's demand curve, that is, the total quantity demanded by the strong and weak demanders ($Q = Q_S + Q_W$) at a given price.

Enter A1 * D1 in cell E1, and so on, via click and drag until cell E15. Column E gives the simple monopolist's total revenue ($TR = P * Q$).

Enter =E2−E1 in cell F2, =E3−E2 in cell F3, =E4−E3 in cell F4, =E5−E4 in cell F5, =(E6−E5)/2 in cell F6, and so on via click and drag, until cell F15. Column F is the simple monopolist's marginal revenue, that is, the additional revenue received from selling another unit of product ($MR = \Delta TR/\Delta Q$). The entries in cells F6 to F15 are divided by 2 because quantity demanded changes by 2 when price drops by a dollar below $10.

Enter 5 in cell G1. Click and drag down to cell G15 to get a column of the firm's fixed cost (FC).

Enter =2 * D1 in cell H1, and so on via click and drag, until cell H15. Column H is the firm's variable cost (VC).

Enter =G1+H1 in cell I1, and so on via click and drag, until cell I15. Column I is the firm's total cost ($TC = FC + VC$).

Enter I2-I1 in cell J2, =I3−I2 in cell J3, =I4−I3 in cell J4, =I5−I4 in cell J5, =(I6−I5)/2 in cell J6, and so on via click and drag, until cell J15. Column J is the firm's marginal cost ($MC = \Delta TC/\Delta Q$). The entries in cells J6 to J15 are divided by 2 because quantity changes by 2 when price drops by a dollar below $10.

Column K is the profit column ($\pi = TR - TC$). Enter =E1−I1 in cell K1, and so on via click and drag, until cell K15. Then search column K for the highest number (or enter =Max(K1:K15) in cell K16 and let the spreadsheet find the highest number). You'll find the maximum profit in the eighth row in cell K8 at 45. This is the same result we attained using the calculus version above.

Now let's do third-degree price discrimination.

Repeat columns A and B starting in cell A17 and B17. Then enter =A17*B17 in cell C17, and so on via click and drag, until cell C31. Column C is the total revenue from the strong demand curve.

Enter =C18−C17 in cell D18, and so on via click and drag, until cell D31. Column D gives the marginal revenue from the strong demand curve.

Enter =2*B17 in cell E17, and so on via click and drag, until cell E31. Column E gives the variable cost of producing product to be sold in the strong market.

Enter =E18−E17 in cell F18, and so on via click and drag, until cell F31. Column F gives the marginal cost incurred in producing product to be sold in the strong market.

Enter $=$ C17$-$E17 in cell G17, and so on via click and drag, until cell G31. Column G gives the firm's variable profit, that is, $TR_S - VC_S$, for the strong market. We then search column G for the highest number, which is 36 in cell G23 with output of 6 and a price of 8. This is the same result found with the calculus. We could also find this result by entering $=$ Max(G17:G31) in cell C32.

Note that the marginal revenue at $Q=6$ is 3 and the marginal cost is 2. From our earlier discussion, we definitely want to sell the sixth unit since the additional cash flowing into the firm (3) exceeds the cash flowing out of the firm (2). The firm would not want to sell a seventh unit in the strong market because the marginal revenue of the seventh unit is 1 and the marginal cost of the seventh unit is 2. Thus, using our rules, six is the optimal number of units for the strong market.

Enter $=-$A18$/$B18 in cell H18, and so on via click and drag, until cell H31. Column H gives the own price elasticity of demand at each point on the strong demand curve. Note that when the monopolist chose the best single price (7), seven units were sold in the strong market and the demand elasticity was -1.

Now we do the same for the weak market.

Repeat columns A (the market price) and C (the weak quantity demanded) starting in cells A33 and B33 but beginning with price 10 and quantity 0. Then enter $=$ A33*B33 in cell C33, and so on via click and drag, until cell C43. Column C is the total revenue from the weak demand curve.

Enter $=$ C34$-$C33 in cell D34, and so on via click and drag, until cell D43. Column D gives the marginal revenue from the weak demand curve.

Enter $=$ 2*B33 in cell E33, and so on via click and drag, until cell E43. Column E gives the variable cost of producing product to be sold in the weak market.

Enter $=$ E34$-$E33 in cell F34, and so on via click and drag, until cell F43. Column F gives the marginal cost incurred in producing product to be sold in the weak market.

Enter $=$ C33$-$E33 in cell G33, and so on via click and drag, until cell G43. Column G gives the firm's variable profit, that is, $TR_W - VC_W$, for the weak market. We then search column G for the highest number, which is 16 in cell G37 with output of 4 and a price of 6. This is the same result found with the calculus. We could also find this result by entering $=$ Max(G33:G43) in cell G44.

Note that these results are similar to those in the strong market. At $Q=4$ marginal revenue is 3 and marginal cost is 2. Whereas at $Q=5$, marginal revenue is 1 and marginal cost is 2. Thus, 4 is the optimal output for managers to sell in the weak market.

Enter $=-$A34$/$B34 in cell H34, and so on via click and drag, until cell H43. Column H gives the own price elasticity of demand at each point on the weak demand curve. Note that when the monopolist chose the best single price (7), three units were sold in the weak market and the demand elasticity was -2.333. This demonstrates the result pointed out in the text, that we tend to raise the price (from 7 to 8) in the least elastic market (strong with elasticity of -1) and lower the price (from 7 to 6) in the most elastic market (weak with elasticity of -2.333).

Adding the two variable profits gives total variable profit ($36 + 16 = 52$). Subtracting the firm's fixed cost of 5 yields the firm's profit of 47, the result of third-degree price discrimination.

APPENDIX: TWO-PART TARIFF WITH INTERSECTING DEMANDS

Managers may find themselves executing a two-part tariff pricing strategy in markets where demand curves intersect. In such a case determining the optimal use price and entry price may entail searching back and forth among the demand curves, as we show in the following example.

There are two types of demanders in our market. Consumer 1 has a demand curve of

$$P_1 = a_1 - b_1 Q_1$$

and consumer 2 has a demand curve of

$$P_2 = a_2 - b_2 Q_2$$

Marginal cost is constant at c.

Managers can estimate the consumer surplus for any demander i when the use fee is set at marginal cost. Consumer surplus when the use fee is equal to marginal cost is

$$CS_i = (a_i - c)^2 / 2b_i$$

where $i = 1, 2$.

One fact managers can estimate is whether double the consumer surplus for the smaller consumer surplus demander is greater than the consumer surplus for the larger consumer surplus demander. If so, then the optimal entry fee *if marginal cost is the use fee* is the consumer surplus of the lower consumer surplus demander. If not, then the optimal entry fee *if marginal cost is the use fee* is the consumer surplus of the higher consumer surplus consumer. However, it is possible that a use fee (P^*) greater than marginal cost will lead to the highest profit.

The profit margin under such a use fee is $P^* - c$. The quantity consumed in market i at price P^* is

$$Q_i = (a_i - P^*)/b_i$$

and therefore the total amount consumed by both consumers at price P^* is

$$Q = [a_1 b_2 + a_2 b_1 - (b_1 + b_2)P^*]/b_1 b_2$$

yielding profit from the use fee of

$$[(a_1b_2 + a_2b_1)(P^* - c) - (b_1 + b_2)P^{*2} + c(b_1 + b_2)P^*]/b_1b_2$$

that is, $(P^* - c)Q$.

The consumer surplus resulting from the choice of P^* as the use fee would be

$$CS_i = (a_i - P^*)^2/2b_i$$

If double the resulting consumer surplus for the demander with the lower consumer surplus exceeds the resulting consumer surplus of the demander with the higher consumer surplus, managers will choose the smaller consumer surplus as the entry fee. How can we determine which consumer surplus is relevant?

Suppose $a_1 > a_2$. We can portray the decision by managers when seeking the best use price greater than marginal cost as dividing the range of $a_2 > P_{Use} > MC$ into regions to determine the relevant entry fee to charge. a_2 is an upper boundary because demander 2 will not participate in the market if the use fee is higher than a_2. MC is a lower boundary because managers will never produce unless the price they can charge for output at least covers marginal cost. When a P_{Use} exists such that $CS_1 = CS_2$, either consumer surplus is the relevant entry fee. Equating the two consumer surplus values gives

$$P = [(a_1b_2 - a_2b_1) \pm \sqrt{(a_1 - a_2)^2b_1b_2} - (a_1 - a_2)^2b_1b_2]^{0.5}]/(b_2 - b_1)$$

where $A = a_1b_2 - a_2b_1$, $B = (a_1 - a_2)(b_1b_2)^{0.5}$, and $C = b_2 - b_1$.

The relationship between CS_1 and CS_2 as a function of use fee (P^*) appears in Figure 9.8 for the case where $(A + B)/C < (A - B)/C$. (This is the case examined in the first example here.)

Between MC and $(A + B)/C$, $CS_2 > CS_1$, so the consumer surplus of consumer 1 (if the optimal use price is in this range) will be charged to both demanders. The entry price will thus be

$$P_{Entry} = (a_1 - P^*)^2/2b_1$$

and the profit from the entry fee will be

$$\pi_{Entry} = (a_1 - P^*)^2/b_1$$

because both demanders will pay it.

The profit earned is

$$\pi = (a_1b_2 + a_2b_1)(P^* - c) - (b_1 + b_2)P^{*2} + c(b_1 + b_2)P^*$$
$$+ (a_1^2b_2 - 2a_1b_2P^* + b_2P^{*2})]/b_1b_2$$
$$\Delta\pi/\Delta P^* = [(a_1b_2 + a_2b_1) - 2(b_1 + b_2)P^* + c(b_1 + b_2) - 2a_1b_2$$
$$+ 2b_2P^*]/b_1b_2 = 0$$

Solving for P^x gives

$$P^* = [a_2 b_1 - a_1 b_2 + c(b_1 + b_2)]/2b_1$$

It must be checked that the resulting P^* lies in the range of

$$MC < P^* < (A + B)/C$$

Between $(A + B)/C$ and a_2, $CS_1 > CS_2$, so the consumer surplus of demander 2 (if the optimal use price is in this range) will be charged to both demanders.

QUANT OPTION

To set the record straight, profit is maximized when

$$d\pi/dP^* = [(a_1 b_2 + a_2 b_1) - 2(b_1 + b_2)P^* + c(b_1 + b_2) - 2a_1 b_2 + 2b_2 P^*]/$$
$$b_1 b_2 = 0$$

The optimal use price in this range will be

$$P^* = [a_1 b_2 - a_2 b_1 + c(b_1 + b_2)]/2b_2$$

Of course we must check that the resulting P^* lies in the range of

$$(A + B)/C < P^* < a_2$$

Consider the following example: $P_1 = 9 - 3Q_1$, $P_2 = 8 - 2Q_2$, and $MC = 2$. Equating consumer surpluses gives

$$(A + B)/C = 3.55 \text{ and } (A - B)/C = 8.45$$

that is, $(-6 + 2.45)/-1 = 6 - 2.45 = 3.55 < (-6 - 2.45)/-1 = 8.45$. So this meets the conditions graphed in Figure 9.8.

Viewing potential use fees where $MC < P^* < (A + B)/C$ gives

$$P^* = (24 - 18 + 10)/6 = 2.67$$

Because $MC = 2$ and $(A + B)/C = 3.55$, the price meets the constraints.

Viewing potential use fees where $(A + B)/C < P^* < a_2$ gives

$$P^* = (18 - 24 + 10)/4 = 1$$

Because $(A + B)/C = 3.55$ and $a_2 = 8$, this price does not satisfy the constraints.

Substituting $P^* = 2.67$ into the profit function here gives a profit of 16.5556. We must still compare this result with pricing the use fee at marginal cost and the

FIGURE 9.8

The Relationship between the Demanders' Consumer Surpluses and the Use Price Chosen

The difference in the consumer surplus of demander 2 and demander 1 varies with the use price. In this example, as the use price increases above marginal cost, demander 1's consumer surplus gets closer to demander 2's consumer surplus until at use price $(A + B)/C$, the two consumer surpluses are equal. As the use price rises above $(A + B)/C$, demander 1's consumer surplus exceeds demander 2's consumer surplus. At use price a_2 until use price a_1, only demander 1 has consumer surplus.

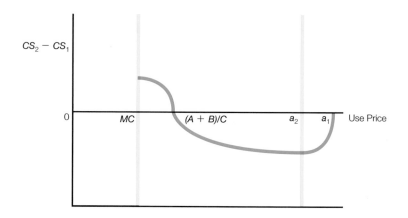

TABLE 9.1

Various Use Price and Entry Price Combinations and Their Resulting Profit

P_{Use}	CS_1	CS_2	π_{Use}	π_{Entry}	P_{Entry}	Consumer Determining Entry Fee	π
2	8.1667	9	0	16.3333	8.1667	1	16.3333
2.5	7.0417	7.5625	2.4583	14.0833	7.0417	1	16.5417
2.67	6.685	7.1111	3.185	13.37	6.685	1	16.5556
3	6	6.25	4.5	12	6	1	16.5
3.5	5.0417	5.0625	6.125	10.0833	5.0417	1	16.2083
3.55051	4.9495	4.9495	6.2667	9.899	4.9495	Either	16.165
4	4.1667	4	7.3333	8	4	2	15.3333
5	2.6667	2.25	8.5	4.5	2.25	2	13
6	1.5	1	8	2	1	2	10
7	0.6667	0.25	5.8333	0.5	0.25	2	6.3333
7.5	0.375	0.0625	4.125	0.125	0.0625	2	4.25
7.93725	0.1882	0.001	2.2896	0.002	0.001	2	2.2915
7.93725	0.1882	0.001	2.0133	0.1882	0.1882	1*	2.2915
7.95	0.1838	0.0006	2.0825	0.1838	0.1838	1*	2.2663

* In these cases only consumer 1 is served.

entry fee equal to either the larger consumer surplus (if it is more than double the smaller consumer surplus) or the smaller consumer surplus (if when doubled, it is more than the larger consumer surplus). As shown in Table 9.1, the best policy *if the firm sets the use fee equal to marginal cost* is to sell to both consumers at an entry fee of 8.1667 yielding a profit of 16.3333. Thus a use fee greater than marginal cost yields the highest profit.

But suppose the producer experimented with use fees (and charged the best resulting entry fee). The results appear in Table 9.1.

As we can see, as price rises above marginal cost, both consumers consume the product with consumer 1's consumer surplus equal to the entry fee. At a use price of 3.55051, the consumer surpluses of each consumer are the same. At use prices higher than 3.55051, both consumers consume the product with consumer 2's consumer surplus equal to the entry fee until the use price reaches 7.93725. At that price, the profit from selling to both at an entry fee equal to consumer 2's consumer surplus equals the profit from selling to just consumer 1 with an entry fee equal to consumer 1's consumer surplus. Obviously this would be true at prices between 8 and 9, but it's best to exclude consumer 2 before the use fee reaches consumer 2's maximum reservation price.

Consider a second example where the second demander's demand is $P_2 = 6 - 2Q_2$. Then $(A + B)/C = -7.35$, which makes no sense, and $(A - B)/C = 7.35$, which exceeds a_2. In this case the graph looks like Figure 9.9.

FIGURE 9.9

A Different Relationship between the Demanders' Consumer Surpluses and the Use Price Chosen

In this case there is no user fee where the consumer surpluses are the same. Here we get a "corner solution," where the optimal use fee is at marginal cost.

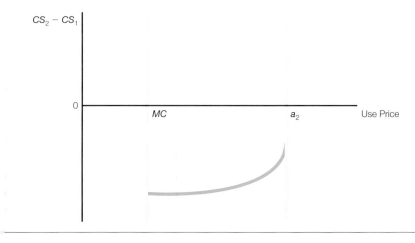

TABLE 9.2

Various Use Price and Entry Price Combinations and Their Resulting Profit

P_{Use}	CS_1	CS_2	π_{Use}	π_{Entry}	P_{Entry}	Consumer Determining Entry Fee	π
2	8.1667	4	0	8.1667	8.1667	1*	8.1667
2.67	6.685	2.7778	1.407	6.685	6.685	1*	8.09
2.95	6.1004	2.2494	1.9158	6.1004	6.1004	1*	8.0163
3	6	2.25	3.5	4.5	4	Either	8
3	6	2.25	2	6	6	1*	8
3.05	5.9004	2.1756	2.0825	5.9004	5.9004	1*	7.9829
4	4.1667	1	3.333	4.1667	4.1667	1*	7.3333
5	2.6667	0.25	4	2.6667	2.6667	1*	6.6667
6	1.5	0	4	1.5	1.5	1*	5.5

* In these cases only consumer 1 is served.

The supporting figures for Figure 9.9 are shown in Table 9.2.

In this case the best solution is to set the use price equal to marginal cost and the entry fee equal to the resulting consumer surplus of consumer 1 and not serve consumer 2. The weaker demand of demander 2 significantly constrains the profitability of the firm.

CHAPTER 10

BUNDLING AND INTRAFIRM PRICING

Another sophisticated pricing strategy used by managers is bundling. **Simple bundling** occurs when managers offer several products or services as one package so consumers do not have an option to purchase package components separately. An example of simple bundling is the inclusion of a service contract with a product. **Mixed bundling** allows consumers to purchase package components either as a single unit or separately. The bundle price is generally less than the sum of the components. Season tickets to sporting events or the value meals of McDonald's are examples of a mixed bundling strategy.

Bundling is best used when there is wide variance in consumers' price sensitivity of demand and when market conditions make it difficult to price discriminate. Managers increase profit by leveraging the different valuations (reservation prices) consumers have for a product. Managers prefer to form bundles so as to create negative correlations across consumers. **Negative correlation** exists when some customers have higher reservation prices for one item in the bundle but lower reservation prices for another item in the bundle, whereas another group of customers has the reverse preferences. By bundling together the products, managers (under certain conditions) can make a greater profit than by selling the products separately.

Consumers often encounter bundling when managers offer distinct goods or services together at a packaged price. Economists distinguish between simple (pure) bundling, when the goods are offered only in the package, and mixed bundling,

Simple bundling When managers offer several products or services as one package so consumers do not have an option to purchase package components separately.

Mixed bundling Allows consumers to purchase package components either as a single unit or separately.

Negative correlation When some customers have higher reservation prices for one item in the bundle but lower reservation prices for another item in the bundle, whereas another group of customers has the reverse preferences.

when the goods have a packaged price as well as stand-alone prices. Examples abound. Entertainers as diverse as professional sports teams and opera companies commonly practice mixed bundling, offering tickets to individual performances as well as season tickets, subscriptions of tickets to multiple (but not all) performances, and other bundles. A record company bundles 12 songs of your favorite recording artist on a CD, and you must buy the CD (the bundle) to obtain the several songs you want (and hence obtain more songs that you do not want as much, if at all). This product is a pure bundle.

THE MECHANICS OF BUNDLING

Why do managers commonly use bundling? One reason is that it can increase the seller's profit if customers have varied tastes. In addition, it is a way to emulate perfect price discrimination when perfect price discrimination is not possible (because knowing individual reservation prices is either too difficult or expensive to pursue) or it is not legal to charge multiple prices for the same product. With a bundle, we need not know the reservation price of each consumer for each good (as in perfect price discrimination) but only the distribution of all consumers' reservation prices over the goods.

Managers need to consider other issues in choosing bundling schemes. For example, is the worth of the bundle to consumers the sum of their reservation prices for the separate goods in the bundle? That is, are the goods independent? This will be our assumption. However, we can easily envision cases of complementarity of the goods, where the goods as a bundle have a value greater than the sum of the separate reservation prices—such as software and hardware. We can also envision cases of goods, where the goods as a bundle have a value less than the sum of their separate reservation prices. And what about demand? We will assume consumers purchase no more than one unit of any good either separately or in a bundle. From the cost side, managers need to consider whether there are economies of scope or scale in the production of two goods. We will assume production costs are the same regardless of whether the goods are produced for sale separately or as a bundle; that is, the cost of a bundle is the sum of the individual costs of the two goods. A last issue is whether the goods are sold in secondary markets. We will assume that consumers do not resell the goods.

Of course managers can always sell the goods as separate items. If managers cannot price discriminate but must charge a single price for each good, we'll assume that price is the simple monopoly profit-maximizing one.

We can investigate the three possible pricing scenarios in the following three figures. Figure 10.1 shows the separate price strategy. Managers choose the optimal simple monopoly prices for good 1 and good 2 (the ones that maximize profit). Call them $p_1^{\#}$ and $p_2^{\#}$ Figure 10.1 shows the resulting consumption behavior of consumers depending on their reservation prices. For example, consumers

STRATEGY SESSION: Bundling Carbon Credits with Gas Sales

Gazprom is a Russian energy firm that sells natural gas to Europe and has profited handsomely. But now it has figured out how to make even more profit. A London subsidiary (Gazprom Marketing and Trading) has invested in a Brazilian biomass power plant (Propower do Brasil) that earns Gazprom Marketing and Trading carbon dioxide emission credits (because biomass uses renewable resources and is "carbon neutral" because it emits as much carbon when used as fuel as was absorbed when it was a crop). Gazprom will then bundle those credits with natural gas and sell the combination as a single product to electric utilities in Europe. The utilities need these credits to burn natural gas.

The ability to make this bundle has come about because of the 1997 Kyoto Protocol on climate change, which gave Russia a massive amount of these credits, and a 2005 European Union program of "cap and trade" that allows "dirty" utilities (heavy polluters) to purchase carbon dioxide credits that permit them to pollute and "clean" utilities (low polluters) to sell pollution credits they don't need. Although Russia

is one of the largest producers of greenhouse gases because of antiquated technology, relatively small investments will enable them to significantly reduce emissions. This gives Gazprom access to a large amount of Russian pollution credits (the Brazilian pollution credits are just Gazprom's test of the bundled market). To facilitate the activity, Gazprom's banking subsidiary has established a carbon trading unit (Carbon Trade and Finance) with Dresdner Bank. Carbon Trade and Finance will then invest in modern efficient equipment at Russian polluting firms and thus earn the credits that Gazprom will use to bundle with its natural gas.

It's estimated that the value of carbon credits in Russia is in the range of $40 to $60 billion. The fly in the ointment? If the Kyoto Protocol is not extended, the carbon credits could be worth nothing.

Source: Andrew E. Kramer, "Russian Energy Giant to Bundle Carbon Credits with Gas Sales," *New York Times*, April 25, 2007, at www.nytimes.com/2007/04/25/business/worldbusiness/25carbon.html.

n the upper right cell buy both goods given their high reservation prices for the oods.

Figure 10.2 shows the strategy of pure bundling. Here managers choose the optimal pure bundle price (the one that maximizes profit). Call it $p_B^\#$. Consumers ocated to the right of the $p_B^\#$ line in Figure 10.2 buy the bundled product.

Figure 10.3 shows the strategy of mixed bundling. Managers choose the optimal pure bundle price ($p_B^\star$), the optimal separate price for good 1 ($p_1^\star$), and the optimal separate price for good 2 ($p_2^\star$); these prices are set to maximize profit. Figure 10.3 shows the resulting consumption behavior of consumers depending on their reservation prices. This is a good example of how managerial actions influence the behavior of consumers. By increasing the purchase options, managers can rack behavior in specific sectors of the market.

The optimal solution is the *greatest profit of the profit-maximizing solutions yielded by separate pricing, pure bundling, and mixed bundling*. The manager

FIGURE 10.1

Price Separately

Whether consumers purchase goods separately depends on their reservation price for the good relative to the prices charged by the seller.

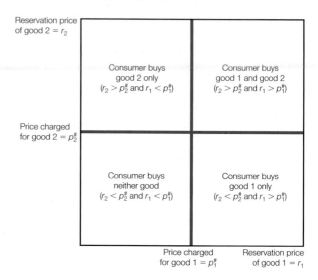

FIGURE 10.2

Pure Bundling

Whether consumers purchase the bundle depends on the sum of their reservation prices for the goods relative to the bundled price charged by the seller.

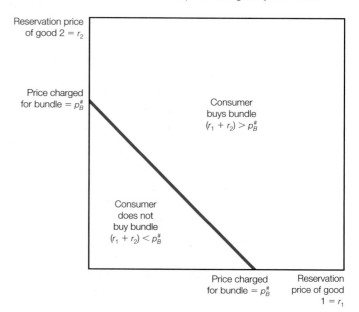

STRATEGY SESSION: Bundling College Textbooks

Sticker shock hit college students (and their parents) a number of years ago in terms of tuition rates and textbook prices, which increased at a rate more than double that of inflation of other goods and services. Textbook costs can reach over $1,000 per year. Legislators, who have children too, have heard from their constituents and have acted.

By the way, don't blame us, your humble authors. If we had our way, textbook publishers would price where the demand elasticity was −1 where total revenue from sales of the book are maximized (because our royalties are a share of total revenue). Publishers, however, wish to maximize profits. This means charging where price equals $[\eta/(\eta+1)]MC$ where elasticity is less than −1 (−1 > η, i.e., demand is elastic), that is, a price higher than when $\eta = -1$. See, we're on your side.

Publishers have found another way to increase profits. They pure bundled the textbook with other items like a study guide, an online laboratory, and so on. Since the publishers could have mixed bundled—

that is, offered the current bundle **and** sold each item separately or just sold each item in the bundle separately and not offered the bundle at all, but rather chose only to pure bundle—pure bundling must have been most profitable and extracted the most consumer surplus from the consumer.

A new federal rule that went into effect in July 2010 now requires publishers to offer the mixed bundle. Some students may opt for the bundle for its convenience. You should never assemble your own bundle by buying each of the components separately—that would cost you more—but you may not want or need all the constituent parts of the bundle, and now you won't need to buy them to get the text.

Source: Tara Siegel Bernard, "How to Find Cheaper College Textbooks," *New York Times*, August 3, 2010, at http://bucks.blogs.nytimes.com/2010/08/03/how-to-find-cheaper-college-textbooks.

chooses the action that maximizes profit. These figures do not show the cost of producing the goods to keep things simple. Obviously, although the figures show the buyers' intentions, their realized transactions are a subset of those shown because certain pricing actions are precluded by the manager's profit-maximizing behavior. Solving for the profit-maximizing solutions for Figures 10.1 and 10.2 is easy because of the more limited choices of consumers. Figure 10.1 considers only individual reservation prices for the goods; and only the sum of each consumer's reservation prices is a candidate price for the pure bundle in Figure 10.2. Any other prices would unnecessarily leave consumer surplus on the table (and a profit-maximizing seller always wants to convert such consumer surplus into producer surplus).

The more difficult calculation is determining the best mixed bundle prices. As we show next, the optimal prices do not have to be a reservation price of a good or a bundle. The solution is derived either by educated trial and error or via a computer program[1] that searches all separate prices and pure bundle prices and

1. Hanson and Martin, "Optimal Bundle Pricing," *Management Science* vol. 36(2), 1990, pp. 155–174, have developed such a program, as have the authors.

FIGURE 10.3

Mixed Bundling

Whether the consumer purchases the goods separately or as a bundle depends on the consumer surplus (the difference between consumers' reservation prices, or sum of their reservation prices, and the price charged by the seller). Consumers choose the goods or bundles that maximize their consumer surplus.

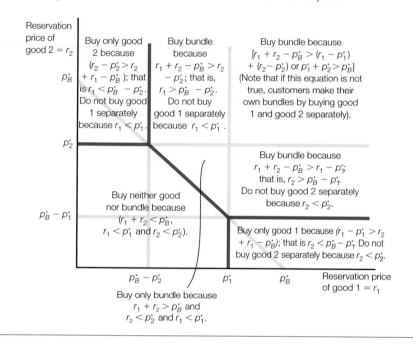

chooses the combination yielding the highest profit. Trial and error can be done in simple cases with few consumers and goods. Cases with many consumers and goods require a computer program. Critical to mixed bundling is creating a credible mixed bundle. **Credibility of the bundle** means that managers correctly anticipate which customers will purchase the bundle or the goods separately.

The following example shows the three types of bundling strategies when reservation prices of consumers are perfectly negatively correlated; that is, all the reservation prices lie on a line of slope -1 in the price space. Note that while the customers have a negative correlation in their reservation prices for the two goods, they exhibit *no* variation in their valuation of the bundle: They all value the bundle at $100. The consumer reservation prices are shown in Table 10.1, and the situation is depicted in Figure 10.4.

Suppose the constant unit cost of production of each good is 1. The separate price, pure bundling, and mixed bundling cases are shown in Tables 10.2, 10.3, and 10.4.

Credibility of the bundle When managers correctly anticipate which customers will purchase the bundle or the goods separately.

TABLE 10.1

Reservation Prices of Good 1 and Good 2 of Consumers A, B, C, and D

Consumer	Reservation Price Good 1	Good 2	Bundle Price
A	90	10	100
B	60	40	100
C	50	50	100
D	10	90	100

FIGURE 10.4

Example of Perfect Negative Correlation of Consumers' Reservation Prices

Consumers A, B, C, and D value each good differently, but all value the bundle of the two goods at $100.

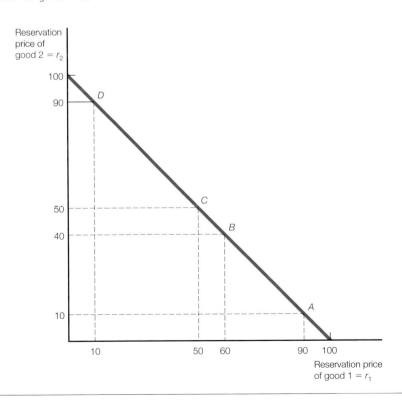

TABLE 10.2

Optimal Separate Prices for Good 1 and Good 2

Consumer	Price 1	Cost/unit	Profit/unit	Number of units	Profit
A	90	1	89	1	89
B	60	1	59	2	118
C	**50**	1	49	3	**147**
D	10	1	9	4	36

Consumer	Price 2	Cost/unit	Profit/unit	Number of units	Profit
A	10	1	9	4	36
B	**40**	1	39	3	**117**
C	50	1	49	2	98
D	90	1	89	1	89

The profit from the best separate price strategy of $P_1 = \$50$ and $P_2 = \$40$ is $264.

TABLE 10.3

Optimal Pure Bundle Price for Consumers A, B, C, and D

Consumer	Bundle Price	Cost/Bundle	Profit/Bundle	Number of Bundles	Profit
A, B, C, D	100	2	98	4	392

The profit from the best pure bundling strategy of $P_{Bundle} = \$100$ is $392.

Managers can always come up with a mixed bundle by pricing the individual goods at prices at which no consumer purchases the good. In some cases, *but not this one*, it is possible to increase profit through mixed bundling. Mixed bundling, therefore, always *weakly dominates* pure bundling.

If we look at mixed bundles where customers actually consume the bundle and at least one of the goods is sold separately, the pricing strategy in Table 10.5 is the best mixed bundle.

Note that consumer A does not consume the bundle because at price $100, she receives no consumer surplus. However, consumer A consumes good 1 at $89.99 because she receives a positive consumer surplus (of $0.01). Likewise, consumer D does not consume the bundle because at price $100, he receives no consumer surplus. However, consumer D consumes good 2 at $89.99 because he receives a positive consumer surplus (of $0.01). We discuss this logic further in another example.

TABLE 10.4

Optimal Mixed Bundle Prices

Consumer	Bundle Price	Cost/Bundle	Profit/Bundle	Number of Bundles	Profit
A, B, C, D	100	2	98	4	392

Consumer	Price 1	Cost/Unit	Profit/Unit	Number of Units	Profit
None	90.01	1	89.01	0	0

Consumer	Price 2	Cost/Unit	Profit/Unit	Number of Units	Profit
None	90.01	1	89.01	0	0

The profit from the best mixed bundling strategy of $P_{Bundle} = \$100$, $P_1 > \$90$, and $P_2 > \$90$ is \$392.

TABLE 10.5

Optimal Mixed Bundle Prices When Consumers Buy Bundle and at Least One of the Separately Priced Goods

Consumer	Bundle Price	Cost/Bundle	Profit/Bundle	Number of Bundles	Profit
B, C	100	2	98	2	196

Consumer	Price 1	Cost/Unit	Profit/Unit	Number of Units	Profit
A	89.99	1	88.99	1	88.99

Consumer	Price 2	Cost/Unit	Profit/Unit	Number of Units	Profit
D	89.99	1	88.99	1	88.99

The profit from the best mixed bundling strategy, where customers actually purchase the bundle and purchase at least one of the separately priced goods of $P_{Bundle} = \$100$, $P_1 = \$89.99$, and $P_2 = \$89.99$, is \$379.98.

In the preceding case, where pure bundling is the best pricing strategy, perfect price discrimination is completely replicated as the manager extracts *all* the consumer surplus from each customer. This goal is called **extraction**. In addition, a manager can also practice **exclusion**: not selling a good to a customer who values the good at less than the cost of producing it. Finally, a manager may want to practice **inclusion**: selling a good to a customer who values the good at greater than the seller's cost of producing the good. Perfect price discrimination extracts all available consumer surplus, does not sell to anyone for less than cost, and sells to everyone who values the good more than cost. Thus perfect price discrimination satisfies all three of the concepts defined here. These three pricing mechanisms (price separately, pure bundling, and mixed bundling) can be compared to perfect price discrimination on the three dimensions of extraction, exclusion, and inclusion.

Pricing separately should always entail exclusion; but because of its single price per good nature, it will not fulfill complete extraction or inclusion (for negatively sloped demand curves). Pure bundling can allow complete extraction (as in the preceding case); but when the sum of all demanders' reservation prices for goods does not lie on a line with a slope of −1 (that is, there is less than perfect negative correlation of reservation prices), extraction is less than complete. Mixed bundling falls someplace between pricing separately and pure bundling.

Pure bundling can also fail inclusion and exclusion. Note how the best price strategy changes when the cost of producing the goods changes. Consider the example just used but with the production cost of each good now at $11 each. Tables 10.6, 10.7, and 10.8 show the solutions for pricing separately, pure bundling, and mixed bundling.

Extraction When the manager extracts the entire consumer surplus from each customer.

Exclusion When the manager does not sell a good to a customer who values the good at less than the cost of producing it.

Inclusion When a manager sells a good to a consumer who values the good at greater than the seller's cost of producing the good.

TABLE 10.6

Optimal Separate Prices for Good 1 and Good 2

Consumer	Price 1	Cost/Unit	Profit/Unit	Number of Units	Profit
A	90	11	79	1	79
B	60	11	49	2	98
C	**50**	11	39	3	**117**
D	10	11	−1	4	−4

Consumer	Price 2	Cost/Unit	Profit/Unit	Number of Units	Profit
A	10	11	−1	4	−4
B	**40**	11	29	3	**87**
C	50	11	39	2	78
D	90	11	79	1	79

The profit from the best separate price strategy of $P_1 = \$50$ and $P_2 = \$40$ is $204.

TABLE 10.7

Optimal Pure Bundle Prices for Consumers A, B, C, and D

Consumer	Bundle Price	Cost/Bundle	Profit/Bundle	Number of Bundles	Profit
A, B, C, D	100	22	78	4	312

The profit from the best pure bundling strategy of P_{Bundle} = $100 is $312.

TABLE 10.8

Optimal Mixed Bundle Prices

Consumer	Bundle Price	Cost/Bundle	Profit/Bundle	Number of Bundles	Profit
A, B, C, D	100	22	78	4	312

Consumer	Price 1	Cost/Unit	Profit/Unit	Number of Units	Profit
None	90.01	11	79.01	0	0

Consumer	Price 2	Cost/Unit	Profit/Unit	Number of Units	Profit
None	90.01	11	79.01	0	0

The profit from the best mixed bundle strategy of P_{Bundle} = $100, $P_1 > 90$, and $P_2 > 90$ is $312.

However, if we look at mixed bundles where customers actually consume the bundle and at least one of the goods sold separately, Table 10.9 shows the best mixed bundle.

In this case the concept of exclusion dominates the concept of extraction. The pure bundle price of $100 completely extracts all consumer surplus. However, the seller sells (in the bundle) good 2 to consumer A, and A values the good at only $10, whereas it costs the seller $11 to produce good 2. Likewise, the seller sells good 1 to consumer D in the bundle, and D values the good at only $10, whereas it costs the seller $11 to produce good 1. It is better for the seller to exclude consumer A from buying good 2 and consumer D from buying good 1. The seller can do that by practicing mixed bundling. The seller sacrifices $10.01 in consumer revenue from each of consumers A and D by switching those consumers from a price of $100 for the bundle to a price of $89.99 for the separate goods (a total of $20.02). But the seller saves $22 in cost by not producing one unit of good 1 and one

TABLE 10.9

Optimal Mixed Bundle Prices When Consumers Buy Bundle and at Least One of the Separately Priced Goods

Consumer	Bundle Price	Cost/Bundle	Profit/Bundle	Number of Bundles	Profit
B, C	100	22	78	2	156

Consumer	Price 1	Cost/Unit	Profit/Unit	Number of Units	Profit
A	89.99	11	78.99	1	78.99

Consumer	Price 2	Cost/Unit	Profit/Unit	Number of Units	Profit
D	89.99	11	78.99	1	78.99

The profit from the best mixed bundle strategy, where customers actually purchase the bundle and at least one of the separately priced goods of $P_{Bundle} = \$100$, $P_1 = \$89.99$, and $P_2 = \$89.99$, is $313.98. Therefore, mixed bundling is the best pricing strategy for the seller.

unit of good 2. This $1.98 difference is the difference in profits between the best pure bundle profit of $312 and the best mixed bundle profit of $313.98. Inclusion and exclusion are practiced perfectly in this case of mixed bundling, but complete extraction is not. In general, optimal pricing solutions among these three methods entail a trade-off among the concepts of extraction, exclusion, and inclusion.

Suppose further that the cost of producing each good is now $55. Tables 10.10, 10.11, and 10.12 show the solutions for pricing separately, pure bundling, and mixed bundling.

The only reason that mixed bundling yields the same profit as separate pricing here is that a bundle price is selected so that no consumer will choose the bundle—that is, a price over $100. In cases where separate pricing is best, we can always price the bundle at a price at which no one will consume it. Therefore mixed bundling weakly dominates pricing separately. Previously we established that mixed bundling weakly dominates pure bundling; technically mixed bundling should be a part of any bundling strategy because the profit from it is always better than or equal to that of pricing separately or pure bundling.

Although pure bundling perfectly extracts all consumer surplus in this perfectly negatively correlated reservation price example when the unit production cost is $55, it fails miserably on exclusion. Many units (five) are sold to customers who value the good at less than its cost of production. Mixed bundling, except at a price that excludes everyone from buying the pure bundle, can do no better than

TABLE 10.10

Optimal Separate Prices for Good 1 and Good 2

Consumer	Price 1	Cost/Unit	Profit/Unit	Number of Units	Profit
A	**90**	55	35	1	**35**
B	60	55	5	2	10
C	50	55	−5	3	−15
D	10	55	−45	4	−180

Consumer	Price 2	Cost/Unit	Profit/Unit	Number of Units	Profit
A	10	55	−45	4	−180
B	40	55	−15	3	−45
C	50	55	−5	2	−10
D	**90**	55	35	1	**35**

The profit from the best separate price strategy of $P_1 = \$90$ and $P_2 = \$90$ is $70.

TABLE 10.11

Optimal Pure Bundle Prices for Consumers A, B, C, and D

Consumer	Bundle Price	Cost/Bundle	Profit/Bundle	Number of Bundles	Profit
A, B, C, D	100	110	−10	4	−40

The best pure bundling strategy is any bundle price over $100. No one will buy the bundle, and the profit is $0.

TABLE 10.12

Optimal Mixed Bundle Prices at Any Pure Bundle Price over $100 (So No Bundle Is Purchased)

Consumer	Price 1	Cost/Unit	Profit/Unit	Number of Units	Profit
A	90	55	35	1	35

Consumer	Price 2	Cost/Unit	Profit/Unit	Number of Units	Profit
B	90	55	35	1	35

The profit from the best mixed bundle strategy of $P_{Bundle} > \$100$, $P_1 = \$90$, and $P_2 = \$90$ is $70.

pricing separately. Pricing separately extracts much of the *profitable* consumer surplus, excludes the right consumers, but does not include consumer B who values good 1 at $60 (the cost of production is $55).

Negative correlation of reservation prices enables a manager to fully extract all consumer surplus with a pure bundle when the cost of production is low. If we increase the production cost while keeping the reservation prices with perfectly negative correlation, initially mixed bundling is the profit-maximizing action; if production costs keep increasing, eventually separate pricing will maximize profit.

But negative correlation is not required to make bundling the best choice. Suppose customers are uniformly distributed over reservation prices for good 1 from $0 to $100 and for good 2 from $0 to $100. This would be a case of zero correlation of reservation prices. There are 10,000 such consumers. To keep things simple, suppose production costs of the goods are $0. Therefore, maximizing the total revenue is the same as maximizing profit.[2]

The best separate prices are $P_1 = \$50$ and $P_2 = \$50$, and the profit is $500,000.[3] This is shown in Figure 10.5.

2. The following examples are from "Bundling: Teaching Note," Harvard Business School, 5-795-168, rev. July 22, 1998.

3. Call the optimal price of good 1 x. Because of the uniform distribution, this also is the optimal price of good 2. When x is chosen, it determines how many customers consume each good. Consider choosing x on the horizontal axis. Everyone to the left of x does not consume good 1, and everyone at and to the right of x consumes good 1. Consider choosing x on the vertical axis. Everyone below x does not consume good 2, and everyone at and above x consumes good 2. The total area of Figure 10.5 is $100 \times 100 = 10,000$. Viewing each of the four areas created, we can calculate the percentage of the total area occupied by each of the subareas. For instance, area A occupies $x^2/10,000$ amount of the total area. Area B occupies $(100 - x)x/10,000 = (100x - x^2)/10,000$ of the total area (as does area D). Area C occupies $(100 - x)(100 - x)/10,000 = (10,000 - 200x + x^2)/10,000$ of the total area. The number of customers in each area is the percentage of the total area times 10,000. The revenue from each area is the number of customers times the price they pay. Therefore, area A generates $0x^2$ in revenue, area B generates $x(100x - x^2)$ in revenue, area C generates $2x(10,000 - 200x + x^2)$ in revenue, and area D generates $x(100x - x^2)$ in revenue, yielding a total revenue (TR) of $20,000x - 200x^2$. We maximize TR by setting $dTR/dx = 20,000 - 400x = 0$ or $x = \$50$. Total profit is $500,000.

FIGURE 10.5

Optimal Separate Prices in the Case of Uniformly Distributed Consumer Reservation Prices

The optimal separate prices when the uniform distribution of consumer reservation prices is between $0 and $100 for both goods are $50 for each good. Profits are $500,000.

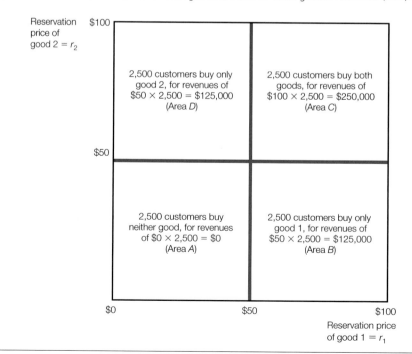

FIGURE 10.6

Optimal Pure Bundle Price in the Case of Uniformly Distributed Consumer Reservation Prices

The optimal pure bundle price when the uniform distribution of consumer reservation prices is between $0 and $100 for both goods is $81.65. Profits are $544,331.05.

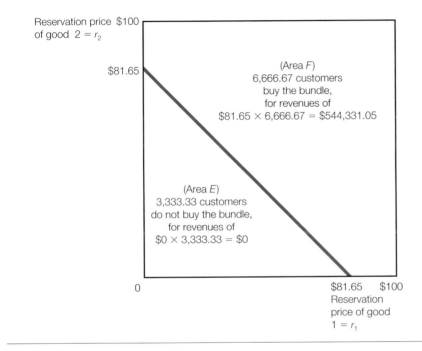

4. Call the optimal price of the bundle y. When the price of the bundle is chosen, it creates a line of slope -1 that connects the vertical axis from point y to the horizontal axis at point y. Area E has an area of $0.5(y)(y) = 0.5y^2$. Its share of the whole area is $0.5y^2/10,000$, and hence it has $0.5y^2$ customers in it. Area F has the remainder of the customers—that is, $10,000 - 0.5y^2$. The total revenue generated from area E is $\$0(0.5y^2) = \$0$, and the total revenue generated from area F is $y(10,000 - 0.5y^2)$. The total revenue (TR) from pure bundling is therefore $10,000y - 0.5y^3$. Maximize TR by setting $dTR/dy = 10,000 - 1.5y^2 = 0$ or $y \approx \$81.65$. Total profit is approximately $544,331.05.

5. Call y the bundle price and x the price of good 1 (and good 2 because of the symmetry). Areas $G + H + I = 0.5y^2$. As shown in the two previous footnotes, these areas represent the number of consumers in the area. Area $H =$ Area $I = 0.5(y - x)(y - x) = 0.5y^2 - xy + 0.5x^2$. Therefore, Area $G = 2xy - 0.5y^2 - x^2$. Area $I +$ Area $J =$ Area $H +$ Area $L = (100 - x)(y - x) = 100y - 100x + x^2 - xy$. Hence, Area $J =$ Area $L = 100y - 100x + x^2 - xy - (0.5y^2 - xy + 0.5x^2) = 100y - 100x - 0.5y^2 + 0.5x^2$. Area $J +$ Area $K +$ Area $L = 10,000 - 0.5y^2$. Area $K = 10,000 - 0.5y^2 - (200y - 200x - y^2 + x^2) = 10,000 - 200y + 200x + 0.5y^2 - x^2$. Consumers in Area $I +$ Area J purchase only good 2 and yield revenues of $x(100y - 100x + x^2 - xy) = 100xy - 100x^2 + x^3 - x^2y$. Consumers in Area $H +$ Area L purchase only good 1 and yield revenues of $x(100y - 100x + x^2 - xy) = 100xy - 100x^2 + x^3 - x^2y$. Consumers in Area K purchase the bundle and yield revenues of $y(10,000 - 200y + 200x + 0.5y^2 - x^2) = 10,000y - 200y^2 + 200xy + 0.5y^3 - x^2y$. Consumers in Area G buy nothing and yield no revenues. Total revenue (TR) is therefore

(Continued)

The best pure bundle price is approximately $81.65, and profit is approximately $544,331.05.[4] This is shown in Figure 10.6. Even without negative correlation, bundling can increase profit over simple monopoly pricing (that is, pricing separately).

The best mixed bundle has a bundle price of approximately $86.19, $P_1 = \$66.67$, and $P_2 = \$66.67$, yielding a profit of approximately $549,201.[5] Therefore, mixed bundling is even better than pure bundling. This is shown in Figure 10.7. So with no negative correlation of reservation prices, the best pricing policy is mixed bundling.[6]

We may also consider quantity discounting as a form of mixed bundling. Suppose that the cost of producing the good is $1. Table 10.13 represents consumers' reservation prices for the first unit of the good and the second unit of the good. Consumers want (at most) two units of the good. Table 10.14 shows the case of separate pricing, and Table 10.15 shows the pure bundling strategy. Finally, Table 10.16 shows the best mixed bundling strategy.

FIGURE 10.7

Optimal Mixed Bundle Pricing in the Case of Uniformly Distributed Consumer Reservation Prices

The optimal mixed bundle pricing when the uniform distribution of consumer reservation prices is between $0 and $100 for both goods is $P_1 = \$66.67$, $P_2 = \$66.67$, and $P_{Bundle} = \$86.19$. Profit is $549,201.

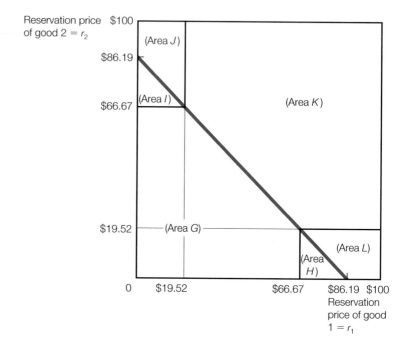

$10,000y - 200y^2 + 400xy + 0.5y^3 - 3x^2y - 200x^2 + 2x^3$. Total revenues are maximized where $\partial TR/\partial x = 0$ and $\partial TR/\partial y = 0$; $\partial TR/\partial x = 400y - 6xy - 400x + 6x^2 = 0$.

This yields $400x - 400y = 6x^2 - 6xy$ or $400(x - y) = 6x(x - y)$, or $6x = 400$, which yields $x = \$66.67$. $\partial TR/\partial y = 10,000 - 400y + 400x + 1.5y^2 - 3x^2 = 0$. Substituting $x = \$66.67$ into $\partial TR/\partial y$ yields $10,000 - 400y + 26,666.67 + 1.5y^2 - 13,333.33 = 1.5y^2 - 400y + 23,333.33 = 0$. Solving via the quadratic formula yields $y = \$86.19$. Substituting $y = \$86.19$ and $x = \$66.67$ into $TR = 10,000y - 200y^2 + 400xy + 0.5y^3 - 3x^2y - 200x^2 + 2x^3 = \$549,201$.

6. Bundling can also work if reservation prices are positively correlated. Consider the case where consumer A values good 1 at 11 and good 2 at 24, consumer B values good 1 at 15 and good 2 at 45, and consumer C values good 1 at 16 and good 2 at 15. The reservation prices are weakly positively correlated (0.037); that is, the slope of a linear regression is 0.214. The cost of good 1 is 5 and the cost of good 2 is 10. The best separate prices of $P_1 = 15$ and $P_2 = 45$ yield a profit of 55. The best pure bundle price is $P_B = 31$, yielding a profit of 48. But the best choice is a mixed bundle of $P_B = 60$, $P_1 = 16$, and not offering good 2 separately. Consumer B buys the bundle, consumer C buys good 1, and consumer A buys nothing. The profit is 56.

We give one final example of bundling to demonstrate how tricky calculating an optimal mixed bundle pricing package can be. The example demonstrates the point made previously about having to consider only customers' reservation prices as candidates for optimal separate prices and only the sum of customers' reservation prices as candidates for pure bundling. It also shows that in mixed bundling, the optimal prices need not be any customer's reservation price (or sum of reservation prices). And the consumer selects the good or bundle that leaves her with the greatest consumer surplus.

The complexity of solving for the optimal bundle is that managers have no $\Delta\pi/\Delta Q = 0$ formula to help derive the optimal pricing scheme. The procedure is more trial and error than derivation. The mixed bundle pricing package consists of prices for individual components and a single price for the product (or service) bundle. A manager can maximize profit even if the prices of the individual goods

TABLE 10.13

Reservation Prices for the First and Second Units of a Good by Consumers A and B

	Reservation Price of Good	
Consumer	First Unit	Second Unit
A	4	1.5
B	3.99	3

TABLE 10.14

Optimal Separate Prices for the Good

Price of Good	Cost/Unit	Profit/Unit	Number of Units	Profit
4	1	3	1	3
3.99	1	2.99	2	5.98
3	1	2	3	**6**
1.5	1	0.5	4	2

So the best separate price is $3, and the profit is $6.

TABLE 10.15

Optimal Pure Bundle Price for Two Units of the Same Good

Price of Bundle	Cost/Bundle	Profit/Bundle	Number of Bundles	Profit
5.5	2	3.5	2	**7**
5.99	2	4.99	1	4.99

So the best pure bundling strategy is a price of $5.5, and the profit is $7.

or the bundle are different from the reservation prices of consumers. This cannot be true when considering just separate pricing or pure bundling. Whether we deal with prices different than reservation prices or their sums depends on trade-offs from the consumers' view of consumer surplus and from the producers' view of producer surplus.

TABLE 10.16

Optimal Mixed Bundling Prices for the Case of a Single Good

Price of Bundle	Cost/Bundle	Profit/Bundle	Number of Bundles	Profit
6.99	2	4.99	1 (B)	4.99

Price of Good	Cost/Unit	Profit/Unit	Number of Units	Profit
4	1	3	1 (A)	3

So the best mixed bundle and the best overall pricing strategy are to price a unit of the good at $4 and a bundle of two goods at $6.99. This yields a profit of $7.99.

Consider the scenario in Table 10.17. There are three consumers (or consumer groups)—A, B, and C, for simplicity, with an equal number of consumers in each group, each wanting no more than one of each good at their reservation price or less—and two goods, X and Y. Both products cost a constant $4 to produce. The best separate prices are shown in boldface in Table 10.18. Therefore, the best separate pricing strategy is price X at $12 and price Y at $8, which yields a profit of $16. The best pure bundling price is shown in Table 10.19 in boldface. The best pure bundle price is $13.33, which yields a profit of $15.99.

Note the negative relationship (correlation) among the customer's reservation prices. Note also that in considering separate prices, you need never consider a nonreservation price as a pricing candidate. For instance, suppose you investigated pricing good X at $5. Two customers will purchase at that price (A and B who have reservation prices of $5.33 and $12, respectively). Your profit with such a price is ($5 − $4)2 = $2. But when you price at $5, you leave consumer surplus on the table. Consumer A is willing to pay $5.33, but you do not ask her to. As a result, you sacrifice $0.33 in profit (not only on customer A but also on customer B if you had offered good X at $5.33). By lowering your price to $5, you pick up no additional sales and sacrifice $0.66 in profit. If you do not charge the reservation prices of the customers, you cannot maximize profit using a separate price strategy. The same is true for pure bundling. Why shouldn't you consider pricing the bundle at $14.50 as one of your candidates? Because at $14.50 you get only customer B to buy the bundle, and she would have purchased the bundle at $15. You would leave consumer surplus on the table.

Consider now a mixed bundling strategy with a bundle price of $13.33, a price of good X at $10.32, and a price of good Y at $10.32. It first might appear that all customers would buy the bundle at $13.33 (because B gets consumer surplus

TABLE 10.17

Consumer Reservation Prices for Good X and Good Y (in Dollars)

| | Reservation Prices for Goods by Consumer | | |
	Good X	Good Y	Both X and Y
Consumer A	5.33	8	13.33
Consumer B	12	3	15
Consumer C	3	11	14

TABLE 10.18

Best Separate Price Strategy

	Cost/Unit	Profit/Unit	Number of Units	Profit
Price of X				
5.33	4	1.33	2	2.66
12.00	4	8.00	1	**8.00**
3.00	4	−1.00	3	−3.00
Price of Y				
8.00	4	4.00	2	**8.00**
3.00	4	−1.00	3	−3.00
11.00	4	7.00	1	7.00

TABLE 10.19

Best Pure Bundling Strategy

Price of Bundle	Cost/Bundle	Profit/Bundle	Number of Bundles	Profit
13.33	8	5.33	3	**15.99**
15.00	8	7.00	1	7.00
14.00	8	6.00	2	12.00

of $15 - $13.33 = $1.67 and C gets consumer surplus of $14 - $13.33 = $0.67). But if the price of X is $10.32, consumer B gets a higher consumer surplus of $12 - $10.32 = $1.68 > $1.67 if she buys good X alone; and if the price of good Y is $10.32, consumer C gets a higher consumer surplus of $11 - $10.32 = $0.68 > $0.67 if she buys good Y alone. But consumer B does not get to consume good Y if she does not buy the bundle, and consumer C does not get to consume good X if she does not buy the bundle—doesn't that count? Yes, but they are still better off with the larger consumer surplus from consuming just one good.

Suppose consumer B has $15. If she buys the bundle for $13.33, she will have consumer surplus of $1.67 and both goods. But if she buys just good X for $10.32, she will have good X and $4.68 left over. She has $1.68 in consumer surplus from good X; and although she does not have good Y, she has $4.68 in cash ($3 of which is not part of the consumer surplus from good X). But $4.68 in cash instead of good Y is attractive to consumer B because good Y is worth only $3 to her. (She has the equivalent of good Y with the $3 in cash that is not associated with the consumer surplus for good X; recall that the definition of reservation price is that a person is exactly indifferent between a good and the amount of the reservation price.) Therefore, $4.68 in cash and good X is a better position for consumer B than $1.67 in cash and both goods (which are worth only $4.67 to her). Analogously, consumer C, starting off with $14, is better off with $3.68 in cash and good Y rather than having $0.67 in cash and both goods (because good X is worth $3 to her).

How much profit do managers earn with such a mixed bundle? Table 10.20 demonstrates the profit improvement to $17.97. The profit of $17.97 dominates the profit of $16 available from the best separate pricing strategy and the profit of $15.99 available from the best pure bundling strategy. The secret is to see if we can pull customers out of the best pure bundling strategy and increase profit with a credible bundle. The best pure bundle yields $5.33 profit per customer. We retain that net profit for customer A and pull customers B and C out at higher profit margins, thus increasing the firm's profit. In the case of separate pricing, we need to ask whether we can put some customer(s) in a bundle and do better. We sacrifice profit margin from consumer B (down from $8 in the best separate price situation), but we more than make up that loss with the tremendous gain on consumers A and C, who were yielding only $4 each under the best separate pricing strategy. (We are down $1.68 from customer B but up $1.33 from customer A and up $2.32 from customer C; so we gain $1.97, the difference between the mixed bundle profit of $17.97 and the best separate price profit of $16.)

If we price good X at $10.34, customer B does not buy it (it yields a consumer surplus of only $12 - $10.34 = $1.66, and she can get $15 - $13.33 = $1.67 by buying the bundle). So pricing good X at $10.34 and the bundle at $13.33 is

TABLE 10.20

Best Mixed Bundling Strategy

Price of Bundle	Cost/Bundle	Profit on Each	Total Number	Total Profit
13.33	8	5.33	1 (consumer A)	5.33

Price of X	Cost/Unit	Profit/Unit	Total Number	Total Profit
10.32	4	6.32	1 (consumer B)	6.32

Price of Y	Cost/Unit	Profit/Unit	Total Number	Total Profit
10.32	4	6.32	1 (consumer C)	6.32
				Sum of Profit
				17.97

not a credible mixed bundle because someone you didn't want to buy the bundle (consumer B) does.

As you can see, mixed bundling need not charge the reservation prices of a consumer for the items. But we see a lot of mixed bundling in the market—so it is important to know that experimentation plays an important role and pure bundling and separate pricing are not always the best strategies.

WHEN TO UNBUNDLE

It is important to remember that the concept of bundling entails a null case of pricing the bundled goods (services) separately. Just because bundling is the optimal pricing strategy at time t does not mean it is the optimal pricing strategy at time $t + 1$. Managers must reassess their markets periodically to see if changed conditions warrant new prices, including an unbundling of commodities.

Table 10.21 shows the reservation prices of consumers A, B, and C for goods X and Y at time t. Consumers want, at most, one of each good. The unit cost of each good is 3, and a bundle of the two goods costs the producer 6. The reservation price of a consumer for a bundle of the goods is the sum of his reservation prices for the goods. The producer cannot price discriminate.

The optimal (profit-maximizing) strategy for the producer under these conditions is to price good X at $P_X = 8.32$, price the bundle at $P_B = 10.33$, and not offer good Y separately. This policy yields a profit of 13.98. The best pure bundle

TABLE 10.21

The Reservation Prices for Consumers A, B, and C for Good X, Good Y, and a Bundle of Good X and Good Y

	Reservation Price		
	Good X	Good Y	Bundle of Good X and Good Y
Consumer A	5	5.33	10.33
Consumer B	3	10	13
Consumer C	9	2	11

would be to offer the bundle at $P_B = 10.33$, yielding a profit of 12.99. The best separate price policy would be $P_X = 9$ and $P_Y = 10$, yielding a profit of 13.

Figure 10.8 shows the best mixed bundling policy versus the best pure bundle and best separate price policies and the use of the method of "crow's feet"[7] to solve the bundling problem.

Pure bundling at $P_B = 10.33$ gives the lowest profit of the three types of pricing at 12.99. Each consumer contributes 4.33 ($= 10.33 - 6$) to the profit. If managers want to pull consumer B out of the bundle by a separate price policy, they will have to offer B a greater consumer surplus than she receives from the bundle (she currently gets 2.67 $= 13 - 10.33$) and so must offer more than 2.67 to pull consumer B from the bundle—this is shown as length b in Figure 10.8). Only good Y is at play here because consumer B is willing to pay the MC only for good X (so managers can't reduce the price and make a profit). Because B will pay 10 for good Y, if managers reduce the price of good Y to $10 - 2.67^+ = 7.33^-$, consumer B will have consumer surplus of $10 - 7.33^- = 2.67^+$; this beats the consumer surplus from the bundle, so she will defect from the bundle. However, this means the profit from consumer B falls to $7.33^- - 3 = 4.33^-$, which is less than before (and without changing consumers A and C's behavior and hence their profit contribution). Thus, managers should not want to pull consumer B from the bundle.

If managers want to pull consumer C out of the bundle by a separate price policy, they will have to offer C a greater consumer surplus than he receives from the bundle (he currently gets 0.67 $= 11 - 10.33$) and so must offer more than 0.67 to pull consumer C from the bundle (this is shown as length c in Figure 10.8). Only good X is in play here because consumer C is not willing to pay the MC for good Y. Because C will pay 9 for good X, if managers reduce the price of good X to $9 - 0.67^+ = 8.33^-$, consumer C will have consumer surplus of $9 - 8.33^- = 0.67^+$; this beats the consumer surplus from the bundle, so he will defect from the bundle. This means the profit from consumer C increases to $8.33^- - 3 = 5.33^-$, which is more (by 0.99^+) than before (and without changing

7. Our former Wharton colleague Matt White introduced us to the "crow's feet" method.

FIGURE 10.8

Depiction of Bundling Problem in Table 10.21

The bundling problem is solved by analyzing the "crow's feet" (the large blue lines) in this figure. The "crow's feet" method is extended when the reservation price of consumer B for good Y increases from 10 to 11.

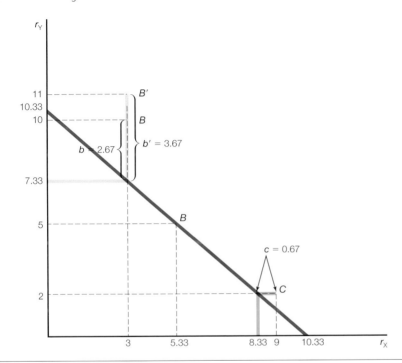

consumers A and B's behavior and hence their profit contribution). Thus managers do want to pull consumer C from the bundle.

Pulling consumer A from the bundle lowers profits from A and also from the other consumers. To pull A from the bundle, suppose P_X is dropped to 5^- and P_Y is dropped to 5.33^- A will buy each good separately, but profit from A drops to $5^- - 3 + 5.33^- - 3 = 4.33^{--}$ (less than before). In addition, consumer B will defect from the bundle (now getting a $10 - 5.33^- = 4.67^+$ consumer surplus from good Y), and consumer C will defect from the bundle (now getting a $9 - 5^- = 4^+$ consumer surplus from good X). Profit from B falls to $5.33^- - 3 = 2.33^-$ (much less than in the bundle), and profit from C falls to $5^- - 3 = 2^-$ (much less than in the bundle). Thus the mixed bundle is much better than the pure bundle priced at $P_B = 10.33$.

How about the separate price solution versus the mixed bundle? Consumer A purchases nothing under the optimal separate price solution of $P_X = 9$ and $P_Y = 10$ and hence contributes nothing to profit. Pulling her into a bundle at

10.33 will increase profit from zero to 4.33. Consumer B buying good Y at 10 contributes 7 to profit, and consumer C buying good X at 9 contributes 6 to profit Figure 10.8 shows that bringing consumer B into the bundle will cause B to contribute 2.67 (length b) less in profit than before ($10.33 - 6 = 4.33$ versus $10 - 3 = 7$). Pricing good X at 8.33^- will keep consumer C from joining the bundle (which he will do if the price of X remains at 9). This decreases the profit from consumer C by 0.67^+, shown as length c in Figure 10.8 ($8.33^- - 3 = 5.33^-$ versus $9 - 3 = 6$). But on net, where does it leave total profit? The mixed bundle increases profit from A by 4.33, decreases the profit from B by 2.67, and decreases the profit from C by 0.67^+ for a net increase in profit of $4.33 - 2.67 - 0.67^+ = 0.99^-$.

Thus Figure 10.8 shows the optimality of the mixed bundle pricing policy of $P_B = 10.33$, $P_X = 8.33^-$, and not offering good Y separately over the best pure bundle strategy of $P_B = 10.33$ and the best separate price strategy of $P_X = 9$ and $P_Y = 10$. Note that the verbal explanation here is shown by the "crow's feet" (the large red and blue lines radiating from the $P_{\text{Bundle}} = 10.33$ line in Figure 10.8).

Suppose demand conditions change. In particular, suppose consumer B's reservation price for good Y increases from 10 to 11 as shown in Figure 10.8 (with the consumer's new position shown as B'). Note that B's reservation price for the bundle has now increased to 14 ($3 + 11$).

If consumer B buys the bundle at 10.33, she gets a consumer surplus of $3.67 (= 14 - 10.33)$ and contributes a profit of $4.33 (= 10.33 - 6)$. However, if managers do not offer the bundle, they will make $8 (= 11 - 3)$ from consumer B by charging B's reservation price for good Y. At the same time, charging consumer C his reservation price of 9 for good X yields a profit of $6 (= 9 - 3)$ from consumer C. Consumer A will buy neither good and hence contributes nothing to profit. However, total profit is now $14 (= 8 + 6)$, which exceeds the profit of pure bundling at $P_B = 10.33$ of 12.99 and the profit of mixed bundling at $P_B = 10.33$ $P_X = 8.33^-$, and not offering good Y separately of 13.99^-. In fact, an increase in consumer B's reservation price for good Y to 10.98^+ will make the unbundling policy the most profitable.

When consumer B was at point B (not B'), the separate price profit was $13.99^- - 13 = 0.99^-$ behind the optimal (mixed bundling) pricing policy. Raising the reservation price of good Y for consumer B by 1 enables managers to profitably change their pricing policy. Again, note that the "crow's feet" tell the same story.

Here's another case where managers will want to unbundle. If consumer C's good X reservation price increases to 10 (and all other consumers' reservation prices remain the same), managers could also unbundle and sell both good X and good Y each at 10 and earn $14 (= 10 - 3 + 10 - 3)$. In fact, any combination of increases in B's reservation price for good Y and C's reservation price for good X greater than 0.98 should cause managers to unbundle the products and just sell each good separately.

Consider the new scenario where B's reservation price for good Y is 11. Suppose a bundle price of 10.33. If consumer B buys the bundle, she receives a consumer surplus of 3.67 ($= 3 + 11 - 10.33$) and yields a profit of 4.33 ($= 10.33 - 6$). To pull B out of the bundle, she'd have to be offered a consumer surplus greater than 3.67. This would entail offering good Y at a price of less than 7.33 (say 7.33^-). Such a price would yield a profit from consumer B of less than the 4.33 available from selling B the bundle at 10.33 ($7.33^- - 3 = 4.33^-$). No other consumption would be affected by dropping the price of good Y to 7.33^-, and profit is reduced by this move.

By taking away the option of the bundle from the mixed bundling scenario and just charging $P_X = 9$ and $P_Y = 11$, Figure 10.8 shows the gain in profit. For B, who bought the bundle when it was available, profit increases from 4.33 ($= 10.33 - 6$) to 8 ($= 11 - 3$) or by 3.67 ($= 8 - 4.33$) or by b' in Figure 10.8. Individual C now buys just good X for 9, yielding a profit of 6 ($= 9 - 3$), whereas under mixed bundling, he bought just good X at 8.33^-, yielding a profit of 5.33^- ($= 8.33^- - 3$). Profit from C has thus increased by 0.67^+ ($= 6 - 5.33^-$) or by c in Figure 10.8. Without the bundle available, A consumes neither good and hence the profit of 4.33 ($= 10.33 - 6$) she contributed to the firm under the mixed bundle has been lost. But the combined increase in profit from B and C of 4.34^+ ($= 3.67 + 0.67^+$) exceeds the loss in profit from A of 4.33, yielding a net gain of 0.01^+ ($= 4.34^+ - 4.33$). This is shown by the difference in the separate price profit of 14 and the mixed bundling profit of 13.99^-.

So although some form of bundling (pure or mixed) will many times increase a firm's profit, unbundling can also increase profit. It all depends on the reservation prices and the costs of production. The diagrammatic technique shows how to measure the conditions under which managers can profitably change prices.

BUNDLING AS A PREEMPTIVE ENTRY STRATEGY

In addition to being a strategy to enhance profits, bundling is also used to deter entry by potential rivals. Suppose managers at the Alpha Company have developed a bundle made up of product W and product S, which they plan to sell for $\$X$. The question for us to answer is this: What is X?

The Beta Company is developing a product (C) that is a close substitute to W. The Gamma Company is developing a product (N) that is a close substitute to S. Managers at both Beta and Gamma want to bring their products to market. Only Alpha has the financial ability to produce both products as a bundle. Alpha's entry cost to the market is 30. It would cost Beta 17 to enter the market, and it would cost Gamma 17 to enter the market. If Alpha managers were to produce each product separately, it would cost them 15 to enter each market. In all cases, these entry costs are independent of the number of units sold. Note that Alpha's entry costs are 15 for each product regardless of whether the product is sold separately or is included in a bundle.

The market for the services provided by W and C, by S and N, and for a bundle that provides both services is presented in Table 10.22. Suppose consumers regard Beta's product C as comparable to Alpha's product W and regard Gamma's product N as comparable to Alpha's product S. Consumers also regard making their own bundle (buying Beta's C and buying Gamma's N) as comparable to Alpha's bundle of W and S. The numbers in the table are the consumers' reservation prices for each product. It costs each producer 2 to distribute each product (and hence it costs Alpha 4 to distribute its bundle).

For simplicity, assume there is one of each consumer type and the table represents the long-run demand for the products. Consumers want, at most, one of each product. The companies cannot form joint ventures. The consumers' reservation prices are shown in Table 10.22.

The goods are perfectly negatively correlated. Normally this suggests a pure bundle strategy. Indeed, if Alpha is the only participant in this market, the pure bundling strategy (with a bundle price of 30) yields all consumers purchasing and a net revenue exclusive of entry costs of $(30 \times 3) - (4 \times 3) = 78$. Alpha's entry costs are 30, yielding a profit of 48. This vastly exceeds the best separate price strategy of $P_W = P_S = 15$, which yields a profit of $(15 \times 4) - (2 \times 4) - (15 \times 2) = 22$, or the mixed bundling strategy of the bundle priced at 30 and $P_W = P_N = 20$, which yields a profit of $[(30 - 4) \times 1] + [(20 - 2) \times 2] - (15 \times 2) = 32$.

But if Alpha faces the entry threat from Beta and Gamma, it cannot price the bundle at 30. If it does, Beta could enter and sell C for as little as $(23/3)$ and make money. Likewise, Gamma could enter and sell N for as little as $(23/3)$ and make money. If both Beta and Gamma priced at $(23/3)$, all three consumers

---

TABLE 10.22

The Reservation Prices for Consumers A, B, and C for Good W or C, Good S or N, and a Bundle of Good W and Good S or a Bundle of Good C and Good N

Consumer Class	Reservation Price for Product W or C	Reservation Price for Product S or N	Reservation Price for bundle W and S or C and N
A	10	20	30
B	15	15	30
C	20	10	30

STRATEGY SESSION: How *The New Yorker* Used Bundling

The New Yorker is a wonderfully written magazine with witty, informative, entertaining articles. But apparently the market for high-quality journalism has fallen on hard times as consumers have switched their cultural and media preferences.

Magazines depend on subscriptions and newsstand sales and, most of all, advertising for their revenues. And advertising revenues depend on the number of magazines sold because advertisers pay more if the circulation to their demographic group is higher.

Over the years, circulation and advertising revenues fell. It appeared that *The New Yorker* could

not cover its costs with its revenues. Thus *The New Yorker's* publisher (Conde Nast) came up with a bundling strategy. Conde Nast also publishes *Architectural Digest* and *Vanity Fair* (which are doing well). The bundling strategy? If a company wanted to advertise in *Architectural Digest* or *Vanity Fair*, it also had to advertise in *The New Yorker*. This proved to be a profitable strategy, and *The New Yorker* is still publishing.

Source: "There's Less Buzz and Less Lunch at *The New Yorker*," *New York Times*, Monday, June 28, 1999.

would purchase C from Beta, giving Beta revenue of 23. Beta's entry cost is 17, and its cost of distributing C to the consumers would be $2 \times 3 = 6$ for a total cost of 23. The same would hold for Gamma. Both Beta and Gamma would be earning a normal profit (and zero excess profit).

If Alpha prices the bundle at slightly less than $(46/3)$, say at $(46^-/3)$, then neither Beta or Gamma can enter the market because neither can cover the $(23/3)$ cost. How will Alpha do? All three consumers will purchase Alpha's bundle at $(46^-/3)$, yielding Alpha revenue of 46^-. Alpha's cost of entry would be $15 \times 2 = 30$, and the cost of distributing the three bundles would be $4 \times 3 = 12$ for a total cost of 42. Profit would be $46^- - 42 = 4^-$. This is a far cry from 48. But it does leave Alpha as the sole producer.

The threat of entry can significantly reduce monopoly profit. But at the same time the use of bundling can preclude entry and keep a profitable market for the bundler.

Despite the lack of a rigorous analytical solution, following a few simple guidelines will help managers construct more effective bundling policies:

1. If goods' reservation prices are positively correlated, pure bundling can do no better than separate pricing (but mixed bundles might).

2. If the marginal cost of producing a good exceeds its reservation price, in general you should think carefully about selling it.[8]

8. Sometimes it may be more profitable to sell a good in a pure bundle even though the reservation price of a bundle buyer for a good in the bundle is less than the cost of producing the good. Consider a firm choosing between only separate pricing and pure bundling. The reservation prices for good 1 and good 2 for consumers A through F are ($70, $30), ($80, $20), ($75, $25), ($75, $15), ($84, $16), and ($90, $10), respectively. The unit cost of production of good 1 is $70 and of good 2 is $20. The optimal separate prices are $P_1 = $80 and P_2 either $30 or $25, yielding a profit of $40. The optimal pure bundling price of $100 yields a profit of $50. Consumers E and F, who buy the bundle, value good 2 at less than its cost and are not excluded because that would decrease the firm's profit. If mixed bundling is allowed, the exclusion problem can be solved. The bundle would be priced at $100, and good 1 would be priced at $83.99. This yields a profit of $57.98, and E and F consume only the good (good 1) they value at greater than cost.

STRATEGY SESSION: When to Unbundle

In July 2011, managers of Netflix unbundled its streaming DVD and its mail DVD plans into two separate product lines, that are priced separately. Previously, the products were only sold as a pure bundle for $9.99/month. Now each product would cost $7.99/month; in other words, making your own bundle cost $15.98.

Initial reaction of Netflix customers seemed to be overwhelmingly negative, with an unscientific survey in *USA Today* claiming that 74% would switch away from Netflix. Netflix managers were stunned by the negative reaction. They claimed to have thought carefully prior to their decision.

Let's use the techniques in the text to see what must be going on to make this a viable strategy for managers. We'll concentrate just on the revenue implications first and then make some cost assumptions. The diagram on the next page shows the price separately and the pure bundling situations.

Under the pure bundling pricing, consumers in areas B, C, D, and E will buy the bundle. Assume there are A consumers in area A, B consumers in area B, and so on. Thus, total revenue from the previous pricing policy is

$$(X) \quad \$9.99B + \$9.99C + \$9.99D + \$9.99E$$

Under the price separately policy, consumers in areas A, B, and C will buy the streaming DVDs and consumers in areas C, E, and F will buy the mail DVDs. Thus, total revenue from pricing separately is

$$(Y) \quad \$7.99A + \$7.99B + \$15.98C$$
$$+ \$7.99E + \$7.99F$$

From a revenue standpoint, Netflix managers chose the correct strategy if $(Y) > (X)$ or

$$\$7.99A + \$7.99B + \$15.98C + \$7.99E + \$7.99F$$
$$> \$9.99B + \$9.99C + \$9.99D + \$9.99E$$

Or $(Z) \quad \$7.99A + \$5.99C + \$7.99F$
$$> \$2B + \$9.99D + \$2E$$

The marginal cost of serving the streaming DVDs is very low. The cost of serving the mail DVDs is higher because of postage and handling. The A demanders never consume mail DVDs, so their impact in (Z) is strictly on the profit side (assuming the marginal cost of serving them is approximately zero). The F customers are new to Netflix, so their net contribution is positive (assuming the $7.99 they pay exceeds the mailing and handling cost). The costs of handling the C customers is the same as before, so the C above represents a profit gain. Thus, the left-hand side of (Z) must only be reduced by the cost of serving the new F customers to change it from a revenue stream to a profit stream. The B, D, and E customers all previously consumed the bundle. Some probably only streamed (most likely the Bs) and some probably only mailed (most likely the Es). To change the left-hand side of (Z) from a revenue stream to a profit stream, we'd have to subtract out the costs of serving the Bs, Ds, and Es.

3. If goods' reservation prices are correlated *perfectly* negatively and the marginal cost of production of the goods is zero, pure bundling is best.

4. If goods' reservation prices are negatively correlated, as the marginal cost of production increases, mixed bundling is likely to be better than pure bundling; and as it increases further, separate pricing is likely to be better.

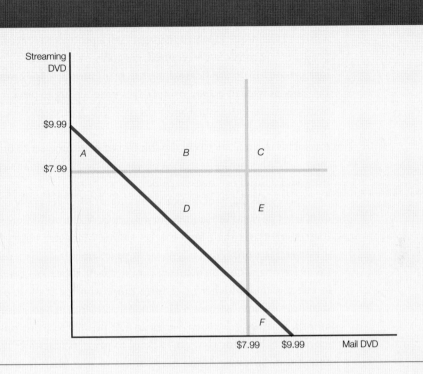

Thus, whether this was a good move or not depends on the number of demanders in each area and the cost of serving them. This is what Netflix managers should have considered in reaching their decision.

Whether they did or not we do not know. We do know managers were forced to publicly reverse the unbundling strategy three months later in October due to a serious drop in demand. Most customers saw the unbundling as a 60% price hike. Even though Reed Hastings, the CEO of Netflix publicly declared the price hike was necessary, the significant drop in demand forced him to rescind it.

Sources: Tiernan Ray, "Netflix Splits Streaming, DVD Plans, $15.98 for Both," *Tech Trader Daily*, July 12, 2011, at http://blogs.barrons.com/techtraderdaily/2011/07/12/netflix-splits-streaming-dvd-plans-15-98-for-both/; Troy Wolverton, "Netflix Reverses Decision to Split Its Video Streaming and DVD Services," *The Mercury News*, October 11, 2011.

But everything really depends on the reservation prices and the costs of production, so remember that intelligent experimentation is the way to solve bundling pricing. The other approach, especially when the demanders or goods are many, is to use a computer program to search all three types of pricing and every price in each type for the profit-maximizing result.

TYING AT IBM, XEROX, AND MICROSOFT

Tying A pricing technique in which managers sell a product that needs a complementary product.

One form of bundling involving complementary products is called **tying**. Tying is a pricing technique in which managers sell a product that needs a complementary product. The consumer is required, generally by contract, to buy the complementary product from the firm selling the main product. For example, an individual can only download a song from iTunes onto an Apple product. Both the United States and the European Union charged that Microsoft uses a tying strategy to force consumers to use its browser product (Internet Explorer) instead of a rival product (Firefox). Microsoft did this by tying the browser to the Windows operating system, then using its market power to force PC manufacturers to package only Internet Explorer on their machines.

Successful implementation of a tying strategy generally requires the exercise of market power. For example, managers of Apple and Microsoft largely control their markets via their high market shares. Managers engage in tying practices for several reasons. First, it is a way of practicing price discrimination. By setting the price of the complementary product well above its cost, managers can get, in effect, a much higher price from those who use it more often. For example, suppose customer A uses a Hewlett-Packard printer to print 10,000 pages per month, whereas customer B uses an HP printer to print only 1,000 pages per month. It is hard for Hewlett-Packard to price its machines to obtain more revenue from customer A, the more intensive user, than from customer B. But if HP can tie the sale of ink cartridges to the sale of its printer, it can get more profit from customer A than from customer B because it makes more on selling cartridges.

Tying has been challenged as a legal business strategy. Until recently, tying was viewed as per se illegal in most U.S. courts. However, recent decisions suggest judges are recognizing the efficiencies generated by the strategy.

For example, tying can lower transaction costs. Most buyers prefer to purchase a "complete" automobile with all necessary equipment such as tires, engine, and seats. Tying is also used to protect product integrity. Managers are able to control quality levels across product components.

Another reason managers use a tying strategy is to maintain their monopoly position. For example, Microsoft has held a market share of over 90% in the PC operating system market since 1991. Even a competitor the size of IBM was forced to quickly withdraw from this market after spending hundreds of millions of dollars on the OS/2 operating system. Netscape was a concern for Microsoft because its product threatened to reduce the number of application programs written for Windows. So Microsoft wanted to exclude Netscape's product. When asked the following question by a government lawyer, a Microsoft executive agreed with the lawyer's assessment:

STRATEGY SESSION: Which is More Expensive: Printers or Ink?

When printers first hit the market, they were expensive. But as more companies produced printers, the price fell. The printer is a one-time expense (for the life of the printer), but the ink cartridges run out of ink and must be replaced. For heavy users, this occurs a lot. So why not entice customers to buy your printer by offering a low price for it, and then after having locked them in, sock it to them by charging high prices for the replacement cartridges, which only work in your printer? This method has been used to sell razors (cheap razor, expensive blades). Well, why wouldn't the customer just refill an empty cartridge with ink? The companies were putting a chip in the cartridges to prevent this, until environmental laws forced recycling of cartridges. Why not use an off-brand cartridge that was engineered for your printer? Because you may be afraid of the off-brand's quality, and you may void the warranty on your printer if you don't use a manufacturer-made cartridge. Hewlett-Packard, with a 40% share of the global market for color printers, had mastered making money from cartridges. One student claims to have bought a new printer when his printer ran out of ink because it was cheaper than buying a new cartridge.

Now Kodak is trying to change all this by introducing an ink-jet printer that costs $50 more than the competitors' printers but uses ink that is much cheaper than the competitors' ink. Xerox has introduced a color printer that costs $900 more than the competition but will produce color pages at the same cost as black and white.

Some experts say that the buyers want low-cost hardware (printers) and control costs by controlling the amount of printing done. Kodak feels that people will print more if the cost of ink comes down and reports that its customers are buying nine cartridges per year, while the industry average is four per year. Kodak said that it listened to its customers, who said that high ink costs caused them to limit printing. This may not be good news for trees, but users seem to be happy. A real estate agency that spent $1 million per year on color printing now reports printing expenses of $200,000.

Source: Claudia H. Deutsch, "In a Switch, Charging More for Printers and Less for Ink," *New York Times*, September 24, 2007, at http://www.nytimes.com/2007/09/24/technology.

And all I am trying to establish is that the reason for that [packaging Internet browser with Windows] was because you believed that if the customer had a choice of the two browsers side by side, the user would, in the vast majority of cases or in the majority of cases, pick Netscape for the reasons that you've identified, correct?[9]

This belief was reiterated in an internal Microsoft e-mail presented at the trial:

It seems clear that it will be very hard to increase browser share on the merits of Internet Explorer alone. It will be more important to leverage

9. From September 21, 1999, trial transcript.

the OS asset to make people—to make people choose Explorer instead of Navigator.[10]

In addition, managers may use a tying strategy to ensure the firm's product works properly and its brand name is protected. To do so, the firm insists that customers use its complementary product. For example, Jerrold Electronics Corporation, which installed community antenna systems, required customers to accept five-year maintenance contracts to avoid breakdowns resulting from improper servicing of its equipment. And McDonald's franchises must buy their materials and food from McDonald's so that the hamburgers are uniform and the company's brand name is not tarnished.

TRANSFER PRICING

In some cases, transactions occur where markets do not exist; many times they involve intrafirm pricing. Say there are two divisions of a firm, where a product required as an input is produced exclusively in an upstream plant for use in a product of a downstream plant. Transfer pricing results from creating an internal market that simulates an external one and allows optimal profit-maximizing decisions by managers in both divisions of the firm. For instance, auto companies purchase inputs from their components' divisions so they can produce automobiles. When an external market exists for the product of the upstream division, the rules for the optimal transfer price determination differ because now the upstream division has the option of selling the product in the external market and the downstream division has the option of purchasing the upstream product in the external market.

Transfer pricing is prevalent. *A recent survey shows that managers in 91% of the Fortune 150 practice transfer pricing and that in one-third of the firms, managers engage in four or more instances per year of intrafirm transactions.*

Consider a multidivisional firm with a downstream monopoly and an upstream provider of a component to the downstream product, such as an engine maker serving a downstream automaker. We assume initially there is no external market for engines; that is, no other engine maker can supply engines to the downstream automaker, nor can any other automaker use the engines of the upstream engine maker. Therefore, managers must decide how many engines and autos to make (these are the same because there is no external market for engines).[11] The downstream operation is subject to the discipline of the market because autos are sold in an external market. But if there is no external market for the upstream product, what price should change hands between the two divisions to pay for the upstream product? This payment, called a **transfer price**, simulates a market where no formal market exists.

Transfer price Payment that simulates a market where no formal market exists.

10. Ibid.
11. For simplicity, we assume that all the upstream product produced during the period must be sold then. In other words, no inventories of the upstream product can be carried over.

In considering transfer pricing policies, managers need to ensure the profit-maximizing (from the point of view of the entire firm) output of the downstream and the upstream output is produced. Then they must ensure the upstream managers have the right incentive to produce the profit-maximizing amount of the upstream product in the most efficient way.

The following notation enables us to view the transfer pricing issues facing managers. The demand curve for the downstream product is

$$P_D = P_D(Q_D)$$

where P_D is the price of the downstream product per unit, Q_D is in units of the downstream product, and the parentheses mean "function of" in this and the next equation. Recall that the impacts of complementary and substitute goods on this demand are subsumed in the intercept of the demand curve, as shown in Chapter 2.

The production function[12] of the downstream operation is defined as

$$Q_D = f(L_D, K_D | Q_U)$$

The production function is like those of Chapter 5, but it is conditional; that is, it states that Q_D can be produced with labor (L_D) and capital (K_D) *given* the critical upstream input Q_U.

This production function yields a downstream cost function of

$$TC_D = TC_D(Q_D | Q_U)$$

which is the total cost of the downstream division *exclusive* of the cost of the upstream operation.

Finally, the total cost of the upstream division is just a function of Q_U; it reads

$$TC_U = TC_U(Q_U)$$

and is typical of the cost functions we developed in Chapter 6.

The profit of the multidivisional firm is

$$\pi = TR_D - TC_D - TC_U \tag{10.1}$$

To maximize profit, we must have $\Delta\pi/\Delta Q_U = 0$. Note that Q_U is the variable that controls what managers do. Without the critical input produced by the upstream division, nothing can be produced in the downstream division. And whatever is produced upstream equals the amount produced downstream; that is, $Q_D = Q_U$ when transfer pricing is done correctly. Although we might be tempted to put a total revenue for the upstream division in equation (10.1) ($TR_U = P_U Q_U$, where P_U would be the transfer price), it would be exactly offset by a cost item for the downstream firm (recall that TC_D is the downstream cost *exclusive* of the cost of the upstream product). Because this nets out to zero, it is not included in equation (10.1).

12. The | is not a division sign in this equation or the next one; rather, it reminds us that the functions are conditional on the amount of Q_U.

If we make the left side of equation (10.1) $\Delta\pi/\Delta Q_U = 0$, we must make the following adjustments to the right side of equation (10.1)

$$\frac{\Delta\pi}{\Delta Q_U} = \left(\frac{\Delta TR_D}{\Delta Q_D}\right)\left(\frac{\Delta Q_D}{\Delta Q_U}\right) - \left(\frac{\Delta TC_D}{\Delta Q_D}\right)\left(\frac{\Delta Q_D}{\Delta Q_U}\right) - \frac{\Delta TC_U}{\Delta Q_U} = 0$$

or

$$\left[\left(\frac{\Delta TR_D}{\Delta Q_D}\right) - \left(\frac{\Delta TC_D}{\Delta Q_D}\right)\right]\left(\frac{\Delta Q_D}{\Delta Q_U}\right) = \left(\frac{\Delta TC_U}{\Delta Q_U}\right)$$ (10.2)

or

$$(MR_D - MC_D)MP_U = MC_U$$ (10.3)

QUANT OPTION

Setting $\partial\pi/\partial Q_U = 0$ will maximize the firm's profit. Thus,

$$\partial\pi/\partial Q_U = (\partial TR_D/\partial Q_D)(\partial Q_D/\partial Q_U) - (\partial TC_D/\partial Q_D)(\partial Q_D/\partial Q_U) - dTC_U/dQ_U = 0$$

or

$$[(\partial TR_D/\partial Q_D) - (\partial TC_D/\partial Q_D)](\partial Q_D/\partial Q_U) = (dTC_U/dQ_U)$$

or

$$(MR_D - MC_D)MP_U = MC_U$$

Note that $(\partial Q_D/\partial Q_U)$ is the marginal product of the upstream product.

Note that $(\Delta Q_D/\Delta Q_U)$ is the marginal product of the upstream product in producing the downstream product.

The intuition of equation (10.3) is straightforward. If managers produce another unit in the upstream operation, they incur an additional cost, MC_U. Producing that additional upstream product enables the conglomerate to produce MP_U more downstream units. Each additional downstream unit produced causes managers to incur additional cost in the downstream plant (MC_D) but also enables them to earn additional revenue (MR_D). If the additional net revenue earned, $(MR_D - MC_D)MP_U$, which is produced as a result of incurring the additional cost upstream, MC_U, exceeds that additional upstream cost, then managers want to produce the additional unit upstream (because profit increases). If it does not, managers do not want to produce the additional unit upstream (because profit decreases). Managers maximize profit when the additional net revenue earned downstream as a result of producing an additional unit upstream just equals the additional cost incurred in producing that unit upstream.

But MP_U equals 1 because every time one more unit is produced upstream, one more unit can be produced downstream. In situations where it would appear that the upstream firm has to produce multiple units to enable one additional unit to be produced downstream, such as four tires being required to produce one car, we treat this by requiring one bundle (of four tires) to be produced upstream in order to produce one car. Obviously the situation can also go the other way—such as one extra steer on an upstream cattle ranch enabling the downstream meat processing division to produce $X(>1)$ steaks. Here producing one more steer lets the conglomerate firm produce one more bundle of (X) steaks.

In the situation when $MP_U = 1$, equation (10.3) becomes

$$MR_D - MC_D = MC_U$$

or

$$MR_D = MC_D + MC_U \qquad (10.4)$$

and the rule becomes our familiar one: The marginal revenue of the product must equal the marginal cost of producing it. That is, the marginal cost of producing the downstream product is the marginal cost of the downstream operation (remember that this excludes the cost of the upstream operation) plus the marginal cost of the upstream product.

Solving equation (10.4) for $Q_U^* = Q_D^* = Q^*$ gives the correct amount of the upstream product and downstream product produced.

Now suppose managers set the transfer price the downstream division pays and the upstream division receives for its upstream product. They tell the upstream division chief that she will receive P_U for every unit she produces. A profit-maximizing division chief (who is now a price taker) maximizes profit by setting $P_U = MC_U$, as was shown in Chapter 7. But what P_U should managers choose? Clearly it is the P_U that results in Q_U^* units being produced. This is shown in Figure 10.9.

What difference does it make what P_U managers choose? Whatever it is, would it not merely cause the upstream division to have $P_U Q_U^*$ in revenues and the downstream division to have $P_U Q_U^*$ in costs? The two terms merely cancel each other out (which is why we left them out of equation (10.1)). From the point of view of the conglomerate, profit is the same. However, *the profit of each division differs.* And because managers' bonuses are often predicated on their division's profit, these managers care about that transfer price. If the conglomerate's managers determine the optimal Q (that is, Q^*) and order both divisions to produce it, then the conglomerate maximizes profit regardless of the transfer price.

But if the managers are trying to maximize firm profit, it is critical that the correct P_U be chosen. If P_U is set too high, the upstream division will produce

FIGURE 10.9

Determination of the Transfer Price, Given No External Market for the Transferred Good

The optimal transfer price, P_U, equals the marginal cost at the optimal output, Q^*.

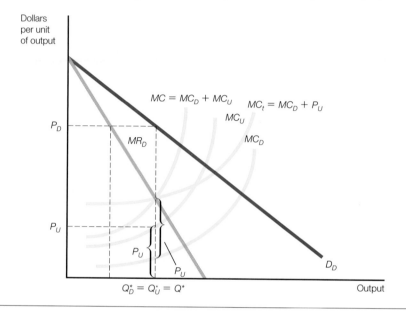

too much of the product (recall that in price-taking situations, the marginal cost is rising). Also, managers of the downstream division will see its marginal cost of producing another unit ($MC_D + P_U = MC_t$) as too high and therefore will produce too little downstream output. Therefore, profit will not be maximized. If P_U is set too low, managers of the downstream division will see their marginal cost of producing another unit as too low and will therefore want to produce more than the optimal output (which they cannot do because the upstream division has produced less of its output).

TRANSFER PRICING: A PERFECTLY COMPETITIVE MARKET FOR THE UPSTREAM PRODUCT

In many cases there is a market outside the firm for the product transferred from one division to the other. If this is true, the output levels of the downstream and upstream divisions no longer need be equal. If the downstream division wants more of the upstream product than is produced by the upstream division, it can buy some from external suppliers. If the upstream division produces more of its product than the downstream division wants, it can sell some to external custom-ers. Assuming the market for the upstream product is perfectly competitive, we can readily determine how managers should set the transfer price.

Figure 10.10 shows the optimal price and output for the firm as a whole. Because there is a perfectly competitive market for the upstream product, managers at the upstream division act as if they see a horizontal demand curve, D_U, where the price is P_U, the price of the upstream product in the external market. To maximize profit, managers at the upstream division should produce the output Q_U, where the marginal cost of the upstream division, MC_U, equals the *externally* determined market price P_U. In this sense the upstream division behaves like a perfectly competitive firm.

To maximize the firm's overall profit, the transfer price should equal P_U, the price of the upstream division in the perfectly competitive market outside the firm. Because managers at the upstream division can sell as much product as they want to external customers at a price of P_U, they have no incentive to sell it at a price below P_U to the downstream division. Similarly, because managers at the downstream division can buy as much of the upstream product as they want from external suppliers at a price of P_U, they have no incentive to buy it from the upstream division at a price above P_U.

FIGURE 10.10

Determination of the Transfer Price, Given a Perfectly Competitive External Market for the Transferred Product

The optimal transfer price, P_U, equals the market price of the transferred product.

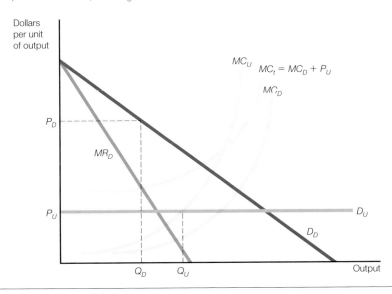

STRATEGY SESSION: Transfer Pricing in Practice

Transfer pricing plays two different roles for managers. One is the proper allocation of resources within a conglomerate business when goods or services are transferred from one division of the conglomerate to another. Since we view prices as a signal to managers as part of the process of how much to produce and how to produce it, we should want those signals to the division managers to be such that the overall profit of the conglomerate is maximized.

With that in mind, Michalski, Bunger, and Stiller investigated the role of transfer prices in a cradle-to-grave analysis from producing hydrogen for fueling automobiles to the retail outlet that would dispense the fuel to automobiles. Unless the process was treated as one system, suboptimal transfer prices at the various handoffs of product through the production and distribution phases would impact the profitability of the whole process (and the profitability of any constituent part). This is not surprising given the analysis in the text.

The other role is in tax policy. On January 20, 2011, Ernst & Young issued its *2010 Global Transfer Pricing Survey: Addressing the Challenges of Globalization*. The main finding from surveying 877 multinational enterprises in 25 countries was that transfer pricing remains the number one challenge for these leading companies. Governments, facing record deficits, are stepping up their scrutiny and enforcement of transfer price practices or introducing transfer pricing rules for the first time. KPMG conducts its own annual survey (*Global Transfer Pricing Review*), and notes that increasing international trade is putting pressure on the industry to standardize transfer pricing rules. The KPMG report is over 200 pages long, documents the policies in 64 countries, and gives snapshots of developments in 35 countries that either have no policies or are just beginning to develop their policies.

Just how well have governments been in stepping up enforcement and stopping the evasion of taxes via the use of transfer prices? A National Bureau of Economic Research paper[a] looks at the use of transfer prices as well as other mechanisms, such as using hybrid entities that are treated as corporations in some countries but flow-through entities in others, to transfer profits from high-tax countries to low-tax countries. The paper finds that in the last 20 years, multinational corporations have taken to "domicile swapping" with a passion. For nine developed countries with sufficient observations over the period from 1989 to 2009, the effective tax rate (ETR) had a mean (and median) decline of 12 percentage points. In Japan, the decline was 22 percentage points; in Switzerland and Great Britain, 15; and in the United States, 12. Bloomberg estimates that Google (domiciled in Bermuda) saved $3.1 billion in the last three years by such maneuvering.

Despite all of this opportunity (ETRs in high-tax countries are double the ETRs in low-tax countries), some companies stay domiciled in high-tax countries. Japanese-domiciled companies face the highest effective tax rate, followed by the United States, France, and Germany. Although the ETR has declined as mentioned above, the rank ordering of countries by ETRs has changed little over time.

[a] Kevin S. Markle and Douglas A. Shackelford, "Cross-Country Comparisons of Corporate Income Taxes," Working Paper No. 16839.

Source: Jan Michalski, Ulrich Bunger, and Christoph Stiller, "Business Analysis of the Hydrogen Refueling Station Infrastructure and the Role of the Transfer Pricing System," *International Journal of Hydrogen Energy* 36 (2011), pp. 8152–8157; Terry Hayes, "Transfer Pricing Remains Key Challenge for MNEs," *Journal of International Taxation* 22, no. 4 (April 2011), p. 8; KMPG, "Global Transfer Pricing Review" at www.snipurl.com/27pakr; Mythili Bhusnurmath, *Economic Times of India* (New Delhi), "MNCs Lower Tax Burden by Swapping Domicile," May 15, 2011, at http://economictimes.indiatimes.com/opinion/policy/mcns-lower-tax-burden-by-swapping-domicile/articleshow/8309924.cms.

Managers at the downstream division, which must buy the upstream product at price P_U regardless of where it comes from, have a marginal cost of MC_t, which is the sum of the downstream division's marginal cost, MC_D, and the market-determined price of the upstream product, P_U. To maximize their own profit, managers at the downstream division must choose the output level, Q_D, where their marginal cost, $MC_t (= MC_D + P_U)$, equals their marginal revenue, MR_D. Figure 10.10 shows that the output of the downstream division, Q_D, is less than the output of the upstream division, Q_U; so the optimal solution in this case calls for the conglomerate's upstream division to sell part of its output (specifically $Q_U - Q_D$ units) to outside customers.[13]

THE GLOBAL USE OF TRANSFER PRICING

Transfer pricing is widespread. Many firms have policies whereby one division can buy another division's product, with the transfer price determined by various means. This observation found support in a 1992 survey of transfer pricing that targeted *Fortune* 500 firms. For domestic interdivisional transfers, the most common methods were the use of market prices, actual or standard full production costs, full production costs plus a markup, and negotiated prices. For international transfers, market-based transfer prices and full production costs plus a markup were the most commonly reported methods. Comparing the results to an earlier survey conducted in 1977, the shift has been to market-based prices in both the domestic and international markets.[14]

Managers use transfer pricing to shift profits between divisions to minimize tax liability. This, done on a state-by-state and country-by-country basis, has caused government officials to investigate transfer pricing as a method of avoiding taxation. A 1999 survey by Ernst & Young showed that the number one international tax issue is transfer pricing. Firms are concerned with double taxation and onerous penalties for noncompliance. Many countries have enacted legislation enabling their tax agencies to intensify their transfer pricing inquiries and regulation enforcement. These countries feel that managers use transfer prices to decrease profit in high-tax countries, transferring this profit to low-tax countries. Items included in transfer pricing are goods, services, property, loans, and leases. Fortunately (and in line with the theory developed in this chapter), survey respondents noted that "the most important factor shaping transfer pricing policies is maximization of operating performance, not optimizing tax arrangements."[15]

Suppose the tax rate in a downstream country is α and the tax rate in an upstream country is β where $\alpha > \beta$. Suppose the case is one of no external market for the upstream product. The after-tax profit in the downstream country is

$$(1 - \alpha)(TR_D - TC_D - P_U Q_U)$$

13. Of course it is not always true that Q_D is less than Q_U. Whether this is the case depends on the shape and position of the marginal cost curves (MC_D and MC_U) and the demand curve as well as the price of the transferred product in the external perfectly competitive market. If $Q_D > Q_U$, the downstream division purchases the required $Q_D - Q_U$ units in the external market at the market-determined price of P_U.
14. Roger Tang, "Transfer Pricing in the 1990s," *Management Accounting* vol. 73(8), pp. 22–26. This 1992 survey replicated one conducted in 1977.

PROBLEM SOLVED: The Orion Corporation

Consider the Orion Corporation, where an upstream chemical division [P] produces a product that it transfers to a downstream marketing division [M] which packages the basic chemical into the final product and sells it to outside customers. To illustrate how managers should calculate the optimal output rates, assume demand and cost conditions are as follows. The demand for the finished product sold by Orion's downstream marketing division is

$$P_M = 100 - Q_M \tag{10.5}$$

where P_M is the price (in dollars per ton) of the finished product and Q_M is the quantity demanded (in millions of tons per year). Excluding the cost of the basic chemical, the marketing division's total cost function is

$$TC_M = 200 + 10Q_M \tag{10.6}$$

where TC_M is the division's total cost (in millions of dollars).

Turning to Orion's upstream production division, its total cost function is

$$TC_P = 10 + 2Q_P + 0.5Q_P^2 \tag{10.7}$$

where TC_P is total production cost (in millions of dollars) and Q_P is the total quantity produced of the basic chemical (in millions of tons per year). As we did earlier, we assume a perfectly competitive market for the basic chemical (the upstream output). Assume that its price in this market is $42 per ton.

Under these conditions, managers can readily determine the optimal rate for each division as well as the proper transfer price for the basic chemical. The production division can sell all the basic chemical that it wants at $42 per ton. Therefore, its marginal revenue equals $42. From equation (10.7), we see that $\Delta TC_P / \Delta Q_P = MC_P = 2 + Q_P$

To find the output that maximizes the production division's profit, managers set its marginal revenue equal to its marginal cost

$$MR_P = 42 = 2 + Q_P = MC_P$$

or

$$Q_P = 40$$

Hence the production division should produce 40 million tons per year of the basic chemical.

QUANT OPTION

Orion's marginal cost is $dTC_P/dQ_P = 2 + Q_P$.

15. "Multinationals Face Greater Transfer Pricing Scrutiny According to New Ernst & Young Survey," *Business Wire*, November 3, 1999.

and the after-tax profit in the upstream country is

$$(1 - \beta)(P_U Q_U - TC_U)$$

The transfer price of the basic chemical should be its price in the perfectly competitive market outside the firm. This market price is $42 per ton, and the transfer price should be the same. Also, we know from our earlier work that the marketing division's marginal cost, MC_t, is the sum of its own marginal marketing cost, MC_M, and the transfer price. That is,

$$MC_t = MC_M + P_U$$

where $P_U = \$42$ and its own marginal marketing cost equals $MC_M = \Delta TC_M/\Delta Q_M$.

From equation (10.6), we see that $\Delta TC_M/\Delta Q_M = MC_M = 10$. Therefore,

$$MC_t = 10 + 42 = 52$$

To maximize the marketing division's profit, managers must set its marginal cost equal to its marginal revenue. The marketing division's total revenue is

$$TR_M = P_M Q_M = (100 - Q_M)Q_M = 100Q_M - Q_M^2$$

The marketing division's marginal revenue is therefore

$$\Delta TR_M/\Delta Q_M = 100 - 2Q_M$$

Setting this expression for its marginal revenue equal to its marginal cost, we find that

$$MR_M = 100 - 2Q_M = 52 = MC_t = MC_M + P_U$$

or

$$Q_M = 24$$

Hence the marketing division should sell 24 million tons per year of the base chemical at a price of $76; that is, $P_M = 100 - 24$.

To sum up, managers at the Orion Corporation's production division should produce 40 million tons per year of the basic chemical. Of this amount, 24 million tons should be transferred to Orion's marketing division at the market price of $42 per ton, and 16 million tons $(40 - 24)$ should be sold externally at the market price of $42 per ton. The transfer price should be the same as the market price: $42 per ton.

QUANT OPTION

Take this at face value.

Orion's marginal cost is $dTC_M/dQ_M = 10$; Orion's marginal revenue is $dTR_M/dQ_M = 100 - 2Q_M$.

Suppose all profits are expressed in the same currency; that is, we have adjusted for exchange rates and the P_U was set to maximize before-tax profit. The overall conglomerate's after-tax profit is

$$(1 - \alpha)(TR_D - TC_D) - (1 - \beta)(TC_U) + (1 - \beta - [1 - \alpha])(P_U Q_U)$$
$$= (1 - \alpha)(TR_D - TC_D) - (1 - \beta)(TC_U) + (\alpha - \beta)(P_U Q_U)$$

Because $\alpha > \beta$, the conglomerate's after-tax profit is higher if P_U is greater. But the optimal before-tax profit-maximizing P_U is what it is (and it could be low).

Suppose the firm, having determined the optimal $Q_D^\star = Q_U^\star = Q^\star$, now creates a "subterfuge P_U" $= P_U^S$ for tax purposes and sets it such that

$$P_U^S = (TR_D - TC_D)/Q_U^\star$$

With this P_U^S, the after-tax profit in the downstream country becomes 0 and the conglomerate's after-tax profit is

$$(1 - \beta)(TR_D - TC_D - TC_U)$$

That is, all corporate profit is taxed at the lowest tax rate. Here we see the motivation of high tax rate countries to look at the transfer price policies of multinational firms.

Just why have transfer prices become so important on the international level? Four basic reasons exist: increased globalization, different levels of taxation in various countries, greater scrutiny by tax authorities, and inconsistent rules and laws in the various tax jurisdictions. Transfer price policies that seem to cause the fewest legal problems in the international scenario are (1) comparable uncontrolled price, in which the prices are the same or similar to "arm's-length" transaction prices; (2) cost-plus prices, in which a markup used in arm's-length transactions is added to the seller's cost of the good or service; and (3) resale price, in which the resale price is used as a base for determining an arm's-length margin for the functions performed by the selling company.[16]

SUMMARY

1. Bundling is a strategy that enables managers to increase profit by selling two or more goods in a bundle. In general, bundling works better if the reservation prices of goods are negatively correlated; that is, one group has a high reservation price for one good and a low reservation price for another good relative to another group. Even so, bundling need not generate more profit relative to pricing each good separately. A pure bundle occurs when the goods are sold only as a bundle. Mixed bundling occurs when goods are sold both as a bundle and at least one good is sold separately. No analytical model is available to solve the bundling pricing problem, so experimentation or a computer model is used. Managers also use bundling as an entry deterrent.

2. Many large firms are multidivisional, and one division sells its product to another division of the firm. To maximize the firm's overall profit, it is important that the price at which this transfer takes place, the so-called transfer

16. Brenda Humphreys, "International Transfer Pricing: More Important Than Ever Before!" *Cost & Management* vol. 68(4), pp. 24–26.

price, be set properly. If there is no market outside the firm for the transferred product, the transfer price should equal the marginal production cost of the transferred product at the optimal output. If the outside market is perfectly competitive, the transfer price should equal the market price. Transfer prices have been used by global firms to transfer profits from high-tax countries to low-tax countries.

PROBLEMS

wwnorton.com/studyspace

1. The Locust Corporation is composed of a marketing division and a production division. The marginal cost of producing a unit of the firm's product is $10 per unit, and the marginal cost of marketing it is $4 per unit. The demand curve for the firm's product is

$$P = 100 - 0.01Q$$

where P is the price per unit (in dollars) and Q is output (in units). There is no external market for the good made by the production division.
   a. How should managers set the optimal output?
   b. What price should managers charge?
   c. How much should the production division manager charge his counterpart in marketing for each unit of the product?

2. The Xerxes Company is composed of a marketing division and a production division. The marketing division packages and distributes a plastic item made by the production division. The demand curve for the finished product sold by the marketing division is

$$P_0 = 200 - 3Q_0$$

where P_0 is the price (in dollars per pound) of the finished product and Q_0 is the quantity sold (in thousands of pounds). Excluding the production cost of the basic plastic item, the marketing division's total cost function is

$$TC_0 = 100 + 15Q_0$$

where TC_0 is the marketing division's total cost (in thousands of dollars). The production division's total cost function is

$$TC_1 = 5 + 3Q_1 + 0.4Q_1^2$$

where TC_1 is total production cost (in thousands of dollars) and Q_1 is the total quantity produced of the basic plastic item (in thousands of pounds). There is a perfectly competitive market for the basic plastic item, the price being $20 per pound.
   a. What is the optimal output for the production division?
   b. What is the optimal output for the marketing division?

    c. What is the optimal transfer price for the basic plastic item?

    d. At what price should the marketing division sell its product?

3. Knox Chemical Corporation is one of the largest producers of isopropyl alcohol, or isopropanol, as it frequently is called. Isopropanol is used to produce acetone, an important industrial chemical; it is also used to make various chemical intermediate products. Because Knox Chemical produces both acetone and these chemical intermediates, it uses much of the isopropanol it makes. One of the many tasks of Knox's product manager for isopropanol is to set transfer prices for isopropanol within the company.

    a. Knox's product manager for isopropanol generally sets the transfer price equal to the prevailing market price. Is this a sensible procedure?

    b. When the production of phenol expands rapidly, a great deal of acetone is produced because it is a by-product of the process leading to phenol. What effect do you think this has on the market price of isopropanol?

    c. In producing a pound of phenol, 0.6 pound of acetone is produced. Are phenol and acetone joint products?

    d. Are they produced in fixed proportions?[17]

4. The reservation prices (in dollars) of three classes of demanders (classes A, B, and C) for Ricky Parton's (a Latin country-western singer) compact discs are given in the table that follows:

Class	CD 1	CD 2
A	11	5
B	8	9
C	9	10

It costs $4 to produce and distribute each compact disc. The company can sell each CD separately, can put them together as a boxed set (that is, as a pure bundle), or can sell them in a mixed bundling format (offer the CDs both separately and as a boxed set). Assume that each demander wants only one of each of the CDs at the reservation price (or at any lower price) and that there are an equal number of demanders in each class. For simplicity, assume that the only costs are those mentioned here.

    a. What pricing method would you advise Ricky's company to use?

    b. How much better (profitwise) is the best pricing method than the second most profitable pricing method?

5. Bob and Ron's Stereo sells televisions and DVD players. They have estimated the demand for these items and have determined that there are three consumer types (A, B, and C) of equal number (assume one for simplicity) that have the following reservation prices for the two products. Bob and Ron's cost

17. For further discussion, see E. R. Corey, *Industrial Marketing: Cases and Concepts,* 3d ed. (Englewood Cliffs, NJ: Prentice-Hall, 1983).

for a TV is 9 and for a DVD player is 9. It will cost Bob and Ron 18 to produce a bundle of one TV and one DVD player.

Consumer	TV	DVD Player
A	28	12
B	29	4
C	30	10

Any consumer's reservation price for a bundle of one TV and one DVD player is the sum of their reservation prices for each item. Consumers will demand (at most) one TV and one DVD player.

a. If Bob and Ron only consider pricing each item separately, pricing a pure bundle, or pricing a mixed bundle as their pricing policy, what price(s) would maximize their profit and what would be their profit?

b. If Bob and Ron were able to perfectly price discriminate (that is charge different prices to different consumers, how much would their profit increase over their optimal profit in part a?

6. The University of Pennsylvania basketball team will play both the University of Kansas and Nowhere University this year on Penn's campus. Kansas is a nationally ranked team, while Nowhere is just plain terrible.

The athletic director traditionally prices each game separately. You approach him and point out that two other pricing options exist. One possibility is to offer a pure bundle, that is, a ticket package containing one Kansas ticket and one Nowhere ticket. The second possibility is a mixed bundle. In this situation, a pure bundle is offered but admissions to the games can also be sold separately. It costs Penn a constant 5 per spectator to produce a game. It would cost Penn 10 to produce a bundle of a Kansas game and a Nowhere game.

Three types of potential spectators exist (A, B, and C). There are an equal number of types (for simplicity, assume one of each type). Their reservation prices for each game are shown below:

Spectator	Kansas	Nowhere
A	40	13
B	49	3
C	3	30

Penn's policy is not to price discriminate. A spectator's reservation price for a bundle of the two games is the sum of their reservation prices for each game. A spectator wants (at most) one admission to each game.

    a. What's your pricing advice to the athletic director (so that the director maximizes Penn's profit)?

    b. Given the current pricing policy of Penn, what's your advice worth to the athletic director?

7. GeeM has a sporty wheel package and a luxury interior package that it is considering offering to its auto buyers. GeeM has estimated that there are three consumer types (A, B, and C—all of equal magnitude—for simplicity, consider it one of each type). Consumers want (at most) one of each package. It costs GeeM 5 to produce a sporty wheel package and 10 to produce a luxury interior package. It will cost GeeM 15 to produce a bundle consisting of both packages

    The following are the consumer reservation prices for each package:

Consumer	Wheels	Interior
A	11	24
B	35	12
C	18	28

A consumer's reservation price for a bundle consisting of sporty wheels and a luxury interior is the sum of the individual component reservation prices GeeM does not price discriminate.

    GeeM has solicited your help in pricing the wheel and interior package. You know that they could sell the packages separately, as a pure bundle, or as a mixed bundle.

    Of those three pricing strategies, which one would maximize GeeM's profit? What are the prices (what is the price) that you suggest? How much better is the best pricing strategy than the second best pricing strategy?

8. Food for Life makes health foods for active, outdoor people. Their three basic products are whey powder, a high protein strength bar, and a meal additive that has the taste and consistency of sawdust. Research shows that consumers fall into two types (A and B) and these are described in the table below by their reservation prices for the products. Each consumer will demand no more than one unit of any product at their reservation price. The consumers will value a bundle of the products at the sum of the constituent reservation prices. Each product costs $3 to produce. A bundle of all three products costs $9 to produce. Food for Life does not price discriminate.

Consumer	Whey	Strength	Sawdust
A	10	16	2
B	3	10	13

There is an equal number of each consumer type (for simplicity, one of each type).

What pricing (profit-maximizing) strategy (among pricing separately, pure bundling, and mixed bundling) would you recommend to Food for Life? Why? Only bundles of all three products need to be considered.

EXCEL EXERCISE: TRANSFER PRICING

Suppose that the demand for the downstream product is given by

$$P_D = 100 - 0.1Q_D$$

The total cost of the downstream division (exclusive of the cost of the upstream input) is

$$TC_D = 5Q_D$$

The total cost of the upstream division is given by

$$TC_U = 20Q_U + 0.05Q_U^2$$

It takes one unit of the upstream input to make one unit of the downstream output; the upstream division cannot sell its product to anyone but the downstream division, and the downstream division can only buy its input from the upstream division. The upstream division's product is unique, and there is no other producer of their product.

The downstream total revenue is

$$TR_D = P_D{}^*Q_D = (100 - 0.1Q_D){}^*Q_D = 100Q_D - 0.1Q_D^2$$

The downstream marginal revenue is

$$MR_D = dTR_D/dQ_D = 100 - 0.2Q_D$$

The downstream marginal cost (exclusive of the cost of the upstream input) is

$$MC_D = dTC_D/dQ_D = 5$$

The upstream marginal cost is

$$MC_U = dTC_U/dQ_U = 20 + 0.1Q_U$$

To maximize profit, the conglomerate firm (combination of upstream and downstream) will set $MR_D = MC_D + MC_U$, that is,

$$MR_D = 100 - 0.2Q_D = 5 + 20 + 0.1Q_U = 25 + 0.1Q_U = MC_D + MC_U$$

or $\qquad 100 - 0.2Q = 25 + 0.1Q$ since $Q_D = Q_U = Q$ because it takes one unit of input to make one unit of output.

Thus $\qquad\qquad\qquad\qquad 0.3Q = 75$

or $\qquad\qquad\qquad\qquad Q = 250$

Substituting $Q = Q_D = 250$ into the downstream demand gives

$$P_D = 100 - 0.1*250 = 100 - 25 = 75$$

Substituting $Q = Q_D = 250$ into the upstream marginal cost function gives the optimal transfer price that the downstream division should pay the upstream division for a unit of the upstream division's output, that is,

$$P_U = MC_U = 20 + 0.1*250 = 20 + 25 = 45$$

The total revenue of the downstream division is

$$TR_D = P_D*Q_D = 75*250 = 18,750$$

The total cost of the downstream division (exclusive of the cost of the upstream division) is

$$TC_D = 5*250 = 1,250$$

The cost of the downstream division of obtaining the input from the upstream division is

$$P_U*Q_U = 45*250 = 11,250$$

The profit of the downstream division is

$$\pi_D = TR_D - TC_D - P_U*Q_U = 18,750 - 1,250 - 11,250 = 6,250$$

The total revenue of the upstream division is

$$TR_U = P_U*Q_U = 45*250 = 11,250$$

The total cost of the upstream division is

$$TC_U = 20Q_U + 0.05Q_U^2 = 20*250 + 0.05*250^2 = 5,000 + 0.05*62,500$$
$$= 5,000 + 3,125 = 8,125$$

The profit of the upstream division is

$$\pi_U = TR_U - TC_U = 11,250 - 8,125 = 3,125$$

The profit of the combined firm is

$$\pi = \pi_D + \pi_U = 6,250 + 3,125 = 9,375$$

Suppose that the transfer price was set at 65 instead of the optimal 45. What would happen? Then the marginal cost of the input to the downstream plant would be 65 and the downstream would optimize where

$$MR_D = 100 - 0.2Q_D = 5 + 65 = 70 = MC_D + MC_U = MC_D + P_U$$

or
$$0.2Q_D = 30$$
or
$$Q_D = 150$$

Substituting $Q_D = 150$ into the downstream demand gives

$$P_D = 100 - 0.1*150 = 100 - 15 = 85$$

The total revenue of the downstream division is

$$TR_D = P_D*Q_D = 85*150 = 12,750$$

The total cost of the downstream division (exclusive of the cost of the upstream input) is

$$TC_D = 5*150 = 750$$

The cost of the downstream division of obtaining the input from the upstream division is

$$P_U*Q_U = 65*150 = 9,750$$

The profit of the downstream division is

$$\pi_D = TR_D - TC_D - P_U*Q_U = 12,750 - 750 - 9,750 = 2,250$$

Managers of the upstream division will only produce 150 units, which is the output demanded by downstream managers. (The output is worthless to managers of external firms.)

The total revenue of the upstream division is

$$TR_U = P_U*Q_U = 65*150 = 9,750$$

The total cost of the upstream division is

$$TC_U = 20Q_U + 0.05Q_U^2 = 20*150 + 0.05*150^2$$
$$= 3,000 + 0.05*22,250 = 3,000 + 1,125 = 4,125$$

The profit of the upstream division is

$$\pi_U = TR_U - TC_U = 9,750 - 4,125 = 5,625$$

The profit of the combined firm is

$$\pi = \pi_D + \pi_U = 2,250 + 5,625 = 7,875$$

By setting the wrong transfer price the combined companies' profits fell by $9,375 - 7,875 = 1,500$.

Here's how we get the same results with a spreadsheet. Suppose the following data was available about the market price and quantity demanded and the upstream costs associated with quantity produced.

These numbers can be derived from the demand curve for the downstream product ($P_D = 100 - 0.1Q_D$) and the total cost curve for the upstream product ($TC_U = 20Q_U + 0.05Q_U^2$). Managers often use such discrete models in estimating demand.

Price	Downstream Quantity Demanded	Upstream Total Cost
100	0	0
95	50	1,125
90	100	2,500
85	150	4,125
80	200	6,000
75	250	8,125
70	300	10,500
65	350	13,125
60	400	16,000
55	450	19,125
50	500	22,500

You know that the marginal cost of the downstream equals its average variable cost equals 5.

Call up your spreadsheet. Enter 100 in cell A1, 95 in cell A2, and so on, until you enter 50 in cell A11.

Enter 0 in cell B1, 50 in cell B2, and so on until you enter 500 in cell B11. Columns A and B give the downstream demand curve.

Enter $=A1*B1$ in cell C1. Then click on the lower right hand corner of cell C1 and drag your mouse until you reach cell C11. Column C will be the total revenue of the downstream division.

Enter $=5*B1$ in cell D1. Then click and drag until cell D11. Column D is the downstream division's total cost (exclusive of the cost of the upstream division).

Enter 0 in cell E1, 1125 in cell E2, and so on, until you enter 22,500 in cell E11. Column E in the upstream total cost.

Enter $=D1+E1$ in cell F1. Then click and drag until you reach cell F11. Column F is the combined firm's total cost.

Enter $=C1-F1$ in cell G1. Then click and drag until you reach cell G11. Column G is the combined firm's profit. Search column G for the highest number (or enter $=Max(G1:G11)$ in cell G12 and let the spreadsheet find it). The highest combined profit will be 9,375 in cell G6. Reading leftward on the sixth row, you will see that this entails producing 250 units (cell B6) and pricing the downstream product at 75 (cell A6).

Enter $=(E2-E1)/(B2-B1)$ in cell H2. Then click and drag until you reach cell H11. The $(E2-E1)$ type of calculation gives the firm's discrete marginal cost for 50 increment increases in output. Dividing E2−E1 by B2−B1 gives an estimate of the per-unit marginal cost in that increment. At the optimal output, the marginal cost for producing the 50 units between 200 and 250 is 2,125. Dividing 2,125 by 50 gives 42.5 as an average marginal cost of producing a unit. The marginal cost of producing the 50 units between 250 and 300 is 2,375. Dividing 2,375 by 50 gives 47.5 as an average marginal cost of producing a unit. Thus, if the upstream transfer price for a unit of upstream product had been set at 47.5, too many units would have been produced (300). But with the transfer price set at 42.5, the optimal 250 units would be produced. Why is our optimal transfer price 42.5, different from the 45 price derived from the above calculus model? This model is discrete in naturel; instead of looking at small changes, our change in demand is in 50 unit intervals. Though, note both models identify optimal upstream and downstream output of 250.

Suppose we had more granular data and knew the upstream cost of producing 249 units was 8,080.05 (as shown in the upstream cost formula at the beginning of the problem). Then the discrete marginal cost of producing the 250th upstream product would be $8,125 - 8,080.05 = 44.95$, which is virtually the 45 shown in the earlier calculus case.

PART 6
THE STRATEGIC WORLD OF MANAGERS

CHAPTER 11

Oligopoly A market with a small
number of firms.

OLIGOPOLY

Now we come to our last market structure, that of oligopoly. An **oligopoly** is a market with a small number of firms. As a general rule, you'd like to manage as an oligopolist; they realize relatively high profits. Think of the U.S. petroleum industry, where a few firms account for most of the industry's refining capacity. Oligopolies are strategically interesting from the managerial view. There is a tight interdependence between managers of rival firms because of the small set of players. This causes managers to explicitly consider the reactions of rivals in formulating pricing policy. When managers at Exxon Mobil raise their price of home heating oil by $0.01 or $0.02 per gallon, they try to anticipate the reaction of rival managers. If rivals decide against such a price increase, it is likely that Exxon Mobil managers will rescind the cut; otherwise, those rivals will capture a significant number of Exxon Mobil customers. In the next chapter, we offer managers game theory as a guide to this process of making strategy.

Oligopolies are global phenomena. For example, the market for commercial aircraft is dominated by Boeing and Airbus. Victoria Thieberger of *The Financial Times* writes about a duopoly in the Australian grocery market. She notes that two companies, Woolworth Ltd. and Wesfarmers Ltd., control over 80% of the grocery sector.[1]

There are many reasons why oligopolists are able to rule markets for scores of years. One is a high entry barrier that managers erect using their cooperative market power. Managers at smaller competitors claimed the grocery duopolists were

1. Victoria Thieberger, "Costco
Plans Australia Foray to Challenge
Duopoly," at www.reuters.com,
June 24, 2008.

410

using their market power to negotiate contracts that discouraged landlords from renting space to them. Thieberger also notes that managers at both companies were part of an inquiry into the setting of eerily similar prices at the rival stores.

Government fiat is another reason for duopolies. The U.S. petroleum industry was once a monopoly controlled by John D. Rockefeller. A brilliant strategist, Rockefeller transformed the industry into a design of his own making. The courts finally tore asunder what rivals could not breach.

A more common reason for oligopolies is economies of scale. Because costs decrease as output expands, only a few firms can survive in the market. Managers of these firms still achieve cost savings even when their output represents a substantial percentage of the market. Scale economies were a large part of Rockefeller's success. Even the courts could not use their power to significantly fragment the industry because of the underlying economics.

The hallmark of oligopoly strategy is its behavorial nature. In contrast to perfect competition or monopoly, for which there is a single unified model, behavior is more varied in oligopolies. This variance in behavior is due to the tight interdependence between market rivals.

COOPERATIVE BEHAVIOR

Conditions in oligopolistic industries tend to encourage cooperation among rival managers. This can increase profit, decrease uncertainty, and raise barriers to discourage others from entering the market. However, maintaining cooperative behavior is difficult. There are usually incentives for cooperative parties to "cheat"; and in most countries formal collusive agreements are not enforceable.

If a collusive arrangement is made openly and formally, it is called a **cartel**. In some countries cartels are legally acceptable; but in the United States most collusive agreements, whether secret or open cartels, were outlawed by the Sherman Antitrust Act (discussed in detail in Chapter 17), which dates back to 1890. But this does not mean the government does not see the cooperative value of oligopolies. Major League Baseball is exempted from the U.S. antitrust laws by an act of Congress. And, governments have allowed international air carriers to form alliances to set prices so managers can use economies of scale to reduce costs.

Cartel When a collusive arrangement is made openly and formally.

If a cartel is established to set a uniform price for a particular (homogeneous) product, what price will managers charge? To answer this question, managers need to estimate the marginal cost curve for the cartel as a whole. If input prices do not increase as the cartel expands, the marginal cost curve is the horizontal summation of the marginal cost curves of the individual firms. Suppose the resulting marginal cost curve for the cartel is as shown in Figure 11.1. If the demand curve for the industry's product and the relevant marginal revenue curve are as shown there, the output that maximizes the total profit of the cartel members is Q_0. Therefore, to maximize profit, the cartel will choose a price of P_0, which is

---

FIGURE 11.1

Price and Output Determination by a Cartel

The cartel chooses a price of P_0 and an output of Q_0.

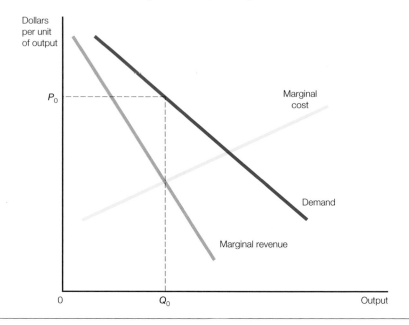

the monopoly price. Note that this price maximizes the profit earned by the cartel, but it says nothing about how this profit is divided among cartel members.

Cartel managers also determine the distribution of sales across members; this is the process that makes cartels rather unstable. If the purpose of the managers is to maximize the profit to the corporate entity, they should allocate sales to cartel members so that the marginal cost of all members is equal (and, in turn, equal to the cartel's marginal revenue). Otherwise cartel managers can increase corporate profit by reallocating output among members to reduce the cost of producing the cartel's total output. If the marginal cost at firm A is higher than that at firm B, cartel managers can increase profit by transferring some production from firm A to firm B.

This allocation of output is unlikely to take place, because allocation decisions are the result of negotiation between members with varying interests and capabilities. This is a political process in which managers have varying amounts of influence. Those with the most influence and the shrewdest negotiators are likely to receive the largest sales quotas, even though this raises the total cartel costs. Also, managers of high-cost firms are likely to receive bigger sales quotas than cost minimization requires because they are usually unwilling to accept the small quotas required by cost minimization. In practice, sales are often distributed in accord with a member's level of sales in the past or the extent of a member's productive capacity. Also, cartel managers might divide a market geographically, with members being given particular countries or regions.

THE BREAKDOWN OF COLLUSIVE AGREEMENTS

Let's formally see why cartels are not stable so managers understand the weakness of a cartel structure. Consider the firm in Figure 11.2. If firm managers chose to leave the cartel, they would face the demand curve of DD' as long as the other firms in the cartel maintained a price of P_0. This demand curve is very elastic; managers can significantly expand sales with a small reduction in price. Even if managers were unable to leave the cartel, they would face the same demand curve if they granted secret price concessions.

The maximum profit of managers who either leave the cartel or secretly lower their price is attained when they sell an output of Q_1 at a price of P_1: This is the output at which marginal cost equals marginal revenue. This price would result in a profit of $Q_1 \times P_1B$, which is generally higher than the profit realized if managers conformed to the price and sales quota dictated by the cartel.[2] Managers who break away from a cartel—or secretly cheat—increase their profit as long as rival managers do not do the same thing and the cartel does not punish this behavior.

FIGURE 11.2

Instability of Cartels

If the firm leaves the cartel, profit equals $Q_1 \times P_1B$, which is generally higher than it would be if the firm adhered to the price and sales quota established by the cartel.

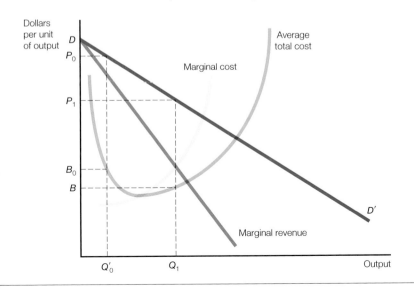

2. At price P_0, the firm's profit is $Q_0' \times P_0B_0$, which is less than $Q_1 \times P_1B$. Because the demand curve is so elastic, total revenues increase significantly as price drops from P_0 to P_1. While the total costs increase as output increases from Q_0' to Q_1, unless they increase very rapidly, the increase in total revenue exceeds the increase in total cost.

But if all managers do this, the cartel disintegrates. Hence there is a constant threat to the existence of a cartel. Its members have an incentive to cheat, and once a few do so, others may follow. Just as is true in relationships, trust is vital to a cartel's existence. As we will see, the incentive to cheat exists even in more informal cooperative endeavors.

PRICE LEADERSHIP

Price leadership In oligopolistic industries, managers at one firm have significant market power and can set their price.

In many oligopolistic industries, managers at one firm have significant market power and can set their price; rivals then follow their lead. This is called the **price leadership** strategy. Examples of industries that have seen the use of this strategy include steel, nonferrous alloys, and agricultural implements. Managers should understand what to consider when setting prices in these markets. We assume the market is composed of a large dominant firm (the price leader) and a number of small firms. Managers at the dominant firm set the price for the market but let the small firms sell all they want at that price. Whatever amount the small firms do *not* supply at that price is provided by the dominant firm.

A new version of price leadership has arisen in the retail sector with the arrival of the "big box" stores. When Wal-Mart or Home Depot come to town, the small retailers, hardware stores, lumber yards, and the like are basically victims of the

---

STRATEGY SESSION: Cranberries: Where 30% of the Market Are Price Takers

The cranberry, that marvelous red berry that helps prevent bladder infections, has lots of vitamin C, and contains antioxidants, is dominated by a giant growers' cooperative—Ocean Spray.

Ocean Spray is the price setter. When Ocean Spray sets a price (with a 60% share of the U.S. cranberry juice market, 70% share of the fresh cranberry market, 70% share of the cranberry sauce market, and an 80% share of the dried cranberry market), the other (nonmember) producers fall into line. Each year, in late September and early October, Ocean Spray sets a price for sales to supermarkets per case of 24 12-ounce bags. This price is based on anticipated and actual supply and demand conditions in the market.

Given the price that Ocean Spray sets, other producers must decide how much of the product they wish to harvest for sale, harvest for use in other products (such as juice), or leave in the bogs.

Thus, Ocean Spray is the price leader, and the remaining 30% of the cranberry growers are followers. Whatever price is set by Ocean Spray, the followers take as given and optimize against that price.

Source: Amanda Hesser, "The Case of the Vanishing Berries," *New York Times*, at www.nytimes.com./2000/11/22/dining/the-case-of-the-vanishing-berries.html; William A. Knudson, "The Economic Impact of Expanded Cranberry Production," The Strategic Marketing Institute Working Paper 01-1208, Michigan State University, circa 2006–2007 and the current website of the Oppenheimer Group, a distributor of cranberries in the U.S. and Canada, at www.oppyproduce.com/print2.cfm?page=cranberries_var, which states that Ocean Spray has 70% share.

prices charged by those big stores. Small stores may try to differentiate with service and high-end items; but anyone who was selling the items sold by Wal-Mart and Home Depot before their arrival must follow the prices of the big guys. Some do and survive, but newspapers are full of stories of the demise of small businesses that cannot compete with the prices and variety of the big box stores.

Managers of a dominant firm can readily determine what price to set. Because managers at the small firms are price takers, they act as if they are in a competitive market, taking the price as given. Hence managers at the small firms should choose output where price equals marginal cost. Therefore a supply curve for all the small firms combined is estimated by *horizontally* summing their marginal cost curves. This supply curve is shown in Figure 11.3. The demand curve facing managers at the dominant firm is derived by subtracting the amount supplied by the small firms at each price from the total amount demanded. Thus the demand curve for the output of the dominant firm, d, is determined by finding the *horizontal* difference at each price between the industry demand curve and the supply curve for all small firms combined.

To illustrate how d is derived, suppose managers at the dominant firm set a price of P_0. The small firms supply R_0, and the total amount demanded is V_0. Therefore the output supplied by the dominant firm is $V_0 - R_0$, which is the quantity d_0 on the d curve at price P_0. In other words, d_0 is set equal to $V_0 - R_0$.

FIGURE 11.3

Price Leadership by a Dominant Firm

Managers at the dominant firm set a price P_1 and supply Q_1 units of the product. The total industry output is D_1.

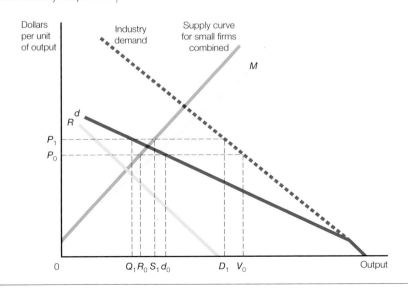

PROBLEM SOLVED: Ghoshal, Inc.: A Numerical Example

To illustrate how managers at a dominant firm can determine the price to maximize profit, consider Ghoshal, Inc., the dominant firm in an industry. The demand curve for this industry's product is

$$Q = 100 - 5P$$

where Q is the quantity demanded and P is the price. The supply curve for the small firms in this industry is

$$Q_S = 10 + P$$

where Q_S is the total amount supplied by all these small firms combined. Ghoshal's marginal cost is

$$MC = (8/3)Q_A \qquad (11.1)$$

where Q_A is Ghoshal's output.

To derive the demand curve for Ghoshal's output, we subtract Q_S from Q, the result being

$$Q_A = Q - Q_S = (100 - 5P) - (10 + P) = 90 - 6P$$
$$P = 15 - (1/6)Q_A \qquad (11.2)$$

Remembering that Ghoshal's total revenue equals PQ_A, Ghoshal's total revenue equals

$$TR = [15 - (1/6)Q_A]Q_A = 15Q_A - (1/6)Q_A^2$$

Therefore, Ghoshal's marginal revenue is

$$\Delta TR_A/\Delta Q_A = MR_A = 15 - (1/3)Q_A \qquad (11.3)$$

To maximize profit, managers at Ghoshal need to produce where marginal revenue in equation (11.3) is equal to marginal cost in equation (11.1):

$$MR_A = 15 - (1/3)Q_A = (8/3)Q_A = MC_A$$

So Q_A must equal 5. Consequently, from equation (11.2), it follows that $P = \$14.17$.

To sum up, if managers at Ghoshal want to maximize profit, they should set their price at $\$14.17$.

QUANT OPTION

Ghoshal's marginal revenue is

$$dTR_A/dQ_A = 15 - (1/3)Q_A$$

The process by which the other points on the d curve are determined is exactly the same; this procedure is repeated at various price levels.

Knowing the demand curve for the output of the dominant firm, d, and the dominant firm's marginal cost curve, M, managers can readily determine the price and output that maximizes their profit. Their marginal revenue curve, R, is derived from the dominant firm's demand curve, d, in the usual way. The optimal output for the dominant firm is the output Q_1, where its marginal cost equals its marginal revenue. This output is achieved if managers set a price of P_1. The total industry output is D_1, and the small firms supply $S_1(= D_1 - Q_1)$.

POSSIBLE BEHAVIOR IN MARKETS WITH FEW RIVALS

As we will see in the next chapter, managers need to anticipate the behavior of others. As the behavior of rivals changes your actions often change. We now examine models of probable behavior among managers of a small number of firms. For clarity, we will explain behavior using two firms. These markets are known as *duopolies*. As we subsequently show, the results are generalizable to larger oligopolistic markets.

The two firms produce an identical product, and managers make their output decisions simultaneously. When rival managers make decisions without knowing the decisions of others, we say decision making is simultaneous. (We will formally define *simultaneous behavior* and *sequential behavior* in the next chapter.) Managers often make simultaneous decisions. When managers engage in a sealed bid auction they make decisions simultaneously. When firms enter the market at the same time and managers design plant capacity without knowing the plans of others, that too is simultaneous.

Later we consider sequential move strategies, where managers know the decisions of others before making their decisions. Managers who take action before others are called *first movers* or *market leaders*. The market leader is able to accelerate before others for several reasons. First movers often see what others don't because of business acumen, because they invent or patent a product or process, or because entrepreneurs see opportunities others do not. It may also be due to luck: Mobile phone franchises were first granted to companies via a government lottery. Also, landing slots at some airports are also allocated using a lottery.

When Rivals Are Few: Price Competition

One common strategy used by managers is that of price competition. Often price competition results in a downward spiral of price cuts, stopped only (sometimes) by the constraint of marginal cost. The great strategist Sun Tzu referred to behavior such as price wars as that of the scorched earth. Managers should try to avoid this behavior.

Consider two firms, A and B, producing identical products in a simultaneous-move scenario. Suppose both firms have identical total cost functions of

$$TC_i = 500 + 4q_i + 0.5q_i^2 \qquad (11.4)$$

where $i = A, B$ and q_i is the output of firm i.

The market demand as seen by managers of both firms is

$$P = 100 - Q = 100 - q_A - q_B \qquad (11.5)$$

where P is the unit price of the product, Q is the quantity demanded at price P, and $Q = q_A + q_B$.

The marginal cost of firm i is

$$MC_i = \Delta TC_i / \Delta dq_i = 4 + q_i \qquad (11.6)$$

STRATEGY SESSION: Warren Buffett and Duopoly

Why did the "sage" of Omaha make Berkshire Hathaway the largest shareholder in the rating agency Moody's? According to testimony Buffett gave to the Financial Crisis Inquiry Commission: "The long term value was . . . the duopoly's . . . incredible pricing power." The other player in this duopoly is, of course, Standard and Poor's. If the ratings agencies make mistakes when rating bonds (in particular, giving them higher ratings than they deserve), Buffett's insurance companies can prosper. For instance, if Buffett's companies get a higher rating, they can borrow money at a lower interest rate helping them on the cost side and attract customers who are searching for a strong, less risky insurance company on the demand side.

The pricing power works like this: States regulate insurance companies, and states specify which rating agencies can rate the insurance company's bonds. They choose from a list generated by the Securities and Exchange Commission showing nationally designated rating agencies. Buffett does not have the option of going to multiple agencies for competitive bids but only to those specified by the insurance regulator, and those agencies are usually Moody's and/or Standard & Poor's and a few others. But Buffett believes that competition would not produce quality ratings, but rather a race to the bottom. He believes that the agencies would compete not only on price

but also on laxity, that is, come with us and we won't be tough in giving you a risk rating, but also that a monopoly would have no reason to compete on price or laxity. Thus Buffett likes the duopoly case because of the profits it generates for Moody's. It turns out that he likes the laxity case too. He states: "What we really hope for is mis-rated securities, because that will give us a chance to make a profit, if we disagree with how the agencies rate them." Of course, there can be legitimate differences in opinion on ratings, but if the profit comes about because a lax agency rates a skunk as a rose, then questions should be asked. That is what the Commission was doing.

From the text, we know that monopolies don't have to compete on price—they determine the price, but there is no reason for them to be strict in the quality of their product (because they have no competition). We've shown that a duopoly could be very competitive and set prices as if they were in a competitive market. But we've also shown that they can behave without colluding and obtain prices and profits close to monopoly results. It is the monopoly end of the spectrum that drove Buffett to Moody's. The two dominant rating agencies have apparently learned to play our duopoly game well.

Source: John Carney, "Warren Buffett's Anti-Competitive Profits," CNBC.com, June 3, 2010, at www.cnbc.com/id/37493375/.

QUANT OPTION

The firm's marginal cost is

$$dTC_i/dq_i = 4 + q_i$$

If managers at both firms want to compete on price, the competition will drive price down to the level of their marginal cost. Managers should never price below marginal cost because the additional revenue made from making the last sale is exceeded by the additional cost of making that sale.

The first good demanded has a reservation price of $99—that is, $100 - 1$. This good would cost each producer $5 (that is, $4 + 1$) to produce. If managers compete on price over this customer, while they could charge as much as $99, they are willing to accept as little as $5. In fact, if there were just this one customer, and they competed on price, we expect the price to be $5. Suppose that managers at firm A offer to sell to the customer at $99 (hoping for a profit of $99 - $5 = $94). Managers at firm B would then offer to sell the product for $98 (hoping for a profit of $98 - $5 = $93). Then managers at A would counteroffer at $97. As you can see, in a series of counteroffers, the price will be bid down to $5. At that price the possibility of a profitable sale by a lower price disappears (any lower price is exceeded by the marginal cost of production).

So we can expect that price equal to marginal cost is the ultimate resolution of this pricing contest. For firm A, this means that

$$P = 100 - Q = 100 - q_A - q_B = 4 + q_A = MC_A$$
$$2q_A = 96 - q_B$$
$$q_A = 48 - 0.5q_B \qquad (11.7)$$

For firm B, it means that

$$P = 100 - Q = 100 - q_A - q_B = 4 + q_B = MC_B$$
$$2q_B = 96 - q_A$$
$$q_B = 48 - 0.5q_A \qquad (11.8)$$

We determine the ultimate result of this pricing game by substituting equation (11.8) into equation (11.7) and solving for q_A (or by substituting equation (11.7) into equation (11.8) and solving for q_B)

$$q_A = 48 - 0.5(18 - 0.5q_A) = 24 + 0.25q_A$$
$$0.75q_A = 24$$
$$q_A = 32$$

Substituting $q_A = 32$ into equation (11.8) gives $q_B = 48 - 0.5(32) = 32$, which should not be surprising (because each firm has identical cost functions). Because each firm produces 32, the total output is 64 ($= Q$). Substituting $Q = 64$ into the market demand function yields a price of $36 ($= 100 - 64$). This also equals each firm's marginal cost, $36 (that is, $4 + 32$). Each firm has a total revenue of $1,152 ($36 \times 32$) and total costs of $1,140 ($= 500 + 4(32) + 0.5(32^2)$), leaving managers at each firm with a profit of $12.[3]

3. If each was a constant-cost firm with an identical marginal cost, price competition would take the price down to that marginal cost and profit would be zero (or minus fixed costs if fixed costs exist). For example, if both firms had a marginal cost of $4, both firms together would produce 96—that is, $4 = 100 - Q$ or $Q = 96$(with each producing 48). Each firm's total revenue would be $192 ($= 4 \times 48$), and both firms would have variable cost of $192 ($= 4 \times 48$). Thus all profit would be lost to competition.

STRATEGY SESSION: Cartels Come in Many Shapes and Sizes

In 1997, every two weeks in Rutherford, New Jersey, 20 shipping line managers met and discussed what they would charge to move cargo across the North Atlantic. Although this meeting could have been composed of the managers of a single ocean shipping line discussing pricing strategy, it was not. Rather, they were executives of 20 different companies. Exempt from the U.S. antitrust laws, they collusively set rates on tens of billions of dollars of cargo. This practice has since been declared illegal, but it demonstrates that, if allowed, many firms would choose to collude rather than to compete.

Their monopoly power was limited because the cartel was unable to control the shipping capacity of its members, and some ocean carriers were not members of the cartel. Nevertheless, it was estimated that the cartel was able to raise rates 18 to 19% above competitive rates. Ah, the power of monopoly.

Of course, the epitome of controlling supply and hence creating monopoly power is the Organization of Petroleum Exporting Countries [OPEC] and its power in the crude oil market. Despite the fact that the 12 nations (Algeria, Angola, Ecuador, Iran, Iraq, Kuwait, Libya, Nigeria, Qatar, Saudi Arabia, United Arab

Emirates, and Venezuela) that make up OPEC supply only approximately 40% of the world's oil production, OPEC dictates the world's price. Other oil producing nations have chosen not to join and/or their antitrust laws prohibit firms from their countries from joining. This remaining 60% of the market is content with OPEC marking prices up considerably over marginal costs (because it yields these countries or firms in these countries handsome profits).

The monopoly power is so substantial because of the strong demand for the product, the relative inelasticity of demand for the product, and the fact that the low-cost producers are members of the cartel. Although the cartel is not perfect (that would be where all producers are members and all their capacity is controlled), the nonmembers are high cost producers (which makes it difficult for them to challenge the cartel—since the cartel could take down prices to drive the high cost producers out of business).

In 2011, there was substantial unrest in the Middle East. While this unrest has substantially impacted Libyan oil production (virtually zero production in summer 2011), as of this writing there has been no impact on production in Algeria (where protests against the

---

4. It is the horizontal summation because we want to measure the additional cost of producing an additional unit of output in the cartel. To produce that additional unit in the cheapest possible way, the cartel would always want to have identical marginal costs for each producer. If the marginal costs were not the same, the cartel could lower its total cost of production by shifting production from the high-marginal-cost firm to the low-marginal-cost firm until their marginal costs were equalized. See the appendix to Chapter 8 and the earlier discussion in this chapter.

When Rivals Are Few: Collusion

What if our two managers both realized the dangers of a price war and instead chose to act cooperatively? How cooperative could they get? Let's take it to the limit and assume they can legally form a cartel. Under these circumstances, the market demand curve is the cartel's demand curve, and the cartel's marginal cost curve is the *horizontal* summation of each firm's marginal cost curve.[4] Rewriting each firm's marginal cost as

$$q_A = -4 + MC_A$$
$$q_B = -4 + MC_B$$

and adding q_A and q_B (that is, summing the marginal costs horizontally—adding up the quantities produced at any given marginal cost), we get government fizzled with announced plans for demo-cratic reforms), Kuwait (where the emir gave people free food and a $4,000 cash grant), Qatar (where things quieted down after calls for protest against the emir), Saudi Arabia (where protests quickly subsided), and the United Arab Emirates (where 160 intellectuals petitioned for comprehensive reform). Of course, given the ongoing activities in Iraq, production there is sub-ject to uncertainty. Most of the remaining countries, such as Nigeria, are not noted for their stability.

But the crisis in the Middle East (with the excep-tion of Libya)—in countries like Egypt, Tunisia, Syria, and Yemen—basically involves countries that are not members of OPEC and are not significant oil producers.

Others have tried to emulate the behavior of OPEC. Brazil and Colombia (both of which have substantial oil production but are not members of OPEC) once looked at their neighbor Venezuela with envy. Venezuela was able to receive a very high price (because of OPEC) relative to the cost of extraction for a black liquid that was turned into energy. Brazil and Colombia noted that they had a product that could be turned into another black liquid that produced energy too—not oil, but coffee. So they formed a coffee cartel.

Ever heard of it? Not likely. It failed miserably. They withheld coffee from the market to raise price (just like cartel theory dictates), but when the price rose, con-sumers switched from coffee to tea and caffeinated colas. Though managers may successfully control supply in a market, they may not be able to exercise their monopoly pricing power if close substitutes exist. Close substitutes dictate that demand is relatively elastic, that is, consumers are price sensitive.

Cartels exist not only for goods, but also for ser-vices. In Germany, a wage-setting cartel is constitu-tionally sanctioned between unions and corporations. The cartel keeps wages high and labor strife low, and ends up costing Germans jobs. This is exactly what we expect a monopoly to do—raise prices (wages) and restrict output (jobs).

Sources: "As U.S. Trade Grows, Shipping Cartels Get a Bit More Scrutiny," *Wall Street Journal*, October 7, 1997; and "Ger-man Wage Pact Ends Up Costing Jobs," *Wall Street Journal*, February 19, 1997.

$$Q = q_A + q_B = -4 + MC_A - 4 + MC_B = -8 + 2MC$$

Rearranging yields

$$2MC = 8 + Q$$
$$MC = 4 + 0.5Q$$

which is the cartel's marginal cost.

The cartel behaves as a monopolist (see Chapter 8 and earlier in this chapter) and sets its marginal revenue equal to its marginal cost. The cartel's total revenue is

$$TR = PQ = (100 - Q)Q = 100Q - Q^2$$

The cartel's marginal revenue is therefore

$$MR = \Delta TR/\Delta Q = 100 - 2Q$$

STRATEGY SESSION: How Seagoing Chemical Haulers May Have Tried to Share the Market

In 2003 Stolt-Nielsen SA, two of its executives, and two subsidiary companies were accused of conspiring to allocate customers, fix prices, and rig bids on contracts in the parcel tanker business. It was alleged that the participants would allocate business on a route-by-route basis, and that Stolt-Nielsen had calculated a table that showed how much better off their revenues would be if they cooperated rather than competed.[a] This accusation occurred after Stolt-Nielsen had gone to the U.S. Department of Justice (DOJ) on January 8, 2003, and confessed to the antitrust violation to which it had been a party. Soon thereafter, the Justice Department entered into a leniency agreement (the amnesty agreement outlined below) with Stolt-Nielsen.

However, on April 8, 2003, the Justice Department told Stolt that it had learned that Stolt-Nielsen had not desisted from illegal activity, and so it arrested the manager of Stolt-Nielsen's tanker trading division. In February 2004, Stolt and the manager brought a civil action suit against the Department of Justice seeking an end to its prosecution. On January 14, 2005, the district court in the Eastern District of Pennsylvania enjoined the Justice Department from terminating Stolt-Nielsen's immunity. The Third Circuit Court of Appeals, however, upheld the ruling in favor of the DOJ. But there's more. The appeal court said that if Stolt-Nielsen asserted the leniency agreement as a defense *after indictment*, then the reviewing court had to consider the agreement anew, determine the date Stolt-Nielsen discovered the conspiracy, consider Stolt-Nielsen's subsequent actions, and decide whether Stolt took prompt and effective action to end their role in the illegal activity. Stolt-Nielsen then asserted the leniency agreement as a defense. After viewing Stolt-Nielsen's actions regarding the above, the Third Circuit ruled that Stolt-Nielsen complied with what the appeal court wanted and dismissed the indictments. The Third Circuit's message was clear: "a deal is a deal" and the Justice Department cannot renege unless it has extraordinary reasons for doing so.[b]

QUANT OPTION

The cartel's marginal revenue is

$$dTR/dQ = 100 - 2Q$$

Setting the cartel's marginal revenue equal to the cartel's marginal cost yields

$$MR = 100 - 2Q = 4 + 0.5Q = MC$$
$$2.5Q = 96$$
$$Q = 38.4$$

Substituting $Q = 38.4$ into the cartel's demand curve gives a price of $61.6 (that is, $100 - 38.4$). The cartel's total revenue is $2,365.44 (that is, 61.6×38.4). Since

Here's a little background. The initial indictment was a surprise because Stolt-Nielsen had entered into an amnesty agreement with the Justice Department's Antitrust Division. Prior to the indictment, Stolt-Nielsen claimed it had ceased its anticompetitive actions and had provided information helpful in the convictions of its co-conspirators (which entailed over $62 million in fines for Odfjell Seachem and Jo Tankers, and jail time for some of their executives). The surprise came because the Justice Department revoked the amnesty agreement. The amnesty program was 13 years old in 2006, and Stolt-Nielsen would be the first revocation. The agreement is designed to encourage whistleblowers to come forward and provide supporting information. This is a first-mover situation: The first firm that comes forth gets the amnesty if it terminates the criminal activity and provides information for the prosecution.

As a result of this case, the Justice Department issued a new leniency letter for firms seeking amnesty for antitrust violations. The Justice Depart-ment has pledged to increase the transparency and predictability of its amnesty program. These changes entail a burden of proof on the amnesty applicant to prove that it has stopped all illegal activity. In addition, the leniency applicant must waive judicial review or pre-indictment leniency revocations.[c]

The amnesty/leniency agreement is an important weapon in antitrust law. It creates an incentive for a firm or an individual to come forward and "spill the beans." Only one firm/individual gets a bite at the apple, so if something is amiss, there is an incentive to move fast. Moving second means prosecution. There is only one winner in this race.

[a] See James Bandle, "How Seagoing Chemical Carriers May Have Tried to Divide Market," *Wall Street Journal*, February 20, 2003.
[b] See the website of the National Association of Criminal Defense Lawyers, at www.nacdl.org/public.nsf/PrinterFriendly/A0807p26?
[c] See "Department of Justice Issues New Antitrust Leniency Letter," December 11, 2008, at www.pepperlaw.com/publications_update.aspx?ArticleKey=1319.

each firm has the same marginal cost equation, each should produce the same amount, 19.2, so that both have a marginal cost of $23.2 (that is, $4 + 19.2$), which, of course, equals the cartel's marginal revenue of 23.2 (that is, $100 - 2(38.4)$). The two firms split the total revenue so that each receives $1,182.72. Each firm has total cost of $761.12 ($= 500 + 4(19.2) + 0.5(19.2^2)$); hence, each firm makes profit of $421.6, a considerable improvement over the $12 made when the firms competed on price. Note the cooperative behavior significantly restricts output (from 64 to 38.4) and significantly increases price (from $36 to $61.6); but as observed in Chapter 8, that is what monopolists do.

When Rivals Are Few: Quantity (Capacity) Competition

Unfortunately, forming a cartel is often illegal. But, strictly competing on price is a lose-lose strategy. So, what are managers to do? Well, they could compete on something other than price. Managers should try to compete on any metric that affects profit and gives them a higher profit relative to competing on price. One metric that jumps to mind is quantity (or production capacity). This type of competition is sometimes called *Cournot*, named after the French economist who initially derived its properties.

Cournot analysis makes the following assumptions: The rival managers move simultaneously, have the same view of the market demand, estimate each other's cost functions, and choose their profit-maximizing output conditional on their rival choosing the same.

It is thought as problematic that rival managers hold the same beliefs regarding demand. Yet, there is evidence that it is more likely to occur than students think. In many situations, government- or trade-association-generated data (macroeconomic and industry-specific variables) are used by all analysts and the corporate intelligence of each firm observes the same economic landscape. Often, managers compete against one another for long periods of time. They often get to know each other through various professional associations. Nevertheless, it is possible for two (or more) managers viewing the same economic data to come up with different conclusions or assessments. With respect to knowing each other's cost functions in some cases, good approximations of adversaries' costs are likely. For instance, in the airline industry, there are only two manufacturers of large aircraft remaining (Boeing and Airbus) and only several producers of small commercial aircraft (for example, Bombardier and Embraer). The carriers are either flying the same aircraft as their adversaries or have "speced" the aircraft (that is, received all the operating characteristics of that aircraft from the manufacturer when the carrier considered purchasing new aircraft). Personnel are unionized (for the most part) and wage rates are well known. All carriers buy fuel, food, and other items from a limited set of suppliers. Therefore, carrier A has a fairly decent estimate of what it costs carrier B to operate its fleet (and vice versa). In addition, executive talent is mobile within the industry, and when executives leave carrier A, they carry knowledge of the company in their heads that can be useful to company B.[5]

The last assumption is that firm A optimizes their quantity (capacity) given that firm B's quantity (capacity) is fixed. This is not as restrictive as it sounds. We first formulate this situation as a series of "what-if" questions. *If my adversary actually is going to produce quantity X, what* quantity would I produce to maximize my profit? Which output you actually choose to produce of all the "what-if" possibilities depends on what you think your adversary will *actually* do (and your adversary is going through the same "what-if" process). By a process of deduction, managers can estimate the most logical output for rivals given profit-maximizing behavior. This is the Cournot solution, and we see that it yields a solution identical to that of game theory (see Chapter 12).

We now view the Cournot solution to the preceding case in two different ways. The first is by following a series of "what-if" scenarios. We deal with the decisions of managers at firm A and treat this as our firm. Clearly, if firm A managers think that managers at firm B will abdicate the market to them, they should

5. We will leave it to your ethics course to debate about what information can be revealed. To see how information is obtained about competitors, see "They Snoop to Conquer," *BusinessWeek*, October 28, 1996. In a classic case of crossing the line, Jose Ignacio Lopez left General Motors in 1992 allegedly carrying a briefcase of GM blueprints to his new job at Volkswagen. You need no ethics course to know that this is wrong. GM sued, and in 1996 the case was settled. Lopez was forced to resign from VW, and VW was required to pay GM $100 million and purchase $1 billion worth of GM auto parts.

behave as a monopolist. Since the monopolist's marginal revenue is the same as the cartel's in the preceding situation (and now firm A's marginal revenue, since it is the only producer in the market), and firm A's marginal cost is $MC_A = 4 + q_A$, managers maximize profit by setting $MR = MC$ or

$$MR_A = 100 - 2q_A = 4 + q_A = MC_A$$
$$3q_A = 96$$
$$q_A = 32$$

So, if $q_B = 0$, the profit-maximizing, optimal-quantity response of firm-A managers is $q_A = 32$.

On the other hand, if managers think their rival will produce 96 units, they will only produce 4 (at most). Rewrite the market demand curve as $Q = 100 - P$. Firm A's *residual* demand curve (i.e., the market demand curve less what managers assume firm B produces), what is left for firm A after firm B managers make their production decision, is

$$q_A = 100 - P - 96 = 4 - P$$
$$P = 4 - q_A$$

Firm-A managers will produce nothing under these circumstances, since the *highest* the price could be is \$4 (when q_A is zero) and the lowest their marginal cost could be is \$4 (when q_A is zero). Therefore, the price could never be equal to or exceed firm A's marginal cost at a positive level of output. Therefore, if $q_B = 96$, the profit-maximizing, optimal-quantity response of firm-A managers is $q_A = 0$.

Suppose firm-A managers think their rival will produce 50 units; that is, $q_B = 50$? Under these circumstances, the residual demand is

$$q_A = 100 - P - 50 = 50 - P$$
$$P = 50 - q_A$$

Firm A's total revenue is $Pq_A = (50 - q_A)q_A = 50q_A - q_A^2$. Hence, marginal revenue is

$$MR_A = \Delta TR_A / \Delta q_A = 50 - 2q_A$$

QUANT OPTION

The firm's marginal revenue is

$$dTR/dq_A = 50 - 2q_A$$

TABLE 11.1

Profit-Maximizing Output Responses of Managers of Firm *A* Given Their Assumptions about Firm *B* Output

If Firm *B* Produces	Then Firm *A* Produces
0	32
50	15.33
96	0

To maximize profit, set $MR_A = MC_A$, or

$$MR_A = 50 - 2q_A = 4 + q_A = MC_A$$
$$3q_A = 46$$
$$q_A = 15.33$$

Therefore, if $q_B = 50$, the profit-maximizing, optimal-quantity response of firm *A* managers is $q_A = 15.33$.

So, we know the optimal profit-maximizing responses for the "what-if" scenarios we investigated (see Table 11.1).

By doing more "what-if" situations, we can complete Table 11.1 for all possible firm *B* outputs between 0 and 96. But, we can get the equivalent of a full table directly with the analysis that follows.

Firm *A* maximizes profit when its total revenue (Pq_A) exceeds its total cost ($500 + 4q_A + 0.5q_A^2$) by the maximal amount. Total revenue is

$$TR = (100 - Q)q_A = (100 - q_A - q_B)q_A = 100q_A - q_A^2 - q_Aq_B$$

Marginal revenue is

$$MR_A = \Delta TR_A / \Delta q_A = 100 - 2q_A - q_B \qquad (11.9)$$

QUANT OPTION

The firm's marginal revenue is

$$\partial TR_A / \partial q_A = 100 - 2q_A - q_B$$

To maximize profit, set $MR_A = MC_A$, or

$$MR_A = 100 - 2q_A - q_B = 4 + q_A = MC_A$$
$$3q_A = 96 - q_B$$
$$q_A = 32 - (1/3)q_B \qquad (11.10)$$

Equation (11.10) is called firm A's reaction function; that is, it identifies for managers the profit-maximizing output to produce *given* the output of rivals at firm B. Every number in the right-hand column of Table 11.1 occurs when the corresponding number on the left-hand side of Table 11.1 is substituted into the reaction function (11.10).

Reaction function A function that identifies for managers the profit-maximizing output to produce given the output of their rivals.

Because firm B has the same cost function as firm A and both face the same market demand curve, firm B's reaction function is

$$q_B = 32 - (1/3)q_A \tag{11.11}$$

We identify how to anticipate the profit maximizing output of a rival by substituting firm A's reaction function (11.10) into firm B's reaction function (11.11) and solving for q_A. Alternatively, we could substitute firm B's reaction function (11.11) into firm A's reaction function (11.10) and solve for q_A. The latter yields

$$q_A = 32 - (1/3)[32 - (1/3)q_A]$$
$$q_A = (96/3) - (32/3) + (1/9)q_A$$
$$(8/9)q_A = (64/3)$$
$$q_A = 24$$

Substituting $q_A = 24$ into firm B's reaction function (11.11) gives

$$q_B = 32 - (1/3)24 = 24$$

Therefore, $Q = q_A + q_B = 48$ and substituting $Q = 48$ into the market demand function gives a price of \$52; that is, $100 - 48$.

Think of it like this: The only way that managers at both firms can maximize profit is if they stay on their reaction functions. Again, this function identifies for managers the profit-maximizing output conditional on the output of their rival. The only way this is possible is if we find the point of intersection between the two functions. This then represents the only quantities where what one manager wants to do is mutually consistent with what the other manager wants to do. This is known as a Nash equilibrium after Nobel laureate John Nash—subject of the book and the movie *A Beautiful Mind*.

Under the Cournot scenario, managers at each firm produce 24 units and the market price is \$52. Each firm's total revenue is \$1,248 (i.e., \$52 × 24), and each firm's total cost is \$884 (that is, $500 + 4(24) + 0.5(24^2)$), so managers at each firm earn a profit of \$364. While this is less than each share of the monopoly (cartel) profit of \$421.6, it is considerably better than what they will earn if they compete on price (\$12). The significance of this is the powerful impact of adding just one more equal producer to a monopoly market. In this case, the price falls by 15.6% (from \$61.6 to \$52) and output increases by 25% (from 38.4 to 48). Hence, adding a competitor can have a significant impact on mitigating the power of a monopolist. Looked at from the other direction, the two firms acting as Cournot quantity competitors can retain 86.3% of the monopoly (cartel) profit and enhance the price-competitive profit slightly over 30–fold.

How can managers get themselves into a Cournot scenario and avoid a price-competitive scenario? Some managers cannot seem to avoid the latter; for example, the airlines constantly seem to engage in price wars, much to the detriment of their profit. On the other hand, managers who learn not to "rock the boat" or to "kill the goose that lays the golden egg" learn to compete on quantity (capacity) and not price. Examples include General Electric and Westinghouse in the marketplace for steam turbine engines and Rockwell International and others in the market for water meters.[6] As can be seen from the preceding, the stakes are high so this quantity (capacity) competition is a strategy worth learning for managers who have only a few market rivals. Figure 11.4 is a picture of the situation just discussed.

FIGURE 11.4

Cournot Reaction Functions for Firms *A* and *B*

A Cournot equilibrium occurs where the two firms' reaction functions intersect. This is the only output combination where both firms' expectations of what the other firm will produce are consistent with their own expectations of their own optimal output. In this case, both firms produce 24 units.

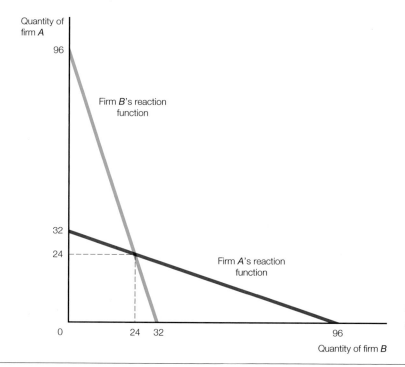

---

6. See Nancy Taubenslag, "Rockwell International," Harvard Business School Case, 9383-019, July 1983.

Such behavior tends to work well when large capital investments must be made. Once the capital investment is made, the quantity to be produced is pretty much determined. Airlines do not practice Cournot competition well because it is easy to change capacity by leasing aircraft (e.g., all of Continental Airlines planes are leased). Oil refining tends to work well because it is difficult to build new refineries (i.e., it's expensive, creates environmental concerns, and no one wants one located near them—the last refinery built in the United States was Marathon-Ashland's Garyville, Louisiana, facility completed in 1976).

The Cournot Scenario with More than Two Firms

Consider a market demand curve $P = a - bQ$ with n identical firms, i.e., $Q_i = Q/n$ where a and b are parameters of the demand function and Q_i is the output of the ith firm. The marginal cost of each firm is $MC_i = c + eQ_i$, where c and e are parameters of the marginal cost function. The market demand curve can be rewritten as

$$P = a - bQ_1 - bQ_2 - \ldots bQ_i - \ldots - bQ_n$$

The total revenue for firm i is

$$TR_i = P \times Q_i = (a - bQ_1 - bQ_2 - \ldots - bQ_i - \ldots - bQ_n)Q_i$$
$$= aQ_i - bQ_iQ_1 - bQ_iQ_2 - \ldots - bQ_i^2 - \ldots - bQ_iQ_n$$

The marginal revenue of firm i is

$$MR_i = \Delta TR_i/\Delta Q_i = a - bQ_1 - bQ_2 - \ldots - 2bQ_i - \ldots - bQ_n$$
$$= a - 2bQ_i - \sum_{k \neq i}^{n} bQ_k = a - 2bQ_i - (n - 1)bQ_i$$

since all firms are the same, $Q_i = Q_k$ for $k \neq c$.

QUANT OPTION

So that we do practice what we preach

$$MR_i = \partial TR_i/\partial Q_i = a - bQ_1 - bQ_2 - \ldots - 2bQ_i - \ldots - bQ_n$$
$$= a - 2bQ_i - \sum_{k \neq i}^{n} bQ_k = a - 2bQ_i - (n - 1)bQ_i$$

Further simplifying the marginal revenue gives $MR_i = a - (n + 1)bQ_i$. To maximize profit, managers will set $MR_i = MC_i$ or

$$MR_i = a - (n + 1)bQ_i = c + eQ_i = MC_i$$

STRATEGY SESSION: The End of a Duopoly?

At the 2011 Paris Air show, Jim Albaugh, the head of Boeing's civil jet division, stated that Embraer (of Brazil), Bombardier (of Canada), Comac (of China), and Irkut (of Russia) are likely to challenge Boeing and Airbus in the duopoly that the two carriers have had in the 100–200 seat aircraft market for the last 15 years. The latter three companies already have aircraft in the development stages and have secured orders. In both the Chinese and the Russian cases, the orders are from domestic carriers in their countries. Albaugh said, "The days of the duopoly with Airbus are over." This was seconded by Tom Enders, Airbus's chief executive. However, Enders added, "The duopoly is over in the 100 to 150 (seat) aircraft segment because this is where the new entrants . . . want to be . . . so that doesn't mean the duopoly is over in the entire range of products."

The significance of the entry into the 100–200 seat market (even at the lower end) is that such sizes dominate the commercial jet market. In the next 20 years, 70% of the market of approximately 25,000 new jets will be in that size range. Enders doubts whether the market can sustain six firms and predicts likely consolidation. And let us not forget that India will have the capability of entering the market in the future. It's also difficult to think that the Chinese won't go after the larger jet market after they cut their teeth on the smaller jets.

But what about the market for jets with fewer than 100 seats (where Boeing and Airbus don't play)? This market includes regional jets and turbo props; it's a triopoly in which Bombardier holds 38% of the market, Embraer holds 36%, and ATR holds 26%. Without turboprops, it's a duopoly of Bombardier and Embraer. The market for engines to power these aircraft is a duopoly between General Electric and Pratt and Whitney, with both at about half the market.

Source: Mark Odell, "Boeing and Airbus Call Time on Duopoly," *Financial Times*, June 21, 2011 at www.ft.com/intl/cms/s/55a1fcf0-9b39-11eo-a254-00144feabdc0,dwp_uuid=890484; Max Kingsley-Jones, "Numbers Game: We crunch the data and analyze how the battle between ATR, Bombardier, and Embraer played out in the space below the mainline jet sector during 2010," *Flight International*, March 29, 2011.

Solving for Q_i gives

$$Q_i = (a - c)/[(n + 1)b + e]$$

Table 11.2 shows the situation when multiple firms (each of which is identical to the two Cournot firms) compete on quantity. Using the formula for Q_i above with $a = 100$, $b = 1$, $c = 4$, and $e = 1$ yields $Q_i = 96/(n + 2)$. Adding a third equal (in cost) competitor to our duopoly drops the price 31.17% from the cartel monopoly price and increases output by 50%. Having eight equal-in-cost competitors in this Cournot situation drops the price by 62.34% relative to the cartel monopoly price and increases output by 100%. Profit becomes negative after three Cournot competitors because of the high level of fixed costs ($500). If the fixed cost were lower (say $50), all situations depicted (except for high values of n) would entail positive profit.

TABLE 11.2

Price, Output, and Profits with Multiple Cournot Competitors

Number of Competitors	Price	Percentage Decrease	Quantity/ Firm	Profit/ Firm	Total Quantity	Percentage Increase
Cartel	61.6		19.2	421.6	32	
2	52	15.58	24	364	48	25
3	42.4	31.17	19.2	52.96	57.6	50
4	36	41.56	16	−116	64	66.67
5	31.43	48.98	13.71	−217.88	68.57	78.57
6	28	54.55	12	−284	72	87.50
7	25.33	58.87	10.67	−329.33	74.67	94.44
8	23.2	62.34	9.6	−361.76	76.8	100
9	21.45	65.17	8.73	−385.75	78.55	104.55
10	20	67.53	8	−404	80	108.33
n	$\dfrac{4n + 200}{n + 2}$		$\dfrac{96}{n + 2}$	$(11{,}824 - 2{,}000n$ $-500n^2)/(n + 2)^2$	$\dfrac{96n}{n + 2}$	
∞	4	93.51	0	−500	96	150

This analysis shows just how the addition of a few entrants in a Cournot situation can bring significant price competition into the market. Even if managers of these entrants have higher costs, they still erode the market power of incumbents and generate significant downward pressure on price.

When Managers Move First: Stackelberg Behavior

Now consider a situation in which managers at one firm are able to implement actions prior to those of rival managers. For example, managers at firm A choose and credibly commit to a capacity decision; managers at firm B know the decision when they choose their own capacity. One behavior is described by Heinrich Freiherr von Stackelberg, and is named after him. How should managers at firm B react to the capacity decision of A managers? Well, if they want to maximize profit, they have to follow their reaction function. This function represents how B managers should act to maximize profit, given the decision of A managers. Managers cannot possibly maximize profit if they are operating off their reaction function. So, managers at firm A can anticipate the capacity choice of B managers.

Therefore, the demand curve firm A faces reads (after substituting firm B's reaction function, equation (11.11), for q_B in the market demand curve, since we can anticipate the decision of B managers)

$$P = 100 - q_A - q_B = 100 - q_A - [32 - (1/3)q_A] = 68 - (2/3)q_A$$

STRATEGY SESSION: Competition among the Few

Below are three related stories about markets in which there is limited competition. Taken together they show that while more competitive markets benefit the consumer, a greater market concentration also carries benefits. The first two stories are about small competitors trying to enter the market and increase competition and their entry strategies when big firms dominant the market.[a] In the third story, competition is being eliminated by a merger that will create a firm with a market share approaching 70% in the Philippine long-distance market.

The world's largest accountancy firms (PricewaterhouseCoopers, Ernst & Young, Deloitte, and KMPG) account for about 90% of the world's large company audit market. There are also smaller rivals clamoring for a chance to increase their participation. They raise issues that a big failure can take out one of the big firms (think Enron taking out Arthur Andersen). Managers at these smaller firms recommend several strategies to make the market more competitive. These include joint auditing (which the big players say will raise the cost of an audit by 20%)

and a mandatory rotating of audits. The pressure is on. The European Union issued a report titled *Audit Policy: Lessons from the Crisis*, and the small firms are hopeful that recommendations (scheduled for November 2011) will open up the market for them.

The second case of increasing competition in markets was discussed in the Strategy Session box on page 418 where we referenced, Warren Buffett's investment in Moody's and his statement that it was a duopoly. While Moody's and Standard & Poor's each have about 40% of the market, a third player, Fitch's, has about 20%. The article refers to the industry as an "oligopoly." Another player, Jules Kroll, wants to enter the market. He previously ran a firm, sold it for $1.9 billion, and started another doing the same thing as the first—sleuthing for one firm on another firm. He feels that he can enter the market because the three major ratings agencies lost their credibility by not performing due diligence on mortgage-backed securities and other structured investments prior to the financial crisis of 2007. He pledges to "look under the covers" when he generates ratings, but he

Firm A's total revenue is $Pq_A = [68 - (2/3)q_A]q_A = 68q_A - (2/3)q_A^2$. The firm's marginal revenue is

$$MR_A = \Delta TR_A/\Delta q_A = 68 - (4/3)q_A$$

QUANT OPTION

Firm A's marginal revenue is

$$dTR_A/dq_A = 68 - (4/3)q_A$$

accepts the historical model in which the issuers of the securities pay the rating agencies. This creates a moral hazard of the firm pandering to the issuer to get the business of rating the issuer's securities. Kroll's target is a 10% market share in five years. The big guys aren't particularly worried, pointing out Kroll's lack of geographical coverage and industry expertise relative to their positions.

Our third case involves the Philippine Long Distance Telephone Company which has acquired Digitel Telecommunications Philippines, resulting in what is being called a duopoly in the wireless segment. So says Justino B. Calaycay, Jr., an analyst at Accord Capital Equities Corporation. The merger will result in the firm controlling 60–70% of the wireless business. Globe Telecom is the other major player. Cid L. Terosa, senior economist at the University of Asia and the Pacific, said the merger had some potentially good points and some bad points. The good points related to economies of scale. The bad points are potential collusive behavior. Calaycay noted that if the two duopolists price competed for consumers'

"peso-votes," it would be good for the consumer. However, if one player got too big, "it might eventually result in a virtual monopoly." Astro C. del Castillo, managing director of the brokerage firm First Grade Holdings, has stated that "Duopoly is an advantage in the Philippines, since it will instill healthy competition between the two dominant firms, as they will compete to provide the most economical and beneficial telecom service for the consumers."

[a] 90% in the case of the top four accountancy firms, and almost 100% in the case of the top three security rating firms—note that usually an 80% share for four firms is the benchmark for very high concentration.

Sources: "Four for All, All for Four," February 25, 2011; *Financial Mail* (South Africa); Janet Morrissey, "A Corporate Sleuth's Eye Turns to Financial Ratings; Experienced Investigator Sees Chance to Compete with the Likes of Moody's," *The International Herald Tribune*, February 28, 2011; J. D. T. Chua, "Popular Economics: When Only Two Firms Control the Market," *Business World* (Philippines), April 26, 2011.

Managers at firm A set marginal revenue equal to marginal cost to maximize profit

$$MR_A = 68 \quad (4/3)q_A - 1 + q_A = MC_A$$
$$(7/3)q_A = 64$$
$$q_A = 27.43$$

Substituting $q_A = 27.43$ into firm B's reaction function yields

$$q_B = 32 - (1/3)27.43 = 22.86$$

Therefore, $Q = q_A + q_B = 50.29$ and substituting $Q = 50.29$ into the market demand curve gives a price of $49.71 (100 - 50.29)$. Firm A's total revenue is $1,363.59 ($49.71 \times 27.43$), and firm A's total cost is $985.88 [500 + 4(27.43) + 0.5(27.43^2)]$; therefore, managers earn a profit of $377.71 (which is $13.71 better than the simultaneous decision of Cournot). As a general managerial rule, if you have the market strength so market rivals cede you the power to move first, use it. Firm B's total revenue is $1,136.33 ($49.71 \times 22.86$), and its total cost is $852.65 (that is, $500 + 4(22.86) + 0.5(22.86^2)$); therefore, the profit is $283.67 (which is $80.33 worse than under Cournot, so, managers at B do pay a penalty for moving second).

The profit situation is exactly reversed if managers at firm B moved first. In this case, where the firms have the same costs, it is worth the same amount for each firm to go first, $94.04 (i.e., the gain from going first plus the loss if the firm moves second). In situations where the firms have different cost functions, the low-cost firm has a greater advantage than the high-cost firm in all the pricing schemes discussed here, including the first-mover situation. Managers at a low-cost firm have the most to gain by moving first. They can even afford to "purchase" the first-mover advantage, outbid the high-cost firm for the patent on the product, or build a bigger plant than the high-cost firm to preempt its output decision.

Let us see how profit changes when managers face different cost functions. The two firms still face the demand curve $P = 100 - q_A - q_B$. But, now, managers at firm A face a cost function $TC_A = 500 + 4q_A + 0.5q_A^2$, while managers at firm B face one of $TC_B = 500 + 10q_B + 0.5q_B^2$ (i.e., firm B has higher costs than firm A). Firm A's reaction function is $q_A = 32 - (1/3)q_B$, and firm B's reaction function is $q_B = 30 - (1/3)q_A$. If you solve for the Stackelberg solution with managers at firm A choosing first, $P = 51.143, $q_A = 28.286$, $q_B = 20.571$ $\pi_A = 433.43, and $\pi_B = 134.78. If you solve for a Stackelberg solution with firm B going first, $P = 51.43, $q_A = 23.714$, $q_B = 24.857$, $\pi_A = 343.55, and $\pi_B = 220.86.

Now we can illustrate how lower costs leverage the advantage of moving first If managers at firm A move first, they earn $\pi_A = 433.43, whereas if they wait for firm B managers to move first, they earn $\pi_A = 343.55. Therefore, managers at firm A gain $433.43 - $343.55 = 89.88 by moving first. If managers at firm B move first, they get $\pi_B = 220.86, whereas if they go second, they earn $\pi_B = 134.78. Therefore, managers at firm B gain $220.86 - $134.78 = 86.08 by moving first. Managers at firm A gain the most from going first. If this were a question of acquiring the patent rights from an inventor, managers at firm A could outbid managers at firm B for the patent (because they can afford to bid up to $89.88, whereas managers at firm B can afford to bid only $86.08). In an ascending auction where all bids are public and the auction ends with the last bid unchallenged, we would expect managers at firm A to acquire the patent and pay a little more than $86.08 for it (because they must only slightly outbid rivals to win the patent).

Oligopoly and competition among the few are so prevalent that these conditions should be studied carefully. For the first time in our analysis of firm behavior *a manager's optimal strategy depends on what she thinks her adversary does*; that is in equation (11.9) the marginal revenue depends not only on what the manager does but also on what the manager's rival does. Hence the price a manager receives for her product depends on both her and her adversary's decisions. This is a chain of reciprocal decisions; that is, my actions depend on your actions, which in turn depend on my actions. Such interdependence of business decisions is typical of most of the economy. This mutual dependence is the basis of the strategy discussed in the game theory chapter (Chapter 12).

DUOPOLISTS AND PRICE COMPETITION WITH DIFFERENTIATED PRODUCTS

Is price competition always a lose–lose situation? We have shown that it is if there is no differentiation between market products. But what if managers can differentiate their products? Is price competition profitable? Let's view two competitors who produce *differentiated but highly substitutable products*. To keep the analysis simple, we'll assume the products have zero marginal cost. The demand for firm 1's product is expressed as

$$Q_1 = 100 - 3P_1 + 2P_2$$

where Q_1 is the quantity of firm 1's product demanded when managers price their product at P_1 per unit and managers at firm 2 price their product at P_2 per unit. Note that as managers at firm 2 price their product higher, the quantity demanded of firm 1's product increases as buyers switch. This shows that differentiation can only mitigate price competition; it is difficult to erase it as a purchase attribute. So again, the demand for firm 1's product depends not only on what managers control (their price) but also on what their rival charges (though they can influence the choices of rivals).

Analogously, the demand for firm 2's product is

$$Q_2 = 100 - 3P_2 + 2P_1$$

Managers at firm 1 want to maximize profit. In this case, this means maximizing the firm's total revenue because unit costs are 0.

As in Cournot, if managers get in a price war, they will compete prices down to marginal costs, and profit will be 0. Again, the price war is lose–lose. But is there a Cournot analog where they compete on price but don't commit economic suicide? There is, and it is called the *Bertrand model*. Firm 1's total revenue is

$$TR_1 = P_1{}^*Q_1 = P_1{}^*(100 - 3P_1 + 2P_2) = 100P_1 - 3P_1{}^2 + 2P_1P_2$$
$$= TR_{11} + TR_{12}$$

where $TR_{11} = 100P_1 - 3P_1{}^2$ and $TR_{12} = 2P_1P_2$.

To maximize total revenue, we form $\Delta TR_1/\Delta P_1 = (\Delta TR_{11}/\Delta P_1) + \Delta TR_{12}/\Delta P_1)$ and set it equal to 0. $\Delta TR_{11}/\Delta P_1$ has the same form as when we did this earlier with respect to ΔQ—that is, $100 - 6P_1$ (same intercept of

100 and double the slope of -3). In the case of $\Delta TR_{12}/\Delta P_1$, call P_1 the initial price and P_1' the new price, so that $\Delta P_1 = P_1' - P_1$. Thus $\Delta TR_{12} = 2P_1'P_2 - 2P_1P_2 = 2P_2(P_1' - P_1) = 2P_2\Delta P_1$, and $\Delta TR_{12}/\Delta P_1 = 2P_2$. So the condition to maximize revenue (profit) for firm 1 will be

$$\Delta TR_1/\Delta P_1 = (100 - 6P_1) + 2P_2 = 0$$

or

$$6P_1 = 100 + 2P_2$$

or

$$P_1 = (50/3) + (1/3)P_2 \qquad (11.12)$$

QUANT OPTION

The revenue [profit]-maximizing condition is

$$\partial TR_1/\partial P_1 = 100 - 6P_1 + 2P_2 = 0$$

In an analogous fashion, the profit-maximizing price for managers at firm 2 is

$$P_2 = (50/3) + (1/3)P_1 \qquad (11.13)$$

Equations (11.12) and (11.13) give us two equations and two unknowns. Substituting (11.13) into (11.12) and solving yields

$$P_1 = (50/3) + (1/3) \times [(50/3) + (1/3)P_1] = (150/9) + (50/9) + (1/9)P_1$$
$$= (200/9) + (1/9)P_1$$

or

$$(8/9)P_1 = 200/9$$

Thus the optimal price for firm 1 managers to charge is $P_1 = 25$. Substituting $P_1 = 25$ in equation (11.13) gives $P_2 = (50/3) + (1/3)25 = 75/3 = 25$. Managers at both firms charge the same price because their differentiation efforts create similar impacts on the demand of others (remember their demand curves with the $+2$ in front of their rival's price). Substituting $P_1 = P_2 = 25$ into firm 1's demand curve gives $Q_1 = 100 - 3 \times 25 + 2 \times 25 = 100 - 75 + 50 = 75$ and analogously, $Q_2 = 75$. Managers at firm 1 earn total revenue (profit) of $TR_1 = P_1 \times Q_1 = 25 \times 75 = 1,875$ and analogously, $TR_2 = 1,875$. That's much nicer than the profit of 0 with the price war. The optimal solution is shown in Figure 11.5.

FIGURE 11.5

Bertrand Reaction Functions and Equilibrium for Firms 1 and 2

A Bertrand equilibrium occurs where the two firms' reaction functions intersect. This is the only price combination at which both firms' expectations of how the other firm will price are consistent with their own expectations of their own optimal price. In this case, both firms will price at 25.

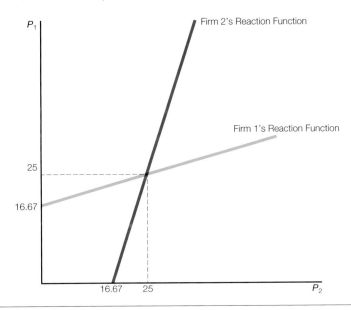

To maximize total revenue (profit), managers will set $\Delta TR/\Delta P_1 = 0$ and $\Delta TR/\Delta P_2 = 0$.

What if the managers at the two firms showed more cooperative behavior and either colluded or merged? Then the combined entity's total revenue would be

$$
\begin{aligned}
TR = TR_1 + TR_2 &= P_1 \times (100 - 3P_1 + 2P_2) + P_2 \times (100 - 3P_2 + 2P_1) \\
&= 100P_1 - 3P_1^2 + 2P_1P_2 + 100P_2 - 3P_2^2 + 2P_1P_2 \\
&= 100P_1 - 3P_1^2 + 100P_2 - 3P_2^2 + 4P_1P_2 \\
&= TR_{11} + TR_{22} + TR_{12}
\end{aligned}
$$

where

$$
\begin{aligned}
TR_{11} &= 100P_1 - 3P_1^2 \\
TR_{22} &= 100P_2 - 3P_2^2 \\
TR_{12} &= 4P_1P_2
\end{aligned}
$$

To maximize total revenue (profit), managers will set $\Delta TR/\Delta P_1 = 0$ and $\Delta TR/\Delta P_2 = 0$.

Analogous to the procedure for deriving equations (11.12) and (11.13), we set

$$
\Delta(TR_{11} + TR_{12})/\Delta P_1 = \Delta TR/\Delta P_1 = 100 - 6P_1 + 4P_2 = 0
$$

or

$$6P_1 = 100 + 4P_2$$

or

$$P_1 = (50/3) + (2/3)P_2 \qquad (11.14)$$

By setting $\Delta(TR_{22} + TR_{12})/\Delta P_2 = \Delta TR/\Delta P_2 = 0$, the optimal price for P_2 is

$$P_2 = (50/3) + (2/3)P_1 \qquad (11.15)$$

QUANT OPTION

To maximize revenue [profit], the firm will set

$$\partial TR/\partial P_1 = 100 - 6P_1 + 4P_2 = 0$$

and

$$\partial TR/\partial P_2 = 100 - 6P_2 + 4P_1 = 0$$

With two equations and two unknowns, we solve by substituting (11.15) into (11.14)

$$P_1 = (50/3) + (2/3)[(50/3) + (2/3)P_1] = (150/9) + (100/9) + (4/9)P_1$$
$$= (250/9) + (4/9)P_1$$

or

$$(5/9)P_1 = 250/9$$

This results in $P_1 = 50$ and $P_2 = 50$. Substituting $P_1 = P_2 = 50$ into firm 1's demand gives $Q_1 = 100 - 3 \times 50 + 2 \times 50 = 100 - 150 + 100 = 50$ and analogously $Q_2 = 50$. Managers at firm 1 earn total revenue (profit) of $TR_1 = P_1 \times Q_1 = 50 \times 50 = 2,500$. Analogously, $TR_2 = 2,500$. Clearly collusion yields better profit, but it is also generally illegal. Managers who choose to compete on prices yield $(1,875/2,500) = 75\%$ of the collusion profit and avoid the price war (as well as jail). Note that turning this around as we did with Cournot, the entry of another competitor reduces prices (in this example by 50%). This is why managers need to think carefully about the effects of competition on variable profit. Competition can allow consumers to keep more consumer surplus and reduce producer surplus. We will further discuss strategic pricing when competition exists among a few firms in Chapter 12.

THE STICKY PRICING OF MANAGERS

The Cournot model explains why price may be "sticky"; that is, managers evolve toward the optimum and stay there. Even in markets with homogeneous products, managers show little incentive to deviate. This is especially true in markets where cost and demand have been stable or easily anticipated and managers have competed for several years. Another behavioral model explains why prices can be sticky even when products are somewhat differentiated.

Consider managers facing a limited number of competitors. They currently price at P_0 and produce Q_0. Should managers increase price, demand will be quite elastic (but not perfectly elastic because with a differentiated product, rival products are not perfect substitutes). Some customers will buy elsewhere when price increases, but other customers have a higher value for the product.

On the other hand, should managers drop their price, they could assume that demand will become less elastic because rivals will also reduce prices to protect their sales. Although lowering the price, *if* no other firm followed suit, might

---

FIGURE 11.6

The Situation of the Kinked Demand Curve

The demand curve kinks at (Q_0, P_0), with the curve being relatively elastic above the kink and relatively less elastic below the kink. The marginal revenue curve is discontinuous at Q_0 (gap BC), and the marginal cost curves intersect the marginal revenue in the gap, leading to marginal revenue equal to marginal cost and yielding an optimal price of P_0 and an optimal quantity of Q_0, despite major shifts in the marginal cost curve.

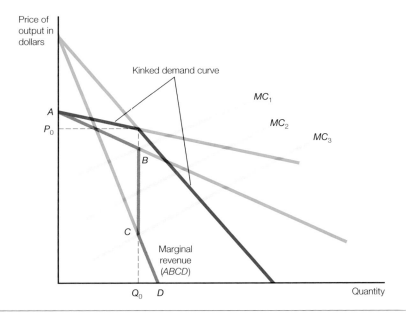

increase sales, when rivals follow a price cut, margins decrease and the increase in sales may not make up the difference.

Hence managers face a kinked demand curve at point (Q_0, P_0), with demand being gently sloped above it and steeply sloped below it. This pattern yields a discontinuous marginal revenue curve (see gap BC in Figure 11.6) at Q_0 (recall that for linear demand curves, the marginal revenue curves have the same dollar axis intercept but fall twice as fast).

Therefore, the marginal cost curves MC_1 and MC_3 (and anything in between, such as MC_2) yield the same price P_0 and quantity Q_0 for the profit-maximizing profit when they intersect the marginal revenue ($ABCD$) in the discontinuity. Thus costs can shift around quite a bit without changing the profit-maximizing price (making it sticky).

SUMMARY

1. Oligopolistic markets are characterized by a small number of firms with a great deal of interdependence, actual and perceived. A good example of an oligopoly is the U.S. oil industry, in which a few firms account for the bulk of the industry's capacity.

2. There is no single model of oligopolistic behavior; behavior depends on the circumstances and expectations. Conditions in oligopolistic industries tend to promote cooperative behavior among rivals, including collusion. Cooperation is easier to attain because the number of firms is small, and managers recognize their interdependence with rivals. The advantages to be derived by managers from collusion seem obvious: increased profit, decreased uncertainty, and a better opportunity to control the entry of new firms. However, collusive arrangements are often hard to maintain because once a collusive agreement is made, any member can increase its profit by cheating on the agreement. Also, cartels may find it difficult to identify a course of action that is agreeable to all members of the industry.

3. Another model of oligopolistic behavior is price leadership. The price leader is the dominant firm in the market. We showed how, under these circumstances, managers of the price leader will set prices to maximize profit. This model also explains pricing in an imperfect cartel (where not all producers are members).

4. When competition among a few firms exists, managers may engage in price competition. This is usually a lose–lose situation because prices are competed down to marginal costs, with severe impact on profit. Cournot competition (competition on quantity or capacity) is a strategy to capture a significant percentage of the high cartel profit and avoid the negative impact on profit of price competition. Cournot behavior exists when managers move simultaneously and engage in what-if moves; for example, what would be my profit-maximizing output response given an output by my rivals? By logically tracing all profit-maximizing responses to rivals' output choices, then putting yourself in their posi-

tion and doing the same analysis for them, behavior can become consistent across all market players. The key to competition among the few is interdependence, where your optimal output is a function not only of what you wish to do but also what your rivals wish to do.

5. If managers at one firm can act before the managers of another firm, Stackelberg behavior can explain the optimal (profit-maximizing) strategy for the first mover and all subsequent movers in this sequential game. In general, first movers see their profit improve relative to the simultaneous-move Cournot situation, and subsequent movers see their profit decrease relative to the Cournot situation. If managers of low-cost firms move first, they earn higher profits than managers of high-cost first movers. If managers can purchase the right to move first, the value they place on this purchase is their profit if they move first minus their profit if they follow.

6. Managers with differentiated products may compete on price and not compete price down to marginal cost. If a limited number of such firms compete, they can determine their and their rivals' reaction functions. Their profit-maximizing price will depend on the prices of rivals as well as their own price. Managers can deduce the optimal price they should charge because they can deduce the optimal prices of rivals. The optimal prices are considerably lower than the price the managers would charge if they formed a cartel and considerably higher than if the managers engaged in a price war.

7. Prices may be sticky (that is, tend to be stable) in oligopolies with differentiated products. This occurs because the demand curve kinks at the current price. The curve is very elastic above the current price because rivals do not follow the price increases of others; whereas it is much less elastic below the current price because rivals are likely to meet any price decreases to protect their sales. The kink in the demand curve leads to a discontinuity in the firm's marginal revenue curve. Therefore, the marginal cost can shift upward or downward considerably but still meet the marginal revenue equals marginal cost condition for profit maximization in the marginal revenue discontinuity—and thus not change the profit-maximizing price and quantity.

PROBLEMS

wwnorton.com/studyspace

1. The Bergen Company and the Gutenberg Company are the only two firms that produce and sell a particular kind of machinery. The demand curve for their product is

$$P = 580 - 3Q$$

where P is the price (in dollars) of the product, and Q is the total amount demanded. The total cost function of the Bergen Company is

$$TC_B = 410Q_B$$

where TC_B is its total cost (in dollars) and Q_B is its output. The total cost function of the Gutenberg Company is

$$TC_G = 460Q_G$$

where TC_G is its total cost (in dollars) and Q_G is its output.

a. If these two firms collude and they want to maximize their combined profit, how much will the Bergen Company produce?

b. How much will the Gutenberg Company produce?

c. Will the Gutenberg Company agree to such an arrangement? Why or why not?

2. The can industry is composed of two firms. Suppose that the demand curve for cans is

$$P = 100 - Q$$

where P is the price (in cents) of a can and Q is the quantity demanded (in millions per month) of cans. Suppose the total cost function of each firm is

$$TC = 2 + 15q$$

where TC is total cost (in tens of thousands of dollars) per month and q is the quantity produced (in millions) per month by the firm.

a. What are the price and output if managers set price equal to marginal cost?

b. What are the profit-maximizing price and output if the managers collude and act like a monopolist?

c. Do the managers make a higher combined profit if they collude than if they set price equal to marginal cost? If so, how much higher is their combined profit?

3. An oligopolistic industry selling a particular type of machine tool is composed of two firms. Managers at the two firms set the same price and share the total market equally. The demand curve confronting each firm (assuming that the other firm sets the same price) follows, as well as each firm's total cost function.

Price (Thousands of Dollars)	Quantity Demanded per Day	Daily Output	Total Cost (Thousands of Dollars)
10	5	5	45
9	6	6	47
8	7	7	50
7	8	8	55
6	9	9	65

a. Assuming that each manager is correct in believing that managers at the other firm will charge the same price as they do, what price should each charge?

b. Under the assumptions in part (a), what daily output rate should managers at each firm set?

4. James Pizzo is president of a firm that is the industry price leader; that is, it sets the price and the other firms sell all they want at that price. In other words, the other firms act as perfect competitors. The demand curve for this industry's product is $P = 300 - Q$, where P is the price of the product and Q is the total quantity demanded. The total amount supplied by the other firms is equal to Q_r, where $Q_r = 49P$. (P is measured in dollars per barrel; Q, Q_r, and Q_b are measured in millions of barrels per week.)

a. If Pizzo's firm's marginal cost curve is $2.96Q_b$, where Q_b is the output of his firm, at what output level should he operate to maximize profit?

b. What price should he charge?

c. How much does the industry as a whole produce at this price?

d. Is Pizzo's firm the dominant firm in the industry?

5. The International Air Transport Association (IATA) has been composed of 108 U.S. and European airlines that fly transatlantic routes. For many years, IATA acted as a cartel: It fixed and enforced uniform prices.

a. If IATA wanted to maximize the total profit of all member airlines, what uniform price would it charge?

b. How would the total amount of traffic be allocated among the member airlines?

c. Would IATA set price equal to marginal cost? Why or why not?

6. In late 1991 two firms, Delta Airlines and the Trump Shuttle, provided air shuttle service between New York and Boston or Washington. The one-way price charged by both firms was $142 on weekdays and $92 on weekends, with lower off-peak advance purchase fares. In September 1991 Delta increased the per-trip shuttle mileage given to members of the Delta frequent-flier program from 1,000 to 2,000 miles, even though actual mileage from New York to either Boston or Washington is about 200 miles. Moreover, Delta also offered an extra 1,000 miles to frequent fliers who made a round-trip on the same day, raising a possible day's total to 5,000 miles. Almost simultaneously, Trump changed the frequent-flier mileage it gave shuttle passengers. (It participated in the One Pass frequent-flier program with Continental Airlines and some foreign carriers.) What sorts of changes do you think Trump made? Why?

7. Two firms, the Alliance Company and the Bangor Corporation, produce vision systems. The demand curve for vision systems is

$$P = 200,000 - 6(Q_1 + Q_2)$$

where P is the price (in dollars) of a vision system, Q_1 is the number of vision systems produced and sold per month by Alliance, and Q_2 is the number of vision systems produced and sold per month by Bangor. Alliance's total cost (in dollars) is

$$TC_1 = 8,000Q_1$$

Bangor's total cost (in dollars) is

$$TC_2 = 12,000Q_2$$

    a. If managers at these two firms set their own output levels to maximize profit, assuming that managers at the other firm hold constant their output, what is the equilibrium price?

    b. What is the output of each firm?

    c. How much profit do managers at each firm earn?

8. In Britain price competition among bookshops has been suppressed for over 100 years by the Net Book Agreement (of 1900), which was aimed at preventing price wars. However, in October 1991 Waterstone and Company began cutting book prices at its 85 British shops. According to Richard Barker, Waterstone's operations director, the decision to reduce the price of about 40 titles by about 25% was due to price cuts by Dillons, Waterstone's principal rival.

    a. According to the president of Britain's Publishers Association, the price-cutting was "an enormous pity" that will "damage many booksellers who operate on very slim margins."[7] Does this mean that price-cutting of this sort is contrary to the public interest?

    b. Why would Dillons want to cut prices? Under what circumstances would this be a good strategy? Under what circumstances would it be a mistake?

9. In the 1960s Procter & Gamble recognized that disposable diapers could be made a mass-market product and developed techniques to produce diapers at high speed and correspondingly low cost. The result was that it dominated the market. According to Harvard's Michael Porter, who made a careful study of this industry, the following were some ways in which Procter & Gamble might have signaled other firms to deter entry.[8]

7. Suzanne Cassidy, "British Book Shops in Price Skirmishes," *New York Times*, October 7, 1991, at www .nytimes.com/1991/10/07/business/ the-media-business-british-book-shops-in-price-skirmishes.html.

8. M. Porter, "Strategic Interaction: Some Lessons from Industry Histories for Theory and Antitrust Policy," in S. Salop, ed., *Strategy, Predation, and Antitrust Analysis* (Washington, DC: Federal Trade Commission, 1981); *New York Times*, April 15, 1993, and March 25, 1995; and *BusinessWeek,* April 26, 1993, and September 19, 1994.

Tactic	Cost to Procter & Gamble	Cost to an Entrant
1. Signal a commitment to defend position in diapers through public statements, comments to retailers, etc.	None	Raises expected cost of entry by increasing probability and extent of retaliation.

2. File a patent suit.	Legal fees	Incurs legal fees plus the probability that P & G wins the suit with subsequent cost to the competitor.
3. Announce planned capacity expansion.	None	Raises expected risk of price-cutting and the probability of P & G's retaliation to entry.
4. Announce a new generation of diapers to be introduced in the future.	None	Raises the expected cost of entry by forcing entrant to bear possible product development and changeover costs contingent on the ultimate configuration of the new generation.

a. In considering these possible tactics, why should managers at Procter & Gamble be concerned about their costs?

b. Why should managers be concerned with the costs to an entrant?

c. By the 1990s Procter & Gamble had to compete with high-quality, private-label diapers (as well as with Kimberly-Clark, which success-fully entered the market in the 1970s). In March 1993 its Pampers brand had about 30% of the market, and its Luvs brand had about 10%. The price of Luvs and Pampers exceeded that of discount brands by over 30%. Should Procter & Gamble have cut its prices?

d. In 1993 Procter & Gamble sued Paragon Trade Brands, a private-label producer, alleging infringement of two patents. Are lawsuits of this kind part of the process of oligopolistic rivalry and struggle?

10. Under which circumstances do managers find it profitable to increase the quality of their products? Do the benefits always exceed the costs? Why or why not?

11. The West Chester Corporation believes that the demand curve for its product is

$$P = 28 - 0.14Q$$

where P is price (in dollars) and Q is output (in thousands of units). The firm's board of directors, after a lengthy meeting, concludes that the firm should attempt, at least for a while, to increase its total revenue, even if this means lower profit.

a. Why might managers adopt such a policy?

b. What price should managers set if they want to maximize total revenue?

c. If the firm's marginal cost equals $14, do managers produce a larger or smaller output than they would to maximize profit? How much larger or smaller?

12. Steve Win has purchased land from the city of Atlantic City in the Marina section. There are stories of a new casino building boom in Atlantic City (MGeeM is also talking about entering, and Gump is opening his fourth casino). Some talk is circulating that Win will subdivide his new land purchase and perhaps three casinos will be built on the site.

Suppose Win subdivides his land into two parcels. He builds on one site and sells the other to another gambling entrepreneur. Win estimates that the demand for gambling in the Marina area of Atlantic City (*after* accounting for the presence of two existing casinos in the Marina and adjusting for the rest of the casinos in Atlantic City) is

$$P = 750 - 5Q$$

where P is the price associated with gambling and Q is the quantity of gambling (think of P as the average amount that a typical patron will net the casino, an amount paid for the entertainment of gambling, and Q as the number of gamblers).

Win, of course, does not sell the other parcel until his casino is built (or is significantly far along); thus he has a first-mover advantage.

Win's total cost TC_W of producing gambling is

$$TC_W = 20 + 40Q_W + 15.5Q_W{}^2$$

where Q_W is the number of gamblers in Win's casino and the total cost (TC_R) of producing gambling for Win's rival is

$$TC_R = 10 + 50Q_R + 20Q_R{}^2$$

where Q_R is the number of gamblers in the rival's casino and

$$Q_W + Q_R = Q$$

Would Atlantic City have done better to sell the land as two separate parcels rather than as a single parcel to Win (given that Win was going to subdivide, Win and his rival could not collude, and Win did not have the ability to produce as a monopolist)? You may assume that Win and his rival could have been Cournot duopolists. If Atlantic City could do better, show why and by how much. Carry all calculations to the thousandths decimal point.

EXCEL EXERCISE: DOMINANT FIRM PRICE LEADER

Suppose that the market demand for a product was expressed as $Q_M = 15{,}000 - 3{,}000P$. The follower firms have a collective marginal cost of $MC_F = 3 + 0.001Q_F$. Because the follower firms will take the price the leader sets as given, follower firms will maximize profits when

$$P = MC_F = 3 + 0.001Q_F$$

or

$$0.001Q_F = -3 + P$$

or

$$Q_F = -3{,}000 + 1{,}000P$$

The leader's residual demand curve is $Q_L = Q_M - Q_F$ or

$$Q_L = 15{,}000 - 3{,}000P - (-3{,}000 + 1{,}000P)$$
$$= 15{,}000 - 3{,}000P + 3{,}000 - 1{,}000P = 18{,}000 - 4{,}000P$$

or

$$4{,}000P = 18{,}000 - Q_L$$

$$P = 4.5 - 0.00025Q_L$$

The leader's marginal revenue is the same intercept and double the slope (as described in the text) and so

$$MR_L = 4.5 - 0.0005Q_L$$

Suppose the leader's marginal cost (and average variable cost) is $MC_L = 2.5 = AVC_L$.
Suppose the leader's fixed cost is $FC_L = 1{,}000$.
To maximize profits, the leader will set $MR_L = MC_L$ or

$$MR_L = 4.5 - 0.0005Q_L = 2.5 = MC_L$$

or

$$0.0005Q_L = 2$$

or

$$Q_L = 4{,}000$$

Substituting $Q_L = 4{,}000$ into the leader's demand curve gives

$$P = 4.5 - 0.00025 * 4{,}000 = 4.5 - 1 = 3.5$$

Substituting $P = 3.5$ into the follower's supply curve gives

$$Q_F = -3{,}000 + 1{,}000 * 3.5 = -3{,}000 + 3{,}500 = 500$$

The leader's total revenue $= TR_L = P*Q_L = 3.5*4{,}000 = 14{,}000$.
The leader's variable cost $= VC_L = AV_L{}^*Q_L = 2.5*4{,}000 = 10{,}000$.
The leader's profit is $= \pi_L = TR_L - VC_L - FC_L = 14{,}000 - 10{,}000 - 1{,}000 = 3{,}000$.

Suppose that we didn't know the above formulas and the calculus rules that lead us to the above optimal behavior by the dominant firm. Instead, we have the following data about estimated market demand and estimated follower supply from the leader firm's marketing group. The leader firm's cost folks tell us that there is a constant marginal cost (= average variable cost) of 2.5, and a fixed cost of 1,000. Can we use a spreadsheet to answer this question? By now, you know the answer is yes.

Price	Market Demand	Follower Supply
5	0	2,000
4.75	750	1,750
4.5	1,500	1,500
4.25	2,250	1,250
4	3,000	1,000
3.75	3,750	750
3.5	4,500	500
3.25	5,250	250
3	6,000	0
2.75	6,750	0
2.5	7,500	0
2.25	8,250	0
2	9,000	0
1.75	9,750	0
1.5	10,500	0
1.25	11,250	0
1	12,000	0
0.75	12,750	0
0.5	13,500	0
0.25	14,250	0
0	15,000	0

Open your spreadsheet. Enter 5 in cell A1, enter 4.75 in cell A2, and so on, until you've entered 0 in cell A21.

Enter 0 in cell B1, 750 in cell B2, and so on, until you've entered 15000 in cell B21. Columns A and B give you the market demand curve.

Enter 2000 in cell C1, 1,750 in cell C2, and so on, until you enter 0 in cell C9. Then click on the lower right-hand corner of cell C9 and drag your mouse down to cell C21. Columns A and C give you the followers' supply curve.

We know that the leader will allow the followers to supply as much as they want *at the price the leader sets*. As can be seen from the table above, at a price of 4.50, the followers will supply exactly what the market demands. At the two prices above 4.50 (4.75 and 5), the followers will supply more than the market demands. Thus, at those prices (4.50, 4.75, and 5), there will be no demand for the leader. However, at prices below 4.5, the followers will provide less than the market demands, and thus the residual will be left for the leader. So here's what we do:

Enter 0 in cell D1, 0 in cell D2, =B3−C3 in cell D3, and so on via click and drag, until cell D21. Column D gives you the leader's quantity demanded at the corresponding price in column A.

Enter =A1*D1 in cell E1, and so on via click and drag, until cell E21. Column E gives the leader's total revenue.

Enter =2.5*D1 in cell F1, = 2.5*D2 in cell F2, and so on via click and drag, until cell F21. Column F is the leader's variable cost.

Enter 1,000 in cell G1, and so on via click and drag, until cell G21. Column G is the leader's fixed cost.

Enter =F1+G1 in cell H1, and so on via click and drag, until cell H21. Column H is the leader's total cost.

Enter =E1−H1 in cell I1, and so on via click and drag, until cell I21. Column I is the leader's profit. Then search column I for the highest value (or put =Max (I1:I21) in cell I22 and let the spreadsheet find the highest value for you). It'll be 3,000 in cell I7. This is the same result obtained by using the calculus-derived formulas. Going leftward on row 7, you will see the leader's output at 4,000, the follower's output at 500, and the optimal market price at 3.5 (as we found above with the calculus-based formulas).

Suppose that some members of the leader's management team had been pressuring the firm to eliminate the follower firms. This could be done by pricing at 3 (note that the follower's supply is zero if the price is 3). This would eliminate competition, increase quantity sold (to 6,000 from 4,000—a 50% increase), and still allow a positive profit margin of 0.5 per unit (=3.0−2.5). However, this would be a drop of 50% from the current profit margin of 1 (=3.5−2.5). Should the management of the leader firm drive out the competitors by pricing at 3? The spreadsheet tells us no. By pricing at 3, the leader's profit falls by a third (from 3,000 to 2,000). The increase in quantity sold is not enough to offset the decrease in profit margin.

It's often the case that the price leader will tolerate fringe players in the market. It's not because the leader is just a nice entity—it's because it's more profitable for the leader to have the fringe there.

EXCEL EXERCISE: COURNOT

Suppose that the market demand for the product was $P = 14 - Q$ or $P = 14 - Q_1 - Q_2$. Each of the two firms has marginal cost (MC) of 2 and average variable cost (AVC) of 2. They also each have fixed cost (FC) of 10.

Firm 1's total revenue is

$$TR_1 = P^*Q_1 = (14 - Q_1 - Q_2)^*Q_1 = 14Q_1 - Q_1^2 - Q_1Q_2$$

Firm 1's marginal revenue is

$$\partial TR_1/\partial Q_1 = MR_1 = 14 - 2Q_1 - Q_2$$

To maximize profit, firm 1 will set marginal revenue equal to marginal cost, that is,

$$MR_1 = 14 - 2Q_1 - Q_2 = 2 = MC_1$$

or $$2Q_1 = 12 - Q_2$$

or $$Q_1 = 6 - 0.5Q_2$$

This is firm 1's reaction function.

In analogous fashion, firm 2's reaction function is $Q_2 = 6 - 0.5Q_1$.

Substituting firm 2's reaction function into firm 1's reaction function gives

$$Q_1 = 6 - 0.5(6 - 0.5Q_1) = 6 - 3 + 0.25Q_1 = 3 + 0.25Q_1$$

or $$0.75Q_1 = 3$$

or $$Q_1 = 4$$

Substituting $Q_1 = 4$ into firm 2's reaction function gives

$$Q_2 = 6 - 0.5{*}4 = 6 - 2 = 4$$

Then $Q = Q_1 + Q_2 = 4 + 4 = 8$.

Substituting $Q = 8$ into the market demand function gives

$$P = 14 - Q = 14 - 8 = 6$$

Thus, each firm makes the following profits.

Total revenue $= P{*}Q = 6{*}4 = 24$
Variable Cost $= AVC{*}Q = 2{*}4 = 8$
Fixed Cost $= FC = 10$
Profit $\pi = TR - VC - FC = 24 - 8 - 10 = 6$

This is the Cournot solution if you know the calculus. But what if you don't know the calculus, and you only have the information that each firm has a marginal cost of 2, an average variable cost of 2, a fixed cost of 10, and that the market demand curve is as below.

Price	Quantity
14	0
13	1
12	2
11	3
10	4
9	5

8	6
7	7
6	8
5	9
4	10
3	11
2	12
1	13
0	14

Let's suppose that you are firm 1. You start by asking yourself "what if" questions. This is scenario planning. Early in the game, you don't know what your adversary is going to do. But you want to consider all possible actions your adversary might take and what profit-maximizing action you would take in response. We'll do that now with a spreadsheet.

Suppose your adversary abdicates the market to you. You then face the market demand curve and act as a profit-maximizing monopolist.

Open your spreadsheet. Enter 14 in cell A1, 13 in cell A2, and so on, until you've entered 0 in cell A15.

Enter 0 in cell B1, 1 in cell B2, and so on, until you've entered 14 in cell B15.

You now have the firm's demand curve in Columns A and B.

Enter =A1*B1 in cell C1. Then click on the lower right-hand corner of cell C1 with your mouse and drag down to cell C15. The result will give you a column of the firm's total revenue.

Enter =2*B1 in cell D1 and then click and drag to cell D15. Column D is the firm's variable cost.

Enter 10 in cell E1 and then click and drag until cell E15. Column E is the firm's fixed cost.

Enter =D1+E1 in cell F1 and then click and drag until cell F15. Column F is the firm's total cost.

Enter =C1−F1 in column G1 and then click and drag down to cell G15. Column G is the firm's profit. Then search column G for the highest number (or enter =Max(G1:G15) in cell G16 and let the spreadsheet find the highest number). This will be 26 in cell G7. Reading leftward in the seventh row, you will see that you will produce 6 units in cell B7. Thus, you have answered one "what-if" question: If my adversary produces 0, I will produce 6.

Let's do another what-if scenario. What if you adversary produces 2? Then what's left for you is the market demand less 2. For instance, at market price 12, 2 goods are demanded. But if your adversary produces 2, there is nothing for you. At market price 11, there are 3 goods demanded. If your adversary produces 2, there is 1 left for you. We continue with this until we get to market price 0. At that price 14 are demanded, but since your adversary is producing 2, there are 12 available to you. So to get your demand curve *given that your adversary is producing two*, we take the market demand curve (Columns A and B), and at any given price, we subtract 2 from the amount in column B. Since that would entail negative quantities for prices 14 and 13 (which makes no sense), we start the process at price 12.

Enter 0 in cell H3, 1 in cell H4, and so on, until you enter a 12 in cell H15. Column A and Column H yield your "residual demand curve," that is, what's left for you of the market demand after your adversary has taken 2.

Enter =A3*H3 in cell I3 and then click and drag to cell I15. Column I is your total revenue at any price when your adversary produces 2.

Enter =10+2*H3 in cell J3 and then click and drag to cell J15. Column J is your total cost.

Enter =I3−J3 in cell K3 and then click and drag to cell K15. Column K is your profit if your adversary produces 2. Search column K for the largest number (or let the spreadsheet do it for you). It will be 15 in cell K8. Looking leftward in the eighth row, you will see that your optimal output (in cell H8) is 5. Thus, if your adversary produces 2, you would produce 5 to maximize your profit.

We continue with another what-if scenario. What if you adversary produces 4? Then what's left for you is the market demand less 4. For instance, at market price 10, 4 goods are demanded. But if your adversary produces 4, there is nothing for you. At market price 9, there are 5 goods demanded. If your adversary produces 4, there is 1 left for you. We continue with this until we get to market price 0. At that price, 14 are demanded, but since your adversary is producing 4, there are 10 available to you. So to get your demand curve given that your adversary is producing 4, we take the market demand curve (Columns A and B), and at any given price, we subtract 4 from the amount in column B. Since that would entail negative quantities for prices between 14 and 11 (which makes no sense), we start the process at price 10.

Enter 0 in cell L5, 1 in cell L6, and so on, until you enter a 10 in cell L15. Column A and Column L yield your "residual demand curve," that is, what's left for you of the market demand after your adversary has taken 4.

Enter =A5*L5 in cell M5 and then click and drag to cell M15. Column M is your total revenue at any price when your adversary produces 4.

Enter =10+2*L5 in cell N5 and then click and drag to cell N15. Column N is your total cost.

Enter =M5−N5 in cell O5 and then click and drag to cell O15. Column O is your profit if your adversary produces 4. Search column O for the largest number (or let the spreadsheet do it for you). It will be 6 in cell O9. Looking leftward in the ninth row, you will see that your optimal output (in cell L9) is 4. Thus, if your adversary produces 4, you would produce 4 to maximize your profit.

What if you adversary produces 6? Then what's left for you is the market demand less 6. For instance, at market price 8, 6 goods are demanded. But if your adversary produces 6, there is nothing for you. At market price 7, there are 7 goods demanded. If your adversary produces 6, there is 1 left for you. We continue with this until we get to market price 0. At that price 14 are demanded, but since your adversary is producing 6, there are 8 available to you. So to obtain your demand curve based on your adversary producing 6, we take the market demand curve (Columns A and B), and at any given price, we subtract 6 from the amount in column B. Since that would entail negative quantities for prices between 14 and 9 (which makes no sense), we start the process at price 8.

Enter 0 in cell P7, 1 in cell P8, and so on, until you enter a 8 in cell P15. Column A and Column P yield your "residual demand curve," that is, what's left for you of the market demand after your adversary has taken 6.

Enter =A7*P7 in cell Q7 and then click and drag to cell Q15. Column Q is your total revenue at any price when your adversary produces 6.

Enter =10+2*P7 in cell R7 and then click and drag to cell R15. Column R is your total cost.

Enter =Q7−R7 in cell S7 and then click and drag to cell S15. Column S is your profit if your adversary produces 6. Search column S for the largest number (or let the spreadsheet do it for you). It will be −1 in cell S10. Looking leftward in the tenth row, you will see that your optimal output (in cell P10) is 3. Thus, if your adversary produces 6, you would produce 3 to maximize your profit. You might wonder why you would produce at all given that your profit is negative. Suppose that the 10 in fixed cost was sunk. Then your variable profit (cash flow under your control) is profit plus fixed cost, which is 9 (=−1 + 10). Thus, you would continue producing.

What if you adversary produces 8? Then what's left for you is the market demand less 8. For instance, at market price 6, 8 goods are demanded. But if your adversary produces 8, there is nothing for you. At market price 5, there are 9 goods demanded. If your adversary produces 8, there is 1 left for you. We continue with this until we get to market price 0. At that price, 14 are demanded, but since your adversary is producing 8, there are 6 available to you. So to get your demand curve given that your adversary is producing 8, we take the market demand curve (Columns A and B), and at any given price we subtract 8 from the amount in column B. Since that would entail negative quantities for prices between 14 and 7 (which makes no sense), we start the process at price 6.

Enter 0 in cell T9, 1 in cell T10, and so on, until you enter a 6 in cell T15. Column A and Column T yield your "residual demand curve," that is, what's left for you of the market demand after your adversary has taken 8.

Enter =A9*T9 in cell U9 and then click and drag to cell U15. Column U is your total revenue at any price when your adversary produces 8.

Enter $=10+2*T9$ in cell V9 and then click and drag to cell V15. Column V is your total cost.

Enter $=U9-V9$ in cell W9 and then click and drag to cell W15. Column W is your profit if your adversary produces 8. Search column W for the largest number (or let the spreadsheet do it for you). It will be -6 in cell W11. Looking leftward in the eleventh row shows you that your optimal output (in cell T11) is 2. Thus, if your adversary produces 8, you would produce 2 to maximize your profit. You might wonder why you would produce at all given that your profit is negative. Suppose that the 10 in fixed cost was sunk. Then your variable profit (cash flow under your control) is profit plus fixed cost, which is 4 ($=-6 + 10$). Thus, you would continue producing.

What if you adversary produces 10? Then what's left for you is the market demand less 10. For instance, at market price 4, 10 goods are demanded. But if your adversary produces 10, there is nothing for you. At market price 3, there are 11 goods demanded. If your adversary produces 10, there is 1 left for you. We continue with this until we get to market price 0. At that price, 14 are demanded, but since your adversary is producing 10, there are 4 available to you. So to get your demand curve given that your adversary is producing 10, we take the market demand curve (Columns A and B), and at any given price, we subtract 10 from the amount in column B. Since that would entail negative quantities for prices between 14 and 5 (which makes no sense), we start the process at price 4.

Enter 0 in cell X11, 1 in cell X12, and so on until you enter a 4 in cell X15. Column A and Column X yield your "residual demand curve," that is, what's left for you of the market demand after your adversary has taken 10.

Enter $=A11*X11$ in cell Y11 and then click and drag to cell Y15. Column Y is your total revenue at any price when your adversary produces 10.

Enter $=10+2*X11$ in cell Z11 and then click and drag to cell Z15. Column Z is your total cost.

Enter $=Y11-Z11$ in cell AA11 and then click and drag to cell AA15. Column AA is your profit if your adversary produces 10. Search column AA for the largest number (or let the spreadsheet do it for you). It will be -9 in cell AA12. Looking leftward in row 12 shows you that your optimal output (in cell X12) is 1. Thus, if your adversary produces 10, you would produce 1 to maximize your profit. You might wonder why you would produce at all given that your profit is negative. Suppose that the 10 in fixed cost was sunk. Then your variable profit (cash flow under your control) is profit plus fixed cost, which is 1 ($=-9 + 10$). Thus, you would continue producing.

What if you adversary produces 12? Then what's left for you is the market demand less 12. For instance, at market price 2, 12 goods are demanded. But if your adversary produces 12, there is nothing for you. At market price 1, there are 13 goods demanded. If your adversary produces 12, there is 1 left for you. We continue with this until we get to market price 0. At that price, 14 are demanded, but since your adversary is producing 12, there are 2 available to you. So to get your demand curve given that your adversary is producing 12, we take the market demand curve (Columns A and B), and at any given price, we subtract 12 from the amount in column B. Since that would entail negative quantities for prices between 14 and 3 (which makes no sense), we start the process at price 2.

Enter 0 in cell AB13, 1 in cell AB14, and 2 in cell AB15. Columns A and AB yield your "residual demand curve," that is, what's left for you of the market demand after your adversary has taken 12.

Enter =A13*AB13 in cell AC13 and then click and drag to cell AC15. Column AC is your total revenue at any price when your adversary produces 12.

Enter =10+2*AB13 in cell AD13 and then click and drag to cell AD15. Column AD is your total cost.

Enter =AC13−AD13 in cell AE13 and then click and drag to cell AE15. Column AE is your profit if your adversary produces 12. Search column AE for the largest number (or let the spreadsheet do it for you). It will be −10 in cell AE13. Looking leftward in the thirteenth row, you will see that your optimal output (in cell AB13) is 0. Thus, if your adversary produces 12, you would produce 0 to maximize your profit. If you produce 0 when your adversary produces 12, you will produce 0 if your adversary produces more than 12.

Now let's summarize what we've found by asking our "what-ifs."

If My Adversary Produces (Q_2)	My Optimal Output is (Q_1)
0	6
2	5
4	4
6	3
8	2
10	1
12	0

From this table, we notice that every time my adversary produces two more, I want to produce one less. We can express this by an equation: $Q_1 = 6 - 0.5Q_2$, or we could plot the above points on a graph with Q_1 on the y axis and Q_2 on the x axis. The y intercept would be a 6 (where $Q_2 = 0$), and the x intercept would be at 12 (where $Q_1 = 0$). The slope is the change in the y axis over the change in the x axis (between any two points—the "rise over the run," i.e., $-6/12 = -0.5$). Thus, the equation of the line we graphed is $Q_1 = 6 - 0.5Q_2$. Notice this is firm 1's reaction function that we derived from the calculus at the beginning of the exercise. We computed it here without any calculus.

We could do the same analysis for my adversary, and we would come up with a comparable table.

If I Produce Q_1	My Adversary's Optimal Output is Q_2
0	6
2	5
4	4
6	3
8	2
10	1
12	0

As above, we can see that when my output goes up by two, my adversary's output goes down by one, or we could graph the points. Either way would lead to firm 2's reaction function of $Q_2 = 6 - 0.5Q_1$.

We can then observe that the only consistent output for each firm that is an equilibrium is for both firms to produce 4. Suppose I produce 6. Then my adversary would want to produce $Q_2 = 6 - 0.5*6 = 6 - 3 = 3$. But then based on his or her reaction function, I would want to produce $Q_1 = 6 - 0.5*3 = 6 - 1.5 = 4.5$. But then based on his or her reaction function, my adversary would want to produce $Q_2 = 6 - 0.5*4.5 = 6 - 2.25 = 3.75$. But if my adversary produced 3.75, then I would want to produce $Q_1 = 6 - 0.5*3.75 = 6 - 1.875 = 4.125$. But then if I produced 4.125, my adversary would want to produce $Q_2 = 6 - 0.5*4.125 = 6 - 2.0625 = 3.9375$. Can you see where this is going? It's taking us to both producing 4—the result we obtained above when we substituted one reaction function into another.

When both produce 4, we calculate the market price of 6 and the profits of each firm at 6 as above.

Suppose that the firms compete on price? They would compete down to marginal cost (=2). The market price would be 2, and the quantity demanded would be $P = 2 = 14 - Q$ or $Q = 12$. If each firm produced 6, its total revenue would be $2*6 = 12$, its variable cost would be $2*6 = 12$, its fixed cost is 10, and each would lose 10. Clearly, Cournot is a lot better (both make 6) than price competition.

What if the firms colluded and formed a cartel? The first seven columns of our spreadsheet showed us that if one firm served the whole market, that firm would price at 8, produce 6 units, and make a profit of 26. If the firms cartelized the market, they would split the output so that each made 3. Each would have total revenue of $8*3 = 24$, each would have total cost of $10 + 2*3 = 16$, and each would make a profit of 8. That is unambiguously better than the Cournot profits of each making 6. Why isn't the monopoly solution stable?

Think of firm 1's reaction function ($Q_1 = 6 - 0.5Q_2$). If I knew my adversary was going to produce 3, would I produce 3? My reaction function tells me the best thing for me to do is $Q_1 = 6 - 0.5*3 = 6 - 1.5 = 4.5$. If this happens,

$Q = Q_1 + Q_2 = 4.5 + 3 - 7.5$ Substituting this into the demand function gives $P = 14 - 7.5 = 6.5$. My total revenue is $6.5*4.5 = 29.25$, my total cost $= 10 + 2*4.5 = 10 + 9 = 19$, and my profit is 10.25, which is better than the 8 I get in our cartel. But if I have figured this out, what has my smart adversary figured out? The same thing. If my adversary produces 4.5, then together we've produced 9. Substituting 9 into the market demand function gives $P = 14 - 9 = 5$. Both of us have total revenue of $5*4.5 = 22.5$, total cost of $10 + 2*4.5 = 10 + 9 = 19$, and profit of 3.5. That's a lot less than the 6 each under Cournot. Unless we can legally sign binding contracts that have both of us making 3 units, the monopoly solution is not stable. Of course, neither is each producing 4.5 units. As shown above, if one firm produces 4.5, the other wants to produce 3.75, and so on, leading us to the Cournot solution of both producing 4.

EXCEL EXERCISE: STACKELBERG

In the Cournot exercise, the market demand was $P = 14 - Q_1 - Q_2$, each firm had a marginal cost (MC) of 2, average variable cost (AVC) of 2, and a fixed cost of 10. We developed each firm's reaction function, that is, $Q_1 = 6 - 0.5Q_2$ and $Q_2 = 6 - 0.5Q_1$.

Suppose that firm 1 has a first-mover advantage. That means that firm 2 will know how much firm 1 has made when firm 2 gets to move. Hence, to maximize their profit, firm 2 will make $Q_2 = 6 - 0.5Q_1$.

Having put itself in firm 2's shoes, firm 1 knows that firm 2 will produce $Q_2 = 6 - 0.5Q_1$. Firm 1 then substitutes for Q_2 in the market demand curve and determines its residual demand curve (i.e., what's left for firm 1 after firm 2 produces $Q_2 = 6 - 0.5Q_1$) is

$$P = 14 - Q_1 - Q_2 = 14 - Q_1 - (6 - 0.5Q_1) = 14 - 6 - Q_1 + 0.5Q_1$$
$$= 8 - 0.5Q_1$$

Firm 1's total revenue is

$$TR_1 = P*Q_1 = (8 - 0.5Q_1)*Q_1 = 8Q_1 - 0.5Q_1^2$$

Firm 1's marginal revenue is

$$MR_1 = dTR_1/dQ_1 = 8 - Q_1$$

To maximize profits, firm 1 will set marginal revenue equal to marginal cost, that is,

$$MR_1 = 8 - Q_1 = 2 = MC_1$$

or
$$Q_1 = 6$$

Substituting $Q_1 = 6$ into firm 2's reaction function gives

$$Q_2 = 6 - 0.5*6 = 6 - 3 = 3$$

Then $Q = Q_1 + Q_2 = 6 + 3 = 9$.

Substituting $Q = 9$ into the market demand curve gives

$$P = 14 - 9 = 5$$

Firm 1's total revenue $= TR_1 = P^*Q_1 = 5^*6 = 30$.
Firm 1's variable cost $= VC_1 = AVC_1{}^*Q_1 = 2^*6 = 12$.
Firm 1's fixed cost $= FC_1 = 10$.
Firm 1's Profit $= \pi_1 = TR_1 - VC_1 - FC_1 = 30 - 12 - 10 = 8$.
Firm 2's total revenue $= TR_2 = P^*Q_2 = 5^*3 = 15$.
Firm 2's variable cost $= VC_2 = AVC_2{}^*Q_2 = 2^*3 = 6$.
Firm 2's fixed cost $= FC_2 = 10$.
Firm 2's Profit $= \pi_2 = TR_2 - VC_2 - FC_2 = 15 - 6 - 10 = -1$.
Firm 2's Variable Profit $= V\pi_2 = TR_2 - VC_2 = 15 - 6 = 9$.

As you can see, it's good to go first since the profit 8 of firm 1 exceeds the simultaneous move profit of Cournot (6). Note also that it's bad to go second, since the profit of −1 of firm 2 is less than the Cournot profit of 6. If the fixed cost was sunk, firm 2 would stay in the market because the controllable cash flow is positive (15 in and 6 out). But if the firm had not yet committed the 10 in fixed cost, it would be a controllable cash flow, and the firm would not enter because cash flow out (16) would exceed cash flow in (15). That would then allow firm 1 to be a single monopolist and produce 6, price at 8, and make the profit of 26 as shown in the first seven columns of the spreadsheet exercise on Cournot.

How can we use a spreadsheet to get the above results? We have derived firm 2's reaction function in the Cournot spreadsheet exercise ($Q_2 = 6 - 0.5Q_1$). But suppose that we didn't know that but only the answers to all the what-if questions we asked in the Cournot exercise. Recall that those questions and answers were as follows:

If I produce Q_1	Then the optimal amount for my adversary to produce (Q_2) is:
12	0
10	1
8	2
6	3
4	4
2	5
0	6

Call up your spreadsheet. Enter 12 in cell A1, 10 in cell A2, and so on, until you enter 0 in cell A7.

Enter 0 in cell B1, 1 in cell B2, and so on, until you enter 6 in cell B7. Columns A and B are firm 2's reaction function.

Enter =14−A1−B1 in cell C1. Then click on the bottom right corner of cell C1 and drag your mouse down to cell C7. This will give you a column of the market price that goes with the corresponding sum of outputs from Columns A and B.

Enter =A1*C1 in cell D1. Then click and drag until cell D7. Column D will give the first mover's (firm 1's) total revenue.

Enter =10+2*A1 in cell E1. Then click and drag until cell E7. Column E will give the first mover's total cost.

Enter =D1−E1 in cell F1. Then click and drag until cell F7. Column F will give the first mover's profit.

Then search column F for the highest number (or let the spreadsheet find it for you by entering =MAX (F1:F7) in cell F8). It will be 8 in cell F4. Reading leftward in row four, you will see in cell A4 that the first mover will produce 6 and in cell B4 that the follower firm will produce 3.

Enter =B1*C1 in cell G1. Then click and drag until cell G7. Column G gives the follower's total revenue.

Enter =10+2*B1 in cell H1. Then click and drag until cell H7. Column H gives the follower's total cost.

Enter =G1−H1 in cell I1. Then click and drag until cell I7. Column I gives the follower's profit. The follower does not get to choose the highest number in column I. Their destiny is sealed when the first mover chooses to produce 6. The follower's profit is found in cell I4 and equals −1.

Enter =10+I1 in cell J1 and click and drag until cell J7. Column J gives the follower's variable profit. The follower gets variable profit of 9 in cell J4 when the first mover chooses output 6.

So we get the same results as the calculus using the spreadsheet.

CHAPTER 12

GAME THEORY

Interactive When the consequence of a manager's decision
depends on both the manager's
own action and the actions of
others.

MAKING STRATEGY AND GAME THEORY

As we have seen, the managerial world is one of interactions with others. In that way, it mirrors life. We now offer a tool to help managers cope with the complexities of managerial life. In fact, it is a tool to help people cope with much of life. Let us explain. We can classify all managerial decisions as either strategic or not. Nonstrategic ones do not involve other people, so their actions need not be considered. For example, managers of a shipping company can generally map the most efficient shipping route without considering what other shipping companies are doing.

Strategic decisions are fundamentally different. Characterized by interactive payoffs, they require a different cognitive frame. Payoffs are **interactive** when the consequence of a manager's decision depends on both the manager's own action and the actions of others. For example, managers decide to enter a new market. Their payoff depends on whether others follow into the market.

So when managers ponder strategic decisions, they must explicitly consider what actions others will take. And optimal choices may change depending on managerial beliefs about others. But if only life were that simple: Others are doing the same thinking about you. And this is just the first link of the expectation chain. Did you ever change a decision because you thought others expected you to take it? Making a strategic decision is like looking at yourself in a hall of mirrors; except in strategy, there are others with you.

460

Game theory helps managers cope with their lives, not solve all their problems. The theory is that of mathematicians who tried to bring order to the complexity of life. Game theory, their organizing framework, can help managers better understand others strategically. Through its use, managers increase their ability to anticipate the actions of others. This ability, in turn, increases the payoffs of managerial decisions—almost as if managers can look into the future.

One rule that is basic to formulating strategy is the direct result of interactive payoffs: the lack of an unconditional optimal strategy. There is no best strategy for all situations; optimality is conditional on situational parameters, many of which are controlled by managers. Though a strategic situation challenges the decision-making skills of managers, it also offers opportunities for managers to change the parameters they control to increase firm payoffs. It is the duty of managers to recognize such opportunities and act accordingly. For example, changing a relationship to the long term from the short can alter the behavior of others (as we show later in this chapter).

Like any long-standing theory, game theory furthers managers' understanding of strategy on several levels. Gravity is a theory that most of us understand, although few can cite its mathematical formula. Game theory is similar in that it illustrates principles that, if followed, will lead to better decisions.

These principles are grounded in Taoist philosophy and were recorded over 2,000 years ago in a series of classic writings, such as *The Art of War*. They are the path to strategy because they should always be followed. The mathematics of game theory clarifies why managers need to follow these principles. Those who follow will make better decisions. The most important principle managers must remember is that they control their strategic environment. Because of interactive payoffs, actions by managers will induce others to change their behavior. As we said, optimality is conditional.

So even managers who simply follow the principles and do not solve for an equilibrium will increase their decision-making ability (though not as much as those who think more rigorously). This greater clarity comes from the visual identification and organization of game parameters.

Because we want to help managers cope better with managerial life, many of the situations we discuss combine conflict with mutual dependence. Such situations are common in the business world—price wars, negotiations, intrafirm relations—and skilled managers understand the relevant considerations.

STRATEGY BASICS

Before we play a game, we need to understand the rules; consider the game of poker. There are many ways to play poker; the rules determine the specific game being played. Game parameters, such as how many cards will be dealt, the betting procedure, and which hands are better than others, define the particular game being played. The same is true for any strategic situation; the rules (parameters) define the game. Hence before managers act, they need to assess and understand the rules.

Sun Tzu said, "Strategy is the Tao of survival or extinction. One cannot but examine it." Assessment is a basic principle. Although this should seem obvious to most managers, empirical evidence shows it is not practiced. For example, the most significant difference between good and bad negotiators is how they prepare for the negotiation. Those with better outcomes prepare more thoroughly.

Game theory provides an assessment framework to help managers. All game theoretic models are defined by a common set of five parameters. Other factors may influence managerial decisions, and game theory usually recognizes these. Here are the defining, common five factors:

1. **The players:** A player is defined as the entity making a decision; entities are either individuals or groups. The decisions of all players determine the outcome. These other entities are in the hall of mirrors with you, looking at the same situation as you but from their viewpoints. Models describe both the identities of the players and their number; changes in either can alter play. Identities are important because of the diversity of the universe. You need to know exactly who is in that hall of mirrors with you. (You cannot know who is playing without a scorecard.) For example, does your behavior change when you are with your parents rather than roommates? How about a total stranger? Most of us act differently if the individual (or group of individuals) with whom we interact changes. The model explicitly recognizes this, so it requires identification. Changes in the number of players can also alter strategies.

2. **The feasible strategy set:** Managers cannot anticipate or assess an action they believe is impossible. So only actions given a nonzero probability of occurring are assessed within a model. These actions constitute the feasible strategy set. Think of it as the potential behavior of others. Behavior not in this set is outside the analytic limits of a particular game model.

It is important for managers to think carefully about the strategy set. Any strategy they don't consider, but is then played by others, puts managers at a strategic disadvantage. From a strategic view, being surprised is bad; it means that others are behaving in ways you did not anticipate. How do you know what to do if you have not assessed the situation?

3. **The outcomes or consequences:** Game models visually represent the intersection of the first two parameters as outcomes. Each player has a feasible strategy set (that is, behavior) comprising individual potential strategies. Each strategy of a player intersects all combinations of the strategies of others to form the outcome matrix. A particular outcome is defined by the strategy choice of each player. Think of the outcome matrix as a crystal ball containing all possible future states. After all players choose and play their strategies, the matrix identifies the

designated state as the future. Like a fortune-teller, game theory tries to predict which state will occur before it is actually realized.

4. The payoffs: A model assigns a payoff for each player to all outcomes. So the payoff for an outcome is expressed as a vector of individual payoffs, and each possible outcome has a corresponding payoff. A player's payoff is based on his or her preferences. An inherent assumption of game theory is that players are rational: They do not wish to harm themselves. Given the choice and all other things equal, they prefer a higher payoff to a lower one. This is another reason why player identities are important. Preferences are subjective: A payoff not highly valued by one player can be highly valued by others.

5. The order of play: Timing is important in both love and war. A model specifies the order in which players reveal their chosen strategies. Models are simultaneous if all managers reveal their strategies without knowing the strategies of others. Simultaneous play is not entirely time dependent. All players need not announce their decisions at precisely the same moment. It is more a matter of information. If all players commit to a strategy before learning the strategies of others, then the game is simultaneous. Nonsimultaneous games are by definition sequential. In any sequential game, the model specifies the order of play.

One way to measure the usefulness of a model is to examine how congruent it is with the real world. Here we summarize the mathematical framework to help managers decide whether it captures the nature of their world. Do managers consider the following in choosing a strategic action?

• How the outcome depends on their actions and the actions of others.
• The identities of others involved in the decisions.
• The order of play.
• How others will react to their decisions.
• The goal to achieve outcomes favorable to their preferences.

We believe most managers would answer these questions in the affirmative. That makes game theory relevant for the managerial world. Game theory formally analyzes what most managers intuitively consider when making strategy. Building a game model requires information managers already know. It asks for a finer partition of the information—a sharpening of managerial strategic focus. The theory's visual representations are tools to help managers with that focus.

VISUAL REPRESENTATION

Game models visualize interactive payoffs (outcomes) as the intersection of individual players' strategies. The representation of these payoffs takes one of two forms: matrix or extensive. The two represent the same information, although

Matrix form Form that summarizes all possible outcomes.

Extensive form Form that provides a road map of player decisions.

sequential games are more easily shown in the extensive form. The **matrix form** summarizes all possible outcomes; the **extensive form** provides a road map of player decisions.

Figure 12.1 represents a matrix form game of the following situation. Managers at two firms, Allied and Barkley, discover they both are planning to launch product development programs for competing products. They can choose to either keep spending at the currently planned level or increase it in hopes of speeding up product development and getting to the market first. Expected profits are a function of the expected development costs and revenues.

Let us see how the matrix addresses the five common parameters:

1. Players: There are two players, Allied and Barkley.
2. Order of play: Simultaneous—each must reach a decision without knowing that of the other.
3. Feasible strategy set: Each player can either maintain the current spending or increase it.
4. Outcomes: Because there are two players, and each has two strategic options, there are four possible outcomes.
5. Consequences: The payoffs are listed for each player within every possible outcome. The convention in game theory is to list the row player's (Barkley) payoff first in each cell and the column player's (Allied) second. So if Allied increases spending but Barkley does not, Allied's expected profit is $3 million and Barkley's is $2 million.

Game trees Games trees are another name for extensive form games and are akin to decision trees.

Extensive form games are also called **game trees**. These are akin to the decision trees we visit in Chapter 14 and are figuratively the same. The fundamental

FIGURE 12.1

A Two-Person Simultaneous Game

		Allied's strategy	
		Spend at current level	Increase spending
Barkley's strategy	Spend at current level	3, 4	2, 3
	Increase spending	4, 3	3, 2

difference between a game tree and a decision tree is one of strategy. A game tree is strategic; a decision tree is not. Decision trees have no interactive payoffs; payoffs are a function of the single individual and nature.

Think of any extensive form game as a decision road map. Just start at the beginning and you cannot get lost. The extensive form gives more details than the matrix form by explicitly stating the timing of choices among players. Extensive form games represent the revelation of a player strategy with decision nodes. The node specifies the player's identity and the feasible strategy set (that is, behavior). The first node (decision) of the game is represented by an open square, all other nodes are shown by a solid square. Lines from each node represent the elements of the feasible strategy set. If other players reveal strategies later in the game, the lines lead from one node to another to show the order of play. If the player is the last to reveal his or her strategy, the lines lead from the node to a payoff schedule.

Figure 12.2 shows an extensive form game representing the following situation. Managers at Allied and Barkley must choose a pricing policy for the new product. They know the other will introduce a similar competing product. Because Barkley is expected to enter the market slightly sooner than Allied, Barkley

---

FIGURE 12.2

Allied–Barkley Pricing: Sequential

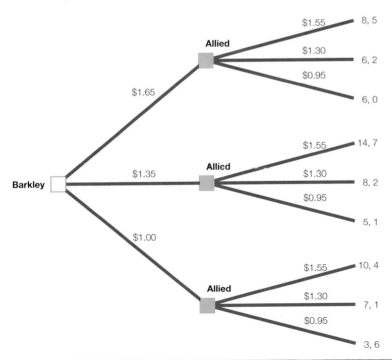

---

managers announce their price first (note the clear square). Managers will choose one of three prices: $1.00, $1.35, or $1.65. Allied managers will reveal their price later. Because Allied is second to market, managers have possible price points of $0.95, $1.30, and $1.55. Payoffs, which represent profits, are a function of costs and revenues.

The extensive form can also show simultaneous games. It does this with information sets. All simultaneous games are played with imperfect information; that is, when revealing his strategy, a player does not know the strategies of all others. This is the nature of simultaneous situations. Figure 12.3 shows the simultaneous version of the situation depicted in Figure 12.2. The only difference between the two figures is the dotted line drawn around the Allied decision nodes. It represents Allied's information set, or knowledge at the time it reveals its strategy. The dotted line signifies that Allied managers know they are at one of the three nodes—but not which one because Barkley managers have not revealed their strategy.

These two types of models show how game theory represents strategic situations. As you see, the information required is not voluminous. But it does require

---

FIGURE 12.3

Allied–Barkley Pricing: Simultaneous

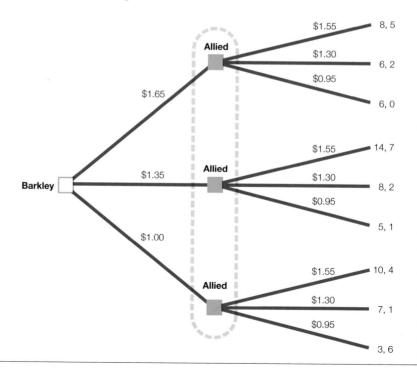

some thought and reflection. The models provide a good organizing framework. They allow managers to communicate more clearly in a common language. The models are good for examining what-if scenarios—a favorite (and helpful) pastime of managers. If this was all they offered, we think the marginal benefits of learning them would far outweigh the marginal costs. But the best is yet to come. These models let managers anticipate the future by predicting the actions of others (and those of the managers themselves). It is important to understand the models' underlying strategic principles. This knowledge gives managers greater insight into human and corporate behavior.

SOLUTION CONCEPTS

How does game theory let managers see the future? It anticipates (correctly) the behavior of others. Using principles of the Taoist tradition, the theory of games adds formal ideas and parameters. How do models anticipate behavior? Unlike crystal balls and tarot cards, the theory provides details of the underlying logic of its predictive power.

Much of the theory's predictive power comes from solution concepts, which are basically rules of behavior. The theory anticipates behavior because it believes individuals act according to prescribed rules. Before we examine some of these rules, we need to understand the concept of an equilibrium.

EQUILIBRIA

Equilibria predict behavior in the following way. In an **equilibrium**, no player has an incentive to unilaterally change his or her strategy. This rule of behavior says little about how individuals arrive at this point; but once there, no one moves unilaterally. So game models predict individual behavior for each player and identify the future (outcome). The concept of an equilibrium holds this behavior in place.

Players do not unilaterally change behavior because they cannot increase their payoff. In an equilibrium, of all possible choices (the feasible strategy set), the present choice rewards players with the highest payoff if no other player changes behavior. In other words, conditional on the choices of others, we are doing the best we can (remember—payoffs are interactive). Thus we assume that behavior is directed by our preferences. We are rational in the sense that we do not want to hurt ourselves and accept a lower payoff. Hence an equilibrium is rational, optimal, and stable. A player's behavior is directed by a preference function. Each player tries to obtain the highest payoff possible, given the actions of others. Once an equilibrium is reached, no player has an incentive to unilaterally change behavior.

Equilibrium When no player has an incentive to unilaterally change his or her strategy.

The growing use of game theory by managers is reflected by articles in the business press that analyze business decisions within a game theory context.

Paul Kerin of *The Australian* uses game theory to analyze a decision by BHP Billiton CEO Marius Kloppers to announce support of a carbon tax in Australia. Kloppers is known to use game theory to analyze acquisitions and other business decisions. Kloppers' support for the tax caught many by surprise. After all, a carbon tax is generally not supported by the CEO of a company that is a major supplier of carbon-related raw materials.

According to Kerin, the key to understanding why Kloppers might support a carbon tax is to think about what alternatives the government might consider. One prominent alternative is the emissions trading scheme (ETS). An ETS creates a market where managers can purchase and sell permits for emissions of specified pollutants. Managers of firms which produce lower levels of emissions than specified can sell some of their extra "credits" to firms that produce emissions above the regulated levels.

If everything was equal, a tax should produce the same results as an ETS. But, there are actually fundamental differences between the two in how they operate. A critical difference is the price setting mechanism. In the ETS market, the price is set by the market. For the carbon tax, the price is set by the government. Clearly, it is easier for Kloppers to influence the political process than try to interfere with the market process. In Kloppers' favor, his lobbyists would be dealing with a new, minority-led government.

From Kloppers' view, another disadvantage of the ETS market is that it reveals information about the marginal cost of cutting emissions. In fact, if efficient, the market-clearing price clearly reflects the marginal cost of abatement. Firms with high marginal costs of abatement will purchase permits or credits while those with low marginal costs will be net sellers. If the government institutes the carbon tax, the government receives no information about the marginal costs of emissions reduction. In fact, the only way they could determine this is to ask managers at each polluting company what their marginal cost is and then identify the firm with the lowest marginal cost. Of course, managers have no incentive to reveal their true marginal cost.

Kloppers also considered that, in the recent Australian election, the Green Party won a significant number of seats. They favor an ETS. Kloppers hoped to forestall their efforts, hence his support for the carbon tax. Supporting the carbon tax also allows Kloppers to truthfully say he is in favor of environmentally-friendly regulations.

DOMINANT STRATEGIES

One way to tame the complexity of strategic thinking is to make it less strategic. What if managers act without regard to the actions of others? This takes managers out of the hall of mirrors and puts them in front of one mirror. Looking back at them are the only people responsible for optimizing payoffs in nonstrategy land: themselves. In these situations, if managers do not choose an optimal strategy, they have only themselves to blame.

But mathematicians cannot ignore the interactivity of life; and life suggests there are times when managers possess an option that is strategically strong rela-

At the time of his announcement some accused Kloppers of not protecting the interests of shareholders. Clearly, those who accused Kloppers did not understand the strategic nature of the situation. Forced to choose between two paths, Kloppers chose the one where he could maintain more control. Frankly, he chose the path that increased firm value.[a]

On October 13, 2009, Dennis Berman of *The Wall Street Journal*, analyzed the proposed Comcast-NBC deal using a game theory model. Developed by Dr. Bueno de Mesquita, the model analyzes a merger situation and predicts outcomes. In analyzing the situation, the model recognizes the complexities of managerial behavior. For example, CEOs may pay a high price to acquire because it is in their interests, not those of the shareholders. The model also accounts for perceived negotiating power among the parties involved.

As a metric of the current state of managerial behavior, de Mesquita has programmed the model to assume all parties are purely self interested. This must be accurate because, according to declassified CIA documents, when CIA personnel "back-tested" predictions, they were correct 9 of 10 times.

One issue the model looked at was the anticipated behavior of a third firm, Vivendi. A large obstacle to the Comcast-GE deal was that Vivendi held a 20% stake in the GE Universal venture. They could sell the shares back to GE or use them to create an IPO. This threat certainly affected the share price negotiation between Vivendi and GE.

Model inputs consisted of both qualitative and quantitative data. For example, the model asked for input on managerial personalities, motives, and bargaining power. Valuation scenarios were created and analyzed.

After conducting the analysis, the model's most likely scenario was for Vivendi to sell its stake to GE at a price slightly below the expected valuation. On December 3, 2009, GE and Vivendi reached a purchase agreement. GE would purchase the 20% for $5.8 billion, slightly lower than the $6 billion many observers expected.[b] This shows the power of game theory to correctly anticipate the future decisions of managers. Used well, game theoretic reasoning is a valuable managerial tool.

[a] Paul Kerin. "A Game Theorist Plays a Trump Card," *The Australian*, September 20, 2010, p. 26.
[b] Dennis Berman. "In NBC Deal, Learn from Game Theory," *The Wall Street Journal*, October 13, 2009, p. C1.

tive to all others. Mathematicians represent these beliefs as **dominant strategies.** A dominant strategy is one whose payoff in any outcome is higher relative to all other feasible strategies.[1] Managers choose dominant strategies to optimize their expected return. Although the strategy choices of others still affect managerial payoffs, thinking about others will not change the managerial decision. A dominant strategy returns a higher payoff than any other strategy across all possible outcomes. Managers should always choose a dominant strategy if it is available.

It is easier to visually represent dominant strategies using the matrix form. Look at Figure 12.1 again. Managers at Allied have a dominant strategy to maintain the current spending level (left column). If managers at Barkley also maintain

Dominant strategies A strategy whose payout in any outcome is higher relative to all other feasible strategies.

1. A strategy is weakly dominant if it does at least as well as any other strategy for some outcomes (it is tied with another for the highest payoff) and better than any strategy for the remaining outcomes. Even if a strategy is only weakly dominant, a player would choose it.

current spending, Allied managers receive a payoff of $4 million (in blue); if Barkley managers increase spending, Allied managers earn $3 million (in blue). Barkley managers also face a dominant strategy: They will increase spending. If Allied managers spend at the current level, Barkley managers earn $4 million; if Allied managers increase spending, Barkley managers earn $3 million.

We can now predict that Allied managers will maintain their current spending and those at Barkley will increase it. We have a dominant strategy equilibrium. Why will this outcome prevail? Because each manager has a dominant strategy and each is always better off playing it. Why won't they change their strategy? Any change in strategy will lead to guaranteed lower payoffs. Domination is the minimum hurdle required of rationality. If you choose dominated strategies when you know dominant ones exist, you are hurting yourself.

Dominant strategies are the stress reducers of the strategic world. They ease the mental cost of decision making and simplify the analytic process. With them, managers can ignore the actions of others. Given the hectic schedules of managers, they are a great time-saver. For example, in Chapter 13 we discuss auctions. Auction design can determine whether a dominant strategy exists for a particular auction. In auctions with no dominant strategy, managers must consider the bids of others in choosing their bids. In ones with a dominant strategy, managers need not. Good strategic managers understand the difference and do not waste time thinking about something irrelevant to a decision.

Not surprisingly, it is dominant to first look for dominant strategies in matrix games. Even if a game is not solvable through dominance, this process eliminates outcomes mapped to dominated strategies; we essentially reduce the set of playable strategies. Recall that no player should ever play a dominated strategy because he or she is always better off playing the dominant one. So we can eliminate dominated strategies from consideration. We never reach those outcomes because no dominated strategy is played. Visually, our outcome matrix is reduced by rows or columns. Mentally, the analysis is simplified because we consider fewer outcomes.

More important strategically, when managers eliminate a strategy, they reduce the set of possible outcomes. This in turn may change a formerly nondominated strategy into a dominated one. This iterative process can proceed until each player is left with only one playable strategy (that is, the situation is dominance solvable).

Figure 12.4 is the matrix form of the game shown in Figure 12.2. Managers can always model strategy as either an extensive or a matrix form game. Each game form is linked to a particular game of the other form with identical players, outcomes, and payoffs. They are like fraternal twins who act identically.

We now look at the strategies for Allied and Barkley managers. Barkley has a dominated strategy: $1.35 dominates $1.00. For any Allied strategy, Barkley managers earn more by pricing at $1.35. If Allied managers price at $0.95, $1.35 earns 5 relative to 3 for $1.00. If they price at $1.30, the ratio is 8 to 7; and if Allied manages to price at $1.55, the ratio is 14 to 10. Barkley managers should never choose

FIGURE 12.4

Matrix Form Representation of Figure 12.2

		Allied's pricing strategies		
		$0.95	$1.30	$1.55
	$1.00	3, 6	7, 1	10, 4
Barkley's pricing strategies	$1.35	5, 1	8, 2	14, 7
	$1.65	6, 0	6, 2	8, 5

$1.00, so we need not further consider its outcomes. This effectively reduces the figure's matrix to that shown in part A of Figure 12.5.

Because we eliminated Barkley's $1.00 strategy as a playable strategy, Allied managers now face a dominated strategy—two in fact: $1.55 dominates both $0.95 and $1.30. Hence the matrix is reduced to that shown in part B of Figure 12.5. Allied managers have only one playable strategy: charging $1.55. Therefore, Barkley managers now face another dominated strategy. Because 14 is greater than 8, Barkley managers will charge $1.35. So this game has a dominant strategy equilibrium: Allied managers will price at $1.55 and Barkley managers will price at $1.35.

Although both this game and the one represented in Figure 12.1 have dominant strategy equilibria, they are solved using different degrees of rationality. Most people view rationality as dichotomous: If you are not rational, you are irrational. But rationality has continuous measures. One such measure is the degree of rationality required to reach an equilibrium. Because of interactive payoffs, we have to worry about not only our own rationality but also the rationality of others. So the degree of rationality measures the number of conjectures required to reach an equilibrium.

For example, in Figure 12.1 managers can solve the game simply by knowing they are rational. If you are rational, choose your dominant strategy. No matter what others do, that is the best response. But this single degree of rationality is not sufficient to ensure that managers reach the equilibrium in Figure 12.4. When dominance is of the iterative variety, managers need to consider the rationality of others.

Let us view the game from the decision viewpoint of Barkley managers. "Well, we know we are rational. We see that $1.00 is dominated, so we will not price at $1.00. Fine; what are our beliefs about the behavior of Allied managers? Will they

---

FIGURE 12.5

Iterative Dominance

A. Barkley's $1.00 strategy is eliminated.

		Allied's pricing strategies		
		$0.95	**$1.30**	**$1.55**
Barkley's pricing strategies	$1.35	5, 1	8, 2	14, 7
	$1.65	6, 0	6, 2	8, 5

B. Allied's $0.95 and $1.30 strategies are eliminated.

		Allied's pricing strategies
		$1.55
Barkley's pricing strategies	$1.35	14, 7
	$1.65	8, 5

---

believe our price of $1.00 is dominated and we will not price there? If so, do Allied managers realize that pricing at $1.55 is a dominant strategy?"

In matrix form games, we measure the degree of rationality by the rounds of iterative dominance needed to reach the equilibrium. The game in Figure 12.4 requires three rounds. It is our experience that many people act rationally for games with a few degrees of rationality, but few people understand games of many degrees.

Life is complex. Domination principles help make managerial life easier. But few games have a dominant strategy equilibrium; interaction with others is generally more complicated. How can managers anticipate behavior in games without a dominant strategy equilibrium?

THE NASH EQUILIBRIUM

That is the question mathematician John Nash asked himself in the early 1950s. His answer is our most widely used solution concept: the Nash equilibrium. Similar to dominance, Nash developed guidelines for behavior that are rational, optimal, and stable. He specified behavior if players lacked a strategy that dominated all others. Here is the intuition underlying Nash's ideas.

A player's objective remains the same whether he has one or more playable strategies: to maximize the payoff. If he must choose among playable strategies, he selects the optimal one. And because payoffs are interactive, he must choose conditional on what he thinks of others. So what rule are the others following? If they are the same (rational), their goals are identical: to maximize their payoffs relative to what others will choose. Hence each will choose the strategy that maximizes his or her payoff, conditional on others doing the same. That is John Nash's prescribed behavior for players with more than one playable strategy.

Nash's concept is more transparent in its mathematical form. Let each of N players identify a strategy $s^\star_i$, where $i = 1, 2, 3, \ldots N$. An outcome represents an array of strategies $s^\star = (s^\star_1, s^\star_2, s^\star_3, \ldots, s^\star_N)$. Let $B_i(s^\star)$ be the payoff to player i when $s^\star$ is chosen, with i being any player, $i = 1, 2, 3, \ldots, N$. Then a Nash equilibrium is an array of strategies such that

$$B_i(s^\star_1, s^\star_2, s^\star_3, \ldots, s^\star_N) \geq B_i(s'_1, s^\star_2, s^\star_3, \ldots, s^\star_N) \quad \text{for all outcomes}$$

The left side of this equation states the existence of an outcome(s), defined by the array of player strategies, where all have a best response to the best responses of others. The right side states that if any player unilaterally changes strategy, she realizes a lower payoff; that is, she chooses a dominated outcome. For a complex and messy process, Nash devised an elegant solution. It treats all with equal rationality and so limits behavior. Dominance is still present, although now conditional. The solution exists for all games with a finite number of players and outcomes.

Dominance is unconditional in dominance-solvable games. We need not speculate about the behavior of others because it makes no difference. But anything less than unconditional dominance requires anticipation. And because payoffs are interactive, this anticipation requires a common vision with others. So Nash prescribes a behavioral rule. Maximize your payoff, conditional on all others doing the same. A Nash solution is dominant, conditional on this rule being followed.

Recall that an equilibrium needs to be rational, optimal, and stable. Nash's solution is rational in the sense that all players follow the prescribed behavior. It is optimal in that all try to maximize their payoffs. And it is stable because no player can unilaterally change strategy and realize a higher payoff.

Figure 12.6 illustrates the following. The numbers represent profits (in millions of dollars). Recall that Barkley entered the market first, followed by Allied. Both firms must now introduce new products. Each can choose one product of several; but because of financial constraints, only one can be supported. Managers at both firms understand this. Their choice to introduce a product is conditional on how they think the other will behave. Nash says that we all behave identically: We maximize payoffs conditional on others doing the same. We will change behavior to obtain a higher payoff but not a lower one.

FIGURE 12.6

New Product Introduction

		Allied		
		Product alpha	Product beta	Product zeta
Barkley	Product lambda	4, 6	9, 8	6, 10
	Product pi	6, 8	8, 9	7, 8
	Product sigma	9, 8	7, 7	5, 5

Look at Figure 12.6. Remember our decision rule: Look for dominated strategies. This is quickly done. Confirm that neither firm has a dominated strategy. Now use the following algorithm. For each strategy, indicate the behavior of the other. For example, if Barkley managers know (with certainty) that Allied will introduce alpha, what will they do? Barkley managers receive 4 if they introduce lambda, 6 if pi, and 9 if sigma (the first numbers in each cell of the product alpha column). Because 9 is the highest of the three payoffs, Barkley managers will introduce sigma if they know Allied will introduce alpha. Write a B in the alpha–sigma outcome. Do the same for strategies beta and zeta. Now follow the same procedure for Allied (the sequence of players makes no difference). For example, if Barkley introduces sigma, what should Allied managers choose? If Allied managers produce alpha, they receive 8, if beta 7, and if zeta 5. So Allied managers will introduce alpha if they know Barkley will introduce sigma. Mark an A in this outcome. Do the same for strategies lambda and pi. The resulting matrix is illustrated in Figure 12.7.

Any cell with an A and a B is a Nash equilibrium. In this game the Nash solution is for Barkley to introduce sigma (and receive 9) and Allied to introduce alpha (and receive 8). Let us understand why this outcome is predicted by Nash An A or B represents a conditional dominant strategy—a best response to a specific strategy of others. A Nash equilibrium is a meeting of the best responses—an outcome where all play conditionally dominant strategies. Beyond the reach of an individual, it is attained by the group.

Each player acts in his or her own best interest and maximizes payoffs. A player not choosing the Nash strategy is playing a dominated one (assuming others play their Nash strategies). Hence no player has an incentive to unilaterally change behavior. For example, as long as Allied produces alpha, Barkley managers want to produce sigma and receive $9 million. If they produce pi, they receive only $6 million, and if

FIGURE 12.7

New Product Introduction with Other's Behavior

		Allied		
		Product alpha	Product beta	Product zeta
Barkley	Product lambda	4, 6	(B) 9, 8	6, 10 (A)
	Product pi	6, 8	8, 9 (A)	(B) 7, 8
	Product sigma	(B) 9, 8 (A)	7, 7	5, 5

lambda, only $4 million. Allied managers face the same scenario: lower payoffs for any change in behavior. Interactive payoffs hold the two hostage to each other.

Recall our example of network economics in Chapter 6. Building a transportation network can be expensive but it does have strategic value. A new entrant has a very difficult task because shippers want to call one carrier who will take any package anywhere. As Fred Smith (the CEO of FedEx) once said: "You don't want to have a yellow phone to call Houston, a green phone to call London, a blue phone to call Los Angeles. . . . You want one color phone to call anywhere. You cannot enter this market piecemeal with just New York to Chicago service when an incumbent can go from New York to anywhere." This is a lesson that successful international giant DHL learned when they attempted to enter the U.S. package freight market. They entered in 2003 by buying Airborne, which had a less-than-complete network that they operated poorly. DHL could not provide the full service that the competitors could. DHL tried to counteract this disadvantage by offering cheaper rates, but this strategy was unsuccessful. The only other entrant into this market has been UPS, but they could piggyback on their already existing and very efficient ground network. Building the network first by FedEx initially lead to a monopoly in the overnight market, then a duopoly when UPS entered. The U.S. Postal Service provides a third player in this market but their network is mandated (and as we are painfully aware, the USPS is hemorrhaging money).

It should be noted that FedEx entered the ground transportation market when interstate motor carriage was deregulated in 1980 and further when intrastate motor carriage was deregulated in 1995. While UPS has integrated its ground and air network, FedEx runs two separate networks. But to this day, FedEx still has the largest market in the air part of the business (where it entered first) and UPS still has the largest market in the ground part of the business (where it entered first).

Let's look at how DHL competed with FedEx and UPS when DHL entered the U.S. domestic market for small package delivery (basically packages weighing up to 150 pounds—average weight much less) in 2002. DHL was (and still is) a powerhouse in international small shipments. FedEx and UPS were firmly established (and highly thought of) by U.S. domestic customers and both serve extensive international markets (just not as well as DHL).

Suppose there are two customers, A and B, of domestic small shipments. If they use FedEx and or UPS, they both profit by 100 Suppose if DHL could actually replicate their international service in the U.S. domestic market, each customer would benefit by 120 if they switched to DHL. However, if one customer used FedEx/UPS and the other used DHL, each customer would have a profit of 90 (the splitting of the market leads to less economies of scale, hence higher unit cost, and hence higher rates). The situation appears in the game theory matrix (Figure 12.8) below.

Using bolds to indicate Customer A's best choice *given* Customer B's choice and underlines to indicate Customer B's best choice *given* Customer A's choice shows two Nash equilibria: the northwest corner with both customers using their current carriers FedEx/UPS and the southeast corner with both customers using DHL. Clearly the southeast corner Nash is superior.

But before DHL entered the market, FedEx/UPS had locked the customers into their respective systems through long term contracts or through inertia (I've always used them). If both shippers would communicate with each other, they would mutually move to the southeast Nash (since 120 > 100). But neither customer would *unilaterally* leave their current provider (because 100 > 90). The difficulty is that there are basically thousands and thousands of system users. So although two can easily say to one another: I'll switch if you switch, for thousands to do so would be very difficult to coordinate. Of course, here's where national media and trade press can help spread the word about the benefits (sort of a Consumer Reports on the small shipments industry).

FIGURE 12.8

Payoffs for Each Customer From Using FedEx/UPS and/or DHL

		Customer B	
		Use FedEx/UPS	Use DHL
Customer A	Use FedEx/UPS	**100**, 100	90, 90
	Use DHL	90, 90	**120**, 120

Is there anything that DHL as a second mover could do by itself to break the stranglehold that FedEx/UPS's first mover advantage had over them? One way is to up the 90 payoff a customer gets from using DHL when the other customer uses FedEx/UPS so that it's over 100 (say 100[+]). This could occur by offering price discounts for DHL services (and DHL did lower prices).

Suppose that a DHL lowering of prices changed the game matrix of Figure 12.8 to that of Figure 12.9 below.

Using the bolds and the underlines as in Figure 12.9 shows now that both Customer A and Customer B have a dominant strategy to switch to DHL. They don't need to coordinate; they just all do what's unilaterally best for themselves and they all switch. The first mover advantage of FedEx/UPS is broken.

If only that was the story for DHL. Alas, it is not. Their service level was so poor that their perceived payoffs to customers did not reach 100[+] even with their rate cuts. Thus the matrix result continued form Figure 12.8. DHL could never again much of a market share in the U.S. domestic small shipments market (perhaps 10% at best and that from customers who cared about price and not service) and lasted only five years in the U.S. market (each year proclaiming that next year they would be profitable and each year losing money which approximated $10 billion from 2003–2008). It is interesting to note that the other major international player (TNT) has shown no interest in entering the U.S. domestic market (presumably because of the cost of building a network and overcoming the first mover advantages of FedEx and UPS).

Networks may be one way or two way (as the phone and FedEx networks above). The pipeline business (oil, oil products, natural gas, water, sewage) are one way networks. Oil flows from A to B in the pipe but there is no return trip. There are limited benefits to existing customers form adding more customers to the current system (unless the current system is undersubscribed). There are some advantages to customers and the pipeline when more customers moving the same product join.

FIGURE 12.9

Payoffs for Each Customer From Using FedEx/UPS and/or DHL after DHL Lowers Rates

		Customer B	
		Use FedEx/UPS	Use DHL
Customer A	Use FedEx/UPS	100, 100	100[+], 100[+]
	Use DHL	100[+], 100[+]	130[+], 130[+]

This is because the various customers product can be co-mingled and the pipeline doesn't have to add separators to keep different products segregated. There are dis-benefits form having too many customers as congestion may develop in the network.

If the number of customers and their flows can be determined *before* the pipeline is constructed, then there are major advantages of adding new customers since a doubling of the pipeline diameter (a major input to the production of the pipeline's services is the amount of steel necessary to construct the pipeline) quadruples the area of the pipeline (the output that the pipeline can produce). This leads to major economies of scale, lowering the unit cost, and potentially lowering the rate. But with the system already in place, congestion raises its ugly head. Think of congestion on existing road networks and airports at rush hour, website crashes when too many people want to access a site at the same time, power failures or brownouts when the temperature skyrockets.

Not only do networks provide the network positive externalities shown above with respect to connectivity, but they can also provide network complementarities. Think of the development of Skype for use on the Internet. Just as with phone service, if there was no one to Skype with, the software would be not valuable. But as the Internet expands, more services will be developed. Here's just a few that have taken hold: Netflix DVD streaming, EBay auctions, online shopping, online dating services, etc, etc.

Think of other network complementarities that have developed because of networks. Electrical networks have generated a vast industry that produces all sorts of electrical appliances. The highway network (which was urged on the government by the auto industry) has grown the automobile industry and all of its complementary industries, e.g., tires, service stations, car detailers, roadside motels, AAA, a pine tree air freshener industry, etc. And as mentioned above, the Internet has lead to a software development industry. The list goes on.

Just one more example to bring the concept of network externalities home. Think of the value of the two way network if you run a dating service. It's hard to sign up the first customer because they'll ask: Who is there for me to date? But when lots are signed up, there are lots times lots minus one potential matches (and that's really a lot). The old method was tedious. You went to a bar and tried you luck or you placed a classified ad and waited for a response (and then you met up in a bar). But now you enter who you are and what you're searching for and you're matched with others who are "compatible." People, of course, lie on these questionnaires (especially about age, height, weight, good looks) but the number of "hookups" are non-trivial and some of the guessing is taken out of the search process. And, of course, the larger the number of subscribers to the dating service (members of the network), the higher is any given subscriber's probability of finding Ms. or Mr. Right. This same principle applies to things like online auctions. The more people that want to sell an item called X, the better it is for buyers of the item and the more people that want to buy a unique item Y, the better it is for the seller of that item.

STRATEGIC FORESIGHT: THE USE OF BACKWARD INDUCTION

A Taoist saying is, "Good strategists take care of the great while the great is small." Good managers use strategic foresight. The ancient Taoists called this the ability to see what others could not see. We define **strategic foresight** as a manager's ability to make decisions today that are rational given what is anticipated in the future. For example, a manager builds extra capacity today because she believes (correctly) that demand will increase in the near future. Strategic foresight is a principle that should always be used. Remember that the decisions of today can never affect your past—only your future. In decision making you always want to look forward. Using strategic foresight also helps managers understand that decisions have both short- and long-term consequences.

Game theory formally models strategic foresight through what is called **backward induction**. In game theory we use backward induction to solve games by looking to the future, determining what strategy players will choose (anticipation), and then choosing an action that is rational, based on these beliefs. Backward induction is most easily seen in extensive form games because of the ability to map the choices of players.

Figure 12.10 shows a game in extensive form. Recall from Figure 12.7 that Barkley managers have chosen to introduce sigma, and Allied managers have chosen to introduce alpha. They must now decide whether to expand their product lines. Either firm's managers have the choice to expand or not. Barkley is the

Strategic foresight A manager's ability to make decisions today that are rational given what is anticipated in the future.

Backward induction Used in game theory to solve games by looking to the future, determining what strategy players will choose (anticipation), and then choosing an action that is rational, based on these beliefs.

FIGURE 12.10

Allied–Barkley Expansion Decision

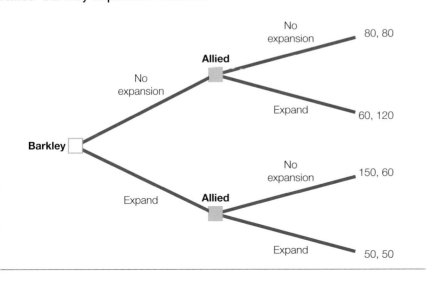

market leader, so assume its managers will reach their decision first. After seeing the decision of Barkley managers, those at Allied decide whether to expand. Payoffs for the four possible outcomes are given in Figure 12.10.

Let us see how a manager with strategic foresight can use backward induction to solve this game. The farthest left decision node represents the decision of Barkley's managers to expand or not. If they decide to expand, Allied's managers face the situation represented by Allied's bottom decision node. If Barkley does not expand, Allied faces the situation represented by the top decision node. Barkley managers use strategic foresight. They want to make a decision today that maximizes their payoff, given their vision of the future. Barkley managers realize that if they expand, Allied will receive a payoff of $50 million if it expands and $60 million if it does not.

Hence Barkley managers anticipate that if they expand, Allied will not. What if Barkley decides not to expand? Allied receives a payoff of $120 million for line expansion and $80 million if it does not expand. Thus, Barkley managers anticipate that Allied will expand if they choose not to. So if they expand, they anticipate a payoff of $150 million (because Allied will not expand). If Barkley does not expand, its managers should anticipate a payoff of $60 million (because Allied will expand). Since $150 million is greater than $60 million, the managers at Barkley know they should expand their product line.

To use backward induction we must come back from the future. We anticipate the future actions of others and then choose actions that are rational, conditioned on our expected behavior of others.

Backward Induction and the Centipede Game

The usefulness of backward induction in strategic thinking is clearly shown in the simple **centipede game**. Many studies have used this game to study whether subjects use and understand backward induction. The game is shown in Figure 12.11.

Two players (*A* and *B*) participate in this sequential game. Player *A* moves first and can choose either down (*D*) or right (*R*). If player *A* chooses *D*, the

Centipede game A sequential game involving a series of decisions that shows the usefulness of backward induction in strategic thinking.

FIGURE 12.11

The Centipede Game

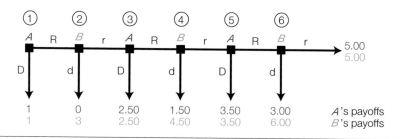

						A's payoffs
1	0	2.50	1.50	3.50	3.00	
1	3	2.50	4.50	3.50	6.00	B's payoffs

game is over and both players receive a payoff of $1. If player *A* chooses *R*, then player *B* faces a similar choice. She can choose *d* or *r*. If player *B* chooses *d*, the game is over; *A* receives a payoff of $0, and *B* receives a payoff of $3. If player B chooses *r*, the game continues, and player *A* chooses either *D* or *R* again. The game continues, until one player chooses down or player *B* is asked to choose for a third time. At this point, if player *B* chooses *d*, *A* receives $3 and *B* receives $6. If player *B* chooses *r* at this point, both players receive $5. Look at Figure 12.11 and assume you are Player *A*. What strategy would you choose?

We solve the game using backward induction. The game is actually a series of six decisions. Player *A* chooses at stages 1, 3, and 5; player *B* chooses at stages 2, 4, and 6. We need to go to the end of the game and work backward from the future. Look at stage 6: Player *B* can choose down and receive $6 or choose right and receive $5. Because $6 is greater than $5, we anticipate that player *B* will choose down. Move backward to stage 5 because we now know the future. Player *A* faces the following. If *A* chooses right, he knows (anticipates correctly) that *B* will choose down, giving *A* a $3 payoff. Or *A* can choose down and receive a payoff of $3.50. Because $3.50 is greater than $3, *A* will choose down at stage 5. What should player *B* choose at stage 4 knowing this? *B* can choose down and receive a payoff of $4.50 or choose right and receive a payoff of $3.50 (because *B* anticipates that *A* will choose down at stage 5). Because $4.50 is greater than $3.50, player *B* will choose down at stage 4. We move backward to stage 3. Player *A* can choose down and receive a payoff of $2.50 or choose right and receive a payoff of $1.50 (since *A* anticipates that *B* chooses down at stage 4). Because $2.50 is greater than $1.50, player *A* will choose down at stage 3. We are now at stage 2. Player *B* can choose down and receive a payoff of $3 or choose right and receive a payoff of $2.50 (since player *A* will choose down at stage 3). So player *B* will choose down at stage 2. Finally we find ourselves in the present; this is decision time. At Stage 1, player *A* can choose down and receive $1 or choose right and receive $0 (because *B* will choose down at stage 2). Player *A* will choose down at stage 1. This is the only rational choice, given our view of the future. Player *A* will choose down at stage 1, and both players will realize a payoff of $1. What the ancients called foresight, game theorists model as backward induction.

Now comes the real question. How do subjects behave while playing the game? Initially few subjects appear to use foresight (or they have a distorted view of the future). Subjects appear to focus on the growing size of the payoffs and try to move down this path. At some late stage, either they choose down or the person they are playing with chooses it. The next time they play, most subjects tend to choose down at an earlier stage (especially those whose partners chose down in the earlier game). By the third or fourth play sequence, most A players are resigned to the fact that they should choose down at stage 1. They do so hesitantly because they still see the path of greater payoffs. But they also know the future. Experience has shown the wisdom of backward induction.

The Credibility of Commitments

Backward induction has many uses. One is to test the credibility of commitments. From threats to promises, epithet slinging to love's rhapsody, we want to know whether we should believe others. When facing these situations, always check credibility first. That is a dominant strategy. Consider only credible commitments. A commitment is **credible** if the costs of falsely sending one are greater than the associated benefits. Managers at a company who proclaim its product is best are not credible. There is little cost to proclaiming this, and associated benefits are high. The managers can make that claim credible by offering a product warranty. A warranty increases the commitment cost (if it is falsely sent). There are many uses for such costs.

Credible commitment When the costs of falsely sending a commitment are greater than the associated benefits.

Consider the following. Recall that Barkley managers expanded their product line but Allied managers have not. Allied's managers decide to counter Barkley's product line extension by dropping the price of their product. However, they are concerned that if they drop their price, Barkley managers will follow with a price cut of their own. In fact, Barkley's managers told a common supplier of both firms that if Allied drops its price, they will drop theirs. What should Allied managers do?

Allied's managers first must consider whether Barkley's threat to drop its price is credible. They can do so by looking at Figure 12.12 and solving the game using backward induction. Barkley managers can either keep their price high or drop it. Allied managers have the same two strategies available to them. What happens if

---

FIGURE 12.12

Does Barkley Have a Credible Threat?

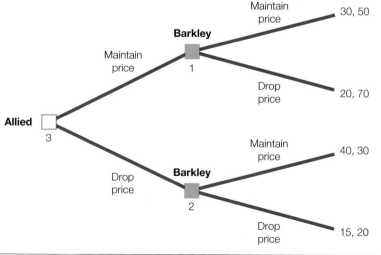

Allied managers drop their price? Those at Barkley can either keep their price high and earn $30 million or drop their price and earn $20 million. Because $30 million is greater than $20 million, Barkley managers should keep their price high if Allied managers reduce their price. What if Allied maintains its price? Barkley managers could keep their price high and earn $50 million or drop their price and earn $70 million. Hence Barkley managers will drop their price if Allied managers maintain their high price. Given that Allied managers can anticipate these actions from those at Barkley, how should Allied managers decide? They should drop their price. Clearly those at Barkley will not drop their price. The threat by Barkley managers to lower price is not credible, so it should be ignored. If forced to carry out the threat, Barkley managers will refuse. To do so would cost them $10 million in lost profit.

The equilibrium just described is a subgame perfect equilibrium. A **subgame** is defined as being a segment of a larger game. The subgames are marked in Figure 12.12. As you can see, within the overall game, the three constitute three separate subgames. In repeated games, all subgame perfect equilibria are also Nash equilibria, although not all Nash equilibria are subgame perfect. Nash equilibria that are based on noncredible threats are not subgame perfect. Formally, we define a subgame perfect equilibrium as a strategy profile s^* in the overall game (D) such that for any history h, the profile s^*_h is a Nash equilibrium for the subgame $D(h)$. Intuitively this says the equilibrium for any subgame is rational, conditional on equilibrium play in the future. For example, in the centipede game, the strategy profile of A choosing D (down) at stage 1 is rational, conditional on what we know will happen in future subgames. So this is a subgame perfect equilibrium.

Subgame A segment of a larger game.

REPEATED GAMES

The business world is characterized by repeated interactions. In many markets, firms and managers compete against each other for decades. Within firms, managers interact with each other over long periods. So how does a perception of future interaction affect behavior? Managers need to understand how the prospect of a future can change player actions. Again we turn to backward induction to help us understand the implications of repeated play.

We illustrate the strategic effect of repeated play using a stylized example from a class of games known as prisoner's dilemmas. Suppose Allied and Barkley produce an identical product. They also have similar cost structures. Managers at both firms must decide whether to price the product high or low. This situation is shown in Figure 12.13.

The Nash equilibrium of this game is for managers at both firms to sell their products at a low price (and earn $3 million). Although both realize they are better off if each maintains a high price, they are afraid that managers at the other firm will then drop the price and steal the market. Hence managers at both firms price low. If Allied and Barkley managers compete in only one market for a single

FIGURE 12.13

Pricing as a Prisoner's Dilemma

		Allied's pricing strategies	
		Price high	Price low
Barkley's pricing strategies	Price high	5, 5	1, 20
	Price low	20, 1	3, 3

instance, we expect both of them to keep prices low. After all, that is the rational choice.

But what if they are rivals for a long time? Instead of playing this pricing game once, they play it multiple times. Should we still expect managers at both firms to price low? Each firm can see it is forfeiting $2 million per period, simply because neither can trust the other to maintain the high price. As Emerson commented, "Distrust is expensive."

Strategically, the key difference between one-shot games and those that are repeated is the presence of a future. A future introduces behavior not possible in a one-shot world. Trust, reputation, promises, threats, and reciprocity need a future to exist. A future also means that payoffs are no longer relegated to the short term because we now face longer-term implications. A betrayal of trust may create gains in the present, but these may be outweighed by future losses.

Models of repeated games reflect and account for this wider range of feasible behavior. They use the idea of a future to construct norms that let players reach mutually beneficial outcomes. For example, in the preceding situation, these norms help maintain an equilibrium where both firms price high. The risk of one firm undercutting the other is mitigated by the threat of future punishment. Of course such threats must be credible. Let us see how these models work.

The first distinction these models make is whether or not the time horizon is finite. Cooperative behavior is easier to maintain in an infinite horizon game because the future always looms. In finite horizon games, the future grows smaller as we approach the last period. So consider an infinite horizon in the game shown in Figure 12.13. If Allied and Barkley managers cooperate and price high, each receives a payoff of 5 per period. One can defect, price low, and earn 20 for a single period. The other will then price low, and each will receive 3 for the rest of the game. So the incremental earnings of 15 (20 − 5) are lost within 8 periods ((5 − 3) × 8). In fact, in an infinite horizon game, no single-period noncooperative payoff will be larger than the sum of cooperative future payoffs.

The long shadow of a future in an infinite horizon game causes the well-known result called the **folk theorem**. This theorem basically states that any type of behavior can be supported by an equilibrium (as long as the players believe there is a high probability that future interaction will occur). The support for a wide range of behaviors occurs because the future always matters in these games; hence credible threats and promises can alter the current behavior of players. Of course this makes it much harder to accurately predict behavior in games with infinite horizons.

Finite horizon games are fundamentally different because as the game progresses, the future necessarily grows shorter. Because behavior in these games is predicated on the use of credible signals of future behavior, their power diminishes as the future grows shorter. And in the last period, signals hold no power because there is no future (the last period of a repeated game is akin to a single shot); hence the Nash equilibrium is identical to that of a one-shot game. In the pricing game, this means that managers at both firms price low. Without the restraint of credible signals and a future, managers should expect others to act opportunistically.

But wait. If we know managers at both firms will price low in the last period, how should this affect their actions in the prior-to-last period? Let us again use backward induction. Is there any strategy managers at either firm can follow to change the low-price outcome of the last period? No: Regardless of the strategies played, managers at both firms will price low. Their strategic fate is sealed. If this is true, the rational strategy is to price low in this period, too. And just as we saw in the centipede game, similar reasoning extends backward to the first period. So the equilibrium in a repeated version of the game is identical to that of a one-shot game. Managers at both firms should price low.

But what about the looming future and the use of credible commitments? Shouldn't that change behavior? Game theorists had similar thoughts, so they developed the theory to account for these factors. This was a more difficult task relative to the infinite horizon game because they had to account for the final period.

One insight recognized by game theorists is that not everyone is opportunistic. What happens if nonopportunistic individuals are in the population and you do not know (with certainty) whether you are playing with one? How does that change predicted managerial behavior?

INCOMPLETE INFORMATION GAMES

This question established a branch of game theory called **incomplete information games (IIG)**. These games loosen the restrictive assumption that all players have the same information. The introduction of incomplete information makes it possible to derive cooperation (price high in Figure 12.13) as an equilibrium

Folk theorem This theorem states that any type of behavior can be supported by an equilibrium (as long as the players believe there is a high probability that future interaction will occur).

Incomplete information games (IIG) A branch of game theory that loosens the restrictive assumption that all players have the same information.

behavior. Now, when we backwardly induct, pricing low is not necessarily the predicted strategy in the last period. Nonopportunistic players may still price high in the last period because they obtain satisfaction from cooperating. They do not care that there is no future; they just want to cooperate. Instead of pricing low from the initial period, players may want to experiment in early periods by pricing high to determine whether they are playing with a nonopportunistic type.

One strategy players may use to experiment is commonly referred to as **tit for tat**. Players using tit for tat cooperate in the first period. In all succeeding periods they mimic the preceding period's strategy of the other player. For example, assume Barkley managers use a tit-for-tat strategy. In period 1 they price high. In period 2 Barkley managers mimic Allied's period 1 strategy. In period 3 they mimic Allied's period 2 strategy. So Barkley managers begin the game by pricing high. They continue to price high as long as Allied managers price high. If Allied managers price low, they price low in the following period and continue to price low until Allied managers price high again. Using this strategy, Barkley managers determine whether those at Allied are opportunistic and, if they are, suffer only one period of low payoffs.

In IIG models, players possess asymmetric information. For example, Barkley managers may know more details about their own cost function than Allied managers know. IIG models summarize this asymmetric information in the form of player types. A *type* consists of player characteristics that are unknown to others. In business, types may consist of competitive attributes, like cost functions. In personal relationships, they may consist of personality traits, like trustworthiness.

Specific types are represented by different payoff (preference) functions. So a low-cost type has a different payoff function than a high-cost type. A simple IIG model is shown in Figure 12.14. Allied managers need to decide whether to enter a product market where Barkley is an incumbent. Allied managers are uncertain of the reaction of Barkley managers if they decide to enter the market. If Barkley managers are "tough," those at Allied expect them to lower their price and defend their market. If Barkley managers are "soft," those at Allied expect them to keep their price high, thereby allowing Allied to enter the market.

When Barkley managers are actually tough (part A of Figure 12.14), the Nash equilibrium is for Allied managers not to enter the market and for those at Barkley to price low. Of course Barkley managers will not have to price low because those at Allied will never enter the market. When Barkley managers are actually soft (part B of Figure 12.14), the Nash equilibrium is for Allied to enter the market and for Barkley to price high (allowing entry). Note that Allied payoffs are identical across parts A and B. The incomplete information is about Barkley managers, not those at Allied. Only the payoffs of Barkley managers change.

So if Allied managers know the true type of Barkley managers, their decision is easy. If Barkley managers are soft, they enter the market; if they are tough they don't. Unfortunately, Allied managers aren't sure which type is true. And knowing this, can Barkley managers influence their beliefs?

Tit for tat Strategy that allows players to cooperate in the first period and in all succeeding periods the players mimic the preceding period's strategy of the other player.

FIGURE 12.14

Tough or Soft Barkley Managers

A. Barkley managers are tough.

Allied's strategies

		Enter the market	Do not enter the market
Barkley's strategies	Fight (price low)	6, 2	8, 3
	No fight (price high)	5, 4	2, 3

B. Barkley managers are soft.

Allied's strategies

		Enter the market	Do not enter the market
Barkley's strategies	Fight (price low)	2, 2	3, 3
	No fight (price high)	4, 4	7, 3

REPUTATION BUILDING

The presence of a future and incomplete information are the necessary ingredients for building reputations. In their presence, a reputation is a rent-generating asset. In the example here, if Barkley managers convince Allied managers they are tough in the early periods of the repeated game, Allied managers will stay out of the market in the later stages.

In game theory, a reputation is simply the history of behavior. Intuitively, reputation-building models parallel the human thought process. When we are unsure about the traits of others, we look to past behavior for clues. We use this information to form probabilistic beliefs regarding the traits of others. "I think I can trust him, but I wouldn't bet my life on it." In effect, we use a reputation model to infer future actions from past behavior. For example, assume a friend asks you to lend her $100. If you have previously lent money to this friend, you

PROBLEM SOLVED: Can Rating Agencies Improve a Bank's Capital Structure?

Suppose banks A and B compete with each other for high-wealth clientele by simultaneously choosing how much capital each should hold. Because of the rich clientele, neither bank is regulated or rated by the industry rating agency Unstandard and Rich (U&R). If both banks choose HIGH capital, then consumers will perceive each to be safe and there will be little systemic risk and both banks will earn profits of 50. If both banks choose LOW capital, each will reduce its cost of capital, but each will be perceived by clients as riskier and each will earn profits of 20. If one bank chooses LOW and the other HIGH, the LOW capital bank will be able to offer more attractive terms and increase its profit to 60, while the HIGH capital bank will earn only 10.

We can use game theory to determine what capital each bank will choose. A's best choices given B's choices are underlined. B's best choices given A's choices are bolded.

Is it possible to change the game in a way that allows the banks to maximize profits, that is, to both choose High capital? Suppose the directors of Bank A realize that, without regulation and rating, clients do not fully realize how risky a bank will be if it carries low capital. With such a LOW rating by U&R, clients would fully realize the true risk and profits would be reduced by 15 from the numbers given above (the profit is 15 lower whatever the strategy chosen by the rival). The profits for HIGH capital are as before. The directors realize that, if they choose to be rated voluntarily, the decision is irreversible and Bank B would be forced to follow. Does the decision by the directors of Bank A to be rated by U&R advantageously change the game for the banks? Indeed, it does, as can be seen in the matrix below where A's best choices given B's choices are underlined. B's best choices given A's choices are bolded.

| | Bank A | |
	HIGH capital	LOW capital
HIGH capital	50, 50	10, _60_
LOW capital	**60**, 10	**20**, _20_

Bank B (left label) · Bank A (top label)

| | | Bank A | |
		HIGH capital	LOW capital
Bank B	HIGH capital	**50**, _50_	**10**, 45
	LOW capital	45, _10_	5, 5

The Nash equilibrium is both banks choosing LOW capital. It's a prisoner's dilemma game. The win-win scenario is both banks choosing HIGH capital; but this scenario will not occur given the dominant strategies of each bank to choose LOW capital.

Bank A would choose to be rated. Bank B would follow. With ratings by U&R, each bank has a dominant strategy to choose high capital. Thus, both Bank A and Bank B make a profit of 50.

The lesson learned is that providing information that is valuable to both the banks and their clients can improve payoffs.

will recall whether she paid you back. You are more likely to lend money to a friend who repaid a previous debt. Why? Because the friend paid back the earlier debt, you perceive a higher probability that he or she will pay back this new debt. If the previous debt was not repaid, you are less likely to lend the person money again.

So in situations with futures and incomplete information, managers need to generate reputations to earn future rents. In all such situations, using backward induction, managers need to consider how current behavior will affect the future. Reneging on a debt has immediate payoffs (the debtor gains the amount lent) and long-term consequences (the lender is less likely to offer money in the future). Although these reputation models are too complex to explain here, the underlying idea is simple. In games with a future, players must consider both the present and the future. The payoff managers generate has two components: the immediate gain and its effect on future gains.

For example, suppose Barkley's managers are actually soft. They still have an incentive to act tough in early periods. Of course this will give them a lower payoff in these early periods (3 in red) than playing their true soft type (4 in red). But if they act tough early, Allied managers might not enter later because they are convinced (at least enough) that Barkley managers are truly tough. This allows Barkley managers to earn 7 in later periods. Note, though, that as the future gets shorter (as it necessarily does in finite horizon games), the value of maintaining a false reputation shrinks. So in these later periods, there is an increasing probability that Barkley managers will reveal their true type to be soft. And in the final period, Barkley managers will definitely reveal they are soft.

Examples of managerial use of reputation building are easily found. From product quality to entry deterrence, corporate culture to honest auditors, these models help explain behavior. For example, long before the recent corporate fraud scandals, game theorists modeled auditing firms as renting their reputations for being honest. The models predicted that any accounting firms involved in fraudulent activities would lose their high-quality reputations, and the value of their names would decrease toward zero. This is exactly what we saw with the implosion of Arthur Andersen after the accounting scandal at Enron.

COORDINATION GAMES

It is often profitable for managers to coordinate actions with others. Although this is certainly true for activity within a firm, it is often true for market strategy. Managers must consider the benefits and costs of coordination efforts. Managing this effort is an important managerial task. Managers engage in many coordination games; it is essential that they understand their payoff structure.

Game models represent coordination games as containing more than one Nash equilibrium. Recognizing the Nash equilibria (that is, the outcomes on which managers want to coordinate) is generally not an issue, but choosing which one to select is. We will see that as game parameters change, the impediments to coordination shift. Game theory visualizes these shifts with changes in the payoff structure.

Matching Games

In matching games, players generally prefer the same outcome. However, there may be impediments to reaching this outcome. Impediments may include the inability to communicate, different ideas about how to reach an objective, or asymmetric information. The game we show in Figure 12.15 concerns coordination of product attributes.

This game has two Nash equilibria. We expect one firm to produce for the consumer market and one for the industry. Though 7, 7 is clearly inferior to 12, 12, it is not ruled out as a Nash equilibrium. However, note that both Allied and Barkley prefer a payoff of 12 to that of 7.

Battle of the Sexes

In this coordination game, players still want to coordinate, but they prefer different outcomes. Because of different preferences, each prefers a payoff not favored by the other. If this game is repeated, players often switch between equilibria so that both gain. However, in one-shot games like Figure 12.16, it is more difficult to predict the outcome.

Similar to the matching game, each wants to enter the submarket not entered by the other, but now the payoffs are not equal. Managers at both Allied and Barkley are better off if they produce a high-end product, so it is not clear on which outcome they will coordinate.

FIGURE 12.15

Product Coordination Game

		Allied's strategies	
		Produce for consumer market	Produce for industrial market
Barkley's strategies	Produce for consumer market	0, 0	7, 7
	Produce for industrial market	12, 12	0, 0

FIGURE 12.16

Battle of the Sexes

		Allied's strategies	
		High-end product	Low-end product
Barkley's strategies	High-end product	0, 0	11, 6
	Low-end product	6, 11	0, 0

Assurance Games

Coordination games like that in Figure 12.17 are also known as stag hunt games. The French philosopher Rousseau tells the story of two hunters (actually poachers) who could coordinate efforts and catch a stag or renege on their agreement and each catch rabbits for himself. Although each prefers to catch the stag, that strategy carries the risk that the other will renege and the first hunter will catch nothing. So players have similar preferences for outcomes but have an associated risk.

Here we model a decision of whether to shift to new standards. Although managers at both firms prefer to shift, there is a risk if one shifts and the other does not. We say the outcome 12,12 is Pareto dominant (both players are better

FIGURE 12.17

Stag Hunt or Assurance Game

		Allied's strategies	
		Stay with old standard	Shift to new standard
Barkley's strategies	Stay with old standard	6, 6	6, 0
	Shift to new standard	0, 6	12, 12

off) but risk dominated (if one chooses to shift and the other does not, the firm shifting receives 0).

First-Mover Games

We can also use coordination games to show the benefits of moving first. Figure 12.18 shows a sequential game in which managers at both firms want to coordinate but each has an incentive to produce a superior product (similar to the battle of the sexes). However, in this game it is possible to move first by speeding up product development. The game shows which firm managers will move first and how much they are willing to pay to speed up the process.

In this game, managers at both firms want to introduce the superior product first. There are two Nash equilibria. Allied managers produce a superior product and those at Barkley produce an inferior one, or vice versa. Once one firm produces a superior product, the other is resigned to producing an inferior product. The question is this: Which firm's managers are willing to pay a higher price to produce the superior product? We can answer this question by looking at the incremental benefits of moving first. The incremental benefit to Allied managers of producing the superior product is the difference in payoff between producing the superior product ($140) and the inferior product ($70). This is a difference of $70. The incremental benefit to Barkley managers of moving first is $110 − $30 or $80. We would predict that Barkley will move first because it is willing to spend up to $80 to move first, whereas Allied will spend only up to $70.

Hawks and Doves

This interesting coordination game has been applied to behavior in both human and animal worlds. Assume two players are locked in a conflict. If both players act

---

FIGURE 12.18

First–Mover Advantage

		Allied's strategies	
		Produce superior product	Produce inferior product
Barkley's strategies	Produce superior product	25, 50	110, 70
	Produce inferior product	30, 140	20, 30

FIGURE 12.19

Hawks and Doves

Country 1 strategy

		Act like a hawk	Act like a dove
Country 2 strategy	Act like a hawk	−1, −1	10, 0
	Act like a dove	0, 10	5, 5

---

like hawks, conflict is inevitable. However, if one acts like a hawk and the other backs down (acting like a dove), conflict is avoided. If both are doves, conflict is not even threatened. The game is shown in Figure 12.19.

There are two Nash equilibria; they require one country to act like a hawk and the other to act like a dove. The issue is which country will back down and act like a dove because this country will suffer a lower payoff.

John Maynard Smith applied similar models to the animal kingdom to model the fighting behavior of animals. One interesting example concerns the behavior of spiders in New Mexico. Webs are a scarce commodity within the spider community because they are difficult to build in the desert. However, a female spider needs a web to lay her eggs. Therefore, female spiders fight (or threaten to fight) over existing webs. They do so by approaching a web and violently shaking it. After each shows this force, one spider (the dove) generally leaves the web to the other spider. Rarely do the spiders actually engage in a physical fight. Smith and other biologists noted that certain physical traits account for which spider is the hawk and which is the dove. For the spiders, the two most important traits appear to be incumbency and weight. The heavier spider usually claims the web, whereas the lighter spider backs down. Smith believes that the violent shaking of the web is actually a credible signal of which spider is the heaviest.

STRICTLY COMPETITIVE GAMES

The games we have just looked at have mixed motives in the sense that conflict interfaces with mutual dependence. However, some games are strictly competitive: Any gain by one player means a loss by another player. The net gain is always zero;

FIGURE 12.20

Advertising Campaigns

		Allied		
		Campaign A	Campaign B	Campaign C
Barkley	Campaign 1	−5, 5	20, −20	−22, 22
	Campaign 2	−3, 3	7, −7	4, −4
	Campaign 3	−4, 4	−6, 6	17, −17

Zero-sum games A competitive game in which any gain by one player means a loss by another player.

what one gains, the other loses. These games are also known as **zero-sum games**. For example, slow-growth (mature) markets are characterized as zero-sum. Because the market size remains fairly constant, any increase in the share of one firm means an identical decrease in the share of another firm. Figure 12.20 shows one such example.

Zero-sum games are still solvable using Nash equilibria. In Figure 12.20 the Nash equilibrium is for Allied managers to use campaign A and Barkley managers to use campaign 2.

SUMMARY

1. Strategic decisions involve interactive payoffs. Because a player's payoff depends on his or her decision and the decisions of others, that player must anticipate the actions of others in formulating an optimal strategy.

2. Game theory is a mathematical framework that can help managers anticipate the actions of others. The theory helps managers represent strategic issues by focusing on the players involved, their feasible strategies, the possible outcomes, and the payoffs associated with those outcomes.

3. In solving games, managers first need to look for dominant strategies. If they exist, managers need not consider the actions of others. Rational players always play their dominant strategy.

4. If dominant strategies do not exist, managers should try to predict the behavior of others using the solution concept of the Nash equilibrium. This concept assumes that all players do the best they can, conditional on all others

doing the best they can. This is the most widely used solution concept in game theory.

5. Managers should use strategic foresight; this is the ability to make decisions today that are rational, conditional on the anticipated future behavior of others. Game theory models this foresight through backward induction. In using backward induction, we go to the end of the game to determine what strategies players will use, then choose an action for the current period that is rational given these future beliefs.

6. Managers must pay attention only to signals that are credible. Game models can determine the credibility of threats, promises, commitments, and the like.

7. Games with a future are called *repeated games*. When a future exists, players may change the strategies they select. Generally speaking, gaining cooperation from others is much easier in a repeated game.

8. Game theorists have developed incomplete information models to look at situations where there is a future and some uncertainty exists about the traits of others. Under these conditions, building a reputation is important because reputations can generate future rents.

9. The ability to coordinate is an important managerial trait. Coordination models help managers better understand the impediments to coordination and the actions necessary to decrease coordination costs.

PROBLEMS

wwnorton.com/studyspace

1. Two soap producers, the Fortnum Company and the Maison Company, can stress either newspapers or magazines in their forthcoming advertising campaigns. The payoff matrix is as follows:

		Maison Company	
		Stress newspapers	Stress magazines
Fortnum Company	Stress newspapers	$8 mm, $9 mm	$7 mm, $8 mm
	Stress magazines	$9 mm, $8 mm	$8 mm, $7 mm

   a. Is there a dominant strategy for each firm? If so, what is it?

   b. What will be the profit of each firm?

   c. Is this game an example of the prisoner's dilemma?

2. The Ulysses Corporation and the Xenophon Company are the only producers of a sophisticated type of camera. They each can engage in either a high or a low level of advertising in trade journals. The payoff matrix is as follows:

		Xenophon Company	
		Low level	High level
Ulysses Corporation	Low level	$12 mm, $13 mm	$11 mm, $12 mm
	High level	$13 mm, $12 mm	$12 mm, $11 mm

a. Will Ulysses engage in a high or a low level of advertising in trade journals?

b. Will Xenophon engage in a high or a low level of advertising in trade journals?

c. Is there a dominant strategy for each firm?

3. The *New York Times* reports that Wal-Mart has decided to challenge Netflix and enter the online DVD-by-mail market. Because of economies of scale, Wal-Mart has a slight cost advantage relative to Netflix. Wal-Mart is considering the use of a limit pricing strategy. It can enter the market by matching Netflix on price. If it does, and Netflix maintains its price, then both firms would earn $5 million. But if Netflix drops its price in response, Wal-Mart would have to follow and would earn $2 million; Netflix would earn $3 million. Or Wal-Mart could enter the market with a price that is below Netflix's current price but above its marginal cost. If it does, Netflix would make one of two moves. It could reduce its price to below that of Wal-Mart. If it does, Wal-Mart will earn a profit of $0, and Netflix will earn a profit of $2 million. Or Netflix could keep its present price. If Netflix keeps its present price, Wal-Mart can keep its present price and earn $6 million (while Netflix earns $4 million). Or Wal-Mart can increase its price and earn $2 million while Netflix earns $6 million.

a. Draw the extensive form of this game and solve it.

b. Draw the game's matrix form and identify any Nash equilibria.

4. Two rival PE firms are interested in funding the same two start-ups. Each would prefer not to get into a bidding war with the other regarding either of the start-ups. Payoffs are given in the following table:

PE Firm A

		Invest Start-up 1	Invest Start-up 2
PE Firm B	Invest Start-up 1	10, 10	60, 40
	Invest Start-up 2	25, 55	20, 20

What are the reservation prices of managers at the two firms? What will bidding look like?

5. Two soft drink producers, York Cola and Reno Cola, secretly collude to fix prices. Each firm must decide whether to abide by the agreement or to cheat on it. The payoff matrix is as follows:

York Cola

		Abide by agreement	Cheat
Reno Cola	Abide by agreement	$29 mm, $29 mm	$26 mm, $30 mm
	Cheat	$30 mm, $26 mm	$28 mm, $28 mm

a. What strategy will each firm choose, and what will be each firm's profit?

b. Does it matter whether this agreement is for one period or for three periods?

c. Is this game an example of the prisoner's dilemma?

6. **Part 1**: Firm A currently monopolizes its market and earns profits of $10 million. Firm B is a potential entrant that is thinking about entering the market. If B does not enter the market, it earns profits of $0, while A continues to earn profits of $10 million. If B enters, then A must choose between accommodating entry and fighting it. If A accommodates, then A earns $5 million and B earns $5 million. If A fights, then both firms lose $5 million. **Draw the game in extensive form and predict the outcome.**

Part 2: Again, consider the above game. Now, suppose the decision of B to enter is reversible in the following way. After B enters the market, and A has decided to either fight or accommodate, B can choose to remain in the market or exit. All payoffs from the above game remain the same. However, if B decides to exit the market, then B suffers a loss of $1 million, while A regains its old profits of $10 million. **Draw the game in extensive form and predict the outcome.**

7. The Rose Corporation is one of two sellers of paint. It pursues a tit-for-tat strategy. However, it has great difficulty in telling whether its rival is secretly cutting its price. What problems is this likely to cause?

8. Consider a father who is trying to discipline his child. The father insists that the child must go with the rest of the family to visit their grandmother. The child prefers to go to the movies with a friend. The father threatens to punish the child if the child doesn't visit the grandmother. If the child goes with the family to visit the grandmother, both the child and the father receive one unit of utility. If the child refuses to go to the grandmother's house, and the father punishes the child, the child receives one unit of utility, and the father receives one unit of utility. If the child refuses to go and the father relents (does not punish), the child receives two units of utility, and the father receives none.
   a. Draw this game in matrix form.
   b. Draw this game in extensive form.
   c. Solve this game via backward induction.

9. The Boca Raton Company announces that if it reduces its price subsequent to a purchase, the early customer will get a rebate so that he or she will pay no more than those buying after the price reduction.
   a. If the Boca Raton Company has only one rival, and if its rival too makes such an announcement, does this change the payoff matrix? If so, in what way?
   b. Do such announcements tend to discourage price cutting? Why or why not?

EXCEL EXERCISE: GAME THEORY

After airline deregulation in the late 1970s, new entrants would enter or consider entering the market. Most new entrants failed, but Southwest, JetBlue, and AirTran (now merged with Southwest) are among the few exceptions. The legacy carriers (those in the market before deregulation) took particular affront when a new entrant attempted to enter or threatened to enter a hub airport of the legacy carrier. Traditionally, the new entrants were undercapitalized and could not tolerate a significant period of losses.

Several carriers entered American Airlines' hub at Dallas-Fort Worth. American had to consider whether to accommodate the entrant or whether to fight the entrant. Suppose the matrix below represents one time period of a potentially multiple-period game.

Potential Entrant

		Enter	Don't Enter
	Accommodate	**2**, *1*	**3**, *0*
American			
	Fight	1, –1	2, 0

Following the analysis in the text, we see that American has a dominant strategy to accommodate. The potential entrant does not have a dominant strategy, but when the entrant puts itself in American's shoes, the potential entrant determines that American has a dominant strategy to let it enter the market. Given that American will let it in, it'll enter (since $1 > 0$).

Did American accommodate entry into Dallas-Fort Worth? No. Because it was a multiple-period game, and American knew these potential entrants could not tolerate many periods of losses (because they were undercapitalized—they did not have "deep pockets"), American fought them. Under the fight scenario, the potential entrant loses −1 each period it is in the market. Suppose the potential entrant can take two periods of losses and then must fold.

If American accommodates the potential entrant, American's profit stream over time is

$$2, 2, 2, 2, 2, 2, 2, \ldots\ldots\ldots\ldots\ldots\ldots$$

If American fights the potential entrant, American's profit stream over time is

$$1, 1, 3, 3, 3, 3, \ldots\ldots\ldots\ldots\ldots\ldots$$

So the question is whether the net present value of the second stream is better than the net present value of the first stream, that is,

$$1, 1, 3, 3, 3, 3, \ldots\ldots > 2, 2, 2, 2, 2, 2, \ldots\ldots\ldots$$

Netting out terms, this becomes

$$0, 0, 1, 1, 1, 1, \ldots\ldots > 1, 1, 0, 0, 0, 0, \ldots\ldots\ldots$$

The discrete discount factor to determine the net present value of cash in period t today is $1/(1 + i)^t$, where i is the discount (think interest) rate. We'll assume the first period in the analysis above is time 0. Thus, the net present value of the question asked above is

$$0 + 0^*[1/(1 + i)^1] + 1^*[1/(1 + i)^2] + 1^*[1/(1 + i)^3]$$
$$+ 1^*[1(1 + i)^4] + \ldots\ldots > 1 + 1^*[1/(1 + i)^1] + 0^*[1/(1 + i)^2]$$
$$+ 0^*[1/(1 + i)^3] + 0^*[1/(1 + i)^4]\ldots\ldots$$

or

$$1^*[1/(1 + i)^2] + 1^*[1/(1 + i)^3] + 1^*[1/(1 + i)^4] + \ldots\ldots$$
$$> 1 + 1^*[1/(1 + i)^1] + 0 + \ldots\ldots$$

or

$$-1 - 1^*[1/(1 + i)^1] + 1^*[1/(1 + i)^2] + 1^*[1/(1 + i)^3] + 1^*[1/(1 + i)^4] + \ldots > 0$$

So what discount rate makes the above equation positive?

This is a job for a spreadsheet. We'll try this out for five periods.

Enter $= -1-1^*(1/(1+A2)^{\wedge}1)+1^*(1/(1+A2)^{\wedge}2)+1^*(1/(1+A2)^{\wedge}3)+1^*(1/(1+A2)^{\wedge}4)$ in cell A1. Then play around with various interest rates until in cell A2 cell A1 reads 0.

If the above periods are years, a yearly interest rate of approximately 17.87% per year will make the equation in cell A1 zero. Internal rates of return for firms in this range are not unusual, so any rate higher than that would make fighting entry a good long-run strategy. We could play the game for fewer periods (which would lead to a higher interest rate answer) or for more years (which would lead to a lower interest rate answer). We could also play with different payoff numbers for American in the above game matrix. The point is that many different what-if scenarios can be calculated quite quickly by using a spreadsheet.

The other benefit of the fight policy is that American gains a reputation that it will fight any entrant. If this reputation sticks, American will not be faced with the 1, 1, 3, 3, 3, ... profit stream scenario but won't have to fight and thus will face a profit stream of 3, 3, 3, 3, 3, ...

TECHNOLOGICAL CHANGE AND INDUSTRIAL INNOVATION

Companies in the United States have traditionally been at the forefront in using new technologies. Their long-term profitability and market successes are often based on new products or processes. Most of these advances in products or processes are the result of an active commitment to devoting resources to research and development. After all, increases in productivity do not occur haphazardly but are the result of active management of the research and development process. This management not only includes the initial development of a product or process but also the implementation issues involved in getting new products to market.

In this appendix, we discuss various models and techniques for measuring productivity and examine several research and developmental models. These models have proven useful in both helping managers oversee research and development programs and bringing new products to market.

TECHNOLOGICAL CHANGE

Technological change—the advance of technology—often takes the form of new methods of producing existing products and new techniques of organization, marketing, and management. Technological change results in a change in the production function. If the production function were readily observable, a

Technological change Results in a change of a firm's production function over time. This can entail existing products produced more efficiently or can result in the availability of new products.

763

comparison of the production function at two different times would provide the manager with a simple measure of the effect of technological change during the intervening period. If there were only two inputs, labor and capital, and constant returns to scale, the characteristics of the production function at a given date could be captured fully by a single isoquant.[1] One could simply look at the changing position of this isoquant to see the effects of technological change. If this isoquant shifted from position A to position B in Figure A.1 during a certain period of time, technological change had less impact during this period than it would have had if the curve had shifted to position C.

Technological change may also result in the availability of new products. DVD players, for example, did not exist several decades ago; now they are commonplace. iPhones and tablets did not exist a decade ago; today, many managers rely on them. Nylon was first brought to market in the 1930s; today it is hard to imagine what life would be like without it. In many cases, the availability of new products can be regarded as a change in the production function, since they are merely more efficient ways of meeting old wants if these wants are defined with proper breadth. This is particularly true in the case of new goods used by firms, which may result in little or no change in the final product shipped to consumers.

FIGURE A.1

Change over a Period of Time in the Position of an Isoquant

If the isoquant shifted from position A to position B, technological change had less impact than if it had shifted to position C.

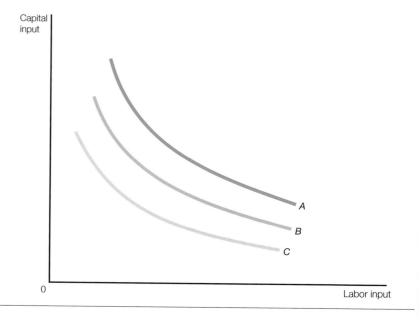

1. Recall that, if there are constant returns to scale, an x percent increase in all inputs results in an x percent increase in output. Hence, if there are constant returns to scale, there is at a given time a unique relationship between capital input per unit of output and labor input per unit of output. This relationship holds for any output and completely summarizes the efficient input combinations.

In other cases, however, the availability of new products cannot realistically be viewed as a change in the production function, since the new products represent an important difference in kind.

LABOR PRODUCTIVITY

Managers have long been interested in productivity—the ratio of output to input. The oldest and most commonly studied productivity measure is labor productivity, output per hour of labor. One determinant of the rate of growth of labor productivity is the rate of technological change: A high rate of technological change is likely to result, all other things being equal, in a high rate of growth of labor productivity. However, the rate of technological change is not the sole determinant of the rate of growth of labor productivity; as a consequence, although labor productivity is often used to measure the rate of technological change, it is in fact an incomplete measure.

Figure A.2 shows how changes in labor productivity can produce false signals concerning the rate of technological change. Suppose the relevant isoquant

---

FIGURE A.2

Productivity Increase without Technological Change

Because labor becomes more expensive relative to capital, labor productivity increases.

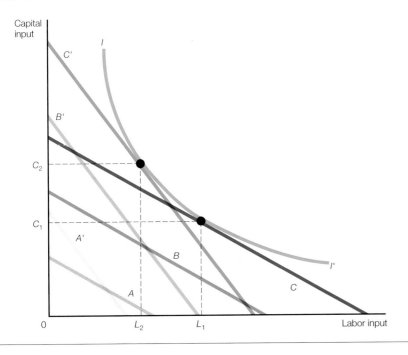

is II' and the input prices at the beginning of the period are such that the isocost curves are A, B, C, and so on. The least-cost combination of inputs is L_1 of labor and C_1 of capital. Now suppose that input prices change and labor becomes more expensive relative to capital; as a result, the isocost curves shift to A', B', C', and so on. Under these new circumstances, the least-cost combination of inputs to produce the same output is L_2 of labor and C_2 of capital. Since output remains constant and labor input decreases, labor productivity increases as a result of the change in input prices. But this productivity increase is not an indication of technological change, there being no change at all in the production function.

TOTAL FACTOR PRODUCTIVITY

Total factor productivity relates changes in the firm's outputs to changes in all the firm's inputs.

A better measure of the rate of technological change is **total factor productivity**, which relates changes in output to changes in both labor and capital inputs, not changes in labor inputs alone. Assume that the production function is of the simple form

$$Q = \alpha(bL + cK) \tag{A.1}$$

where Q is the quantity of output, L is the quantity of labor, K is the quantity of capital, and b and c are constants. Dividing both sides of equation (A.1) by $(bL + cK)$

$$\frac{Q}{bL + cK} = \alpha \tag{A.2}$$

which is total factor productivity. In this simple case, changes in total factor productivity measure changes in efficiency.

If a firm uses more than two inputs, total factor productivity equals

$$\frac{Q}{a_1 I_1 + a_2 I_2 + \ldots + a_n I_n} \tag{A.3}$$

where I_1 is the amount of the first input used, I_2 is the amount of the second input used, . . . , and I_n is the amount of the nth input used. In calculating total factor productivity, firms often let a_1 equal the price of the first input, a_2 equal the price of the second input, . . . , and a_n equal the price of the nth input in some base period, as we shall see next. The principal advantage of total factor productivity over labor productivity is its inclusion of more types of inputs, not labor alone. It otherwise shares many of the limitations of labor productivity. Note that $\sum_i P_i X_i$, where P_i is unit input cost and X_i is amount of input used, is just the firm's total cost (TC). Then Q/TC is just the inverse of the firm's average total cost (ATC). To maximize productivity, minimize ATC. But firms want to maximize profits. That rarely occurs when firms minimize ATC.

Firms calculate total factor productivity to measure changes over time in the efficiency of their operations. It is important for a firm's managers to be aware of the extent to which productivity has increased in response to new techniques and other factors.

To calculate the changes in total factor productivity for a firm or plant over a period of time, managers must obtain data concerning the quantities of output and inputs utilized in each period. For example, suppose that the Landau Company uses three inputs—labor, energy, and raw materials. In 2012, it uses 10,000 hours of labor, 100,000 kilowatt-hours of energy, and 5,000 pounds of materials to produce 400,000 pounds of output. In 2013, it uses 12,000 hours of labor, 150,000 kilowatt-hours of energy, and 6,000 pounds of materials to produce 700,000 pounds of output. What is total factor productivity in each year?

As a first step toward answering this question, we must get data concerning the price of each input in some base period, say, 2012. Suppose that the price of labor is $8 per hour, the price of a kilowatt-hour of energy is $0.02, and the price of a pound of materials is $3. Then, inserting these figures into the expression in (A.3), we find that total factor productivity in 2012 is

$$\frac{400,000}{8(10,000) + 0.02(100,000) + 3(5,000)} = 4.12$$

and total factor productivity in 2013 is

$$\frac{700,000}{8(12,000) + 0.02(150,000) + 3(6,000)} = 5.98$$

Therefore, from 2012 to 2013, total factor productivity increased by 45%—from 4.12 to 5.98.

Note that the base-year input prices are used for all years, not just the base year. For example, the 2012 input prices would be used for all years, not just 2012, in the case of the Landau Company. In this way, we hold constant input prices and do not let changes in them over time affect our results.[2]

USING TOTAL FACTOR PRODUCTIVITY TO TRACK FACTORY PERFORMANCE

To illustrate how changes in total factor productivity can be used to track factory performance, consider a manufacturing plant studied by Harvard's Robert Hayes, Steven Wheelwright, and Kim Clark.[3] Figure A.3 shows the behavior of total factor productivity in this plant during a 10-year period. As you can see, total factor productivity increased at a healthy pace up to 1976. This was the period during which the plant was started up. Because it takes time for a factory to operate properly, one would expect that total factor productivity would increase substantially in this startup phase.

2. Of course, this does not mean that the value of total factor productivity is not affected by the base-year prices. For example, if the price of labor in the base period were $10 (rather than $8) per hour, our results would be different. But changes *over time* in input prices are not allowed to influence our results.

3. R. Hayes, S. Wheelwright, and K. Clark, *Dynamic Manufacturing* (New York: Free Press, 1988).

FIGURE A.3

Total Factor Productivity, Actual Manufacturing Plant

Total factor productivity increased up to 1976, but in 1982 was only slightly higher than in 1976.

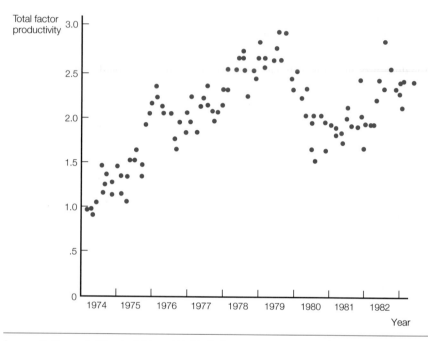

Source: R. Hayes, S. Wheelwright, and K. Clark, *Dynamic Manufacturing*. (New York: Free Press, 1988).

From 1977 to 1983, there was no evidence of any strong, persistent increase in total factor productivity. Instead, there was an increase in 1977 to 1979, a fall in 1979 to 1980, and an increase in 1981 to 1982. In 1982, total factor productivity was only somewhat higher than in 1976. The data in Figure A.3 indicate that this factory experienced little in the way of technological change from 1977 to 1983. Hayes, Wheelwright, and Clark report that these data triggered an investigation of the causes for this poor performance, which indicated that it was due in considerable part to the way the factory managed equipment introductions.[4] Obviously, this information was of use to the firm's top managers.

In passing, note the fact that total factor productivity fell during 1979 to 1980 does not mean that there was negative technological change then. If the factory's sales decreased during this period, perhaps because of cyclical factors, this could cause such a decline in total factor productivity. Also, it sometimes takes time for new equipment to reach its full efficiency. When equipment is first used, productivity may fall temporarily because of "teething" problems.

4. Ibid.

RESEARCH AND DEVELOPMENT: A LEARNING PROCESS

Particularly in science-based industries like electronics and chemicals, a firm's success depends on the extent and nature of the research and development that it carries out. Research and development encompasses work of many kinds. Basic research is aimed purely at the creation of new knowledge, applied research is expected to have a practical payoff, and development is aimed at the reduction of research findings to practice. Inventions can occur in either the research phase or the development phase of organized research and development activity.

Chance plays a crucial role in research and development, and a long string of failures frequently occurs before any kind of success is achieved. A research or development project can be regarded as a process of uncertainty reduction, or learning. Suppose, for example, a manager who is trying to fabricate a part can use one of two alloys and it is impossible to use standard sources to determine their characteristics. Suppose that strength is of paramount importance and the manager's estimates of the strengths of the alloys, alloy X and alloy Y, are represented by the probability distributions in part A of Table A.1. If the manager was forced to make a choice immediately, she would probably choose alloy Y, since she believes there is better than a 50–50 chance that alloy Y will turn out to be stronger than alloy X.

However, there is a good chance that this decision might turn out to be wrong, with the consequence that the part would be weaker than if alloy X had been used. Therefore, the manager may decide to perform a test prior to making the selection. On the basis of the test results, the manager formulates new estimates, represented by the probability distributions in part B of Table A.1. These probability

TABLE A.1

Subjective Probability Distribution of Strength of Alloys X and Y

| | Probabilities | | | |
| | A. Before test | | B. After test | |
Extent of strength	Alloy X	Alloy Y	Alloy X	Alloy Y
Exceptionally high	0.20	0.30	0.10	0.10
Very high	0.40	0.50	0.20	0.80
High	0.20	0.10	0.60	0.10
Medium	0.10	0.05	0.10	0.00
Low	0.10	0.05	0.00	0.00
Total	1.00	1.00	1.00	1.00

distributions show less dispersion than the distributions in part A; in other words, the manager believes she is able to pinpoint more closely the strength of each alloy in part B than in part A. Because of the tests, the manager feels more certainty concerning which alloy will prove stronger.

PARALLEL DEVELOPMENT EFFORTS

Research and development is more risky than most other economic activities. Many development projects use parallel efforts to help cope with the uncertainty. For example, in the development of the atomic bomb, there were several methods of making fissionable materials and no consensus among scientists as to which of these alternatives was the most promising. To make sure that the best one was not discarded, all methods were pursued in parallel. The wisdom of this decision was borne out by the fact that the first method to produce appreciable quantities of fissionable material was one considered relatively unpromising early in the development program's history.

How can a firm's managers tell whether it is optimal to run parallel research and development efforts? What factors determine the optimal number of parallel efforts? Suppose that a firm can select x approaches, spend C dollars on each one over a period of n months, choose the one that looks most promising at the end of the period, and carry it to completion, dropping the others. Suppose that the only relevant criterion is the extent of the development costs, the usefulness of the result and the development time, assumed to be the same regardless of which parallel effort is pursued. For further simplification, suppose that all approaches look equally promising. Under these circumstances, the optimal value of x (the number of parallel research and development efforts) is inversely related to C and directly related to the amount learned in the next n months. As the cost of running each effort increases, the optimal number of parallel efforts decreases. As the prospective amount of learning increases, the optimal number of parallel efforts goes up.

To illustrate why it is sometimes cheaper to run parallel development efforts, consider a case in which each approach has a 50–50 chance of costing $5 million and a 50–50 chance of costing $8 million. Since we assume that all approaches are equally promising, these probabilities are the same for all approaches. The expected total cost of development is the sum of the total costs of development if each possible outcome occurs times the probability of the occurrence of this outcome. If a single approach is used, the expected total costs of development are

$$0.5(\$5 \text{ million}) + 0.5(\$8 \text{ million}) = \$6.5 \text{ million} \tag{A.4}$$

since there is a 0.5 probability that total costs with any single approach will be $5 million and a 0.5 probability that they will be $8 million.

If two approaches are run in parallel and if the true cost of development using each approach can be determined after C dollars are spent on each approach, the expected total costs of development are

$$0.25(\$8 \text{ million}) + 0.75(\$5 \text{ million}) + C = \$5.75 \text{ million} + C \qquad \text{(A.5)}$$

If each approach is carried to the point at which C dollars have been spent on it, the cheaper approach is chosen at that point (the other approach is dropped). Why? Because there is a 0.25 probability that total costs with the better of the two approaches will be $8 million and a 0.75 probability that they will be $5 million. In addition, there is the certainty that a cost of C will be incurred for the approach that is dropped. (The C dollars spent on the project that is not dropped are included in its total costs, given previously.) The reason why there is a 0.25 chance that total costs with the better of the two approaches is $8 million is that this will occur only when the total cost of both approaches turns out to be $8 million—and the probability that this will occur is 0.5 times 0.5, or 0.25. Comparing equation (A.4) with equation (A.5), it is obvious that the expected total cost of development is lower with two parallel approaches than with a single approach if C is less than $750,000.

More generally, if the probability is P that the development cost will be C_1 and $(1 - P)$ that it will be C_2 (where $C_2 < C_1$), the expected cost if a single approach is used is

$$PC_1 + (1 - P)C_2$$

If two approaches are run in parallel, the expected cost is

$$P^2C_1 + (1 - P^2)C_2 + C$$

which is less than the cost of a single approach if

$$C < (1 - P)(P)(C_1 - C_2) \qquad \text{(A.6)}$$

Therefore, if the inequality in (A.6) holds, two parallel approaches result in a lower expected cost than a single approach.

WHAT MAKES FOR SUCCESS?

Even companies in the same industry may differ markedly in their ability to make research and development (R and D) pay off commercially. During a four-year period, for instance, three evenly matched chemical companies found the proportion of their R and D expenditures that earned a profit to be 69%, 54%, and 39%, respectively. These differences are too large to be attributed to errors of measurement or definition. What can explain them?[5]

An R and D project's likelihood of economic success is the product of three factors: (1) the probability of technical success, (2) the probability of

5. For references and sources of information for the data presented in this and the next three sections, see E. Mansfield, "How Economists See R and D," *Harvard Business Review*, November–December 1981. Also, see K. Clark and T. Fujimoto, *Product Development Performance* (Boston: Harvard Business School Press, 1991); R. Stobaugh, *Innovation and Competition* (Boston: Harvard Business School Press, 1988); and E. Mansfield, *Innovation, Technology, and the Economy* (Aldershot, U.K.: Elgar, 1995).

commercialization (given technical success), and (3) the probability of economic success (given commercialization). One econometric study shows that all three of these probabilities are directly related to how quickly an R and D project is evaluated for its economic, as opposed to technical, potential. Also, in those companies whose R and D staff members do not work closely or responsively with the marketing staff, the integration of R and D activity with market realities is haphazard, belated, or both. Commercially successful innovation depends on just this sort of integration. Numerous case studies of successful and unsuccessful innovation come to the same conclusion: The closer is the link between marketing and R and D, the greater is the probability of commercialization (given technical completion).

Consider, by way of illustration, the experience of three chemical companies of roughly the same size and level of R and D expenditure that underwent reorganization at roughly the same time. In two of them, the reorganization produced a closer integration of R and D with marketing by improving the channels of communication between them as well as by noticeably increasing marketing's input to R and D decision making. In the third, however, integration decreased; R and D paid even less attention to marketing than it had before the reorganization.

Data on the probability of commercialization (given technical completion) of 330 R and D projects in these companies (projects carried out anywhere from three to seven years before reorganization to five to eight years after it) are highly suggestive. They show an increase of about 20 percentage points for the two companies that more closely linked R and D with marketing and a decrease of about 20 percentage points for the third.

More generally, a substantial portion of a company's R and D efforts may lie fallow because other parts of the company do not make proper use of them. One survey of executive opinion has noted the widely held belief that the economic success rate of R and D projects would increase by half if marketing and production people fully exploited them. If this figure is anywhere close to the truth, the faulty interface between R and D and the other functions has a very serious effect on the productivity of industrial R and D.

PROJECT SELECTION

However well-founded the fears of excessively detailed control, some managerial oversight of R and D is essential. To make effective use of its R and D capacity, a company must spell out its business objectives and communicate them to its scientists and engineers. Research, after all, makes sense only when undertaken in areas relevant to economic goals.

Simply taking on a team of scientists and allowing them to do research in their favorite fields may produce novel results but results that are unlikely to have much immediate commercial value. Most companies, therefore, have found it worthwhile to make economic evaluations of both project proposals and continuing projects. Without question, these evaluations are useful, since they force managers to make their assumptions explicit. Research suggests that the sooner such evaluations are carried out, the greater a project's chances of ultimate commercial success.

The nature of these evaluations is different for a research lab rather than a development project. As a project moves from the laboratory toward the market, it receives more intensive scrutiny from both the technical and economic angles. In the early research phase, the screening of proposals probably is quick and informal, since costs at this stage are still low and predicting outcomes is very difficult. But, as projects enter the development phase, where costs and predictability are higher, they require a far more detailed process of economic evaluation.

Managerial economists have developed a number of more or less sophisticated models to help solve these problems of evaluation. Some employ relatively straightforward adaptations of capital budgeting techniques. For example, the net present value or internal rate of return (concepts developed in a basic course in finance) of each project may be calculated and compared. The more complicated versions of these models have not found extensive use, for the following

---

STRATEGY SESSION: Parallel Development Efforts at IBM

The IBM Corporation, which spends billions of dollars per year on research and development, is one of the world's leading high-technology companies. Nonetheless, IBM, like other firms, must face the fact that R and D is a risky activity: It is not able to predict with confidence whether a particular R and D project will be successful. Recognizing this fact, parallel development efforts have played a major role in IBM's history, as indicated by the following quotation from one IBM manager:

Parallel projects are crucial—no doubt of it. When I look back over the last dozen products we've introduced, I find in well over half the instances the big development project that we "bet on" via the system came a cropper somewhere along the line. In every instance—and we've gone back and taken a look and I do mean

every—there were two or three (about five once) other small projects, you know, four-to-six person groups, two people in one instance, who had been working on parallel technology or parallel development efforts. It had been with scrounged time and bodies. But that's a time-honored thing. We wink at it. It pays off. Looking at the projects where the initial bets failed, the subsequently developed project came in ahead of the original schedule in three instances. It's just amazing what a handful of dedicated people can do when they are really turned on. Of course they had an advantage. Since they were so resource-constrained, they had to design a simple product in the first place.[a]

[a] Bartlett, *Cases in Strategic Management.* (Dryden Press, 1988).

reasons: (1) Many of the models fail to recognize that R and D is essentially a process of buying information, unsuccessful projects can provide valuable information, and as a result, the real task is to facilitate sequential decision making under conditions of uncertainty. (2) Application of the more-sophisticated models is not cheap. (3) Perhaps most important, the models often rest on overly optimistic estimates that are not very reliable—estimates that reflect both the uncertainty of the undertaking and the desire by researchers and others to "sell" projects to top management.

INNOVATION

An **innovation** occurs when an invention is applied for the first time.

An invention, when applied for the first time, is called an **innovation**. The distinction between an invention and an innovation becomes somewhat blurred in cases like DuPont's nylon, in which the inventor and the innovator are the same firm. In these circumstances, the final stages of development may entail at least a partial commitment to a market test. However, in many cases, the firm that is the inventor is not in a position to—and does not want to—apply its invention, because its business is invention, not production; because it is a supplier, not a user, of the equipment embodying the innovation; or for some other reason. In these cases, the distinction remains relatively clear-cut.

Regardless of whether the break between invention and innovation is clean, innovation is a key stage in the process leading to the full evaluation and utilization of an invention. The innovator—the firm that is first to apply the invention—must be willing to take the risks involved in introducing a new and untried process, good, or service. In many cases, these risks are high. Although R and D can provide a great deal of information regarding the technical characteristics and cost of production of the invention—and market research can provide considerable information regarding the demand for it—many areas of uncertainty can be resolved only by actual production and marketing of the invention. By obtaining needed information regarding the actual performance of the invention, the innovator plays a vital social role.

TIME-COST TRADE-OFFS

For a particular innovator, there is likely to be a time-cost trade-off function, like that in Figure A.4. If the firm cuts the total time taken to develop and introduce the innovation, it incurs higher costs. As the development schedule is shortened, more tasks must be carried out concurrently rather than sequentially, and since each task provides information useful in carrying out the others, there are more false starts and wasted designs. Also, diminishing returns set in as more and more technical workers are assigned simultaneously to the project.

FIGURE A.4

Time-Cost Trade-off Function and Optimal Duration of the Project

The optimal duration of the project is t^* years.

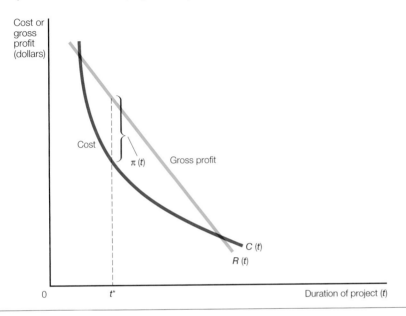

Faced with this time-cost trade-off function, how quickly should the firm develop and introduce the innovation? Clearly, the answer depends on the relationship between the present value of profit (gross of innovation cost) from the innovation and how quickly the firm develops and introduces it. (For a detailed discussion of the concept of present value, see Appendix C.) If $R(t)$ is the present value of gross profit if the duration of the project is t years and the time-cost trade-off function is $C(t)$, profit equals

$$\pi(t) = R(t) - C(t) \tag{A.7}$$

and the first-order condition for profit maximization is

$$\frac{\Delta C}{\Delta t} = \frac{\Delta R}{\Delta t} \tag{A.8}$$

In Figure A.4, the optimal duration of the project is t^* years, since $\pi(t)$, which is the vertical difference between $R(t)$ and $C(t)$, is greatest when this is the duration of the project.

To illustrate, consider the Hanover Company, which wants to develop a new plastic. Its vice president for research and development believes that the time-cost trade-off function for this project is

$$C = 520 - 100t + 5t^2$$

where C is cost (in thousands of dollars) and t is the duration of the project (in years). This equation assumes that $t \geq 1$, since it is believed that the project cannot be carried out in less than a year. Hanover's president believes that

$$R = 480 - 20t$$

where R is the present value of profit (gross of innovation cost) from the innovation (in thousands of dollars). Since

$$\frac{\Delta C}{\Delta t} = \frac{\Delta(520 - 100t + 5t^2)}{\Delta t} = -100 + 10t$$

$$\frac{\Delta R}{\Delta t} = \frac{\Delta(480 - 20t)}{\Delta t} = -20$$

it follows from equation (A.8) that the firm should choose t so that

$$-100 + 10t = -20$$
$$t = 8$$

QUANT OPTION

The profit for period t is

$$\pi(t) = R(t) - C(t)$$

The first order condition for profit maximization is

$$\frac{d\pi(t)}{dt} = \frac{dR(t)}{dt} - \frac{dC(t)}{dt} = 0$$

or

$$\frac{dR}{dt} = \frac{dC}{dt}$$

If $C = 520 - 100t + 5t^2$

and $R = 480 - 20t$

then $\dfrac{dC}{dt} = -100 + 10t$

and $\dfrac{dR}{dt} = -20$

then $\dfrac{dC}{dt} = -100 + 10t = -20 = \dfrac{dR}{dt}$

or $10t = 80$

or $t = 8$

In other words, the Hanover Company should carry out the project in about eight years.

THE LEARNING CURVE

In many industries, technological change is due in considerable part to the learning and on-the-job experience that occurs as a firm produces more and more of a given item. Therefore, holding the firm's output rate constant, its average cost declines with increases in its cumulative total output (that is, the total number of items of this sort that it has produced in the past). For example, production of the first 100 machine tools of a particular type may require about 50% more hours of labor than production of the second 100 machine tools of this type, even though the number of machine tools produced per month remains about the same. Thus, the average cost of this machine tool falls substantially as cumulative total output grows.

One should distinguish between cost reductions due to learning and those due to greater current output. Holding constant the number of these machine tools produced by this firm in the past, it is quite possible that the average cost of producing such a machine tool during the current period declines as more of them are produced. But, this is different from learning. Holding constant the number of such machine tools produced currently, if the average cost is inversely related to the firm's previous total output of this machine tool, this is due to learning.

Managers, economists, and engineers often use the learning curve to represent the extent to which the average cost of producing an item falls in response to increases in its cumulative total output. Figure A.5 shows the learning curves for two actual products: a piece of optical equipment (produced by Optical Equipment Company) and a portable turbine (produced by Solar International, Inc.). As you can see, learning results in major reductions in the average cost of both products. Of course, these cost reductions are not automatic: They occur only if workers and managers strive for increased efficiency. But for many products of this sort, a doubling of cumulative output tends to produce about a 20 or 30% reduction in average cost.

APPLICATIONS OF THE LEARNING CURVE

Many firms adopted pricing strategies based on the learning curve. Consider the case of Texas Instruments, a major producer of semiconductor chips and other electronic products. When the semiconductor industry was relatively young, Texas Instruments priced its product at less than its then-current average costs to increase its output rate and its cumulative total output. Believing that the learning curve was relatively steep, it hoped that this would reduce its average costs to such an extent that its product would be profitable to produce and sell at this low price.

FIGURE A.5

Learning Curves

Average cost declines with increases in cumulative total output.

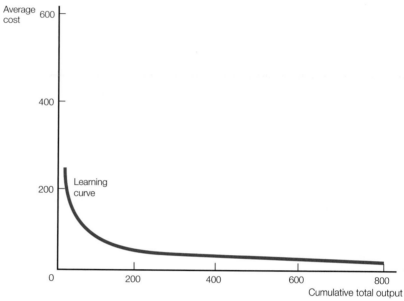

A. Optical equipment produced by Optical Equipment Company

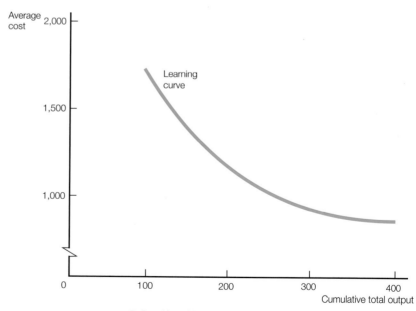

B. Portable turbine produced by Solar International, Inc.

This strategy was extremely successful. As Texas Instruments continued to cut its price, its rivals began to withdraw from the market, its output continued to go up, its costs were reduced further, and its profits rose.[6]

The learning curve is expressed as

$$C = aQ^b \qquad \text{(A.9)}$$

where C is the input cost of the Qth unit of output produced. If this relationship holds exactly, a is the cost of the first unit produced. The value of b is negative, since increases in cumulative total output reduce cost. If the absolute value of b is large, cost falls more rapidly with increases in cumulative total output than it would if the absolute value of b were small. Taking logarithms of both sides of equation (A.9)

$$\log C = \log a + b \log Q \qquad \text{(A.10)}$$

In this logarithmic form, b is the slope of the learning curve.

To estimate the learning curve from historical data concerning cost and cumulative output, one can use the regression techniques in Chapter 4. As shown in equation (A.10), $\log C$ is a linear function of $\log Q$. Therefore, to estimate a and b, we can regress $\log C$ on $\log Q$. (In other words, $\log C$ is the equivalent of Y in Chapter 4, and $\log Q$ is the equivalent of X.) Of course, the values of a and b vary from product to product and firm to firm.

To illustrate how the learning curve can be used in specific cases, suppose that the controller of the Killian Company, a maker of a particular type of machine tool, finds that, for her firm, the learning curve (in logarithmic form) is

$$\log C = 4.0 - 0.30 \log Q$$

where C is expressed in dollars. (That is, $\log a = 4.0$ and $b = -0.30$.) From this equation, she can estimate how much the cost per unit will go down in the future. For example, if she wants to estimate the cost of the 100th machine tool of a particular type, the answer is

$$\log C = 4.0 - 0.30 \log 100 = 4.0 - 0.30(2) = 3.4$$

Since the antilog of 3.4 is 2,512, the answer is that the cost will be $2,512.

HENRY FORD'S MODEL T AND DOUGLAS AIRCRAFT'S DC-9

The learning curve is nothing new. Between 1908 and 1923, the price of Henry Ford's famous Model T automobile fell from over $3,000 to under $1,000, owing in considerable measure to cost reductions due to learning. Ford worked hard to push costs down in this way. Standardization was increased. His product line was less diverse than those of his competitors, and model improvements occurred

6. For a classic paper concerning learning curves, see K. Arrow, "The Economic Implications of Learning by Doing," *Review of Economic Studies*, June 1962, Vol. 29(3), pp. 155–173. The Boston Consulting Group was a leading advocate of its application to corporate planning.

less frequently. The production throughput time was reduced, and the division of labor was increased.

However, not all firms have been as successful as the Ford Motor Company in reducing costs in this way. In cases in which labor turnover is high or a firm cannot obtain workers with the necessary skills, expected cost reductions due to learning may not materialize. For example, when Douglas Aircraft planned the production of the DC-9 airframe, it anticipated little problem in getting qualified workers. But when the time came, the labor market was so tight in Los Angeles that Douglas soon lost 12,000 of the 35,000 workers it hired. The result was that, contrary to the firm's expectations, costs did not fall as a result of learning, substantial losses were incurred, and the firm was forced into a merger (resulting in McDonnell Douglas, which is now part of Boeing).[7]

DIFFUSION MODELS

Another type of technological forecasting technique is based on the use of econometric diffusion models, which analyze the rate at which an innovation spreads. Although these models forecast the diffusion of new processes and products already in existence rather than the occurrence of future inventions, this limitation may be less important than it seems, since the inventions that already occurred are sometimes all that really matter in the short and the intermediate runs. In part, this is because it frequently takes a long time for an invention to be commercially introduced. For example, it took about nine years before catalytic cracking, a major innovation in oil refining, was first used.

The diffusion process, like the earlier stages in the creation and assimilation of new processes and products, is essentially a learning process. However, rather than being confined to a research laboratory or a few firms, the learning takes place among a considerable number of users and producers. When the innovation first appears, potential users are uncertain of its nature and effectiveness, and they tend to view its purchase as an experiment. Sometimes, considerable additional research and development is required before the innovation is successful; sometimes, despite attempts at redesign and improvement, the innovation never is a success. Information regarding the existence, characteristics, and availability of the innovation is circulated by the producers through advertisements and sales representatives; information regarding the reaction of users to the innovation tends to be circulated informally and through the trade press.

Figure A.6 illustrates an important aspect of the process by which new techniques spread throughout an industry. The figure shows the probability that a firm not using an innovation will adopt it in the next few months and is influenced by the proportion of firms in the industry already using it. Specifically, as the number of firms adopting an innovation increases, the probability of its adoption by a nonuser increases. This is because the risks associated with its introduction grow

7. J. Macklin, "Douglas Aircraft's Stormy Flight Path," *Fortune*, December 1966.

FIGURE A.6

Relation between Probability of a Nonuser's Adopting a Process Innovation and the Proportion of Firms Already Using the Innovation

This relationship tends to be direct.

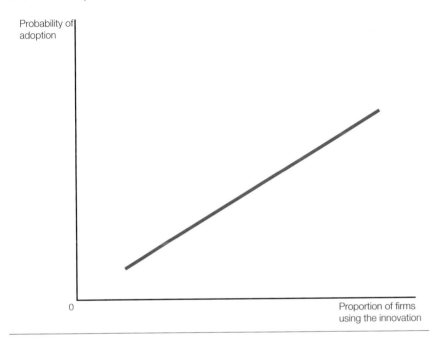

smaller, competitive pressures mount, and bandwagon effects increase as experience and information regarding an innovation accumulate.

Other important aspects of the diffusion process are brought out by Figure A.7. Panel A shows that the probability that a nonuser will adopt the innovation is higher for more profitable innovations than for less profitable innovations, holding constant the proportion of firms in the industry already using it. The more profitable the investment in an innovation promises to be, the greater is the probability that a firm's estimate of its potential profitability compensates for the risks involved in its installation.

Panel B of Figure A.7 shows that the probability a nonuser will adopt the innovation is higher for innovations requiring fairly small investments, holding constant the proportion of firms in the industry that are already using it (and the profitability of the innovation). This is because firms are more cautious before committing themselves to large, expensive projects; and they have more difficulty in financing them.

FIGURE A.7

Effect of Profitability of the Innovation and the Size of Investment Required to Adopt the Innovation on Probability of Adoption

This probability tends to be directly related to profitability and inversely related to the size of the investment.

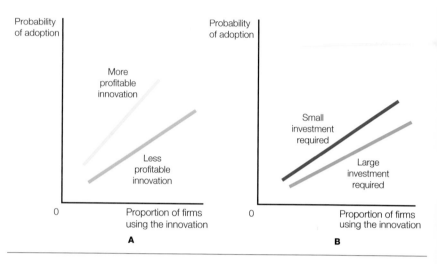

If the relationship in Figure A.6 holds, it can be shown that $P(t)$, the proportion of firms using the innovation, increases in accord with the S-shaped growth curve shown in Figure A.8. The formula for this growth curve (often called the *logistic curve*) is

$$P(t) = \frac{1}{1 + e^{-(A+Bt)}} \tag{A.11}$$

where A and B are parameters that vary from innovation to innovation and t represents time. Whether the diffusion process goes on slowly, as in curve L in Figure A.8, or quickly, as in curve M, depends on the profitability of the innovation and the size of investment it requires. This model has much in common with the models used by epidemiologists to represent the spread of contagious diseases. Firms in a wide variety of industries have found that it can explain reasonably well the available data concerning the diffusion process.[8]

8. See E. Mansfield, *Industrial Research and Technological Innovation* (New York: Norton, 1968); E. Mansfield et al., *The Production and Application of New Industrial Technology* (New York: Norton, 1977); V. Mahajan and Y. Wind, eds., *Innovation Diffusion Models of New Product Acceptance* (Cambridge, MA: Ballinger, 1986); and E. Mansfield, "Contributions of New Technology to the Economy," in *Technology, R and D, and the Economy*, ed. Bruce Smith and Claude Barfield (Washington, DC: Brookings Institution and American Enterprise Institute, 1996).

FORECASTING THE RATE OF DIFFUSION OF NUMERICALLY CONTROLLED MACHINE TOOLS

To illustrate the use of diffusion models for forecasting, consider a study carried out for the Small Business Administration to forecast the percentage of firms in the tool and die industry that would be using numerically controlled machine

FIGURE A.8

Growth over a Period of Time in the Proportion of Firms Using the Innovation

Both growth curves L and M are S-shaped.

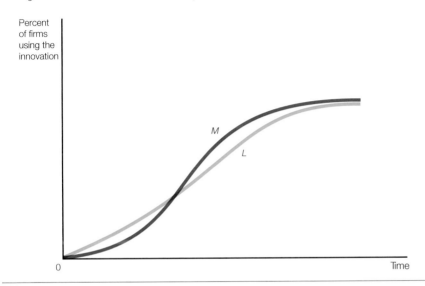

tools two years after the time of the study.[9] When the study was carried out, about 20% of the firms in the National Tool, Die, and Precision Machining Association were using numerically controlled machine tools. To use the model described in the previous section, data were obtained, both from a mail survey and an interview study, of the past growth over time in the percentage of tool and die firms using such machine tools. Based on these data, and using the regression techniques in Chapter 4, estimates of A and B in equation (A.11) were made. To see how these estimates were calculated, note that equation (A.11) implies that

$$\ln \{P(t)/[1 - P(t)]\} = A + Bt \tag{A.12}$$

Thus, A and B can be estimated by regressing $\ln \{P(t)/[1 - P(t)]\}$ on t.[10] (The natural logarithm of any number, say, Y, is designated $\ln Y$.)

Given estimates of A and B, equation (A.11) can be used to forecast $P(t)$ for future values of t. On the basis of the interview data, the model forecasted that about 33% of the firms would be using numerically controlled machine tools. On the basis of mail-survey data, the model forecasted that about 37% of the firms would be using them.

To see how these forecasts compare with those obtained on the basis of other methods, two alternative types of forecasts were made. First, the firms—both in interviews with a carefully selected sample of industry executives and in the

9. See Mansfield et al., *The Production and Application of New Industrial Technology.*
10. This is only a rough estimation technique, but it is adequate for present purposes.

PROBLEM SOLVED: Information Technology and Productivity Growth

The U.S. Bureau of Labor Statistics reports the annual output per worker in the United States increased by 4.8% in 2002, and over 5% in 2003. During the 1980s and 1990s the annual growth in output per worker was less than 2.7%. While many articles attribute this productivity increase to the expanded use of information technology (IT), recent research shows that technology alone only accounts for a small percentage of the increase. More important than technology is how managers re-design their work processes around the technology.

Professors Eric Brynjolfsson of MIT and Lorin Hitt of the The Wharton School studied over 1,100 large U.S. corporations. They concluded the critical question facing managers should not be, "Does IT pay off," but "How can we best use computers?" They found that complementary organizational capital assets coupled with IT provide most of the increases in productivity. These complementary assets include human capital, training, work processes and routines, knowledge transfer, and corporate culture and value. For every dollar invested in IT hardware, companies spend up to nine dollars on these complementary assets. Their conclusion is that IT does not in itself produce productivity gains, rather it is the management around the use of IT that produces the gains.

For example, they examined the use of IT in both Wal-Mart and K-Mart. They found that while Wal-Mart did have a greater use of IT per employee, the bigger differences were in how the organization is designed around IT. Decision making in Wal-Mart is more decentralized, there is a greater use of teams, and compensation is more performance based.

Technological advances like electric motors and robotics essentially replaced the brawn of humans. Computers are different since they do not replace the decision-making abilites of humans, rather they complement those abilities. In fact, studies find companies that use IT extensively employ workers who are better trained, educated, and skilled. These companies leverage this combination of computers and cognitive power by empowering employees through the use of intranets and database sharing. They also motivate their employees to make good decisions by structuring performance based incentive systems.

While IT itself holds the potential for increased productivity within a firm, this potential is only realized when managers take the appropriate actions to re-design organizational assets to complement the technology. Brynjolfsson and Hitt suggest a set of organizational design changes to enhance the productiivy of IT systems. These include:

- automation of routine tasks
- use of highly skilled employees
- decentralized decision making
- more efficient information flow
- greater use of performance based incentives

Sources: Steve Lohr. "Technology and Worker Efficiency," *New York Times*. February 2, 2004 at www.nytimes.com/2004/02/02/technology/02new.html; Erik Brynjolfsson, "The IT Productivity Gap," ebusiness.mit.edu/erik/Optimize/pr_roi.html.

mail survey of the industry—were asked whether they planned to begin using numerical control in the next two years. Since considerable lead time is required in obtaining numerical control, it seemed reasonable to suppose that their replies would have some forecasting value. The results of the interviews indicated that

TABLE A.2

Alternative Two-Year Forecasts of the Percentage of Firms in the U.S. Tool and Die Industry Using Numerical Control, and the Actual Percentage

Type of forecast	Based on interview data	Based on mail survey
Model	33	37
Plans of tool and die firms	33	43
Median forecast by machine tool builders	30	30
Actual percentage	37	37

about 16% of nonusers planned to use numerical control; the results of the mail survey indicated that this was the case for 28% of the nonusers. Therefore, the forecast was 33%, based on the interview data, or 43%, based on the mail survey.

Second, forecasts were obtained from the machine tool builders, the firms presumably closest to and best informed about the market for numerically controlled machine tools. About 25 of the 150 members of the National Machine Tool Builders Association provided forecasts. The results showed a considerable amount of variation, but the median forecast was about 30%.

How accurate were these forecasts? Which forecasting approach was most accurate? Table A.2 shows that the model's forecast based on the data from the mail survey was almost precisely correct and that the model's forecast based on the interview data was off by only 4 percentage points. Regardless of whether we look at results based on the interview data or the mail survey data, the model forecasts better than the other two techniques. Moreover, it forecasts better than simple extrapolation by "naive" models.[11] Certainly, this is encouraging. On the basis of these and other results, it appears that this simple model may be of use in forecasting the rate of diffusion. Of course, this does not mean that it is anything more than a crude device or that it can be applied in situations in which its basic assumptions do not hold. But it does mean that, used with caution, the model may perform at least as well as other commonly used forecasting devices.

SUMMARY

1. Technological change is the advance of technology; it often results in a change in the production function for an existing product or in a new product. The rate of technological change is often measured by changes in productivity. Changes in total factor productivity are often used by firms to measure changes in efficiency.

11. Specifically, the model forecast better than naive models that assumed that the increase in the percentage of firms using numerical control would be the same amount, in absolute or relative terms, during the next two years as it had been during the previous two years.

2. Research and development can be regarded as a process of uncertainty reduction, or learning. Chance plays a large role in research and development, and many projects use parallel efforts to help cope with uncertainty. Techniques are presented in this chapter to indicate when parallel efforts should be used.

3. An R and D project's likelihood of economic success is the product of three factors: the probability of technical success, the probability of commercialization (given technical success), and the probability of economic success (given commercialization). All three seem to be directly related to how quickly an R and D project is evaluated for its economic, as opposed to only technical, potential.

4. To promote successful R and D, there must be a strong link between R and D and marketing personnel and project selection techniques must be effective. However, this does not mean that more complicated quantitative selection techniques need be used.

5. For a particular innovation, there is likely to be a time-cost trade-off function. If the firm cuts the total time taken to develop and introduce the innovation, it incurs higher costs. Time-cost trade-off functions vary from firm to firm, because some firms are more adept and experienced than others in developing and introducing a particular innovation. The optimal duration of the project is the time interval where the discounted gross profits exceed the discounted cost by the maximum amount.

6. In many industries, there is a learning curve, which shows the extent to which the average cost of producing an item falls in response to increases in its cumulative total output. This learning curve plays an important role in pricing. For example, Texas Instruments successfully priced its product at less than its then-current average cost to move quickly down the learning curve. Regression techniques can be applied to estimate the learning curve for a particular product.

7. As the number of firms adopting a new process increases, the probability of its adoption by a nonuser increases. Also, the probability that a nonuser will adopt the innovation is higher for more-profitable innovations than for less-profitable innovations and for innovations requiring small investments than for those requiring large investments. A model based on these propositions can sometimes be of use in forecasting the rate of diffusion of an innovation.

PROBLEMS

 wwnorton.com/studyspace

1. The Monroe Corporation uses three inputs: labor, energy, and materials. In 2011, it used 20,000 hours of labor, 50,000 kilowatt-hours of energy, and 10,000 pounds of materials to produce 200,000 pounds of output. In 2012, it used 30,000 hours of labor, 100,000 kilowatt-hours of energy, and 14,000 pounds of materials to produce 300,000 pounds of output. In 2011, the price of labor was $10 per hour, the price of a kilowatt-hour of energy was $0.02, and the price of a pound of materials was $5.

a. What was the total factor productivity in 2011?
b. What was the total factor productivity in 2012?
c. What is the base year in the preceding calculations?

2. The chief scientist at the Roosevelt Laboratories estimates that the cost (in millions of dollars) of developing and introducing a new type of antiulcer drug equals

$$C = 100 - 19t + 0.5t^2, \quad \text{for } 1 \le t \le 6$$

where t is the number of years taken to develop and introduce the new drug. The discounted profit (gross of innovation cost) from a new drug of this type (in millions of dollars) is estimated to equal

$$R = 110 - 15t, \quad \text{for } 1 \le t \le 6$$

a. The managers of the Roosevelt Laboratories are committed to developing and introducing this new drug within six years, and it is impossible to develop and introduce it in less than one year. What project duration would minimize cost?
b. Why does R decline as t increases?
c. What is the optimal project duration? Why?

3. The Flynn Company produces a particular type of commercial truck. Its chief engineer regresses the logarithm of the input cost of the Qth truck produced on the logarithm of Q, the result being

$$\log C = 5.1 - 0.25 \log Q$$

where C is input cost (in dollars).
a. What is the estimated input cost of the 100th truck produced?
b. What is the estimated input cost of the 200th truck produced?
c. By what percentage does unit input cost decline if output is doubled (from 100 to 200 trucks)?

4. The Martin Company's president wants to estimate the proportion of chemical firms that will be using a particular new process in 2012. One of her assistants regresses $\ln \{m(t)/[n - m(t)]\}$ on t where $m(t)$ is the number of chemical firms using this process in year t and n is the total number of chemical firms that can use this process. Measuring t in years from 1994, the regression is

$$\ln \left[\frac{m(t)}{n - m(t)} \right] = -4.0 + 0.22t$$

a. Prove that, if the proportion of chemical firms using the new process increases in accord with the logistic curve in equation (A.11), $\ln \{m(t)/[n - m(t)]\}$ is a linear function of t.
b. On the basis of the preceding regression, can you estimate A and B (the parameters of the logistic curve in equation (A.11))? If so, how?

    c. Forecast the percentage of chemical firms using the new process in 2012.

5. In the aircraft industry, many studies indicate that a doubling of cumulative output results in about a 20% reduction in cost. If the cost of the 30th unit produced of a particular aircraft is $12 million, what is the cost of the 60th unit produced? Of the 120th unit produced?

6. The Bureau of Labor Statistics produced data showing that output per hour of labor in blast furnaces using the most up-to-date techniques has sometimes been about twice as large as the industry average.

    a. How can such large differences exist at a given time? Why don't all firms continually adopt the most up-to-date techniques?

    b. Should firms always adopt techniques that maximize output per hour of labor? Why or why not?

    c. Should firms adopt techniques that maximize output per dollar of capital? Why or why not?

7. The Russell Corporation is trying to develop an engine that will emit fewer pollutants. There are two possible approaches to this technical problem. If either one is adopted, there is a 50–50 chance that it will cost $2 million to develop the engine and a 50–50 chance that it will cost $1 million to do so.

    a. If the firm chooses one of the approaches and carries it to completion, what is the expected cost of developing the engine?

    b. If the two approaches are run in parallel and the true cost of development using each approach can be determined after $150,000 has been spent on each approach, what is the expected cost of developing the engine? (Note that the total cost figure for each approach, if adopted, includes the $150,000.)

    c. Should parallel approaches be used?

8. To help decide whether particular R and D projects should be carried out, some firms compare the estimated cost of each project with the estimated profits it will earn. To carry out such an analysis, the firm's personnel must estimate how much the R and D project would cost if it were carried out. In one major drug firm, the frequency distribution of 49 projects by the ratio of actual to estimated cost is as follows:

Actual cost divided by estimated cost	Number of projects
Less than 1.01	6
1.01 and under 2.01	24
2.01 and under 3.01	16
3.01 and under 4.01	3

a. If this firm were using this technique to help determine whether particular R and D projects should be carried out, what problems would be encountered?

b. How might the firm try to cope with these problems?

9. The Monroe Corporation wants to develop a new process that would reduce its costs by 10%. There are two ways to go about developing such a process. If the first way is adopted, there is a 0.6 probability that it will cost $5 million to develop the process and a 0.4 probability that it will cost $3 million to do so. If the second way is adopted, there is a 0.7 probability that it will cost $3 million and a 0.3 probability that it will cost $5 million.

a. If the first way is adopted, what is the expected cost of developing the new process?

b. If the second way is adopted, what is the expected cost?

c. If the two approaches can be run in parallel and the true cost of development using each approach can be determined after $500,000 has been spent on each approach, what is the expected cost? (Assume that the outcomes of the two approaches are independent. Also, note that the total cost figure for each approach, if adopted, includes the $500,000.)

10. On the basis of past growth of the percentage of firms in the machinery industry using robots, this percentage can be approximated by

$$P(t) = \frac{1}{1 + e^{-(-6.1+0.41t)}}$$

where $P(t)$ is this percentage and t is measured in years from 1990.

a. During which year did about 25% of the firms in the machinery industry use robots?

b. During which year did 50% of the firms in this industry use robots?

BUSINESS AND ECONOMIC FORECASTING

Many corporations have corporate economists or hire consulting firms to forecast sales or profits. These forecasts can be done on a short-term basis, for example, next quarter, or on a longer-term basis, for the next year, five years, or ten years. Security analysts forecast quarterly and yearly earnings, and one can hear their consensus via First Call before earnings are about to be released. Popular business press publications, like *Bloomberg BusinessWeek* and the *Wall Street Journal*, offer similar results. The Federal Reserve and the Department of Commerce also conduct business forecasts as do trade associations for their industries.

Managers of all sorts are routinely involved in decision making that is informed by forecasts. Sales forecasts, for instance, may dictate raw material orders, production run schedules, and hiring decisions. An organization's mid-level managers are likely to make these decisions. On the other hand, long-term growth forecasts for an industry may entail capital expansion or disinvestment of assets, decisions likely to be made by higher-level managers within the organization, most likely with the board of directors' approval.

In this appendix, we take up the techniques used by many business and economic forecasters. As you work through these subjects, keep in mind that economic forecasting is not an exact science. Too many variables exist to precisely model the economic system or even a small part of it. Even so, most corporations prefer rigorous data to intuition or hunch (and, in fact, managers have a fiduciary responsibility to the owners of the firm to practice due diligence in following rational procedures for decision making).

As we shall see, regression plays a major role in many of these forecasting techniques, including the econometric models that are the staple of the leading private and public economic forecasters.

SURVEY TECHNIQUES

One of the simplest forecasting devices is to survey firms or individuals to determine what they believe will occur. Consider the surveys carried out to forecast firms' expenditures. For example, the U.S. Department of Commerce and the Securities and Exchange Commission conduct surveys of business intentions to buy plant and equipment. Still other surveys are aimed at measuring consumer intentions. The Survey Research Center at the University of Michigan and other such groups provide information on planned purchases of automobiles, appliances, and housing. Also, they indicate the extent of consumer confidence in the economy, which is an important factor influencing consumers' spending decisions. Surveys of this type are of value in forecasting the sales of many products. They provide a wealth of information to the forecaster.

At least two types of information can be obtained from surveys. First, they can provide us with the respondent's forecast of some variable over which he or she has no control. For example, the University of Michigan obtains data from consumers concerning their forecasts of the rate of inflation. Second, surveys can provide us information concerning what people or firms believe they will do. For example, the National Federation of Independent Business surveys firms to determine whether, and to what extent, they plan to increase their prices.

Suppose a survey is used to forecast some variable, such as the sales of a particular firm. How can we determine how reliable this forecasting technique seems to be? One commonly used measure of the size of the forecast error is the root-mean-squared forecast error, which is defined as

$$E = \left(\sum_{i=1}^{n} (Y_i - F_i)^2 / n \right)^{0.5}$$

where F_i is the ith forecast, Y_i is the corresponding actual value, and n is the number of forecasts for which we have data concerning the size of the forecast errors. Therefore, if the forecasts for 2011, 2012, and 2013 are \$110 million, \$120 million, and \$130 million, and if the actual values are \$105 million, \$122 million, and \$127 million, respectively, the root-mean-squared forecast error equals

$$\sqrt{\frac{(105 - 110)^2 + (122 - 120)^2 + (127 - 130)^2}{3}} = 3.56$$

or $3.56 million dollars. This measure of forecast error is used to evaluate forecasts, no matter whether they are based on surveys or other techniques. Clearly, the lower is the root-mean-squared forecast error, the better the forecasting technique.

TAKING APART A TIME SERIES

Although surveys are of considerable use, most major firms seem to base their forecasts in large part on the quantitative analysis of economic time series. The classic approach to economic forecasting, devised primarily by economic statisticians, was essentially descriptive. It assumed that an economic time series could be decomposed into four components: trend, seasonal variation, cyclical variation, and irregular movements. More specifically, it assumed that the value of an economic variable at a certain time could be represented as the product of each of these four components. For example, the value of a company's sales in January 2011 was viewed as equal to

$$Y = T \times S \times C \times I \tag{B.1}$$

where T is the trend value of the firm's sales during that month, S is the seasonal variation attributable to January, C is the cyclical variation occurring that month, and I is the irregular variation that occurred then.[1] Each of these components is defined next.

Trend

A trend is a relatively smooth long-term movement of a time series. For instance, the civilian labor force of the United States increased rather steadily between 1948 and 2011, as shown in Figure B.1. Hence, there has been an upward trend in the U.S. civilian labor force. Of course, not all trends are upward. The trend in farm employment in the United States has generally been downward, as shown in Figure B.2.[2] Whether upward or downward, the trend of a time series is represented by a smooth curve. In equation (B.1), T is the value of the firm's sales predicted for January 2011, on the basis of such a curve.

Seasonal Variation

In a particular month, the value of an economic variable is likely to differ from what would be expected on the basis of its trend because of seasonal factors. For example, consider the sales of a firm that produces Christmas trees. Since the demand for Christmas trees is much higher in the winter than in the summer, one would expect that the monthly time series of the firm's sales would show a pronounced and predictable seasonal pattern. Specifically, sales each year would tend to be higher in December than during the rest of the year. As we shall see, it is possible to calculate *seasonal indexes* that estimate how much each month departs from what would be expected on the basis of its trend. In equation (B.1), we must multiply the trend value T by the seasonal index S to allow for the effect of this seasonal variation.

1. In some versions of this model, the components are added rather than multiplied. That is, it is assumed that

$$Y = T + S + C + I$$

where Y is the value of the time series.

2. In still other cases, the trend is horizontal; that is, there is no upward or downward tendency in the time series. In these cases, it is often said that there is no trend.

FIGURE B.1

Civilian Labor Force of the United States, 1948–2011

This series exhibits a strong upward trend.

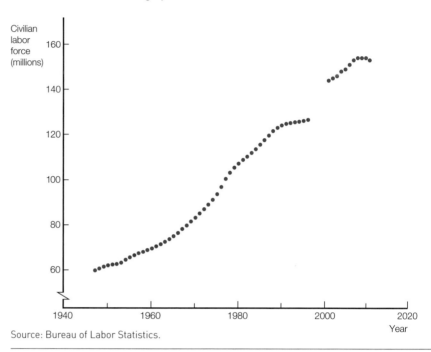

Source: Bureau of Labor Statistics.

Cyclical Variation

Another reason why an economic variable may differ from its trend value is that it may be influenced by the so-called business cycle. The general tempo of economic activity in our society has exhibited a cyclical nature, with booms being followed by recessions and recessions being followed by expansions. These cycles have not been regular or consistent (which is one reason why many economists prefer the term *business fluctuations to business cycles*); but unquestionably there has been a certain cyclical ebb and flow of economic activity, which has been reflected in a great many time series. For this reason, $T \times S$ is multiplied by C, which is supposed to indicate the effect of cyclical variation on the firm's sales in equation (B.1).

Irregular Variation

Once it has been multiplied by both S and C, the trend value T has been altered to reflect seasonal and cyclical forces. But in addition to these forces, *a variety of short-term, erratic forces is also at work*. Their effects are represented by I. Essen-

FIGURE B.2

Farm Employment in the United States, 1947–2011

This series exhibits a strong downward trend.

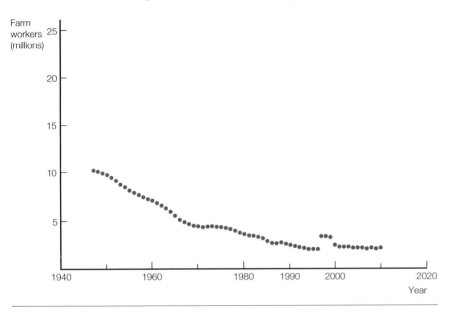

tially, *I* reflects the effects of all factors other than the trend, seasonal variation, and cyclical variation. According to the classic model, these irregular forces are too unpredictable to be useful for forecasting purposes.

HOW TO ESTIMATE A LINEAR TREND

Managerial economists have carried out many studies to estimate the trend, seasonal variation, and cyclical variation in particular economic time series. In this and the following sections of this appendix, we encounter the methods used to estimate a trend; in subsequent sections, we take up seasonal and cyclical variation. First, we consider the case in which the long-term overall movement of the time series seems to be fairly close to linear. For example, this seems true for the sales of the ABC Corporation during the period 1997 to 2011. (These sales are plotted in Figure B.3.) In a case in which the trend seems to be linear, analysts frequently use the method of least squares to calculate the trend. In other words, they assume that, if the long-term forces underlying the trend were the only ones at work, the time series would be approximately linear. Specifically, they assume that

$$Y_t = A + Bt \qquad \text{(B.2)}$$

FIGURE B.3

Linear Trend in Sales, ABC Corporation, 1997–2011

The ABC Corporation's sales have risen rather steadily throughout the period.

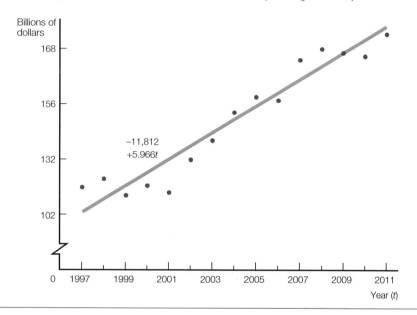

where Y_t is the trend value of the variable at time t. (Note that t assumes values like 2009 or 2010 if time is measured in years.) The **trend value** is the value of the variable that would result if only the trend were at work. The deviation of Y, the actual value of the variable, from the trend value is the **deviation from trend**.

> The **trend value** is the value of Y_t that would result if only the trend existed

> The **deviation from trend** is the difference of the actual value of Y_t and the value of Y_t assumed from equation (B.2).

To illustrate the calculation of a linear trend, we examine the ABC Corporation's annual sales from 1997–2011. Since sales in year t is the dependent variable and t is the independent variable, it follows from our discussion in Chapter 4 that

$$b = \frac{\sum_{t=t_0}^{t_0+n-1}(S_t - \overline{S})(t - \overline{t})}{\sum_{t=t_0}^{t_0+n-1}(t - \overline{t})^2} \tag{B.3}$$

and

$$a = \overline{S} - b\overline{t} \tag{B.4}$$

where S_t is sales (in billions of dollars) in year t, t_0 is the earliest year in the time series (that is, 1997), $t_0 + n - 1$ is the latest year in the time series (that is, 2011), b is an estimate of B, and a is an estimate of A.

Inserting the data underlying Figure B.3 into equations (B.3) and (B.4), we find that the trend line is

$$S_t = -11{,}812 + 5.966t \qquad\qquad \text{(B.5)}$$

This trend line is plotted in Figure B.3.

HOW TO ESTIMATE A NONLINEAR TREND

Many time series do not exhibit linear trends. In some such cases, a quadratic function of time provides an adequate trend. Such a trend can be represented as

$$Y_t = A + B_1 t + B_2 t^2$$

To estimate A, B_1, and B_2, we can use the multiple regression techniques described in Chapter 4. As indicated there, standard computer programs are available to make these computations. The regression contains two independent variables: t and t^2. Whether a quadratic trend is more appropriate than a linear trend can be determined by seeing whether it fits the data significantly better than a linear trend.

FIGURE B.4

Exponential Trend, Assuming $\beta = 1.5$, $\alpha = 1$

Many time series have exponential trends.

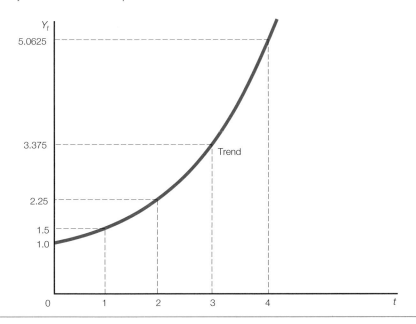

For many variables, an exponential curve provides a better-fitting trend than a quadratic curve. The equation for such a trend (shown in Figure B.4) is

$$Y_t = \alpha\beta^t \tag{B.6}$$

where Y_t is the trend value of the time series at time t. A trend of this sort seems to fit many business and economic time series. It represents a situation in which the variable grows at a constant percentage rate per year. Therefore, if a firm's sales grow at about 5% per year, they are likely to exhibit an exponential trend.

If there is an exponential trend, we can take logarithms of both sides of equation (B.6)

$$\log Y_t = A + Bt \tag{B.7}$$

where $A = \log \alpha$, and $B = \log \beta$. Since equation (B.7) is linear, we can estimate A and B by the method of least squares. Then, we can take antilogs of A and B to estimate α and β, the unknown coefficients in equation (B.6). (The average rate of increase of Y_t equals $\beta - 1$.)[3] In this way, we can estimate the nonlinear trend shown in equation (B.6).

SEASONAL VARIATION

Many time series consist of monthly or quarterly rather than annual data. For such time series, managerial economists and decision makers must recognize that seasonal variation is likely to be present in the series. Seasonal variation in many economic time series is due to the weather. For example, sales of soft drinks are higher in the summer than in the winter. In other cases, such as sales of Christmas trees, seasonal variation is due to the location of a specific holiday (Christmas) on the calendar. Still other reasons for seasonal variation are the fact that some industries tend to grant vacations at a particular time of year, taxes have to be paid at certain times of the year, or schools tend to open at particular times of the year.

Managerial economists have devised methods for estimating the pattern of seasonal variation in a particular time series. In other words, they can determine the extent to which a particular month or quarter is likely to differ from what would be expected on the basis of the trend and cyclical variation in the same series. (In terms of the traditional model in equation (B.1), they can determine the value of S for each month or quarter.) For example, the marketing vice president for a manufacturer of soft drinks may tell the company's board of directors that U.S. production of soft drinks tends in June to be 5.9% higher than what the trend and cyclical variation in soft drink production would indicate. Or she may tell them that U.S. production of soft drinks in December tends to be 7.0% lower than the trend and cyclical variation would indicate.

3. If Y grows at a constant rate of $100r\%$ per year,

$$Y_t = Y_0(1 + r)^t$$

where Y_0 is the value of Y in some base year (say 2010) and Y_t is its value t years after the base year. Taking logarithms of both sides of this equation,

$$\log Y_t = \log Y_0 + [\log (1 + r)]t$$

Therefore, $\log (1 + r)$ equals B, and the antilog of B (which is β) equals $(1 + r)$. Consequently, $r = \beta - 1$. In other words, as stated in the text, the average rate of increase of Y_t (which is r) equals $\beta - 1$. (Mathematical review: If X is the logarithm of Y, Y is called the antilog of X.)

TABLE B.1

Seasonal Variation in Production of Soft Drinks in the United States

Month	Seasonal index	Month	Seasonal index
January	93.4	July	112.4
February	89.3	August	113.4
March	90.7	September	108.3
April	94.9	October	103.9
May	99.0	November	95.8
June	105.9	December	93.0

The seasonal variation in a particular time series is described by a figure for each month, the **seasonal index,** *which shows the way in which that month tends to depart from what would be expected on the basis of the trend and cyclical variation in the time series.* For example, Table B.1 shows the seasonal variation in U.S. production of soft drinks. January's production tends to be about 93.4% of the amount expected on the basis of trend and cyclical variation, February's production tends to be about 89.3% of this amount, March's production tends to be about 90.7% of this amount, and so on. Figures of this sort can be used in a number of ways. *One important application is to forecast what the time series will be in the future.* For example, suppose that on the basis of the trend and cyclical variation, it appears likely that about 30 million gallons of soft drinks will be produced next January. If this is the case, a reasonable forecast of actual January production is 0.934 (30 million) = 28.02 million gallons, since January's production tends to be 93.4% of the amount expected based on trend and cyclical variation.

The **seasonal index** shows the deviation of a particular month's value from the value attributed to the trend and cyclical variation alone.

CALCULATION OF SEASONAL VARIATION

One way of calculating the seasonal variation in a time series is to use regression techniques. Suppose, for example, that a business analyst has a time series composed of quarterly values; that is, each observation pertains to the first, second, third, or fourth quarter of a year. If the analyst believes that the time series has a linear trend, he or she may assume that the value of the observation at time t equals

$$Y = A + B_1 t + B_2 Q_1 + B_3 Q_2 + B_4 Q_3 + e_t \qquad (B.8)$$

where Q_1 equals 1 if time t is the first quarter and 0 otherwise, Q_2 equals 1 if time t is the second quarter and 0 otherwise, Q_3 equals 1 if time t is the third quarter and 0 otherwise, and e_t is an error term.

It is important to understand the meaning of B_1, B_2, B_3, and B_4 in equation (B.8). Clearly, B_1 is the slope of the linear trend, but what are B_2, B_3, and B_4? The answer is that B_2 *is the difference between the expected value of an observation in the first quarter and the expected value of an observation in the fourth quarter when the effects of the trend are removed.* (The **expected value** of an observation is its long-term mean value. To find its expected value, one multiplies each possible value of the observation by the probability of this value, and sums up the results.) To see that this is true, note that, if an observation pertains to time t, the first quarter of a particular year, its expected value equals

$$A + B_1 t + B_2$$

according to equation (B.8). Similarly, if an observation pertains to time $t + 3$, the fourth quarter of the same year, its expected value equals

$$A + B_1(t + 3)$$

according to equation (B.8). Therefore, the difference between the expected value of an observation in the first quarter and the expected value of an observation in the fourth quarter equals

$$(A + B_1 t + B_2) - [A + B_1(t + 3)] = B_2 - 3B_1$$

And, if we remove the effects of the trend (which is responsible for the last term on the right, $3B_1$), this difference equals B_2; this is what we set out to prove. When the effects of the trend are removed, one can show in the same way that B_3 is the difference between the expected value of an observation in the second quarter and the expected value of an observation in the fourth quarter, and B_4 is the difference between the expected value of an observation in the third quarter and the expected value of an observation in the fourth quarter.

Consequently, if equation (B.8) is valid, the analyst can represent the seasonal variation in the time series by the three numbers B_2, B_3, and B_4. To estimate each of these numbers, ordinary multiple regression techniques can be used. The dependent variable is Y, and the independent variables are t, Q_1, Q_2, and Q_3. The last three independent variables (Q_1, Q_2, and Q_3) are dummy variables. (A dummy variable is a variable that can assume only two values: 0 or 1.) Using the regression methods described in Chapter 4, the constants in equation (B.8) (A, B_1, B_2, B_3, and B_4) can be estimated by the ordinary least-squares technique.

When using this procedure, the analyst assumes that seasonal effects are added to the trend value, as shown in equation (B.8). This differs from the traditional model in equation (B.1), where it is assumed that seasonal effects multiply the trend value (see footnote 1). The former assumption is appropriate in some cases, whereas the latter assumption is appropriate in others. Techniques based on both assumptions are useful.[4]

The **expected value** of an observation is its long-term mean value.

4. To calculate the seasonal variation based on the latter assumption, a four-quarter—or 12-month if the data are monthly—moving average can be used. For the details, see any business statistics book.

PROBLEM SOLVED: Forecasting the Demand for Blood Tests

North Carolina Memorial Hospital (now part of University of North Carolina Hospitals) has been interested in forecasting the number of blood tests it will perform. A simple model has been constructed that assumes that the number of tests per month increases according to a linear trend, and that the seasonal variation can be represented in the way described in equation (B.9). In other words, it is assumed that

$$Q = A + B_1 t + B_2 M_1 + B_3 M_2 + \ldots + B_{12} M_{11} + e_t,$$

where Q is the number of blood tests performed at the hospital in month t, M_1 equals 1 if month t is January and 0 otherwise, . . . , M_{11} equals 1 if month t is November and 0 otherwise, and e_t equals an error term. Therefore, B_2 is the difference between January and December in the expected number of tests, B_3 is the difference between February and December in the expected number of tests, and so on (when the effects of the trend are removed).

(a) Indicate how one can estimate the values of A, B_1, B_2, . . . , B_{12}. (b) Potential patients are reluctant to seek medical care during the Christmas holidays. Would you expect B_2 to be positive or negative? Why? (c) According to the hospital, the model forecasts "are being used to plan vacation schedules for employees and to order supplies for the tests." Why would forecasts of this sort be useful for these purposes? (d) Forecasts based on this simple model have been reported to be "excellent." Forecasting errors have averaged only about 4.4%. On the other hand, forecasts based on exponential smoothing (a technique described in the appendix on page 819) did not perform so well. Do you think that a model of this sort will always outperform exponential smoothing?

SOLUTION (a) The values of these parameters can be estimated by calculating a multiple regression, where Q is the dependent variable and t, M_1, M_2, . . . ,M_{11} are the independent variables. (b) Positive, because B_2 is the difference between January and December in the expected number of tests when the effects of the trend are removed. Because patients tend not to want such tests during the holidays, December would be expected to be below January in this regard. (c) If one can forecast the demand for blood tests, it is possible to estimate the number of employees and the quantity of supplies needed at various times. Clearly, this information is useful in scheduling vacations and purchases, among other things. (d) No. In some cases, one forecasting technique works well; in others, it works less well. No technique is universally better than the others discussed in this appendix.

To illustrate how this regression procedure can be used to estimate the seasonal variation in monthly data, suppose you have monthly data concerning the sales of a particular firm. If there is a linear trend, you can assume that

$$Y = A + B_1 t + B_2 M_1 + B_3 M_2 + \ldots + B_{12} M_{11} + e_t \qquad \text{(B.9)}$$

where Y is the firm's sales in month t, M_1 equals 1 if month t is January and 0 otherwise, M_2 equals 1 if month t is February and 0 otherwise, . . . , M_{11} equals 1 if month t is November and 0 otherwise, and e_t equals an error term. Using ordinary multiple regression techniques, you can estimate $A, B_1, B_2, \ldots, B_{12}$. The estimates of $B_2, B_3, \ldots, B_{11}$, and B_{12} indicate the seasonal variation in the firm's sales. In particular, B_2 is the difference between January and December in the expected value of sales, B_3 is the difference between February and December in the expected value of sales, and so on, until B_{12} is the difference between November and December in the expected value of sales (when the effects of the trend are removed).

CYCLICAL VARIATION

The **business cycle** or **business fluctuations** reflect the periodic ups and downs experienced by an economy. It can be measured with any economic variable but the fluctuation of GDP over time is the most common.

Time series in business and economics frequently exhibit cyclical variation, such variation often being termed the **business cycle**. To illustrate what we mean by the business cycle or **business fluctuations**, we look at how national output has grown in the United States since 1980. Figure B.5 shows the behavior of gross domestic product (GDP) in constant dollars in the United States since 1980. Clearly, output has grown considerably during this period; indeed, GDP is more than three and a half times what it was 30 years ago. But this growth has not been steady. While the long-term trend has been upward, there have been periods, such as 1981–1982, 1990–1991, and 2008–2009 when national output declined.

The **full-employment level** of GDP is the total amount of goods and services that could have been produced if there had been full employment.

The **full-employment level** of GDP is the total amount of goods and services that could have been produced if there had been full employment. Figure B.5 shows that national output tends to rise and approach (and perhaps exceed)[5] its full-employment level for a while, then falters and falls below this level, then rises to approach it once more, then falls below it again, and so on. For example, output fell far below the full-employment level in the recession of 2008–2009 but was at this level when the economy was booming in the mid-2000s. This movement of national output is sometimes called the *business cycle*, but it must be recognized that these "cycles" are far from regular or consistent.

The **trough** of the business cycle is where GDP is lowest relative to full-employment GDP.

The **expansion** phase of the business cycle is when GDP rises (such as after reaching the trough).

Each cycle can be divided by definition into four phases, as shown in Figure B.6. *The* **trough** *is the point where national output is lowest relative to its full-employment level.* **Expansion** *is the subsequent phase during which national output rises. The* **peak** *occurs when national output is highest relative to its full-employment level. Finally,* **recession** *is the subsequent phase during which national output falls.*[6]

The **peak** of the business cycle is where GDP is highest relative to full employment GDP.

The **recession** phase of the business cycle is when GDP falls (such as after reaching the peak).

Many business and economic time series go up and down with the business cycle. For example, industrial output tends to be above its trend line at the peak of the business cycle and tends to fall below its trend line at the trough. Similarly, such diverse series as the money supply, industrial employment, and stock prices reflect the business cycle. However, not all series go up and down at exactly the same time. Some turn upward before others at a trough, and some turn downward before others at a peak. As we shall see, the fact that some time series tend to precede others in cyclical variation sometimes is used to forecast the pace of economic activity.

5. During a period of inflationary pressure, national output may exceed its full-employment level.
6. The peak and trough may also be defined in terms of deviations from the long-term trend of GDP rather than in terms of deviations from the full-employment level of GDP.

FIGURE B.5

Gross Domestic Product (GDP) (1987 Dollars), United States, 1980–2010

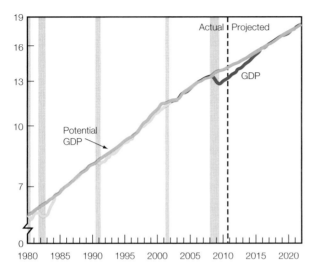

Source: Congress of the United States, Congressional Budget Office, The Budget and Economic Outlook: Fiscal Year 2011 to 2021, January 2011, p. 28.

FIGURE B.6

Four Phases of Business Fluctuations

The peak occurs when national output is highest relative to its full-employment value; the trough occurs when national output is lowest relative to its full-employment value.

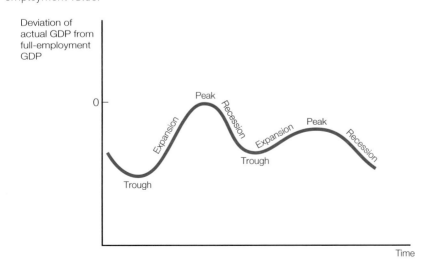

ELEMENTARY FORECASTING TECHNIQUES

In general, all forecasting techniques are extremely fallible, and all forecasts should be treated with caution. Nonetheless, businesses and government agencies have no choice but to make forecasts, however crude. Since firms, governments, and private individuals must continually make decisions that hinge on what they expect will happen, they must make implicit forecasts even if they do not make explicit ones. Therefore, the central question is how best to forecast, not whether to forecast. In this section, we present some elementary forecasting techniques that are commonly applied. Even among small firms, evidence indicates that about three-quarters of the firms use techniques of this sort. However, these techniques should be viewed as crude first approximations rather than highly sophisticated methods. More sophisticated techniques are taken up subsequently.

The simplest type of forecasting method is a straightforward extrapolation of a trend. For example, let us return to the ABC Corporation. At the end of 2011, suppose that ABC Corporation managers wanted to forecast its 2012 sales. During the period 1997–2011, we know from our earlier discussion that the firm's sales could be represented (approximately) by the trend line

$$S_t = -11{,}812 + 5.966t$$

where t equals the year in question. To forecast its 2012 sales, the ABC Corporation could simply insert 2012 for t in this equation. Thus, the forecast for 2012 is

$$-11{,}812 + 5.966(2012) = 191.6$$

or 191.6 billion dollars. As shown in Figure B.7, this forecast is a simple extension, or extrapolation, of the trend line into the future.

Decision makers often need forecasts of monthly rather than annual amounts. In such cases, it is necessary to recognize that seasonal variation, as well as trend, is likely to affect the value for a particular month. To see how a forecast can be made under such circumstances, consider a clothing manufacturer that wants to forecast its sales during each month of 2012. On the basis of data for each month during the period 1981 to 2011, the firm determines that its sales seem to conform to the trend

$$S_t = 12{,}030 + 41t$$

where S_t is the trend value of the firm's monthly sales (in thousands of dollars) and t is time measured in months from January 2011. If this trend continues, the expected sales for each month in 2012 would be as shown in the second column of Table B.2. But this ignores whatever seasonal variation exists in the firm's sales. To include seasonal variation, suppose that the clothing manufacturer's marketing manager analyzes past sales data and finds that the monthly seasonal index for

FIGURE B.7

Simple Trend Extrapolation to Forecast 2012 Sales of the ABC Corporation

The forecast is $191.6 billion.

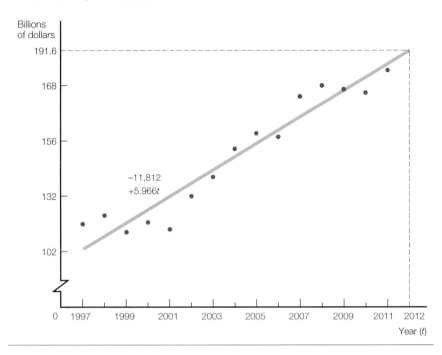

sales is as shown in the third column of Table B.2. (Seasonal effects here are multiplicative, not additive.) If this seasonal pattern continues in 2012 as in the past, we would expect that actual sales each month would equal the trend value (in the second column) times the seasonal index (in the third column) divided by 100. The result, which is shown in the fourth column of Table B.2, is a forecast that includes both the trend and the seasonal variation.

Needless to say, this entire procedure is simply a mechanical extrapolation of the firm's sales data into the future. The assumption is made that the past trend and the past seasonal variation will continue. Moreover, it is assumed that the trend and seasonal variation are the predominant factors that will determine sales in the coming months. The validity of this assumption depends on many considerations, including the extent to which the time series in question (in this case, sales) is affected by cyclical factors and the extent to which the economy is likely to change its cyclical position. In the next section, we turn our attention to a particular method of forecasting business fluctuations.

HOW LEADING INDICATORS ARE USED

Managers and analysts want to modify their forecasts to reflect prospective overall changes in economic activity. For example, if the president of the clothing firm in Table B.2 is convinced that a serious depression will occur 2012, he is likely to modify the forecasts in Table B.2 accordingly. But how does the president of the clothing firm—or anyone else—predict whether there is going to be a depression? There are a variety of ways of doing this, all of which are very imperfect. In this section, we discuss an essentially empirical approach, reserving a discussion of more sophisticated techniques for a later section.

> **Leading indicators** are certain economic series that typically go up or down before GDP does.
>
> A **leading series** are variables that go down before the peak and up before the trough.
>
> A **coincident series** are variables that go down at the peak and up at the trough.
>
> A **lagging series** are variables that go down after the peak and up after the trough.

One of the simplest ways to forecast business fluctuations is to use **leading indicators**, which are certain economic series that typically go down or up before gross domestic product does. The National Bureau of Economic Research carries out detailed and painstaking examinations of the behavior of various economic variables over a long period of time and attempts to find out whether each variable turns downward before, at, or after the peak of the business cycle and whether it turns upward before, at, or after the trough. Variables that go down before the peak and up before the trough are called **leading series**. Variables that go down at the peak and up at the trough are called **coincident series**. Variables that go down after the peak and up after the trough are called **lagging series**.

TABLE B.2

Forecast of Sales of Clothing Manufacturer, 2012

Month	Forecast trend value of sales[a]	Seasonal index	Forecast sales (reflecting both trend and seasonal variables)[a]
January	12,522	90	11,270
February	12,563	80	10,050
March	12,604	80	10,083
April	12,645	90	11,380
May	12,686	110	13,955
June	12,727	120	15,272
July	12,768	80	10,214
August	12,809	110	14,090
September	12,850	120	15,420
October	12,891	100	12,891
November	12,932	100	12,932
December	12,973	120	15,568

[a]Expressed in units of $1,000.

According to the bureau, some important leading series are new orders for durable goods, the average workweek, building contracts, stock prices, certain wholesale prices, and claims for unemployment insurance. These are the variables that tend to turn downward before the peak and upward before the trough.[7] Coincident series include employment, industrial production, corporate profits, and gross domestic product, among many others. Some typical lagging series are retail sales, manufacturers' inventories, and personal income.

These leading series—or leading indicators, as they often are called—are used frequently as forecasting devices. There are sound economic reasons why these series turn downward before a peak or upward before a trough: In some cases, leading series indicate changes in spending in strategic areas of the economy, while in others, they indicate changes in managers' and investors' expectations. To guide business executives in their planning, it is important to try to spot turning points—peaks and troughs—in advance. This, of course, is the toughest part of economic forecasting. Economists sometimes use leading indicators as evidence that a turning point is about to occur. If a large number of leading indicators turn down, this is viewed as a sign of a coming peak. The upturn of a large number of leading indicators is thought to signal an impending trough.

Experience with leading indicators has been only partially successful. The economy has seldom turned downward in recent years without a warning from these indicators, but unfortunately these indicators have turned down on a number of occasions—in 1952 and 1962, for example—when the economy did not turn down subsequently. Therefore, leading indicators sometimes provide false signals. Also, in periods of expansion, they sometimes turn downward too far ahead of the real peak. And in periods of recession, they sometimes turn upward only a very short while before the trough, so that we turn the corners before anything can be done. Nonetheless, leading indicators are not worthless; they are watched closely and used to supplement other, more sophisticated forecasting techniques.

Students interested in learning more about these leading indicators should visit the website of The Conference Board (www.conference-board.org). The Conference Board is a nonprofit organization that provides economic reports and data about business issues and sponsors the business cycle indicators website. The website not only shows a time series for the leading indicators but also discusses their implications for the U.S. economy. In addition, the site reports the leading indicators for other countries.

HOW ECONOMETRIC MODELS ARE USED

Managers and analysts have tended in recent years to base their forecasts more and more on multiple regression techniques and multiequation models. Increased emphasis has been put on the construction and estimation of an equation or system of equations to show the effects of various independent variables on the

7. Of course, claims for unemployment insurance turn upward before the peak and downward before the trough.

variable or variables one wants to forecast. For example, one may want to estimate the quantity of automobiles produced by U.S. auto firms next quarter. According to a study published by the Federal Reserve Bank of New York, the following regression equation is useful for this purpose

$$A = -22,302 + 12.9D - 97.8I - 19.9R + 230P + 6.0N$$

where A is the quantity of autos produced quarterly, D is real disposable income, I is the prime interest rate, R is the inventory-sales ratio, P is the auto price, and N is the nonauto price level. To forecast the quantity of autos produced quarterly, one estimates the values of the independent variables and inserts them into this equation.

PROBLEM SOLVED: Forecasting Shipments of Cement by CEMCO

CEMCO, a small cement producer, has used an econometric model to forecast its sales and profits. According to this model, national cement shipments depend on the amount of residential construction and business fixed investment. Assuming its price is unchanged, CEMCO's shipments of cement are assumed to depend on national cement shipments. Holding national cement shipments constant, CEMCO can increase its shipments by reducing its price. However, its rivals are likely to meet such a price cut, whereas they are less likely to match a price increase.

This year, CEMCO shipped 453,000 tons of cement. Based on this model and alternative assumptions concerning the firm's future price, the forecasted shipments for next year and the year after next were as follows (in thousands of tons):

Assumed future change in CEMCO's price	Next year	Year after next
No price change	468	457
10% price increase	306	296
10% price decrease	473	459

(a) As stated, the firm's model assumes that (1) national cement shipments depend on the amount of residential construction and business fixed investment, and (2) its shipments depend on national cement shipments (if its price does not change). Does it appear that the company expected both residential construction and business fixed investment to be higher in the year after next than in next year? Why or why not? (b) With regard to increases in price, does the demand for the firm's cement seem to be price elastic or price inelastic? Explain. (c) Does the price elasticity of demand seem to be lower for price decreases than for price increases? Is this reasonable? Why or why not?

SOLUTION (a) No. If the company had expected both residential construction and business fixed investment to be higher in the year after next than in next year, it would have forecasted an increase in national cement shipments, which in turn would have implied an increase in CEMCO's cement shipments (assuming no price change). In fact, as shown in the table, it forecasted that its cement shipments would be lower in the year after next than in next year. (b) Price elastic. A 10% increase in price seems to reduce shipments by about one-third. (c) Yes. It seems reasonable if, as stated, the firm's rivals are likely to meet a price reduction but unlikely to meet a price increase.

Multiequation models have been used to forecast many variables, such as gross domestic product. The Wharton model, a pioneer in this field, contained hundreds of equations variously intended to explain the level of expenditures by households, the level of business investment, aggregate output and employment, and wages, prices, and interest rates. The forecasts produced by the Wharton model (and other large models like it) have been followed closely by major business firms and government agencies. Indeed, some firms (like General Electric) have constructed their own multiequation models. Of course, this does not mean that these large models have an unblemished forecasting record; on the contrary, they, like all other forecasting techniques, are quite fallible. However, these models continue to be used in business and government.

Both the single-equation model used to forecast the quantity of autos produced and the Wharton model, with its hundreds of equations, are examples of econometric models. An **econometric model** is a system of equations (or a single equation) estimated from past data used to forecast economic and business variables. The essence of any econometric model is that it blends economic theory with modern statistical methods.

An **econometric model** is a system of equations estimated from past data used to forecast economic and business variables.

THE PURVERE CORPORATION: A NUMERICAL EXAMPLE

To illustrate the nature of multiequation econometric models, consider the Purvere Corporation, a seller of aircraft. Purvere's total revenues come from three sources: the sale of the equipment, servicing the equipment, and the sale of accessories to customers who buy equipment or have it serviced. On the basis of regression analysis, Purvere's managers have found that its revenues from each of these sources can be represented by the following three equations

$$E_t = 100 - 4P_t + 0.02G_t \tag{B.10}$$
$$S_t = 10 + 0.05E_{t-1} \tag{B.11}$$
$$A_t = 25 + 0.1Y_t \tag{B.12}$$

where E_t is the company's revenue from equipment sales in year t, P_t is the price of its equipment, G_t is gross domestic product (in billions of dollars), S_t is its revenue from servicing its equipment, A_t is its revenue from accessory sales, and Y_t is its total sales (which equal $E_t + S_t + A_t$). The values of E_t, S_t, A_t, and P_t are expressed in millions of dollars.

According to equation (B.10), Purvere's equipment sales are inversely related to its price and directly related to gross domestic product. According to equation (B.11), its service revenues are directly related to its equipment sales during the previous year (because the equipment is serviced about a year after it is bought). According to equation (B.12), its revenue from accessory sales is directly related to its total sales.

Purvere's president wants to use this model to forecast next year's total sales, which equal (in year t)

$$Y_t = E_t + S_t + A_t = (100 + 10 + 25) - 4P_t + 0.02G_t + 0.05E_{t-1} + 0.1Y_t$$

Therefore

$$(1 - 0.1)Y_t = 135 - 4P_t + 0.02G_t + 0.05E_{t-1}$$

or

$$Y_t = \frac{1}{0.9}(135 - 4P_t + 0.02G_t + 0.05E_{t-1}) \qquad \text{(B.13)}$$

This equation can be used to forecast next year's value of Y if we know the price of Purvere's equipment next year, the value of GDP next year, and the firm's revenues from equipment sales this year. Suppose that price will be 10 and that this year's equipment sales will be 100. Then

$$Y_t = \frac{1}{0.9}(135 - 4(10) + 0.05(100) + 0.02G_t)$$

$$= \frac{1}{0.9}(100 + 0.02G_t)$$

To forecast Y_t, we must know G_t, the value of gross domestic product next year. Obviously, the best we can do is to utilize the best available forecast of next year's GDP. Suppose that Purvere's president decides to rely on the forecast of a large econometric model (like Wharton's), which is that GDP next year will be about $6,250 billion. If so, his sales forecast for next year would be

$$Y_t = \frac{1}{0.9}[100 + 0.02(6,250)] = \frac{1}{0.9}(225) = 250$$

or $250 million.

Note that Purvere's president links his company model in equations (B.10) to (B.12) to the large econometric model, which is providing the forecasted value of G_t. This is frequently the way managers have used the forecasts of macroeconomic models like the Wharton model.

Before leaving this example, it is important to recognize that it is highly simplified. Firms frequently use multiequation models containing many variables, not just the handful contained in equations (B.10) to (B.12).

"STUDY YOUR RESIDUALS"

Before concluding this appendix, it is important to consider Nobel laureate Paul A. Samuelson's well-known statement: "To the scientific forecaster I say, 'Always study your residuals.'" What Samuelson meant was that, in evaluating any forecasting technique, it is useful to calculate the difference between each observation and what the technique predicts this observation will be. These differences—or residuals—are very useful in indicating whether your forecasting technique excludes some important explanatory variables and whether its assumptions are valid.

To illustrate, suppose you are using an econometric model to forecast your firm's sales and the difference between each year's sales and what this model predicts these sales to be is as shown in Figure B.8. To improve this technique, you should think hard about why the model made the errors that it did. Based on Figure B.8, it might occur to you, for example, that many of the years when the residuals were large and positive were years when your firm had an unusually large sales force and that many of the years when the residuals were large and negative were years when your firm had an unusually small sales force. If the size of your firm's sales force is not included as an independent variable in your model, there may be good reason to include it.

By continually studying your forecasting errors and improving your forecasting techniques, significant progress can be made. Although it generally is unrealis-

---

FIGURE B.8

Residuals from Sales Forecasting Model

The years (1999 and 2007) when the residuals are large and negative are ones when the sales force was small; the years (2003 and 2010) when they are large and positive are ones when the sales force was large.

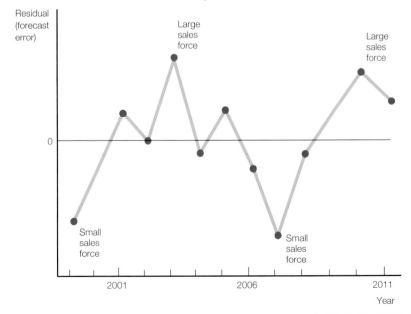

tic to expect business and economic forecasts to be very precise, they are likely to be considerably more trustworthy than forecasts that are not based on the principles of managerial economics.

SUMMARY

1. Although surveys are of considerable use, most major firms seem to base their forecasts in large part on the quantitative analysis of economic time series. The classical approach to business forecasting assumes that an economic time series can be decomposed into four components: trend, seasonal variation, cyclical variation, and irregular movements.

2. If the trend in a time series is linear, simple regression may be used to estimate an equation representing the trend. If it seems to be nonlinear, a quadratic equation may be estimated by multiple regression or an exponential trend may be fitted. An exponential trend is appropriate when the variable increases at a relatively constant percentage rate per year. To fit such a trend, we use the logarithm of the variable, not the variable itself, as the dependent variable in the regression.

3. The seasonal variation in a particular time series is described by a figure for each month (the seasonal index) that shows the extent to which that month's value typically departs from what would be expected on the basis of trend and cyclical variation. Such seasonal indexes, together with the trend, can be useful for forecasting. Regression analysis, including dummy variables, can be employed to estimate seasonal indexes.

4. Cyclical variation, as well as trend and seasonal variation, is reflected in many time series. Variables that go down before the peak and up before the trough are called *leading indicators*. If a large number of leading indicators turn downward, this is viewed as a sign of a coming peak. If a large number turn upward, this is thought to signal an impending trough. Although these indicators are not very reliable, they are watched closely and are used to supplement other, more-sophisticated forecasting techniques.

5. The simplest kind of forecasting method is a straightforward extrapolation of a trend. To allow for seasonal variation, either multiplicative or additive seasonal effects can be included. This entire procedure is simply a mechanical extrapolation of the time series into the future.

6. In recent years, managerial economists have tended to base their forecasts less on simple extrapolations and more on equations (or systems of equations) showing the effects of various independent variables on the variable (or variables) one wants to forecast. These equations (or systems of equations), are called *econometric models*. Examples are the models used by CEMCO and General Electric, as well as the model of auto output published by the Federal Reserve Bank of New York.

PROBLEMS

wwnorton.com/studyspace Ⓢ

1. The following seasonal index was calculated for the room occupancy of a motel located on a major interstate highway in the Southeast. The motel's customers are largely tourists and commercial truckers who regularly travel this highway. This index is based on actual data.[8]

January	74.8	July	116.8
February	79.8	August	117.4
March	92.9	September	105.4
April	108.8	October	103.7
May	107.5	November	100.3
June	112.0	December	80.6

   a. Is there pronounced seasonal variation in this motel's business? All other things equal, by what percentage, on the average, does room occupancy in the peak month exceed that in the lowest month?

   b. What factors would you expect to be responsible for the observed seasonal variation? In calculating the seasonal index, it was assumed that the index for a particular month like January was the same from year to year. Some observers have questioned whether this assumption is correct, given that a recession occurred in 2008 and 2009. Why might the recession have changed the pattern of seasonal variation?

   c. If you were the motel's manager, how might a seasonal index of this sort be of use? Be specific.

2. The Carbide Corporation's sales during the period 1997 to 2012 follow:

Year	Sales (billions of dollars)	Year	Sales (billions of dollars)
1997	1.5	2005	2.7
1998	1.6	2006	2.9
1999	1.6	2007	3.0
2000	1.7	2008	3.0
2001	1.9	2009	3.3
2002	2.1	2010	3.9
2003	2.2	2011	5.3
2004	2.5	2012	5.7

8. B. Bettegowda, "Calculation of Seasonal Index for Motel Room Occupancy," National Technological University, 1991, found at drgeorgejohnny.com/multimedia/lecture/ . . . /07/.doc.

a. Fit a linear trend line to these data.
b. Fit an exponential trend line to these data.
c. Assume that in 2020, Carbide's sales are $9.994 billion. Suppose that in 2012, both the linear trend line and the exponential trend line had been used to forecast the firm's 2020 sales. Which forecast would have been more accurate?
d. Assume that in 2025, Carbide's sales are $9.508 billion. Suppose that in 2012, both the linear trend line and the exponential trend line had been used to forecast the firm's 2025 sales. Which forecast would have been more accurate?

3. The Milton Company's statistician calculates a seasonal index for the firm's sales; the results are shown in the second column. The firm's monthly 2011 sales are shown in the third column.

Month	Seasonal index	2011 sales (millions of dollars)
January	97	2.5
February	96	2.4
March	97	2.7
April	98	2.9
May	99	3.0
June	100	3.1
July	101	3.2
August	103	3.1
September	103	3.2
October	103	3.1
November	102	3.0
December	101	2.9

a. If one divides each month's sales figure by its seasonal index (divided by 100), it is said to be "deseasonalized." That is, the seasonal element is removed from the data. Why is this true?
b. Calculate deseasonalized sales figures for 2011.
c. Why would the managers of the Milton Company want deseasonalized sales figures?

4. The equation describing the sales trend of the Secane Chemical Company is

$$S_t = 21.3 + 1.3t$$

where S_t is the sales (in millions of dollars per month) of the firm and t is time measured in months from January 2012. The firm's seasonal index of sales is

January	103	May	101	September	121
February	80	June	104	October	101
March	75	July	120	November	75
April	103	August	139	December	78

a. Construct a monthly sales forecast for the firm for 2013.

b. Why would the managers of the Secane Chemical Company want monthly sales forecasts of this kind?

5. On October 4, 2011, the U.S. Department of Commerce announced that the index of leading indicators rose 0.6% in August 2011.

a. During August, the average workweek rose. Is the average workweek among the leading indicators? If so, did its increase help to raise the index?

b. During August, stock prices rose. Is the level of stock prices among the leading indicators? If so, did its increase help to raise the index?

6. The Allen Company's monthly sales have the following trend

$$C_t = 4.12 + 0.32t$$

where C_t is the sales (in millions of dollars per month) of the firm and t is time measured in months from July 2004. The firm's seasonal index of sales is

January	81	May	137	September	79
February	98	June	122	October	101
March	102	July	104	November	74
April	76	August	101	December	125

a. Construct a monthly sales forecast for the firm in 2012.

b. The firm's president feels strongly that a recession will occur in late 2012. Would this influence your answer to part a? If so, how?

7. The sales of Sears, Roebuck were as follows during 1978 to 1990:

Year	Sales (billions of dollars)	Year	Sales (billions of dollars)
1978	22.9	1985	40.7
1979	24.5	1986	42.3
1980	25.2	1987	45.9
1981	27.4	1988	50.3
1982	30.0	1989	53.8
1983	35.9	1990	56.0
1984	38.8		

a. Calculate a linear trend based on these data.
b. Sears, Roebuck's sales in 1991 were about $57.2 billion. If you had used a least-squares trend line based on 1978 to 1990 data to forecast its 1991 sales, how big a forecasting error would have resulted?
c. In 1992, Sears, Roebuck's sales were $52.3 billion. If you had used a least-squares trend line based on 1978 to 1990 data to forecast its 1992 sales, how big a forecasting error would have resulted?

8. In the Wharton econometric model, housing starts (divided by the number of households) were specified to be a function of (1) the mortgage rate, (2) a consumer sentiment index, (3) capacity utilization, (4) the occupancy rate, and (5) deposit inflows into savings intermediaries.
a. Indicate why each of these five variables might be expected to influence the number of housing starts.
b. What factors influence these five variables? What sort of multiequation system might be constructed for forecasting purposes?

9. A firm's sales from 1986 to 2012 were as follows:

Year	Sales (billions of dollars)	Year	Sales (billions of dollars)
1986	2.2	2000	4.9
1987	2.6	2001	6.2
1988	3.0	2002	7.2
1989	3.5	2003	7.7
1990	3.3	2004	8.4
1991	3.5	2005	8.4
1992	4.1	2006	8.8
1993	4.3	2007	9.6
1994	4.2	2008	10.5
1995	4.5	2009	11.9
1996	4.2	2010	13.9
1997	4.5	2011	14.1
1998	4.8	2012	15.7
1999	4.9		

a. Using the method of least squares, derive a linear trend.
b. Plot the firm's sales against time. Also, plot the trend line derived in part a against time. (Time here is the year to which the sales figure pertains.)
c. Does a visual inspection of how well the linear trend fits suggest that an exponential trend would do better? That a quadratic trend would do better?
d. Using this linear trend, what would have been the sales forecast for the firm in 2015?

APPENDIX: EXPONENTIAL SMOOTHING AND FORECASTING

A frequently used method of calculating a trend is by **exponential smoothing**. According to this method, *the trend value at time t is a weighted average of all available previous values, where the weights decline geometrically as one goes backward in time.* As an illustration, suppose that a firm has been in existence for five years and its sales have been $2 million, $6 million, $6 million, $4 million, and $8 million (see Figure B.9). Then, the trend value in the fifth year would be a weighted average of $2 million, $6 million, $6 million, $4 million, and $8 million, where the weights decline geometrically as we go backward in time. Specifically, the weight attached to the observation at time t equals θ, the weight attached to the observation at time $t - 1$ equals $(1 - \theta)\theta$, the weight attached to the observation at time $t - 2$ equals $(1 - \theta)^2\theta$, the weight attached to the observation at time $t - 3$ equals $(1 - \theta)^3\theta, \ldots$, and the weight attached to the observation at the earliest relevant time (time 0) equals $(1 - \theta)^t$. Clearly, the weights decline geometrically as one goes backward in time; that is, the weight attached to the observation at time $t - 1$ is $(1 - \theta)$ times the weight attached to the observation at time t; the weight attached to the observation at time $t - 2$ is $(1 - \theta)$ times the weight attached to the observation at time $t - 1$; and so on.

> **Exponential smoothing** occurs when the trend value at time t is a weighted average of all available previous values (where the weights decline geometrically as one goes backward in time).

FIGURE B.9

Sales of Firm, Actual and Exponentially Smoothed
Year 1 is the firm's first year in existence, year 2 is its second year, and so on.

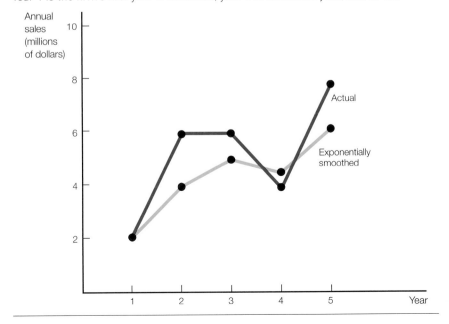

To calculate an exponentially smoothed time series, choose a value of θ, which is designated the **smoothing constant.** If we choose a value of 0.5 for θ, the exponentially smoothed value of the firm's sales in each of the five years is

The **smoothing constant** is an arbitrary value (between 0 and 1) chosen by a manager which determines the weight a manager assigns to an observation at time t. This, in turn, determines the weight assigned to each observation in previous periods.

$$S_0 = 2$$
$$S_1 = (0.5)(6) + (1 - 0.5)(2) = 4$$
$$S_2 = (0.5)(6) + (1 - 0.5)(0.5)(6) + (1 - 0.5)^2(2) = 5$$
$$S_3 = (0.5)(4) + (1 - 0.5)(0.5)(6)$$
$$+ (1 - 0.5)^2(0.5)(6) + (1 - 0.5)^3(2) = 4.5$$
$$S_4 = (0.5)(8) + (1 - 0.5)(0.5)(4) + (1 - 0.5)^2(0.5)(6)$$
$$+ (1 - 0.5)^3(0.5)(6) + (1 - 0.5)^4(2) = 6.25$$

where S_0 is the exponentially smoothed value of the firm's sales in the first year of its existence, S_1 is this value in the second year, S_2 the value in the third year, and so on. Figure B.9 shows both the original time series and the exponentially smoothed time series.

To compute the value of such a smoothed time series at time t, all you really need is the value of the smoothed time series at time $t - 1$ and the actual value of the time series at time t. This is because the smoothed value of the time series at time t is a simple weighted average of the smoothed value at time $t - 1$ and the actual value at time t. If S_t is the smoothed value at time t

$$S_t = \theta Y(t) + (1 - \theta)S_{t-1} \tag{B.14}$$

where $Y(t)$ is the value of the time series at time t.[9] So, to calculate an exponentially smoothed time series, you do not need to keep all the previous values of the actual time series; *all you need to keep is the value of the exponentially smoothed series in the previous period.* From this information alone (together with the current value of the series and the smoothing constant), you can calculate the smoothed value of the series in the current period. For instance, consider the firm in the previous paragraph. If the firm's sales in its sixth year of existence are $10 million, the smoothed value of sales for the sixth year is

$$(0.5)(10) + (1 - 0.5)(6.25) = 8.125$$

or $8.125 million.

9. Let us prove that equation (B.14) is true. If $Y(t)$ is the actual value of the time series at time t, then equation (B.14) implies that

$$S_t = \theta Y(t) + (1 - \theta)S_{t-1}$$
$$= \theta Y(t) + (1 - \theta)[\theta Y(t - 1)$$
$$+ (1 - \theta)S_{t-2}]$$
$$= \theta Y(t) + (1 - \theta)\theta Y(t - 1)$$
$$+ (1 - \theta)^2[\theta Y(t - 2)$$
$$+ (1 - \theta)S_{t-3}]$$
$$\vdots$$
$$= \theta Y(t) + (1 - \theta)\theta Y(t - 1)$$
$$+ (1 - \theta)^2\theta Y(t - 2)$$
$$+ \ldots + (1 - \theta)^t Y(0)$$

Since the right-hand side of the last line is equivalent to the definition of an exponentially smoothed time series in the first paragraph of this appendix, it follows that equation (B.14) is true.

In choosing the value of the smoothing constant θ, you must pick a number between 0 and 1. (In other words, $0 \leq \theta \leq 1$.) If θ is close to 1, past values of the time series are given relatively little weight (compared with recent values) in calculating smoothed values. If θ is close to 0, past values of the time series are given considerable weight (as compared with recent values) in calculating smoothed values. If the time series contains a great deal of random variation, it is often advisable to choose a relatively small value of θ, since this results in relatively little weight put on $Y(t)$, which is influenced more than S_{t-1} by this variation. On the other hand, if one wants the smoothed time series to reflect relatively quickly whatever changes occur in the average level of the time series, the value of θ should be set at a high level.

Forecasting Based on Exponential Smoothing

Exponential smoothing is also used for forecasting purposes. When used in this way, the basic equation for exponential smoothing is

$$F_t = \theta A(t - 1) + (1 - \theta)F_{t-1} \qquad \text{(B.15)}$$

where $A(t - 1)$ is the actual value of the time series at time $(t - 1)$ and F_t is the forecast for time t. Because the forecast is being made at time $(t - 1)$, the actual value of the time series at this time is known. The forecast for time t is simply a weighted average of the actual value at time $(t - 1)$ and the forecasted value for time $(t - 1)$, where the actual value is weighted by θ and the forecasted value is weighted by $(1 - \theta)$. It can readily be demonstrated that the forecast for time t is the weighted sum of the actual values prior to time t, where the weight attached to each value declines geometrically with the age of the observation.

To see how exponential smoothing can be used for forecasting purposes, we return to the firm in Figure B.9, which had been in existence for five years. Sales during the first year were $2 million, and we assume that the firm's sales forecast for the first year was also $2 million. What will be its sales forecast for the second year? To make such a forecast, the firm begins by choosing a value for the smoothing constant θ. (Values of 0.3 or less are often used.) Suppose that a value of 0.2 is chosen. Then the forecast for the second year is $0.2(2) + 0.8(2) = 2$, or $2 million. Since the firm's actual sales in the second year turn out to be $6 million, its sales forecast for the third year will be $0.2(6) + 0.8(2) = 2.8$, or $2.8 million. Since the firm's actual sales in the third year turn out to be $6 million, its sales forecast for the fourth year will be $0.2(6) + 0.8(2.8) = 3.44$, or $3.44 million. And so on. Exponential smoothing is often used in this way to make forecasts, particularly where there is a need for a cheap, fast, and rather mechanical method to make forecasts for a large number of items. For example, to implement various kinds of inventory control models, demand forecasts for hundreds or thousands of items may be required.

DISCOUNTING AND PRESENT VALUES

When a manager chooses between two courses of action, *A* and *B*, he or she is choosing between the cash flows resulting if *A* is chosen and the cash flows if *B* is chosen. These cash flows generally occur over a number of periods. For example, if *A* is chosen, the manager may experience an outflow of $1 million this year and an inflow of $300,000 during each of the next five years. On the other hand, if *B* is chosen, the manager may experience an outflow of $1 million this year and an inflow of $250,000 for each of the next six years. How can a manager compare these two alternatives?

To answer this question, it is convenient to begin by pointing out one of the basic propositions in managerial economics: *A dollar received today is worth more than a dollar received a year from today.* Why? Because one can always invest money that is available now and obtain interest on it. If the interest rate is 6%, a dollar received now is equivalent to $1.06 received a year hence. Why? Because if you invest the dollar now, you'll get $1.06 in a year. Similarly, *a dollar received now is equivalent to* $(1.06)^2$ *dollars two years hence.* Why? Because if you invest the dollar now, you'll get 1.06 dollars in a year, and if you reinvest this amount for another year at 6%, you'll get $(1.06)^2$ dollars.

More generally, suppose you can invest at a compound rate of *i*% per year. What is the *present value*—that is, the value *today*—of a dollar received *n* years hence? Based on the foregoing argument, its present value is

$$\frac{1}{(1 + i)^n} \qquad \text{(C.1)}$$

Thus, if the interest rate is 0.10 and if $n = 4$ (which means that the dollar is received in four years), the present value of a dollar equals

$$\frac{1}{(1 + 0.10)^4} = \frac{1}{1.4641} = \$0.683$$

In other words, the present value of the dollar is 68.3 cents.

To see that this answer is correct, let's see what would happen if you invested 68.3 cents today. As shown in Table C.1, this investment would be worth 75.1 cents after one year, 82.6 cents after two years, 90.9 cents after three years, and 1 dollar after four years. Thus, 68.3 cents is the present value of a dollar received four years hence, because if you invest 68.3 cents today, you will have exactly 1 dollar in four years.

Table E.1 shows the value of $1/(1 + i)^n$, for various values of i and n. For example, according to this table, the present value of a dollar received ten years hence is 46.3 cents if the interest rate is 0.08. To see this, note that the figure in Table E.1 corresponding to $n = 10$ and $i = 0.08$ is 0.46319.

Using this table, you can readily determine the present value of any amount received n years hence, not just 1 dollar. If you receive R_n dollars n years hence, the present value of this amount is

$$\frac{R_n}{(1 + i)^n} \tag{C.2}$$

Thus, to determine the present value of R_n, all that you have to do is multiply R_n by $1/(1 + i)^n$. Since Table E.1 provides us with the value of $1/(1 + i)^n$, this is a simple calculation.

To illustrate, suppose you will receive $10,000 ten years hence and the interest rate is 0.12. According to equation (C.2), the present value of this amount equals $10,000[1/(1 + i)^n]$. Since Table E.1 shows that $1/(1 + i)^n = 0.32197$ when $n = 10$ and $i = 0.12$, the present value of this amount is $10,000(0.32197) = \$3,219.70$.

TABLE C.1

Value of 68.3 Cents Invested at 10% Interest

Number of years hence	Return received	Value of investment
1	68.301(0.10) = 6.830¢	68.301 + 6.830 = 75.13¢
2	75.131(0.10) = 7.513¢	75.131 + 7.513 = 82.64¢
3	82.643(0.10) = 8.264¢	82.645 + 8.265 = 90.91¢
4	90.907(0.10) = 9.091¢	90.909 + 9.091 = 100.00¢

PRESENT VALUE OF A SERIES OF PAYMENTS

As pointed out at the beginning of this appendix, managers generally must consider situations in which cash flows occur at more than a single time. For example, investment in a new machine tool is likely to result in a cash outflow now and a series of cash inflows in the future. To determine the present value of such an investment, it is convenient to begin by considering the simple case in which you receive $1 per year for n years, the interest rate being i. More specifically, the n receipts of $1 occur one year from now, two years from now, . . . , and n years from now. The present value of this stream of $1 receipts is

$$\frac{1}{1 + i} + \frac{1}{(1 + i)^2} + \cdots + \frac{1}{(1 + i)^n} = \sum_{t=1}^{n} \frac{1}{(1 + i)^t} \tag{C.3}$$

For example, the present value of $1 to be received at the end of each of the next five years, if the interest rate is 0.10, is

$$\sum_{t=1}^{5} \frac{1}{(1 + 0.10)^t} = \frac{1}{(1 + 0.10)} + \frac{1}{(1 + 0.10)^2} + \frac{1}{(1 + 0.10)^3}$$

$$+ \frac{1}{(1 + 0.10)^4} + \frac{1}{(1 + 0.10)^5} = 0.90909 + 0.82645$$

$$+ 0.75131 + 0.68301 + 0.62092 = \$3.79 \tag{C.4}$$

To obtain each of the terms on the right in equation (C.4), we use Table E.1. For example, the final term on the right is 0.62092, which is the present value of a dollar received five years hence (if the interest rate is 0.10), according to Table E.1.

Table C.2 shows that $3.79 is indeed the present value of $1 to be received at the end of each of the next five years, if the interest rate is 0.10. As you can see, if you invest $3.79 at 10% interest, you will be able to withdraw $1 at the end of each year, with nothing left over or lacking. Since analysts frequently must calculate the present value of a dollar received at the end of each of the next n years, the expression in equation (C.3)

$$\sum_{t=1}^{n} 1/(1 + i)^t$$

has been tabled; the results are shown in Table E.2. For example, if you receive $1 at the end of each of the next ten years, and if the interest rate is 0.06, the present value is $7.36. To see this, note that the figure in Table E.2 corresponding to $n = 10$ and $i = 0.06$ is 7.3601.

More generally, if you receive R dollars at the end of each of the next n years, and if the interest rate is i, the present value is

$$\sum_{t=1}^{n} \frac{R}{(1 + i)^t} = R \sum_{t=1}^{n} \frac{1}{(1 + i)^t} \tag{C.5}$$

TABLE C.2

Demonstration that $3.79 (Invested at 10% Interest) Provides Exactly $1 at the End of Each of the Next Five Years

Number of years hence	Return received	Amount withdrawn	Net Value of investment
1	$3.790(0.10) = $0.3790	$1.00	$3.790 + 0.3790 − 1.00 = $3.169
2	3.169(0.10) = 0.3169	$1.00	3.169 + 0.3169 − 1.00 = 2.486
3	2.486(0.10) = 0.2486	$1.00	2.486 + 0.2486 − 1.00 = 1.735
4	1.735(0.10) = 0.1735	$1.00	1.735 + 0.1735 − 1.00 = 0.909
5	0.909(0.10) = 0.0909	$1.00	0.909 + 0.0909 − 1.00 = 0

Thus, the present value of $5,000 to be received at the end of each of the next five years, if the interest rate is 0.08, is $5,000(3.9927) = $19,963.5, since Table E.2 shows that the value of $\sum_{t=1}^{n} 1/(1 + i)^t = 3.9927$, when $n = 5$ and $i = 0.08$.

Finally, we must consider the case in which there is a series of unequal, not equal, payments. Suppose that a payment is received at the end of each of the next n years, that the amount received at the end of the tth year is R_t, and that the interest rate is i. The present value of this series of unequal payments is

$$\sum_{t=1}^{n} \frac{R_t}{(1 + i)^t} \tag{C.6}$$

Table E.1 can be used to help carry out this computation. For example, suppose that $i = 0.10$, that $n = 3$, and that the amount received at the end of the first year is $3,000, the amount received at the end of the second year is $2,000, and the amount received at the end of the third year is $1,000. Table C.3 shows how to calculate the present value of this series of unequal payments, which in this case equals $5,131.48.

THE USE OF PERIODS OTHER THAN A YEAR

Thus far, we have assumed the interest or return from an invested amount is paid annually. In other words, we have assumed that a dollar invested at the beginning of a year earns interest of i% at the end of that year. In many situations, this is not correct. Instead, interest, dividends, or other returns from an investment may be received semiannually, quarterly, monthly, or even daily. Because you earn a return in the next period on the return received in this period, the results differ from those given in previous sections of this appendix.

TABLE C.3

Present Value of Stream of Unequal Payments, Where $i = 0.10$ and $n = 3$

Number of years hence	(1) Amount received R_t	(2) $\dfrac{1}{(1 + 0.10)^t}$	(1) × (2) Present value of amount received
1	$3,000	0.90909	$2,727.27
2	2,000	0.82645	1,652.89
3	1,000	0.75131	751.31
			Total $5,131.48

If interest is received *semiannually*, the present value of a dollar received n years hence is

$$\frac{1}{(1 + i/2)^{2n}} \tag{C.7}$$

where i is the annual interest rate. To understand this expression, note that the interest rate for each semiannual period is $i/2$, and that there are $2n$ semiannual periods in n years. Bearing this in mind, this expression can be derived in the same way as expression (C.1).

If interest is received *quarterly*, the present value of a dollar received n years hence is

$$\frac{1}{(1 + i/4)^{4n}} \tag{C.8}$$

where i once again is the annual interest rate. To see why this is true, note that the interest rate for each quarterly period is $i/4$, and that there are $4n$ quarterly periods in n years. Bearing this in mind, this expression can be derived in the same way as expression (C.1).

More generally, suppose that interest is received c times per year. Under these circumstances, the present value of a dollar received n years hence is

$$\frac{1}{(1 + i/c)^{cn}} \tag{C.9}$$

Table E.1 can be used to determine present values under these circumstances. To evaluate expression (C.9), let the interest rate be i/c, and let the number of years be cn; using these values, Table E.1 gives the correct answer. Thus, the present value of 1 dollar to be received 3 years hence, where the interest rate is 8% paid quarterly, can be obtained by finding in the table the present value of 1 dollar to be received 12 years hence where the interest rate is 2%. Specifically, the answer is 78.849 cents.

DETERMINING THE INTERNAL RATE OF RETURN

Previous sections of this appendix have been concerned entirely with determining the present value of a stream of cash flows. While this is of great importance in managerial economics, it also is important to calculate the internal rate of return—the interest rate that equates the present value of the cash inflows with the present value of the cash outflows. Put differently, the internal rate of return is the interest rate that makes the present value of a stream of cash flows equal zero. In other words, we want to find i where

$$R_0 + \frac{R_1}{1 + i} + \frac{R_2}{(1 + i)^2} + \cdots + \frac{R_n}{(1 + i)^n} = 0$$

or

$$\sum_{t=0}^{n} \frac{R_t}{(1 + i)^t} = 0 \qquad\qquad \text{(C.10)}$$

To solve equation (C.10) for i, it often is necessary to use trial and error (if you do not have access to a computer or calculator). The first step is to make a rough estimate of the value of i that will satisfy equation (C.10). The second step is to adjust this estimate. If the present value based on the original estimated rate of interest is *positive, increase* the value of i. If the present value based on the original estimated rate of return is *negative, reduce* the value of i. The third step is to continue to adjust this estimate until you find the value of i that will satisfy equation (C.10).

As an illustration, consider the following stream of cash flows: $R_0 = -\$5,980$, $R_1 = \$3,000$, $R_2 = \$2,000$, and $R_3 = \$2,000$. As a first step, we estimate (roughly) that the internal rate of return is in the neighborhood of 8%. As Table C.4 shows, the present value of this stream of cash flows, given that the interest rate is 8%, is $100.12, which is positive. Thus, a higher value of i must be tried. We choose 9%. As Table C.4 shows, the present value of this stream of cash flows, given that the interest rate is 9%, is virtually zero. Thus, the internal rate of return is 9%.

If the cash flows (in years other than year 0) are all equal, there is a simpler way to determine the internal rate of return. Under these circumstances, equation (C.10) can be written

$$R_0 + \sum_{t=1}^{n} \frac{R}{(1 + i)^t} = 0$$

TABLE C.4

Determination of the Internal Rate of Return

		i = 8%		i = 9%	
Year t	Cash flow R_t	$\dfrac{1}{(1 + i)^t}$	Present value	$\dfrac{1}{(1 + i)^t}$	Present value
0	−$5,980	1.00000	−$5,980	1.00000	−$5,980
1	$3,000	0.92593	$2,777.78	0.91743	$2,752.29
2	2,000	0.85734	1,714.68	0.84168	1,683.36
3	2,000	0.79383	1,587.66	0.77228	1,544.37
Total			100.12		0.02

where R is the cash flow in years 1 to n. Thus,

$$\sum_{t=1}^{n} \frac{1}{(1 + i)^t} = \frac{-R_0}{R} \tag{C.11}$$

Since we are given the value of $-R_0/R$, we can find the value of i in Table E.1 where the entry in the nth row equals $-R_0/R$. This value of i is the internal rate of return.

To illustrate, suppose that a machine tool costs $10,000, and that it will result in a cash inflow of $2,500 for each of the next six years. Since $R_0 = -\$10,000$ and $R = \$2,500$, the value of $-R_0/R$ is 4. Looking in the row of Table E.2 where $n = 6$, we look for the interest rate where the entry in the table is 6. Since the entry is 3.9976 when $i = 13\%$, the internal rate of return is about 13%.

Finally, it is worth pointing out that if an investment yields an infinite series of equal cash flows, the present value of this series is

$$\sum_{t=1}^{\infty} \frac{R}{(1 + i)^t} - R \sum_{t=1}^{\infty} \frac{1}{(1 + i)^t} = \frac{R}{i} \tag{C.12}$$

For example, if an investment yields a perpetual annual return of $4,000 per year, and if the interest rate is 8%, the present value of this perpetual stream of returns equals $4,000/0.08 = \$50,000$.

ANSWERS TO SELECT END-OF-CHAPTER PROBLEMS

CHAPTER 1

1. Yes.

3.

Number of years in the future	Profit (millions of dollars)	$\dfrac{1}{(1+i)^t}$	Present value
1	8	0.90909	7.27272
2	10	0.82645	8.26450
3	12	0.75131	9.01572
4	14	0.68301	9.56214
5	15	0.62092	9.31380
6	16	0.56447	9.03152
7	17	0.51316	8.72372
8	15	0.46651	6.99765
9	13	0.42410	5.51330
10	10	0.38554	3.85540
			Total 77.55056

Thus, the answer is $77.55056 million.

5. a. He will receive $80(50)(\$5) = \$20,000$, from which he must pay $3,000 for the umbrellas and $3(\$3,000) = \$9,000$ for rent. Thus, his accounting profit equals $\$20,000 - \$3,000 - \$9,000$ or $8,000.

  b. Since he could earn $4,000 doing construction work, his economic profit is $8,000 − $4,000 = $4,000. (For simplicity, we ignore the fact that he could have earned interest on the money he invested in this business during the summer.)

CHAPTER 2

1. a. If $Q = 20$, $P = 2,000 − 50(20) = 1,000$. Thus, price would have to equal $1,000.

 b. Since $500 = 2,000 − 50Q$, $Q = 1,500/50 = 30$. Thus, it will sell 30 per month.

 c. Because $Q = (2,000 − P)/50 = 40 − 0.02P$, $dQ/dP = −0.02$. Thus

$$\left(\frac{P}{Q}\right)\left(\frac{\partial Q}{\partial P}\right) = -0.02\frac{500}{30} = -0.33$$

 d. If $-0.02\dfrac{P}{(2,000 − P)/50} = -1$

$$-0.02\frac{50P}{2,000 − P} = -1$$

$$P = 2,000 − P$$

$$= 2,000/2 = 1,000$$

  Thus, if price equals $1,000, the demand is of unitary elasticity.

3. a. $\dfrac{\partial Q}{\partial P}\left(\dfrac{P}{Q}\right) = \dfrac{-3(10)}{500 − 3(10) + 2(20) + 0.1(6,000)}$

$$= \frac{-30}{500 − 30 + 40 + 600} = \frac{-30}{1,110}$$

 b. $\dfrac{\partial Q}{\partial I}\left(\dfrac{I}{Q}\right) = \dfrac{0.1(6,000)}{1,110} = \dfrac{600}{1,110}$

 c. $\dfrac{\partial Q}{\partial P_r}\left(\dfrac{P_r}{Q}\right) = \dfrac{2(20)}{1,110} = \dfrac{40}{1,110}$

 d. Population is assumed to be essentially constant (or to have no significant effect on Q, other than via whatever effect it has on per capita disposable income).

6. a. Because there are lots of very close substitutes for a particular brand, but not for cigarettes as a whole. It appears that the elasticity was less than −2.

 b. No. More will be said about estimating demand functions in Chapter 4.

8. No. The fact that the elasticity of demand with respect to advertising is relatively low (0.003) does not necessarily mean that an additional dollar spent on advertising would not be profitable, or that the last dollar spent was not profitable.

9. a. −3.1.

 b. Decreases.

c. 2.3.

d. 0.1.

e. The quantity demanded will increase by 10%. (Note that Q in this problem is defined as quantity demanded *per capita.*)

CHAPTER 3

3.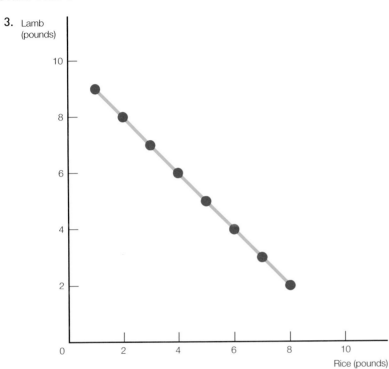

5. His budget line is as follows:

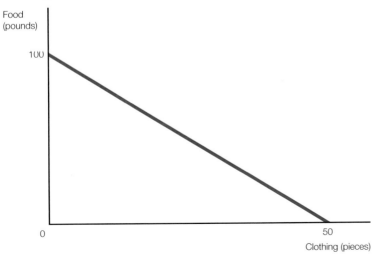

7. Maria will maximize utility at point A, where she purchases 15 units of both chips and salsa. Note that her indifference curves are 90-degree angles.

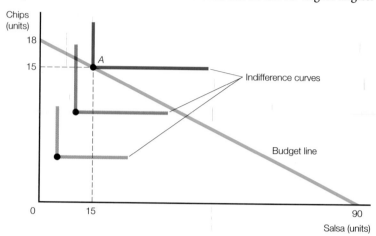

9. Since her marginal rate of substitution of opera tickets for movie tickets equals 5, and since the ratio of the price of an opera ticket to the price of a movie ticket is 10, it is impossible for her to set the marginal rate of substitution equal to the price ratio. She can increase satisfaction by substituting movie tickets for opera tickets because she is willing to give up only 5 movie tickets to get an extra opera ticket, but she has to give up 10 movie tickets to get an extra opera ticket. Thus, she will spend the entire $300 on movie tickets; she will buy 50 of them.

11. a. 150 miles **b.** 300 miles **c.** Yes. -0.5. **d.** $3 billion.

CHAPTER 4

1. a. The evidence appears to be very strong that increases in the firm's advertising expenditure do have a positive effect on the quantity demanded of the firm's product.

b. $Q = -104 + 3.2(5,000) + 1.5(20) + 1.6(1,000) - 2.1P$

$= 17,526 - 2.1P$

Thus

$$P = \frac{17,526 - Q}{2.1} = 8,346 - 0.476Q$$

c. From the answer to part b

$Q = 17,526 - 2.1P$

Thus, if $P = 500$

$Q = 17,526 - 2.1(500) = 16,476$

d. Since R^2 equals 0.89, the regression equation seems to fit the data quite well. However, we have no way of knowing (from the information given here) whether the error terms are serially correlated or a nonlinear equation fits significantly better.

3. **a.** Let profit equal Y and sales equal X. Plotting Y against X, we get the following:

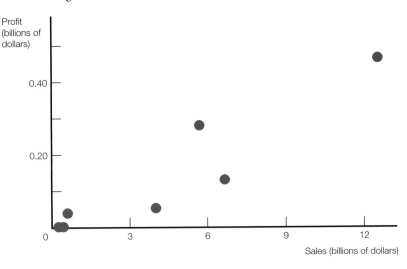

$\Sigma X = 30.0$; $\Sigma Y = 0.94$; $\Sigma X^2 = 248.72$; $\Sigma XY = 8.307$; $n = 7$; $\Sigma Y^2 = 0.3030$.

$$b = \frac{7(8.307) - (30)(0.94)}{7(248.72) - 30^2} = \frac{58.149 - 28.200}{1,741.04 - 900} = \frac{29.949}{841.04} = 0.0356$$

$a = 0.134 - (0.0356)(4.286) = 0.134 - 0.153 = -0.019$

The regression line is $\hat{Y} = -0.019 + 0.0356X$

b. $-0.019 + 0.0356(2) = -0.019 + 0.071 = 0.052$. Thus, the answer is about 0.05 billion dollars.

c. No. Prices and costs will be different in 2001 than in 1980.

5. **a.** 40.833.

b. -1.025.

c. 0.006667.

d. 0.916.

e. 1.361.

f. Less than 0.001.

g. Less than 0.001.

h. 0.244.

i. The average relationship is $C1 = 40.8 - 1.02\,C2 + 0.00667\,C3$. This relationship seems to fit the data quite well, R^2 being 0.916. There is a very small probability that the estimated effect of C2 (price) is due to chance, but a much higher probability (0.244) that the effect of C3 (disposable income) could be due to chance.

7. a. Let General Electric's profits be Y and gross domestic product be X. If we plot Y against X, we get the following graph:

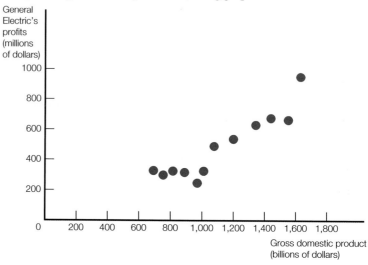

To calculate a and b, we can compute the following:

	X	Y	X²	Y²	XY
	688	355	473,344	126,025	244,240
	753	339	567,009	114,921	255,267
	796	361	633,616	130,321	287,356
	868	357	753,424	127,449	309,876
	936	278	876,096	77,284	260,208
	982	363	964,324	131,769	356,466
	1,063	510	1,129,969	260,100	542,130
	1,171	573	1,371,241	328,329	670,983
	1,306	661	1,705,636	436,921	863,266
	1,407	705	1,979,649	497,025	991,935
	1,529	688	2,337,841	473,344	1,051,952
	1,706	931	2,910,436	866,761	1,588,286
Sum	13,205	6,121	15,702,585	3,570,249	7,421,965
Mean	1,100.42	510.08			

The results are

$$b = \frac{12(7,421,965) - (13,205)(6,121)}{12(15,702,585) - 13,205^2}$$

$$= \frac{89,063,580 - 80,827,805}{188,431,020 - 174,372,025}$$

$$= \frac{8,235,775}{14,058,995} = 0.586$$

and

$a = 510.08 - (0.586)(1,100.42) = 510.08 - 644.85 = -134.77$

Thus, the slope equals 0.586, and the intercept equals -134.77 millions of dollars.

b. On the average a \$1 increase in the GDP seems to be associated with a \$0.000586 increase in General Electric's profits (recalling that GDP is measured in billions of dollars, while General Electric's profits are measured in millions of dollars).

c. The forecast equals $-134.77 + 0.586(2,000) = -134.77 + 1,172 = 1,037.23$. That is, it equals 1,037.23 million dollars.

d. $r^2 = 0.90$.

e. No. No. A nonlinear relationship might be as good or better.

f. If nothing else is available, this model may be serviceable, but it is so crude that it is difficult to believe that the analyst could not improve upon it by taking other independent variables into account.

9. a. Taking antilogs

$Q = 102P^{-0.148}Z^{0.258}$

$\partial Q/\partial P = -0.148(102P^{-1.148}Z^{0.258}) = -0.148\ Q/P$

Since the price elasticity of demand equals $(\partial Q/\partial P)(P/Q)$, it follows that the price elasticity of demand equals -0.148.

b. $\partial Q/\partial Z = 0.258(102P^{-0.148}Z^{-0.742}) = 0.258\ Q/Z$.

Since the cross elasticity of demand equals $(\partial Q/\partial Z)(Z/Q)$, it follows that the cross elasticity of demand equals 0.258.

c. The regression seems to provide a good fit. The fact that $\bar{R}^2$ equals 0.98 means that 98% of the variation in log Q can be explained by the regression (see the chapter appendix). See Figure 5.6.

11. a. No.

b. The market supply curve for wine.

CHAPTER 5

1. a. To see whether 400 hours of skilled labor and 100 hours of unskilled labor are the optimal input combination, the Elwyn Company should pick an input combination where

$$\frac{MP_S}{P_S} = \frac{MP_U}{P_U}$$

where MP_S is the marginal product of skilled labor, MP_U is the marginal product of unskilled labor, P_S is the price of skilled labor, and P_U is the price of unskilled labor. Since $P_S = 10, P_U = 5$, and

$$MP_S = \frac{\partial Q}{\partial S} = 300 - 0.4S$$

$$MP_U = \frac{\partial Q}{\partial U} = 200 - 0.6U$$

it follows that the Elwyn Company should pick an input combination where

$$\frac{300 - 0.4S}{10} = \frac{200 - 0.6U}{5}$$

or

$1,500 - 2S = 2,000 - 6U$

$S = -250 + 3U$

Thus, 400 hours of skilled labor and 100 hours of unskilled labor are not the optimal input combination, because, if $S = 400$ and $U = 100$, this equation does not hold.

b. If a total of $5,000 is spent on skilled and unskilled labor,

$10S + 5U = 5,000$,

since $P_S = 10$ and $P_U = 5$. From the answer to part a, we know that $S = -250 + 3U$.

Solving these two equations simultaneously, $S = 392.9$ and $U = 214.3$. Thus, to maximize output, Elwyn should hire about 393 hours of skilled labor and about 214 hours of unskilled labor.

c. $MP_U \cdot P$ must equal P_U, where P is the price of the product. (Under present circumstances, the marginal revenue product of unskilled labor equals $MP_U \cdot P$, and the marginal expenditure on unskilled labor equals P_U.) Thus, since

$P = 10, P_U = 5$ and $MP_U = 200 - 0.6U$

$10(200 - 0.6U) = 5$

$\qquad\qquad U = 332.5$

To maximize profit, Elwyn should hire 332.5 hours of unskilled labor. (Note that we no longer assume that a total of $5,000 is spent on labor. Thus, the answer is different from that in part b.)

2. a. No.

b. 50 pounds, since half of these amounts (that is, 50 pounds of hay and 125.1 pounds of grain) results in a 25-pound gain.

c. $-(125.1 - 130.9)/(50 - 40) = 0.58$.

d. No, because it is impossible to tell (from the information given in the question) how much hay and grain can be used to produce a 25-pound gain after the advance in technology.

4. a. No.

b. General farms.

c. No.

6. a&b. The average and marginal products of grain when each amount is used are calculated as follows:

Amount of grain	Average product	Marginal product
1,200	5,917/1,200 = 4.93	
		$\dfrac{7,250 - 5,917}{1,800 - 1,200} = 2.22$
1,800	7,250/1,800 = 4.03	
		$\dfrac{8.379 - 7,250}{2,400 - 1,800} = 1.88$
2,400	8,379/2,400 = 3.49	
		$\dfrac{9.371 - 8,379}{3,000 - 2,400} = 1.65$
3,000	9,371/3,000 = 3.12	

c. Yes. The marginal product of grain decreases as more of it is used.

7. a. To minimize cost, the manager should choose an input combination where $MP_L/P_L = MP_K/P_K$, where MP_L is the marginal product of labor, MP_K is the marginal product of capital, P_L is the price of labor, and P_K is the price of capital. Since

$$MP_L = \frac{\partial Q}{\partial L} = 5K \quad \text{and} \quad MP_K = \frac{\partial Q}{\partial K} = 5L$$

it follows that

$$\frac{5K}{1} = \frac{5L}{2}$$

or $K = L/2$. Since $Q = 20$, $K = 4/L$. Thus

$$\frac{L}{2} = \frac{4}{L} \quad \text{or} \quad L^2 = 8$$

which means that the firm should use $2(2)^{0.5}$ units of labor and $(2)^{0.5}$ units of capital.

b. If the price of labor is $2 per unit, the optimal value of K is 2, and the optimal value of L is 2. Thus, output per unit of labor is 20/2, or 10, whereas it formerly was $20/2 \times 2^{0.5}$ or $10/2^{0.5}$. Thus, output per unit of labor will rise.

c. No, because a 1% increase in both K and L results in more than a 1% increase in Q.

CHAPTER 6

1. a. It is the cheapest of these three ways of making steel. Using this method, cost per ton is $310.34, as compared with $368.86 and $401.73 with the other methods.

b. If the price of scrap rises, the cost of producing steel based on the electric-furnace continuous-casting route will increase, because this route uses scrap. Thus, the cost advantage of this route will be reduced if the price of scrap goes up.

   c.   It suggests that U.S. steel producers may have a hard time competing with steel producers in low-wage countries.

   d.   If each figure is the minimum value of long-run average cost for a particular technique, it also equals the long-run marginal cost for the technique, since marginal cost equals average cost when the latter is a minimum.

3. a.   If Q is the sales volume,

$$Q(\$200) - \$5,000 = \$10,000,$$

so Q must equal 75.

   b.   Since $Q(\$250) - \$5,000 = \$10,000$, Q must equal 60.

   c.   Since $Q(\$265) - \$5,000 = \$10,000$, Q must equal 56.6.

5. The table is as follows:

Total fixed cost	Total variable cost	Average fixed cost	Average variable cost
50	0	—	—
50	25	50	25
50	50	25	25
50	70	$16^2/_3$	$23^1/_3$
50	85	$12^1/_2$	$21^1/_4$
50	100	10	20
50	140	$8^1/_3$	$23^1/_3$
50	210	$7^1/_7$	30

7. a.   Yes. Since $(\partial TC/\partial Q)(Q/TC) = \alpha_1$, this is true.

   b.   Yes. If $\alpha_1 < 1$, a 1% increase in output results in a less than 1% increase in total cost, so average cost falls with increases in output; in other words, there are economies of scale. If $\alpha_1 > 1$, a 1% increase in output results in a more than 1% increase in total cost, so average cost increases with increases in output; in other words, there are diseconomies of scale.

   c. $$\frac{TC}{P_K} = \alpha_0 Q^{\alpha_1} \left(\frac{P_L}{P_K}\right)^{\alpha_2}$$

and

$$\log\left(\frac{TC}{P_K}\right) = \log \alpha_0 + \alpha_1 \log Q + \alpha_2 \log\left(\frac{P_L}{P_K}\right)$$

If this is treated as a regression equation, one can estimate the value, using the regression technique discussed in Chapter 4, subject to the caveats concerning various kinds of possible errors cited there.

9. a.   Since marginal cost equals $dTVC/dQ$, it equals

$$MC = 50 - 20Q + 3Q^2$$

It is a minimum when

$$\frac{dMC}{dQ} = -20 + 6Q = 0, \quad \text{or} \quad Q = 20/6$$

b. Average variable cost equals

$$AVC = \frac{TVC}{Q} = 50 - 10Q + Q^2$$

It is a minimum when

$$\frac{dAVC}{dQ} = -10 + 2Q = 0, \quad \text{or} \quad Q = 5$$

c. If $Q = 5$, average variable cost equals $50 - 10(5) + 5^2 = 25$. Marginal cost equals $50 - 20(5) + 3(5^2) = 25$. Thus, marginal cost equals average variable cost at this output level.

11. a. Using equation (6.6), $S = (23,000 + 11,000 - 30,000)/30,000 = 0.13$.

 b. Production facilities used to make one product sometimes can be used to make another product, and by-products resulting from the production of one product may be useful in making other products.

CHAPTER 7

1. a. Since average cost (AC) must be a minimum, and since

$$AC = \frac{25,000}{Q} + 150 + 3Q$$

$$\frac{dAC}{dQ} = \frac{-25,000}{Q^2} + 3 = 0$$

Thus, $Q = \left(\frac{25,000}{3}\right)^{0.5} = 91.3$, and

$$AC = 25,000/91.3 + 150 + 3(91.3) = 697.7$$

so the price must be $697.7, since in long-run equilibrium, price equals the minimum value of average cost.

 b. 91.3 units.

3. a. Marginal cost equals

$$MC = \frac{dTC}{dQ} = 4 + 4Q$$

Setting marginal cost equal to price, we have

$$4 + 4Q = 24$$
$$4Q = 20$$
$$Q = 5$$

Thus, the optimal output rate is 5.

b. Profit equals total revenue minus total cost. Since total revenue equals $24Q$, profit equals

$\pi = 24Q - 200 - 4Q - 2Q^2 = -200 + 20Q - 2Q^2$

Because $Q = 5$

$\pi = -200 + 20(5) - 2(5)^2 = -200 + 100 - 50 = -150$

Thus, the firm loses $150 (which is less than if it shuts down).

5. a. The White Company's marginal cost is $dTC/dQ = MC = 20 + 10Q$. Equating this to the market price $= P = 50$ and solving yields the optimal output Q, i.e., $P = 50 = 20 + 10Q = MC$ or $10Q = 30$ or $Q = 3$.

b. The White Company's total revenue (TR) is $TR = P^*Q = 50^*3 = 150$. The White Company's total cost (TC) is $TC + 1,000 + 20^*3 + 5^*3^*3 = 1,000 + 60 + 45 = 1,105$. The White Company's economic profit is $TR - TC = 150 - 1,105 = -955$.

c. The White Company's average total cost (ATC) is $ATC = TC/Q = (1,000/Q) + 20 + 5Q = (1,000/3) + 20 + 5^*3 = 333.33 + 20 + 15 = 368.33$.

d. The industry is not in equilibrium because the firms in the industry are losing money. In the long run, we would expect some firms to leave the industry such that in the long run, the typical firm would have long run average cost equal to long run marginal cost and no economic profits being made by any firm.

CHAPTER 8

1. a. Marginal revenue $= 100 - 2Q$; marginal cost $= 60 + 2Q$. Thus, if marginal revenue equals marginal cost, $100 - 2Q = 60 + 2Q$, so $Q = 10$.

b. Since $P = 100 - Q$, P must equal 90 if $Q = 10$. Thus, he should charge a price of $90.

3. a. Since $P = (8,300 - Q)/2.1 = 3,952 - 0.476Q$

$MR = 3,952 - 0.952Q$

b. $MC = 480 + 40Q$. If $MC = MR$

$480 + 40Q = 3,952 - 0.952Q$

$40.952Q = 3,472$

$Q = 84.8$

Thus, the firm would produce 84.8 lasers per month. If $Q = 84.8$, $P = 3,952 + 0.476(84.8) = 3,912$. Thus, the price should be $3,912.

c. The firm's monthly profit equals

$84.8(3,912) - [2,200 + 480(84.8) + 20(84.8)^2] = \$145,012.80$

5. a. If the firm is producing 5 units in the first plant, the marginal cost in the first plant equals $20 + 2(5)$, or 30. Thus, if the manager is minimizing costs, marginal cost in the second plant must also equal 30; this means that

$10 + 5Q_2 = 30$

$Q_2 = 4$

Thus, the second plant must be producing 4 units of output.

b. Since $MC_1 = MC_2 = MC$ and the firm's output, Q, equals $Q_1 + Q_2$

$Q_1 = (MC_1/2) - 10$

$Q_2 = (MC_2/5) - 2$

$Q = Q_1 + Q_2 = 0.7MC - 12$

$MC = (1/0.7)(Q + 12)$

c. No, because we do not have information concerning the fixed costs of each plant. But you can determine average variable cost.

7. a. It probably tended to increase because high profits induced entry. Also, the recent recession may have resulted in more demand for the services of pawnshops.

b. No. It is likely to be an oligopoly, since there generally is not a very large number of pawnshops in a small city.

c. Apparently not, but licensing requirements may exist.

9. a. The total revenue (TR) for diamonds is $TR_Z = P_Z{}^*Q_Z = (980 - 2Q_Z)^* Q_Z = 980Q_Z - 2Q_Z{}^2$. The marginal revenue for diamonds is $dTR_Z/dQ_Z = MR_Z = 980 - 4Q_Z$. The marginal cost for diamonds is $MC_Z = dTC/dQ_Z = 50 + Q_Z$. To maximize profit, the monopolist sets $MR_Z = MC_Z$ or $MR_Z = 980 - 4Q_Z = 50 + Q_Z = MC_Z$ or $5Q_Z = 930$ or $Q_Z = 186$. Substituting $Q_Z = 186$ into the demand function yields $P_Z = 980 - 2^*186 = 980 - 372 = 608$. Consumer surplus (CS) is then $CS_Z = 0.5^*(980 - 608)^*186 = 0.5^*372^*186 = 34,596$. Total revenue is $TR_Z = 608^*186 = 113,088$. Variable cost is $VC_Z = 50^*186 + 0.5^* 1686^*186 = 9,300 + 17,298 = 26,598$. So variable cost profit = producer surplus $= PS_Z = TR_Z - VC_Z = 113,088 - 26,598 = 86,490$. Social welfare is $CS_Z + PS_Z = 34,596 + 86,490 = 121,086$.

b. If De Beers acts as a perfect competitor, they would set price $= P_Z = MC_Z$ or $P_Z = 980 - 2Q_Z = 50 + Q_Z = MC_Z$ or $3Q_Z = 930$ or $Q_Z = 310$. Substituting $Q_Z = 310$ into the demand function gives $P_Z = 980 - 2^*310 = 980 - 620 = 360$. Consumer surplus (CS) is then $CS_Z = 0.5^*(980 - 360)^*310 = 0.5^*620^*310 = 96,100$. Total revenue is $TR_Z = 360^*310 = 111,600$. Variable cost is $VC_Z = 50^*310 + 0.5^* 310^*310 = 15,500 + 48,050 = 63,550$. So variable cost profit = producer surplus $= PS_Z = TR_Z - VC_Z = 111,600 - 63,550 = 48,050$. Social welfare is $CS_Z + PS_Z = 96,100 + 48,050 = 144,150$.

c. Social welfare increases by $144,150 - 121,086 = 23,064$.

11. a. To earn 20% on a total investment of $250,000, profit must equal $50,000 per year. Thus, if the plant operates at 80% of capacity (and managers sell 10,000 units), managers must set a price of $15 per unit. (Since average cost equals $10, profit per unit will be $5, so total profit per year will be $50,000.)

b. From the information given, there is no assurance that managers can sell 10,000 units per year if they charge a price of $15 per unit.

c. Unless the markup bears the proper relationship to the price elasticity of demand, the manager probably is sacrificing profit.

13. a. Backus' total revenues equal

$$TR = P_X Q_X + P_Y Q_Y = (400 - Q_X)Q_X + (300 - 3Q_Y)Q_Y$$

and since $Q_Y = 2Q_X$

$$TR = (400 - Q_X)Q_X + (300 - 6Q_X)(2Q_X)$$
$$= 400Q_X - Q_X^2 + 600Q_X - 12Q_X^2 = 1,000Q_X - 13Q_X^2$$

Thus, the firm's profit equals

$$\pi = 1,000Q_X - 13Q_X^2 - 500 - 3Q_X - 9Q_X^2$$
$$= -500 + 997Q_X - 22Q_X^2$$

Setting $d\pi/dQ_X = 997 - 44Q_X = 0$, we find that the profit-maximizing value of $Q_X = 997/44 = 22.66$. Thus, Backus should produce and sell 22.66 units of product X and 45.32 units of product Y per period of time.

b. The price of product X must be $400 - 22.66 = \$377.34$, and the price of product Y must be $300 - 3(45.32) = \$164.05$.

We have assumed that Backus sells all that it produces of both products. The marginal revenue of product X equals $400 - 2(22.66) = 354.68$, and the marginal revenue of product Y equals $300 - 6(45.32) = 28.09$. Since both are nonnegative, this assumption is true if Backus maximizes profit.

CHAPTER 9

1. a. The recommendation is not correct. Profit maximization requires the marginal revenue (MR) in each market be the same and equal to marginal cost. Using the relationship that $MR = P(1 + [1/\eta])$, $MR_J = P_J(1 + [1/\eta_J]) = P_J(1 + [1/-4]) = P_J(1 - [1/4]) = 0.75P_J$, $MR_{US} = P_{US}(1 + [1/\eta_{US}]) = P_{US}(1 + [1/-2]) = P_{US}(1 - [1/2]) = 0.5P_{US}$, and $MR_E = P_E(1 + [1/\eta_E]) = P_E(1 + [1/(2 - 4/3)]) = P_E(1 - [3/4]) = 0.25P_E$, where $J =$ Japan, $US =$ United States, and $E =$ Europe. Thus, profit maximization requires $MR_J = MR_{US} = MR_E$ or $0.75P_J = 0.5P_{US} = 0.25P_E$. $0.75P_J = 0.75*\$1,000 = \$750$, $0.5P_{US} = 0.5*\$2,000 = \$1,000$, and $0.25P_E = 0.25*\$3,000 = \$750$. Since $MR_J = MR_{US} = MR_E$ does not hold, this is not a profit maximizing pricing policy.

b. Since the US price is too high (see a. above), we should not be surprised that the sales (Q) in the US are below expectations.

c. The decision to lower the price in the US to $1,500 results in $MR_J = MR_{US} = MR_E$ since $MR_{US} = 0.5P_{US} = 0.5*1,500 = 750$. We cannot tell if this is a wise decision because we don't know if the marginal cost of the Ridgeway Corporation is 750.

d. We do not know if the Ridgeway Corporation is maximizing profit because we don't know their marginal cost. Profit maximization requires $MR_J = MR_{US} = MR_E = MC$.

3. a. The firm's profit equals $P_C Q_C + P_M Q_M - TC$, or

$$\pi = (495 - 5Q_C)Q_C + (750 - 10Q_M)Q_M - 410 - 8(Q_C + Q_M)$$

Thus

$$\frac{\partial \pi}{\partial Q_C} = 495 - 10Q_C - 8 = 0$$

$$\frac{\partial \pi}{\partial Q_M} = 750 - 20Q_M - 8 = 0$$

Consequently, $Q_C = 48.7$ and $Q_M = 37.1$, so

$P_C = 495 - 5(48.7) = 251.5$

b. $P_M = 750 - 10(37.1) = 379$.

c. Yes. Under these circumstances,

$$Q_C = \frac{495 - P}{5} \quad \text{and} \quad Q_M = \frac{750 - P}{10}$$

so

$$Q = Q_C + Q_M = 174 - 0.3P$$

and

$$P = (174 - Q)/0.3 = 580 - {}^{10}\!/_3 Q$$

Thus

$$\pi = (580 - {}^{10}\!/_3 Q)Q - 410 - 8Q$$
$$= -410 + 572Q - {}^{10}\!/_3 Q^2$$

If π is a maximum

$$\frac{\partial \pi}{dQ} = 572 - {}^{20}\!/_3 Q = 0$$

so $Q = 572(3/20) = 85.8$

Consequently

$$\pi = -410 + 572(85.8) - {}^{10}\!/_3(85.8^2) = 24{,}128.8$$

which compares with

$$\pi = [495 - 5(48.7)]48.7 + [750 - 10(37.1)]37.1 - 410$$
$$- 8(48.7 + 37.1)$$
$$= 251.5(48.7) + 379(37.1) - 1{,}096.4$$
$$= 12{,}248.05 + 14{,}060.9 - 1{,}096.4 = 25{,}212.55$$

which is the value of profits when price discrimination is allowed.

So profits decrease by $1,083.75.

CHAPTER 10

3. a. Yes. As stressed earlier, to maximize the firm's overall profit, the transfer price should equal the price of the product in the external (competitive) market.

b. When the production of phenol increased, the supply of acetone increased, since acetone is a by-product. Thus, since less isopropanol was demanded to make acetone, the demand curve for isopropanol shifted to the left (as shown below), and the price of isopropanol declined (from P_0 to P_1).

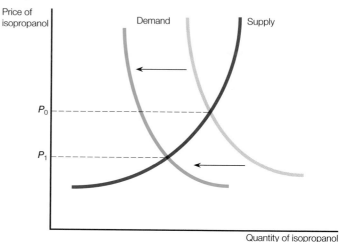

c. Yes.

d. Yes.

CHAPTER 11

1. a. They would want to set marginal revenue equal to the marginal cost of each firm, but this is impossible since Bergen's marginal cost is $410 and Gutenberg's marginal cost is $460. Because Bergen's marginal cost is always less than Gutenberg's, it will produce all the output. Equating its marginal cost to marginal revenue (MR)
$$MR = 580 - 6Q = 410$$
so $Q = 170/6$. This is the output Bergen would produce.

b. Nothing.

c. Not unless Gutenberg receives an attractive share of the profit from Bergen's output even though it produces nothing.

3. a. $9,000. **b.** 6.

5. a. To find the profit-maximizing price, the IATA should construct the marginal cost curve for the cartel as a whole. Then, as shown in Figure 11.2, it should determine the amount of traffic (which is the output of this industry) where marginal revenue equals marginal cost. The price that will elicit this level of traffic is the profit-maximizing price.

b. If IATA wants to maximize profit, it will allocate this traffic among the airlines in such a way that the marginal cost of all airlines is equal. (However, for reasons discussed on page 408, it may not want to maximize profit.)

c. No. This would not maximize profit.

7. a. Letting Alliance's profit be π_1

$\pi_1 = Q_1[200,000 - 6(Q_1 + Q_2)] - 8,000\,Q_1$

Letting Bangor's profit be π_2

$\pi_2 = Q_2[200,000 - 6(Q_1 + Q_2)] - 12,000\,Q_2$

If Alliance maximizes its profit, assuming that Bangor will hold its output constant

$$\frac{\partial \pi_1}{\partial Q_1} = 192,000 - 6Q_2 - 12Q_1 = 0$$

If Bangor maximizes its profit, assuming that Alliance will hold its output constant

$$\frac{\partial \pi_2}{\partial Q_2} = 188,000 - 6Q_1 - 12Q_2 = 0$$

Solving these equations simultaneously, $Q_1 = 196,000/18 = 10,888.89$, and

$Q_2 = (188,000 - 196,000/3)/12 = 122,667/12 = 10,222.22$

so

$P = 200,000 - 6(10,888.89 + 10,222.22) = \$73,333.33$

b. Alliance's output is 10,888.89, and Bangor's output is 10,222.22.

c. Alliance's profit is $10,888.89(73,333.33 - 8,000)$, or approximately $711.41 million.

Bangor's profit is $10,222.22(73,333.33 - 12,000)$, or approximately $626.96 million.

9. a. Obviously, Procter and Gamble must be concerned with its own costs. If it adopts a tactic that is far more costly to itself than to a potential entrant, it may cost more than it is worth. If the costs of the strategy outweigh the benefits, Procter and Gamble, on net, will lose.

b. The point of these tactics is to raise the cost to a potential entrant, thus discouraging entry.

c. Whether Procter and Gamble should have cut its price depends on whether the discount brands (and Kimberly-Clark, which had become a major rival) would cut their prices in response, and by how much. In fact, Procter and Gamble did reduce its price substantially (by 16% in the case of Luvs). According to the chairperson of Procter and Gamble, "We believe our profits are going to grow because we're going to get volume back."

d. Yes. Procter and Gamble wanted to reduce what it regarded as improper imitation of its technology. On the other hand, firms that are sued often regard such suits as attempts to intimidate them.

11. **a.** The size of a firm is often measured by its total revenue. Perhaps a firm might feel that a higher total revenue would make the firm more visible to investors and customers. Also, its managers may be more interested in the growth of the firm than in profits. (However, they are likely to feel that profits should not fall below some minimum level.)

b. To maximize its total revenue, it should set

$$\frac{d(PQ)}{dQ} = \frac{d(28Q - 0.14Q^2)}{dQ} = 28 - 0.28Q = 0$$

Thus, Q should equal 100, and P should equal $14.

c. If it maximizes profit, it sets
$$MR = 28 - 0.28Q = 14 = MC$$
so $Q = 50$. Consequently, the firm produces 50,000 units more than it would if it maximized profit.

CHAPTER 12

1. **a.** Yes. Fortnum should focus on magazines, and Maison should focus on newspapers.

b. Fortnum's profit is $9 million, and Maison's profit is $8 million.

c. No.

3. **a.**

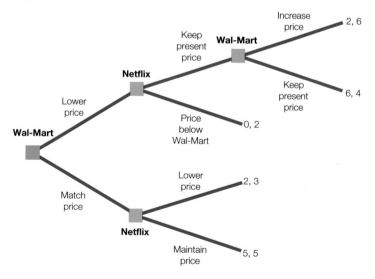

Using backward induction, the equilibrium is for Wal-Mart to lower price, Netflix to keep its present price, and Wal-Mart to respond by keeping its present price. The final payoff to Wal-Mart is 6, and Netflix receives 4.

b.

	Netflix			
	Maintain Price; Price Below Wal-Mart	Maintain Price; Keep Present Price	Lower Price; Price Below Wal-Mart	Lower Price; Keep Present Price
Wal-Mart Match Price	(W)5, 5(N)	5, 5(N)	(W)2, 3	2, 3
Keep Present Price If Lower Price	0, 2	(W)6, 4(N)	0, 2	(W)6, 4(N)
Increase Price If Lower Price	0, 2	2, 6(N)	0, 2	2, 6(N)

In matrix form, we find the Nash equilibria of the game's subgames. Using backward induction in (a), we found the subgame perfect Nash equilibrium.

5. a. Each firm will choose to cheat on the agreement. They will each earn $28 million.

b. No, as long as the horizon is finite, behavior will not change.

c. Yes, this is an example of prisoner's dilemma.

7. If Rose cannot ascertain the strategy of its rival then it cannot implement a tit-for-tat strategy because it will not know which strategy to play. A tit-for-tat strategy requires a player to mimic the strategy played by a rival in the previous period. For example, if Rose's rival played cheat in period n, then Rose would choose cheat in period $n + 1$.

CHAPTER 13

1. Expected value or $EV(\$45) = 1{,}750(\$40.5)(.35) + 1{,}975(\$40.5)(.20) + 2{,}220(\$40.5)(.30) + 2{,}445(\$40.5)(.15)$

$EV(\$45) = \textbf{\$24,806.25} + \textbf{\$15,997.50} + \$26{,}973 + \$14{,}853.38$ or $\$82{,}630.13$.

$EV(\$50) = 1{,}200(\$45)(.35) + 1{,}415(\$45)(.20) + 2{,}001(\$45)(.30) + 2{,}305(\$45)(.15)$

$EV(\$50) = \$18{,}900 + \$12{,}735 + \textbf{\$27,013.50} + \textbf{\$15,558.75}$ or $\$74{,}207.25$

$EV(\text{auction}) = \$24{,}806.25 + \$15{,}997.50 + \$27{,}013.50 + \$15{,}558.75 = \$83{,}376$

So, the value of information $= \$83{,}376 - \$82{,}630.13 = \$745.87$

3. a. The mean value is 51.

b. $z = (80 - 51)/19.85 = 1.46099$; using a standard z table, a z-score of 1.46099 is equivalent to an area under a normal distribution and to left of 80 equal to .9280. Hence the probability of a reservation price being less than 80 is approximately 93%.

5. If they choose to price their PSLs at $6,000, their expected revenue is: $58,802,000 + $58,800,000 + **$60,000,000** = $177,602,000. If they choose to price their PSLs at $7,000, their expected revenue is: **$60,214,000** + 58,803,500 + 56,000,000 = 175,017,500. If they choose to price their PSLs at $8,000, their expected revenue is: $56,030,000 + **$61,610,500** + $50,000,000 = $167,640,500. So, if they set the price and don't use an auction, they should charge $6,000/PSL. If the Eagles use a modified Dutch auction, then their expected revenue is: $60,214,000 + $61,610,500 + $60,000 = $181,824,500. So relative to setting a price of $6,000/PSL, the auction would increase expected revenue by $4,222,500. But since auction costs are $5,100,000, the Eagles are better off pricing the PSLs at $6,000.

CHAPTER 14

1. **a.** The expected present value is $10.7 million, the standard deviation is approximately $5.06 million, and the coefficient of variation is 47.3%.
   b. The expected present value is $10 million, the standard deviation is approximately $1.67 million, and the coefficient of variation is 16.7%.
   c. Investment X.
   d. Investment Y, since she is a risk averter (as indicated by the fact that U increases at a decreasing rate as P rises). Investment Y may have a lower expected present value, but it has a lower standard deviation than investment X and, more importantly, investment X's expected utility is less than investment Y's, i.e., $E(U_X) = 29.902 < 30 = E(U_Y)$.

3. No, because no probability distribution of the outcome has been given.

5. **a.** 3.   **b.** −0.6.   **c.** −1.2.

7. **a.**

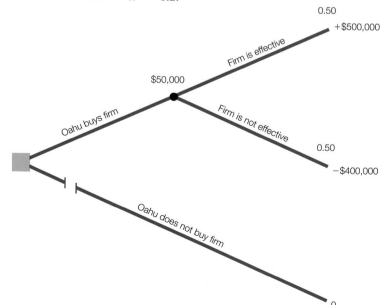

b. There is only one: whether to buy the firm or not.

c. There is only one: whether the firm becomes an effective producer of washing machine parts or not.

d. Yes, it should buy the firm.

e. (1) Yes.

(2) Three mutually exclusive outcomes are: (a) The firm becomes an effective producer of washing machine parts; (b) The firm does not become an effective producer of washing parts and is sold to the Saudis; (c) The firm does not become an effective producer of washing machine parts and cannot be sold to the Saudis.

(3) The probability of the first outcome (in part 2) is 0.5, the probability of the second outcome is 0.5(0.2), or 0.1, and the probability of the third outcome is (0.5)(0.8), or 0.4.

(4) The extra profit to Oahu from the first outcome is $500,000; the extra profit from the second outcome is $100,000; the extra profit from the third outcome is −$400,000.

f. Oahu should buy the firm. The expected extra profit if it does so is 0.5($500,000) + 0.1($100,000) + 0.4(−$400,000) = $100,000.

g. (1) If the extra profit if the firm is made into an effective producer of washing machine parts is $400,000 or less, the decision will be reversed. Put differently, if the *error* was an *overstatement* of this extra profit by $100,000 or more, the decision will be reversed.

(2) If the extra profit if the firm is made into an effective producer of washing machine parts is $300,000 or less, the decision will be reversed. Put differently, if the *error* was an *overstatement* of this extra profit by $200,000 or more, the decision will be reversed.

9. a.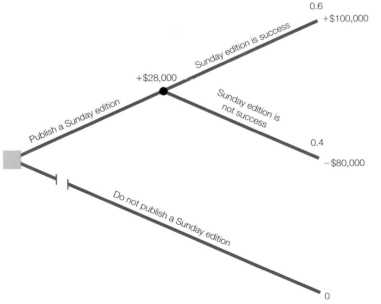

If the publisher is risk neutral, she wants to maximize expected profit. Thus, she should publish the Sunday edition.

b. Whether to publish the Sunday edition is a decision fork. Whether it is a success, if published, is a chance fork.

CHAPTER 15

1. a. Flat salary:

If effort is low, utility = 758.29. If effort is high, utility = 658.29. The manager chooses low effort since it gives higher expected utility. Your expected profit will be 0.3($5 million) + 0.4($10 million) + 0.3($15 million) − $0.575 million = $9.425 million.

b. Six percent of profit:

Expected utility of manager with

Low effort is $0.3\sqrt{0.06(\$5 \text{ million})} + 0.4\sqrt{1.06(\$10 \text{ million})} + 0.3\sqrt{0.06(15 \text{ million})} = 758.76$

High effort is $-100 + 0.3\sqrt{0.06(\$7 \text{ million})} + 0.4\sqrt{0.06(\$12 \text{ million})} + 0.3\sqrt{0.06(\$17 \text{ million})} = 736.82$

The manager chooses low effort since it gives higher expected utility. Given the manager's choice of low effort, your expected profit will be the expected profit of $10 million minus 6% of $10 million which is {0.3($5 million) + 0.4($10 million) + 0.3($15 million)} (1 − 0.06) = $9.4 million.

c. Five hundred thousand dollars plus half of profits in excess of $15 million:

Expected utility of manager with

Low effort is $\sqrt{(\$0.5 \text{ million})} = 707.11$

High effort is $-100 + 0.7\sqrt{(\$0.5 \text{ million})} + 0.3\sqrt{1/2(\$17 \text{ million} - \$15 \text{ million}) + \$0.5 \text{ million}} = 762.40$

The manager chooses high effort since it gives higher expected utility. Your expected profit will be the expected profit of $12 million minus expected compensation which is {$0.5m + 0.3(0.5($2m))} = $800,000. {0.3($7m) + 0.4($12m) + 0.3($17m)} − $0.8m = $11.2 million. You will choose the third plan (c) since it gives highest profit after deducting the manager's compensation.

3. If the manager does not work hard, she will receive

$[100]^{0.5} = 10$

If the manager works hard, she will receive

$[100 + x(1,500 - 1,300)]^{0.5} - 1$

To calculate the minimum level of x necessary to ensure that the expected compensation will be higher with hard work, set the expected utility with hard work equal to that without hard work:

$[100 + x(1{,}500 - 1{,}300)]^{0.5} - 1 = 10$

$[100 + x(1{,}500 - 1{,}300)]^{0.5} \quad = 11 \qquad$ (square both sides to get)

$[100 + x(1{,}500 - 1{,}300)] \quad = 11^2 = 121$

$x = \dfrac{121 - 100}{1{,}500 - 1{,}300} = 0.105$

Thus, if the manager gets a little over 10.5% of equity in excess of 1,300, she will work hard.

5. **Total value of firm:**

$$V = 500 + 300 - 700\left(\frac{0.2}{1 + s}\right) - s = 800 - \frac{140}{1 + s} - s$$

To calculate the value of s that maximizes total value, set the derivative of value with respect to s equal to zero

$$\frac{dV}{ds} = \frac{140}{(1 + s)^2} - 1 = 0$$

So, $s = 10.832$.

Therefore, the value of firm is

$$800 - \frac{140}{11.832} - 10.832 = 777.34$$

Division 1 is riskless and has a stand-alone value of 500. Since all the risk comes from division 2, we must consider the chosen level of safety of this unit as a stand-alone entity. In calculating this value recollect that its value is 300 if no liability arises. However, if a loss of 700 occurs, it simply cannot pay more than the original 300 stand-alone value (because of limited liability). So, the stand-alone value of division 2 is

$$300 - 300\left(\frac{0.2}{1 + s}\right) - s = 300 - \frac{60}{1 + s} - s$$

Set the derivative equal to zero to maximize the division 2 stand-alone value

$$\frac{dV}{ds} = \frac{60}{(1 + s)^2} - 1 = 0. \text{ So, } s = 6.746$$

So, the stand-alone value of division 2 is

$$300 - \frac{60}{7.746} - 6.746 = 285.51$$

Total value with split up

$500 + 285.51 = 785.51$

So the gain from split up is $785.51 - 777.34 = 8.17$

7. There is an asset-substitution problem. To show this, we should value the firm as a whole, and each of the stakeholders' claims, first assuming A is chosen and then assuming B is chosen. We can then see which project selection leads to the higher value of equity. This is the one shareholders would naturally favor.

Value of the firm if project A is chosen:

First, note the value of the firm is either 720 (300 from existing operations and 420 from the new project) or 1020 (600 from existing operations and 420 from the new project) depending on the success of existing operations. This value must be divided up by first paying off old debt, next new debt, and finally equity.

Value of the firm	$0.5(720 + 1020) = 870$
Old debt	$0.5(250 + 250) = 250$
New debt	$0.5(400 + 400) = 400$
Equity	$0.5(70 + 370) = 220$

Value of the firm if project B is chosen:

The value of the firm will be either 300, 600, 1000, or 1300. These figures come from the different combinations of the two possible values for the existing operations (300 and 600) and the two values for the new project (0 and 700).

Value of the firm	$0.25(300 + 600 + 1000 + 1300) = 800$
Old debt	$0.25(250 + 250 + 250 + 250) = 250$
New debt	$0.25(50 + 350 + 400 + 400) = 300$
Equity	$0.25(0 + 0 + 350 + 650) = 250$

Shareholders would like to choose B after they had creditors' money. But since investors would pay only 300 for new debt, this cannot be funded. So neither project can be undertaken if debt financing is used. The analysis can be repeated using equity financing for the new project. The values of the firm will be the same as above, but these will be allocated first to the existing debt (for which 250 is owing) and any residual will accrue to equity.

Value of the firm if project A is chosen:

Value of the firm	$0.5(720 + 1020) = 870$
Old debt	$0.5(250 + 250) = 250$
Equity	$0.5(470 + 770) = 620$

Value of the firm if project B is chosen:

Value of the firm	$0.25(300 + 600 + 1000 + 1300) = 800$
Old debt	$0.25(250 + 250 + 250 + 250) = 250$
Equity	$0.25(50 + 350 + 750 + 1050) = 550$

Now, shareholders will naturally choose the higher net present value project A since it has the higher equity value. The asset-substitution problem is solved.

CHAPTER 16

1. First, note that buyers will not be willing to pay $10,000 for any used car since there is a chance that it is a lemon. So the obvious price to contemplate is a price reflecting the average quality; i.e., there is a 75% chance the car will be "good" and worth $10,000 and a 25% chance the car will be "bad" and worth $5,000.

Average value $(.75)(\$10,000) + (0.25)(\$5,000) = \$8,750$

But, sellers of high quality cars, knowing their vehicles are really worth $10,000, will not be willing to sell at this price. So, only sellers of low quality vehicles will offer their cars for sale. But buyers can anticipate that only low quality cars will be offered, therefore they will only be willing to pay $5,000 for any secondhand Corolla on the secondhand market. Thus, only low quality cars are sold and the price is $5,000.

3. Form the following table if all are considering buying insurance:

Group	Initial Car Value	Ending Car Value If Accident	Probability of Accident	Expected Claim
A	10,000	5,000	0.2	1,000
B	10,000	5,000	0.3	1,500
C	10,000	5,000	0.4	2,000

Thus, if all purchased insurance, the expected claims would be $1,000 + 1,500 + 2,000 = 4,500$ and hence the premium would have to be $4,500/3 = 1,500$. But this requires that ALL types buy the policy. Let's see if they will.

Would A buy insurance if the premium was 1,500? If A self insures (does not buy insurance), his/her expected utility would be

$EU_a = 0.8(10,000)^{0.5} + 0.2(5,000)^{0.5} = 0.8(100) + 0.2(70.711) = 80 + 14.142 = 94.142$

If A buys a full coverage policy for 1,500, A's expected utility will be

$EU_a = (10,000 - 1,500)^{0.5} = (8,500)^{0.5} = 92.195$

Thus, A will self insure since $94.142 > 92.195$

Thus, the premium cannot be 1,500 since A is not buying insurance.

So, if the type A's drop out of the insurance pool, we are left with the B's and C's. If only B and C are interested in buying, the expected claims are $1,500 + 2,000 = 3,500$ and the premium must be $3,500/2 = 1,750$.

But would B buy insurance at the premium of 1,750? If B self insures, their expected utility would be

$EU_b = 0.7(10,000)^{0.5} + 0.3(5,000)^{0.5} = 0.7(100) + 0.3(70.711) = 70 + 21.213 = 91.213$

If B buys a full coverage policy for 1,750, B's expected utility will be

$EU_b = (10,000 - 1,750)^{0.5} = (8,250)^{0.5} = 90.830$

Thus, B will self insure since $91.213 > 90.830$.

Thus, the premium cannot be 1,750 since B is not buying insurance.

If only C is interested in buying insurance, then the premium must be 2,000. If C self insures, their expected utility would be

$EU_c = 0.6(10,000)^{0.5} + 0.4(5,000)^{0.5} = 0.6(100) + 0.4(70.711)$

$= 60 + 28.284 = 88.284$

If C buys a full coverage policy for 2,000, C's expected utility will be

$EUc = (10,000 - 2,000)^{0.5} = (8,000)^{0.5} = 89.443$

Since $89.443 > 88.284$, C will buy the insurance for a premium of 2,000. However, No-State can sell the policy for a higher price. Type C's certainty equivalent will be $(88.284)^2 = 7,794.11$. Thus, Type C's would be willing to pay up to $10,000 - 7,794.11 = 2,205.89$ for such a policy. Since the question required that the premium must be sufficient to cover expected claims and the expected claims for type C's are

$0.4(5,000) = 2,000$, a premium of 2,205.90 would certainly fill the bill.

5. The following table charts the maximum price people are willing to pay.

Formula =

$1.1(x)(\$50,000)$ for less risk averse

$1.3(x)(\$50,000)$ for more risk averse

	Poor health Life expectancy = 9 years	Good health Life expectancy = 11 years
Less risk averse Pay up to 1.1 times expected value	495,000	605,000
More risk averse Pay up to 1.3 times expected value	585,000	715,000

At a price of $550,000, the product will be purchased by all those in good health and the more risk averse in poor health.

The expected profit can now be calculated

More risk averse in poor health: (50 times $550,000) − (50 times 9 times $50,000) = $5,000,000

Less risk averse in good health: (50 times $550,000) − (50 times 11 times $50,000) = $0

More risk averse in poor health: (50 times $550,000) − (50 times 11 times $50,000) = $0

TOTAL PROFIT = $5,000,000

CHAPTER 17

1. a. It equaled $27.5 + 21.9 + 18.5 + 9.3 = 77.2\%$. Yes.

   b. It was $27.5 + 21.9 + (18.5 + 7.3) + 9.3 = 84.5\%$ if we simply combine United's and Pan Am's shares to approximate United's postpurchase share.

3. a. If $P = 480$, $Q = 260$, according to the demand curve. Thus, the firm's total revenue equals 260(480) thousand dollars, or $124,800,000. The

firm's total cost equals $50 + 0.25(260) = \$115,000,000$. Thus, the firm's accounting profit is $9,800,000; this means that its rate of return is 9.8%.

b. If it were deregulated, it would maximize

$$\pi = (1/1{,}000)[Q(1{,}000 - 2Q)] - 50 - 0.25Q$$
$$= -50 + 0.75Q - 0.002Q^2.$$

Setting $d\pi/dQ = 0.75 - 0.004Q = 0$, $Q = 187.5$. Thus, under deregulation

$$\pi = -50 + 0.75(187.5) - 0.002(187.5^2) = \$20.3125 \text{ million}$$

So, the difference is $20.3125 - \$9.8 = \$10.5125$ million.

5. a. $220/250 = 88\%$.

b. Yes, because it is dominated by a few firms.

c. $225/250 = 90\%$.

d. $140/145 = 97\%$.

7. a. No. If price is set equal to $1, 12 firms of optimal size can exist in the market.

b. Eight.

9. a. Because the commission tries to provide the firm with a "fair" rate of return on its investment.

b. Because this increase reduced the firm's profit.

c. See pages 652 to 656.

CHAPTER 18

1. a. Since the cost per patient-day $(Y) = C/X$, the desired relationship is

$$Y = \frac{4{,}700{,}000}{X} + 0.00013X$$

b. To find the value of X that minimizes the value of Y, we set the derivative of Y with respect to X equal to zero

$$\frac{dY}{dX} = -\frac{4{,}700{,}000}{X^2} + 0.00013 = 0$$

Thus, $X = \left(\dfrac{4{,}700{,}000}{0.00013}\right)^{0.5}$ or approximately 190,141.6476 patient-days.

c. Since $d^2Y/dX^2 = 2(4{,}700{,}000)/X^3$, d^2Y/dX^2 must be positive (since X is positive). Thus, Y must be a minimum, not a maximum, at the point where $dY/dX = 0$.

3. a. $5{,}000 - \$3{,}000$.

b. 7 units per day.

c. No, because profit is higher at 9 units per day than at 7 units per day.

5. a. Since marginal cost equals $4 + 16Q$, it is 164 when $Q = 10$.

b. $4 + 16(12) = 196$.

c. $4 + 16(20) = 324$.

7. **a.** 6

    b. $24X$

    c. $48X^2$

    d. $8/X^3$

9. **a.** 2

    b. $12X^2$

    c. $0.8Z^{0.2}X^{-0.2} = 0.8\dfrac{Y}{X}$

    d. $-3Z/(4 + X)^2$

11. **a.** $\partial C/\partial X_1 = -3 + 4X_1 + X_2 = 0$

      $\partial C/\partial X_2 = -4 + 6X_2 + X_1 = 0$

    Solving these two equations simultaneously

    $X_1 = 14/23$ and $X_2 = 13/23$

    b. The answer will not change.

13. **a.** The Lagrangian function is $L_{TC} = 7X_1^2 + 9X_2^2 - 1.5X_1X_2 + \lambda(10 - X_1 - X_2)$. Thus

    $\partial L_{TC}/\partial X_1 = 14X_1 - 1.5X_2 - \lambda = 0$

    $\partial L_{TC}/\partial X_2 = 18X_2 - 1.5X_1 - \lambda = 0$

    $\partial L_{TC}/\partial \lambda = 10 - X_1 - X_2 = 0$

    From the first two of these equations, it follows that $X_1 = (195/155)X_2$, which, together with the third equation, implies that $X_1 = 195/35$ and $X_2 = 155/35$.

    b. Yes.

    c. If we substitute 195/35 for X_1, and 155/35 for X_2 in either of the first two equations, we find that $\lambda = 71.36$, which is the marginal cost of a rug at the cost-minimizing combination of types that total ten rugs per day.

APPENDIX A

1. **a.** $\dfrac{200,000}{10(20,000) + 0.02(50,000) + 5(10,000)} = \dfrac{200,000}{251,000} = 0.797$

    b. $\dfrac{300,000}{10(30,000) + 0.02(100,000) + 5(14,000)} = \dfrac{300,000}{372,000} = 0.806$

    c. The base year is 2000.

3. **a.** $\log C = 5.1 - 0.25 \log 100$

          $= 5.1 - 0.25(2)$

          $= 4.6$

    Thus, $C = 39,811.$

    b. $\log C = 5.1 - 0.25 \log 200$

          $= 5.1 - 0.25 (2.30)$

          $= 4.525$

Thus, $C = 33,497$
  c. $1 - 33,497/39,811 = 16\%$.
5. $9.6 million. $7.68 million
7. a. $0.5(\$1\text{ million}) + 0.5(\$2\text{ million}) = \$1.5\text{ million}$.
  b. $0.75(\$1\text{ million}) + 0.25(\$2\text{ million}) + \$150,000 = \$1.4\text{ million}$. This assumes that whether each approach costs $1 million or $2 million is independent of what the other approach costs. Also, the total cost figure for each approach, if adopted, includes the $150,000. Thus only the $150,000 spent on the aborted approach is lost. The $150,000 spent on the approach that is adopted is part of the total cost figure given in the problem.
  c. Comparing the answers to parts a and b, parallel approaches result in lower expected cost.
9. a. $0.6(\$5\text{ million}) + 0.4(\$3\text{ million}) = \$4.2\text{ million}$.
  b. $0.7(\$3\text{ million}) + 0.3(\$5\text{ million}) = \$3.6\text{ million}$.
  c. $0.18(\$5\text{ million}) + 0.82(\$3\text{ million}) + \$500,000 = \$3.86\text{ million}$.

APPENDIX B

1. a. Yes. Room occupancy in August tends to be about 57% greater than in January.
  b. There are more tourists in the summer than in the winter. Because of the recession, there may have been fewer tourists, and hence the seasonal variation may have been less pronounced during the recession than before it.
  c. It might be of use in scheduling labor inputs and in ordering supplies. Certainly, the manager would want to take proper account of this seasonal variation in his or her hiring and purchasing decisions.
3. a. Because the seasonal index shows by what percent sales for a particular month tend to be above or below normal.
  b. Deseasonalized sales are as follows:

January	$2.5/0.97 = \$2.58$ million	July	$3.2/1.01 = \$3.17$ million
February	$2.4/0.96 = \$2.50$ million	August	$3.1/1.03 = \$3.01$ million
March	$2.7/0.97 = \$2.78$ million	September	$3.2/1.03 = \$3.11$ million
April	$2.9/0.98 = \$2.96$ million	October	$3.1/1.03 = \$3.01$ million
May	$3.0/0.99 = \$3.03$ million	November	$3.0/1.02 = \$2.94$ million
June	$3.1/1.00 = \$3.10$ million	December	$2.9/1.01 = \$2.87$ million

  c. Because they want to see how sales are changing, when the seasonal factor is deleted.
5. a. Yes. Yes.
  b. Yes. Yes.

7. a. $S_t = -5,744 + 2.9143t$

  b. The forecast would have been $-5,744 + 2.9143(1991) = 58.4$ billion dollars, so the forecasting error would have been about 2%.

  c. The forecast would have been $-5,744 + 2.9143(1992) = 61.3$ billion dollars, so the forecasting error would have been about 17%.

9. a. Let $t' = 0$ when $t = 1963$. Let y be General Electric's sales.

t'	y	t'^2	y^2	$t'y$
-13	2.2	169	4.84	-28.6
-12	2.6	144	6.76	-31.2
-11	3.0	121	9.00	-33.0
-10	3.5	100	12.25	-35.0
-9	3.3	81	10.89	-29.7
-8	3.5	64	12.25	-28.0
-7	4.1	49	16.81	-28.7
-6	4.3	36	18.49	-25.8
-5	4.2	25	17.64	-21.0
-4	4.5	16	20.25	-18.0
-3	4.2	9	17.64	-12.6
-2	4.5	4	20.25	-9.0
-1	4.8	1	23.04	-4.8
0	4.9	0	24.01	0.0
1	4.9	1	24.01	4.9
2	6.2	4	38.44	12.4
3	7.2	9	51.84	21.6
4	7.7	16	59.29	30.8
5	8.4	25	70.56	42.0
6	8.4	36	70.56	50.4
7	8.8	49	77.44	61.6
8	9.6	64	92.16	76.8
9	10.5	81	110.25	94.5
10	11.9	100	141.61	119.0
11	13.9	121	193.21	152.9
12	14.1	144	198.81	169.2
13	15.7	169	246.49	204.1
Sum 0	180.9	1,638	1,588.79	734.8
Mean 0	6.7			

$$b = \frac{734.8 - (180.9)(0)}{1,638 - (0)(0)} = \frac{734.8}{1,638} = 0.449$$

$a = 6.7 - (0.449)(0) = 6.7$

Thus, the trend is $6.7 + 0.449t'$.

b. The graph is as follows:

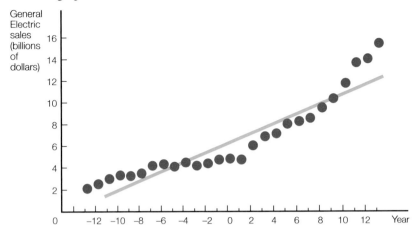

c. It appears from the graph that the trend may be curvilinear, and that an exponential or quadratic trend might do better.

d. The forecast would be $6.7 + 0.449(31) = 20.619$ billion dollars, which was only about 30% higher than actual sales in 1976. In fact, GE's sales were about \$60 billion in 1994, which indicates how poor linear extrapolations of this sort can be, particularly when one is using them to forecast many years (18 years in this case) into the future.

APPENDIX E

TABLES

TABLE E.1

Value of $\dfrac{1}{(1 + i)^n}$

					Value of i					
n	1%	2%	3%	4%	5%	6%	7%	8%	9%	10%
1	.99010	.98039	.97007	.96154	.95233	.94340	.93458	.92593	.91743	.90909
2	.98030	.96117	.94260	.92456	.90703	.89000	.87344	.85734	.84168	.82645
3	.97059	.94232	.91514	.88900	.86384	.83962	.81639	.79383	.77228	.75131
4	.96098	.92385	.88849	.85480	.82270	.79209	.76290	.73503	.70883	.68301
5	.95147	.90573	.86261	.82193	.78353	.74726	.71299	.68058	.64993	.62092
6	.94204	.88797	.83748	.79031	.74622	.70496	.66634	.63017	.59627	.56447
7	.93272	.87056	.81309	.75992	.71063	.66506	.62275	.58349	.54705	.51316
8	.92348	.85349	.78941	.73069	.67684	.62741	.58201	.54027	.50189	.46651
9	.91434	.83675	.76642	.70259	.64461	.59190	.54393	.50025	.46043	.42410
10	.90529	.82035	.74409	.67556	.61391	.55839	.50835	.46319	.42241	.38554
11	.89632	.80426	.72242	.64958	.58468	.52679	.47509	.42888	.38753	.35049
12	.88745	.78849	.70138	.62460	.55684	.49697	.44401	.39711	.35553	.31683
13	.87866	.77303	.68095	.60057	.53032	.46884	.41496	.36770	.32618	.28966
14	.86996	.75787	.66112	.57747	.50507	.44230	.38782	.34046	.29925	.26333
15	.86135	.74301	.64186	.55526	.48102	.41726	.36245	.31524	.27454	.23939
16	.85282	.72845	.62317	.53391	.45811	.39365	.33873	.29189	.25187	.21763
17	.84436	.71416	.60502	.51337	.43630	.37136	.31657	.27027	.23107	.19784
18	.83602	.70016	.58739	.49363	.41552	.35034	.29586	.25025	.21199	.17986
19	.82774	.68643	.57029	.47464	.39573	.33051	.27651	.23171	.19449	.16354
20	.81954	.67297	.55367	.45639	.37689	.31180	.25842	.21455	.17843	.14864
21	.81143	.65978	.53755	.44883	.35894	.29415	.24151	.19866	.16370	.13513
22	.80340	.64684	.52189	.42195	.34185	.27750	.22571	.18394	.15018	.12285
23	.79544	.63414	.50669	.40573	.32557	.26180	.21095	.17031	.13778	.11168
24	.78757	.62172	.49193	.39012	.31007	.24698	.19715	.15770	.12640	.10153
25	.77977	.60953	.47760	.37512	.29530	.23300	.18425	.14602	.11597	.09230

TABLE E.1 (continued)

Value of $\dfrac{1}{(1+i)^n}$

					Value of i						
n	11%	12%	13%	14%	15%	16%	17%	18%	19%	20%	24%
1	.90090	.89286	.88496	.87719	.86957	.86207	.85470	.84746	.84043	.83333	.8065
2	.81162	.79719	.78315	.76947	.75614	.74316	.73051	.71818	.70616	.69444	.6504
3	.73119	.71178	.69305	.67497	.65752	.64066	.62437	.60863	.59342	.57870	.5245
4	.65873	.63552	.61332	.59208	.57175	.55229	.53365	.51579	.49867	.48225	.4230
5	.59345	.56743	.54276	.51937	.49718	.47611	.45611	.43711	.41905	.40188	.3411
6	.53464	.50663	.48032	.45559	.43233	.41044	.38984	.37043	.35214	.33490	.2751
7	.48166	.45235	.42506	.39964	.37594	.35383	.33320	.31392	.29592	.27908	.2218
8	.43393	.40388	.37616	.35056	.32690	.30503	.28478	.26604	.24867	.23257	.1789
9	.39092	.36061	.33288	.30751	.28426	.26295	.24340	.22546	.20897	.19381	.1443
10	.35218	.32197	.29459	.26974	.24718	.22668	.20804	.19106	.17560	.16151	.1164
11	.31728	.28748	.26070	.23662	.21494	.19542	.17781	.16192	.14756	.13459	.0938
12	.28584	.25667	.23071	.20756	.18691	.16846	.15197	.13722	.12400	.11216	.0757
13	.25751	.22917	.20416	.18207	.16253	.14523	.12989	.11629	.10420	.09346	.0610
14	.23199	.20462	.18068	.15971	.14133	.12520	.11102	.09855	.08757	.07789	.0492
15	.20900	.18270	.15989	.14010	.12289	.10793	.09489	.08352	.07359	.06491	.0397
16	.18829	.16312	.14150	.12289	.10686	.09304	.08110	.07073	.06184	.05409	.0320
17	.16963	.14564	.12522	.10780	.09293	.08021	.06932	.05998	.05196	.04507	.0258
18	.15282	.13004	.11081	.09456	.08080	.06914	.05925	.05083	.04367	.03756	.0208
19	.13768	.11611	.09806	.08295	.07026	.05961	.05064	.04308	.03669	.03130	.0168
20	.12403	.10367	.08678	.07276	.06110	.05139	.04328	.03651	.03084	.02608	.0135
21	.11174	.09256	.07680	.06383	.05313	.04430	.03699	.03094	.02591	.02174	.0109
22	.10067	.08264	.06796	.05599	.04620	.03819	.03162	.02622	.02178	.01811	.0088
23	.09069	.07379	.06014	.04911	.04017	.03292	.02702	.02222	.01830	.01509	.0071
24	.08170	.06588	.05322	.04308	.03493	.02838	.02310	.01883	.01538	.01258	.0057
25	.07361	.05882	.04710	.03779	.03038	.02447	.01974	.01596	.01292	.01048	.0046

TABLE E.2

Value of $\sum_{t=1}^{n} \dfrac{1}{(1 + i)^t}$

	Value of i									
n	1%	2%	3%	4%	5%	6%	7%	8%	9%	10%
1	.9901	.9804	.9709	.9615	.9524	.9434	.9346	.9259	.9174	.9091
2	1.9704	1.9416	1.9135	1.8861	1.8594	1.8334	1.8080	1.7833	1.7591	1.7355
3	2.9410	2.8839	2.8286	2.7751	2.7233	2.6730	2.6243	2.5771	2.5313	2.4868
4	3.9020	3.8077	3.7171	3.6299	3.5459	3.4651	3.3872	3.3121	3.2397	3.1699
5	4.8535	4.7134	4.5797	4.4518	4.3295	4.2123	4.1002	3.9927	3.8896	3.7908
6	5.7955	5.6014	5.4172	5.2421	5.0757	4.9173	4.7665	4.6229	4.4859	4.3553
7	6.7282	6.4720	6.2302	6.0020	5.7863	5.5824	5.3893	5.2064	5.0329	4.8684
8	7.6517	7.3254	7.0196	6.7327	6.4632	6.2093	5.9713	5.7466	5.5348	5.3349
9	8.5661	8.1622	7.7861	7.4353	7.1078	6.8017	6.5152	6.2469	5.9852	5.7590
10	9.4714	8.9825	8.7302	8.1109	7.7217	7.3601	7.0236	6.7101	6.4176	6.1446
11	10.3677	9.7868	9.2526	8.7604	8.3064	7.8868	7.4987	7.1389	6.8052	6.4951
12	11.2552	10.5753	9.9589	9.3850	8.8632	8.3838	7.9427	7.5361	7.1601	6.8137
13	12.1338	11.3483	10.6349	9.9856	9.3935	9.8527	8.3576	7.9038	7.4869	7.1034
14	13.0088	12.1062	11.2960	10.5631	9.8986	9.2950	8.7454	8.2442	7.7860	7.3667
15	13.8651	12.8492	11.9379	11.1183	10.3796	9.7122	9.1079	8.5595	8.0607	7.6061
16	14.7180	13.5777	12.5610	11.6522	10.8377	10.1059	9.4466	8.8514	8.3126	7.8237
17	15.5624	14.2918	13.1660	12.1656	11.2740	10.4772	9.7632	9.1216	8.5435	8.0215
18	16.3984	14.9920	13.7534	12.6592	11.6895	10.8276	10.0591	9.3719	8.7556	8.2014
19	17.2201	15.2684	14.3237	13.1339	12.0853	11.1581	10.3356	9.6036	8.9501	8.3649
20	18.0457	16.3514	14.8774	13.5903	12.4622	11.4699	10.5940	9.8181	9.1285	8.5136
21	18.8571	17.0111	15.4149	14.0291	12.8211	11.7640	10.8355	10.0168	9.2922	8.6487
22	19.6605	17.6581	15.9368	14.4511	13.1630	12.0416	11.0612	10.2007	9.4424	8.7715
23	20.4559	18.2921	16.4435	14.8568	13.4885	12.3033	11.2722	10.3710	9.5802	8.8832
24	21.2435	18.9139	16.9355	15.2469	13.7986	12.5503	11.4693	10.5287	9.7066	8.9847
25	22.0233	19.5234	17.4181	15.6220	14.9039	12.7833	11.6536	10.6748	9.8226	9.0770

TABLE E.2 (continued)

Value of $\sum_{t=1}^{n} \dfrac{1}{(1 + i)^t}$

					Value of i						
n	11%	12%	13%	14%	15%	16%	17%	18%	19%	20%	24%
1	.9009	.8929	.8850	.8772	.8696	.8621	.8547	.8475	.8403	.8333	.8065
2	1.7125	1.6901	1.6681	1.6467	1.6257	1.6052	1.5852	1.5656	1.5465	1.5278	1.4568
3	2.4437	2.4018	2.3612	2.3126	2.2832	2.2459	2.2096	2.1743	2.1399	2.1065	1.9813
4	3.1024	3.0373	2.9745	2.9137	2.8550	2.7982	2.7432	2.6901	2.6386	2.5887	2.4043
5	3.6959	3.6048	3.5172	3.4331	3.3522	3.2743	3.1993	3.1272	3.0576	2.9906	2.7454
6	4.2305	4.1114	3.9976	3.8887	3.7845	3.6847	3.5892	3.4976	3.4098	3.3255	3.0205
7	4.7122	4.5638	4.4226	4.2883	4.1604	4.0386	3.9224	3.8115	3.7057	3.6046	3.2423
8	5.1461	4.9676	4.7988	4.6389	4.4873	4.3436	4.2072	4.0776	3.9544	3.8372	3.4212
9	5.5370	5.3282	5.1317	4.9464	4.7716	4.6065	4.4506	4.3030	4.1633	4.0310	3.5655
10	5.8892	5.6502	5.4262	5.2161	5.0188	4.8332	4.6586	4.4941	4.3389	4.1925	3.6819
11	6.2065	5.9377	5.6869	5.4527	5.2337	5.0286	4.8364	4.6560	4.4865	4.3271	3.7757
12	6.4924	6.1944	5.9176	5.6603	5.4206	5.1971	4.9884	4.7932	4.6105	4.4392	3.8514
13	6.7499	6.4235	6.1218	5.8424	5.5831	5.3423	5.1183	4.9095	4.7147	4.5327	3.9124
14	6.9819	6.6282	6.3025	6.0021	5.7245	5.4675	5.2293	5.0081	4.8023	4.6106	3.9616
15	7.1909	6.8109	6.4624	6.1422	5.8474	5.5755	5.3242	5.0916	4.8759	4.6755	4.0013
16	7.3792	6.9740	6.6039	6.2651	5.9542	5.6685	5.4053	5.1624	4.9377	4.7296	4.0333
17	7.5488	7.1196	6.7291	6.3729	6.0472	5.7487	5.4746	5.2223	4.9897	4.7746	4.0591
18	7.7016	7.2497	6.8389	6.4674	6.1280	5.8178	5.5339	5.2732	5.0333	4.8122	4.0799
19	7.8393	7.3650	6.9380	6.5504	6.1982	5.8775	5.5845	5.3176	5.0700	4.8435	4.0967
20	7.9633	7.4694	7.0248	6.6231	6.2593	5.9288	5.6278	5.3527	5.1009	4.8696	4.1103
21	8.0751	7.5620	7.1016	6.6870	6.3125	5.9731	5.6648	5.3837	5.1268	4.8913	4.1212
22	8.1757	7.6446	7.1695	6.7429	6.3587	6.0113	5.6964	5.4099	5.1486	4.9094	4.1300
23	8.2664	7.7184	7.2297	6.7921	6.3988	6.0442	5.7234	5.4321	5.1668	4.9245	4.1371
24	8.3481	7.7843	7.2829	6.8351	6.4338	6.0726	5.7465	5.4509	5.1822	4.9371	4.1428
25	8.4217	7.8431	7.3300	6.8729	6.4641	6.0971	5.7662	5.4669	5.1951	4.9476	4.1474

TABLE E.3

Areas under the Standard Normal Curve

This table shows the area between zero (the mean of a standard normal variable) and z. For example, if $z = 1.50$, this is the shaded area shown below, which equals .4332.

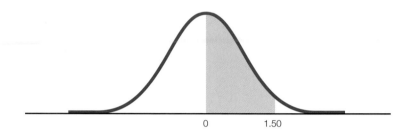

z	.00	.01	.02	.03	.04	.05	.06	.07	.08	.09
0.0	.0000	.0040	.0080	.0120	.0160	.0199	.0239	.0279	.0319	.0359
0.1	.0398	.0438	.0478	.0517	.0557	.0596	.0636	.0675	.0714	.0753
0.2	.0793	.0832	.0871	.0910	.0948	.0987	.1026	.1064	.1103	.1141
0.3	.1179	.1217	.1255	.1293	.1331	.1368	.1406	.1443	.1480	.1517
0.4	.1554	.1591	.1628	.1664	.1700	.1736	.1772	.1808	.1844	.1879
0.5	.1915	.1950	.1985	.2019	.2054	.2088	.2123	.2157	.2190	.2224
0.6	.2257	.2291	.2324	.2357	.2389	.2422	.2454	.2486	.2517	.2549
0.7	.2580	.2611	.2642	.2673	.2704	.2734	.2764	.2794	.2823	.2852
0.8	.2881	.2910	.2939	.2967	.2995	.3023	.3051	.3078	.3106	.3133
0.9	.3159	.3186	.3212	.3238	.3264	.3289	.3315	.3340	.3365	.3389
1.0	.3413	.3438	.3461	.3485	.3508	.3531	.3554	.3577	.3599	.3621

TABLE E.3 (continued)

Areas under the Standard Normal Curve

z	.00	.01	.02	.03	.04	.05	.06	.07	.08	.09
1.1	.3643	.3665	.3686	.3708	.3729	.3749	.3770	.3790	.3810	.3830
1.2	.3849	.3869	.3888	.3907	.3925	.3944	.3962	.3980	.3997	.4015
1.3	.4032	.4049	.4066	.4082	.4099	.4115	.4131	.4147	.4162	.4177
1.4	.4192	.4207	.4222	.4236	.4251	.4265	.4279	.4292	.4306	.4319
1.5	.4332	.4345	.4357	.4370	.4382	.4394	.4406	.4418	.4429	.4441
1.6	.4452	.4463	.4474	.4484	.4495	.4505	.4515	.4525	.4535	.4545
1.7	.4554	.4564	.4573	.4582	.4591	.4599	.4608	.4616	.4625	.4633
1.8	.4641	.4649	.4656	.4664	.4671	.4678	.4686	.4693	.4699	.4706
1.9	.4713	.4719	.4726	.4732	.4738	.4744	.4750	.4756	.4761	.4767
2.0	.4772	.4778	.4783	.4788	.4793	.4798	.4803	.4808	.4812	.4817
2.1	.4821	.4826	.4830	.4834	.4838	.4842	.4846	.4850	.4854	.4857
2.2	.4861	.4864	.4868	.4871	.4875	.4878	.4881	.4884	.4887	.4890
2.3	.4893	.4896	.4898	.4901	.4904	.4906	.4909	.4911	.4913	.4916
2.4	.4918	.4920	.4922	.4925	.4927	.4929	.4931	.4932	.4934	.4936
2.5	.4938	.4940	.4941	.4943	.4945	.4946	.4948	.4949	.4951	.4952
2.6	.4953	.4955	.4956	.4957	.4959	.4960	.4961	.4962	.4963	.4964
2.7	.4965	.4966	.4967	.4968	.4969	.4970	.4971	.4972	.4973	.4974
2.8	.4974	.4975	.4976	.4977	.4977	.4978	.4979	.4979	.4980	.4981
2.9	.4981	.4982	.4982	.4983	.4984	.4984	.4985	.4985	.4986	.4986
3.0	.4987	.4987	.4987	.4988	.4988	.4989	.4989	.4989	.4990	.4990

Source. This table is adapted from National Bureau of Standards, *Tables of Normal Probability Functions*, Applied Mathematics Series 23, U.S. Department of Commerce, 1953.

TABLE E.4

Values of *t* That Will Be Exceeded with Specified Probabilities

This table shows the value of *t* where the area under the *t* distribution exceeding this value of *t* equals the specified amount. For example, the probability that a *t* variable with 14 degrees of freedom will exceed 1.345 equals .10.

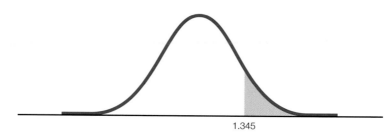

1.345

Degrees of freedom	Probability						
	.40	.25	.10	.05	.025	.01	.005
1	0.325	1.000	3.078	6.314	12.706	31.821	63.657
2	.289	0.816	1.886	2.920	4.303	6.965	9.925
3	.277	.765	1.638	2.353	3.182	4.541	5.841
4	.271	.741	1.533	2.132	2.776	3.747	4.604
5	0.267	0.727	1.476	2.015	2.571	3.365	4.032
6	.265	.718	1.440	1.943	2.447	3.143	3.707
7	.263	.711	1.415	1.895	2.365	2.998	3.499
8	.262	.706	1.397	1.860	2.306	2.896	3.355
9	.261	.703	1.383	1.833	2.262	2.821	3.250
10	0.260	0.700	1.372	1.812	2.228	2.764	3.169
11	.260	.697	1.363	1.796	2.201	2.718	3.106
12	.259	.695	1.356	1.782	2.179	2.681	3.055
13	.259	.694	1.350	1.771	2.160	2.650	3.012
14	.258	.692	1.345	1.761	2.145	2.624	2.977
15	0.258	0.691	1.341	1.753	2.131	2.602	2.947
16	.258	.690	1.337	1.746	2.120	2.583	2.921
17	.257	.689	1.333	1.740	2.110	2.567	2.898
18	.257	.688	1.330	1.734	2.101	2.552	2.878
19	.257	.688	1.328	1.729	2.093	2.539	2.861
20	0.257	0.687	1.325	1.725	2.086	2.528	2.845
21	.257	.686	1.323	1.721	2.080	2.518	2.831
22	.256	.686	1.321	1.717	2.074	2.508	2.819
23	.256	.685	1.319	1.714	2.069	2.500	2.807
24	.256	.685	1.318	1.711	2.064	2.492	2.797

TABLE E.4 (continued)

Values of *t* That Will Be Exceeded with Specified Probabilities

This table shows the value of *t* where the area under the *t* distribution exceeding this value of *t* equals the specified amount. For example, the probability that a *t* variable with 14 degrees of freedom will exceed 1.345 equals .10.

Degrees of freedom	Probability						
	.40	.25	.10	.05	.025	.01	.005
25	0.256	0.684	1.316	1.708	2.060	2.485	2.787
26	.256	.684	1.315	1.706	2.056	2.479	2.779
27	.256	.684	1.314	1.703	2.052	2.473	2.771
28	.256	.683	1.313	1.701	2.048	2.467	2.763
29	.256	.683	1.311	1.699	2.045	2.462	2.756
30	0.256	0.683	1.310	1.697	2.042	2.457	2.750
40	.255	.681	1.303	1.684	2.021	2.423	2.704
60	.254	.679	1.296	1.671	2.000	2.390	2.660
120	.254	.677	1.289	1.658	1.980	2.358	2.617
∞	.253	.674	1.282	1.645	1.960	2.326	2.576

Source: *Biometrika Tables for Statisticians* (Cambridge, U.K.: Cambridge University, 1954).

TABLE E.5

Value of an *F* Variable That Is Exceeded with Probability Equal to .05

	Degrees of freedom for numerator								
	1	2	3	4	5	6	7	8	9
1	161.4	199.5	215.7	224.6	230.2	234.0	236.8	238.9	240.5
2	18.51	19.00	19.16	19.25	19.30	19.33	19.35	19.37	19.38
3	10.13	9.55	9.28	9.12	9.01	8.94	8.89	8.85	8.81
4	7.71	6.94	6.59	6.39	6.26	6.16	6.09	6.04	6.00
5	6.61	5.79	5.41	5.19	5.05	4.95	4.88	4.82	4.77
6	5.99	5.14	4.76	4.53	4.39	4.28	4.21	4.15	4.10
7	5.59	4.74	4.35	4.12	3.97	3.87	3.79	3.73	3.68
8	5.32	4.46	4.07	3.84	3.69	3.58	3.50	3.44	3.39
9	5.12	4.26	3.86	3.63	3.48	3.37	3.29	3.23	3.18
10	4.96	4.10	3.71	3.48	3.33	3.22	3.14	3.07	3.02
11	4.84	3.98	3.59	3.36	3.20	3.09	3.01	2.95	2.90
12	4.75	3.89	3.49	3.26	3.11	3.00	2.91	2.85	2.80
13	4.67	3.81	3.41	3.18	3.03	2.92	2.83	2.77	2.71
14	4.60	3.74	3.34	3.11	2.96	2.85	2.76	2.70	2.65
15	4.54	3.68	3.29	3.06	2.90	2.79	2.71	2.64	2.59
16	4.49	3.63	3.24	3.01	2.85	2.74	2.66	2.59	2.54
17	4.45	3 59	3.20	2.96	2.81	2.70	2.61	2.55	2.49
18	4.41	3.55	3.16	2.93	2.77	2.66	2.58	2.51	2.46
19	4.38	3.52	3.13	2.90	2.74	2.63	2.54	2.48	2.42
20	4.35	3.49	3.10	2.87	2.71	2.60	2.51	2.45	2.39
21	4.32	3.47	3.07	2.84	2.68	2.57	2.49	2.42	2.37
22	4.30	3.44	3.05	2.82	2.66	2.55	2.46	2.40	2.34
23	4.28	3.42	3.03	2.80	2.64	2.53	2.44	2.37	2.32
24	4.26	3.40	3.01	2.78	2.62	2.51	2.42	2.36	2.30
25	4.24	3.39	2.99	2.76	2.60	2.49	2.40	2.34	2.28
26	4.23	3.37	2.98	2.74	2.59	2.47	2.39	2.32	2.27
27	4.21	3.35	2.96	2.73	2.57	2.46	2.37	2.31	2.25
28	4.20	3.34	2.95	2.71	2.56	2.45	2.36	2.29	2.24
29	4.18	3.33	2.93	2.70	2.55	2.43	2.35	2.28	2.22
30	4.17	3.32	2.92	2.69	2.53	2.42	2.33	2.27	2.21
40	4.08	3.23	2.84	2.61	2.45	2.34	2.25	2.18	2.12
60	4.00	3.15	2.76	2.53	2.37	2.25	2.17	2.10	2.04
120	3.92	3.07	2.68	2.45	2.29	2.17	2.09	2.02	1.96
∞	3.84	3.00	2.60	2.37	2.21	2.10	2.01	1.94	1.88

Degrees of freedom for denominator

TABLE E.5 (continued)

Value of an *F* Variable That Is Exceeded with Probability Equal to .05

					Degrees of freedom for numerator					
	10	12	15	20	24	30	40	60	120	∞
1	241.9	243.9	245.9	248.0	249.1	250.1	251.1	252.2	253.3	254.3
2	19.40	19.41	19.43	19.45	19.45	19.46	19.47	19.48	19.49	19.50
3	8.79	8.74	8.70	8.66	8.64	8.62	8.59	8.57	8.55	8.53
4	5.96	5.91	5.86	5.80	5.77	5.75	5.72	5.69	5.66	5.63
5	4.74	4.68	4.62	4.56	4.53	4.50	4.46	4.43	4.40	4.36
6	4.06	4.00	3.94	3.87	3.84	3.81	3.77	3.74	3.70	3.67
7	3.64	3.57	3.51	3.44	3.41	3.38	3.34	3.30	3.27	3.23
8	3.35	3.28	3.22	3.15	3.12	3.08	3.04	3.01	2.97	2.93
9	3.14	3.07	3.01	2.94	2.90	2.86	2.83	2.79	2.75	2.71
10	2.98	2.91	2.85	2.77	2.74	2.70	2.66	2.62	2.58	2.54
11	2.85	2.79	2.72	2.65	2.61	2.57	2.53	2.49	2.45	2.40
12	2.75	2.69	2.62	2.54	2.51	2.47	2.43	2.38	2.34	2.30
13	2.67	2.60	2.53	2.46	2.42	2.38	2.34	2.30	2.25	2.21
14	2.60	2.53	2.46	2.39	2.35	2.31	2.27	2.22	2.18	2.13
15	2.54	2.48	2.40	2.33	2.29	2.25	2.20	2.16	2.11	2.07
16	2.49	2.42	2.35	2.28	2.24	2.19	2.15	2.11	2.06	2.01
17	2.45	2.38	2.31	2.23	2.19	2.15	2.10	2.06	2.01	1.96
18	2.41	2.34	2.27	2.19	2.15	2.11	2.06	2.02	1.97	1.92
19	2.38	2.31	2.23	2.16	2.11	2.07	2.03	1.98	1.93	1.88
20	2.35	2.28	2.20	2.12	2.08	2.04	1.99	1.95	1.90	1.84
21	2.32	2.25	2.18	2.10	2.05	2.01	1.96	1.92	1.87	1.81
22	2.30	2.23	2.15	2.07	2.03	1.98	1.94	1.89	1.84	1.78
23	2.27	2.20	2.13	2.05	2.01	1.96	1.91	1.86	1.81	1.76
24	2.25	2.18	2.11	2.03	1.98	1.94	1.89	1.84	1.79	1.73
25	2.24	2.16	2.09	2.01	1.96	1.92	1.87	1.82	1.77	1.71
26	2.22	2.15	2.07	1.99	1.95	1.90	1.85	1.80	1.75	1.69
27	2.20	2.13	2.06	1.97	1.93	1.88	1.84	1.79	1.73	1.67
28	2.19	2.12	2.04	1.96	1.91	1.87	1.82	1.77	1.71	1.65
29	2.18	2.10	2.03	1.94	1.90	1.85	1.81	1.75	1.70	1.64
30	2.16	2.09	2.01	1.93	1.89	1.84	1.79	1.74	1.68	1.62
40	2.08	2.00	1.92	1.84	1.79	1.74	1.69	1.64	1.58	1.51
60	1.99	1.92	1.84	1.75	1.70	1.65	1.59	1.53	1.47	1.39
120	1.91	1.83	1.75	1.66	1.61	1.55	1.50	1.43	1.35	1.25
∞	1.83	1.75	1.67	1.57	1.52	1.46	1.39	1.32	1.22	1.00

Degrees of freedom for denominator (left axis label)

Source: *Biometrika Tables for Statisticians.*

TABLE E.6

Value of an *F* Variable That Is Exceeded with Probability Equal to .01

	Degrees of freedom for numerator								
	1	2	3	4	5	6	7	8	9
1	4052	4999.5	5403	5625	5764	5859	5928	5982	6022
2	98.50	99.00	99.17	99.25	99.30	99.33	99.36	99.37	99.39
3	34.12	30.82	29.46	28.71	28.24	27.91	27.67	27.49	27.35
4	21.20	18.00	16.69	15.98	15.52	15.21	14.98	14.80	14.66
5	16.26	13.27	12.06	11.39	10.97	10.67	10.46	10.29	10.16
6	13.75	10.92	9.78	9.15	8.75	8.47	8.26	8.10	7.98
7	12.25	9.55	8.45	7.85	7.46	7.19	6.99	6.84	6.72
8	11.26	8.65	7.59	7.01	6.63	6.37	6.18	6.03	5.91
9	10.56	8.02	6.99	6.42	6.06	5.80	5.61	5.47	5.35
10	10.04	7.56	6.55	5.99	5.64	5.39	5.20	5.06	4.94
11	9.65	7.21	6.22	5.67	5.32	5.07	4.89	4.74	4.63
12	9.33	6.93	5.95	5.41	5.06	4.82	4.64	4.50	4.39
13	9.07	6.70	5.74	5.21	4.86	4.62	4.44	4.30	4.19
14	8.86	6.51	5.56	5.04	4.69	4.46	4.28	4.14	4.03
15	8.68	6.36	5.42	4.89	4.56	4.32	4.14	4.00	3.89
16	8.53	6.23	5.29	4.77	4.44	4.20	4.03	3.89	3.78
17	8.40	6.11	5.18	4.67	4.34	4.10	3.93	3.79	3.68
18	8.29	6.01	5.09	4.58	4.25	4.01	3.84	3.71	3.60
19	8.18	5.93	5.01	4.50	4.17	3.94	3.77	3.63	3.52
20	8.10	5.85	4.94	4.43	4.10	3.87	3.70	3.56	3.46
21	8.02	5.78	4.87	4.37	4.04	3.81	3.64	3.51	3.40
22	7.95	5.72	4.82	4.31	3.99	3.76	3.59	3.45	3.35
23	7.88	5.66	4.76	4.26	3.94	3.71	3.54	3.41	3.30
24	7.82	5.61	4.72	4.22	3.90	3.67	3.50	3.36	3.26
25	7.77	5.57	4.68	4.18	3.85	3.63	3.46	3.32	3.22
26	7.72	5.53	4.64	4.14	3.82	3.59	3.42	3.29	3.18
27	7.68	5.49	4.60	4.11	3.78	3.56	3.39	3.26	3.15
28	7.64	5.45	4.57	4.07	3.75	3.53	3.36	3.23	3.12
29	7.60	5.42	4.54	4.04	3.73	3.50	3.33	3.20	3.09
30	7.56	5.39	4.51	4.02	3.70	3.47	3.30	3.17	3.07
40	7.31	5.18	4.31	3.83	3.51	3.29	3.12	2.99	2.89
60	7.08	4.98	4.13	3.65	3.34	3.12	2.95	2.82	2.72
120	6.85	4.79	3.95	3.48	3.17	2.96	2.79	2.66	2.56
∞	6.63	4.61	3.78	3.32	3.02	2.80	2.64	2.51	2.41

Degrees of freedom for denominator (left axis label)

TABLE E.6 (continued)

Value of an *F* Variable That is Exceeded with Probability Equal to .01

		Degrees of freedom for numerator									
		10	12	15	20	24	30	40	60	120	∞
Degrees of freedom for denominator	1	6056	6106	6157	6209	6235	6261	6287	6313	6339	6366
	2	99.40	99.42	99.43	99.45	99.46	99.47	99.47	99.48	99.49	99.50
	3	27.23	27.05	26.87	26.69	26.60	26.50	26.41	26.32	26.22	26.13
	4	14.55	14.37	14.20	14.02	13.93	13.84	13.75	13.65	13.56	13.46
	5	10.05	9.89	9.72	9.55	9.47	9.38	9.29	9.20	9.11	9.02
	6	7.87	7.72	7.56	7.40	7.31	7.23	7.14	7.06	6.97	6.88
	7	6.62	6.47	6.31	6.16	6.07	5.99	5.91	5.82	5.74	5.65
	8	5.81	5.67	5.52	5.36	5.28	5.20	5.12	5.03	4.95	4.86
	9	5.26	5.11	4.96	4.81	4.73	4.65	4.57	4.48	4.40	4.31
	10	4.85	4.71	4.56	4.41	4.33	4.25	4.17	4.08	4.00	3.91
	11	4.54	4.40	4.25	4.10	4.02	3.94	3.86	3.78	3.69	3.60
	12	4.30	4.16	4.01	3.86	3.78	3.70	3.62	3.54	3.45	3.36
	13	4.10	3.96	3.82	3.66	3.59	3.51	3.43	3.34	3.25	3.17
	14	3.94	3.80	3.66	3.51	3.43	3.35	3.27	3.18	3.09	3.00
	15	3.80	3.67	3.52	3.37	3.29	3.21	3.13	3.05	2.96	2.87
	16	3.69	3.55	3.41	3.26	3.18	3.10	3.02	2.93	2.84	2.75
	17	3.59	3.46	3.31	3.16	3.08	3.00	2.92	2.83	2.75	2.65
	18	3.51	3.37	3.23	3.08	3.00	2.92	2.84	2.75	2.66	2.57
	19	3.43	3.30	3.15	3.00	2.92	2.84	2.76	2.67	2.58	2.49
	20	3.37	3.23	3.09	2.94	2.86	2.78	2.69	2.61	2.52	2.42
	21	3.31	3.17	3.03	2.88	2.80	2.72	2.64	2.55	2.46	2.36
	22	3.26	3.12	2.98	2.83	2.75	2.67	2.58	2.50	2.40	2.31
	23	3.21	3.07	2.93	2.78	2.70	2.62	2.54	2.45	2.35	2.26
	24	3.17	3.03	2.89	2.74	2.66	2.58	2.49	2.40	2.31	2.21
	25	3.13	2.99	2.85	2.70	2.62	2.54	2.45	2.36	2.27	2.17
	26	3.09	2.96	2.81	2.66	2.58	2.50	2.42	2.33	2.23	2.13
	27	3.06	2.93	2.78	2.63	2.55	2.47	2.38	2.29	2.20	2.10
	28	3.03	2.90	2.75	2.60	2.52	2.44	2.35	2.26	2.17	2.06
	29	3.00	2.87	2.73	2.57	2.49	2.41	2.33	2.23	2.14	2.03
	30	2.98	2.84	2.70	2.55	2.47	2.39	2.30	2.21	2.11	2.01
	40	2.80	2.66	2.52	2.37	2.29	2.20	2.11	2.02	1.92	1.80
	60	2.63	2.50	2.35	2.20	2.12	2.03	1.94	1.84	1.73	1.60
	120	2.47	2.34	2.19	2.03	1.95	1.86	1.76	1.66	1.53	1.38
	∞	2.32	2.18	2.04	1.88	1.79	1.70	1.59	1.47	1.32	1.00

Source: *Biometrika Tables for Statisticians.*

TABLE E.7

Values of d_L and d_U for the Durbin–Watson Test

A. Significance level = .05

	k = 1		k = 2		k = 3		k = 4		k = 5	
n	d_L	d_U	d_L	d_U	d_L	d_U	d_L	d_U	d_L	d_U
15	1.08	1.36	0.95	1.54	0.82	1.75	0.69	1.97	0.56	2.21
16	1.10	1.37	0.98	1.54	0.86	1.73	0.74	1.93	0.62	2.15
17	1.13	1.38	1.02	1.54	0.90	1.71	0.78	1.90	0.67	2.10
18	1.16	1.39	1.05	1.53	0.93	1.69	0.82	1.87	0.71	2.06
19	1.18	1.40	1.08	1.53	0.97	1.68	0.86	1.85	0.75	2.02
20	1.20	1.41	1.10	1.54	1.00	1.68	0.90	1.83	0.79	1.99
21	1.22	1.42	1.13	1.54	1.03	1.67	0.93	1.81	0.83	1.96
22	1.24	1.43	1.15	1.54	1.05	1.66	0.96	1.80	0.86	1.94
23	1.26	1.44	1.17	1.54	1.08	1.66	0.99	1.79	0.90	1.92
24	1.27	1.45	1.19	1.55	1.10	1.66	1.01	1.78	0.93	1.90
25	1.29	1.45	1.21	1.55	1.12	1.66	1.04	1.77	0.95	1.89
26	1.30	1.46	1.22	1.55	1.14	1.65	1.06	1.76	0.98	1.88
27	1.32	1.47	1.24	1.56	1.16	1.65	1.08	1.76	1.01	1.86
28	1.33	1.48	1.26	1.56	1.18	1.65	1.10	1.75	1.03	1.85
29	1.34	1.48	1.27	1.56	1.20	1.65	1.12	1.74	1.05	1.84
30	1.35	1.49	1.28	1.57	1.21	1.65	1.14	1.74	1.07	1.83
31	1.36	1.50	1.30	1.57	1.23	1.65	1.16	1.74	1.09	1.83
32	1.37	1.50	1.31	1.57	1.24	1.65	1.18	1.73	1.11	1.82
33	1.38	1.51	1.32	1.58	1.26	1.65	1.19	1.73	1.13	1.81
34	1.39	1.51	1.33	1.58	1.27	1.65	1.21	1.73	1.15	1.81
35	1.40	1.52	1.34	1.58	1.28	1.65	1.22	1.73	1.16	1.80
36	1.41	1.52	1.35	1.59	1.29	1.65	1.24	1.73	1.18	1.80
37	1.42	1.53	1.36	1.59	1.31	1.66	1.25	1.72	1.19	1.80
38	1.43	1.54	1.37	1.59	1.32	1.66	1.26	1.72	1.21	1.79
39	1.43	1.54	1.38	1.60	1.33	1.66	1.27	1.72	1.22	1.79
40	1.44	1.54	1.39	1.60	1.34	1.66	1.29	1.72	1.23	1.79
45	1.48	1.57	1.43	1.62	1.38	1.67	1.34	1.72	1.29	1.78
50	1.50	1.59	1.46	1.63	1.42	1.67	1.38	1.72	1.34	1.77
55	1.53	1.60	1.49	1.64	1.45	1.68	1.41	1.72	1.38	1.77
60	1.55	1.62	1.51	1.65	1.48	1.69	1.44	1.73	1.41	1.77
65	1.57	1.63	1.54	1.66	1.50	1.70	1.47	1.73	1.44	1.77
70	1.58	1.64	1.55	1.67	1.52	1.70	1.49	1.74	1.46	1.77
75	1.60	1.65	1.57	1.68	1.54	1.71	1.51	1.74	1.49	1.77
80	1.61	1.66	1.59	1.69	1.56	1.72	1.53	1.74	1.51	1.77
85	1.62	1.67	1.60	1.70	1.57	1.72	1.55	1.75	1.52	1.77
90	1.63	1.68	1.61	1.70	1.59	1.73	1.57	1.75	1.54	1.78
95	1.64	1.69	1.62	1.71	1.60	1.73	1.58	1.75	1.56	1.78
100	1.65	1.69	1.63	1.72	1.61	1.74	1.59	1.76	1.57	1.78

TABLE E.7 (continued)

Values of d_L and d_U for the Durbin–Watson Test

B. Significance level = .025

n	k = 1		k = 2		k = 3		k = 4		k = 5	
	d_L	d_U	d_L	d_U	d_L	d_U	d_L	d_U	d_L	d_U
15	0.95	1.23	0.83	1.40	0.71	1.61	0.59	1.84	0.48	2.09
16	0.98	1.24	0.86	1.40	0.75	1.59	0.64	1.80	0.53	2.03
17	1.01	1.25	0.90	1.40	0.79	1.58	0.68	1.77	0.57	1.98
18	1.03	1.26	0.93	1.40	0.82	1.56	0.72	1.74	0.62	1.93
19	1.06	1.28	0.96	1.41	0.86	1.55	0.76	1.72	0.66	1.90
20	1.08	1.28	0.99	1.41	0.89	1.55	0.79	1.70	0.70	1.87
21	1.10	1.30	1.01	1.41	0.92	1.54	0.83	1.69	0.73	1.84
22	1.12	1.31	1.04	1.42	0.95	1.54	0.86	1.68	0.77	1.82
23	1.14	1.32	1.06	1.42	0.97	1.54	0.89	1.67	0.80	1.80
24	1.16	1.33	1.08	1.43	1.00	1.54	0.91	1.66	0.83	1.79
25	1.18	1.34	1.10	1.43	1.02	1.54	0.94	1.65	0.86	1.77
26	1.19	1.35	1.12	1.44	1.04	1.54	0.96	1.65	0.88	1.76
27	1.21	1.36	1.13	1.44	1.06	1.54	0.99	1.64	0.91	1.75
28	1.22	1.37	1.15	1.45	1.08	1.54	1.01	1.64	0.93	1.74
29	1.24	1.38	1.17	1.45	1.10	1.54	1.03	1.63	0.96	1.73
30	1.25	1.38	1.18	1.46	1.12	1.54	1.05	1.63	0.98	1.73
31	1.26	1.39	1.20	1.47	1.13	1.55	1.07	1.63	1.00	1.72
32	1.27	1.40	1.21	1.47	1.15	1.55	1.08	1.63	1.02	1.71
33	1.28	1.41	1.22	1.48	1.16	1.55	1.10	1.63	1.04	1.71
34	1.29	1.41	1.24	1.48	1.17	1.55	1.12	1.63	1.06	1.70
35	1.30	1.42	1.25	1.48	1.19	1.55	1.13	1.63	1.07	1.70
36	1.31	1.43	1.26	1.49	1.20	1.56	1.15	1.63	1.09	1.70
37	1.32	1.43	1.27	1.49	1.21	1.56	1.16	1.62	1.10	1.70
38	1.33	1.44	1.28	1.50	1.23	1.56	1.17	1.62	1.12	1.70
39	1.34	1.44	1.29	1.50	1.24	1.56	1.19	1.63	1.13	1.69
40	1.35	1.45	1.30	1.51	1.25	1.57	1.20	1.63	1.15	1.69
45	1.39	1.48	1.34	1.53	1.30	1.58	1.25	1.63	1.21	1.69
50	1.42	1.50	1.38	1.54	1.34	1.59	1.30	1.64	1.26	1.69
55	1.45	1.52	1.41	1.56	1.37	1.60	1.33	1.64	1.30	1.69
60	1.47	1.54	1.44	1.57	1.40	1.61	1.37	1.65	1.33	1.69
65	1.49	1.55	1.46	1.59	1.43	1.62	1.40	1.66	1.36	1.69
70	1.51	1.57	1.48	1.60	1.45	1.63	1.42	1.66	1.39	1.70
75	1.53	1.58	1.50	1.61	1.47	1.64	1.45	1.67	1.42	1.70
80	1.54	1.59	1.52	1.62	1.49	1.65	1.47	1.67	1.44	1.70
85	1.56	1.60	1.53	1.63	1.51	1.65	1.49	1.68	1.46	1.71
90	1.57	1.61	1.55	1.64	1.53	1.66	1.50	1.69	1.48	1.71
95	1.58	1.62	1.56	1.65	1.54	1.67	1.52	1.69	1.50	1.71
100	1.59	1.63	1.57	1.65	1.55	1.67	1.53	1.70	1.51	1.72

TABLE E.7 (continued)

Values of d_L and d_U for the Durbin–Watson Test

C. Significance level = 0.01

n	k = 1 d_L	k = 1 d_U	k = 2 d_L	k = 2 d_U	k = 3 d_L	k = 3 d_U	k = 4 d_L	k = 4 d_U	k = 5 d_L	k = 5 d_U
15	0.81	1.07	0.70	1.25	0.59	1.46	0.49	1.70	0.39	1.96
16	0.84	1.09	0.74	1.25	0.63	1.44	0.53	1.66	0.44	1.90
17	0.87	1.10	0.77	1.25	0.67	1.43	0.57	1.63	0.48	1.85
18	0.90	1.12	0.80	1.26	0.71	1.42	0.61	1.60	0.52	1.80
19	0.93	1.13	0.83	1.26	0.74	1.41	0.65	1.58	0.56	1.77
20	0.95	1.15	0.86	1.27	077	1.41	0.68	1.57	0.60	1.74
21	0.97	1.16	0.89	1.27	0.80	1.41	0.72	1.55	0.63	1.71
22	1.00	1.17	0.91	1.28	0.83	1.40	0.75	1.54	0.66	1.69
23	1.02	1.19	0.94	1.29	0.86	1.40	0.77	1.53	0.70	1.67
24	1.04	1.20	0.96	1.30	0.88	1.41	0.80	1.53	0.72	1.66
25	1.05	1.21	0.98	1.30	0.90	1.41	0.83	1.52	0.75	1.65
26	1.07	1.22	1.00	1.31	0.93	1.41	0.85	1.52	0.78	1.64
27	1.09	1.23	1.02	1.32	0.95	1.41	0.88	1.51	0.81	1.63
28	1.10	1.24	1.04	1.32	0.97	1.41	0.90	1.51	0.83	1.62
29	1.12	1.25	1.05	1.33	0.99	1.42	0.92	1.51	0.85	1.61
30	1.13	1.26	1.07	1.34	1.01	1.42	0.94	1.51	0.88	1.61
31	1.15	1.27	1.08	1.34	1.02	1.42	0.96	1.51	0.90	1.60
32	1.16	1.28	1.10	1.35	1.04	1.43	0.98	1.51	0.92	1.60
33	1.17	1.29	1.11	1.36	1.05	1.43	1.00	1.51	0.94	1.59
34	1.18	1.30	1.13	1.36	1.07	1.43	1.01	1.51	0.95	1.59
35	1.19	1.31	1.14	1.37	1.08	1.44	1.03	1.51	0.97	1.59
36	1.21	1.32	1.15	1.38	1.10	1.44	1.04	1.51	0.99	1.59
37	1.22	1.32	1.16	1.38	1.11	1.45	1.06	1.51	1.00	1.59
38	1.23	1.33	1.18	1.39	1.12	1.45	1.07	1.52	1.02	1.58
39	1.24	1.34	1.19	1.39	1.14	1.45	1.09	1.52	1.03	1.58
40	1.25	1.34	1.20	1.40	1.15	1.46	1.10	1.52	1.05	1.58
45	1.29	1.38	1.24	1.42	1.20	1.48	1.16	1.53	1.11	1.58
50	1.32	1.40	1.28	1.45	1.24	1.49	1.20	1.54	1.16	1.59
55	1.36	1.43	1.32	1.47	1.28	1.51	1.25	1.55	1.21	1.59
60	1.38	1.45	1.35	1.48	1.32	1.52	1.28	1.56	1.25	1.60
65	1.41	1.47	1.38	1.50	1.35	1.53	1.31	1.57	1.28	1.61
70	1.43	1.49	1.40	1.52	1.37	1.55	1.34	1.58	1.31	1.61
75	1.45	1.50	1.42	1.53	1.39	1.56	1.37	1.59	1.34	1.62
80	1.47	1.52	1.44	1.54	1.42	1.57	1.39	1.60	1.36	1.62
85	1.48	1.53	1.46	1.55	1.43	1.58	1.41	1.60	1.39	1.63
90	1.50	1.54	1.47	1.56	1.45	1.59	1.43	1.61	1.41	1.64
95	1.51	1.55	1.49	1.57	1.47	1.60	1.45	1.62	1.42	1.64
100	1.52	1.56	1.50	1.58	1.48	1.60	1.46	1.63	1.44	1.65

Source: J. Durbin and G. S. Watson, "Testing for Serial Correlation in Least Squares Regression," *Biometrika 38* (June 1951).

INDEX